NYC ACCESS®

Orientation

A thorough description of **New York City** might exhaust the largest vocabulary: sophisticated and brutal, exhilarating and oppressive, earthy and aloof. A city of dynamic contrasts, New York showcases them all. The purpose of this guide is to locate the best of the city and to lay it out in a systematic way so the visitor can gather it all in.

Begin with homework. Map out specific routes. Remember that Manhattan is mostly a simple grid of numbered streets and avenues—north, south, east and west are all you really need. Should you require help, New Yorkers are, contrary to popular myth, quite friendly and happy to assist when asked for directions and recommendations—it's simple street smarts to ask the right question of the right person. Like any large city, this is not a place in which you want to wander about looking helpless.

New York often seems relentless and chaotic to a new visitor, but a little sensitivity to its shifting rhythms is all that's required to sort out what's right for you and what's not. Again, contrary to what you may have heard, New York is a good deal safer than many other American cities. But it is a *big* city, and where official guidelines are exhausted, common sense should prevail.

Finally, you might want to dispel the notion of *covering a lot of ground* when you plan a day trip. One of New York's great distinctions is its astounding number of choices, rivaling any other city in the world. You may well find yourself immersed in a single neighborhood for longer than you had planned. New York presents this pleasant dilemma for the visitor who wants to see everything quickly. So start early. Or stay longer. Better still, come back again.

Airports

John F. Kennedy International Airport

The area's largest airport is located about 15mi east of Manhattan in the borough of Queens and, depending on traffic, traveling time into Manhattan can take anywhere from 45min to 1½ hr. Most transatlantic flights, as well as many domestic flights, arrive and depart here. Terminals are connected by shuttle buses.

JFK Airport Information

Airport Information	718/656.4520
Airport Emergency	718/656.4333
Airport Police	718/656.4668
Customs	718/917.1648
Dental Service	718/656.4747
Ground Transportation	800/247.7433
Immigration	718/917.1688
Lost & Found	718/656.4120
Lost or damaged baggage:	See airline reps.
Medical Clinic	718/656.5344
Paging	call individual airline
Parking Availability	718/656.5699
Travelers Aid	718/656.4870
ATMs:	Citibank, American Express

Rental Cars

Call for shuttle on red phone in any terminal

Avis	718/244.5400
Budget	718/656.6010
Dollar	718/656.2400
Hertz	718/656.7600
National	718/632.8300

Getting into town from JFK The best way into Manhattan by car is to take the Van Wyck Expwy to the Grand Central Pkwy, which connects with the Long Island Expwy. Those going to downtown Manhattan (or to Brooklyn) should exit the LIE onto the Brooklyn Queens Expwy. The BQE, in turn, feeds into the Williamsburg, Manhattan and Brooklyn bridges. For Midtown destinations, continue on the LIE, which connects with the Queens-Midtown Tunnel.

Other possibilities:
Carey Transportation, Inc, buses (718/632.0500) depart JFK every 30min, 6AM-11:30PM. All buses stop at Grand Central Terminal and Port Authority. (The last departure from Grand Central to JFK is midnight.) Travel time is about 1hr. Helicopter flights can be arranged through several companies. **New York Helicopter** (800/645.3494) offers a total of fifteen 10min shuttles, running from 8:40AM until 9PM, from the TWA terminal to the E 34th St Heliport. Limousine service may be obtained at booths within individual terminals.

La Guardia Airport
Closer to Manhattan—8mi NE, about a 30min drive—in NW Queens. Most airlines serving other American cities use the 2-level main terminal. Delta Airlines has its own terminal, and the Pan Am and Eastern shuttle flights serving Boston and Washington DC use separate buildings. Terminals are connected through shuttle buses.

Getting into town from La Guardia If you're traveling by car, you could take Grand Central Pkwy to the Triborough Bridge, then travel south on the FDR Dr. Or, if you wish to save the toll and the time, get off the Van Dam St exit just before the Triborough Bridge, turn south on Van Dam/21st St, and you'll meet up with the Queensborough Bridge (59th St Bridge) going into Manhattan. If your destination is downtown (SoHo or Wall St), take the Brooklyn-Queens Expwy to the Williamsburg Bridge, which exits at Delancey St.

Other possibilities:
Triborough Coach (718/335.1000) runs a 24hr bus

service from La Guardia's main terminal to the Jackson Heights 74th St subway station in Queens for connections into Manhattan. The trip takes about 45min. **Carey Transportation, Inc** (718/632.0500), runs buses between La Guardia and Manhattan every 20min from 6AM to midnight. Limousine service may be obtained at booths within individual terminals. The **Pan Am Water Shuttle** (800/543.3779) is a high-speed boat that departs the Marine Air Terminal several times each morning and in the early evening. Stops: 34th St at the East River (about a 35min trip); Pier 11, Wall St at South St (45min, approximately).

Newark International Airport
Local traffic snafus are making Newark a more popular choice, especially if your final destination is the West Side or downtown Manhattan. Located on Newark Bay, 16mi SW of Manhattan (30min-1hr traveling time), it has one international and 2 domestic terminals, with shuttle bus connections.

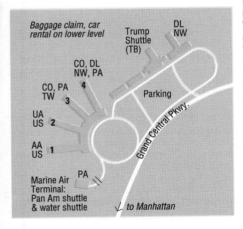

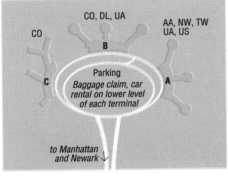

LGA Airport Information
Airport Information	718/476.5000
Airport Police; Lost & Found	718/476.5115
Customs	718/476.5561
Ground Transportation	800/247.7433
Lost or damaged baggage:	See airline reps. in baggage claim area
Paging	call individual airline
ATMs:	Cirrus, NYCE

Rental Cars
Lower level by baggage claim
Avis	718/507.3600
Budget	718/639.6400
Dollar	718/779.5600
Hertz	718/478.5300
National	718/803.4101

EWR Airport Information
Airport Information	201/961.2000
Airport Police/Lost & Found	201/961.2230
Customs & Immigration	201/645.6105
Ground Transportation	800/247.7433
Medical Clinic	201/961.2525
Paging	call individual airline
Parking Availability	201/961.2013

Rental Cars
In baggage claim area. 7AM-midnight
Avis	201/961.4300
Budget	201/961.2990
Hertz	201/621.2000
National	201/622.1270

Getting into town from Newark Airport The route in by car is fairly straightforward, allowing you to take the New Jersey Tpk and follow the signs to either the Holland Tunnel (downtown) or the Lincoln Tunnel (Midtown). Note: traffic can be a problem at any hour in New York, and only a very few taxi drivers know the city street shortcuts off the highway. Common sense rules still apply, and you should not be easily persuaded to venture forth in a taxi.

Other possibilities:
New Jersey Transit (201/460.8444) offers 24hr bus service every 15-30min to Port Authority. **Olympia Trails** (964.6233) runs buses from Newark to 1

Orientation

World Trade Center (M-F 6AM-9:15PM; Sa-Su, holidays 7AM-9PM) and 41st St at Park Ave and 34th St at 8th Ave every 20-30min daily from 5AM-11PM. The ride lasts from 30 to 45min. Limousine service may be obtained at booths within individual terminals. **New York Helicopter** (800/645.3494) offers six 10min shuttles, running on the hour from 2-7PM, from Continental Terminal C to the E 34th St Heliport.

Airlines

Air Canada (AC)	869.1900
Air France (AF)	247.0100
Air India (AI)	751.6200
Alitalia (AZ)	582.8900
American Airlines (AA)	800/433.7300
American West (HP)	800/247.5692
British Airways (BA)	800/247.9297
Continental Airlines (CO)	319.9494
Delta Airlines (DL)	239.0700
El Al Airlines (LY)	768.9200
Finnair (AY)	889.7070
Icelandair (FI)	967.8888
Japan Air Lines (JL)	838.4400
KLM Royal Dutch Airlines (KL)	759.3600
Lufthansa (LH)	718/895.1277
Northwest (NW)	
Domestic	736.1220
International	563.7200
Pan Am (PA)	800/327.6580
Scandinavian Airlines (SK)	718/657.7700
Swissair (SR)	718/995.8400
Trump Shuttle (TB)	800/247.8786
TWA (TW)	
Domestic	290.2121
International	290.2141
United Airlines (UA)	800/241.6522
USAir (US)	736.3200

212 area code unless otherwise noted

For further information on traveling to, from and between the 3 airports: 800/247.7433

Getting Around Town

Perhaps the most crucial element of your stay here is mastery of the city's transportation services and routes. The 5 major ways of getting around are subway, bus, taxi, car service and foot. Of the 5, walking is the most highly recommended, and sometimes the quickest. Manhattan is laid out in a rather easy-to-grasp grid of north/south avenues and east/west numbered streets. Bear in mind that 5th Ave is the dividing line between east and west. Below Houston St, the numbers end, and parts of downtown (Greenwich Village in particular) can get a little tricky, since the streets there were laid out during the time of the horse-drawn carriage.

The **subway**, despite the fact that it's loud, dirty and often crowded, is the most efficient way to move longer distances within Manhattan. Actually, most of the graffiti-riddled cars have been replaced with sleeker, modern cars that are air conditioned in the summer and heated in winter.

Consult the subway map in this book (see page 8); the system is complicated and not immediately decipherable. Entrance to the system requires the purchase of a token, which allows you to travel its length and breadth (and to make connections), and is available at token booths at most stations. It's wise to purchase tokens in ten-packs if you're planning to ride often. The subway system is open 24hr, although at night it can be a lonesome wait.

Buses are a lot slower, but you have the satisfaction of seeing where you're going. A sign on the front of each bus gives its route number and final destination, and stops are clearly marked on the street, sometimes with maps showing the route served (although not every bus serves every stop). In addition to the longer-distance routes that run on the north-south avenues, there are many crosstown bus routes. (Request a transfer from the driver when you get on, so that if you're going, say, north and then west across town, you don't have to pay a second fare on the crosstown route, or vice-versa.) During rush hours, buses marked *Limited* function like express subway lines and stop only at major intersections. Exact change or a token is required.

There are nearly 12,000 licensed **taxis** in New York City—a meaningless number if you can't find one when you need one. Licensed cabs are bright yellow and signal their availability through a light on the roof. Cabs may be hailed anywhere on the street, except for crosswalks and intersections, and by law they are supposed to take you wherever you wish to go—but be forewarned, New York cab drivers are an independent bunch. The taxi rates are posted on the side of the cab, or sometimes stickered inside, and after 8PM there is a nighttime surcharge. A cab ride in New York can be colorful, amusing and efficient, or hellish and frustrating, depending on the traffic and the driver.

Car services and so-called *gypsy cabs* (generally owner-operated, and not as strictly controlled as licensed cabs) have sprung up in town simply because yellow cabs will often not go where you wish to go—particularly to the outerboroughs, or to Harlem and Washington Heights. Or you may find yourself visiting until a late hour and wish to have a car at your door rather than have to find one on the avenue. Car services and gypsy cabs are noted by their *livery* license plates. Car services are listed in the *Yellow Pages* and gypsy cabs can be hailed on the street—if you have to. Negotiate the fare *before* you reach your destination.

Drinking Bar hours vary (all are closed before noon on Sunday), but the legal limit for closing is 4AM. On Sunday, restaurants may not serve alcohol until noon, and liquor stores are closed, but beer, which is sold in food stores, may be purchased after noon. The legal drinking age is 21, and many bars, restaurants and clubs require ID.

Hours It's a good idea to call ahead to find out if a particular restaurant or shop will be open the day and time you plan to visit. This book provides the days of the week that shops and restaurants are closed, per information available at press time, but keep in mind this information may change with the seasons, the economy or even the whim of the owner. Since museums, galleries and historical sites tend to have somewhat dependable schedules, we have provided their hours of business. However, it is best to call ahead.

Money Deak-Perera and a number of foreign banks in New York (Bank Leumi, for instance) will exchange foreign currency at current market rates. Traveler's checks may be purchased at most commercial banks.

Newspapers and Periodicals There are 4 daily papers—*The New York Times, The New York Post, The Daily News* and *Newsday*—and a number of weekly publications, including *New York Magazine, The New Yorker* and *The Village Voice*, that have excellent listings and information.

Phone As of this writing, it costs 25 cents to make a local call from a pay phone. Manhattan and the Bronx are in the 212 area code; Brooklyn, Queens and Staten Island calls require dialing the 1.718 prefix before calling, although they are still local calls.

Smoking It is illegal to smoke on all public transportation, in the lobbies of office buildings, enclosed public places, taxis, in designated areas of theaters and restaurants and in most shops and markets.

David Macaulay from *Up & Down*

Street Smarts Cities attract every type of person, and that includes the worst. It is perhaps less a commentary about New York than about our times to say that you have to be alert on the street (and in buildings, the subways, etc.) and try not to advertise helplessness, naiveté or confusion, or else you may attract some unsolicited assistance from someone who will only help him- or herself. **Common sense dos and don'ts:** Don't display your good jewelry on the subway. Don't make eye contact with people who impart a sense of danger or derangement, even though they may seem exotic to you. (View the scene from a safe distance, if you must.) Carry your purse

with the clasp side against your body. Don't carry your wallet in a back pants pocket or in a way that causes it to bulge. Don't let strangers carry packages for you. If you see trouble coming, avoid it.

Tipping A 15-20 percent gratuity is standard. In restaurants, most people simply double the sales tax. Taxi drivers are tipped 15 percent of the meter reading. Hotel bellhops and station porters expect $1 for each bag they carry. A tip is a reward for service; if you don't get it, don't pay for it.

It's Always Been New York City... and It Always Will Be

♦ Headquarters for 117 *Fortune 1000* companies (nearly 3 times more than any other city in the nation)

♦ 5000 law firms

♦ 7000 insurance carriers

♦ 94 institutions of higher learning, serving more than 379,000 students

♦ The 3 national television networks

♦ The New York and The American Stock Exchanges, and The Commodity Exchange

♦ 24 industrial parks

♦ 2 major airports

♦ 578 miles of waterfront

♦ The 2 national weekly news magazines

♦ Over 350 million sq ft of office space

♦ Hub of region whose 20 million people have a disposable income of $150 billion

♦ 1600 data processing firms

♦ 6 of the country's *Big Eight* accounting firms

♦ 14,000 restaurants

♦ 30 major department stores

♦ The Yankees, the Mets, the Rangers and the Knicks

♦ 238 theaters

♦ 150 museums

♦ A public transit system serving approximately 6 million riders a day

♦ 1400 advertising agencies

♦ The nation's largest metropolitan labor force

♦ 1300 engineering firms

Alliance for New York City Business

Phonebook
All numbers are in 212 area code unless otherwise noted.

Emergency
Ambulance	**911**
Fire	**911**
Police	**911**
Animal Medical Center	838.8100
Arson Hotline	718/403.1300
ASPCA	876.7700
Child Abuse and Maltreatment Reporting Center	800/342.3720
Coast Guard	668.7936

Orientation

Deaf Emergency Teletypewriter (police, fire and ambulance services)	800/342.4357
Dental	679.3966
Doctor	718/238.2100
Electrical Emergency	683.8830
FBI	553.2700
Lost and Found:	
Bus and Subway	718/330.3000
Taxi	869.4513
NYC Transit Authority (subway and bus information)	718/330.1234
Poison Control	340.4494
State Police–New York City	488.2710

General Information
Dow Jones Report	976.4141
Road Conditions	566.3406
Time	976.1616
Weather	976.1212
Western Union	800/325.6000

Recreation
Municipal Art Society	935.3960

Service
Able Messengers	687.5515
Cycle Messengers	925.5900
Kaufman Pharmacy (24 hr)	755.2266
Night & Day Locksmith	722.1017
Village Copy Center	924.3456
Mid City Duplicating	687.6699

Auto Rental
Avis	800/331.1212
Budget	800/527.0700
Dollar	800/365.5276
Hertz	800/654.3131
National	800/227.7368
Thrifty	800/367.2277

Auto Service
AAA Highway Condition	757.2000
AAA Road Service	757.3356

Bus Service
George Washington Bus Station	564.1114
Greyhound	971.6363
New York Bus Service	994.5500
Port Authority Bus Terminal	564.8484

Car Service
Carmel	662.2222
Davel	645.4242
Minute Man	718/899.5600

Ferry Service (To and From Manhattan)
Pan Am Water Shuttle	800/543.3779
Port Imperial (Weehawken NJ)	201/902.8850
Staten Island (St. George, Staten Island)	806.6940
Statue of Liberty and Ellis Island	269.5755

Helicopter Service
Island Helicopter	925.8807
New York Helicopter	800/645.3494
Wall Street Helicopter	943.5959
Jet Aviation Executive Air Fleet	868.1122

Heliports
Pan Am Metroport	880.6234
Port Authority W 30th St Heliport	563.4442

Limousine Service
Carey	582.6875
Fugazy	661.0100
London Towncars	988.9700

Rail Service
Amtrak	736.4545
JFK Express (Train to the Plane)	718/858.7272
Long Island Railroad	718/454.5477
Metro North	532.4900
Metropolitan Transportation Authority	878.7000
NJ Transit (Bus and Train)	201/460.8444
PATH Line	466.7649
Transit Authority	718/330.1234

Taxi/Car Service
All City Transportation	402.4747
Intra-boro	344.4763
NYC Limousine & Taxi Commission	869.4110

Manhattan Address Locator

To locate avenue addresses, take the address, cancel the last figure, divide by 2, then add or subtract the key number below. The answer is the nearest numbered cross street, approximately. For example, to find the cross street to 1650 Broadway, take half of 165 (roughly 83) and subtract 30 as indicated below. The answer is 53rd St.

To find addresses on numbered cross streets, remember–numbers above 8th St increase east or west from 5th Ave, which runs north-south. Below 8th St, Broadway is the dividing line.

Aves A, B, C, D,	Add 3	Ave of the Americas (6th Ave)	Subt. 12	Ft. Washington Ave	Add 158
1st Ave	Add 3	7th Ave	Add 12	Lenox Ave	Add 110
2nd Ave	Add 3	Above 110 St	Add 20	Lexington Ave	Add 22
3rd Ave	Add 10	8th Ave	Add 10	Madison Ave	Add 26
4th Ave	Add 8	9th Ave	Add 13	Manhattan Ave	Add 100
5th Ave		10th Ave	Add 14	Park Ave	Add 35
Up to 200	Add 13	Amsterdam Ave	Add 60	Pleasant Ave	Add 101
200-400	Add 16	Audubon Ave	Add 165	Riverside Dr (up to 165th St)	
400-600	Add 18	Broadway (23-192 Sts)	Subt. 30		Divide house number by 10
600-775	Add 20	Columbus Ave	Add 60		and Add 72
775-1286		Convent Ave	Add 127	St. Nicholas Ave	Add 110
Cancel last figure and subt. 18		Central Park West		Wadsworth Ave	Add 173
1286-1500	Add 45	Divide house number by 10		West End Ave	Add 60
Above 200	Add 24	and Add 60		York Ave	Add 4
		Edgecombe Ave	Add 134		

6

New York Speak

In George Orwell's *1984*, society is undermined by a language called *newspeak*, a series of sophisticated words and phrases that actually mean nothing at all.

New Yorkers have taken the opposite tack by cultivating a series of crude and simple phrases that, once understood, speak volumes. Here, then, is a simple guide to some of the more trenchant vocabulary:

Greetings and Such

Yo—could mean *Pardon me, Watch it, you,* or *Pleased to see you, my good man.*

How'm I doin'?—phrase used by mayoral incumbents when conducting street polls.

Watcha closin' doors—courtesy warning sometimes given to subway passengers by their conductor. Followed by shouts of *Yo!* when passengers are still boarding.

Cuisine

grab a slice—to purchase and consume pizza.

the original Ray's—refers to a famed establishment on 6th Ave at 11th St, whose name has since been used by dozens of imitators. See *grab a slice.*

a shmear—refers to a small portion of cream cheese to be smeared upon a bagel.

a regular—a cup of coffee with milk, no sugar.

a black—a cup of coffee with sugar, no milk.

wait on them—contrary to popular practice, something that waiters tell *customers* to do, as in *You're gonna have to wait on them fries.*

Geography

the Deuce—42nd St.

the Island—Long Island. Not used to refer to Staten Island. Never, but never used to refer to Manhattan.

Martha—the lower level of the George Washington Bridge.

uptown—when used in Greenwich Village or points south, refers to the area above 14th St.

upstate—anywhere north of New York City, within New York State.

over there—New Jersey.

Consumerism

Bloomie's—Bloomingdale's, as in *I saw her in Bloomie's.* Not to be confused with underwear.

boom box—portable stereo the size of a station wagon. The louder it is, the closer it must be held to one ear.

standing on line—known everywhere else in the world as *standing in line.*

fashion victim—someone whose clothes and makeup are too trendy to wear anywhere but in front of a fountain, with 2 other fashion victims.

East Village type—the flip side of *fashion victim;* someone whose clothes and makeup are too repellent to wear anywhere but on Avenue D.

sample sales—sales of leftover or sample merchandise held by manufacturers in the Garment District. Although some *garmentos* like to keep the best sales a secret (more for them), they are often advertised to the public in the back of *New York Magazine* and on flyers handed out on the street or adhered to lampposts and mailboxes.

can't afford not to buy—sales pitch. See introduction.

Lotto fever—an affliction that compels people to wait hours on line for a 1-in-26-million chance at wealth, although it's more likely they'll be crushed by a meteor while watching *Jeopardy* that night. Its seriousness increases as the jackpot grows.

two-fer—a theater coupon that entitles the bearer to 2 tickets for the price of one (plus a surcharge) to the show for which the two-fer is issued. Available next to the register at many stores; in addition, there's usually a good supply at the Convention and Visitors Bureau at Columbus Circle.

Orientation

Our Fair Streets

Don't Block the Box—warning to drivers meaning *Do not drive into the intersection until there is room to cross it.*

gridlock—the traffic jam that results when someone blocks the box.

Don't Even THINK of Parking Here—courteous street sign provided by the city. Usually ignored.

alternate parking—rules in which the side of the street one may park on is determined by the hour and day of the week.

bridge-and-tunnel people—commuters from New Jersey and Long Island. See *over there*

No Radio—posted on car windows as an appeal to thieves who might be tempted to break in without first checking to see that the radio has been removed.

New York, Home Style

A couple who recently won a free night at one of New York's most famous hotels were pleased to find their suite furnished with a bar, a refrigerator and cable TV. After availing themselves of these amenities, they found a price sheet on top of the refrigerator. Everything they had used was extra—a 3oz can of peanuts had just cost them $13! Welcome to Hospitality.

Due to unconscionable hotel expenses, many travelers have turned to bed-and-breakfasts. A time-honored tradition in Europe, these services are becoming increasingly popular here, placing out-of-town visitors in the homes of accommodating New York hosts. Beyond the attraction of saving money, most B&B guests enjoy meeting new people in the relaxed atmosphere of a home—a setting that can make a world of difference to travelers who find the city daunting.

Here are some of the B&B services with listings in the New York area. Since B&Bs are not hotels, you must call or write well in advance of your arrival:

Abode Bed & Breakfast, Ltd. PO Box 20022, New York NY 10028. 472.2000

Bed & Breakfast USA Old Sheffield Rd, South Egremont MA 01258. 413/528.2113, 800/255.7213

City Lights Bed & Breakfast PO Box 20355, Cherokee Station, New York NY 10028. 737.7049

New World Bed & Breakfast 150 5th Ave, Suite 711, New York NY 10011. 675.5600, 800/443.3800

Urban Ventures, Inc. PO Box 426, New York NY 10024. 594.5650

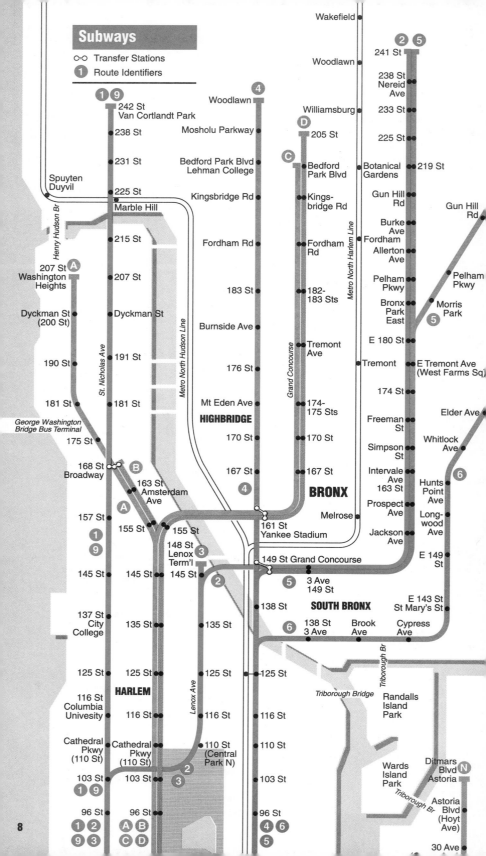

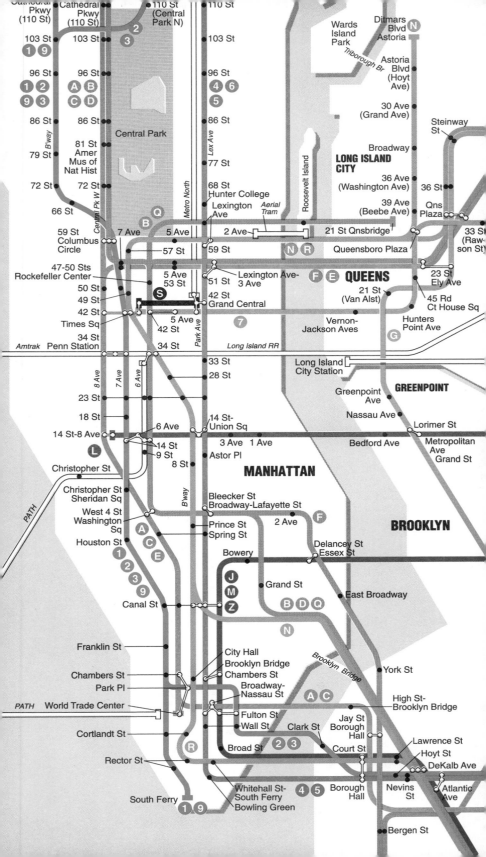

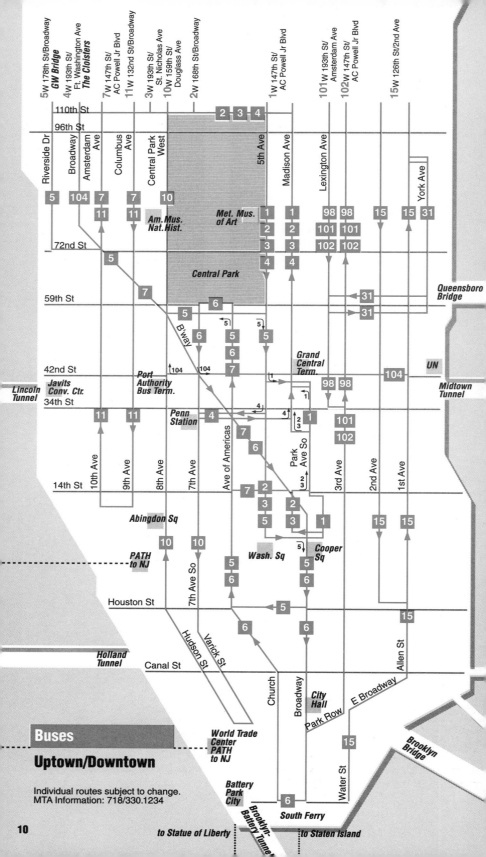

Buses

Uptown/Downtown

Individual routes subject to change.
MTA Information: 718/330.1234

10

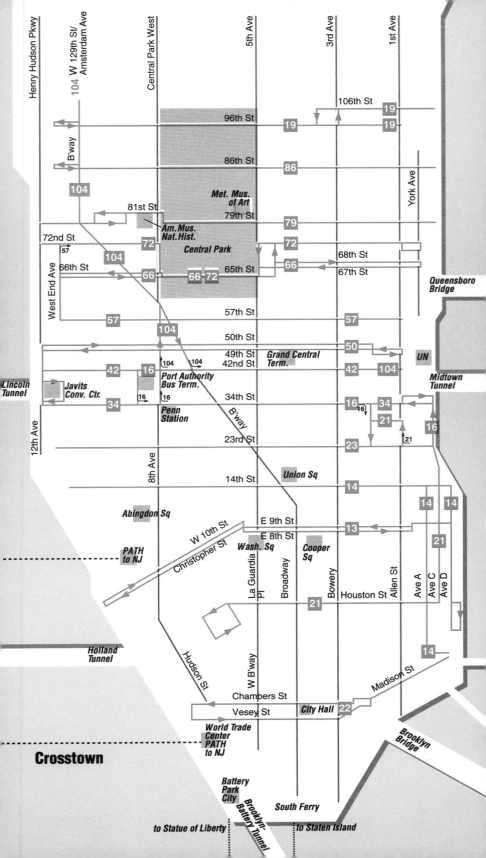

Year-Round New York City

January Ice Capades, Madison Square Garden; National Boat Show, Jacob Javits Center; Winter Antiques Show, Seventh Regiment Armory; *it's time to buckle down to work after the holidays*

February Chinese New Year, Chinatown; Westminster Kennel Club/Westminster Dog Show, Madison Square Garden; Black History Month, events in all boroughs; Annual Exhibition, National Academy of Design; Washington's Birthday Parade, 5th Ave; *spend the day visiting museums to shake off the winter blues*

March Ringling Bros. and Barnum & Bailey Circus, Madison Square Garden; St. Patrick's Day Parade, 5th Ave; American Cup Gymnastics, Madison Square Garden; Flower Show of the Horticultural Society of New York, Hudson Exhibition Pier near 53rd St; Golden Gloves finals, Madison Square Garden; Greek Independence Day Parade, 5th Ave; National Invitational Basketball Tournament, Madison Square Garden; Circle Line Cruise begins seasonal operations, W 42nd St at the Hudson River; *watch for slush puddles as you step off the curb*

April Easter Parade, 5th Ave; Greater New York International Automobile Show, Madison Square Garden; Easter lily display, Channel Gardens, Rockefeller Center; Orchid Show, New York Botanical Garden, the Bronx; Cherry Blossom Festival, Brooklyn Botanic Garden; Great Easter Egg Event, Bronx Zoo; Annual Flower Show, Macy's; New York City Ballet spring season begins, State Theater, Lincoln Center; Mets season opens, Shea Stadium, Queens; Yankee season opens, Yankee Stadium, the Bronx; *enjoy the smell of blooming honeysuckle in Central Park*

May American Youth Hostels Five Borough Bike Tour, begins and ends at Battery Park; Washington Square Outdoor Art Show, University Pl; Rose Week and Orchid Show, New York Botanical Garden, the Bronx; city beaches open; SoHo Festival; Martin Luther King Jr., Parade, 5th Ave; Memorial Day Parade, 5th Ave; Ninth Avenue International Festival, 35th-57th Sts; *get to a theater early to see the premiere of one of this summer's big movies*

June Guggenheim Concerts, Damrosch Park, Lincoln Center, and Seaside Park, Brooklyn; Metropolitan Opera/New York Philharmonic concerts, city parks; Belmont Stakes, Belmont Park, Long Island; *take an early evening stroll through Greenwich Village*

July Mostly Mozart concerts, Avery Fisher Hall, Lincoln Center; American Crafts Festival, Lincoln Center; Shakespeare in the Park, Delacorte Theater, Central Park; *watch the Independence Day fireworks from a high rooftop*

August Lincoln Center Out-of-Doors Festival, Lincoln Center Plaza; US Open Tennis Championships, Flushing Meadows, Queens; *have a sunset picnic in Riverside Park*

September New York Philharmonic season opens, Avery Fisher Hall, Lincoln Center; San Gennaro Festival, Little Italy; Washington Square Outdoor Art Show, University Pl; New York Film Festival, Alice Tully Hall, Lincoln Center; Jets football season opens, Giants Stadium, Meadowlands NJ; Giants football season opens, Giants Stadium, Meadowlands NJ; New York Is Book Country fair, 5th Ave, 48th-57th Sts; Metropolitan Opera opens, Metropolitan Opera House, Lincoln Center; Edgar Allan Poe Birthday Celebration, 84th St at West End Ave; *take a boat ride around Manhattan and enjoy the cool air*

October Ice-skating season begins, Rockefeller Center; thoroughbred racing opens at Aqueduct Racetrack, Queens; Halloween Parade, Greenwich Village; Columbus Day Parade, 5th Ave; Rangers hockey season opens, Madison Square Garden; *watch as the leaves turn and begin to fall in Battery Park*

November National Horse Show, Giants Stadium, Meadowlands NJ; New York City Ballet fall season begins, State Theater, Lincoln Center; Collegiate basketball season opens, Madison Square Garden; New York Marathon, begins at the Verrazano Bridge toll plaza; Thanksgiving Day Parade, Broadway; Virginia Slims Women's Tennis Championships, Madison Square Garden; Veterans' Day Parade, 5th Ave; The Magnificent Christmas Spectacular, featuring the Rockettes, Radio City Music Hall, Rockefeller Center; *spend an afternoon browsing in unusual shops for rare holiday gifts*

December Lighting of the Christmas tree at Rockefeller Center; Nabisco Masters Tennis Championship, Madison Square Garden; Special Christmas Star Show, Hayden Planetarium; Hannukah candle lightings at City Hall; New Year's Eve celebrations throughout the city, including the midnight run in Central Park; *watch young parents teaching their children to ice-skate at Rockefeller Center*

Cityscape

Dyckman House 1785
Broadway & 207th St.

Morris-Jumel Mansion 1765
Edgecombe Ave. & W 160th St.

Bronx

Hamilton Grange 1801
287 Convent Ave.

125th St

New Jersey

Manhattan

Broadway

5th Ave

Park Ave

Cityspire
156 W 56th St.
802' / 72 stories

Gracie Mansion 1799
East End Ave. @ 86th

Equitable Center
787 7th Ave.
750' / 58 stories

Exxon Building
1251 6th Ave.
750' / 54 stories

One Astor Plaza
1515 Broadway
730' / 54 stories

Citicorp Center
Lexington & 53rd
914' / 59 stories

One Worldwide Plaza
350 W 50th St.
778' / 47 stories

GE Building
570 Lexington Ave.
850' / 70 stories

One Penn Plaza
250 W 34th St.
764' / 54 stories

42nd St

Empire State Building
350 5th Ave.
1250' / 102 stories

34th St

Old Merchant's House 1832-33
29 E 4th St.

Stuyvesant-Fish House 1803-04
21 Stuyvesant St.

Colonnade Row 1822-23
428 Lafayette St.

Daniel Leroy House 1832
20 St. Mark's Place

14th St

203 Prince St. 1833-34

Stephen van Rensselaer House 1816
141 Mulberry St.

Sullivan St. Houses 1818; 1832

James Brown House 1817
362 Spring St.

Houston St

Edward Mooney House 1785-89
18 Bowery

Woolworth Building
233 Broadway
792' / 60 stories

World Trade Center
Church & Vesey Sts.
1350' / 110 stories

Henry St. Settlement Houses 1827; 1834

51 Market St. House 1824-25

Harrison St. Town Houses 1797-1828
317 Washington St.

2 White St. House 1809

World Financial Center
739' / 54 stories

One Liberty Plaza
Broadway & Cortlandt St.
743' / 50 stories

Shrine of the Blessed Elizabeth Seton 1793
7 State St.

Lower Manhattan

It all began in **Lower Manhattan**, bounded by **Chambers St** and the **East** and **Hudson** rivers. Here, at the confluence of these majestic rivers, the earliest explorers —Giovanni Verrazano, Esteban Gómez and Henry Hudson—first touched land.

And it was here, in 1664, that the Dutch set up **Fort Amsterdam** to protect the southern perimeter of their settlement, called *Nieuw Amsterdam*. The skyscrapers and canyons of today's **Financial District** stand where once the tiny Dutch settlement, and later the prime residential enclave of post-Revolutionary New York, flourished.

The narrow alleys of the Financial District are a reminder of the scale of colonial America. But, except for a few fragments of old foundations, not a single building erected during the 40 years of Dutch rule remains. When the British Army withdrew in 1783 after 7 years of occupation, the village of New York—which covered 10 blocks north from the Battery—lay almost totally in ruins. But once New York City pulled itself together and began to push north, it grew in swift strides. Two blocks of low-rise commercial buildings from this early surge of development have survived: the **Fraunces Tavern** block and **Schermerhorn Row**.

When **City Hall**, the one still in use today, was being built in 1811 on the northern-most fringe of town, it seemed economically prudent to face the north side with common brownstone instead of marble, because no one ever expected the building to be seen from that side. But by 1820, New York City had expanded another 10 to 15 blocks, and by 1850, the limits had pushed 2 miles north to 14th St. A fire in 1835 leveled most of Lower Manhattan, but even that didn't halt the expansion of what had become the leading commercial center and port in the new country after the War of 1812. Pearl St, on the original shoreline of the East River, was replaced with landfill by Water St, then Front St, and finally South St, where by the 1820s a thick forest of masts congested the port. The **South Street Seaport Museum** evokes that era of sea power. By 1812, lawyers, insurance companies, merchants and financiers were crowding out the families in the Financial District, whose symbolic and geographic center became the intersection of Broad and Wall Sts (so called because of the wooden wall that was the northern fortification of *Nieuw Amsterdam*). The construction of the new **Merchants' Exchange** in 1836 speeded up the area's transition to a commercial district.

Today you can visit the current commodities and stock exchanges, but in the limestone-and-glass caverns of Wall St only a few of the old public buildings remain: **Federal Hall**, the former **US Custom House** on Bowling Green, the famous **Trinity Church** (an 1846 incarnation, several times removed from the original), and the less well-known but earlier **St. Paul's Chapel**. A 20th-century masterpiece worth going out of your way to look at is the **Woolworth Building**.

Whitehall conjures up Dutch governor **Peter Stuyvesant's** mansion (renamed by his English replacement), which was on

Whitehall St. **Bowling Green**, a cattle market in Dutch days, and then a green for bowling and recreation at the center of a desirable residential area, is now an egg-shaped park at the foot of Broadway, with new neighbors but with its 1771 fence still intact. And the **Civic Center**—the cluster of old and new government buildings, some handsome, some horrendous, just north of the Financial District—has become the western boundary of Chinatown.

Created by landfill, the present **Battery Park** offers cooling breezes, welcome greenery and a panoramic view of **New York Harbor**. It's the jumping-off spot for the ferries to **Liberty Island**, **Ellis Island** and **Staten Island**, the best sightseeing buy for close-ups of the *Statue of Liberty* and the New York City skyline. The Observation Deck at the **World Trade Center** can't be beat for an aerial perspective of Manhattan Island and surrounding territory. Nearby, 2 massive developments, **Battery Park City** and the **World Financial Center**, symbolize Lower Manhattan's emergence as the new epicenter of downtown activity.

1 Ellis Island National Monument (1898, Boring & Tilton) On 1 January 1892, when a boat carrying 148 steerage passengers from the SS *Nevada* pulled into the new pier at Ellis Island, **Annie Moore**, a 15-year-old girl from Ireland, stepped ashore and became the first immigrant to set foot on the island. More than 16 million souls followed in her footsteps before it was closed in 1932. In 1907, its peak year, 1,285,349 people were admitted. The original station burned to the ground in 1897, and the present complex of buildings was already decaying during the WWII years when German aliens were imprisoned there. When it finally closed in 1954, vandals moved in and did their best to destroy what was left. In September 1990, after 8 years of restoration (at a cost of $156 million, with much of the funding spearheaded by **Lee Iacocca**), the main building opened as a museum. The fate of the other 32 buildings is undetermined, although plans to turn the hospital (where immigrants with contagious diseases were held) into an international conference center have been discussed.

On Ellis Island:

Ellis Island Museum of Immigration
Visitors can now follow the footsteps of their ancestors upon arrival in America: from the **Baggage Room**, where they dropped off what were often all of their worldly belongings; to the **Registry Room**, where they underwent 60-second medical and 30-question legal examinations; and on to the **Staircase of Separation**, which led to the ferryboats that transported the immigrants who were granted admittance (98 percent of those who arrived here) to either Manhattan or New Jersey, where they would then catch trains to points farther west. Also on view are exhibitions tracing the immigration experience: *Treasures from Home* contains personal property brought here by immigrants; the *American Immigrant Wall of Honor*, running along the sea wall overlooking the *Statue of Liberty* and the Manhattan skyline, lists the names of more than 200,000 immigrants who passed through Ellis Island. (Another wall is in the making to accommodate the overwhelming response to the museum's call for names.) In the **Oral History Studio** visitors are given the opportunity to listen to immigrants reminisce about their experiences here. The **Ellis Island Family History Center**, scheduled to open in 1992, will provide visitors with computerized access to the records of 17 million immigrants who landed on Ellis Island and other New York ports. *An RSW recommendation.* ◆ Free. Daily 9AM-5PM. Closed 25 Dec. 363.3267. Ferry from Castle Clinton in Battery Park: Fee (combination ticket to the *Statue of Liberty* available) Daily 9AM-4PM. 269.5755

1 Statue of Liberty National Monument (1886, **Frédéric Auguste Bartholdi**; pedestal, **Richard Morris Hunt**) Her official name is *Liberty Enlightening the World.* The figure alone (supported by a steel skeleton engineered by **Gustave Eiffel**) is 151ft high, not counting the pedestal, which adds another 89ft. It is a full 30ft taller than the Colossus of Rhodes, one of the Seven Wonders of the Ancient World. It is interesting to note that Bartholdi's orginal idea was to place a statue of a peasant woman holding the Lamp of Progress to Asia at the entrance to the Suez Canal—an idea that was rejected by the sultan of Egypt. When Bartholdi came to the New World from France looking for a site for *Liberty*, he traveled up and down the Eastern Seaboard and as far west as Salt Lake City, but he never for a moment seriously considered any place but Bedloe's Island, which he saw as his ship sailed into New York Harbor.

Bartholdi placed her carefully. As a ship rounds the Narrows between Brooklyn and Staten Island, she first appears on portside, striding forward in a gesture of welcome. Then, as it passes directly in front of her, she is suddenly erect and saluting. It is an optical illusion, but one of the most impressive in the world.

The island, which was renamed **Liberty Island** in 1956, was used as a quarantine station in the early 18th century, and after 1811 was the site of **Fort Wood**, which is the star-shaped structure that forms the pedestal's base. In the years between, it was a popular place for hanging pirates.

Since the statue's restoration (completed 1986), climbing the spiral staircase to its crown is easier than it had been for 100 years, but there are still 171 steps to climb after the 10-story elevator ride. The view is worth the climb, but the panorama on the ground is impressive too, as is the outlook from the promenade around the top of the pedestal, just under Miss Liberty's feet. The line to go up to the crown can be quite long. You may be turned away if you arrive after 2PM, so plan to visit in the morning. ♦ Liberty Island

Within the *Statue of Liberty*:
The Statue of Liberty Museum
Chronicles the panorama of immigration beginning with the arrival of the Dutch. The museum also contains exhibitions on the statue itself, including the torch, which was re-created and replaced during the 1986 restoration. ♦ Free. Daily 9AM-5PM. 363.3200. Ferry service is from Castle Clinton in Battery Park; frequency varies according to season. Fee. Daily 8:30AM-5PM. 269.5755

2 Battery Park The Dutch began rearranging the terrain the moment **Peter Minuit** bought Manhattan from the Indians in 1626. When they dug their canals and leveled the hills, they dumped the dirt and rocks into the bay. Over the next 300 years or so, more than 21 acres were added to the tip of the island, creating a green buffer between the harbor and the dark canyons of the Financial District. The park takes its name from a line of cannons that once overlooked the harbor. Despite its bellicose name, it has always been a place for those **Herman Melville** described as *...men fixed in ocean reveries.* ♦ Southern tip of Manhattan

Lower Manhattan

Within Battery Park:
Staten Island Ferry This must-do trip for visitors provides an excellent visual orientation to New York City. The ferry leaves from the southern tip of Manhattan, weaves through harbor traffic—from tug to sailboat, yacht to cruise ship—and travels past the *Statue of Liberty* and Ellis Island to the NE edge of Staten Island, then back again. En route, passengers have a glorious view of the city's celebrated skyline. The price, although recently doubled to 50 cents, is still one of the great bargains of our day! ♦ South St at State St

R. O. Blechman

Verrazano Monument (1909, **Ettore Ximenes**) During the celebration of the **Hudson-Fulton Festival**, an extravaganza marking the 300th anniversary of **Henry Hudson's** trip up the river, New York's Italian-Americans placed this heroic group at the edge of the harbor. It commemorates their countryman, who got here first. It should be noted that the female figure representing Discovery is trampling a book labeled *History*.

Castle Clinton National Monument (1811, **John McComb Jr.**) Originally **West Battery**, a defense post housing 28 cannons within 8ft-thick walls. It faced **Castle William** on **Governors Island**, and the pair were fortified to block the harbor from enemy attack. John McComb

Lower Manhattan

Jr. designed the original building, which fell into disuse when no enemy appeared. As an entertainment emporium called **Castle Garden**, the structure was redesigned and the main hall was used for the American premiere of singer **Jenny Lind**, presented by showman **P.T. Barnum**. For several years, it was the **Emigrant Landing Depot**, processing over 7 million immigrants before giving up that role to Ellis Island. In one of its final incarnations—1896 to 1941—the building housed the **New York Aquarium** (now at Coney Island in Brooklyn). Finally, as need for repairs became apparent and its historical importance was realized, the building was designated a National Landmark and renovations were begun. It has been restored as a fort and also serves as an information center and a ticket office for the **Statue of Liberty Ferry**, which leaves Battery Park daily on the hour (more often during the summer). ♦ Daily 8:30AM-5PM (State St at West St) 344.7220

Battery Park Control House (1905, **Heins & LaFarge**) One of 2 surviving ornate entrances to the original IRT Subway (the other is at 72nd St and Broadway), the term *control house* was coined by engineers who designed them to control crowds coming and going in 2 directions at once. ♦ State St at Battery Pl

3 Church of Our Lady of the Rosary (1800, **John McComb Jr.**) This pair of Georgian townhouses was restored in 1965 as a shrine church dedicated to **St. Elizabeth Ann Seton**, the first American-born saint, who lived here in 1801. The exteriors were faithfully returned to their original condition, giving us a small reminder of the character of this entire neighborhood at the beginning of the 19th century. ♦ Daily 6:30AM-6PM. 7-8 State St (Water St)

3 New York Unearthed In the fall of 1990, a permanent archaeological display (administered by the **South Street Museum**) opened in an annex behind 17 State St. Visitors enter at street level, where they view 10 dioramas, created by graphic designer **Milton Glaser**, that hold items like medicine vials, crucibles, cannon balls, bottles, all excavated on or near this site. On the lower level, museumgoers may board the **Unearthing New York Systems Elevator**, which takes them on a simulated dig, 4 centuries back into New York history. ♦ Closed Sa-Su. 17 State St (Water St) 669.9416

4 Peter Minuit Plaza A small park honoring the man who bought Manhattan from the Indians for a small price. The flagpole is a memorial to the first Jewish settlers, who arrived in 1654. They had been expelled from Portugal to a Dutch colony at Recife in Brazil, but were driven from there in a Portuguese conquest. On the way back to Holland, their ship was attacked by pirates, and the survivors were taken to the nearest Dutch colony, *Nieuw Amsterdam*, where they were allowed to stay. ♦ South St at State St

5 Battery Maritime Building (1906, **Walker & Gillette**) The sheet-metal-and-steel facade of this Beaux-Arts ferry terminal has been painted green to simulate copper. Before the Brooklyn Bridge was built, there were 17 ferry lines between Lower Manhattan and Brooklyn. One of them operated out of this terminal until 1938. Today it houses the small fleet of white ferries that serves Governors Island. ♦ 11 South St (Whitehall St)

6 Governors Island When the Dutch arrived here in 1624, they established their first toehold on what they called *Nut Island*. The British established their own governor here even before the Dutch governor surrendered New Amsterdam to them in 1665. Among the other historic landmarks on the island, in addition to the British **Governor's Mansion**, is the 1840 **Admiral's House**, the home of the commanding general of the army garrison stationed here from 1790 until 1966. Governors Island is now the headquarters of the US Coast Guard, which has overall responsibility for all the waterways in the country east of the Continental Divide.

The island is an idyllic place with sweeping lawns and fine old houses on traffic-free roads, a few hundred yards from the tip of Manhattan. But, alas, as a government reservation, it is closed to the public except for one day a year, usually in May or June, when they polish up the brass and welcome visitors for the annual open house. For further information, call the Support Center New York, Special Services. ♦ 668.3402

We have honored our heroes with parades along lower Broadway since Colonial times. **President Theodore Roosevelt** was the first to be showered with ticker tape, as part of his welcome home from an African safari in 1910. Flags flew and paper cascaded from every window of every building, except one. The building at 26 Broadway, across from Bowling Green, didn't even raise a flag that day. It was the home of **John D. Rockefeller's** Standard Oil, involved at the time in an antitrust suit instigated by the old *Rough Rider* himself. These days, the tons of ticker tape that once filled the air have been replaced by less festive, heavier computer printouts.

Restaurants/Nightlife: Red   **Hotels:** Blue
Shops/Parks: Green   **Sights/Culture:** Black

7 Fraunces Tavern (1907, **William Mersereau**) This Georgian brick building, built in 1719, became the tavern of **Samuel Fraunces** in 1763, and was made famous when **George Washington** said farewell to his officers here on 4 December 1783. Washington returned 6 years later to old City Hall, 5 blocks away, to take the oath of office as the first president of the new nation. The building was refurbished in 1927 in the spirit and style of the period rather than as an accurate restoration. ♦ 54 Pearl St (Broad St)

Within Fraunces Tavern:

Fraunces Tavern Restaurant ★★$$
Wood-burning fireplaces, a warm Colonial atmosphere and an all-American menu make this one of the better spots for downtown dining. ♦ American ♦ Closed Sa-Su. Reservations recommended. 269.0144

Fraunces Tavern Museum Permanent and changing exhibitions of decorative arts, period rooms, paintings, prints and manuscripts from 18th- and 19th-century America. ♦ Admission. M-F 10AM-4PM. 425.1778

KP-C

8 United States Custom House (1907, **Cass Gilbert**) This building has been called one of the finest examples of the Beaux-Arts style in New York City, and it is instantly apparent why. The granite facade is surprisingly delicate, despite Ionic columns with Corinthian capitals along the face, and an ornate frieze. Four monuments, representing Africa, Asia, Europe and America are **Daniel Chester French** and **Adolph Weinman**'s contribution to the magnificence that, despite the building's name and purpose, is somehow very un-American in

style. **Reginald Marsh** painted the murals in the wonderful oval rotunda. In 1992, the **National Museum of the American Indian** will open a permanent exhibition space here. ♦ Broadway at Bowling Green

9 Bowling Green In 1734, a group of citizens leased the space facing the Custom House as a bowling green, for an annual rent of one peppercorn. In the process, it became the city's first park. In 1729, the park was embellished with an equestrian statue of England's **King George III**, which was demolished by a crowd that assembled here to listen to a reading of the Declaration of Independence on 9 July 1776. The statue was melted down to make bullets that, according to some contem-

porary accounts, were responsible for the killing of 400 British soldiers during the war that followed. ♦ Broadway at Battery Pl

9 The Charging Bull In response to the stock-market crash of 1987, **Arturo DiModica** sculpted this 3.5-ton bronze bull—one of the emblems of the business community—to attest to the *vitality, energy and life of the American people in adversity*. Its future at this site is uncertain. ♦ Bowling Green

10 Whitehall Building (1903, **Henry J. Hardenbergh**; rear section 1910, **Clinton & Russell**) A 1930s real-estate guide said that the tenants of this building, which at the time included the **Internal Revenue Service, Quaker Oats** and the **Bon Ami Cleanser Co**, had ...*an intimate relationship with the landlord*, and no one ever moved out. There has been some turnover since the guide was written, but tenants are still (understandably) reluctant to give up what may be the best of all harbor views. ♦ 17 Battery Pl (West-Washington Sts)

In primeval Manhattan, a 60ft deep spring-fed pond, which the Dutch named **Der Kolck** (Rippling Water), covered the area from present-day Duane to White, and Baxter to Lafayette Sts. For many years it was the city's best source of drinking water. A fountain at one end, known as teawater, became the source of the city's first bottled water in the 1780s. In 1791, after slaughterhouses and tanneries managed to pollute the pond, the city decided to fill it in, a project that took 10 years. The landfill provided a site for New York's first outdoor circus in 1811, but eventually became the poor people's Coney Island, attracting what **Mayor Philip Hone** called *unbreeched little tatterdemalions* and other outcasts of society. At the nearby intersection of Baxter and Worth Sts was the infamous Five Points, considered the worst slum New York has ever produced. For a 15-year period, the former Coulter's Brewery on the present site of the New York County Courthouse, averaged 15 murders each and every night. Reformers eventually managed to cool it down, but there are New Yorkers alive today who remember when it wasn't safe to come near this neighborhood. When the New York-born gangster **Al Capone** was led off to prison on tax evasion charges in the 1930s, he said, *I shoulda never left Five Points*.

11 Downtown Athletic Club (1926, **Starrett & Van Vleck**) The arched ground-floor arcade and the window treatment of this Art Deco masterpiece are perfection itself. And the interior (**Barnett-Phillips**) is even better. The rooms are reminiscent of a 1920s ocean liner. In addition to an enclosed roof garden, the building originally contained a miniature golf course. Off-limits to women until 1978, the club now boasts a coed, cross-cultural membership. ♦ 19 West St (Morris St) 425.7000

12 Brooklyn-Battery Tunnel (1949, **Ole Singstad**) In the early 1930s, builder **Robert Moses** announced that he was going to construct a bridge between Lower Manhattan and

Lower Manhattan

Brooklyn to connect his Long Island parkway system with his West Side Highway, which reached a dead end at Battery Park. Preservationists were appalled, and even **Eleanor Roosevelt** got into the act when she wrote: *Isn't there room for some consideration of the preservation of one of the few beautiful spots that still remain to us on an overcrowded island?* City officials, noting that the city would lose $29 million a year in real-estate taxes, also opposed it. The battle raged until 1939, when **President Roosevelt** stepped in and denied federal funds for the project. The bridge became a tunnel, and Battery Park was saved. But Moses got his revenge by keeping most of the park enclosed behind a construction fence for more than 4 years, even though there was no construction going on behind it. When the tunnel finally opened, it carried more than 15 million cars in its first year. ♦ West St (Morris-Rector Sts) Manhattan to Hamilton Ave, Brooklyn

---

The neighborhood of Water Street abounds in lodging houses for sailors, dance houses and various other low places of amusement. Brothels of the worst description swarm in all directions. At night, the noisy disturbances make the darkness hideous, and are of such frequency that none can hope for a night's rest. The use of deadly weapons, too, is so common that murder provokes no sentiment of horror among the denizens of Water Street. And if they have homes, what are they? The men are often confirmed drunkards and unable to support their families honestly; the women—oh, horrible thought!—earning the wages of sin with the consent of their husbands; the children literally brought up in the gutter; the whole family huddled together at night on bare boards in one ill-built, badly ventilated and filthy room where any pretense at decency is impossible.

Anonymous, 1874

Going down Wall Street you pass what looks like an alley called New Street. The street is hardly new. The name was bestowed in 1647 because the street was the first in this part of town laid out by the new English government. **Joyce Gold**, *From Windmills To The World Trade Center*, 1982

13 26 Broadway (1885; altered 1922, **Carrère & Hastings**) This graceful giant, which curves to follow the street line, was the most important business address in the world for a half century. It was where **John D. Rockefeller** said that he had revolutionized the way of doing business ...*to save ourselves from wasteful conditions and eliminate individualism.* There is no denying he accomplished his goal, and at the same time built one of the world's greatest fortunes behind these walls—the headquarters of **Standard Oil**. When the Supreme Court dissolved the trust in 1911, the building became home to **Socony Mobil**, one of the new companies that rose from the ashes. ♦ Bowling Green

14 Delmonico's ★★$$ (1891, **James Brown Lord**) This is the last remaining reminder of **Lorenzo Delmonico**, one of the great restaurateurs of New York's gilded age, who began his career here in 1825. It was originally restricted to men, and only socially prominent men at that. Delmonico claimed, but never proved, that the columns flanking the doorway came from Pompeii. The restaurant is as elegant as ever, and the food—solid fare, like steaks and chops—is well-prepared. ♦ Continental ♦ Closed Sa-Su. 56 Beaver St (William St) Jacket, tie and reservations required. 422.4747

15 India House (1854, **Richard J. Carman**) A beautiful brownstone building built as headquarters for the **Hanover Bank**. At other times it was used as the **New York Cotton Exchange** and the main office of **W.R. Grace and Co.** It is now a private club. ♦ 1 Hanover Sq (Pearl-Stone Sts)

16 Hanover Square Named for the English royal family of the **Georges**, this was once a small London-style park at the center of a residential neighborhood. Homeowners included **Captain William Kidd**. He was considered a solid citizen in New York, but the British had a different point of view. They hanged him for piracy in 1701. He has gone down in popular history as the most bloodthirsty of pirates, and even today people poke around beaches along the coast in hopes of finding the fabulous treasure he supposedly buried. The square was also the home of New York's first newspaper, the *New-York Daily Gazette*, established in 1725. **George E. Bissell**'s statue of **Abraham de Peyster**, a one-time mayor of the city, was moved here from Bowling Green. ♦ Stone-Pearl Sts

17 United States Assay Office (1930, **James A. Wetmore**) This is a division of the US Mint for refining gold and silver bullion and melting down old coins. It is also a storehouse that contains about 55 million troy ounces of gold, worth more than $2 billion at the official government price. ♦ Old Slip (Front-Water Sts)

18 HRC Tennis Nonmembers are allowed to reserve tennis courts 24 hours in advance, but should be prepared to pay high rates for the privilege, especially during the peak hours—after 5PM during the week. ♦ Wall Street Piers 13, 14. 422.9300

19 Sloppy Louie's ★★★$$$ Before the renaissance of South Street Seaport forced **Louie** to clean up his act and raise his prices, this was a no-nonsense restaurant catering to the people who worked in the area's markets. The quality is still good enough for the most demanding fishmonger; it's just more genteel. ♦ Seafood ♦ 92 South St (Fulton-John Sts) 509.9694

19 Sweets ★$$$ This restaurant has been here on the 2nd floor of an old Schermerhorn building since 1842. When the area was restored, they spruced the place up a bit but didn't change their hours, and, like the fish market, they are still closed weekends. I think it is the freshest seafood you can eat. ♦ Seafood ♦ Closed Sa-Su. 2 Fulton St (South St) 344.9189

20 Fulton Fish Market (1907) The present home of this venerable institution, established here in 1821, was called the **Tin Building** by old salts who remembered the wooden building it replaced. The market was originally located here to serve fishing boats, but today the catch arrives in refrigerated trucks. Daytime visitors find it a quiet place, but it is a place of frantic activity between midnight and 8AM. Early risers can watch the activity wind down by taking guided tours at 6AM on the first and 3rd Thursday of each month; reservations required. ♦ South St at Fulton St. Tour information 669.9416

21 South Street Seaport Museum (Schermerhorn Row, 1811; Market Building, 1983; Pier 17 1985, The Rouse Co.; primary architects, **Ben Thompson Associates**) In the days of sailing ships, most of the port's activities were along this stretch of the East River, which has been re-created as a museum of ships. With the coming of steamships, the deeper piers on the Hudson River took away the traffic, and the East River piers went into decline. In 1967, a group of preservation-minded citizens banded together to buy some of the rundown waterfront buildings and began acquiring a collection of historic ships. Twelve years later, commercial interests

moved in and provided funds to restore the old buildings and add some new ones. The result, thanks to the ingenuity of architects **Ben** and **Jane Thompson**, is a mix of old and new made to look old. In many ways more a shopping center than a historic site, it has nonetheless revitalized a derelict neighborhood, transforming it into one of New York's most fascinating enclaves. It is especially active after 5PM, when young Wall Streeters drift by for an after-work drink in surroundings dramatically different from their high-tech offices. The streets within the Seaport are paved with stones often called Belgian blocks. Before the days of asphalt, most of the city's streets were made of these stones, which arrived here as ballast in the

holds of tall-masted sailing ships. ♦ Water St-East River (Dover-Fletcher Sts) 669.9400

Within South Street Seaport:

Titanic Memorial Lighthouse This structure originally overlooked the harbor from the Seamen's Church Institute on Water St at Cuyler's Alley. It is a memorial to the 1500 who died when the White Star Line's *Titanic* struck an iceberg in 1912. It was moved here in 1976 to mark the entrance to the Seaport. The black ball suspended above it was a time signal that was dropped from the top of the pole each day at noon, giving everyone in the neighborhood a reliable means of synchronizing his or her watch. ♦ Fulton St at Water St

Brookstone The ultimate hardware store, with one of each tool or gadget in stock displayed like an *objet d'art* next to a card describing its virtues. Each is the best in its class. You pick up a clipboard when you enter and write down your order as you go. At the end, it is delivered via a dumbwaiter from the loft above. ♦ 18 Fulton St (Front-Water Sts) 344.8108

Museum Gallery The scene of changing exhibitions covering America's nautical heritage, housed in a former warehouse built in 1868. The **Melville Research Library** is upstairs; open by appointment only. ♦ Admission. Daily 10AM-5PM. 213 Water St (Fulton St) 669.9420

Abercrombie & Fitch Sports clothing and equipment since 1892. ♦ 199 Water St (Fulton St) 809.9000

Strand Bookstore The downtown branch of New York's landmark bookstore stocks a large selection of new books at huge discounts, plus remainders and review copies. ♦ 159 John St (Front St) 809.0875

Museum Books and Charts Store New York's best source for fiction and nonfiction on ships of all kinds and the waters they sail—not to mention rare prints and ship models and otherwise hard-to-find books on New York City and its history. ♦ 209 Water St (Fulton St) 669.9453

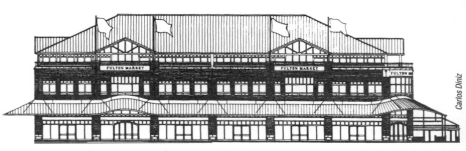

Carlos Diniz

Fulton Market A reconstruction of an 1882 structure that once housed a fresh produce and meat market. The things sold there were brought over from Long Island farms on the

Fulton Ferry, which connected Fulton St in Manhattan with Fulton St in Brooklyn. The new building houses shops and restaurants, including many stalls selling fresh food in imitation of the old market. ◆ 11 Fulton St (South-Front Sts) 608.2920

The Ships Visiting ships make Piers 15, 16 and 17 an always changing experience, but the Seaport's permanent collection includes 2 tall ships: *Peking,* a steel-hulled, 4-masted bark built in 1911, and *Wavertree,* an iron full-rigged ship built in 1885. They are open to the public every day 10AM-5PM (later in summer), as is *Ambrose,* the steel lightship that was anchored at the entrance to the harbor from 1908 until 1963, when she was replaced by a permanent tower. Boarding tickets, available on Pier 16 and at the **Visitors** Center at Fulton and Water Sts, allow admission to all exhibition galleries and daily changing events. Other ships in the South Street Seaport fleet: the working tugboat *W.O. Decker,* the steam ferryboat *Maj. Gen. William H. Hart* and the schooner *Lettie G. Howard. Pioneer,* a former cargo schooner, makes daytime and twilight sails in the harbor. Hours vary according to season. Reservations can be made within 14 days of a sail; unreserved tickets are sold each day starting at 10AM at Pier 16 (669.9400). I recommend the special exhibitions scattered throughout the Seaport, as well as the special holiday events. Two separate walking tours guide you to them. ◆ Daily 10AM-5PM. East River (South-Fulton Sts) 669.9400

Jan Hird Porkorny, Architects & Planners

Schermerhorn Row (1812) A restoration of a row of Federal-style warehouses and counting houses built by **Peter Schermerhorn**. At various times in their history, the buildings were used as stores, taverns, rooming houses and hotels. Greek Revival cast-iron storefronts

were added later when the Fulton Ferry brought more stylish customers into the area. The upper floors are the least altered from the original, but the mansard roof at the western end was added in 1868 when 2 Fulton St was the Fulton Ferry Hotel. The ground floor currently houses a variety of interesting shops, including **The Nature Company, The Body Shop** and **The Sharper Image.** ◆ Fulton-South Sts

Seaport Line Harbor Cruises The sidewheeler *Andrew Fletcher* and the steamboat *DeWitt Clinton* take 90-minute cruises April to October at varying times during the day, and in the evening they take longer music cruises with live entertainment. ◆ Tickets available at Pier 16. 964.9082

Pier 17 The stepped plaza overlooking the East River is the best part of this festive pier, which contains shops and restaurants in several varieties and price ranges. The **Brooklyn Bridge** frames the ever-changing view of the waterborne traffic, and in spite of the crowds, it is one of the city's more relaxing experiences. ◆ South St (Fulton-Beekman Sts)

22 Bridge Cafe $$ It can't be just the cachet of dining in a City Hall hangout that draws customers from all over town to this Franco-Italo-American bistro set in such an out-of-the-way place. The brick-walled bar/dining room, noisy and friendly, has a certain simple waterfront charm. The food is good, but not worth a cab ride. Stop in only if you're already in the neighborhood. ◆ International ◆ 279 Water St (Dover St) 227.3344

Most shipping these days is done by air, but the **Port of New York**, which handles more than 150 million tons a year, is far and away the most important seaport in America. New York Harbor is at the apex of a triangle that extends more than 100 miles to the east and south like a giant funnel. The Hudson River, once connected to the Great Lakes by the Erie Canal, gives access to inland America and the East River and, with 771mi of shoreline, offers more space for anchorage than any other port in the US.

Manhattan's first office building was a reed-thatched structure built in 1625 for the **Dutch West India Company**. It stood on Whitehall St between Bridge and Pearl Sts.

Restaurants/Nightlife: Red	Hotels: Blue
Shops/Parks: Green	Sights/Culture: Black

23 Brooklyn Bridge (1869–1883, John A. Roebling and Washington Roebling) This milestone in civil engineering is now more than a century old. An esthetic masterpiece as well as a structural one, the Brooklyn Bridge gets its dynamic tension from the massive strength of its great stone pylons and Gothic arches contrasted with the intricate web of its woven suspension cables. In 1855, John Roebling's proposal for a bridge across the East River was met with derision, but far-sighted residents of Brooklyn (still a separate city) pushed the idea after the Civil War. The Roebling family's fate was inextricably tied up with that of the bridge. John Roebling died as the result of an accident on a Brooklyn wharf before work on the bridge began, but his son, Washington Roebling, carried on, even when he got the bends during construction and became partially paralyzed for the rest of his life. The Brooklyn Bridge was the first bridge to use steel cables. For 20 years, it was the world's longest suspension bridge; for many more its span was the world's longest. The subject of many poems, paintings, paeans of praise and bad jokes, the bridge still gives a special uplift to the bicyclists, walkers and marathoners who cross it. ◆ Park Row, Manhattan to Cadman Pl, Brooklyn

24 127 John Street A huge electric display clock designed by **Corchia-de Harak Associates**, in addition to the nearby colorful steel patio furniture, adds a touch of whimsy to the Water St street-scape. ◆ View from Water St (Fulton-Pearl Sts)

Lower Manhattan

Verrazano-Narrows Bridge:
Completed 1964; center span 4260'; total length 6690'; maximum clearance above water 228'

Brooklyn Bridge:
Completed 1883; center span 1595'6"; total length 3455'6"; maximum clearance above water 133'

Manhattan Bridge:
Completed 1909; center span 1470'; total length 2920'; maximum clearance above water 135'.

Williamsburg Bridge:
Completed 1903; center span 1600'; total length 2793'6"; maximum clearance above water 135'.

Queensborough Bridge:
Completed 1909; major span 1182'; total length 3724'; maximum clearance above water 135'.

George Washington Bridge:
Completed 1931; center span 3500'; total length 4760'; maximum clearance above water 212'.

San Francisco's Golden Gate Bridge:
Completed 1936; center span 4199'; total length 6460'; maximum clearance above water 222'.

AAG

25 Wall Street Plaza (1973, **I.M. Pei & Associates**) This white-aluminum-and-glass structure richly deserved the award presented by the American Institute of Architects for its classical purity, rather rare in the new buildings in this area. The 1974 sculpture in its plaza, by **Yu Yu Yang**, consists of a stainless-steel slab with an opening that faces a polished disk. It is a memorial to the Cunard liner *Queen Elizabeth*, whose history is outlined on a nearby plaque. ◆ 88 Pine St (Water-Front Sts)

26 74 Wall Street (1926, **Benjamin Wistar Morris**) The nautical decoration around the arched entrance of this solid-looking building is a reminder that it was built for the **Seamen's Bank for Savings**, the second oldest savings

bank in the city. It was chartered in 1829 as a financial haven for sailors, who usually arrived in the port with their pockets full of back pay accumulated while they were out at sea. The official address of the property was 76 Wall St, but before it was changed, superstitious seamen refused to leave their money there because the numbers added up to 13. ◆ Pearl St

27 55 Wall Street (1836, **Isaiah Rogers**; remodeled and expanded 1907, **McKim, Mead & White**) One of the first buildings in the area after the *Great Fire of 1835* leveled 700 structures between Wall and South Sts, Coenties Slip and Broad St. It was built as a 3-story trading hall for the **Merchants' Exchange**, and later became the **Custom House**. After the turn of the century, its height was doubled and it became the headquarters of **First National City Bank**, which still maintains an impressive-looking branch here under its new name, **Citibank**. ◆ William-Hanover Sts

28 Bank of New York (1927, **Benjamin Wistar Morris**) The bank has occupied several buildings on this site since its founding by **Alexander Hamilton** in 1784. **Commodore Vanderbilt** used one of them as his banking headquarters. The present Georgian building is easily one of the most attractive in the area, with tall, arched windows and a broken pediment framing a handsome galleon lantern. ◆ 48 Wall St (William St)

29 30 Wall Street (1921, **York & Sawyer**; additions 1955, **Halsey, McCormack & Helmer**) When this structure was built as the **US Assay Office**, the facade of its predecessor, the **Bank of the United States** (1826, **Martin E. Thompson**), was dismantled and eventually reconstructed in the American Wing of the **Metropolitan Museum of Art**. ◆ Nassau-William Sts

29 40 Wall Street (1929, **H. Craig Severance** and **Yasuo Matsui**) This tower was built at the same time as the Chrysler Building uptown, and was secretly designed to be 2ft higher, which would have made it the tallest in the world. (But the Chrysler's builders outfoxed the bankers with a secret plan of their own.

They pushed a 123ft stainless-steel spire through a hole in their roof.) This was the headquarters of the **Bank of the Manhattan Company**, which eventually merged with the **Chase National Bank**. The **Manhattan Co.** was founded in 1799 by **Aaron Burr**, who was blocked by political rivals when he tried to charter a bank. Instead, he received legislative permission to establish a water company. In the charter's fine print, he was granted the power to loan money to property owners who wanted to connect their buildings to his wooden water mains. Before he had dug up too many streets, Burr abandoned the water business and became what he had always wanted to be: a banker. ◆ William-Nassau Sts

29 Federal Hall National Memorial (1842, **Town & Davis**; interior, **John Frazee** and **Samuel Thompson**) This Americanization of the Parthenon is one of New York City's finest examples of Greek Revival architecture and a fitting National Landmark. At the front of the building, **John Quincy Adams Ward**'s statue of **George Washington** marks the spot where the Revolutionary War general became the country's first president. The building served as the US governmental seat in the days when New York City was the nation's capital. Doric columns 32ft high span the building's face. Enter for a self-guided tour of the building as well as exhibitions organized by both the **Historic Hudson Valley** and the **Museum of the American Constitutional Government**. ◆ 15 Pine St, also 26 Wall St (Nassau St) 344.3830

30 Morgan Guaranty Trust Company (1913, **Trowbridge & Livingston**) If ever a single man epitomized the American capitalist, **J.P. Morgan** (1837–1913) was that man. **John Pierpont Morgan Jr.**, who took control of the empire the year this building was built, like his father, was apparently not without enemies. On 16 September 1920, at the height of the lunch hour, a carriage parked on Wall St suddenly exploded, killing 33 people, as well as the horse, and injuring 400. The marble walls of the building still have scars from the disaster. No reason was ever determined, and the owner of the carriage was never found. ◆ 23 Wall St (Broad St)

Wall Street's first financier was probably Frederick Philipse, whose house was at the northern end of New Amsterdam. Indian wampum, made from Long Island clam shells, was the legal tender of the colony, and in 1665, Philipse bought several barrels of it, creating an artificial shortage. Anyone who needed any wampum to settle debts and continue in business had to buy it from Philipse, at his rates.

New York City's skyline was seriously altered during WWII, when there was a 15-story dimout limit.

Restaurants/Nightlife: Red   **Hotels:** Blue
Shops/Parks: Green   **Sights/Culture:** Black

31 New York Stock Exchange (1903, **George B. Post**; upper section 1923, **Trowbridge & Livingston**) The NYSE's giant portico, colonnade and sculptures express austerity and security—key design goals of the early 1900s. The solemn facade masks the leading-edge technology that drives the exchange today. That technology, integrated with the judgment and skills of the trading floor's professionals, provides investors with the broadest, most open and most liquid equities market in the world. Before entering the gallery that overlooks the trading floor, visitors go through an exhibition area that includes visual presentations and frequent lectures on the history and workings of the institution. A multilingual, prerecorded explanation of what's happening 3 floors below is provided from a glass-enclosed gallery overlooking the floor. The tickets required for tours (M-F 9:15AM-3PM) are dispensed at 20 Broad St; try to arrive before noon as there are a limited number of tickets. ◆ Free. Visitors Gallery M-F 9:15AM-3:45PM. 20 Broad St. 3rd floor. 656.5168

32 Bankers Trust Building (1912, **Trowbridge & Livingston**) The pyramid on top of this 31-story tower became the corporate symbol of **Bankers Trust**, and remained its logo even after the bank moved its main headquarters up to 280 Park Ave in 1963. ◆ 16 Wall St (Nassau St)

Within Bankers Trust:

La Tour D'Or ★$$$ A dramatic restaurant in the 31st-floor space that was once a *pied-à-terre* for **J.P. Morgan**. The views extend in every direction, but the best is from the comfortable bar that overlooks the harbor and the *Statue of Liberty*. The Monday and Tuesday buffet lunches are popular among Wall Streeters. I always order the medallion of pork with Black Forest mushrooms. ◆ French ◆ Closed Sa-Su. 233.2780

33 Irving Trust Company Building (now The Bank of New York) (1932, **Voorhees, Gmelin & Walker**) **Ralph Walker**'s only skyscraper, is built on what was called the most expensive piece of real estate in the world in the 1930s. He said his design was one of superimposed rhythms, a steel frame draped outside with rippling curtains of stone. The gold, red and orange Art Deco mosaics, created by **Hildreth Meière**, in the banking room off Wall St make a visit rewarding even if you are not a depositor. ◆ 1 Wall St (Broadway)

34 Bank of Tokyo Trust (1895, **Bruce Price**; alterations 1975, **Kajima International**) The modernization has taken place behind Price's

pillars. The 8 Greek ladies, by **J. Massey Rhind**, still guard the building from their perch on the 3rd floor. Look further up and you'll find more of them on an even higher perch. ◆ 100 Broadway (Pine St)

35 Waldenbooks This branch of the national chain is spacious, and many of its departments are separated by alcoves. Especially strong in business, technology and science. Also, wide selections in cooking, history and sports. Many remainder and sale books. ◆ Closed Sa-Su. 57 Broadway (Exchange Pl) 269.1139

36 Trinity Church (1846, **Richard Upjohn**) This historic, architectural and religious monument, with its strong, square tower punctuated by an exclamation point spire, has the good fortune to stand at the head of Wall St. The shaded, grassy cemetery—a welcome open space in this neighborhood—offers a noontime haven for office workers. The cemetery came first, and such notables as **Alexander Hamilton, William Bradford** and **Robert Fulton** are buried here (marked by placards that are especially helpful when gravestone inscriptions have worn away). This is the third Trinity Church on this site. The original was built in 1698, and paid for by taxation of all citizens, regardless of religion, because the Church of England was the official religion of the colony. It burned in 1776. The second was demolished in 1839. The present Trinity was designed in 1846; **Richard Morris Hunt**'s brass doors were added later. The **Chapel of All Saints**, designed by **Thomas Hash**, was built in 1913; the **Bishop Manning Memorial Wing**, by **Adams & Woodbridge**, in 1965. In 1989, in an effort to restore the building to its original appearance, workers began the time-consuming process of steaming away a layer of parafin that was mistakenly applied to the building in the 1920s to keep it from crumbling; beneath the parafin are layers of coal dust and pollutants that have made this building blacker than many other historic buildings. The result, rosy sandstone as Upjohn had intended, is quite a surprise to the thousands of Wall Streeters who, everyday for years, had been walking past what they believed to be a very dark building. Work is expected to be completed by November 1991. ♦ Services: M-F 8AM, noon; Sa 9AM, noon; Su 9, 11:15AM. Museum: free. M-F 9-11:45AM, 1-3:45PM; Sa 10AM-3:45PM; Su 1-3:45PM. Broadway at Wall St. 602.0800

37 American Stock Exchange (1930, **Starrett & Van Vleck**) Known until 1953 as the *Curb Exchange*. Before 1921, its brokers stood at the corner of Wall and Broad Sts and communicated with one another through hand gestures. ♦ 86 Trinity Pl (Thames-Rector Sts) 306.1000

Lower Manhattan

37 Syms Located in the heart of the Financial District, this famous discount house is primarily for men and women who like to dress in a middle-of-the-road style. Sizes range from lean and trim to 46 portly, at discounts of 30-50 percent. Unlike most other discount stores, Syms leaves the original labels on the stock, and each price tag shows both the nationally advertised price and Syms' price. There are double-breasted and single-breasted suits in conservative pinstripes, herringbones and Harris tweeds, double-pleated slacks as well as jeans, and all the accessories to go with them. But the greatest strength is the shirt department, which takes up nearly the entire 2nd floor. You can't beat the selection or the prices—everything from Viyella and pure cotton to cotton/poly for the drip-dry set. Finally, on the 3rd and 4th floors are the women's departments, which feature designer suits, dresses, separates and coats. ♦ Closed M. 42 Trinity Pl (Rector St) 797.1199

Most visitors to the World Trade Center are perfectly satisfied to look out at the view from the Observation Deck. There are a few intrepid souls, however, for whom the towers represent an invitation to perform a dangerous feat. On 7 August 1974, circus performer **Philipe Petit** took a 45min walk on a 131ft steel cable running from the North to the South Tower. When asked why, he explained: *When I see 3 oranges, I have to juggle, and if I see 2 towers, I have to walk.* In July 1975, **Owen Quinn**, a skydiver and dock builder, dove from the 110th floor of the North Tower. At about the 60th floor, after he had gained enough momentum, he opened his parachute. The entire trip took 2 minutes. On 27 May 1977, a mountain climber named **George Willig** scaled the South Tower in a 3¹/₂ hr climb. *I thought I'd like to try it, he said. RSW: I was having lunch at Windows the day of Willig's climb. There was great excitement—what started as a quiet murmuring from table to table, waiter to waiter, suddenly escalated to swarms of police and reporters.*

The World Trade Center has more than a half-million sq ft of glass.

38 Trinity and **U.S. Realty Buildings** (1906, **Francis H. Kimball**) The Trinity Building replaced Richard Upjohn's 5-story 1840 building of the same name, which was the first office building in the city. After the present Gothic structure was built, its developers, **US Realty Company**, acquired a similar 50ft plot next door and constructed an identical 21-story building for their own use, with a shared service core along Thames St. Fantastic creatures sporting lions' heads and eagles' wings watch as you approach the entrance to the Trinity Building. ♦ 111 and 115 Broadway (Cedar St)

39 Equitable Building (1915, **Ernest R. Graham**) A massive structure that is noteworthy not for any particular stylistic qualities, but for its size, which changed the history of building in New York. This 40-story block contains 1.2 million sq ft of office space on a site of slightly less than one acre. The public outcry when it was completed in 1915 caused the creation of the 1916 zoning laws, the first ever in the country, to ensure a minimum of light and air on city streets in the future. ♦ 120 Broadway (Pine-Cedar Sts)

40 Marine Midland Bank (1967, **Skidmore, Owings & Merrill**) One of Lower Manhattan's more successful modern-style steel-and-glass high rises. This sleek black building has an appropriateness of scale, largely due to a spandrel design that helps it fit into its older, more ornate surroundings. A vermilion cube by sculptor **Isamu Noguchi** enlivens the plaza. ♦ 140 Broadway (Liberty St)

41 Chase Manhattan Bank (1960, **Skidmore, Owings & Merrill**) Built as a catalyst to revitalize the aging Wall Street area, the bank's aluminum-and-glass face rises an impressive 813ft, and it is still a fittingly imposing base for the Rockefeller banking empire. The designers gave the tower a trend-setting feature—its large plaza, with *A Group of Four Trees* by **Jean Dubuffet** and a sunken sculpture garden by **Isamu Noguchi**. ♦ 1 Chase Manhattan Pl (Liberty-Nassau Sts)

42 Federal Reserve Bank of New York (1924, **York & Sawyer**) This is the banker's bank, where the nations of the world maintain the balance of trade by the storage and exchange of gold, which is housed on 5 underground floors. The riches inside the building are represented on the outside in the best Renaissance style, with **Samuel Yellin**'s finely detailed ironwork adding to the serene beauty of the limestone-and-sandstone facade. Free tours of the gold vaults are available on a limited basis, weekdays. Reservations are required at least one week in advance. ♦ 33 Liberty St (William-Nassau Sts) 720.6130

43 Louise Nevelson Plaza A small triangular park with large steel sculptures created by the late artist **Louise Nevelson**. A popular lunch spot. ♦ Bounded by Maiden Ln, Liberty and William Sts

43 Whitney Museum of American Art The Whitney's downtown branch hosts temporary exhibitions of contemporary American art. ♦ Closed M. 33 Maiden Ln. Lower Level of Federal Plaza. 570.3600

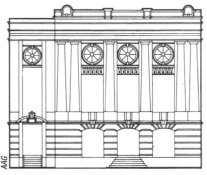

44 Chamber of Commerce of the State of New York (1901, **James B. Baker**) An ornate Beaux-Arts edifice, ponderous from its heavy stone base to its massive top, with Ionic columns adding to its almost predatory look. ♦ 65 Liberty St (Liberty Pl)

45 McDonald's $ You'll know that this is not your typical home of the golden arches as soon as the tuxedo-clad doorman welcomes you and leads you to the glass-and-wood-dining room, where a pianist is serenading diners. The food is standard McDonald's fare, except espresso and cappuccino are served from silver trays and pastries come from **Dumas**, an Upper East Side bakery. Worried about the market? A Dow Jones ticker tape looms above. ♦ Fast food ♦ 160 Broadway (Fulton St-Maiden Ln) 285.9026

The **Trinity Building** stands on the site of the **King's Arms Tavern**, a favorite watering hole in English Colonial days. Its owner, **Roger Baker**, was fined and tried for treason when he claimed that the English king's nose was made of wax. In 1702, not long after he became Royal Governor, **Lord Cornbury** rode his horse into the bar and ordered a whiskey for himself and water for the beast, then he clattered out, breaking chairs and tables on the way. Cornbury was **Queen Anne**'s cousin, so his eccentricities were overlooked. But New Yorkers knew they had their hands full when his first speech was about the great beauty of his wife. He was especially entranced by her ears, and commanded every man in the room to feel them for himself. The local citizenry was scandalized when he appeared around town wearing his wife's clothing, an affectation he explained was quite proper since he was the representative of the Queen, whom he felt he closely resembled. During a yellow fever epidemic, Cornbury moved to Jamaica (Queens), where the local Presbyterians offered him the use of their parsonage. He repaid them by confiscating their church and all their property and giving it to the Anglican Church. In spite of his profit-making schemes, Cornbury owed money to hundreds of his cousin's subjects and was eventually thrown into debtors' prison, where he stayed for nearly a year before sailing quietly back to London.

46 Century 21 A larger version of the Brooklyn discount department store. Three bustling floors of top-quality housewares, clothing, toys and electronics with popular labels intact. Even Wall Street loves a bargain. Opens at 7:45AM. ♦ Closed Su. 22 Cortlandt St (Broadway-Church St) 227.9092

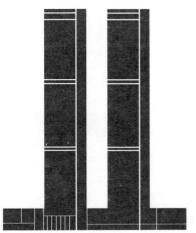

47 World Trade Center (1962–77, **Minoru Yamasaki & Associates** and **Emery Roth & Sons**) The World Trade Center consists of 6 buildings—the towers, 3 low plaza buildings and the 22-story **Vista Hotel**—which form a semicircle around a 5-acre plaza. All buildings are connected at ground level by the concourse, a vast shopping mall and pedestrian walkaround filled with 60 shops, banks and the concourse restaurants and gathering places. The twin monolithic towers are, at 110 stories, the highest and most prominently sited of any buildings in the city, rising as an architectural gateway to Lower Manhattan. The World Trade Center offers 9.5 million sq ft of office space, and is home to more than 1200 trading firms and organizations. Some 50,000 people work in the complex, and over 80,000 visitors come daily. Almost 2000 cars can park in the underground garages, and it is a major station for city subway and PATH lines. ♦ Church St (Liberty-Vesey Sts)

Within the World Trade Center:

The Observation Deck Floor-to-ceiling windows at the top of 2 WTC, the more southerly of the twin towers, are marked with unobtrusive diagrams to explain what you are seeing. The walls behind you on all 4 sides of the building display the history of world trade. The view from the deck has been called the best in the world, but if you want a better one, take the escalator up to the rooftop promenade. Another thrill: take the 1 1/4-mile, 58-second elevator ride from the mezzanine level of 2 WTC to the 107th floor. Tickets are sold on the mezzanine level of 2 WTC. ♦ Admission. Daily 9:30AM-9:30PM. Check for holiday schedule. 466.7377

WINDOWS ON THE WORLD

The Restaurant at Windows on the World ★$$$$ **Warren Platner** designed this spectacular terraced restaurant at the top of 1 WTC so that every table has an unobstructed view to the south and east. The menu changes frequently, and traditional international selections are augmented by sophisticated original creations like fricassee of lobster with spinach and cucumbers, or sautéed venison with juniper berries, wild mushrooms and galette potatoes. I particularly like the wine list, which

Lower Manhattan

offers more than 600 choices. ♦ Continental ♦ Jacket, tie and reservations required. 938.1111

The Hors d'Oeuvrerie at Windows on the World ★$$ A place to sip a cocktail, snack on a wide assortment of delicacies, listen to piano music from 4:30PM, dance from 7:30PM until 1AM, and marvel at the view to the south and west. ♦ International ♦ Jacket required. Reservations recommended for Su brunch. 938.1111

Cellar in the Sky ★★★★$$$$ A small, 40-seat area at Windows on the World, where there are no windows, but a wonderful experience that more than makes up for it. A 7-course prix-fixe dinner, with appropriate wines, is served here each evening. The menu, which changes biweekly, includes heavenly entrees like steamed salmon with tomato-and-champagne sauce, and lobster surrounded by pasta topped with pesto. The service is attentive, and background music is provided by a classical guitarist. ♦ Continental ♦ Closed Su. Jacket, tie and reservations required. 938.1111

Skydive $$ An informal restaurant with a view from the 44th floor of 1 WTC, featuring omelets to order and a free buffet every night. Live music Wednesday and Friday. ♦ American ♦ Closed Sa-Su. 938.1958

Classic Books A wide selection of fact, fiction, travel and business titles, plus several tables of remainders. ♦ 133 WTC. Concourse. 466.0668

Benjamin Book & Co. Given the location, it's no wonder this bookseller specializes in business and computer titles. An interesting and helpful array of travel books is here too, as well as a full range of fact and fiction. ♦ Closed Su. 408 WTC. Concourse. 432.1103

The hole dug for the **World Trade Center** towers required the removal of 1.2 million cubic yards of earth, later used to create part of Battery Park City. It is estimated that on a clear day the twin towers of the World Trade Center can be seen from as far away as 53 miles. From the towers, one can, theoretically, see equally as far.

The Market Restaurant ★$$$ A restaurant of the sort that existed a century ago, featuring generous cuts of meat, fresh seafood and vegetables and an outstanding wine list in a modern setting on the concourse level near the PATH station. ♦ American ♦ 938.1155

The Big Kitchen ★$ A collection of 8 different fast-food kiosks arranged on the concourse level like a big street fair, serving everything from hamburgers to fresh oysters. ♦ International ♦ 938.1153

Subway Stations IRT, BMT and IND lines all stop here. See page 8 for more information.

PATH Station The Port Authority-operated PATH (Port Authority Trans-Hudson) rapid rail transit line, serving Hoboken, Newark, Jersey City and Harrison NJ, has its downtown terminus here. ♦ PATH Sq (lowest level)

TKTS Half-price day-of-performance tickets available for evening performances of Broadway and Off Broadway shows. Wednesday, Saturday and Sunday matinee tickets sold from 11AM-5:30PM the day before the performance. ♦ M-F 11AM-5:30PM; Sa 11:30AM-3:30PM. 2 WTC. Mezzanine. 354.5800. Also at: Broadway at 47th St

Commodities Exchange Four different exchanges trading in gold, silver, coffee, cotton and other commodities in a frenzied setting, somewhat like an auction. Watch the activity from a glass-enclosed balcony overlooking the trading floor. ♦ M-F 9:30AM-3PM. 4 WTC. 9th floor. 938.2018

In 1798, when the **Park Theater** opened around the corner in what is still known as **Theater Alley**, the east side of City Hall Park became New York's theater district. The stretch of Park Row between Ann and Frankfort Sts also became the headquarters of the city's newspapers. At the beginning of the 20th century, when there were 14 dailies in New York, 12 were published in this 3-block stretch. The proximity of the theaters was only one reason. Having City Hall across the street was another, as was the nearness of the Financial District. But possibly most significant of all was Park Row's convenience to the nearby seaport. Arriving ships from abroad provided the only source of international news. In the 1860s, a steam engine located on Spruce St between William and Nassau Sts provided power through a series of India rubber belts that ran over streets and through backyards and alleys. 41 Park Row (1889, **George B. Post**), between Beekman and Spruce Sts, was once the home of *The New York Times*. The 1872 statue of **Benjamin Franklin**, who described himself in his own epitaph as a printer, marks the little triangle once known as **Printing House Square**, now called **Pace University Plaza**.

Austin J. Tobin Plaza The 5-acre space between the towers is graced with a fountain that surrounds a 25ft bronze construction by **Fritz Koenig**. The granite pyramid at the entrance is by **Masyuki Nagare**, and the stainless-steel abstract sculpture is by **James Rosati**. There is an **Alexander Calder** stabile just outside on Church St. Other sculpture is often temporarily displayed on the windy plaza, which is frequently used as a setting for concerts and other events. Other works of art commissioned for the World Trade Center include **Louise Nevelson's** *Sky-Gate New York* on the mezzanine of 1 WTC, and a 3-ton tapestry by **Joan Miró**, which hangs in the mezzanine of 2 WTC.

Vista International Hotel $$$$ (1981, **Skidmore, Owings & Merrill**) This sleek yet welcoming Hilton International, with views of the Hudson River from the highest floors, is packed during the week with businesspeople who want proximity to Wall St and the World Trade Center, and on weekends, with visitors who want to be near the sights and charms of Old New York. Free weekend shuttle buses uptown make it a pleasure to venture out of the neighborhood, too. A fitness center provides a free indoor swimming pool, jogging track, sauna and exercise rooms (fee for racquetball and massage). The business center offers secretarial services, personal computers and cellular phones. An added tariff buys a room or suite on one of the Executive Floors, with access to a special lounge for complimentary cocktails, as well as breakfast and other perks. The adjacent concourse of the World Trade Center is a bazaar of stores and restaurants. There's a comfortable spot in the lobby for express breakfast or lunch, and the **Tall Ships Bar** (drinks, piano music, hearty potpies and sandwiches), which becomes a jammed singles bar after work. ♦ 3 WTC. 938.9100, 800/HILTONS

Within the Vista International Hotel:

American Harvest ★★$$$ This brave attempt at translating American regional dishes into fine restaurant fare is often quite successful. Appetizers, vegetables and desserts are notably delectable, and are served in plush, elegant and quiet contemporary/traditional surroundings. Polite, eager service. Good American wine list. Complimentary parking. ♦ American ♦ Closed Sa-Su. 2nd floor. Jacket required. 432.9334

Greenhouse Bar and Restaurant
★★★$$ The skylight roof allows an unusual view of the World Trade Center twin towers soaring above, and lets the sun stream through to the beautifully planted gardenlike room set with rattan chairs. Good salad plates, omelets, unusual sandwiches, moderately priced main courses, unique breads and tempting desserts make it one of the best informal hotel restaurants. The wine bar, with tastes by the glass served at the table by a knowledgeable sommelier, is an added attraction. Excellent for breakfast, lunch, snacks. ♦ American ♦ 2nd floor. 938.9100

48 Battery Park City (Master plan 1979, **Cooper, Eckstut Associates**) When this eclectic complex of 14,000 rental and cooperative apartments is finally complete, it will support a population larger than that of Bozeman MT (the residential population will be approximately 25,000). The total development cost of this 92-acre landfill site adjacent to the Financial District is estimated at $4 billion, including the privately financed 1.5-billion-dollar World Financial Center. The master plan divides the blocks into parcels, with individual developers for each one, thus avoiding a superblock appearance. About 30 percent of the site is open park land—parks are linked by the 1.2mi landscaped waterfront. **The Espla-**

nade (landscape architects: **Stanton Eckstut**, Liberty St-West Thames St; Stanton Eckstut, **Susan Child Associates**, artist **Mary Miss**, South Cove; **Carr, Lynch, Hack & Sandell**, North Cove Yacht Harbor-Chambers St), which extends the entire length of the site, provides a perfect place to relax and watch the river traffic. Access for the handicapped has been incorporated into the overall design.

The first completed section was **Gateway Plaza** (1982), a trio of 34-story towers and three 8-story buildings that provide 1712 residential units. The structures, designed by **Jack Brown** and **Irving Gershorn**, were begun before the master plan was established. Developed by **Marina Towers Association**, the Gateway was fully occupied by 1983.

The architects who worked on **Rector Place** (1988), the second phase of residential construction, include **Charles Moore, Ulrich Franzen, Conklin Rossant** and **Mitchell Giurgola** and **Davis Brody & Associates**. Developed under the master plan, this 9-acre plot contains 2200 apartments grouped around the one-acre, landscaped Rector Park (landscape architects, **Vollmer Associates**).

The third phase, **Battery Place** (scheduled for a mid-1990s completion), consists of 2800 residential units on 9 parcels located between Rector Pl and Pier A. The architects involved in the initial 3 buildings are **The Ehrenkrantz Group & Eckstut; Gruzen Samton Steinglass;** and **James Stewart Polshek & Partners**. The southern end of this area will include the **Museum of Jewish Heritage**; a hotel; the largest residential building in this complex; as well as **South Gardens**, a 3-acre park designed by architect **Alexander Cooper**, landscape architect **Nicholas Quennell** and artist **Jennifer Bartlett**.

At the northernmost tip of the complex is an 8-block area that runs from the World Financial Center to Chambers St. A new **Stuyvesant High School**, expected to open in 1991, is being designed by **Alexander Cooper & Partners**. ♦ Pier A (Battery Park-Chambers St)

Winter Garden Courtyard by Carlos Diniz

49 World Financial Center (1981, **Cesar Pelli & Associates**) More than 8 million sq ft of office, retail and recreational space have been created here on landfill produced by the construction of the World Trade Center across West St. There are four 33- to 50-story office towers, two 9-story buildings designated as gatehouses, a 4-acre plaza and a glass **Winter Garden**, whose most dramatic feature is 16 palm trees, each a uniform 45ft high. Tenants include **Bally of Switzerland, Caswell-Massey, Godiva Chocolatier, Manufacturers Hanover Trust, Rizzoli International Bookstore** and **Plus One Fitness Clinic**. The **Courtyard**, a 2-level outdoor piazza, houses 4 international restaurants and cafes. The **World Financial Center Plaza** is a stellar example of public space design: 3 ½ beautifully landscaped acres of park land on the Hudson River with 2 twin soft reflecting pools. The WFC presents an ongoing series of music, dance and theater events as well as visual arts installations, and is world headquarters for companies like **American Express, Merrill Lynch** and **Dow Jones**. ◆ Daily 7AM-1AM. West St (Vesey-Liberty Sts)

Standouts among the restaurants and stores:

Hudson River Club ★★$$$ The menu specializes in food from the Hudson River Valley: trout, shad roe and smokehouse products, as well as regional wines. The clublike atmosphere, with its plush banquette seating and armchairs, has a breathtaking view of North Cove Harbor Marina and the *Statue of Liberty*. Three dining rooms accommodate 190 people; there are also private dining areas that seat from 10 to 200. ◆ American ◆ 4 WFC. Upper level. Reservations recommended. 786.1500

Restaurants/Nightlife: Red	**Hotels**: Blue
Shops/Parks: Green	**Sights/Culture**: Black

Le Pactole ★$$$$ This 10,000sq ft restaurant features the talents of French chef **Willi Kraus**, formerly of Le Perigord. For the adventurous, a tournabroche—a spit-roasting machine from France—is used to prepare grilled game birds, lamb and whole pineapples roasted with honey. Included are a lounge area, where lighter fare can be had, and separate banquet facilities for business clients, with amenities like telex and fax machines and audio and video facilities. On weekends, there is dancing in a private dining room. A gourmet shop delivers meals to offices and homes in the Wall Street area. Gigantic windows overlook the Hudson.
♦ French ♦ 2 WFC. 2nd level. Reservations recommended. 945.9444

Pipeline ★★$$ Designed by **Sam Lopata** to look like an oil refinery, this vast space seats 120 indoors and 150 more outside. The interior features brightly colored pipes, catwalks, ladders and a great video/jukebox system. Chef **Gonzalo Figueroa** creates dishes like corn chowder, and penne with tuna and white-bean salad; for dessert, the chocolate truffle cake and bread pudding are musts. Also featured is what Pipeline calls *Battery Park Picnic Baskets*, which, as you've probably guessed, are special lunch and dinner takeout boxes.
♦ American ♦ 2 WFC. Ground floor. Reservations recommended. 945.2755

Au Mandarin $ An authentic Mandarin menu, popular at lunch. ♦ Mandarin ♦ Winter Garden. Ground floor. 385.0310

Donald Sacks ★$ Good potpies, salads and grilled sandwiches are served at this outpost of SoHo's famed takeout shop. Here, you can relax in the elegant mahogany-and-marble room while contemplating an unexpected river view. I always sit by the windows. ♦ American ♦ 2 WFC. Courtyard. Lunch reservations recommended. 619.4600

Barneys New York Architect **Peter Marino** designed the 10,000sq ft men's store overlooking the Hudson. Keeping its Wall Street clientele firmly in mind, Barneys features fine collections of sportswear, outerwear, furnishings, formal wear, shoes and a special shirting collection from **Truzzi**. During Special Designer Weeks, when different designers are featured, the store makes made-to-measure clothing available at the ready-to-wear-cost.
♦ 2 WFC. Upper level. 945.1600. Also at: 7th Ave at 17th St. 929.9000

Mark Cross A quality accessory store that carries a full range of signature luggage, billfolds, handbags, desk sets and jewelry boxes.
♦ 2 WFC. Upper level. 945.1411. Also at: 645 5th Ave. 421.3000

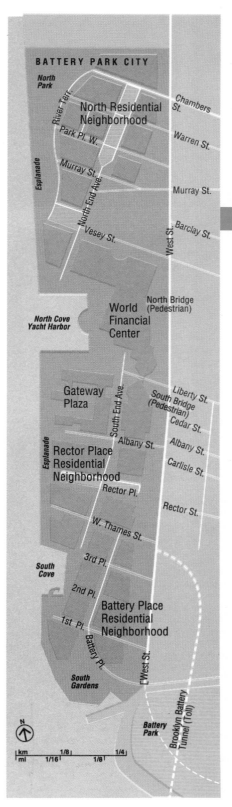

BATTERY PARK CITY

North Park

River Terr.

North Residential Neighborhood

Chambers St.

Park Pl. W.

Warren St.

Esplanade

Murray St.

North End Ave.

Murray St.

West St.

Barclay St.

Vesey St.

North Bridge
(Pedestrian)

World Financial Center

North Cove Yacht Harbor

Liberty St.

Gateway Plaza

South End Ave.

South Bridge (Pedestrian)

Cedar St.

Esplanade

Albany St.

Albany St.

Rector Place Residential Neighborhood

Carlisle St.

Rector Pl.

Rector St.

W. Thames St.

3rd Pl.

South Cove

2nd Pl.

Battery Place Residential Neighborhood

1st Pl.

Battery Pl.

West St.

South Gardens

Brooklyn Battery Tunnel (Toll)

N

Battery Park

km
mi   1/16   1/8   1/8   1/4

Tahari Tahari's full line of sophisticated clothing for women, including scarves, jewelry and handbags. The shop also contains antiques from **Ellie Tahari**'s collection. ♦ 2 WFC. Upper level. 945.2450. Also at: 802 Madison Ave. 535.1515

CD Street Lots of CDs—which you can listen to on the headphones that hang from the wall—and fast, computer-aided service. Audio equipment and accessories too. ♦ 4 WFC. Lobby. 587.0093

Gallery of History Documents autographed by the famous—from a signed photograph of the *Rolling Stones* to a draft of **Albert Einstein**'s first relativity treatise. ♦ Winter

Lower Manhattan

Garden. Ground floor. 945.1000

50 195 Broadway (1917, **William Welles Bosworth**) There are more columns on the facade of this building, built as headquarters for the **American Telephone & Telegraph Co**, than on any other building in the world. And there are even more inside; the lobby is like some ancient Athenian temple. The ornamental panels over the Broadway entrance, as well as the bronze seals on the lobby floor and the other interior decorative elements are by **Paul Manship**, whose best-known work in New York is the *Prometheus* fountain in Rockefeller Plaza. When AT&T moved uptown to Madison Ave at 55th St in 1984, it took along **Evelyn Longman**'s sculpture *Spirit of Communication*, which had been on the pinnacle of this building for more than 65 years. ♦ Dey-Fulton Sts

When the first burials took place in St. Paul's and Trinity churchyards, they provided employment for gentlemen licensed by the city as **Inviters to Funerals**. Dressed in somber black, with long black streamers attached to their stovepipe hats, they marched in pairs from house to house extolling the virtues of the recently deceased. As they walked through the streets, one tolled a bell and the other pounded the pavement with a long black pole. They served as masters of ceremonies at the funeral itself, and their fee was determined by the turnout. At the gravesite, the 12 pallbearers were given souvenir spoons engraved with figures of the 12 apostles, which were usually so badly cast they were known as monkey spoons. Female relatives were given a mourning brooch or ring, which had a compartment containing strands of the deceased's hair. If they were burying a bald man, it was the hair of his nearest male relative. Spoons, brooches and rings were all sold by the Inviters, who also earned a fee for supervising the party that followed every funeral. The quality of the wine served was a tribute in itself, and many people stored away the best they could afford to be used at their own funerals. When a person became mortally ill, a different pair of licensed professionals, known as **Comforters of the Sick**, were hired by relatives to spend as many hours as were needed reading scriptures, singing hymns and otherwise preparing the doomed soul for an easy entry into heaven.

51 St. Paul's Chapel (1766, **Thomas McBean**) This is Manhattan's only remaining pre-Revolutionary War church. We're lucky it survived 1776's *Great Fire*, because it's not only a rare Georgian architectural gem, but is also important historically. Said to be the most impressive church in the colony when built, St. Paul's grandeur loses nothing in the shadow of that neighboring temple of commerce, the World . Trade Center. It's humbling to remember that in 1750 this site was a wheat field, that the cemetery once extended to the Hudson River and that **George Washington** came here to pray after his swearing-in as the country's first president. McBean's plan for St. Paul's was much influenced by **St. Martin-in-the-Fields** in London, designed by his teacher, **James Gibb**. The interior, lit by Waterford crystal chandeliers, is one of the city's best. Come here for the free concerts of classical and church music Monday and Thursday at 12:10PM, or for services weekdays 1:05PM and Sunday 8AM. ♦ Broadway (Church-Fulton Sts) 602.0800

52 New York County Lawyers' Association (1930, **Cass Gilbert**) Among the beautiful rooms is a 2nd-floor assembly hall that is an exact copy of the main room of Philadelphia's **Independence Hall**. ♦ 14 Vesey St (Church St-Broadway)

53 Pace University (1970, **Eggers & Higgins**) Originally founded as an accounting school, Pace now offers courses in the arts and sciences as well as business, education and nursing. The welded copper sculpture on the facade, by **Henri Nachemia** represents *The Brotherhood of Man*. ♦ Nassau St (Frankfort-Gold Sts)

54 Woolworth Building (1913, **Cass Gilbert**) One of the city's most dramatic skyscrapers was designed as the headquarters of **Frank Woolworth**'s chain of five-and-dime stores. The building is a Gothic celebration inside and out, with picturesque details enhancing the forceful massing and graceful vertical thrust, which culminates in a perfectly composed crown. Inside, the lobby features a soaring glass mosaic ceiling and marble walls awash with more Gothic detail. An added surprise—it seems that Gilbert was an architect with a sense of humor! In the lobby you will find caricature bas-reliefs, including one of Gilbert himself with a model of the building and another of Frank Woolworth counting nickels and dimes. The Woolworths were so pleased with Gilbert's work that they payed for it in cash ($1.5 million) and maintain an office here. Worth a visit. ♦ 233 Broadway (Barclay St-Park Pl)

55 City Hall and City Hall Park (1802–11 **Mangin and McComb**) Surprisingly, New York City is still doing business (with a little help from the nearby Municipal Building) in the same building that was its headquarters in 1811. This elegant, scaled-down palace, a winning entry in a design competition, suc-

Boss Tweed began his political career in 1848 as the organizer of the **Americus Volunteer** Fire Company, whose unusually large fire engine was painted with the head of a tiger. The fire company was associated with **Tammany Hall**, and it was an easy step from one to the other. By 1853, Tweed had become a congressman. By 1867, he was powerful enough to overthrow Reform mayor **Fernando Wood** and put his own man,

George Opdyke, in charge at City Hall. In 1868, he became **Grand Sachem of Tammany Hall**, which gave him back-room control over the state as well as the city. Attacks by cartoonist **Thomas Nast** in *Harper's Weekly* led to his downfall in 1873. He was convicted, but jumped bail and slipped away to Spain, where he was captured by police who recognized him from the Nast cartoons. He died in prison 3 years later.

cessfully combines the Federal style with French Renaissance details. The central hall has a sweeping twin-spiral marble staircase under a splendid dome, making it the perfect setting for public functions and grand entrances. Kings, poets and astronauts have been received here. Upstairs, the grand **City Council Chamber** (also used by the Board of Estimate) and the **Governor's Room**, now a portrait gallery with paintings by **Sully, Trumbull, Inman** and others, are worth a visit. And there are always exhibitions with historical or artistic themes. Interiors were restored and refurbished between 1902 and 1920, and the exterior was restored and repaired by **Shreve, Lamb and Harmon** in 1959. What is known today as **City Hall Park** has always been the city's village green or town common. The park, equally grand in scale, sets off the mass of City Hall. ◆ M-F 9AM-5PM. City Hall Park (Broadway-Park Row)

Tammany was the popular name for the Democratic political machine that ruled Manhattan for nearly a century. The **Tammany Society**, also known as the Columbian Order of New York City, was formed about 1786. By the mid 1830s, what began as a basically social organization championing reforms for the common man, mushroomed into an unstoppable political force, a vehicle for the rich and powerful that fostered corrupt bosses like **William Marcy Boss Tweed**. After state investigations (1930-31) headed by **Samuel Seabury**, Tammany was defeated in the 1932 elections. Though it resurfaced briefly following WWII, it disappeared entirely in the late '60s, during the mayoralty of **John Lindsay**.

55 New York City Courthouse (1872, John Kellum) Known as the **Tweed Courthouse** because Tammany Hall chieftain **William Marcy Tweed** escalated its cost to 52 times the appropriated amount, most of which went into his own bank account. Because of the scandal, the building became a symbol of graft and has always been something of a municipal stepchild. Recent attempts to restore it have been half-hearted, but it has been saved from destruction. The original building had a grand staircase in front, removed in 1955 to make room for widening Chambers St. The result is a blank space that ruins the facade. ◆ 52 Chambers St (Broadway-Centre St)

56 Ecco ★$$$ None of the downtown funkiness you'd expect in this neighborhood. Carved mahogany, beveled mirrors and the 2-story-high tin ceiling provide a clubby, 19th-century atmosphere. The waiters bustle through the mixed crowd of Wall Streeters and art dealers. I suggest you stick with pasta and dessert. ◆ Italian ◆ 124 Chambers St (W. Broadway-Church St) Reservations recommended. 227.7074

On 16 December 1835, fire engulfed Lower Manhattan, scorching everything south of Wall Street and east of Broadway. Over 650 buildings were burned. The conflagration took nearly 20 hours to bring under control; final loss of property was some $20 million.

Restaurants/Nightlife: Red   **Hotels:** Blue
Shops/Parks: Green   **Sights/Culture:** Black

57 Ellen's Cafe and Bake Shop ★$ Ellen Hart Sturm, a former Miss Subway beauty queen, runs this bustling upscale cafe and bakery across from City Hall. The walls are lined with photos of former Miss Subways; Ellen sponsors yearly reunions for these beauties. Try the Mayor's Special (toasted Thomas' English Muffin halves layered with tuna salad and tomato slices, topped with melted cheese). Be sure to save room for Ellen's pecan pie. ♦ American ♦ Closed Su. 270 Broadway (Chambers St) 962.1257. Also: Ellen's Stardust, 1377 6th Ave. 307.7575

58 Surrogate's Court (1911, **John R. Thomas** and **Horgan & Slattery**) Monumental sculp-

Lower Manhattan

tures, including a pair by **Philip Martiny** at the entrance, one representing Britannia (an English soldier and a maiden), the other America (an Indian and a Pilgrim), along with an array of cherubs, eagles, festoons, ship prows and shields, let you know something important is going on here. The French Empire facade, reminiscent of the Paris Opera, is only the beginning. The interior has a mosaic ceiling by **William de Leftwich Dodge**, marble walls and floors and allegorical reliefs. The huge double stairway is yet another touch borrowed from the Opera. Intended to be the last resting place of important city records, the building also serves as the Surrogate's Court. Over the years this became its primary function, as the need grew for more space to probate wills and administer guardianships and trusts. ♦ 31 Chambers St (Centre St)

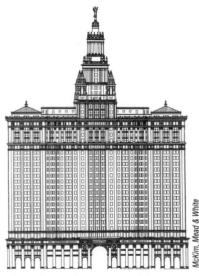

McKim, Mead & White

59 Municipal Building (1914, **McKim, Mead & White**) This Neoclassical skyscraper was created to house city government offices. The building straddles a city street and coexists quite happily with neighboring, smaller City Hall without upstaging it. The almost Baroque confection is topped with a fanciful cluster of colonnaded towers capped by **Adolph Weinman**'s gilded statue. ♦ 1 Centre St (Chambers St)

60 Police Plaza (1973, **M. Paul Friedberg**) At 3 full acres, this is the largest public plaza in New York. On the south side is a prison window from the 1763 **Rhinelander Sugar Warehouse**, which was on this site until 1895. (The original building was used by the British to house American prisoners of war during the Revolution.) The 5 interlocking oxidized-steel disks, a 1974 creation by **Bernard Rosenthal**, represent the 5 boroughs of the city. Just beyond, an 8ft waterfall marks the entrance to a multilevel parking garage under the plaza. ♦ Chambers St (pedestrian mall between Municipal Building and Police Headquarters)

61 St. Andrew's Church (1939, **Maginnis & Walsh, Robert J. Reiley**) A Roman Catholic church established here in 1842 to minister to the needs of Irish immigrants. Its mission has changed along with the neighborhood. In the late 18th century, it offered a 2:30AM Mass for night workers from nearby newspaper offices, and later became the first to offer a noon Mass for business people. ♦ 20 Cardinal Hayes Pl (Pearl Street) 962.3972

62 United States Courthouse (1936, **Cass Gilbert and Cass Gilbert Jr.**) Another Lower Manhattan structure trying to be a temple. This civic building presents a traditional, stately image with rows of Corinthian columns as a base for a tower crowned with a gold pyramid. ♦ 40 Centre St (Foley Square)

63 New York County Courthouse (1926, **Guy Lowell**) A National Landmark, this hexagon-shaped building won a 1912 competition. The Roman style of this building—particularly the Corinthian portico—works much better here than at the neighboring US Courthouse. ♦ 60 Centre St (Pearl St)

64 Jacob K. Javits Federal Building (1967, **Alfred Easton Poor** and **Kahn & Jacobs**) The smaller building on the left houses the US Customs Court, and the taller one with the strange windows is filled with government offices. ♦ 26 Federal Plaza (Duane-Worth Sts)

Like other cities that have them, New York is made workable, if not always delightful, by its subways. They support the city's buried life by moving millions of people a day through commercial corridors on more than 800 miles of track, most of them underground. But despite their obvious importance, the subways today have no enthusiastic partisans. No one admits to liking them. Subways are suffered, endured, blamed, feared. Noisy, dirty, uncomfortable, they are nevertheless still fast; and they make life and work here possible for travelers who descend twice a day to depths they never dreamed of.
Ralph Caplan, writer and design consultant

Restaurants/Nightlife: Red   Hotels: Blue
Shops/Parks: Green   Sights/Culture: Black

Barbara Kirshenblatt-Gimblett
Folklorist, Tisch School of the Arts,
New York University

Fresh-smoked mozzarella, still warm and milky, from **Joe's Latticini** on Thompson St.

Silvery glints in **Lower East Side** skies as pigeon flyers exercise their birds.

Hall of the American Indian at the **American Museum of Natural History**.

The elusive aroma of vanilla, rotten eggs, almonds, turpentine and old shoes exuded by durian in **Chinatown** as the thick prickly skin splits and exposes the coveted creamy fruit.

Fourteenth Street from river to river.

Reading Yiddish books salvaged from Hitler's Europe at the **YIVO Institute for Jewish Research** in the ballroom of the old Vanderbilt mansion on 5th Ave.

Thirty varieties of local apples at the Union Square **Greenmarket** in late September.

Seeing what people will put on their heads at the **Easter Parade** on 5th Ave.

Whatever the **Wooster Group** is currently performing.

The sizzle, smoke and shredded red paper left on the streets of **Chinatown** after lion dancing and firecrackers have ushered in the lunar year.

Genroku Sushi (366 5th Ave), for conveyor belt service.

Spotting fuzzy dice, palm crosses (during the Easter season), collections of air freshener, magnetic saints, lucky charms and other dashboard ornaments in parked cars.

Thanking André Soltner after lunch at **Lutèce**.

Statue of Puck on the **Puck Building**, built in 1885.

Looking into storefront workshops in the fur district near Penn Station, where furriers prepare pelts on large tables under frosty blue lights, as if suspended in a mammoth ice cube.

Dusk on a summer weekend in **Washington Square Park**, the best live show in town.

Rummaging through old prints at **Pageant Book and Print Shop**.

Rustic Korean stews and incendiary homemade pickles at **Woo Chon Restaurant** (5 W 36th St)—open 24 hours.

Marks of the hand on the city—chalk lines on the asphalt for skelly and hopscotch, painted signs for shoe repair and fish shops, barber poles.

Kitchen Arts and Letters, a close-focus bookshop for the food obsessed.

Walking Tour C of **Greenwich Village** in the *AIA Guide to New York City* on an autumn evening.

Kasuri (indigo ikat) pants and jackets at **Kimono House** on Thompson St.

A taxi up the **East River** on a clear day for a sequence of grand vistas.

Speed chess, backgammon and shoe shines on 42nd St, outside the **New York Public Library**, in nice weather.

Edna Lewis' crabcakes at **Gage & Tollner**.

Guiness World Records Exhibit Hall for tacky displays of the unbelievable—a latter-day dime museum.

Watching **D&G** bakers slide loaves shaped by hand into a turn-of-the-century coal-fired brick oven in a tenement basement on Mulberry St at midnight.

Fred Ferretti
A *Gourmet at Large* Columnist, *Gourmet* Magazine

A bowl of fresh and thick barley soup with mushrooms in **Ratner's Dairy Restaurant** on the Lower East Side. With onion rolls.

The cooking, on any day, in the very best of the city's French restaurants—**Lutèce**, where André Soltner remains, after a quarter-century, a municipal trea-

sure; **La Reserve**, an outpost of elegant restraint under Jean-Louis Missud; and **Montrachet**, where Debra Ponzek creates the most intense of flavors.

Some of the best Italian cooking, in a place overrun by Italian restaurants, in of all places, **Le Cirque**, where Sirio Maccioni is gradually teaching his bright young French chef, Daniel Boulud, the niceties of La Cucina Rustica.

There is nothing better than a hot dog, boiled on a street cart, served with a lot of mustard and a bit of sauerkraut, and eaten while sitting with **General Sherman** at the entrance to **Central Park**.

The 100-year-old Spanish tiles, the Tiffany lamp, the marble statuary, the lure of the city's most romantic restaurant, **Café Nicholson**.

Breakfast, lunch or dinner, provided they have slabs of that rough country pâté, the best around, at **Café des Artistes**, just outside Central Park's western border.

The upper right-field stands of **Yankee Stadium** on a hot Sunday afternoon with a cold beer, hoping that Don Mattingly will hit one near you.

Is there a better sandwich in the world than corned beef on rye from the **Carnegie Deli**? No, no, absolutely no.

A seat halfway up the orchestra of the **Metropolitan Opera House** in Lincoln Center, listening to Pavarotti singing songs from Naples, with handkerchief. No better concert seat, no better concert.

The best steak in the city at **Sparks Steak House**, with a selection from what may well be New York's best list of American wines.

Henry Wolf
Photographer

Taking a cab up **Park Ave** at 2AM, making 15 blocks on one light, easy.

Jim Mullen's Restaurant—a lively, congenial place to eat and look at models, politicians, yuppies, Wall Streeters and taste good, reasonable food. Chicken potpie, mashed potatoes and chocolate brownies.

Weyhe Bookstore—slightly dusty, slow help, but wonderful art books, often rare, out-of-print volumes. Nothing like it in New York.

Chinatown/ Lower East Side/ Little Italy

In New York's early days, the swampy territory just northeast of City Hall was considered worthless. But as waves of immigrants began arriving in the middle of the 18th century, the former marshes became quite valuable to the real-estate developers who packed the newcomers into crowded tenements. The distinct ethnic flavors of **Chinatown**, the **Lower East Side** and **Little Italy** were established as each group settled the area roughly bounded by the **East River** and **Lafayette, Chambers** and **Houston Sts.**

Nearly every part of New York has metamorphosed several times during the last 2 centuries. But in this area, only the faces of the people have changed. During the 1860s, thousands of Germans arrived, forcing the long-settled Irish farther uptown. Between 1881 and 1910, 1.5 million Jews fled Rumania, Hungary and Russia, creating the largest Jewish settlement in the world on Manhattan's Lower East Side. Italians, Greeks, Poles and Turks were among the other settlers.

The neighborhood continues to be a first stop for newly arrived immigrants—today's predominantly Hispanic population fills streets that carry the legacy of the Jews they replaced. The southwestern portion is a magnet for Chinese immigrants, who began arriving from San Francisco during the 1870s, and since the immigration laws were changed in the mid 1960s, the neighborhood has welcomed more of them than ever.

Today its more than 150,000 Chinese residents make it the largest Chinese community outside of China. The need for more living space has caused new arrivals to cross Canal St into the enclave traditionally reserved for immigrants from Naples and Sicily. The result is that the neighborhood called Little Italy is now filled with sweatshops and other businesses identified by Chinese ideograms. (Distressed about this situation, Italian community leaders have requested that signs along Mulberry Street be posted only in Roman letters.)

Chinatown is a neighborhood that thrives on street life. Don't expect quaintness. Except for pagoda tele-

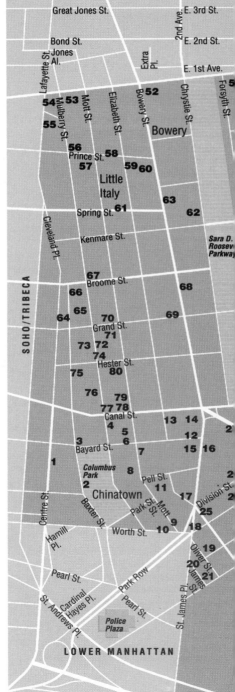

phone booths, what you will find is poverty hidden behind warrens of shops selling exotic vegetables, bargain basement Chinese clothing and housewares, and Formica and vinyl restaurants, many of which prepare wondrous dishes. (When he retired as food critic for *The New York Times*, **John Canaday** identified his favorite New York restaurant as Chinatown.)

The largest crowds appear on **Chinese New Year's**, in January or February, when a parade snakes through the streets and revelers toss firecrackers and throng the restaurants.

The **Lower East Side** is roughly the area below Houston St east of the Bowery to the East River. During the 1880s and '90s, immigrants from Eastern Europe flooded into the airless red-brick tenements. At the turn of the century, this was the world's largest Jewish settlement, a slum that later became a center of culture and community (documented by **Irving Howe** and others), spawning many writers, businessmen and intellectuals. Most of the upwardly mobile Jewish immigrants left as quickly as possible, and now the Lower East Side is home to blacks, Chinese and Puerto Ricans. Although many synagogues remain empty, the old crowd comes back for a steak at **Sammy's Famous Roumanian Jewish Steakhouse** or to shop. **Orchard St** is still discount heaven for everything from fabrics to designer dresses. In observation of the Sabbath, most nonreligious sites on the Lower East Side are closed from sundown Friday to sundown Saturday.

Mulberry St is the main drag of **Little Italy** (the area bounded by Canal, Lafayette and Houston Sts and the Bowery), a bustling residential area filled with neighborhood stores and old

Italian social clubs. Former residents and visitors come for the food—to buy salamis, cheeses and pastas, to dine in plentiful restaurants, to linger over an espresso and pastry in a *caffè*. The area was settled mainly between 1880 and 1924 by immigrant families. Many have moved on, but they always come back —especially for the **Feast of San Gennaro**, a week-long religious celebration held each September that is famous for its eating, drinking and merrymaking.

1 Criminal Courts Building (1939, **Harvey Wiley Corbett**) Called the *Tombs* after its Egyptian Revival ancestor across the street, this giant ziggurat is the third Manhattan jail, the last before prisoners were housed at Riker's Island. It is an elegant Art Moderne structure (you'll recognize Corbett's hand in Rockefeller Center). In its day, the Tombs' 835-cell jail was considered a standard for penal reform: each cell housed only one prisoner. ♦ 100 Centre St (Leonard-White Sts)

2 Columbus Park The only real open space in Chinatown provides a setting for ballplaying and outdoor entertainment. It is a staging area for the dragon dancers during Chinese New Year's. It replaces **Mulberry Bend**, once a redlight district and a part of the 19th-century slum neighborhood known as **Five Points**. ♦ Worth-Bayard Sts (Mulberry-Baxter Sts)

3 Thailand Restaurant ★$ It's not much to look at, but this place serves some of the best and cheapest Thai food in town. ♦ Thai ♦ 106 Bayard St (Baxter St) No credit cards. 349.3132

4 New Grand Fortune ★★$ Beautifully prepared dim sum, but not as extensive a selection as at the Silver Palace. At lunchtime, the downstairs dining room is very busy with local mothers and their kids. At the upstairs counter, you have to know what to order. ♦ Dim sum ♦ 194 Canal St (Mulberry St) No credit cards. 267.2221

4 Kamman Food Products, Inc. An astonishing selection of fresh vegetables, dried fish of all kinds, herbs, teas, noodles and, in the basement, kitchenware. The barbecued ducks and chickens are delicious. ♦ 200 Canal St (Mulberry St) 571.0330

5 Mee Heung Chow Mein Co. You can't go in, but do take a look. Noodles for most of the restaurants in the area are made in the back all day and night. You might even spy a few men intensely playing *mah-jongg*. If it's very late, and you're lucky, someone may even come out and give you a bag of those wonderful crunchy noodles. ♦ 75 Mott St (Canal-Bayard Sts) 962.6894

5 Mon Bo ★$ Some of the best plain Cantonese cooking in Chinatown. Large enough to accommodate groups, and interesting enough to satisfy purists. Highlights: clams with black-bean sauce; the *subgum* pot, a casserole brimming with meat, fish and vegetables; and the barbecued spare ribs, plain and wonderful. ♦ Cantonese ♦ 65 Mott St (Canal-Bayard Sts) No credit cards. 964.6480

6 Saigon Restaurant ★★$$ The decor is dreadful, but the food is authentic Vietnamese; the appetizers and soups are best: crisp spring rolls, shrimp with sugar cane, cold shrimp-and-pork roll, seafood and chicken soups with lemon grass. A favorite among lawyers and judges who work at the nearby courthouses. ♦ Vietnamese ♦ 60 Mott St (Bayard St-Bowery) 227.8825

6 Tai Hong Lau ★$ Inexpensive, authentic Cantonese cooking. Try the winter melon treasure, a curved piece of white melon atop a mixture of mushrooms, roast duck, chicken, pork and shrimp, surrounded by broccoli florets. ♦ Cantonese ♦ 70 Mott St (Bayard St) No credit cards. 219.1431

6 Eastern States Buddhist Temple of America, Inc. The sparkling gold Mountain of Buddhas in the window beckons strollers into this neighborhood temple. There are over 100 statue Buddhas and other religious articles in the back. For a song, you can either pick up a fortune (not in a cookie) or buy a bottle of Mazola Oil to offer at the elaborate shrine. Neighborhood worshippers come here to pay respects and light incense. ◆ 64B Mott St (Canal-Bayard Sts) 966.4653

6 Wonton Garden ★$ A fine place for the many varieties of Cantonese noodle dishes, especially wonton noodles in chicken broth with roast pork and various Chinese vegetables. ◆ Cantonese ◆ 52-56 Mott St (Bayard St) No credit cards. 966.4886

7 New Lin Heong ★$ Greasy spoon Chinese —heavy on the oyster sauce and sweet-and-sour—but popular because of the low prices, generally good-humored staff and heaping plates of delicious *chow fun*. Also try the big batter-dipped fried fantail shrimp. Long lines and fast turnover on weekends. ◆ Cantonese ◆ 69 Bayard St (Mott St) No credit cards. 962.8195

7 Bo Ky Restaurant ★$ The specialty of this restaurant, owned by **Chiu Chow** people from Vietnam, is the big bowls of steaming hot rice noodles topped with shrimp, fish, shrimp balls or sliced roast duck. ◆ Vietnamese ◆ 80 Bayard St (Mott St) No credit cards. 406.2292

8 Lung Fong Bakery Best bakery in Chinatown, although most of these beautiful sweets are an acquired taste. For the unadventurous, however, there are huge, meltingly good almond and walnut cookies. ◆ 41 Mott St (Pell St) 233.7447

9 20 Mott Street ★★$$ As close to the Hong Kong eating experience as it is possible to find in New York. Ask for the baked conch stuffed in its own shell. Also have dim sum, some of the best around. ◆ Cantonese ◆ Park Row. 964.0380

9 Peking Duck House ★★$$ The main reason to stop here is the Peking duck, enough for 6 as an appetizer or light bite. The laboriously crisped duck is carved tableside in home style (with the flesh clinging to the skin) rather than the more usual banquet style (skin only).

Served with the traditional accompaniments: thin pancakes in which to roll the duck, slivered cucumbers and the scallion brush with which to swab the duck with *hoisin* sauce. Before the duck arrives, have an order of steamed pork dumplings. ◆ Peking/ Szechuan ◆ 22 Mott St (Park Row-Pell St) 962.8208

9 Chinatown Fair An amusement arcade filled with the usual (pinball machines and the latest video games) and the unusual—a live chicken who challenges you to a game of tic-tac-toe. ◆ 8 Mott St (Pell St-Chatham Sq)

10 Hunan Garden ★★$$ A friendly restaurant with a large and interesting menu that includes spicy Hunan specialties along with Cantonese fare. Gather several friends together and call ahead for the special Chinese banquet.

Chinatown/Lower East Side/Little Italy

◆ Hunan/Cantonese ◆ 1 Mott St (Chatham Sq) 732.7270

11 Doyers Street A narrow little street with a wishbone-shaped curve that was once known as *Bloody Angle*. Opium dealers who thrived here in the last century lured their competitors here, where they could be ambushed beyond the blind turn. ◆ Pell St at Bowery

11 Nam Wah Tea Parlor ★$ The oldest and most colorful Hong Kong dim sum parlor. Funky fun, but not as good as some others. Lo mein and wonton soup are also available. ◆ Dim sum ◆ 13 Doyers St (Pell St-Bowery) No credit cards. 962.6047

11 Viet-Nam ★★$ With patience and perhaps a few wrong turns, you'll be glad you sought this place out. The flashing sign will signal that you're in the right place and, after the descent down the steep stairs, you'll have some of the best Vietnamese food in the city. What they save on the decor (linoleum, paneling and plastic plants), they put into the food— the menu lists some 100 items. Start with any of the perfectly done egg rolls; try the chicken with lemon grass for Vietnamese food at its most authentic. ◆ Vietnamese ◆ 11 Doyers St (Pell St-Bowery) 693.0725

11 Yun Luck Rice Shop ★$ Most of the items listed on the extensive menu are in Chinese. If I see something that looks good on another table, I ask a waiter about it; they are all friendly and helpful. *Chow fun* (wide rice noodles) is always good. ◆ Cantonese ◆ 17 Doyers St (Pell St-Bowery) No credit cards. 571.1375

The **New York City Landmarks Preservation Commission** was established in 1965, 2 years after the demolition of **Pennsylvania Station**. The commission protects buildings of historic, cultural and esthetic value to the city.

Restaurants/Nightlife: Red   **Hotels:** Blue
Shops/Parks: Green   **Sights/Culture:** Black

12 First Taste ★★★$$$ Probably the best Hong Kong cuisine (if not the best of any cuisine) in Chinatown is served in this charming new restaurant where the staff speaks English and is more than willing to explain each dish. Appetizers: broiled eel shish kabob, cold jelly fish topped with baby squid or chicken or beef consommé, double boiled and baked. Entrees: soft, silky bean curd steamed with fresh scallops and crisp salt-baked chicken with spicy ginger sauce. Dessert: hot red-bean soup or lotus seeds in a cool natural broth with rock sugar. I suggest you go with a group—there will be more plates to taste from. ◆ 53 Bayard St (Bowery-Elizabeth Sts) 962.1818

13 Oriental Town Seafood ★★$$$ This place is always packed; don't be surprised when they seat strangers at your table just to make

Chinatown/Lower East Side/Little Italy

sure the place is filled to the gills. But the seafood here is so good, you won't mind feeling like a sardine. ◆ Cantonese/seafood ◆ 14 Elizabeth St (Canal-Bayard Sts) No credit cards. 619.0085

13 Lin's Sister Associates Corp. A Chinese drugstore carrying herbs, vitamins, various traditional medicines. If you're feeling poorly, stop in for a detailed consultation and prescription from an herbalist. Could be in the form of a tea, capsules or poultice. ◆ 18A Elizabeth St (Bayard St) 962.5417

13 King Fung ★★$$ A combination of every Chinese restaurant you've ever been to: the decor is replete with lanterns, lions on pedestals, fan-shaped windows and dragons. Everything is done with care—there are tablecloths and full sets of utensils on the tables. The food is excellent and beautifully presented. ◆ Cantonese ◆ 20 Elizabeth St (Canal St) Credit cards at dinner only. 964.5256

14 Phoenix Garden ★★$$ Not too much to look at, but the best and most sophisticated Cantonese restaurant in Chinatown. It makes no culinary concessions to Western tastes and, unlike most restaurants in this part of town, has maintained its high quality for many years. Prices are—justifiably—slightly more uptown than in the rest of the neighborhood. Try the pepper-and-salty shrimp or Phoenix special roast squab. ◆ Cantonese ◆ 46 Bowery (Bayard-Canal Sts) 233.6017

14 Silver Palace ★★$$$ This bustling dining room is best for dim sum. Regular customers get preference when the line gets long, which it regularly does on Sunday. Point to what you

want off the carts rolling by, and keep eating. Bills are totaled by the record of empty plates. ◆ Cantonese ◆ 50 Bowery (Bayard-Canal Sts) Credit cards Su and at dinner only. 964.1204

14 Vegetarians Paradise ★$ Funny vegetarian versions of iron steak and Peking duck made out of bean curd, taro root, etc. Not a speck of meat in this restaurant. ◆ Vegetarian/Chinese ◆ 48 Bowery (Canal St) 571.1535

14 Yuet Tung ★★$$ A fine place for the hearty food of Southern China's **Hakka** people. Wonderful bean curd stuffed with chopped shrimp and fresh, long-cooked bacon, and served with preserved vegetables. ◆ Southern Chinese ◆ 40 Bowery (Bayard St) 608.6383

14 Hee Seung Fung (HSF) ★$$ There are often long lines because they are unusually welcoming to Westerners. It's less risky than usual to order dim sum here, as the restaurant offers a photographic guide to the 75 available varieties. You can't go wrong with the *harkow* (steamed shrimp dumpling). ◆ Dim sum ◆ 46 Bowery (Bayard-Canal Sts) 374.1319

15 Noodle Town ★$ One of the best of the noodle houses for curried Singapore-style noodles, pan-fried Cantonese noodles served with different meats and that thick rice porridge the Cantonese call *congee*. ◆ Cantonese ◆ 28 1/2 Bowery (Pell St) 349.0923

16 Confucius Plaza (1976, **Horowitz & Chun**) At odds with its smaller 19th-century neighbors, this huge, chunky modern building solves a pressing need for more living space. It also houses a public school. ◆ Bowery (Division St-Manhattan Bridge)

17 Edward Mooney House (1789) The oldest Federal-style house in Manhattan was modified in 1971 to become a busy branch of the New York Off-Track Betting Corp, which has since moved on to larger quarters. ◆ 18 Bowery (Doyer St)

18 Chatham Square The monument in the traffic island at the center of the square is the **Kim Lau Memorial** (1962, **Poy G. Lee**), dedicated to Chinese-American war dead. ◆ Bowery (E. Broadway-Park Row)

18 Manhattan Savings Bank A mock Chinese temple serves as the Chinatown branch of the bank, and brightens up the square. ◆ 17 Chatham Sq

19 Mariners' Temple (1842, **Minard Lafever**) A brownstone Greek temple, originally called the **Oliver Street Church**, which served sailors based at the nearby East River piers. It is now a Baptist church serving a widely varied community. ◆ 12 Oliver St (Henry St)

20 First Shearith Israel Cemetery (1683–1828) Near **Chatham Square**, which it once covered, it is the surviving fragment of the **Congregation Shearith Israel's** first burial ground (there are 2 more), the oldest Jewish cemetery in Manhattan. The most ancient gravestone is dated 1683. Shearith Israel, started by early Portuguese and Spanish settlers in 1654, is now uptown at a synagogue on Central Park West. ♦ 55 St. James Pl (Oliver-James Sts)

21 St. James Roman Catholic Church (1837, **Minard Lafever**) A Greek Revival-style Roman Catholic church that is an interesting neighbor to the nearby Mariners' Temple. ♦ 32 James St (St. James Pl-Madison St)

22 Originally **William Clark House** (1824) While this house—and especially the entrance—would appear to epitomize all the elegance of the Federal style, there is a twist: it is one of the very few known to have 4 floors (2 or 3 were preferred). ♦ 51 Market St (Monroe-Madison Sts)

23 Nice Restaurant ★★★$$$ One of Chinatown's better Cantonese restaurants, with excellent barbecued duck, a selection of quite good dim sum and a cold dessert of melon and tapioca. ♦ Cantonese ♦ 35 E. Broadway (Catherine-Market Sts) 406.9510

24 Hwa Yuan ★$$ Best Szechuan restaurant in Chinatown, and as such, the nondescript room is often very crowded. Try anything on the extensive menu, but if you want your food authentically fiery, ask for it that way. Even dishes marked hot here are acceptable to timid palates. ♦ Szechuan ♦ 40 E. Broadway (Catherine St) 966.5534

25 Golden Unicorn ★★★$$$ Larger and more elegant than the typical storefront kitchen-cum-restaurant generally found in Chinatown. This one feels like a real restaurant, done up in sleek black and peach with lots of mirrors. You'll even find your napkin folded in your glass. It has been discovered by families who come to sample an amazing array of daytime dim sum, so be sure to get in early. Dinner is equally good, and interestingly enough, the nonspicy dishes are better than the hot ones. I usually start with tasty fried dumplings, then move on to egg foo yung, which is very good here. ♦ Cantonese ♦ 18 E. Broadway (Bowery-Chrystie St) 2nd floor. 941.0911

26 Canton ★$$ Popular with uptowners, but the food is dramatically uneven. Have the owner, **Eileen**, order for you. ♦ Cantonese ♦ Closed M-Tu. 45 Division St (Manhattan Bridge) No credit cards. 226.4441

26 Great Shanghai ★★$$ It has been here forever, but has recently been given a more modern look—you know: pink and gray and neon. But the food is pure Chinatown. Skip the appetizers and share as many main dishes as there are in your party. You won't be disappointed if you don't restrict yourself to one item. ♦ Shanghai ♦ 27 Division St (E. Broadway-Bowery) 966.7663

26 Triple 8 Palace Restaurant ★★★$$$ Ignore the awful decor because this is one of the best (and largest) restaurants in Chinatown. Excellent appetizers include steamed dumplings, fresh oyster pancakes, moist, tender soy chicken and abalone and vegetable soups. Hordes of workers come here for lunch for the best dim sum around;

crowded on weekends as well. Located on the top floor of a new mall within the approaches to the Manhattan Bridge. ♦ Hong Kong ♦ 59 Division St (under Manhattan Bridge) 941.8886

27 Manhattan Bridge (1905, **Gustav Lindenthal**; arch and colonnade, **Carrère & Hastings**) The elaborate approach from Canal St is a shadow of its former self. But the quality still shows. Originally known as the **Court of Honor**, the bridge was designed so that vehicles would pass under a triumphal arch. Brooklyn-bound streetcars were forced to go around the arch, and the subway was hidden underneath it. The **Daniel Chester French** sculptures (representing *Manhattan* and *Brooklyn*) that originally flanked the arch were moved to the front of the Brooklyn Museum in

1963. ♦ Canal St at Bowery, Manhattan to Tillary St at Flatbush Ave, Brooklyn

28 Eldridge Street Synagogue (1887, **Herter Bros.**) Congregation **K'hal Adath Jeshurun Anshe Lubz** built this as the first Orthodox synagogue in the area during a time when other congregations were transforming Christian churches for their own use. Grand in scale, the main sanctuary was an opulent room with brass chandeliers and an ark imported from Italy. The building fell into disrepair over the years—although the congregation has never missed a Sabbath—and is currently being restored to its original splendour; in the spring of 1991 it will open as a center for the celebration of American Jewish history. Comedian **Eddie Cantor** spent his boyhood in a building across the street. (He answered to the name **Edward Iskowitz** back then.) ♦ 12 Eldridge St (Forsyth-Canal Sts) 219.0888

29 Originally **S. Jarmulovsky's Bank** (1895) It was established in 1873 to serve the non-English-speaking immigrants coming to the Lower East Side. With the onset of WWI, many depositors withdrew money to send home—causing runs on the bank, then riots outside its doors. On *Black Tuesday* (4 August 1914, just 2 years after this building was completed), Jarmulovsky's Bank, along with some other local banks, was closed for insolvency. Architecturally, its claim to fame is the quasi religious-looking structure atop its 12 stories. ♦ 54-58 Canal St (Orchard St)

30 Harry Zarin Co. Fabric Warehouse Decorator fabrics at super prices. You can find everything from opulent silk brocades to mattress ticking—and you don't have to be a decorator either. ♦ Closed Sa. 72 Allen St (Grand St) 226.3492

Restaurants/Nightlife: Red **Hotels:** Blue
Shops/Parks: Green **Sights/Culture:** Black

41

30 Fishkin Women's sportswear by **Adrienne Vittadini, Jones New York** and **Basco** (Barneys' private label), handsome boots and shoes by **Via Spiga** and **Nickels**, plus lots of silk and cashmere at a 20-percent discount. ◆ Closed Sa. 314 Grand St (Allen St) 226.6538/9

30 A.W. Kaufman Luxurious lingerie from a variety of designers, including **Christian Dior, Mary McFadden** and **Lejaby**, snugly packed into this narrow shop. ◆ Closed Sa. 73 Orchard St (Grand St) 226.1629

31 Ezra Cohen Fine linens for bed and bath, such as **Wamsutta**'s pure cotton sheets and flower-sprigged designs by **Laura Ashley**, discounted here by 20 to 40 percent. ◆ Closed Sa. 307 Grand St (Allen St) 925.7800

31 Leslie's Bootery for Men and Women Fashionable footwear at a 30-percent discount.

Chinatown/Lower East Side/Little Italy

Women's shoes include bare sandals, espadrilles, pumps and knee-high gleaming calfskin boots, depending on the season. The men's stock includes loafers, wingtips and sport shoes. ◆ 319 Grand St (Orchard St) 431.9196

32 Sunray Yarns A full array of yarns, including **Paton, Lion Brand, Bernat** and **Missoni**, plus their own brand, which they sell to the designers on Seventh Avenue. ◆ Closed Sa. 349 Grand St (Essex St) 475.9655

33 Guss Pickle Products The oldest purveyor of pickles in New York, and still the best. You can get a kosher dill sour enough to make your face pucker. The sauerkraut, pickled peppers and tomatoes are terrific, as well. They're all displayed in the shop and on the sidewalk out front in brine-filled barrels. ◆ Closed Sa. 35 Essex St (Grand-Hester Sts) 254.4477

34 Seward Park (1900) Two blocks of tenement buildings were removed to provide this 3-acre breathing space (named for **William H. Seward**, governor of New York, a US senator and Lincoln's secretary of state). In its early days, it was a gathering place for immigrants looking for daily work. Its southern and western edges are the site of a regular Sunday flea market, during which elderly people use the benches to sell *tchotchkes* (knickknacks), usually quite useless things, like socks that don't match and watches that don't tell time. But the prices are good, and the bargaining an entertainment in itself. ◆ Canal St (E. Broadway-Essex St)

35 Educational Alliance (1891, **Arnold Brunner**) America's first settlement house, founded in 1889 by so-called *uptown Jews*, who felt an obligation to help their coreligionists in the downtown ghetto and to stem possible anti-Semitism. It held classes to Americanize youngsters, and provided exercise and bathing facilities. It also gave assistance to women whose husbands had deserted them, which was common among immigrant families. Among the young people the Alliance served was **Arthur Murray**, who learned to dance here. ◆ 197 E. Broadway (Jefferson St)

36 Ritualarium (1904) The former **Arnold Toynbee Hall** of the **Young Men's Benevolent Association** was converted to a *mikvah*, a ritual bath for Orthodox Jewish women. They are required to attend in preparation for marriage, and on a monthly basis after that. Because the Scriptures command that the water be pure, rainwater is collected in cisterns. Tours are given by appointment. Call **Mrs. Bormiko** at 674.5318 for information. ◆ 313 E. Broadway (Grand St) 475.8514

37 Bialystoker Synagogue (1826) Originally the **Willett Street Methodist Episcopal Church**, it was purchased by the Congregation Anshei Bialystok in 1905. It is the oldest structure housing a synagogue in New York. ◆ 7 Willett St (Grand-Broome Sts)

38 Louis Abrons Arts Center (1975, **Prentice & Chan, Ohlhausen**) This performing- and visual-arts complex is part of the **Henry Street Settlement**, a social service agency that has operated on the Lower East Side since 1893. Among its programs are arts workshops, professional performances and exhibitions—all meant to help participants develop a form of self-expression through the arts and an appreciation of the cultural diversity of New York City. Contains 3 theaters: the **Recital Hall**, the **Experimental Theater** and the **Henry DeJur Playhouse**. ◆ Seats 99, 146, 340. 466 Grand St (Pitt-Willett Sts) 598.0400

39 Williamsburg Bridge (1903, **Leffert L. Buck**) This second bridge to span the East River changed Williamsburg in Brooklyn from a resort area to a new home for immigrants from the Lower East Side. The bridge is unusual in that there are no cables on the land side of the steel towers, robbing it of some of the soaring grace of a full suspension span. ◆ Delancey St at Clinton St, Manhattan to Washington Plaza, Brooklyn

40 Streit's Matzoth Company The only Manhattan producer of the unleavened bread used during Passover. Watch the huge sheets of matzah as they pass by the windows on conveyor belts. ◆ 150 Rivington St (Suffolk St)

40 Schapiro's House of Kosher and Sacramental Wines Tour the only still-operating winery in the city on Sunday, 11AM-5PM, or during the week by appointment. ◆ Nominal fee. 126 Rivington St (Suffolk St) 674.4404

41 Ratner's ★$$ Its glory days far behind, this New York institution is now more a cultural than a gustatorial experience. All the standard Jewish dairy dishes are listed, but few are worth the inevitable heartburn. It's best to soak in the *Yiddishkayt* over a bowl of soup, a plate of pan-fried cheese or potato blintzes, or the deep-fried *pirogen*. ◆ Jewish dairy ◆ Closed Sa. 138 Delancey St (Norfolk-Suffolk Sts) No credit cards. 677.5588

42 Economy Candy Company People with a longing for some good, old-fashioned penny candy will find it here. But though the prices are good, a penny won't go very far. It has been here since 1937, selling candy of all kinds as well as dried fruits, nuts, coffees, teas and other delicacies. When you stop in, ask for the mail order catalog. ♦ 108 Rivington St (Essex-Ludlow Sts) 254.1832

43 Bernstein-on-Essex Street $$ A kosher Chinese experience in which veal and fin fish are translated into pork and seafood dishes. The rest remains hardcore American shopping center Chinese. ♦ Kosher/Chinese ♦ 135 Essex St (Rivington-Stanton Sts) 473.3900

44 The Hat/El Sombrero $ Not the best Mexican food but a real neighborhood hangout. Try nachos *traditionales* and a frosty margarita, and soak in the local color. ♦ Mexican ♦ 108 Stanton St (Ludlow St) 254.4188

44 The Ludlow Street Cafe A relaxed upbeat cafe with live music at about 10PM nightly. Go on Monday for *Beat Rodeo*, a lively country-rock band whose members love to keep the audience happy, especially the would-be rock 'n' rollers who join in from time to time. ♦ Cafe ♦ 165 Ludlow St (E. Houston-Stanton Sts) 353.0536

44 Max Fish A jukebox keeps the beat at this bright (vibrant paintings cover white walls), popular (the crowd spills onto the sidewalk) club, filled with the young and attractive. Pinball, billiards and cheap beers. ♦ Ludlow St (E. Houston-Stanton Sts) No phone

45 Katz's Delicatessen ★$ Famous old delicatessen. Have a look (the *Send a salami to your boy in the Army* sign is a relic of WWII), take a ticket when you come in, then pick up some sausages or a warm brisket on rye. Site of the memorable deli scene in the 1989 film *When Harry Met Sally*. Worth a visit. You can be waited on at the tables to the left as you enter, or serve yourself by ordering at the counter. ♦ Deli ♦ 205 E. Houston St (Ludlow St) No credit cards. 254.2246

46 Russ & Daughters A shopping mecca—you should pardon the expression—for serious connoisseurs of lox and bagels and cream cheese, not to mention smoked Nova Scotia salmon (called *Novie* in these parts), golden smoked whitefish, unctuous sable carp, tart-crisp herring, salads, dried fruits, nuts and other foods that many native New Yorkers call appetizing. *An RSW recommendation.* ♦ 179 E. Houston St (Orchard-Allen Sts) 475.4880

47 Orchard Street The old pushcarts are gone, but bargain hunters still flock to Orchard St, a seething indoor-outdoor bazaar of discount dresses, coats, shoes, linens, fabrics and accessories piled on tables and hanging from clotheslines. More than 300 stores line Orchard and surrounding streets from Houston to Canal Sts on the Lower East Side. On Sunday, the streets are closed to traffic, and the latest from **Ralph Lauren** to **Charles Jourdan** is hawked from the sidewalks. This kind of shopping is not for the faint of heart, but if you go prepared for the rough and tumble of bartering and remember that not all stores take credit cards or have gracious salespeople, you can turn up some jewels among the *schlock*—and have fun too. Go weekdays if you can. Sunday is insane, and many stores are closed on Saturday. One of New York's musts. ♦ Canal-Houston Sts

Chinatown/Lower East Side/Little Italy

47 Anna Z High-fashion European clothing for women, including designs by **Bill Kaiserman** and **Malisy Gilbert Basson**, at 20 percent off retail. ♦ 143 ½ Orchard St (Rivington St) 533.1361

47 Giselle Sportswear Better American sportswear for women, including warm, wooly alpaca jackets and soft leather jackets and pants at 25 percent off. ♦ Closed Sa. 143 Orchard St (Rivington St) 673.1900

48 Tobaldi American and European high-fashion men's clothes are discounted 20 percent. Merchandise includes tweed jackets, leather jackets, pure cotton shirts, silk ties and bikini underwear. ♦ Closed Sa. 83 Rivington St (Orchard St) 260.4330

48 Fine & Klein An extensive collection of high-end handbags, briefcases and accessories, including the latest from **Carlos Falchi, Enny and Lisette** (sometimes **Valentino** and **Givenchy** too). Good discounts and gracious service at this Orchard St institution. Upstairs, at **Lea's**, enjoy a 30-percent discount on women's clothing from designers like **Albert Nippon** and **Louis Feraud**. ♦ 119 Orchard St (Rivington-Delancey Sts) 674.6720

49 Beckenstein There is a roughly 15-percent discount here on an enormous and excellent collection of fabrics, including men's shirting of pure cotton, cashmere, mohair and silk charmeuse. ♦ Closed Sa. 130 Orchard St (Rivington-Delancey Sts) 475.4525. Also at: 125 Orchard St. 475.4653

Every street in Chinatown is filled with exotic mystery, but East Broadway, with its comparatively wide sidewalks, is a good place to drink in the atmosphere. Among the street's attractions are several theaters displaying films from China. Most soundtracks are in Mandarin, the language of China's North and West, which is unintelligible to natives of Canton. But the ideograms used in the subtitles are the same for every dialect. Many Chinatown residents, including waiters and chefs, communicate with one another in writing.

Restaurants/Nightlife: Red   **Hotels:** Blue
Shops/Parks: Green   **Sights/Culture:** Black

50 Originally **Congregation Adath Jeshurun of Jassy Synagogue** This 1903 building was also the home of the First Warsaw Congregation. Now abandoned, it still projects a rich and distinctive image with its collage of architectural styles. ♦ 58-60 Rivington St (Allen-Eldridge Sts)

51 **Yonah Schimmel** ★$ A dumpy old storefront serving knishes, but best known for clabbered milk (yogurt) and borscht, the same Jewish specialties they've been dishing up since the turn of the century. ♦ Snacks ♦ 137 E. Houston St (1st-2nd Aves) 477.2858

52 **Irreplaceable Artifacts** Lighting fixtures, architectural antiques, garden ornaments and interesting junk from Europe, Canada, South America and the United States are sold under a tent at this corner and in 2 showrooms: 7

Chinatown/Lower East Side/Little Italy

floors at 14 2nd Ave and 3 floors (specializing in antique bars and restaurant equipment) at 259 Bowery. ♦ SE corner of Bowery and Houston St. 982.5000

53 **Knitting Factory** ★$$ A vital 2-level performance spot with an impressive weekly roster of performances—everything from jazz to poetry readings to the latest performance art. Performances daily. ♦ Cover. 47 E. Houston St (Mott-Mulberry Sts) 219.3055

Courtesy Puck Bldg.

54 **Puck Building** (1885; addition 1892, **Albert Wagner**) A dominant Romanesque Revival building that reflects the influence of the Chicago School in its bold and vibrant use of brickwork. It was once the home of the humor magazine *Puck*, whose spirit remains in the 2 larger-than-life statues perched on 3rd-floor ledges at the NE corners. The interior of this great building has been renovated as commercial condominiums for art galleries, workshops and design offices. The Puck's opulent rooms are also rented out for weddings and celebrations of all kinds. ♦ 295-309 Lafayette St (E. Houston St)

55 **Urban Archaeology** Owner **Gil Shapiro** has moved his seemingly infinite collection of architectural ornaments, display cases, lighting fixtures and much, much more into unique and immense quarters—a 4-story former candy factory. Interior designer **Judith Stockman** revamped all 50,000sq ft, a process that included sandblasting candy off the walls. Two lovely sky-lit areas show off cast-iron

furniture, garden accessories and vintage motorcycles. Wholesale and retail. ♦ 285 Lafayette St (E. Houston-Prince Sts) 431.6969

56 **Do Kham** Clothing, jewelry and accessories from Tibet and the Himalayas, some designed by the amiable store owner, **Phlegye Kelden**, a former Tibetan monk. Check out his chic fake- and genuine-fur hats. ♦ 51 Prince St (Lafayette-Mulberry Sts) 966.2404

56 **Old St. Patrick's Cathedral** (1815, **Joseph Mangin**; restoration 1868, **Henry Englebert**) When the new cathedral at 5th Ave and 50th St was consecrated in 1879, this became a Roman Catholic parish church serving a predominantly Irish neighborhood. It was New York's first Gothic Revival building. Sadly, its historic facade was badly altered after an 1866 fire. ♦ 264 Mulberry St (E. Houston-Prince Sts)

57 **Old St. Patrick's Convent and Girls' School** (1826) A beautiful Federal doorway framed with Corinthian columns makes this unusually large Federal-style building a treasure. ♦ 32 Prince St (Mott St)

58 **Lunch For Your Ears** Cutting-edge record store that specializes in foreign and independent labels on CD. The owner (who comprises the entire staff) will let you listen before buying. ♦ 25 Prince St (Mott-Elizabeth Sts) 941.1774

59 **Le Poeme** $ A comfy tearoom and bakery serving natural Corsican and French specialties. Live music Thursday-Saturday evenings. ♦ Cafe ♦ 14 Prince St (Elizabeth St) 941.1106

60 **Connecticut Muffin Co.** Fresh-baked goods and a friendly staff. Try a banana-nut muffin or cheddar cheese scone. ♦ 10 Prince St (Elizabeth St-Bowery) 925.9773

61 **Just Shades** A shop that sells nothing but lampshades. In stock are shades of string, parchment, silk and burlap; others can be custom-ordered. ♦ Closed W. 21 Spring St (Mott-Elizabeth Sts) 966.2757

62 **Sammy's Famous Roumanian Jewish Steakhouse** ★★★$$$ The best Jewish restaurant in the city, although not kosher. The room is low-down and tacky. The so-called entertainment—an electric piano and a comic who thinks he's **Henny Youngman**—is so bad it's good. If you are unfamiliar with the cuisine, order almost everything the waitress tells you to, but in only half the quantity she recommends. Among these are likely to be chopped liver (yes, you do want the works to put on it: chicken cracklings and shredded black radishes with onion, laced with chicken fat), *kishke* and unborn eggs. And those are just the appetizers. For a main course, Rumanian tenderloin steak, a rib steak, fried breaded veal chop or boiled beef with mushroom-barley gravy will do fine. And you must have, on the side, mashed potatoes with fried onions, and *kasha varnishkes* (that's buckwheat groats with bowtie macaroni). Portions are large, the food is authentically heavy (even without liberal pourings from the pitcher of chicken fat on the table) and the bill mounts up quickly. If you have room left for any of the weighty baked desserts, you'll get what you deserve. Better you should have prunes. Or try an egg cream, the classic New York *digestif*. Management supplies a container of milk, a bottle of Fox's U-Bet chocolate syrup and the seltzer. You mix: syrup, about a quarter of a glass of milk to taste, seltzer to fill. Stir well for a nice foam. You'll definitely want to try this place—once. ♦ Eastern European/Jewish ♦ Entertainment nightly. 157 Chrystie St (Delancey-Rivington Sts) Reservations required. 673.0330

63 Mazer Store Equipment Co. This is where **Craig Claiborne, Mimi Sheraton, Lauren Bacall** and **Stockard Channing** buy their Garland restaurant-style stoves. Mazer not only discounts the stove, which now comes with porcelainized oven walls, back and roof, but arranges for the oven to be installed and burners to be adjusted. Service is what distinguishes this store from others of its kind. ♦ Closed Sa-Su. 207 Bowery (Delancey St) 674.3450

64 The Police Building (1909, **Hoppin & Koen**; restoration 1988, **Ehrenkranz Group & Eckstut**; interiors, **dePolo/Dunbar**) A commanding presence with an imposing dome as a symbol of authority, this was the main headquarters of the **New York City Police Department** for nearly 65 years. The new copper dome was done by the French artisans brought here to restore the *Statue of Liberty's* copper flame. The interior has been converted into 55 cooperative apartments. ♦ 240 Centre St (Grand-Broome Sts)

65 Benito I and **Benito II** ★$$ The original owners of this pair of small trattorias sold out and moved off to LA. The restaurants are no longer related, but the tradition lingers on, and either one is a good choice for a hearty low-cost Italian meal. ♦ Neapolitan ♦ Benito I: 174 Mulberry St (Broome-Grand Sts) No credit cards. 226.9171; Benito II: 163 Mulberry St (Broome-Grand Sts) No credit cards. 226.9012

66 Grotta Azzurra ★★$$ The kitsch of dining in an ersatz blue cave may appeal to some, but the food may not appeal to many. Chicken cacciatore is a safe bet; avoid the seafood. The best things about it—the portions are ample, you don't need a reservation and it's fun! The Italian equivalent of Sammy's Famous Roumanian Jewish Steakhouse. ♦ Neapolitan ♦ 387 Broome St (Mulberry St) No credit cards. 226.9283

66 Caffè Roma ★★$ Knowledgeable New Yorkers favor this old bakery and coffeehouse over the slicker Ferrara. No redecorating was necessary to make this place look authentic. It just is. ♦ Bakery/cafe ♦ 385 Broome St (Mulberry St) No credit cards. 226.8413

Chinatown/Lower East Side/Little Italy

67 Road to Mandalay ★★$$ A cozy restaurant, where all the food is good, but the noodle dishes are particularly special. ♦ Thai/Burmese ♦ 380 Broome St (Mott-Mulberry Sts) 226.4218

68 New York Gas Lighting Company One of the few lighting stores that does not blind you with wattage. This 70-year-old store takes its name from its authentic open-flame gas lights. It also offers an array of handsome fixtures that includes opalescent chandeliers from Czechoslovakia, lamps made from antique ginger jars and the Hunter wood ceiling fan. ♦ 145 Bowery (Broome St) 226.2840

69 Bowery Savings Bank (1894, **McKim, Mead & White**) A double treat. Outside, the Roman columns attached to a Renaissance facade are somehow apropos on the edge of Little Italy. Inside, another treat in the opulent interior detailing. Both are worth a look. ♦ 130 Bowery (Grand-Broome Sts)

The Police Building

70 Pearl River Chinese Products A store to satisfy any Sinophile's passion for clothing and housewares. Pearl River carries cotton T-shirts, silk jackets, pillowcases, sheets and bedspreads in pastel pinks, blues and yellows embroidered with flowers and animals. For Chinese cooking, an easy-to-use wok with a wooden handle is another find. ♦ 200 Grand St (Mott St) 966.1010

70 Villa Pensa ★★$$$ Established in 1898, this is Little Italy's oldest Italian restaurant.

Chinatown/Lower East Side/Little Italy

Rudolf Valentino and **Enrico Caruso** sought it out for its spaghetti and, in more recent years, **Billy Joel** dashed off a song called *Big Man on Mulberry Street* at one of its tables. ♦ Neapolitan ♦ 198 Grand St (Mulberry-Mott Sts) 966.5620

71 Ferrara $ A slick emporium with an extensive take-home department featuring a wide variety of Italian pastries, cookies and candies. The espresso bar is one of the city's more popular places for cappuccino and the like. In nice weather the bar extends out onto the sidewalk, where there is also a counter dispensing very authentic Italian gelati. ♦ Bakery/cafe ♦ 195 Grand St (Mulberry-Mott Sts) No credit cards. 226.6150

71 E. Rossi & Co. A crowded store selling bocci balls, pasta machines, T-shirts, Italian greeting cards, cookbooks in both Italian and English, religious statuary and, my favorite item, big buttons reading, *Kiss me, I'm Italian.* ♦ 191 Grand St (Mulberry St) 966.6640

72 Angelo's of Mulberry Street $$ An old Little Italy stand-by that might be a bit too touristy, but churns out consistently decent southern Italian food. ♦ Southern Italian ♦ 146 Mulberry St (Grand-Hester Sts) 966.1277

73 Ristorante Taormina ★★$$ With its blond wood and peach furnishings, exposed brick walls, large windows and graceful tall plants, this attractive restaurant would be more at home further uptown than in Little Italy. But, surprisingly, the difference is not unwelcome here. Begin a delightful dining experience with the excellent stuffed artichokes. Any of the veal entrees is quite good, as are most of the items on the Neapolitan menu. An added bonus: you never know who may be at the next table. The famous, and infamous, pass through Taormina. ♦ Neapolitan ♦ 147 Mulberry St (Grand-Hester Sts) 219.1007

Label **Vishinsky**, inventor of an early automatic bagelmaker, claimed that the first New York bagel emerged from 15 Clinton St in 1896.

73 S.P.Q.R $$$ A grand and gorgeous multi-level room, but the kitchen is perpetually troubled. Stick to simple stuff and you'll eat decently. ♦ Neapolitan ♦ 133 Mulberry St (Grand-Hester Sts) 925.3120

73 Umberto's Clam House $$ A landmark because a famed underworld figure was assassinated here, but the seafood with hot, medium or mild sauce is probably better at Vincent's. ♦ Clam bar ♦ 129 Mulberry St (Hester St) No credit cards. 431.7545

74 Caffe Napoli ★$ You'll feel like you're at a sidewalk cafe even when you're sitting inside. Take a cue from the locals, who come here for dessert rather than going to the more famous Ferrara. If you get stumped trying to decide which of the marvelous-looking pastries in the glass case you want, you can't go wrong if you choose a cannoli. ♦ Cafe ♦ 191 Hester St (Mulberry St) No credit cards. 226.8705

74 Forzano Italian Imports Inc. If you want a souvenir from Little Italy, you can buy it here. The speakers pipe Italian music onto the street, and this place does indeed carry a large selection of Italian records and tapes —and just about everything else. You'll find espresso-makers in every shape, size and price, and a variety of meat grinders, as well as more kitschy fare, such as T-shirts proclaiming your Italian heritage and devil horns to hang over your rear-view mirror to—you guessed it—keep bad luck away. ♦ 128 Mulberry St (Hester St) 925.2525

74 Restaurant Puglia ★$$ A rambling, no-nonsense place serving generous portions of spaghetti with parmigiana specialties at long tables that patrons share in the European style—the young crowd sings along to the live music. The homemade wine, which comes in odd bottles, isn't like anything you'll find in local wine stores. ♦ Southern Italian ♦ Closed M. 189 Hester St (Mulberry-Mott Sts) No credit cards. 966.6006

75 Ceramica Classic Italian patterns appear on imported linens, mosaics and earthenware—the Rafaelesco, a dragon pattern Rafael used on many of his frames, is particularly beautiful. Everything is handmade for the store. ♦ Closed M. 182 Hester St (Mulberry-Baxter Sts) 966.3170

76 Il Cortile ★$$ The lines to get in may be too long, the rooms may be too noisy, the waiters too harried. Still, the food is fresh and cooked well, and the room is beautifully decorated. ♦ Northern Italian ♦ 125 Mulberry St (Hester-Canal Sts) 226.6060

76 Lo Spuntino ★★$ Small, narrow and tiled in white, Lo Spuntino is not as flashy as the rest of the cafes on Mulberry St. The hand-painted sign and the gorgeous desserts in the window will let you know you are in the right place. An assortment of mousses is always available (pumpkin, pear, white-chocolate almond), as well as standard Italian pastry fare—cannolis, eclairs, etc. Try the special *torta di Lo Spuntino.* ◆ Cafe ◆ Hours vary. 117 Mulberry St (Hester-Canal Sts) Unlisted phone

77 Luna ★$ The feel is more oversized kitchen than touristy restaurant. The hallway that leads you to the dining room gives a full view of the kitchen—if you peek in, you'll know that you're not going to be served anything these cooks wouldn't eat themselves. Despite, or perhaps because of, the haphazard mix of tables and booths, propped-up photographs and occasionally gruff service, the experience is authentic—and filling. Worth a visit. ◆ Southern Italian ◆ 112 Mulberry St (Hester-Canal Sts) No credit cards. 226.8657

78 Oriental Pearl ★$$$ Suggested from the extensive menu at this large, dull-looking restaurant are the Peking spare ribs and the steamed flounder or shrimp with walnuts. One of the few restaurants where you can order stewed and roasted geese. ◆ Cantonese ◆ 103 Mott St (Canal St) 219.8388

79 Wong Kee ★$ Fresh, very good food at prices that will make you wonder how they stay in business. Try the boiled, skinless chicken breast, roast duck, scrambled eggs with pork, wonton and cabbage soup, glazed pork, any wide rice noodles. I think you're better off if you skip the chef's suggestions. ◆ Cantonese ◆ 113 Mott St (Hester-Canal Sts) No credit cards. 226.9018

79 Chao Chow ★$$ Perhaps the best example of *lo soi* duck to be had in New York. The duck is cooked in cinnamon, 8-star anise and nutmeg, a sauce that becomes richer from repeated use. ◆ Northern Chinese ◆ 111 Mott St (Hester St) No credit cards. 226.2590

80 Pho Bânc Restaurant ★$ Authentic Vietnamese cooking with especially well done whole shrimp summer rolls and sugar paste on sugar cane. A plate of exotic lettuces and an array of sauces accompany the meal. ◆ Vietnamese ◆ 117 Mott St (Hester-Canal Sts) 966.3797. Also at: 3 Pike St. 233.3947; 8 Chatham Sq. 587.0870

80 Vincent's Clam Bar $$ A city institution. Fresh seafood on hard bread with a choice of hot, medium or mild tomato sauce. Hot is for serious masochists, of which there appear to be many. ◆ Seafood ◆ 119 Mott St (Hester St) 226.8133

BIG APPLE BLUES
The cabbie is having a bad day.
Been in this can for 12 hours, he says.
And shoots across Fifty-Seventh Street
    yelling
at a mother with a baby in her arms.
Keep jaywalking, lady, the baby's life ain't
    worth much.
It is fall and the leaves in Central Park are
    rust gold.
The air smells of chestnuts and rain.
My wife ran off with a stockbroker.
He lights a cigar.
The flags are flapping like gull wings in front
of the Metropolitan. A lady in a sable coat is
walking an afghan on a grey suede leash.
Two models pose
by the Monkey Cage in the Zoo. A tiny boy in
a school uniform is buying a hot pretzel.
Left me with three kids sleeping on the floor of
my studio in Queens.
A pretty blond is doing double axels in
    Rockefeller Center.
Two ladies from Great Neck are having
    lunch at the Palm Court
and raving about *Cats.*
A quartet of students plays Vivaldi for quarters
    in front of Bergdorf's.
Jane Fonda is signing books at Doubleday.
What way is that to raise kids? They think
    pizza is health food.
Two businessmen in cashmere overcoats chat
    as they enter La Côte Basque for lunch.
A Japanese couple is buying a solid gold
    watch at Tiffany.
Schoolchildren stand in line at the Whitney.
The Rockettes are kicking 6 inches over
    their heads at Radio City.
I should take them to my sister in Orlando, get
some sunshine and fresh fruit into 'em.
Tourists go to Mass at St. Peter's. A young
    couple jogs by the East River.
The Russian Embassy is having a party.
A pink-headed crazy drags a duffel bag down
    Fifth Avenue.
Someday, he says, slamming to a stop in
    front of Grand Central
I'll sell this heap and get out of this goddamn
city.

                      Gloria Nagy

10 Terrific Things for Kids

9 Hear your favorite author reading from your favorite book at **Books of Wonder** or at **Eeyore's**.

10 Produce your own newscasts and public affairs programs at the Time Warner Center for Media at the **Children's Museum of Manhattan**.

1 Young audiences are encouraged to participate when the **Little People's Theater Company** stages favorites like *Humpty Dumpty Falls in Love* at the Courtyard Playhouse.

2 Feel like a shrimp under the 10-ton blue whale, or get lost in the stars at the planetarium, both at the **American Museum of Natural History**.

3 Little sweet teeth will love the fabulously tasty *Bocce Ball* (Italian ice cream covered with chocolate), but even the simple 2-scoop cone is grand when eaten at **Rumpelmayer's**.

4 The **New York City Ballet**'s *Nutcracker Suite* brings dancing toy soldiers, evil mice and sugarplum fairies to Lincoln Center.

5 The New York Philharmonic's **Young People's Concerts** at Avery Fisher Hall include talks to introduce kids to classical music.

6 Getting into the **Brooklyn Children's Museum** through a 180ft tunnel and waterway is half the fun!

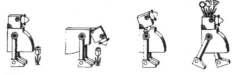

7 You can climb up on a mushroom and join Alice, the Cheshire Cat and the Mock Turtle at José de Creeft's statue overlooking **Central Park's Conservatory Water**.

8 One of the best ways to enjoy Lower Manhattan is with a view from the river of a replica of an 18th-century steamboat at the **South Street Seaport**.

The 5-borough **NYC Marathon** is a great family activity: everyone who finishes is a winner.

NYC Marathon Route: 26.2 miles

20 mi. — Bronx
La Guardia Airport
95
Central Park
Finish — 25 mi. / 15 mi.
Queens
278
495
New York
3
New Jersey
Hudson River
Manhattan
East River
10 mi.
1/9
Jersey City
478
Prospect Park
78
Statue of Liberty Natl. Mon.
5 mi.
Upper New York Bay
Brooklyn
Staten Island Ferry Plaza
278
Staten Island
Start

km	2|	4|	6|	8|
mi	1|	2|	3|	4|	5|

Underground New York City

New York City has long had a catacomb of caverns, tunnels, tubes and viaducts weaving through the city's substructure.

Many were planned and built over 150 years ago and function as effectively today as they ever did (such as some wood-lined aqueducts). But others became redundant, unnecessary or politically expendable, and were sealed off and forgotten.

The discovery in 1980 of an 1840s railroad tunnel in Brooklyn was hailed as an archaeological find by its 22-year-old discoverer, in the face of city bureaucrats denying they ever lost it. Indeed, it is considered the world's first subway tunnel (London built the first subway system 20 years later). It is one-half mile long and 21ft wide, and is supported by a brick archway 18ft high. It pioneered the *cut-and-cover* technique still used in subway construction, and was the first to use ventilation shafts. Even more interesting is its history, pocketed with covert uses, after the community forced its closure after only 11 years' use. Legends have it infested with smugglers, bootleggers, mushroom growers and legions of spies from the Civil War and both World Wars.

But Brooklyn has no monopoly on vast, empty, underground caverns. They are literally underfoot wherever you walk. Innumerable ancient water tunnels, some up to 20ft in diameter, crisscross the boroughs, especially Manhattan. An obsolete automobile tube crosses upper Manhattan to the George Washington Bridge. The Transit Authority can only guess at the number of abandoned subway stations and tunnels; a recent estimate described 23 stations and around 5 1/2 miles of unused tunnels. When the baseball Giants moved to San Francisco in 1958, a subway line to the Polo Grounds was closed, stations and all. (There is also an abandoned elevated station in Brooklyn standing poised, waiting for tracks to be built to it.) As recently as 1974, 4 separate sections totaling almost a mile of the unfinished 2nd Ave line were sealed up. Water is pumped out of these sections daily, while the city scrambles quietly to rent the space or find some use for it.

But practical use of these lost spaces is rare: the Metropolitan Museum uses an ancient, 4-block-long aqueduct of unknown lineage beneath its building for general storage; Columbia University uses a maze of old coal transportation tunnels for building access and new utility systems (and the students used them to invade the university during the 1968 riots); and the city uses one abandoned subway station for a transit museum—easily one of New York City's best kept secrets.

But generally, the underground remains a mysterious, vaguely creepy netherworld. Something you enter only when you absolutely have to. I mean, how can you trust an underworld that shoots steam at you through holes in the street?

Peter Bradford

Drawing by Edward Koren from Up & Down

Although you probably won't encounter one, we thought you'd be interested in knowing that underground New York is home to millions of Norway rats. These creatures, who average 18in from nose to tail and weigh in at about a pound, can and will eat practically anything, as well as chew their way through such seemingly impenetrable substances as lead insulation and cinder blocks. In addition to their powerful jaws and stomachs, they breed like—you guessed it—rats!

SoHo/TriBeCa

The name **SoHo** was coined to define the district **South of Houston St**, not to honor the neighborhood in London. Combined with the wedge-shaped territory known as **TriBeCa** (city departmentese for **Triangle Below Canal St**), it includes the area bounded by **Houston, Lafayette** and **Chambers Sts** and the **Hudson River**.

There is nothing neat and prettied-up about SoHo, in spite of its soaring prices. White-on-white galleries and chic buildings occupy grimy streets so broken that the 19th-century cobblestones show through the ravaged asphalt. The district has had a checkered past. It was occupied by Indians during the 17th century (that's who the famous wall of Wall St was supposedly protecting the early settlers from, although it was really meant to protect them from the British), then by farms and estates between New York City and the outlying suburb of Greenwich Village. In the early part of the 19th century, the land was bought up for houses (the oldest one still standing, at 107 Spring St, dates from 1806), and from the 1840s to 1860s it was the center of the city, with the major department store, **Lord & Taylor**, on Grand St, and the city's principal hotel, **The American House**, at Spring St and West Broadway.

Industry followed, housed in those fantasies of American business—prefabricated cast-iron buildings fashioned to look literally like temples of commerce. By the 1960s, light industry had moved on, and **Robert Moses**, the city's master builder, viewed SoHo as a wasteland of useless industrial buildings that he wanted to level and replace with the Lower Manhattan Expwy. When that plan was abandoned in the mid 1960s, SoHo was discovered by artists looking for large, cheap studio space. Avant-garde galleries, one-of-a-kind boutiques and nouvelle cuisine restaurants followed close behind. Today SoHo continues to hold its own as an alternative to the art world of Madison Ave. The neighborhood is saturated with a mix of original ideas and junk, sheer exuberance and exhibitionism. When planning this walk remember that many of the shops, restaurants and galleries do not open until 11 or noon, are closed on Monday and during the month of August.

TriBeCa, unlike SoHo, retains much of the industrial bohemian quality that once characterized the entire complex of cast-iron architecture between Houston and Chambers Sts. Because this neighborhood overlaps the City Hall area with its enormous daytime working population, it has been more successful in resisting the tide of fad enterprise. Greek coffeeshops, shoe repairs, pet shops, and appliance and camera stores enliven commercial streets little changed since the 1930s.

Art and commerce have, of course, transformed TriBeCa, but they have not overwhelmed it. With easy access to Chinatown and Lower Manhattan, it remains a uniquely New York neighborhood, artistic and ethnic.

---

1 Cheese of All Nations More than 1000 types of cheese sold, from countries as far away as Algeria and Yugoslavia (no Zaire). Two dozen bries, fetas, Jarlsbergs. Jammed at lunch by nearby office workers. ♦ Closed Su. 153 Chambers St (W. Broadway-Greenwich St) 732.0752

2 P.S. 234 (1988, **Richard Dattner**) Too bad all schools aren't as well designed (some of the architectural elements seem to come straight out of a child's imagination), or as nicely sited. Be sure to study the fanciful fence, by artist **Donna Dennis**, that encloses the schoolyard. ♦ Greenwich St (Warren-Chambers Sts)

3 Washington Market Park Progress has reduced the former Washington Market to this little park. In its day, the market extended up along the river from Fulton St into this neighborhood. Even Washington St, which once formed its spine, has been reduced to a 2-block-long thoroughfare between Murray and Chambers Sts. The old market was essentially a produce exchange (now centered at Hunt's Point in the Bronx), but it was also a distribution point for the imported foods that are being rediscovered in gourmet shops. It was a wholesale market, but many New York households took advantage of the opportunity to

Grove St.
Barrow St.
Commerce St.
Cornelia St.
Morton St.
Bedford St.
Bleecker St.
Carmine St.
Leroy St.
Walker Park
Clarkson St.
7th Ave.
Downing St.
Varick St.
W. 3rd St.
Bleecker St.
La Guardia Pl.
Avenue of the Americas (6th Ave.)

New York University

GREENWICH VILLAGE

E. 4th St.
E. 3rd St.

E. Houston St.
Lafayette St.

W. Houston St.
130   129
Hudson St.
Greenwich St.
King St.
Charlton St.
Vandam St.
Spring St.
78   79
Renwick St.

SoHo

81   128   127   126   123   122   121   120   118   113
125   124   119   116   115   112   109
86   87   117   114   111   110   108
85   90   91   96   97   103   104   107
88   92   94   95   102   105   106
84   89   93   99   98   101
82   83   77   71   60   51   Spring St.   50
MacDougal St.
Sullivan St.
Thompson St.
W. Broadway
Wooster St.
Greene St.
Mercer St.
Prince St.

80   76   75   72   70   61   59   58   52   49   48   Broome St.
73   69   62   57   53   47   46
34   68   56   54   45
Dominick St.
Broome St.
Watts St.   74   67   63   44   43   Grand St.
Canal St.   36   37   66   65   64   55   38   42   Howard St.
35   39
to Holland Tunnel (Toll)
to Holland Tunnel (Toll)
Watts St.
33   Washington St.
Desbrosses St.
Vestry St.   32
Laight St.
Hubert St.

TriBeCa

Canal St.   40   41
Lispenard St.
Varick St.
6th Ave.

West St.
Collister St.
31
Beach St.
21
N. Moore St.   20
Franklin St.
18   16   14   13
Harrison St.   15
17
19   Jay St.   Staple St.
Greenwich St.
4   Duane St.   6   7
5
3
1
2
Chambers St.
Ericsson Pl. St.

26
22   24
23   25

30   Walker St.
29
Church St.   27
White St.
28
Franklin St.
Broadway
Cortland Alley
Lafayette St.

Leonard St.   12   Catherine Ln.
Worth St.
11
Thomas St.
10
9
8   Duane St.
Reade St.

River Terr.   Chambers St.
North End Ave.

LOWER MANHATTAN

W. Broadway
Warren St.
Church St.
Murray St.
Park Pl.
Broadway
Centre St.

Park Pl. W.
Murray St.

N.Y. City Courthouse

City Hall

CHINATOWN/LOWER EAST SIDE/LITTLE ITALY

km   1/8   1/4
mi   1/16   1/8

N

stock their own larders. The park that remains is one of Manhattan's better play areas for young children. It is clean, safe and, from a kid's point of view, great fun. ♦ Chambers St at Greenwich St

4 Independence Plaza (1975, **Oppenheimer, Brady & Vogelstein, John Pruyn**) Forty floors of middle-income housing a little off the beaten path and with great views of the river. ♦ Greenwich St (Duane-N. Moore Sts)

5 Tommy Tangs ★★$$$ Local restaurant critics have given high marks to the Thai cuisine served here. A correspondent for *The Bangkok Post* said that Tommy Tang is the best Thai chef in America. The staff will guide you through the intricacies of the menu. ♦ Thai ♦ Closed Su. 323 Greenwich St (Reade-Duane Sts) 334.9190

6 Bouley ★★★★$$$$ Chef/owner **David Bouley** has put together an outstanding French menu. My favorites: a pastiche of 3

SoHo/TriBeCa

salads (hot goose foie gras, grilled shrimp, wild mushrooms); roast Maine lobster served in its own consommé with crisp asparagus, winter mint and fresh black truffles; sautéed Maine sea scallops with potato crusts. The

BOULEY

handsome Provençal interior was designed by Bouley and architect **Kevin White**. The prix-fixe luncheon and dinner menus are good first-time choices. Some say a table here is the best to be had in Manhattan. ♦ French ♦ Closed Su. 165 Duane St (Greenwich-Hudson Sts) Jacket, tie and reservations required. 608.3852

7 NeoPersona Gallery Contemporary painting and sculpture by emerging and blue-chip American and European artists. ♦ Tu-F 11AM-6PM; Sa noon-6PM; also by appointment. 51 Hudson St (Duane St) 406.9835

7 Duane Park Cafe ★★$$$ You'll let out a sigh of relief the moment you set foot inside this comfortable restaurant. It's not only pretty in here (thanks to designer **Andrew Ong**), it's quiet. Once seated, you'll discover the menu, a creative mix of **K-Paul's, Hubert's** and **Marcella Hazan** (the 2 head chefs have logged time with each of the above). Menu standouts include sweetbreads accompanied by wild mushrooms and polenta, grilled tuna with olive paste and a gorgeous pear hazelnut tart. ♦ Continental ♦ Closed Su. 157 Duane St (W. Broadway-Hudson St) Reservations required. 732.5555

8 Delphi $ Greek cooking served in large portions at incredibly low prices makes this bustling taverna particularly appropriate for families. The daily special is usually very fresh broiled fish. ♦ Greek ♦ 109 W. Broadway (Reade St) 227.6322

9 Shoe Steal Discontinued shoe styles at amazing savings. Sacha London, Charles Jourdan and Nickels labels have been discovered here among the hodgepodge of not-so-beautiful shoes. ♦ Closed Su. 116 Duane St (W. Broadway) 964.4017

9 Le Zinc ★$$$ This used to be a popular watering hole among the beautiful people but is now more of a neighborhood restaurant. Try the pâté at the bar if you don't want a full meal. ♦ French ♦ Closed Su. 139 Duane St (Church St-W. Broadway) Reservations recommended. 732.1226

10 The Odeon ★★$$$ A good choice for a late-night drink if what you have in mind is a place to sit and schmooze. When it first opened, this neon-lit room was the hottest spot downtown—to the art community what Le Cirque is to international cafe society. The pretentions of the kitchen and the sometimes uppity staff turn off serious diners, though trend-spotters search here for the occasional celebrity. Excellent espresso. ♦ American/French ♦ 145 W. Broadway (Thomas St) Reservations recommended. 233.0507

11 American Telephone & Telegraph Long Lines Building (1974, **John Carl Warnecke & Associates**) Almost windowless (except for the high, squared portholes), this edifice houses electronic wizardry for communications. Texturized pink Swedish granite contrasts with vertical stripes of a beige granite used for, um, decoration. ♦ Church St (Thomas-Worth Sts)

12 The Clocktower (1870, **Griffith Thomas**; expanded 1890, **McKim, Mead & White**) Sponsored by the Institute for Contemporary Art, this nonprofit sibling of **P.S. 1 Museum**, the exhibition space in Long Island City, is situated in the high-ceilinged tower room of a former office building. The institute is dedicated to supporting new and experimental projects and artists working in areas not covered by established museums. ♦ Suggested contribution. Th-Su noon-6PM. 108 Leonard St (Broadway) 233.1096

13 Aux Delices des Bois Stop in for your own supply of the same mushrooms that the chefs at **China Grill** and **21** will be cooking with tonight; shiitake, crimini, portobello, enoki, chanterelle and lobster are among the varieties that **Amy** and **Thierry Farge** import from all over the world. ♦ Closed Sa-Su. 4 Leonard St (W. Broadway-Hudson St) 334.1230

14 Nautical Chart Supply Co. This supplier to the big shipping companies now makes his nautical wares available to the general public. Everything from a laminated card explaining basic knots and how to tie them to sailing directions to Scotland, the *Modern Marine Engineers Manual* and marine barometers. ♦ Closed Su. 90 Hudson St (Harrison St) 925.8849

There 504.3mi of sidewalk in New York City.

15 Puffy's Tavern Retaining the atmosphere of a speakeasy, which it was during Prohibition, this pre-TriBeCa bar pulls you in from the street to have a beer, hang out and listen to the jukebox with the after-work crowd and neighborhood regulars. ♦ 81 Hudson St (Harrison St) 766.9159

16 Chanterelle ★★★$$$$ Young chef **David Waltuck**, acclaimed as a fresh, unspoiled genius, attracted fashionable uptown crowds to the dining room he and his wife, **Karen**, established on Grand St. Now they flock here, a pretty space designed by **Bill Katz**, where little has changed but the address. The food is quite original, artfully presented and always delicious. The seafood sausages are justifiably renowned. Alas, they don't serve breakfast anymore. ♦ French ♦ Closed M, Su. 6 Harrison St (Hudson St) Reservations required. 966.6960

16 New York Mercantile Exchange (1884) Another headquarters, like the one at 628 Broadway, for the big dealers in dairy and poultry products. The main offices used to be uptown, but this great old building, closer to the actual markets, is where the action was at the turn of the century. ♦ 6 Harrison St (Hudson St)

16 Just Kidding The cotton children's clothing, most of which is made downstairs in the basement or by artists in the neighborhood, is wonderful, but owner **Margaret Owen**'s most effective marketing tool may be the play area in the back: little ones beg to stay longer. ♦ Closed Su. 22 Harrison St (Staple-Hudson Sts) 219.0035

16 The Sporting Club ★$$ A sports fanatic's dream. Up to 6 different events are piped in by satellite onto screens in every corner of the room; the main event is shown on a 10x10ft screen above the bar. A glance at the patented electronic scoreboard will tell you the status of every pro and college game being played that day. You may even catch a TV sports crew taping a fan reaction spot at the bar. The menu is made up of appropriately named dishes—try the *Willie Mays Catch* or the *Steak Lamotta*. ♦ Continental ♦ 99 Hudson St (Franklin-Leonard Sts) Reservations required for major sporting events. 219.0900

17 A.L. Bazzini Company The largest dried fruit and nut suppliers in the city for over 100 years. To your right as you enter are shelves filled with exotic condiments and spices. Upstairs you'll find the aromatic peanuts that are dry-roasted, plus a full array of gourmet treats, including great coffee beans. I always order a cappuccino to go on my way out. ♦ 339 Greenwich St (Jay St) 334.1280

18 How's Bayou $$ You can dig right into the warm chips and tasty (though not spicy) salsa while waiting for a frozen margarita. But don't fill up on the starters—entrees are generous. Keep the beads they give you when you walk in—10 sets get you a free drink. The music is a tad too loud, but goes well with the upbeat atmosphere. ♦ Cajun ♦ 355 Greenwich St (Harrison St) No credit cards. 925.5405

18 Tribeca Grill ★★$$$ **Drew Nietorent**, owner of **Montrachet**, one of the city's best restaurants, has teamed up with **Robert De Niro** to open this

loftlike restaurant in the former Martinson Coffee Building. The first-rate bistro fare includes roast monkfish with wild mushrooms, barbecued duck with Chinese overtones and sautéed red snapper. Desserts are a must, especially the chocolate cake. Sketches and paintings by Mr. DeNiro's father, **Robert**, adorn the walls. The mahogany bar is the original bar from Maxwell's Plum. Mr. DeNiro has converted the warehouse into a film production center. Tenants include **Steven Speilberg, Brian De Palma** and **Martin Scorsese**. ♦ American ♦ 375 Greenwich St (Franklin St) 941.3900

19 Harrison Street Row (1828; restored 1975, **Oppenheimer, Brady & Vogelstein**) Almost a stage set, this row of impeccably restored Federal houses acts as an antidote to the massive apartment houses above it. ♦ 37-41 Harrison St (Greenwich St)

20 Riverrun Cafe ★$$ One of the first restaurants in TriBeCa, it's a neighborhood staple for decent food and a comfortable place to sit, eat and talk without feeling hassled. The colorful map outside will help you find your way to your next downtown destination. ♦ Continental ♦ 176 Franklin St (Hudson-Greenwich Sts) 966.3894

One man's junk is another man's treasure, and you can find outstanding examples of both along Canal St between Broadway and 6th Ave. The selections range from used clothing to seemingly useless pieces of electronic equipment, plumbing supplies and other assorted gadgets and hardware. It costs nothing to look at, and very little to buy the endlessly fascinating things you see here. The street was originally a wide drainage ditch carrying polluted water from the Collect Pond (eventually filled to become the Foley Square area) over to the Hudson River. Citizen complaints about the stench and the mosquito problem led to the filling of the ditch—which the city preferred to call a canal—in 1820.

20 Cafe Americano ★$$$ This eye-catching restaurant is open and airy, and the decor, service and food are all quite pleasant. But it doesn't attract the crowd it used to. Its owners have resorted to making up postcards telling patrons which celebrities have been there—they should know that this will surely keep the rich and famous away. ♦ Italian ♦ Closed Su. 105 Hudson St (Franklin St) 219.8802

21 Commodities A natural foods supermarket with a large stock of organic and otherwise healthy comestibles, as well as bodycare products, cookbooks and health food for your pet. An extensive variety of flour, rice, cereal, beans and pasta is sold in bulk from rows of wooden bins. ♦ 117 Hudson St (N. Moore St) 334.8330

22 Walkers $ Run by the people who own **The Ear Inn**. Have a drink with police officers from the 1st Precinct finishing up their shifts or chat with the other friendly folk over free, after-5

SoHo/TriBeCa

munchies. ♦ American ♦ 16 N. Moore St (Varick St) 941.0142

23 Franklin Street Potters Watch potters create in this working studio and gallery, formerly a cheese store. All of the wares are lead-free and microwave- and dishwasher-safe. ♦ 151 Franklin St (Hudson St-W. Broadway) 431.7361

24 two eleven ★$$$ A longtime artists' hangout that isn't bohemian in the slightest. On the contrary, it's exactly what you'd expect a TriBeCa restaurant to be. High ceilings and fans, greenery, subdued colors and interesting music add to the hushed, intense atmosphere. The outdoor cafe is quite popular in the warmer months. ♦ Continental ♦ 211 W. Broadway (Franklin St) 925.7202

24 El Teddy's ★★$$$ Inside the 3-story building topped with a lifesize replica of the *Statue of Liberty*'s crown are old-fashioned booths, vintage 1940s wallpaper and a neon fish tank, among other eclectic touches. The cuisine is basic Mexican fare. Check out the margaritas—the best in town. ♦ Mexican ♦ 219 W. Broadway (White-Franklin Sts) 941.7070

24 Artists Space One of the most original, and certainly one of the most successful of the alternative space galleries. A perennial springboard for new talent, they also award grants and maintain a file of about 3000 artists, which is used by collectors, curators and architects in search of an artist who falls into a specific category: conceptual, feminist, under 35, etc. ♦ Tu-Sa 11AM-6PM. 223 W. Broadway (Franklin-White Sts) 226.3970

25 Franklin Furnace Call it an alternative art space or an experimental outpost, but this is the country's largest collection of published art works: books, periodicals, postcards, pamphlets and cassette tapes, displayed in temporary installations using text and image.

Performances by artists January-June, September-December. ♦ Free. Tu-F 11AM-6PM; Sa noon-6PM. 112 Franklin St (W. Broadway-Church St) 925.4671

MONTRACHET

26 Montrachet ★★★$$$ The establishment is very French, which means that the setting is very stylish (**Spanier & Dennis** did the interior) and the food very good. Chef **Debra Ponzek** is producing wonderfully imaginative contemporary fare that fans say is among the best in the area. Respected for its extensive and well-chosen wine list. Depending on who you are or who the staff thinks you are not, the service can be somewhat haughty. I always sit in one of the interior dining rooms. ♦ French ♦ Closed Su. 239 W. Broadway (White St) Reservations recommended. 219.2777

26 White Street An eclectic range of styles reflects the history of the TriBeCa cast-iron district. There are more attractive streets nearby, but none more typical. Contrast the authentic Federal details of No. 2 (built as a liquor store in 1809), the artful stonework of No. 10 (designed by **Henry Fernbach** in 1869) and the mansard roofline of No. 17. The upper stories of Nos. 8 and 10 are shorter than the lower floors—a favorite Renaissance Revival device that makes the buildings appear taller. ♦ W. Broadway-Church St

26 SoHo Photo Gallery The oldest and largest cooperative gallery for photographers in the US. ♦ Tu 7-9PM; F-Su 1-6PM. 15 White St (W. Broadway-Church St) 226.8571

26 Alternative Museum Two spacious galleries in a cast-iron building house a museum founded and operated by artists for nonestablished artists. Poetry readings and concerts—folk, jazz, traditional—with the emphasis on the international and unusual. ♦ Free. Tu-Sa 11AM-6PM. 17 White St (Church St) 966.4444

27 Arqua ★★$$$ A typical late-1980s' chic New York City restaurant: a cavernous room, deafening acoustics, minimalist decor, snippy service, beautiful people. But the food is good, and most enjoyable at lunchtime, when you can actually hear your companion. ♦ Italian ♦ Closed Su. 281 Church St (White St) Reservations recommended. 334.1888

28 Let There Be Neon The creations of founder **Rudi Stern**, one of America's foremost neon artists. They include clocks, tables, chairs, windows, signs, stage sets and interiors, all in neon. He has neon-lit fish tanks, and has made signs for dentists (one says *Roots*, the other *Gums*). Stern is the author of *Let There Be Neon*, a pictorial history of the medium. ♦ Closed Sa-Su. 38 White St (W. Broadway-Church St) 226.4883

Restaurants/Nightlife: Red
Shops/Parks: Green
Hotels: Blue
Sights/Culture: Black

29 Barocco ★★$$$ No one seems to care that they are practically sitting on the laps of their neighbors in this sparse but lively trattoria; the diners are too happy in the knowledge that they are among the chic-est and most with-it of the downtown crowd. To satisfy your palate as well as your ego, have the delicious pan-roasted quail and some *fettunta* (garlic bread) with any of the excellent homemade pastas. Portions are extremely generous. One of my favorite restaurants. ◆ Italian ◆ 301 Church St (Walker St) Reservations recommended. 431.1445

30 HOME for contemporary theatre and art Gallery and performance space for new and emerging (aka struggling) artists. Performances nightly at 8PM. ◆ Gallery Tu-Su 11AM-8PM. 44 Walker St (Church St-W. Broadway) 431.7434

31 Royal Canadian Pancake House & Restaurant ★$ Fifty-four varieties of pancakes, 18 kinds of waffles, 12 variations of French toast, all worth the caloric splurge, and what a splurge it is: each pancake measures 8 1/2in in diameter! Expect a line on weekends. ◆ 145 Hudson St (Beach-Hubert Sts) 219.3038

31 Thai House Cafe ★$ Small, unassuming and generic-looking. But if you can stand the Muzak, you'll enjoy excellent authentic Thai food and friendly, helpful service. ◆ Thai ◆ Closed Su. 151 Hudson St (Hubert St) No credit cards. 334.1085

32 Jan Weiss Gallery Weiss, a quantitative investment analyst-turned-art collector shows the work of contemporary American, Australian and European artists. ◆ M-F by appointment; Sa 1-6PM. 98 Laight St (Greenwich St) 925.7313

Capsouto Frères

33 Capsouto Frères ★★$$ One of the first trend-setting TriBeCa restaurants to attract a citywide clientele. The *frères* (brothers) are almost always on hand to make their guests welcome. Drop in at the bar for a midafternoon cup of espresso, or linger over a long dinner. The menu reflects French and American styles, and there are always some interesting surprises and good desserts. ◆ French ◆ 451 Washington St (Watts St) Reservations required F-Su. 966.4900

34 Holland Tunnel (1927) The world's first underwater tunnel for vehicles, the Holland dips nearly 100ft below the surface of the Hudson River. The tunnel is about 29ft wide with a 12ft ceiling. Its north tube is 8558ft long, and its south tube stretches 8371ft. One of the major problems of the tunnel's construction was ventilation: 42 huge fans at each end provided the solution. **Clifford M. Holland** was the engineer who masterminded this building marvel, and the feat secured his

name in New York—and American—history. ◆ Canal St, Manhattan to 12th St, Jersey City

35 Nosmo King ★★$$ In this out-of-the-way, oddly comfortable place, you can indulge in the pleasures of denial and gratification simultaneously: wade into the excesses of gourmet organic and vegetarian cuisine and come out healthy. Exotic mushrooms, seared tuna, Chinese chardonnay and dairyless desserts are available—and delicious. But no butter, no meat and no smoking. Ask for a booth. ◆ Haute Organic ◆ Closed M. 54 Varick St (Canal St) 966.1239

36 Triplets Roumanian Restaurant ★★$$$ Don't be misled by the decidedly un-Rumanian decor; the food is as authentic as it gets this side of the Danube. And as you may have guessed, it's owned and run by identical triplets (brothers) with a fascinating history—they were separated at birth and reunited at age 19. On weekend nights, you'll feel like a

tagalong at cousin Sophie's wedding. Stuffed cabbage and professional egg creams made at your table. ◆ Rumanian ◆ Closed M. 11-17 Grand St (6th Ave) Reservations required. 925.9303

37 Moondance Diner ★$ A real diner with gussied-up diner food, in keeping with the creative atmosphere of the neighborhood. Soups, burgers and sandwiches are best bets. Barbecued chicken is moist, tender and wonderfully sloppy. The coffee, laced with cinnamon, is served as it should be—in a pitcher. Good wine bargains. Great breakfasts. ◆ American ◆ 80 6th Ave (Grand St) No credit cards. 226.1191

38 Greene Street These 5 cobblestoned blocks are in the heart of the **SoHo Cast-Iron Historic District** (designated in 1973), an area taken over by textile manufacturing and other light industry after the retail and entertainment center of the city moved north in the mid-19th century. The 50 cast-iron buildings still intact on Greene St were built between 1869 and 1895. Functionally, cast iron anticipated modern steel-frame building techniques, but decoratively it was used to imitate styles and manners of traditional masonry construction. Designers particularly loved ornate Renaissance and Neoclassical motifs, which they altered with a free and fantastical hand. The 2 outstanding buildings on this street—both in excellent condition—are by **J.F. Duckworth** Nos. 28-30 (1872), a magnificently mansarded representative of the Second Empire style with leafless Corinthian columns, and Nos. 72-76 (1873), also Corinthian, but here treated in an Italianate manner with a pedimented porch and porticoes all the way up the projecting center bays. The building was built for the **Gardner Colby Company**, whose initials appear on the pilasters. Also noteworthy are the arched lintels and columns, with their egg-and-dart motifs, of Nos. 114-120, designed in 1882 as a branch of a department store; the Ionic capitals turned sideways at Nos. 132-134, 136 and 138 (1885); and all of the extraordinarily ornate No. 31 (1876). Of course, all here is not necessarily iron. Several masonry buildings of the same period sport decorative ironwork—Nos. 42-44 and 84-86, for example—and one is, well, paint. The brick side wall on the corner is graced by **Richard Haas'** trompe l'oeil mural (1975) that mimics the cast-iron facade of the building. Many interior spaces remain intact as well. Perhaps the easiest to visit, and ones that best demonstrate the expansive qualities of a loft space, are galleries such as No. 142. ♦ Canal-W. Houston Sts

38 Zero A showroom for Zero, the Italian high-tech, modular display system. The huge display in the front of the shop is a piece of art-

SoHo/TriBeCa

work in itself. ♦ 89 Grand St (Green St) 925.3615

38 Yohji Yamamoto Themes of recent collections by this talented Japanese designer have included turn-of-the-century Eastern Europe and haute couture with an asymetrical twist. The prices are high, but the shop is worth a visit even if only to see the iron, rolled-steel and bronze fixtures designed in London by **Antony Donaldson.** ♦ 103 Grand St (Mercer St) 966.9066

39 Ronald Feldman Fine Arts Inc. This gallery's eclectic and challenging stable includes American, European and Soviet artists. ♦ M by appointment; Tu-Sa 10AM-6PM. 31 Mercer St (Canal-Grand Sts) 226.3232

39 Museum of Holography If you've never been able to understand holograms—3-D images recorded by laser light—you will after a visit to these remarkable exhibitions. *Holo* means whole, *gram* means message. The medium is the whole message in this case: you will have to decide for yourself if it is also an art form. ♦ Admission. Daily 11AM-6PM. 11 Mercer St (Canal-Grand Sts) 925.0581

40 Industrial Plastic Supply Co. A sprawling loft space filled with plastic of every description and color, and they'll cut any of it to any size without charge. Resins and rubber for mold-making, picture frames, mirrors, decorative accessories and lots of things you never knew could be made of plastic. ♦ Closed Su. 309 Canal St (Broadway-Mercer St) 226.2010

41 Pearl River Mart This Chinese department store stocks Chinese imports, including groceries and a good selection of kimonos. I like to wander around here; I always come away with something. ♦ 277 Canal St (Broadway) 2nd, 3rd floors. 431.4770

42 443 Broadway (1860, **Griffith Thomas**) In a neighborhood of iron buildings pretending to be stone, this 5-story building is the real thing; and it's a real beauty, once you get past the altered ground floor. The building next door, at 447, built at the same time, is also stone, but its storefront is iron, right out of **Daniel Badger's** catalog. ♦ Howard-Grand Sts

43 Amsterdam's ★$$ This always jumping 2-tier restaurant includes a long bar along one side and an open grill on the other. Best bets are the chicken and seafood. ♦ American ♦ 454 Broadway (Grand St) Reservations recommended. 925.6166. Also at: 428 Amsterdam Ave. 874.1377

44 L'Ecole ★★$$ (1880, **John Correja**) **Jacques Pepin,** author and cooking school director, is dean of culinary education at the **French Culinary Institute,** whose students run this restaurant. There is some good cooking to be had here; particularly recommended are the regional dinners that they prepare from time to time. Like all student-operated restaurants though, it sometimes has its off days. ♦ French ♦ Closed Su. 462 Broadway (Grand St) 219.8890

45 Pony Circus, Ltd. Lots of 19th-century (some 18th-century) oak furniture, plus cash registers, stained-glass windows, old signs and Tiffany lamps are packed—chairs even hang from the ceiling—into this big antique shop. A fascinating place to browse, even if you're not buying. A popular stop for set designers. Call for an appointment. ♦ Closed Su. 476 Broadway (Grand-Broome Sts) 925.7589

45 478 Broadway (1874, **Richard Morris Hunt**) Of all the cast-iron buildings in New York, the magazine *Architectural Record* hailed this one as the *most serious attempt to utilize the almost unlimited strength of the material.* ♦ Grand-Broome Sts

Within 478 Broadway:

Pure Madderlake An eclectic, spirited shop with 3 personalities: a florist specializing in fresh flowers that grow in English gardens; a home furnishings boutique stocked with antique furniture and a wide variety of tabletop items, including an exclusive line of crystal from Vienna; and a professional photography studio in the back. ♦ 941.7770

46 486 Broadway (1883, **Lamb & Rich**) This titanic former home of the Mechanics Bank combines Romanesque and Moorish elements in brick, stone and terra cotta. Look up at the mansard roof with its projecting windows and small cupolas. ♦ Broome St

47 Haughwout Building (1857, **John Gaynor**) A cast-iron Italian palazzo, famous as the building that contained New York's first elevator, a reminder of which is a little rusting sign over the door just to the left of the main entrance. The store is now the **SoHo Mill Outlet**, and the building itself is in a sinful state of disrepair. In better days it was **E.V. Haughwout's** cut glass and silver store. ♦ 490 Broadway (Broome Sts)

48 Canal Jean Co. The original home of surplus chic, it's much more than just jeans. Shop here for the SoHo look without flattening your wallet. ♦ 504 Broadway (Broome-Spring Sts) 226.1130

49 495 Broadway (1893, **Alfred Zucker**) Proof that hope springs eternal: this handsome brick-and-stone structure with fine iron panels replaced an 1860 cast-iron building at almost the same time the district began heading for its decline. ♦ Broome-Spring Sts

49 521-523 Broadway (1854) Nothing but this section remains of the luxurious **St. Nicholas Hotel**, which once extended along Broadway, Mercer and Spring Sts. Its original frontage on the 3 streets was 750ft. Inside, the rugs, tapestries, crystal chandeliers and beveled mirrors made it a tourist attraction even among visitors who couldn't afford to stay there. The hotel's dining rooms accommodated 600, and there was usually a line outside. Its bridal suite, filled with satin and lace, rich rosewood and crystal, was said to have been designed to intimidate newlyweds, but it attracted them by the score, and for 30 years was considered the best possible place to begin a happy marriage. **Long Island Fabrics,** on the ground floor of 521, stocks a good selection of African prints (925.4488) ♦ Broome-Spring Sts

49 Mattawan Even if you're not in the market for a down comforter, a quilt or a blanket (all home furnishings are 100% natural), stop in anyway to see the beautiful interior and tin ceiling in this 1897 building. ♦ 491 Broadway (Broome-Spring Sts) 226.5825

50 Spring Street Natural ★★$$ Steamed brussels sprouts with melted Jarlsberg and seasoned bread crumbs; pumpkin ravioli with scallions, red peppers, pine nuts, curry and cream; and any one of the several varieties of fresh fish are winning choices here. The light-filled interior is strewn with plants. ♦ American ♦ 62 Spring St (Lafayette St) 966.0290

51 Art et Industrie The art here is not just to look at, but to use. On the other hand, if you have no immediate use for some of these pieces, it's worthwhile to stop in for a look around. ♦ Closed M, Su. 106 Spring St (Mercer St) 431.1661

51 Jacques Carcanagues Jewelry, textiles, furniture, sculpture and ritual objects from around the world. ♦ Closed M. 114 Spring St (Mercer-Greene Sts) 925.8110

51 Evergreen Antiques Scandinavian country furniture and accessories. ♦ Closed Su. 120 Spring St (Mercer-Greene Sts) 966.6458

52 Michael Carey American Arts & Crafts A good selection of pottery, lighting, furniture by **Gustave Stickley** (1858-1942) and other period designers. ♦ Closed M, Su. 77 Mercer St (Broome-Spring Sts) 226.3710

52 The Enchanted Forest This bewitching shop looks like a miniature set for a fantasy adventure. Beasts, books and handmade toys

are part of the celebration. ♦ 85 Mercer St (Broome-Spring Sts) 925.6677

52 Leekan Designs The always exotic window invites you in to peruse. Antique jade and porcelain, wood carvings, silk rugs, embroidered hangings, wedding baskets, inexpensive folk art and other treasures imported from China and Southeast Asia. ♦ 93 Mercer St (Broome-Spring Sts) 226.7226

53 The Smiths A great rectangular loft space shows off classic clothing with a twist: a strategically placed belt turns a workaday suit into a stylish day-into-night outfit; a cropped, hand-knit sweater dresses up a simple linen skirt. Great care is taken with alterations. ♦ 454 Broome St (Mercer St) 431.0038

54 Friends of Figurative Sculpture A friendly gallery featuring bronze sculptures of the human figure in a variety of sizes. ♦ Sa 1-6PM; also by appointment. 53 Mercer St (Grand-Broome Sts) 226.4850

54 Marianne Novobatzky Women's clothing designed by Novobatzky for urban living with an attention to detail rarely found in today's high-speed world. If you don't find the perfect fit or color in her ready-to-wear collection, a new garment will be custom-stitched for you in her workshop downstairs. All of the display pieces in the shop were sculpted by Marianne's boyfriend, artist **John Ittner**. ♦ 65 Mercer St (Broome St) 431.4120

55 Niall Smith Antiques A popular haunt for designers and collectors from all over the world in search of Neoclassical European furniture dating from 1800-1830. ♦ Closed Su. 96 Grand St (Green-Mercer Sts) 941.7354

On 21 January 1908, the first ordinance banning smoking was passed—not surprisingly, this ordinance applied to women only.

56 **SoHo 20 Gallery** A cooperative of women artists with group and individual shows. ♦ Tu-Sa noon-6PM. 469 Broome St (Greene St) 226.4167

57 **Brooke Alexander Editions** Longtime champions of the graphic image, **Brooke** and **Carolyn Alexander** have opened the roomy, light-filled space that every print maven dreams about. Featured are American prints since 1960 by such contemporary masters as **Johns, Lichtenstein** and **Judd** as well as a selective inventory of works by younger artists and distinctive Europeans. ♦ Tu-Sa 10AM-6PM. 476 Broome St (Greene-Wooster Sts) 4th floor. 925.4338

58 **Luna D'Oro** Jewelry, handicrafts and furnishings from South and Central America. ♦ 66 Greene St (Broome-Spring Sts) 925.8225

58 **The Second Coming** Home furnishings, furniture, apparel and jewelry that was fashionable in the 1940s and '50s. Among the

SoHo/TriBeCa

selections are overstuffed Art Deco furniture, dresses in black rayon and velvet and printed fabrics. The building, one of 4 on the street designed by **Isaac Duckworth** in 1873, was called the *King of Greene St*. (*The Queen* is 28 Greene St.) This one is a masterpiece of French Second Empire in cast iron. ♦ 72 Greene St (Broome-Spring Sts) 431.4424

59 **5&10-No Exaggeration** $$ The antiques in this vintage 1940s jazz club are all for sale. The food is OK; come for the entertainment. ♦ American ♦ 77 Greene St (Broome-Spring Sts) Reservations required F-Sa. 925.7414

59 **Heller Gallery** One of the most important representatives of the modern glass movement, this always interesting gallery usually has 2 solo shows and a monthly overview. ♦ Tu-Sa 11AM-6PM; Su noon-5PM. 71 Greene St (Broome-Spring Sts) 966.5948

59 **Craft Caravan, Inc**. Traditional African handicrafts plus some interesting household items in a display case up front—*Beauty Pagent* talc powder and *Elephant Powder* laundry detergent, for instance. ♦ Closed M. 63 Greene St (Broome-Spring Sts) 431.6669

60 **Platypus** All sorts of housewares, from designer kettles and flatware (**Alessi, Michael Graves, Aldo Rossi**) to wicker furniture and antiques (18th- and 19th-century pine armoires, cupboards, cribs). Stop in for Godiva chocolates as well. ♦ 126 Spring St (Greene St) 219.3919

60 **Penny Whistle Toys** The downtown branch of this refreshing toy store has new and old-fashioned board games, indoor gyms, costumes and rattles for infants—all lovingly assembled by owner **Meredith Brokaw**, wife of the well-known TV anchor.

♦ Closed M. 132 Spring St (Greene-Wooster Sts) 925.2088. Also at: 1283 Madison Ave. 369.3868; 448 Columbus Ave. 873.9090

60 **Jaap Rietman** Just one flight up, an unsurpassed source for the best books and periodicals on art, architecture and photography. The staff is knowledgeable, and the atmosphere conducive to browsing—it's actually encouraged. I often retreat here on rainy days. ♦ Closed Su. 134 Spring St (Greene-Wooster Sts) 2nd floor. 966.7044

60 **Peter Roberts Antiques** Specialist in American Arts and Crafts furniture and accessories. ♦ 134 Spring St (Greene-Wooster Sts) 226.4777

60 **Laurence Miller Gallery** Works by photography greats **Lee Friedlander** and **Helen Levitt** hang beside those of younger shutterbugs, all chosen with Miller's customary discretion. ♦ Tu-Sa 10AM-6PM. 138 Spring St (Greene-Wooster Sts) 3rd floor. 226.1220

61 **Printed Matter Bookstore at Dia** This nonprofit art center specializes in books made by artists, which means the artist has been directly involved with the conceptualization, design and production of the work. The average price per book is $10—choose among 4000 titles by 2500 artists—making them one of very few bargains in the art world. ♦ Tu-Sa 10AM-6PM. 77 Wooster St (Broome-Spring Sts) 925.0325

62 **59 Wooster Street** (1890, **Alfred Zucker**) Originally a warehouse, this 6-story building dominates the corner where it stands. Its mass is relieved by arched, iron-rimmed windows on its Broome St facade, and by highly sculptural reliefs scattered over its surface. The seemingly random play between the rough-hewn masonry, smooth brickwork and crenolated roofline (look hard, and you'll see hand-size human faces way up top) somehow pulls the building together and gives it an oddly noble presence. Best seen from the south side of Broome St. ♦ Broome St

Within 59 Wooster Street:

Brooke Alexander In luxurious quarters designed by the English architect **Max Gordon, Carolyn** and **Brooke Alexander** feature painting and sculpture by some of the most vigorous talents, including **Jane Dickson, Yvonne Jacquette** and **Tom Otterness**. ♦ Tu-Sa 10AM-6PM. 2nd floor. 925.4338

New York's first subway (1 car, seating 22 passengers) was fueled by a blast of air from a huge steam-driven fan, which would suck the car back when it reached the end of the line. It traveled 10 miles an hour and ran under Broadway from Warren to Murray Sts, a distance of 312ft. It was conceived and constructed in 1870 by **Alfred Ely Beach**, a publisher and the inventor of the typewriter.

Restaurants/Nightlife: Red Hotels: Blue
Shops/Parks: Green   Sights/Culture: Black

62 Sura Kayla Dried, silk and fresh flowers, candles, antique and vintage knicknacks, custom-made furniture (pine dining and end tables with white birch legs, for example) and gift ideas galore. They also do party planning. ♦ 484 Broome St (Wooster St) 941.8757

63 The Drawing Center An important nonprofit exhibition space for unaffiliated artists, as well as exceptional scholarly shows of work on paper from historical and contemporary periods. Excellent catalogs. The elegant space was designed by **James Stewart Polshek** in 1986. ♦ Tu, Th-Sa 10AM-6PM; W 11AM-8PM. 35 Wooster St (Grand-Broome Sts) 219.2166

63 Performing Garage Home to one of America's oldest experimental theater companies, **The Wooster Group.** Founded in 1967 by director **Richard Schechner** and under the direction of **Elizabeth LeCompte**, the company redefines traditional notions of storyline, thematic content and performance structure. ♦ Seats 120. 33 Wooster St (Grand-Broome Sts) 966.3651

64 Lucky Strike $$ A very popular late-night SoHo hangout. The food is good, if boring—except for the French fries, which are excellent. Airy, comfortable, unpretentious. ♦ Continental ♦ 59 Grand St (Wooster St-W. Broadway) 941.0479

64 La Jumelle $$ La Jumelle means *the twin*—this twin's twin is **Lucky Strike**, just 2 doors down. Both are charmingly frumpy bars-cum-restaurants with their bistro menus written on blackboards. The clientele is young, trendy Upper West Side on a trip to SoHo. ♦ French ♦ 55 Grand St (Wooster St-W. Broadway) 941.9651

65 Jour et Nuit ★★★$$ With all those beautiful people streaming in here, concentrating on the food at this popular bistro is difficult—but really worth the effort. Try the shellfish soup, foie gras on toast with fig confit, and salmon tuna carpaccio. Try to sit upstairs by all means. A good spot for a SoHo lunch. Reservations are a must. ♦ French ♦ 337 W. Broadway (Grand St) 925.5971

66 Tamu Indonesian Rijsttafel ★★$$ Indonesia is such a diverse country, it isn't easy to pinpoint a national cuisine. But the Dutch colonists favored *rijsttafel*, a meal based on rice with an array of small dishes of chicken, seafood, meat, vegetables and condiments. This is the best example of how it should be prepared and presented. ♦ Indonesian ♦ 340 W. Broadway (Grand St) Reservations recommended. 925.2751

CINCO·DE·MAYO

67 Cinco de Mayo ★$$ Sunny Mexico lands in SoHo with authentic home-cooked specialties. Chicken in chili-and-pumpkin seed sauce and *taquitos de moronga* (small corn shells filled with slivers of grilled sausage and spices) are a far cry from most New York Tex-Mex. ♦ Mexican ♦ 349 W. Broadway (Grand-Broome Sts) Reservations recommended. 226.5255. Also at: 45 Tudor City Pl. 661.5070

68 The Cupping Room Cafe $$ Waffles with berries, giant muffins (the whole wheat is addictive), bagels with fixings and a choice of terrific coffees and teas draw a fiercely loyal crowd. A very popular (standing-room-only) Saturday and Sunday brunch spot. Live jazz Thursday-Saturday evenings. ♦ Continental ♦ 359 W. Broadway (Broome

SoHo/TriBeCa

St) Dinner reservations recommended. 925.2898

68 Kenn's Broome Street Bar $ This 1825 building was altered in 1868 to become a boarding house and a saloon. The hamburgers served here today come on pita bread. There are other trendy touches, but your grandfather would still recognize the bar, which hasn't changed much in all these years. ♦ American ♦ 363 W. Broadway (Broome St) No credit cards. 925.2086

69 Amazonas ★$$ Better food can be found elsewhere, but the Brazilian cocktails, interesting music and amusing late-night crowd are worth coming for. ♦ Brazilian ♦ 492 Broome St (Wooster St-W. Broadway) Reservations required F-Sa. 966.3371

70 Gemini GEL at Joni Weyl New and vintage prints from the venerable LA workshop, including editions by **Ellsworth Kelly**, **Roy Lichtenstein** and **Robert Rauschenberg**, can be viewed by appointment. ♦ 375 W. Broadway (Broome-Spring Sts) 2nd floor. 219.1446

Only a few areas remain to remind us of the once predominant Federal-style brick row house. The **Charlton-King-Vandam Historic District** (1828-34), a 4-block area (bounded by 6th Ave and Houston, Varick and Vandam Sts) was developed primarily by **John Jacob Astor**. It has the city's largest concentration of these old homes and was designated a National Landmark in 1966. There is a fine example of the period in the unbroken row on the north side of Vandam St. A larger row along Charlton's north side includes the noteworthy Nos. 37 and 39, along with 4 Greek Revival replacements. King St mixes Federal with a potpourri of later styles. At the corner of King and MacDougal Sts is one of the few 19th-century storefronts left in the city. ♦ Vandam-Houston Sts (6th Ave-Varick St)

70 Betsy Senior Contemporary Prints
Senior maintains a select inventory of prints
from small American publishers, as well as
new editions by rising stars. ♦ By appointment. 375 W. Broadway (Broome-Spring Sts)
2nd floor. 941.0960

70 SoHo Emporium A frightening gaggle of
some 40 independent boutiques selling everything from furs to jewelry, and crafts to crystal. Should you be in need of advice—a way
out, perhaps—there is even a fortuneteller.
♦ 375 W. Broadway (Broome-Spring Sts)
966.7895

70 Portico Owner **Steven Werther** travels far
and wide to find craftspeople who meet his
meticulous standards of construction. Among
the pieces that have made the grade are handmade reproductions of Shaker furniture,
Mexican and Argentinian antiques and dishes
and glassware from Italy. In the middle of the
store—it stretches all the way to Wooster St

SoHo/TriBeCa

—is a pleasant cafe setting where you can sit
and relax with a cappuccino or a cup of tea
(try one from the United Society of Shakers in
Maine). ♦ 379 W. Broadway (Broome-Spring
Sts) 941.7800

70 O.K. Harris Works of Art A SoHo landmark
for 20 years, this gallery is a record-setter
with more than 70 artists represented, and an
average of 50 exhibitions each year in its
11,000sq ft spread. **Ivan Karp**, an early champion of Pop Art, is the gallery's founder and
chief point man. ♦ Tu-Sa 10AM-6PM. 383 W.
Broadway (Broome-Spring Sts) 431.3600

71 New Deal ★$$ This smart-looking restau-

rant was formerly called
WPA, and the black-and-
white murals by the late
George Stavrinos (best-
known for his fashion illus-
trations for Bergdorf's)
evoke the period when the
Works Progress Administra-
tion was among the agencies
that were part of President
Roosevelt's New Deal. The
murals alone are worth a
visit, as is the food—safari fanatics take note:
New Deal's annual Game Festival includes
snake, beaver, lion, elk, buffalo and giraffe.
Another reason to drop in is the live jazz (no
minimum, no cover) presented every night in
the small front bar. ♦ Continental ♦ 152
Spring St (Wooster St-W. Broadway)
431.3663

72 Think Big If you can find a use for a 6ft-long
pencil or a wristwatch too big for King Kong,
more power to you. This famous store has a
whole line of outsize items that will make you
feel like a Lilliputian. ♦ 390 W. Broadway
(Broome-Spring Sts) 925.7300

72 D.F. Sanders Until recently one of the
biggest and best high-tech houseware and
design stores. You could find state-of-the-art
vacuum cleaners, as well as exclusives like
pure cotton shag bathroom rugs. Lets hope
they come to their senses. ♦ 386 W. Broad-
way (Broome-Spring Sts) 925.9040

72 Barolo ★$$$ Italian food with excellent
pasta and broiled fresh fish is served in this
enormous restaurant, probably the largest in
SoHo. Go and see the 9 magnificent matching
cherry trees in the garden; this is where the
action is anyway. Those in-the-know go elsewhere for dessert. ♦ Italian ♦ 398 W. Broadway (Spring-Broome Sts) 226.1102

73 Papers Etc. A source for lush, handmade
papers, cards and gifts. ♦ 510 Broome St (W.
Broadway-Thompson St) 431.7720

73 Betina Riedel Comfortable women's
clothes featured in the designer's own store.
♦ Closed M. 508 Broome St (W. Broadway-
Thompson St) 226.2350

74 Manhattan Brewing Co. $$ This massive
building was once a Con Edison power sta-
tion, but it's now a restaurant and the fourth
largest microbrewery in the country. All of the
beers are available in the **Tap Room**, which
features the huge copper vats used in beer-
making. Call for brewery tour information.
♦ Continental ♦ Closed M. 40 Thompson St
(Broome St) Reservations recommended for
dinner F-Sa. 219.9250

75 Victoria Dinardo A millinery designer who
will make a unique *chapeau* especially for you.
♦ Closed M-Tu except by appointment. 68
Thompson St (Broome-Spring Sts) 334.9615

75 Il Bisonte Fine handcrafted Florentine hand-
bags, portfolios, luggage and accessories.
♦ 72 Thompson St (Broome-Spring Sts)
966.8773

What's a Manhattan Special?
It's not an express bus from Brooklyn. And it has noth-
ing to do with the subways. But it's been a part of New
York City since 1885. Described as *The World's Most
Delicious Coffee Soda*, the Manhattan Special is a
hand-brewed concoction of freshly roasted coffee
beans and 100% granulated sugar (practically un-
heard of in the beverage industry today). It also comes
in sugar- and caffeine-free. The result is a lusty
espresso coffee soda that's well-worth sampling, a
special New York taste treat!

76 Classic Toys Put together your own private army, create a miniature zoo or mount a wee Wild West show from this imaginative collection. ◆ Closed M-Tu. 69 Thompson St (Broome-Spring Sts) 941.9129

76 Strand & Lowe Jewelry, furnishings, folk art and unusual objects from 1900-1960. ◆ Closed M. 75 Thompson St (Broome-Spring Sts) 925.0932

77 Berrys ★$$ A convivial bistro that has become established as an in-place for Sunday brunches. It is noisy, dark (it has a certain Victorian appeal) and crowded, but cozy and friendly as well. The food is well-prepared and the menu imaginative. ◆ American ◆ 180 Spring St (Thompson St) Reservations recommended; required for Su brunch. 226.4394

78 The Ear Inn ★$ Built in 1817, now a designated Landmark of the City of New York. You can easily picture the seafaring rowdies who once frequented this dark and dusty bar and restaurant. There are poetry readings on weekends, and regulars say it has the best jukebox in town. Off the beaten path (the original shoreline of the river used to be only 5ft away from the entrance), but worth it. ◆ American ◆ 326 Spring St (Washington-Greenwich Sts) 226.9060

78 Bell Caffe $ A new hangout for neighborhood artists—who want to keep it a secret. The table you're sitting at, as well as most everything else here, was probably saved from destruction when co-owner **Kurt** found it on the street. The food is okay (homemade breads, soups, vegetable pies) but the scene is more the point. ◆ Closed M. 310 Spring St (Renwick St) 334.BELL

79 Castillo Cultural Center Progressive, independent cultural center encompassing a performance space, gallery, publishing house, photo lab and video lab. One notable performance included a live hair montage—3-dimensional environments created on top of peoples' heads. ◆ M-Sa 10AM-10PM; Su noon-6PM. 500 Greenwich St (Spring-Canal Sts) 941.5800

80 New York City Fire Museum The Fire Department's own collection of apparatus and memorabilia dating back to colonial times is combined here with that of the **Home Insurance Co**. This is the largest exhibition of its kind in the country, and if you have youngsters in tow they won't complain a bit about the long walk west when they discover this is

the destination. ◆ Voluntary contribution. Tu-Sa 10AM-4PM. 278 Spring St (Varick-Hudson Sts) 691.1303

81 Sam Flax Warehouse Outlet Twenty to 60 percent off merchandise from this chain of art- and office-supply stores. ◆ 233 Spring St (6th Ave-Varick St) 675.3486

82 Cafe ★★$$$ An interesting newcomer on a corner that sees a lot of restaurants come and go. There's a lovely terrace on the 6th Ave side; cafe tables for lunch on Spring St; and inside, an elegant dining room decorated with medieval religious antiques. I have high hopes for Cafe; it's off to a very good start. ◆ Cafe/French ◆ Closed M. 210 Spring St (6th Ave) 274.0505

83 Spring Street Garden The always charming window displays show off just some of the exotica within—unusual varieties of tulips (the French Parrot Tulip is stupendous), miniature roses and all sorts of dried flowers.

Delivery within Manhattan. ◆ Closed M, Su. 186 ¹/₂ Spring St (Thompson-Sullivan Sts) 966.2015

84 Mezzogiorno ★$$$ Roberto **Magris** designed this airy restaurant, which, during the warmer months, opens out onto the sidewalk. I think coal-oven pizzas and carpaccio—shaved raw beef with your choice of accompaniments—are the things here, though you can't go  wrong with pasta. Just one caveat: unless the staff knows you, the service can be a bit haughty. ◆ Italian ◆ 195 Spring St (Thompson-Sullivan Sts) No credit cards. 334.2112

84 Nick & Eddie ★$$$ An old-fashioned neighborhood restaurant where locals meet in the late afternoon; uptowners, in search of the *SoHo experience*, arrive later. The dependable American menu includes marinated swordfish on grilled sourdough bread, fresh salads, steaks and French fries served in old-fashioned paper cones and juicy hamburgers. ◆ American ◆ 203 Spring St (Sullivan St) 219.9090

85 Peter Fox Shoes All Peter Fox designs, inspired by Victorian and medieval styles, are handmade (except for the stitching of the sole to the leather) in Italy. Check next door for the full line of wedding styles; bridal customers have included supermodel **Paulina Porizkova** and model-turned-actress **Phoebe Cates**. ◆ 105 Thompson St (Spring-Prince Sts) 431.6359

85 Ecco Shoes Classically avant-garde women's footwear and bags. If you're hankering for ankle-high boots, this is the place. Good sales. ♦ 111 Thompson St (Spring-Prince Sts) 925.8010

85 Omen ★$$ A quiet restaurant that has cultivated a loyal following. First-timers should try omen—Japanese noodles, served with a variety of toppings and flavorings—a perfect introduction to the extensive menu. ♦ Japanese ♦ Closed M. 113 Thompson St (Prince St) Reservations recommended. 925.8923

86 Le Erbe An intimate shop selling all-natural herbal products from Italy for the face, body

and hair. ♦ Closed M, Su. 196 Prince St (Sullivan St) 966.1445

86 Raoul's ★$$$ Solid bistro fare, as French as you can get in SoHo: a cold sweetbread salad, steak au poivre, duck breast with green peppercorns. A maître d' with personality, attentive service and an always interesting crowd. ♦ French ♦ 180 Prince St (Thompson-Sullivan Sts) Reservations required. 966.3518

86 Hans Koch Ltd. Fine belts and handbags. If nothing suits your fancy, Mr. Koch will whip up something that will. ♦ 174 Prince St (Thompson-Sullivan Sts) 226.5385

87 Milady ★$ This neighborhood bar underwent a face-lift of sorts not too long ago. They changed the name and the decor, but the clientele is basically the same—local types who come for a beer and conversation. Simple entrees, great burgers and salads. ♦ American ♦ 162 Prince St (Thompson St) 226.9340

87 Vesuvio's Bakery This charming storefront has been selling chewy loaves of bread, breadsticks and the most addictive pepper biscuits since 1928. If you want to catch up on neighborhood goings-on, speak to owner **Anthony Dapolito**: he's one of SoHo's genuinely concerned citizens. A SoHo landmark. ♦ Closed Su. 160 Prince St (W. Broadway-Thompson St) 925.8248

88 Peter Hermann The finest handbags, belts and luggage in the world, mostly from Europe, although when the American goods are up to par it does carry them. ♦ 118 Thompson St (Spring-Prince Sts) 966.9050

88 Anvers Belgian designer **Anne Kegels**' sober designs suit busy women who need versatile clothing that can be dressed up or down for the occasion. ♦ 110 Thompson St (Spring-Prince Sts) 219.1308

88 Bébé Thompson Designer clothes for children, including imported handmade cotton and wool outfits that will still be in style long after they have been outgrown. ♦ 98 Thompson St (Spring-Prince Sts) 925.1122

89 Spring Street Books In addition to newspapers and cards, this top-notch bookstore has a good selection of foreign magazines, small press publications and remainders. The late hours (until midnight Friday and Saturday nights) are a boon to last-minute gift shoppers. ♦ 169 Spring St (W. Broadway-Thompson St) 219.3033

89 Ad Hoc Softwares Owners **Julia McFarlane** and **Judith Auchincloss** scour the marketplace for a wide range of bed and bath items, including unbleached, chemical-free linen and cotton sheets from Austria and West Germany, Italian and French waffle towels, high-quality blankets from Europe as well as Africa and India. There's a broad selection of French and English bodycare products. Well-made small gift items also. ♦ 410 W. Broadway (Spring St) 925.2652

90 Harriet Love This is the shop that originally made antique clothes fashionable, and it's still the best in the business. (The owner is the author of *Harriet Love's Guide to Vintage Chic*.) Many of the clothes—all in mint condition—date from the 1940s and '50s, a few go back even further. Harriet Love also stocks vintage jewelry, alligator- and crocodile-skin bags and brand new clothing with a vintage feel. ♦ Closed M. 412 W. Broadway (Spring-Prince Sts) 966.2280

90 La Bagagerie Two floors of luscious, high-quality leather handbags, briefcases, totes, belts and luggage. ♦ 412 W. Broadway (Spring-Prince Sts) 941.1172

90 Paracelso A moderately priced source for women's clothes in natural fibers. The styles—many from India—are casual and loose-fitting. ♦ 414 W. Broadway (Spring-Prince Sts) 966.4232

91 420 West Broadway A heavy-hitter building, housing 2 of SoHo's most prestigious galleries, **Leo Castelli** and **Sonnabend**, as well as several others. ♦ Spring-Prince Sts

Within 420 West Broadway:

Charles Cowles Gallery Contemporary painting, sculpture and ceramics by a wide ranging stable that includes many West Coast artists. ♦ Tu-Sa 10AM-6PM. 5th floor. 925.3500

49th Parallel Funded by the Canadian government, this gallery is devoted exclusively to that country's contemporary artists. ♦ Tu-Sa 10AM-6PM. 4th floor. 925.8349

Sonnabend Gallery Ileana Sonnabend's celebrated and highly respected eye has drawn in such Americans as **Robert Morris**, who shares the floor with an ever growing list of distinguished Europeans, including **Jannis Kounellis, Gilbert & George** and **Anne and Patrick Poirier**. ♦ Tu-Sa 10AM-6PM. 3rd floor. 966.6160

Leo Castelli Gallery A must-see on anyone's SoHo circuit, Castelli's extraordinary gallery features a veritable Who's Who of Abstract Expressionist and Pop artists, many of whom have shown with Castelli since the early 1960s. **Jasper Johns, Ellsworth Kelly** and **Ed Ruscha** are but a few of the gallery regulars. ♦ Tu-Sa 10AM-6PM. 2nd floor. 431.5160

Germans van Eck This ambitious Dutch-born dealer boasts a healthy mix of eccentric American and European painters and sculptors. ♦ Tu-Sa 10AM-6PM. Ground floor. 219.0717

Marilyn Pearl Gallery A transplant from uptown who seems a bit out of place in the SoHo bustle. Contemporary and historical exhibitions. ♦ Tu-Sa 10AM-6PM. Ground floor. 966.5506

91 **Vucciria** ★$$$ SoHo art folk come here for Sicilian home cooking and warm, friendly service. On a good night, the chicken with sausage and mushrooms and the *penne* with eggplant are excellent, as is the angel hair pasta with seafood. Ask for a seat along the north wall. ♦ Italian ♦ 422 W. Broadway (Spring-Prince Sts) 941.5811

91 **Joovay** Fine cotton and silk lingerie, sleepwear and a good selection of toiletries. ♦ 436 W. Broadway (Spring-Prince Sts) 431.6386

92 **Dapy** Take the boredom out of TV-watching with a transparent set that lets you see what's going on inside. Or decorate your living space with a Volkswagen *Bug* stereo system. Lots of smaller, less expensive toys, like dancing Coke cans too. ♦ 431 W. Broadway (Spring-Prince Sts) 925.5082

92 **Nancy Hoffman Gallery** Hoffman's generous space is the backdrop for easygoing paintings and works on paper by such Realists as **Joseph Raffael** and **Peter Plagens**, as well as oils on canvas by **Rafael Ferrer** and others. ♦ Tu-Sa 10AM-6PM. 429 W. Broadway (Spring-Prince Sts) 966.6676

92 **Beau Brummel** Though most of the men's clothing and accessories sold here today are by European designers, **Ralph Lauren** began his career designing ties for Beau Brummel. ♦ 421 W. Broadway (Spring-Prince Sts) 219.2666

92 **Mary Boone** A much publicized upstart in the early 1980s heyday of Neo-Expressionism, Boone has settled into the establishment with a solid roster of American and mid-career European artists. **Eric Fischl, David Salle** and **Julian Schnabel** (who has since moved on to the Pace Gallery) are among her successes. ♦ Tu-Sa 10AM-6PM. 417 W. Broadway (Spring-Prince Sts) 431.1818

92 **415 West Broadway** There are 8 galleries, including **Witkin** and **Maxwell Davidson**, in this impressive 6-story building with a simple cast-iron storefront. ♦ Spring-Prince Sts

Within 415 West Broadway:
Maxwell Davidson Gallery This seasoned dealer, formerly on upper Madison, hosts a

variety of artists, with an emphasis on Realism. ♦ Tu-Sa 10AM-6PM. 5th floor. 925.5300

Witkin Gallery The focus is on vintage and contemporary photography by such artists as **Berenice Abbott, Evelyn Hofer, George Tice** and **Jerry N. Uelsmann**. Also new, rare and out-of-print books on photography. ♦ Tu-F 11AM-6PM; Sa noon-6PM. 4th floor. 925.5510

92 **Robert Lee Morris** Morris designs the jewelry in this special, much imitated shop, as well as the sculptures of incomplete torsos upon which he drapes his creations. Look through the window—it's all on spectacular display. ♦ 409 W. Broadway (Spring-Prince Sts) 431.9405. Also at: 550 Madison Ave. 593.3388

93 **The Irish Secret** Tradition is here, but so is innovation, in fashions by contemporary Irish designers. Beautifully tailored dresses in silk, linen, cotton or wool. ♦ Closed M. 155 Spring St (Wooster St-W. Broadway) 334.6711

93 **Morgane Le Fay** The window here is always austere and monochromatic. What changes, and what is featured, is the clothing of **Liliana Ordas**—flowing dresses, coats, capes, skirts in a wide range of wool flannels, wool crepes, jerseys and velvets. ♦ 151 Spring St (Wooster St-W. Broadway) 925.0144

93 **Putumayo** Each season owner **Dan Storper** and his team, inspired by the traditional styles of a foreign country, design a new collection of these moderately priced, comfy clothes. Interior designer **Susan Brynner** redecorates the shop in the same spirit, making each visit, if not a shopping spree, an interesting experience. Recent inspiration has come from Scandinavia, Greece, Morocco and India. ♦ 147 Spring St (Wooster St-W. Broadway) 966.4458

93 Ron Fritts Painter-turned-designer Fritts offers spectacular fabrications of textures and colors in clothes made to travel well. ♦ 145 Spring St (Wooster St-W.Broadway) 219.1064. Also at: 698 Madison Ave. 758.2732

93 Tennessee Mountain ★$$ The smells (which waft down Spring St) are better than the food—ribs, fried chicken and vegetarian chili—but the frozen margaritas will put you in the proper mood. ♦ American ♦ 143 Spring St (Wooster St) Reservations recommended. 431.3993

94 101 WOOSTER STREET The law firm of **Dolgenos Newman & Cronin** maintains this contemporary art exhibition right in their workspace. With the assistance of a professional curator, they show art that might not make it into a commerical gallery due to lack of marketability. Exhibitions that focus on socially relevant issues, such as the UN Decade for Women, are featured. ♦ Sa-Su

SoHo/TriBeCa

noon-6PM. 101 Wooster St (Spring-Prince Sts) 925.2800

95 T&K French Antiques Among the direct imports from France are copper bathtubs, ornate bird cages and fine antique furniture. ♦ Closed Su. 120 Wooster St (Spring-Prince Sts) 219.2472

95 Comme des Garçons Japanese couturier **Rei Kawakubo** designs trendy clothes under the Comme des Garçons label. She also designed this stark showroom to function as a dramatic setting for her exotic line. A truly Minimalist experience. Don't miss the men's clothing on the lower level. ♦ 116 Wooster St (Spring-Prince Sts) 219.0661

95 Detour The accent is on femininity in this collection of mostly European clothing. Detour sells men's clothing at 425 W. Broadway. ♦ 114 Wooster St (Spring-Prince Sts) 219.8183

96 Michelle Nicole Wesley A charming little lingerie shop that also sells very feminine sportswear and dresses and an eclectic assortment of tabletop items and antiques. ♦ 126 Prince St (Greene-Wooster Sts) 334.1313

96 Otto Once you spring for the shoes, you'll have to pick up a couple of pairs of socks. Take your time, the selection is vast. ♦ 124 Prince St (Greene-Wooster Sts) 925.6641

96 Reinstein/Ross A shop devoted entirely to the exquisite jewelry created by **Susan Reinstein**. Multicolored sapphires and 22K gold, often alloyed in subtle colors, most of which she has developed herself. ♦ Closed M. 122 Prince St (Greene-Wooster Sts) 226.4513. Also at: 29 E 73rd St. 772.1901

96 Donald Sacks ★★$ A quaint old storefront serving homey sandwiches, soups and salads to go. I'm especially fond of the curried

chicken. ♦ Takeout ♦ 120 Prince St (Greene-Wooster Sts) 226.0165. Also at: 220 Vesey St (World Financial Center) 619.4600

agnès b.

96 agnès b. French designer who takes classics for men, women and children—such as V-necked sweaters, cotton T-shirts and long-collared shirts—and makes them modern. How does she do it? She takes the sweater and makes the V neck lower and sexier, stripes the T-shirts in fresh colors like baby blue and maroon and wakes up the stuffy men's shirt with black-and-white checks. The children's line is sold uptown in her shop at 1063 Madison Ave. ♦ 116-18 Prince St (Greene-Wooster Sts) 925.4649

96 SoHo Center for Visual Artists Funded by the **Aldrich Museum of Contemporary Art**, the center's purpose is to provide one-time group shows for emerging artists not currently represented by local commercial galleries. ♦ Tu-Sa noon-6PM. 114 Prince St (Greene-Wooster Sts) 226.1995

96 Tootsi Plohound You'd probably never guess that a store with a name like this sells unusual and unusually good women's shoes. For equally interesting men's shoes, check out Tootsi's other half, **Otto**, just up the street. ♦ 110 Prince St (Greene-Wooster Sts) 925.8931

96 130 Prince Street (1989, **Lee Manners & Associates**) This new *PoMo* building is home to English jewelry designer **Stuart Moore's** shop of sophisticated *bijoux*, plus 8 art galleries—**Louver, Lohring Augustine, Perry Rubenstein, Christine Burgin, Andrea Rosen, Petersberg, Victoria Munroe** and **Tony Shafrazi**—each of which commissioned their own architect to design the space according to their specifications. ♦ Wooster St

Within 130 Prince Street:

Victoria Munroe Gallery Contemporary paintings, sculpture and works on paper by American artists, including abstract and representational works. The spectacular space was designed by **Joel Sanders** and **Ernie Guenzburger**. ♦ Tu-Sa 10AM-6PM. 4th floor. 226.0040

Louver Gallery Contemporary painting and sculpture from **Peter Shelton, David Nash, Tony Bevam** and **Pieter Laurens Mol**, among others. ♦ Tu-Sa 10AM-6PM. 2nd floor. 925.9205

Stuart Moore The right jewelry shop to visit if you are in the market for exceptionally well-made (expensive) jewelry in 18K gold or platinum. Custom work is the specialty, and the mark-up on gemstones exceeding $6000 in cost is only 20 percent—a bargain, if you can afford it. ♦ Closed M. Ground floor. 941.1023

97 David Beitzel Gallery Beitzel's eye is broad-ranging, and he tends to favor emerging artists who work in highly individual idioms. ♦ Tu-Sa 10AM-6PM. 104 Prince St (Greene St) 219.2863

97 Annina Nosei Gallery A champion of contemporary American and international artists (who come from as far away as Argentina and Zaire). ♦ Tu-Sa 10AM-6PM. 100 Prince St (Mercer-Greene Sts) 431.9253

97 Fanelli Cafe ★$$ A holdover from the district's days as a neighborhood of factories. Still a good choice for those in search of a terrific hamburger and fries, and a favorite among factory workers as well as arty newcomers. The service could be a little more genteel, but the place doesn't invite kid gloves. Be sure to admire the beautiful glass door. ♦ American ♦ 94 Prince St (Mercer St) No credit cards. 226.9412

98 Jay Gorney Art A trendy venue for contemporary painting and sculpture, with a more than ample dose of late-1980s marketing savvy. ♦ Tu-Sa 10AM-6PM. 100 Greene St (Spring-Prince Sts) 966.4480

98 Wolfman-Gold & Good Company Tableware and home accessories. Very white. Very expensive. ♦ 116 Greene St (Prince St) 431.1888

98 Buffalo Chips Bootery After 17 years on their feet as hairdressers, **Ron Tassely** and **Paul Greyshock** turned their passion for cowboy boots (and their desire to find a comfortable pair) into a business. Working with the **Hyer** boot company, they have designed a fashionable line of podiatrist-approved cowboy boots with steel-reinforced arches and low, tapered heels for proper support. If you can't find a pair that you like among the 50 or so on display, they'll be glad to do a custom design. They also sell artwork and jewelry by Southwestern artists. ♦ 116 Greene St (Prince St) 274.0651

98 110 Greene Street (1908, **William J. Dilthy**) The sign says this is The SoHo Building, but long before anyone ever thought of calling this neighborhood SoHo, it was an annex of the **Charles Broadway Rouss Department Store** that thrived over on Broadway. ♦ Spring-Prince Sts

99 SoHo Kitchen and Bar $$ Pizzas and fries,

another theatrical interior by owner **Tony Goldman** (dramatic lighting, immense canvases, black ceiling) and Manhattan's longest wine list (96 wines, 14 champagnes). Oenophiles: don't miss the *flights of wines*—a heady experience in which 4 to 8 wines within a specific category are sampled in 2 1/2-oz increments. ♦ American ♦ 103 Greene St (Spring-Prince Sts) 925.1866

99 Jekyll & Hyde The fine fabrics and quality tailoring of the outstanding men's suits, fine belts and shoes you'll find here will hardly bring out the best in you. In fact, you'll probably like the transformation. ♦ 93 Greene St (Spring-Prince Sts) 966.8503

99 Zona One of the very best reasons to visit SoHo. **Louis Sagar**'s high-ceilinged, wonderfully airy space is as much a gallery as a store: **Paolo Soleri**'s bells, garden tools, furniture of the Southwest, terra cotta and other well-designed housewares from the Great American Desert (and all over the world) are displayed with great care and imagination—qualities every store should aim for. It's worth buying something just to get it gift-wrapped. ♦ Closed M. 97 Greene St (Spring-Prince Sts) 925.6750

99 Barbara Gladstone Gallery Gladstone's elegant 2-tiered space allows her to mount dual exhibitions from an ever increasing

stable of European and American artists. **Vito Acconci, Anish Kapoor, Rosemarie Trockel** and **Genny Holzer** are part of her distinguished roster. ♦ Tu-Sa 10AM-6PM. 99 Greene St (Spring-Prince Sts) 431.3334

99 Greene Street Restaurant ★$$$ The imaginative food and the contemporary, drummerless jazz are only part of the attraction put together by owner **Tony Goldman**. Other aspects are the vast duplex space, the professional staff, the handsome and stylish clientele and the decor: mural by **Françoise Schein**, chairs by **David Uts**, plants by **Chris** and graphics by **Susan Hunt Yule**. The music goes until 12:30AM. At least stop in for a drink. ♦ American ♦ 101 Greene St (Spring-Prince Sts) Reservations required F-Sa. 925.2415

100 The Grass Roots Gallery de Artes Populares **Margery Nathanson** stocks this basement-level shop with Latin American and Haitian folk art, textiles, pottery, masks and jewelry. Margery's husband, **Larry**, is the green thumb behind the cornucopia of plants for sale at **the grass roots garden** upstairs. ♦ Closed M, Su. 131 Spring St (Greene-Wooster Sts) 431.0144

100 Manhattan Bistro ★$$ The best choices here are the homey French specialties—slow-cooked stews and small steaks with sensational skinny fries. Relax with a glass of wine and indulge in the sport of people-watching. ♦ French ♦ 129 Spring St (Greene-Wooster Sts) Dinner reservations required. 966.3459

101 **101 Spring Street** (1871, **N. Whyte**) A sensitive approach to the use of cast iron as complex ornament. The ground floor is completely unchanged. ◆ Mercer St

102 **A Photographer's Place** This shop buys and sells photographic books, antiques and prints. ◆ 133 Mercer St (Spring-Prince Sts) 431.9358

102 **Alaia New York** Artist **Julian Schnabel** devised this stark interior to show off **Azzedine Alaia**'s famous body-hugging fashions, which hang on a couple of strategically positioned clothing racks. Note the artfully undulating, barely finished floor. ◆ Closed M. 131 Mercer St (Spring-Prince Sts) 941.1166

103 **Little Singer Building** (1904, **Ernest Flagg**) In a letter to *The Sun*, at the time he designed this 12-story building for the **Singer Sewing Machine Co**, Flagg said, *I believe tall buildings will shortly become unsafe. As an architect, I will never have anything to do with*

SoHo/TriBeCa

buildings of this kind. A year later he began work on the big Singer Building, a 41-story, 612ft tower on Broadway at John St, which was demolished in 1967, leaving this as a monument to what was lost. ◆ 561-63 Broadway (Spring-Prince Sts)

104 **560 Broadway** A fine old structure remodeled to house several distinguished galleries. ◆ Prince St

Within 560 Broadway:

Salvatore Ala American, British and European artists, with an emphasis on sculpture. Always off the beaten track, and always worth a look. ◆ Tu-Sa 10AM-6PM. 3rd floor. 941.1990

Max Protetch

Max Protetch Gallery The primary commercial outlet in New York for drawings by such distinguished architects as **Louis I. Kahn, Frank Lloyd Wright, Michael Graves, Aldo Rossi** and **Rem Koolhaas**, Protetch also exhibits painting, ceramics and sculpture. It's well worth a visit to his spacious quarters. ◆ Tu-Sa 10AM-6PM. 2nd floor. 966.5454

Diane Brown Gallery Contemporary sculpture is this gallery's strength. ◆ Tu-Sa 10AM-6PM. 2nd floor. 219.1060

Wolff Gallery An ambitious East Village transplant featuring painting and sculpture by young up-and-comers. ◆ Tu-Sa 10AM-6PM. 2nd floor. 431.7833

Also within 560 Broadway:

Dean & DeLuca The ultimate and original high-tech grocery housed in a block-long, 9700sq ft space. Wonderful kitchenware, cookbooks and all you would ever want to eat from the world's gastronomic centers—all displayed with extraordinary panache. Added

bonuses: a coffee bar, a butcher, a fishmonger and a full range of takeout dishes. Certain to become one of the must-see places for anyone passionate about food. Espresso bar opens daily at 8AM. ◆ Ground floor. 431.8350

104 **Duggal Downtown** This extension of the W 20th St branch is where the professional photographers in the neighborhood come for their film and processing needs. It's a huge space with a continually changing photography exhibition along the right-hand wall and windows through which you can watch the technicians work. ◆ 560 Broadway (Spring-Prince Sts) 431.5582. Also at: 9 W 20th St. 924.7777

105 **P.P.O.W** The adventuresome young partners, **Penny Pilkington** and **Wendy Olsoff** (hence the name PPOW), pride themselves on their preference for individuals over trends. They show **David Wojnarowicz** and **Erika Rothenberg** as well as installation work (built environments) by **TODT**. ◆ Tu-Sa 10AM-6PM. 532 Broadway (Spring-Prince Sts) 3rd floor. 941.8642

106 **New York Open Center** Each year the Center offers hundreds of workshops, courses, lectures and performances that explore spiritual and social issues, psychology, the arts—in short, all aspects of traditional and contemporary world culture. Check out the bookstore for the latest literature on all the above. ◆ 83 Spring St (Crosby St) 219.2527

107 **Savoy** ★★$$$ A new restaurant run by chef **Peter Hoffman** and his wife, pastry chef **Suzan Rosenfeld**. Highlights of the eclectic menu include cold barley soup with yogurt, grilled sardines over simmered onions, salted crusted duck, and poached monkfish with chanterelles and lotus leaf. I never leave without a slice of chocolate hazelnut orange torte. ◆ Continental ◆ Closed Su. 70 Prince St (Broadway-Lafayette St) 219.8570

108 **280 Modern** Decorative arts with an emphasis on designer furniture from the 1920s to the '60s. A good selection of original works by the late **Piero Fornasetti** and new pieces from his son's company in Milan. ◆ 280 Lafayette St (E. Houston-Prince Sts) 941.5825

108 **Secondhand Rose** Antiques dealer **Suzanne Lipshutz** (aka Secondhand Rose) fills 5000sq ft with treasures from the 1920s to the '70s. Her impressive stock ranges from custom-made leather furniture to architectural fragments. ◆ Closed Su. 270 Lafayette St (Prince St) 431.7673

Restaurants/Nightlife: Red   **Hotels:** Blue
Shops/Parks: Green   **Sights/Culture:** Black

109 Barbara Flynn Gallery A spirit of invention pervades this gallery, formerly Art Galaxy. Artists represented include the technological wizards **Kristin Jones** and **Andrew Ginzel**. ♦ Tu-Sa 10AM-6PM. 113 Crosby St (Prince-E. Houston Sts) 966.0426

110 568-578 Broadway A boon for art lovers is the proliferation of gallery clusters in fine old Broadway buildings. This real-estate trend makes life easy for the browser, rain or shine. This dual-entry structure now houses so many galleries that it has been dubbed *The Mall* by artworld locals. ♦ Prince-W. Houston Sts

Within 568-578 Broadway:

Lorence Monk Gallery Among the complex's first tenants, these serious dealers have tripled their exhibition space to encompass most of the south building's top floor. Shows of young artists alternate with scholarly exhibitions of master graphics. ♦ Tu-Sa 10AM-6PM. 568 Broadway. 11th floor. 431.3555

Curt Marcus Gallery Contemporary American and European artists in all mediums. ♦ Tu-Sa 10AM-6PM. 578 Broadway. 10th floor. 226.3200

Castelli Graphics Prints, drawings and photographs by many of the artists represented by Leo Castelli Gallery (**Roy Lichtenstein** and **Jasper Johns**, for example) as well as artists from their own stable, such as **Robert Cumming**. ♦ Tu-Sa 10AM-6PM. 578 Broadway. 3rd floor. 941.9855

Crown Point Press The New York gallery for San Francisco's preeminent etching workshop. ♦ Tu-F 9:30AM-5:30PM; Sa 10AM-6PM. 568 Broadway. 1st floor. 226.5476

111 Uzzolo Eleven thousand square feet filled with black-and-white high-tech furniture, lighting, housewares and gifts. ♦ 565 Broadway (Prince St) 219.2225

TheNewMuseum
OF CONTEMPORARY ART

112 The New Museum of Contemporary Art Founder/director **Marcia Tucker** is the force behind this unique institution. She not only shows artists who have trouble getting a foot in the museum establishment's door: she shows all aspects of their work. As many as 3 or 4 shows are mounted at one time, often including videos and installations. The changing storefront installations are one of lower Broadway's great attractions. ♦ Voluntary contribution. W-Th, Su noon-6PM; F-Sa noon-8PM. 583 Broadway (Prince-Houston Sts) 219.1222

112 The Cockpit Re-creations of the vintage goatskin and horsehair jackets preferred by daring young men in their flying machines are available here along with what The Cockpit calls current issue. Everything to do with flying, from B-17 flight bags to shorts made from Flying Tigers briefing maps, to books,

watches, patches, gloves and boots. If the selection overwhelms you, ask for their mail order catalog. ♦ 595 Broadway (Prince-Houston Sts) 925.5455, 800/354.5514

113 Tansuya Corporation The Japanese word *tansu* means cabinet, and you can have one custom-made and lacquered here. They also build modern and traditional Japanese-style furniture, trays and lacquered boxes. Each piece is an original, and many are accented in gold and other colors. ♦ 159 Mercer St (Prince-Houston Sts) 966.1782

113 Distant Origin A clone of the incomparable Zona around the corner on Wooster St. Still, an impressive selection of Southwestern paintings, pillows, pottery and furniture east of Santa Fe. ♦ Closed M. 153 Mercer St (Prince-W. Houston Sts) 941.0025

113 After the Rain A grownup's fantasy of kaleidoscopes, art glass, tapestries and handmade jewelry. Sister store of **The Enchanted Forest**.

♦ 149 Mercer St (Prince-W. Houston Sts) 431.1045

114 Jerry's $ A bustling lunch spot for SoHo's working population, especially the gallery crowd—Jerry used to own the frame shop down the street. Fresh salads, sandwiches, daily soups. The dinnertime tempo is considerably slower. ♦ American ♦ 101 Prince St (Mercer-Greene Sts) 966.9464

114 Edward Thorp Gallery Thorp's affinity for landscape painting with a twist is clear in the work of artist **April Gornik.** He also represents **Deborah Butterfield**, who sculpts horses out of found objects. Frequent large group shows. Above the Prince St post office. ♦ Tu-Sa 10AM-6PM. 103 Prince St (Mercer-Greene Sts) 431.6880

115 Back Pages Antiques An impressive collection of classic Wurlitzer jukeboxes, working slot machines, Coca-Cola vending machines, player pianos, pool tables and advertising signs. Everything here has been lovingly restored. Even the mooseheads seem to have a new lease on life. If you have a party room, you can furnish it from here. ♦ 125 Greene St (Prince-W. Houston Sts) 460.5998

116 Phyllis Kind Gallery An eclectic collection of contemporary paintings and *outsider* art by American and international artists. ♦ Tu-Sa 10AM-6PM. 136 Greene St (Prince-W. Houston Sts) 925.1200

Seventy-five percent of New York City's restaurants change hands or close before they are 5 years old.

116 **John Weber** A longtime artworld fixture, Weber has supplemented his distinguished roster of Minimal and Conceptual artists, including **Sol LeWitt** and the estate of **Robert Smithson**, with some bright new—and off-beat—talent. ◆ Tu-Sa 10AM-6PM. 142 Greene St (Prince-W. Houston Sts) 3rd floor. 966.6115

116 **Sperone Westwater** The New York home to many of Italy's most innovative artists, including **Mario Merz** and *the three C's* (**Sandro Chia, Francesco Clemente, Enzo Cucchi**), this gallery also boasts an impressive roster of other European and American talents. ◆ Tu-Sa 10AM-6PM. 142 Greene St (Prince-W. Houston Sts) 2nd floor. 431.3685

116 **The Pace Gallery** The downtown branch of the blue-chip gallery. The vast space provides a dramatic backdrop for large-scale paintings and sculpture. ◆ Tu-Sa 10AM-6PM. 142 Greene St. (Prince-W. Houston Sts) Ground floor. 431.9225

SoHo/TriBeCa

116 **Barbara Toll Fine Arts** This gallery's adventuresome point of view always warrants a look in from Greene St. All mediums, including large installation works by Scottish artist **David Mach**. ◆ Tu-Sa 10AM-6PM. 146 Greene St (Prince-W. Houston Sts) 431.1788

116 **Metro Pictures** An odd, somewhat dated assortment of painters and photographers, but home to the many-guised self-portraitist **Cindy Sherman**, one of the 1980s true originals. ◆ Tu-Sa 10AM-6PM. 150 Greene St (Prince-W. Houston Sts) 925.8335

117 **Dean & DeLuca Cafe** An airy, white-brick space provides a refreshing backdrop for a peaceful breakfast, lunch or snack at this cafe run by the gourmet food emporium at Broadway and Prince. I often come here on Sunday morning to read the paper (thoughtfully provided by D&D) and drink cappuccino. ◆ 121 Prince St (Wooster-Greene Sts) 254.8776

117 **Whole Foods** A full selection of everything you need for a sound body and soul: vitamins, grains, fresh fish, organic vegetables, cosmetics and an impressive assortment of books to tell you what you should be doing with all these things. ◆ 117 Prince St (Green-Wooster Sts) 673.5388

117 **Prince Street Bar & Restaurant** ★$ The faithful clientele come as much for the lively bar scene as for the fairly standard burgers, salads and sandwiches. ◆ American ◆ 125 Prince St (Wooster St) 228.8130

118 **Paula Cooper Gallery** A SoHo pioneer nearly 2 decades ago, Cooper has built a stable of remarkable winners, including **Jennifer Bartlett, Jonathan Borofsky, Elizabeth Murray** and **Joel Shapiro**. ◆ Tu-Sa 10AM-6PM. 155 Wooster St (Prince-W. Houston Sts) 674.0766

118 **147 Wooster Street** (1876, **Jarvis Morgan Slade**) If this were a cast-iron facade, it would be a landmark of the art, but the arched storefront decorated with bands of fleur-de-lis and other floral motifs is all hand-carved in marble. Only the cornice is iron. ◆ Prince-W. Houston Sts

118 **Dia Center for the Arts** *The New York Earth Room*, a permanent installation by conceptual artist **Walter da Maria**, has become a SoHo fixture. ◆ W-Sa noon-6PM. 141 Wooster St (Prince-W. Houston Sts) 473.8072

119 **Susan P. Meisel Decorative Arts** Twentieth-century decorative arts, including hand-painted English pottery created by **Clarice Cliff** between 1928 and 1938, '50s Mexican sterling silver jewelry, and vintage watches. ◆ Closed M, Su. 133 Prince St (Wooster St-W. Broadway) 254.0137

119 **Louis K. Meisel** Meisel championed the Photorealists back in the 1970s, and has stuck to his convictions despite the art world's ever changing tides. ◆ Tu-Sa 10AM-6PM. 141 Prince St (Wooster St-W. Broadway) 677.1340

VICTORIA FALLS

120 **Victoria Falls** Whether the clothes are new or old (the stock is split half-and-half), Victoria Falls maintains its point of view, which is to offer exquisitely detailed clothes that are either of the Victorian era or inspired by it. There are linen blouses, dresses from the 1920s and antique Oriental robes and shawls. ◆ 451 W. Broadway (Prince-W. Houston Sts) 254.2433

120 **SoHo Wine & Spirits** This may very well be the most civilized, not to mention best-stocked, small wine store in town. But there is no wine snobbery in this well-organized, well-designed outlet. It also carries the world's great spirits, including the city's most extensive choice of single malt Scotch whiskeys. ◆ Closed Su. 461 W. Broadway (Prince-W. Houston Sts) 777.4332

120 **Yoshi** A unique store that features the latest fashions from an international set of young designers, including **Faycolamor** from France, **Gemmakahng** from New York and Englishman **Jasper Conran**. To top it off, there is a particularly wonderful selection of *chapeaux* from 14 different designers, including a squash-hat made of rayon cording by French designer **Jacques LeCorre**. ◆ 461 W. Broadway (Prince-W. Houston Sts) 979.0569

Perhaps the most distinguishing feature of the city's streets in the 1880s was the mass of telephone and telegraph wires overhead. After the blizzard of 1888 they were placed underground.

120 I Tre Merli ★★$$ The exposed brick walls give this Italian restaurant and wine bar a quiet charm. Though the service is inattentive at best, the food—especially the raw artichoke salad—is quite good. During the summer, the tables spill out onto West Broadway. ◆ Italian ◆ 463 W. Broadway (Prince-Houston Sts) Reservations recommended. 254.8699

120 Amici Miei A new Italian restaurant-cum-cafe with a lovely terrace looking onto greenery rather than Houston St traffic. Handsome Italian waiters and struggling actors serve classic Italian fare: good mozzarella, excellent pasta, the usual scaloppini dishes, heavy Italian pastries and excellent espresso. ◆ Italian ◆ 475 W. Broadway (W. Houston St) 533.1933

121 Gallery of Wearable Art Everything here makes a statement. Whether it is a statement you'd care to make about yourself is something you'll have to decide. A unique collection of wedding gowns and bridal accesories. ◆ 480 W. Broadway (Prince-W. Houston Sts) 212.GALLERY

121 If Boutique Designer clothes by **Thierry Mugler, Jean Paul Gaultier, Romeo Gigli** and **Moschino**, accessories by **Johnny Farah**, terrific belts, shoes and jewelry. Best feature: the sales here are real sales. ◆ 474 W. Broadway (W. Houston St) 533.8660

121 Rizzoli Bookstore of SoHo One of the best sources of fine art books, foreign magazines, and music recordings. ◆ 454 W. Broadway (Prince-W. Houston Sts) 674.1677. Also at: 250 Vesey St. 385.1400; 31 W 57th St. 759.2424

122 Betsey Johnson For more than 2 decades, Johnson's fashion statements have been providing the youthful with a statement of their own. ◆ 130 Thompson St (Prince-W. Houston Sts) 420.0169. Also at: 251 E 60th St. 319.7699; 248 Columbus Ave. 362.3364

122 Eileen Lane Antiques Specializing in Scandinavian and Biedermeier and Art Deco furniture and lighting. ◆ 150 Thompson St (Prince-W. Houston Sts) 475.2988

123 Belgis Freidel Gallery Rare posters and turn-of-the-century prints, including the work of **Henri de Toulouse-Lautrec** and **Pierre Bonnard**. ◆ Tu-Su noon-6PM. 131 Thompson St (Prince-W. Houston Sts) 475.0248

123 Opal White Edwardian and Victorian clothing, including a wide selection of antique wedding dresses. ◆ By appointment only. 131 Thompson St (Prince-W. Houston Sts) 677.8215

124 Untitled This tiny wedge of a store sells all sorts of art and photography postcards, wrapping and note papers, calendars and a small selection of books and periodicals. ◆ 159 Prince St (W. Broadway-Thompson St) 982.2088. Also at: 680 Broadway. 254.1360

125 Madeline's/Patisserie M. Lanciani ★★$ A charming French bakery and seafood restaurant. One of the better places for a champagne brunch. ◆ Continental ◆ Closed M. 177 Prince St (Thompson-Sullivan Sts) Reservations recommended. 477.2788

125 Raoul's Boucherie & Charcuterie An old-fashioned place with a tin ceiling and black-and-white tiles on the floor. The spe-

cialty is homemade sausages. It also features very good deli fare, which you can eat on the premises or take with you. ◆ 179 Prince St (Thompson-Sullivan Sts) 674.0708

125 Elephant & Castle $$ For a handsome price, one of the best hamburgers in town can be had here. Omelets are recommended too. Try the hefty bowl of hot Indian pudding with Häagen-Dazs vanilla ice cream, a meal in itself. ◆ American ◆ 183 Prince St (Thompson-Sullivan Sts) 260.3600

126 Depression Modern Owner **Michael Smith** likes to redecorate his shop, and does so every Saturday with the Moderne furniture of the '30s and '40s that he spends the rest of the week restoring to its original perfect condition. ◆ Closed M-Tu. 150 Sullivan St (Prince-W. Houston Sts) 982.5699

126 Joe's Dairy There are about 3 storefronts left to give an indicator of the old Italian-American enclave along Thompson and Sullivan Sts. Joe's Dairy, with its checkered tile floor and sweating glass cases, is one of them. Parmigiana Reggiano is hewn from fragrant wheels, sweet ricotta is drawn from moist, cool places. A few times a week intense acrid smoke pours from its basement door—mozzarella *afumicato* is being made. ◆ Closed M. 156 Sullivan St (Prince-W. Houston Sts) 677.8780

Restaurants/Nightlife: Red   Hotels: Blue
Shops/Parks: Green   Sights/Culture: Black

For a short-lived period in the mid 1970s, the **Metropolitan Transit Authority** offered a half-fare schedule on weekends and holidays.

127 Provence ★★★$$$
Michel and Patricia Jean's
Provençal bistro has a lot
going for it: a creamy and
potent fish soup, a heady
onion tart, roasted chicken
in garlic, rabbit paillard (my
favorite), perfectly charred
crème brûlée, a trendy
crowd and, of course,
French waiters. When it's
warm, the garden is lovely
for lunch or an early dinner.
♦ French ♦ 38 MacDougal St (Prince St) Reservations required. 475.7500

128 Souen Downtown $$ This pretty, airy
Japanese-style room serves heavy, barely-
seasoned brown rice, soba noodles and veg-
etable specialties. ♦ Macrobiotic ♦ 210 6th
Ave (Prince St) 807.7421. Also at: 2444
Broadway. 787.1110; 28 E 13th St. 627.7150

129 S.O.B's Sounds of Brazil $$$ This casual
restaurant, specializing in Bahian and Brazilian
food, becomes a late-evening showcase for
salsa, samba, reggae and whatever else is
currently being imported from the Caribbean,
South America and Africa. For lunch or dinner,
try *Carmen Miranda's Favorite*—shrimp
cooked in a spicy sauce with chunks of fresh
pineapple, all served in a pineapple boat. But
the *caipirinha*, a sweet and sour Brazilian
cocktail, keeps them coming back. ♦ Brazilian
♦ Cover. Closed Su. 204 Varick St (W. Hous-
ton St) Dinner reservations required.
243.4940; advance tickets 947.5850

130 375 Hudson Street Say the word advertis-
ing, and Madison Ave naturally comes to
mind. But most advertising agencies are
located downtown, including **Saatchi &
Saatchi**, the world's largest advertising
agency holding company, which occupies this
building. Most of its neighbors are printing
companies. ♦ W. Houston St

Thaddeus Hyatt dramatically changed the sidewalks
of New York in 1845, when he invented iron vault cov-
ers with glass inserts that allowed daylight to filter into
building basements. Before electric lights, basement
space was all but useless. Cast-iron buildings incorpo-
rated Hyatt's invention into light platforms that were
raised a step or 2 off the sidewalk so window shop-
pers could indulge themselves without stopping pe-
destrian traffic on narrow sidewalks. The platforms
usually had round, pink-tinted translucent windows on
the risers of the steps to allow light into the below-
ground floor. Most of them have either been removed,
paved over or turned into truck loading docks. But
some, including the vault cover in front of 87-89
Greene St, are waiting to be rediscovered.

In February of 1989, 18,900 potholes were created in
New York's streets, considerably fewer than in
February of 1988, when the city reported 33,000.

Corky Pollan
Contributing Editor, *New York* Magazine

The **Frick Collection**—this is probably on everyone's
list of favorites, but where else in New York can you
view some of the greatest works of art without having
to jockey for position? The Frick is such a quiet
haven.

The **Seal Pond** at the renovated **Central Park Zoo**.

Lunch at the **Post House** for old-world elegance and
service.

Tea at the **Mayfair Regent** for soothing teas,
delectable sandwiches and comforting sofas.

The **Conservatory Garden** any spring day.

The **Museum of the City of New York** for its
enchanting collection of antique and vintage dolls,
dollhouses and toys.

Lower Broadway on a Saturday or Sunday to catch
the hottest and trendiest fashion looks.

Rizzoli, even when you're not in the market for a
book.

Little Rickie on 1st Ave for nostalgic toys from the
'50s and '60s.

Drinks at the **Top of the Tower** at sunset—one of the
city's most romantic spots.

Betsy Carter
Editor-in-Chief, *New York Woman*

The trains in the **Citicorp Building** at Christmas.

Any night submerged in the magic of *Phantom of the
Opera*.

The lobby of the **NBC building**, where ushers urge
you to be in the studio audience for game shows.

Looking out on the city from the **Rainbow Room**.

Outside the **New York Times building** when the
trucks unload the gigantic rolls of newsprint.

The **Penguin Department** of the boutique zoo at
Central Park.

The singing clock at **F.A.O. Schwarz**.

The express line at **Food Emporium** when there's
nobody on it.

Browsing the **Fragrance Shoppe** on E 7th St—it's
like wandering through a beautiful, aromatic
dollhouse.

Studying the dessert tray at **Rumpelmayer's**.

The **Greenmarket** at Union Square.

Sitting in the **Ziegfeld Theater** just as the lights go
down.

The smell of bagels brewing at **Ess a Bagel** (1st Ave
at 9th St).

Watching the boats from the **South Street Seaport**.

The discount flower markets that line **6th Ave** for 5 or
6 blocks.

The **Cloisters** and vicinity.

Howard J. Rubenstein
Public Relations,
Howard J. Rubenstein Associates, Inc.

Peter Luger restaurant. The best steak in town.

The city skyline—a triumph of engineering, architecture and the human spirit.

Carnegie Deli. A New York landmark.

The **Four Seasons.** Unrivaled decor.

Ellis Island. Where it all started for millions of Americans.

Trump Tower. A must to see and shop.

Empire State Building Observatory. Stunning views.

Central Park. For running, views, boating.

Apollo Theater. Great fun.

City Hall. Architectural heights.

Brooklyn Botanic Garden. New, exciting look.

Shea Stadium. Best game in town.

Union Square. Resurgent neighborhood; farmer's market.

Whitney Museum. Alive with exciting art.

New-York Historical Society. A great building and collection, and now also host to the Jewish Museum, which is temporarily closed during its expansion.

Battery Park City. Great design, spectacular vistas.

Lights of **Times Square** at night. Still quintessential New York.

Yankee Stadium. For baseball and baseball history.

Ralph Destino
Chairman of the Board, Cartier Inc.

Shopping along **Madison Avenue** on a Saturday afternoon in the fall, or walking through **Central Park** on any afternoon in the spring.

Dinner at **Gino's** on a Sunday night, making certain to order the secret sauce with the pasta.

Lunch or dinner at **21**; there is nothing like it anywhere else in the world.

Any excuse to go to the **Rainbow Room**, where every view is breathtaking, inside or out.

A leisurely sail around Manhattan in the late afternoon. No one would ever tire of these wonderful sights. (If the Forbes family doesn't invite you on their *Highlander II*, then do it on the **Circle Line**.)

Sampling any of the creative dishes at **Sam's Cafe**...and rediscovering each time you go that the owner, Mariel Hemingway, is every bit as sweet and nice as she looks in her movies.

Food shopping at **Zabar's**—this surely is New York—and coming away with twice as much stuff as you set out to buy.

Making sure that every month contains one each of the following: a hamburger at **P.J. Clarke's**; a veal chop at **Elaine's**; a chicken potpie at **Jim McMullen's**; fettuccine at **Vico**; crème brûlée at **Le Cirque**; anything at all at the **Four Seasons**.

Patricia Jean
Restaurant Owner, Provence

The **Frick Collection.** Because it feels grand and special and I can never walk by without going in.

The **Greenmarket** at Union Square. There the city and country really meet. Because it's really seasonal produce from the region. Because you can't beat the bread from **Boiceville** or the tomatoes from Long Island (no, not New Jersey).

Horseback riding in **Central Park**, ice-skating at **Rockefeller Center**, and looking up at the buildings around and feeling a sense of solitude.

Florent for onion soup and tripe at 2 in the morning. As close as you get to Paris without losing New York.

The food stores, especially **Dean & DeLuca** and **Jefferson Market**.

SoHo's streets before the stores and galleries open. It has the best neighborhood feeling in all New York, and it all changes after noon.

SoHo/TriBeCa

Dinner at the **River Café** at sunset because there's not a more beautiful and edifying view around!

Saturday afternoon gallery-hopping.

The flowers everywhere, but especially at the market on 28th St.

The feeling that anything is possible (this feeling comes and goes, but I've only ever had it in New York).

Three Lives Company Bookstore—the best bookstore ambience in New York; owned and operated by people, not corporate entities.

Nancye L. Green
Designer, Donovan and Green

The **West Side** from about 23rd St down, filled with the kinds of shops, galleries and restaurants that feel like the real New York—or at least New York the way I like it. Idiosyncratic, authentic, high energy. Friendly and unexpectedly good neighborhood places. Streets that are filled with the people who live there.

In Chelsea, **Chelsea Central** is a neighborhood treasure. Wonderful food, inviting atmosphere, easy to take.

All the way downtown, a great Sunday outing, walking along the river, lunch at the **Hudson River Club** in the World Financial Center. It's a treat inside and out for shopping, eating and strolling.

What I really love about New York is the surprises. One great one for me, **Tartine**, an extraordinarily authentic French bistro in Park Slope, Brooklyn. Great French food, lovely California wines and the intimacy and unpretentiousness that is so absent from a lot of the newer trendy restaurants.

For those with children—a fantastic park—**Washington Market Park**. Combine it with an outing to **Battery Park City** and you feel like New York is still a place to live!

New York City on Screen

The City goes out of its way to court the film industry, providing a special mayor's office as an industry liaison, police protection to stars and production crews, and even helping to arrange scenes ranging from helicopter chases to historical location settings.

The number of feature films shot here has quadrupled since 1977, and movie, TV and commercial production ranks among the city's top 5 growth industries.

New York was a booming film production city even before the sunny skies of Hollywood began to woo producers and filmmakers west in the early 1900s. **D.W. Griffith** loved to shoot here; **Mack Sennett's Keystone Cops** ran rampant through Coney Island. It is no wonder then that many visitors to movieland's Gotham get a feeling of *déjà vu*. Here are a few of the movies and locations you may remember:

1941 *Citizen Kane* rallies political support at **Madison Square Garden** in **Orson Welles'** classic.

1942 **Alfred Hitchcock's** chilling *Saboteur* includes a dangling climax from the *Statue of Liberty's* crown.

1945 **Ray Milland** seeks solace at **Bellevue Hospital** after enduring *The Lost Weekend* ◆ A troubled family discovers that *A Tree Grows in Brooklyn*.

1947 **Macy's** Santa Claus proves he's real to a jury and to young **Natalie Wood** in *Miracle on 34th Street*.

1949 In the quintessential New York picture, *On the Town*, **Frank Sinatra, Gene Kelly** and **Ann Miller** dance from **Wall Street** to **Rockefeller Center**.

1953 **Fred Astaire** and **Cyd Charisse** go *Dancing in the Dark* through **Central Park** in *The Band Wagon* ◆ **Richard Widmark** stars in the Cold War thriller *Pickup on South Street*, whose location shots include the **Bowery**.

1954 **Judy Holliday** and **Jack Lemmon** reside at 115 W 69th St in *It Should Have Happened to You*.

1957 **Tony Curtis** and **Burt Lancaster** dine at **21** in *The Sweet Smell of Success*.

1961 Director **Robert Wise** shoots the opening scene of *West Side Story* between Amsterdam and West End Aves at 68th St ◆ **Audrey Hepburn** and **George Peppard** find love (and silver toenail clippers) on 5th Ave in *Breakfast at Tiffany's*.

1963 *America, America*, **Elia Kazan's** portrayal of immigration to the US, incorporates **Ellis Island** locales.

1966 **Astor Place** plays host to the wedding party in the film version of **Mary McCarthy's** novel, *The Group*.

1967 Newlyweds **Jane Fonda** and **Robert Redford** meet in **Washington Square** in *Barefoot in the Park* ◆ **Harren High School** at 59th St and 10th Ave hosts the teenagers of *Up the Down Staircase* (and the kids looking for *Fame* some 13 years later).

1968 *Funny Girl* **Barbra Streisand** shares the spotlight with the *Statue of Liberty* ◆ **Dustin Hoffman** and **Jon Voight** jam up traffic at 58th St and 6th Ave in *Midnight Cowboy* ◆ **Spanish Harlem** hostility creates controversy for production crews and star **Richard Widmark** in the tough-cop story *Madigan* ◆ **Frank Sinatra** and **Lee Remick** meet at the **Columbia Law Library** in *The Detective*.

1969 Director **Gene Kelly** and crew convert the village of **Garrison's Landing** to 1890 **Yonkers** for *Hello, Dolly!*

1971 The *Panic in Needle Park* strikes heroin addicts at Broadway and Amsterdam Ave ◆ Unforgettable cop *Popeye Doyle* (**Gene Hackman**) chases drug smugglers along Brooklyn's **Stillwell Ave** to discover *The French Connection*.

1973 **Al Pacino** fights corruption in the NYPD in *Serpico*, with location shots at **New York University** ◆ A slice-of-life look at 3 losers in **Little Italy** is provided by *Mean Streets*, with **Robert De Niro**.

1974 **De Niro** returns to **Little Italy** as young mob boss *Don Corleone* in *The Godfather, Part II* ◆ Extortionists demand $1 million for the lives of subway passengers on the **Pelham Bay Line** in *The Taking of Pelham 1-2-3*.

1975 **Al Pacino** and 2 cohorts turn a simple Manhattan bank robbery into a *Dog Day Afternoon* ◆ **Jack Lemmon** and **Anne Bancroft** are victims of the vicious city in *Prisoner of Second Avenue*.

1976 *Next Stop, Greenwich Village* captures the lure of artsy bohemia for a Brooklyn boy ◆ **Robert De Niro** finds his own way of cleaning up New York's crime-ridden streets in **Martin Scorsese's** *Taxi Driver*.

1977 **Woody Allen** grows up under the **Cyclone** roller-coaster at **Coney Island** in *Annie Hall* ◆ **Liza Minelli's** the singer, **Robert De Niro's** the sax player and this is the town in *New York, New York* ◆ **John Travolta** escapes his futureless reality as a disco dance king in *Saturday Night Fever*. His identity crisis reaches a climax atop the **Verrazano-Narrows Bridge** when a friend falls to his death ◆ Unexpected and totally unwelcome, **Richard Dreyfuss** moves into **Marsha Mason's** apartment at 78th St and Amsterdam Ave in *The Goodbye Girl*.

1978 **Christopher Reeve**, that *Superman*, disguises himself as a mild-mannered reporter at the *Daily Planet*. The actual **New York Daily News Building** is used ◆ Yellow linoleum tile transforms the **Brooklyn Bridge** into Oz in *The Wiz*, with **Diana Ross** ◆ **Jill Clayburgh** portrays the trauma of becoming *An Unmarried Woman* on the **Upper East Side**.

1979 **Dustin Hoffman** drops his son off at school (**P.S. 6** on Madison Ave at 81st St), while his soon-to-be-ex-wife **Meryl Streep** watches from across the street at **The Copper Lantern**, in *Kramer vs. Kramer* ◆ Hippies dance through **Central Park** in Milos Forman's film version of *Hair* ◆ **Woody Allen's** tribute to *Manhattan* features a tour of the **Hayden Planetarium**.

1980 **Dustin Hoffman** shocks **Sydney Pollack** in the **Russian Tea Room**, as *Tootsie* drops in for lunch.

1981 Paul Newman is a policeman overwhelmed by out-of-control crime in *Fort Apache, The Bronx*. ◆ Dudley Moore questions his date's profession just a bit too loudly in the Oak Bar at the Plaza in *Arthur*.

1982 Meryl Streep and Kevin Kline live together in a Victorian house in Flatbush (101 Rugby Rd) in *Sophie's Choice* ◆ Peter O'Toole tests the firehose by rappelling down the side of the Waldorf-Astoria in *My Favorite Year*.

1983 Four thousand extras attend a protest staged at Union Square for *Daniel*, Sidney Lumet's adaptation of E.L. Doctorow's novel ◆ In *Splash*, mermaid Daryl Hannah tries to tell Tom Hanks her name while shopping at Bloomingdale's. The resulting fish-squeal shatters every TV set in the store. She later chooses the name *Madison* while walking down that avenue with him.

1984 Suburban housewife Rosanna Arquette finds unexpected adventure in Battery Park, with Madonna in *Desperately Seeking Susan* ◆ Ghostbusters Bill Murray, Dan Aykroyd and Harold Ramis move into (and blow the roof off of) the 8 Hook and Ladder Firehouse in TriBeCa.

1985 This time Rosanna Arquette is the adventurous one, leading Griffin Dunne to SoHo and the most hellish date of his life in *After Hours* ◆ At the Brooklyn Heights Promenade, Jack Nicholson debates whether he should marry Kathleen Turner, or ice her, in *Prizzi's Honor*.

1987 Paul Hogan resides at the Plaza while visiting from Down Under, in *Crocodile Dundee* ◆ Cher is *Moonstruck* on the streets of Brooklyn.

1988 Michael J. Fox finds the New York fast lane to be moving just a little too fast in the film version of Jay McInerney's novel, *Bright Lights, Big City* ◆ In *Big*, Tom Hanks and Robert Loggia perform a charming impromptu musical number at F.A.O. Schwarz.

1989 Bernadette Peters portrays an aspiring hat designer lost in the artificiality of the SoHo art world in the film version of Tama Janowitz's *Slaves of New York* ◆ In Rob Reiner's *When Harry Met Sally*, Sally demonstrates to Harry the art of sexual deception while they are sharing a meal together at Katz's Delicatessen on the Lower East Side ◆ Woody Allen studies life, death and infidelity against the backdrop of the New York City skyline in *Crimes and Misdemeanors*.

1990 Gerard Depardieu woos Andie MacDowell in Peter Weir's tale of love-after-marriage, *Green Card* ◆ Sherman McCoy's world of Upper East Side privilege is shattered after a hellish ride through the Bronx in *Bonfire of the Vanities* ◆ Audiences get an unglamorous view of the Mafia in Martin Scorsese's *GoodFellas*.

1991 Barbra Streisand and Nick Nolte portray a New York psychiatrist and a high school football coach from South Carolina who discover that beyond their differences lie the commonalities of human joy and suffering, in the film version of Pat Conroy's best-selling novel, *Prince of Tides*.

...and in Song

Sidewalks of New York—James Blake and C. Lawlor

The Streets of New York—Victor Herbert and Henry Blossom

Autumn in New York—Vernon Duke

New York, New York—Betty Comden, Adolph Green and Leonard Bernstein

Lonely Town—Comden, Green and Bernstein

Christopher Street—Comden, Green and Bernstein

When I'm Out with the Belle of New York—Johnny Mercer and Harry Warren

I Happen to Like New York—Cole Porter

Manhattan—Cole Porter

Give It Back to the Indians—Gordon Jenkins

Lullaby of Broadway—Harry Warren and Al Dubin

Forty-Second Street—Warren and Dubin

She's a Latin from Manhattan—Warren and Dubin

Manhattan Serenade—Lewis Alter and Harold Adamson

Springtime in Manhattan—Anthony Sciletta and Alice Reach

Carry Me Back to Old Manhattan—George Cory and Douglas Cross

Take Me Back to Manhattan—Cole Porter

Give My Regards to Broadway—George M. Cohan

Broadway Melody—Nacio Herb Brown and Arthur Freed

Broadway Rhythm—Brown and Freed

Slumming on Park Avenue—Irving Berlin

Fifth Avenue—Harry Warren and Mark Gordon

Slaughter on Tenth Avenue—Richard Rodgers

Chinatown, My Chinatown—Jean Schwartz and William Jerome

Rose of Washington Square—Ballard MacDonald and James Hanley

Sunday in the Park—Harold Rome

Saturday Night in Central Park—Richard Lewis and Arnold Horwitt

Bojangles of Harlem—Jerome Kern and Dorothy Fields

Stompin' at the Savoy—Chick Webb and Benny Goodman

Don José from Far Rockaway—Harold Rome

Nesting Time in Flatbush—Jerome Kern and P.G. Wodehouse

I Have Grown to Love New York—Howard Dietz and Vernon Duke

On Broadway—Barry Mann, Cynthia Weill, Jerry Leiber and Mike Stoller

59th Street Bridge Song—Paul Simon and Art Garfunkel

New York State of Mind—Billy Joel

Dirty Blvd.—Lou Reed

Greenwich Village

Although it has been officially a part of Manhattan for so many years, **Greenwich Village** (bounded by the **Hudson River, Broadway, Houston** and **14th Sts**) is still very much a town-within-a-city. And not a homogeneous one at that. It is home to students of **New York University**, actors in Off Broadway theaters, jazz musicians, the calm of **Morton St** and the hustle of **Bleecker St**. It is radical and old guard, grand and glitzy, authentic and ersatz. It arouses fanatical loyalty among its residents, who fight among themselves about social and political issues of the day, but also fight to maintain the Village's human scale and history.

In the 1790s, the country estates were sold off in lots or subdivided and developed by large landholders. Weavers, sailmakers and craftsmen moved into rows of modest homes along streets laid out following the boundaries of the old estates and travelers' paths. Later, when a grid was established for new streets in Manhattan, it was too late to change the Village's crazy maze of thoroughfares.

The growth of Greenwich Village, which was far removed from the city's congestion, was stimulated by influxes of New Yorkers fleeing epidemics of

smallpox, yellow fever and cholera that ravaged New York in the 1790s and early 1800s. Hastily built houses and hotels arose to accommodate them. Bank St is named for Wall Street banks that opened here along with other commercial ventures during the severe epidemic of 1822.

In the 1830s, prominent families began to build townhouses at **Washington Square**, which had become a public park in 1828. New York society took over 5th Ave and the side streets from University Pl to 6th Ave. But the fashionable set always moves on to ever more desirable pastures, and soon the Washington Square elite had gravitated to **Gramercy Park, Madison Square** and upper 5th Ave. By the late 1850s, the Village was solidly built up and settled into a quiet backwater of middle-class, old-line Anglo-Dutch families. Warehouses and industrial plants proliferated along the Hudson River, and commercial development began to the east and north. But the Village always retained its residential character. In the '80s and '90s, Irish and Chinese immigrants moved in, while Italians populated the tenements built south of Washington Square.

Houses from all periods remain in the Village, but of the brownstones that once lined 5th Ave from Washington Sq to Central Park in what was called

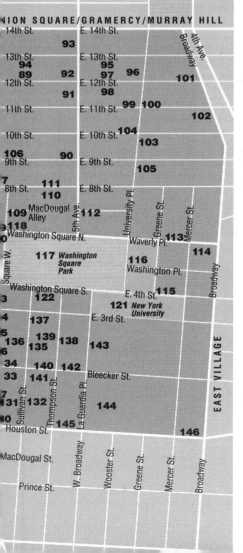

Two Miles of Millionaires, only one remains. One of the first brownstone mansions in the Italianate style, it was built in 1853 at 47 5th Ave for **Irad Hawley**, president of the Pennsylvania Coal Company. **The Salmagundi Club**, the city's oldest club for art and artists (founded in 1870), moved into the brownstone in 1917, and opens its doors for exhibitions from time to time.

As the high rollers moved out, their big houses were divided into flats and studios and their stables into houses. The cheap rents appealed to writers **Edgar Allan Poe, Horace Greeley, Walt Whitman, Mark Twain** and **Edna St. Vincent Millay**, who at one time occupied the narrowest house in the city—just $9^1/2$ ft wide—at $75^1/2$ Bedford St; painters of the Hudson River School, **Bierstadt, Church, Kensett** and **La Farge**; Impressionists **Ernest Lawson** and **Robert Henri**; and members of the early 20th-century Ashcan School, **Glackens, Sloan** and **Hopper**. Greenwich Village became the American bohemia before WWI. After the war, it continued to be a magnet for those looking for sexual freedom, radicalism and revolt in the arts and politics. **Upton Sinclair** founded the **Liberal Club** on MacDougal St. The **Washington Square Players** (later to become the **Theater Guild**) organized in 1917.

The following year, the **Provincetown Players**, the company that gave **Eugene O'Neill** his first chance, opened in the Village; the company is still putting on plays at the **Provincetown Playhouse** on MacDougal St.

In the '30s, the Village was home not only to bohemians, but also to old families, white-collar workers and the families of Irish and Italian blue-collar workers. After WWII, the Beat Generation and the hippies found the Village. Commercialism and developers got their hooks in too. Although residents have fought hard to keep the community the way it was, apartment houses and high rises have made inroads. Some of the development, such as **Westbeth**, a Bell Telephone Laboratories building recycled as housing for artists, has been fairly sensitive. One of the Village's largest landowners, **Sailors' Snug Harbor**, however, has been criticized for some of the decisions it has made for its 21 acres of leased land near Washington Sq. In 1801, **Captain Robert Richard Randall** deeded the land and a small cash gift for the purpose of establishing a home for retired seamen, which is now in North Carolina and financed by the returns on the Greenwich Village holdings. **Trinity Parish**, the other large landowner with deeds from the same period, is usually given high marks for helping to maintain the character of the Village.

Today, every style of 18th- and 19th-century architecture, culture and history can still be found (often intermingled), from the gracious Classical houses on

the north side of Washington Sq, where **Henry James** and **Edith Wharton** lived, to converted stables in MacDougal Alley behind them, where in the 1900s sculptors **Jo Davidson** and **Gertrude Vanderbilt Whitney** and actor **Richard Bennett** occupied houses. A Village church, such as **Judson Memorial**, designed by **McKim, Mead & White**, may be known as much for its experimental theater as for its historical or architectural value. NYU now has colleges and schools at its Washington Sq campus. **The New School for Social Research**, America's first university for adults, is still championing social causes and offering a dazzling variety of night-school courses. The New School and **Parsons School of Design** formed a partnership that broadens the excellent curriculum of both schools. History is everywhere—in bars like the **Minetta Tavern** on MacDougal St, filled with photos and memorabilia from earlier days, or the **Cedar Tavern** on University Pl, where Abstract Expressionists **Jackson Pollock**, **Franz Kline** and **Larry Rivers** used to hang out. At the **Gansevoort Market**, the city's wholesale meat market, you can imagine what it was like when **Herman Melville** worked as a customs inspector for 19 years at what was then the **Gansevoort Dock**.

R A K E L

◆ ◆ ◆ ◆ ◆

1 Rakel ★★$$$ The sight of the white baby grand piano just past the entrance establishes the tone of this dramatic, multileveled restaurant. The artful setting, in turn, shows off the *très* fashionable diners, as if the trompe l'oeil ceiling and the Issey Miyake suits were designed in tandem. The menu doesn't sway from this theme—the creative combinations are exciting and satisfying, starting with the complimentary quiche or sashimi. The wine list is surprisingly reasonable. The piano is put to good use with music nightly, jazz on weekends. ◆ French ◆ 231 7th Ave So (Clarkson St) Reservations required. 929.1630

2 Carmine Street Public Pools Don't be confused by the name: these indoor and outdoor public pools aren't actually on Carmine St anymore, thanks to a zoning law that created Clarkson St out of the west half of Carmine. Nonmembers are permitted to swim in the outdoor pool, only. Call for hours, and bring a padlock. ◆ Clarkson St at 7th Ave So. 397.3107

3 Café Español $$ Welcome in an area that is resisting pretentiousness less and less. Spanish cuisine served in an authentic Catalan atmosphere at reasonable prices. ◆ Spanish ◆ 63 Carmine St (7th Ave So) 675.3312

3 Mostly Magic Nightclub/theater featuring magic, comedy and music; Saturday afternoon magic shows for children. ◆ Shows: Tu-Th 9PM; F 9, 11PM; Sa 2, 9, 11PM. 55 Carmine St (Bedford St-7th Ave So) 924.1472

4 Cent' Anni ★$$$ At times this seems like one of the best informal Italian restaurants in town, and at one time it was, but it can be disappointing. The quasi-Florentine menu features an extraordinary minestrone, a few outstanding pasta dishes and a huge Tuscan-style porterhouse steak. Skip dessert. Service is friendly and efficient, if somewhat chaotic on a busy night. ◆ Italian ◆ 50 Carmine St (Bedford St) Reservations recommended. 989.9494

4 46 Carmine Street Jackson Pollock lived in an apartment in this building between 1932 and 1933 while studying at the Art Students League. ◆ Bleecker-Bedford Sts

5 House of Oldies An incredible collection of rare and out-of-circulation rock 'n' roll and R&B LPs, including 10,000 rock 'n' roll 78s and over a million 45s. Additional stock is sent up from the basement via a dumbwaiter. ◆ Closed Su. 35 Carmine St (6th Ave-7th Ave So) 243.0500

5 Village Flute & Sax Shop Doctor Rich repairs woodwind instruments for some of the best in the business. You can take lessons here, buy or sell a musical instrument or just drop by and see a genuine craftsman at work. ◆ Closed Su. 35 Carmine St (6th Ave-7th Ave So) 243.1276

5 Church of Our Lady of Pompeii (1927, **Matthew Del Gaudio**) The gilded marble interior convinces you this structure might have been picked up intact from the hills of Italy. The illusion goes further than that—some services are conducted in Italian. The square across the street is named for **Father Antonio Demo**, who served this parish from 1901 until 1936. ◆ 25 Carmine St (6th Ave-7th Ave So)

6 New York Public Library, Hudson Park Branch (1905, **Carrère & Hastings**) The original building, by the same architects as its big brother up on 5th Ave, was expanded in 1935 at about the same time the **Carmine Street Pool** was added behind it. The library's **Early Childhood Resource and Information Center**, a facility for small children and their parents, is located here. Hours may change due to budget cuts. ◆ Tu 10AM-6PM; W, F noon-6PM; Th noon-8PM; Sa noon-5PM. 66 Leroy St (7th Ave So-Hudson St) 243.6876

6 Anglers & Writers ★$ 1930s literary Paris is recaptured in this cozy, unpretentious cafe/tearoom owned by mother-and-son team **Charlotte** and **Craig Bero**. Mismatched English and Austrian china, turn-of-the-century American country furniture and shelves of books—with an emphasis on **Hemingway, Fitzgerald** and fly fishing—create an ideal atmosphere for writing in a journal, reading (or writing) a novel, reminiscing with friends

or gazing out the large picture windows, which overlook James J. Walker Park and the Hudson River. ◆ Cafe ◆ 420 Hudson St (St. Luke's Pl) 675.0810

7 Village Atelier ★$$ The farmhouse setting is an appropriate backdrop for the regional American food served here. The roast chicken stuffed with apples, prunes, sausage and wild rice is outstanding, as are the freshwater fish dishes. ◆ American ◆ Closed Su. 436 Hudson St (Morton St) Reservations required. 989.1363

8 Mary's ★$$$ There are few vestiges of the old Greenwich Village, but Mary's certainly qualifies—except that the attitude and the prices have more of a modern edge. The rooms are still charming—especially the upstairs salon; I think it's worth the wait. And the food—Mary's does wonders with chicken—harkens back to Mama's kitchen. Side-street location is a bit of a hunt. ◆ Italian ◆ 42 Bedford St (7th Ave So) Reservations required. 243.9755

Greenwich Village

9 75 ¹/₂ Bedford Street Built in 1873, this 9 ¹/₂ft wide building is thought to be the narrowest in the city, and was the last New York City residence of **Edna St. Vincent Millay** and her husband, **Eugen Boissevain**. No. 77 next door, built in 1800, is the oldest house in the Village. ◆ Commerce St

9 Cherry Lane Theater (1846) Originally built as a brewery, this building was converted to a theater (founded by **Edna St. Vincent Millay**) for avant-garde productions in 1924. *Godspell* had its world premiere here. ◆ Seats 184. 38 Commerce St (Bedford-Barrow Sts) 989.2020

9 Blue Mill Tavern $ Villagers cherish it for its determined plainness and dependably ordinary food. ◆ Portuguese/American ◆ 50 Commerce St (Bedford-Barrow Sts) 243.7114

9 Shopsin's $ A general store turned into a highly personal kitchen that turns out an amazing array of dishes with a home-cooked feeling. The chef and his wife, who are always on hand, and the children, who are always underfoot, make this place seem like a community hangout, if not downright communal. The place can look like a mess—just like home. ◆ American ◆ Closed Sa-Su. 63 Bedford St (Commerce-Morton Sts) 924.5160

10 39 and 41 Commerce Street (1831) A well-preserved pair of mansard-roofed houses with a central garden. An apocryphal but oft-repeated tale is that they were built by a sea captain for his 2 unmarried daughters, who were not on speaking terms. ◆ Bedford-Barrow Sts

Restaurants/Nightlife: Red   Hotels: Blue
Shops/Parks: Green   Sights/Culture: Black

11 St. Luke-in-the-Fields (1822, **James N. Wells**) The simple Federal-style building, restored after a 1981 fire, still has the feeling of a country church. **St. Luke's School**, one of the city's most highly respected Episcopal parochial schools, was established in 1945. The thrift store next door is a tad more expensive than you'd expect, but well stocked. ◆ 487 Hudson St (Barrow-Christopher Sts)

12 Crystal Gardens Quartz, minerals, medicine jewelry, seminars, consultations and an interesting newsletter written by co-owner **Connie Barrett**. A recent issue featured an article about medicine cards, native American tools of divination. I send my spiritually inclined friends here. ◆ 21 Greenwich St (Christopher-W 10th Sts) 727.0692

12 LainaJane Galleria Silk and cotton lingerie, kimonos, PJs and his-and-her boxer shorts—all reasonably priced. ◆ Closed Su. 150 W 10th St (Waverly Pl-Greenwich St) 727.7032

13 Grove Court (1854) Between 10 and 12 Grove St, at the middle of what some consider

Greenwich Village

to be the most authentic group of Federal-style houses in America, you can find one of the most charming and private enclaves in Manhattan. These 6 brick-fronted buildings were built as houses for working men when the court was known as *Mixed Ale Alley*. ◆ Closed M. Bedford-Hudson Sts

14 Chumleys $$ A speakeasy during the 1920s (the anonymous building has the advantage of a back exit to Barrow St), it still doesn't have a sign. Villagers who want to make a real impression enter through the back door. It's a cozy, convivial place with working fireplaces and wooden benches deeply carved with customers' initials. The food isn't terrific, but it's a great place to stop for a drink. ◆ American ◆ 86 Bedford St (Barrow-Grove Sts) 675.4449

15 Pink Teacup $$ Longtime regulars of what was once downtown's only soul food shack have been disappointed that the Teacup pulled up stakes and moved to a slicker location around the corner from its original site on Bleecker St. It's still the only *echt* soul food restaurant in the Village, and if you like smothered porkchops, collard greens, black-eyed peas and smooth banana pudding, they now come as gentrified as the hamburgers and pizzas in other places. ◆ Southern ◆ 42 Grove St (Bleecker-Bedford Sts) No credit cards. 807.6755

16 Courtyard Playhouse The **Little People's Theater Company** entertains children and their parents with plays like *Humpty Dumpty Falls in Love*, *Cinderella* and *Wilbur the Christmas Mouse*. They do 8 shows per season, beginning the week after Labor Day and running through the 3rd week of June. Reservations are a must. ◆ Seats 74. 39 Grove St (Bleecker St) 765.9540

16 Collage ★$$ A small neighborhood restaurant with a lovely garden. The eclectic cuisine *à la française* includes excellent coq au vin and seared tuna plus a *tarte aux pommes extraordinaire*. ◆ French ◆ 314 Bleecker St (Grove St) 645.1612

17 Chez Michellet $$ This charming and intimate French-style bistro is always packed with a neighborhood crowd. Especially good are the roasted chicken, steak and French fries. A place to watch. ◆ French ◆ 90 Bedford St (Grove St) 242.8309

17 Twin Peaks In 1925, **Clifford Reed Daily** transformed this very conventional 1830 residence into a fairy-tale fantasy as a reaction against the mediocrity of Village architecture. Pseudo-Tudor details trim the stucco facing, and an unorthodox flap acts as a front cornice (there's an attic room behind it). It's not great architecture, but it is great fun. ◆ 102 Bedford St (Grove-Christopher Sts)

18 Lucille Lortel Theatre Formerly the **Theatre De Lys**, this house was a major boost to Off Broadway in the 1950s, when a revival of the Brecht-Weill classic *The Threepenny Opera* was staged here. It was later renamed for its distinguished owner, **Lucille Lortel**, who produced *Brecht on Brecht* and **John Dos Passos'** *USA*. More recently, it was the home to the hugely successful *Steel Magnolias* during its 2 1/2-year run. ◆ Seats 299. 121 Christopher St (Bleecker-Hudson Sts) 924.8782

18 McNulty's Tea and Coffee Company Exotic coffees (from China, Sumatra, Indonesia) and teas (over 250 varieties) since 1895; the experience shows. ◆ 109 Christopher St (Bleecker-Hudson Sts) 242.5351

19 Li-Lac Chocolates Somewhat drab from the outside, but a chocolate addict's dream-come-true inside. Stop by and sample their wares; the Jordan Crackers (milk- or dark-chocolate covered soda biscuits) are excellent companions for a walk around the Village. Pick up a chocolate Empire State building for a chocoholic back home. ◆ 120 Christopher St (Bleecker-Bedford Sts) 242.7374

19 Pot Belly Stove Restaurant $ If you feel like having a hamburger, an omelet or a salad at 3AM, this is one of the better places to satisfy the urge. ◆ American ◆ 94 Christopher St (Bleecker-Bedford Sts) No credit cards. 243.9614

20 Tekk Billiards There's no bar and no food (except for vending machine offerings), and the only music is a blaring radio. But there are pool tables, lots of them, in this popular hangout for the college-age (and under) crowd. Open until the wee hours. ◆ 75 Christopher St (7th Ave So-Bleecker St) 463.9282

21 La Vie en Rose It's just roses here, and all different kinds: lavender, jacaranda, African. Check out *The Ten Commandments for a Better Rose Life* before leaving with your bouquet. ◆ 82 Christopher St (Bleecker St-7th Ave So) 366.4010, 800/8.ROSE85

22 Grove Decoys Both antique and new duck decoys are part of this extensive collection, which also includes bird carvings and rare fish decoys. ♦ 49 Grove St (Bleecker St-7th Ave So) 924.4467

22 Grove Street Café ★$$$ A place that's easy to fall in love with—the charming, softly lit room is conveniently located near all the Village theaters. The mostly very good nouvelle cuisine is priced more fairly than at places of a similar ilk. Service is better too. The BYO wine policy helps keep the tab in line. ♦ French ♦ Closed Su. 53 Grove St (Bleecker St-7th Ave So) Reservations recommended. No credit cards. 924.9501

22 Fukuda ★$$ A small, cozy restaurant with an outstanding sushi bar. ♦ Japanese ♦ 61 Grove St (7th Ave So-Bleecker St) Reservations recommended. 242.3699

23 Christopher Park Until the Parks Department put a sign near the entrance, everyone thought this was Sheridan Sq. The confusion began when the IRT Sheridan Sq subway stop was opened in 1918, and was compounded when **Joseph Pollia**'s statue of the Civil War general was placed here (possibly by mistake) in 1936. ♦ 7th Ave So (Grove-Christopher Sts)

23 Sheridan Square Because there is another park closer to the Sheridan Sq subway stop, which is around the corner, Sheridan Sq is at the same time one of the best-known and hardest-to-find spots in all of Greenwich Village. The community garden in the center yielded rare archaeological treasures when it was created in the early 1980s. It was the only spot in Manhattan that hadn't been disturbed since Indians lived here. ♦ W 4th St (Washington Pl-7th Ave So)

23 The Ridiculous Theatrical Company The late great **Charles Ludlam** felt that farce, parody and travesty were essential ingredients for comic drama. They still are—Ludlam's virtuosic company continues the tradition with such delights as a severely adapted *A Tale of Two Cities*. ♦ Seats 155. 1 Sheridan Sq (W 4th St at 7th Ave So) 691.2271

24 Actor's Playhouse One of the high spots on the Off Broadway theater scene since it raised its first curtain in 1940. Productions have included *10% Review* and *The Good and Faithful Servant*. ♦ Seats 165. 100 7th Ave So (Bleecker-Grove Sts) 691.6226

24 Sweet Basil The giants of the jazz world— **Doc Cheatham, Chico Hamilton, Dakota Staton** and others—perform here regularly. Good salads and stir-fry dishes. ♦ Cover. Shows nightly 10PM, midnight. 88 7th Ave So (Bleecker-Grove Sts) 242.1785

Among the famous New Yorkers who have called the serene **St. Luke's Place** home are **Mayor Jimmy Walker, Sherwood Anderson, Marianne Moore** and **Theodore Dreiser**.

Restaurants/Nightlife: Red   **Hotels:** Blue
Shops/Parks: Green   **Sights/Culture:** Black

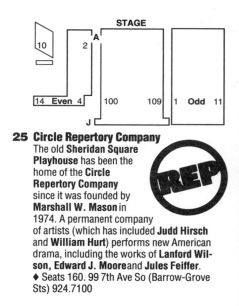

25 Circle Repertory Company The old **Sheridan Square Playhouse** has been the home of the **Circle Repertory Company** since it was founded by **Marshall W. Mason** in 1974. A permanent company of artists (which has included **Judd Hirsch** and **William Hurt**) performs new American drama, including the works of **Lanford Wilson, Edward J. Moore** and **Jules Feiffer**. ♦ Seats 160. 99 7th Ave So (Barrow-Grove Sts) 924.7100

26 One If By Land, Two If By Sea ★★$$$$ (1834) There is no sign outside this charming restaurant, but don't give up. Once you've found it, you'll never forget it. There is a large bar and a working fireplace just inside the door. The 2-level interior is romantically candlelit, and the food (beef Wellington is the thing here) is beautifully prepared. ♦ American ♦ 17 Barrow St (W 4th St-7th Ave So) Reservations required. 228.0822

27 Manhattan Chili Company ★$ When you're in the mood for a good bowl of chili, go no further. It comes in a wide range of spices; there's even vegetarian chili for those watching their cholesterol levels. If I happen to be with someone who's not a chili fan, there are plenty of other Southern fixin's to keep them happy. The beer is, wisely, inexpensive—I always need more than one to wash down the Texas Chain Gang chili (classification: *hot hot*). Terrific for catered parties. *An RSW recommendation*. ♦ Southern/Mexican ♦ 302 Bleecker St (7th Ave So) 206.7163

28 Ottomanelli's Meat Market If you're a long way from home, you're probably not in the market for fresh game or a fine veal roast. But there aren't many butcher shops like this one anymore. Drop in to see what you're missing. ♦ Closed Su. 285 Bleecker St (Jones St-7th Ave So) 675.4217

28 Second Childhood Antique toys and other artifacts of childhood squeezed into a tiny storefront. ♦ Closed Su. 283 Bleecker St (Jones St-7th Ave So) 989.6140

28 Vanessa ★$$$ Stylish and popular, Vanessa became an almost instant sensation. Sadly, although it is fashionably creative, not all the food equals the beauty of the dining room. ♦ American ♦ 289 Bleecker St (7th Ave So) 243.4225

29 Aphrodisia Over 800 different herbs and spices. Scoop your choice into a small paper bag and label with the name and price. A good selection of books for healthy living. ♦ 282 Bleecker St (7th Ave So) 989.6440

29 John's Pizzeria ★$ Some years ago, **Woody Allen** wrote in *The New Yorker* that John's makes the best coal-oven pizza in New York. Even if you have to wait in line to find out for yourself—and you will—you'll agree it was worth it. ♦ Italian ♦ 278 Bleecker St (Morton St-7th Ave So) 243.1680

Greenwich Village

30 Cucina Stagionale ★$ The menu is basic Italian with a twist (try the eggplant mani-cotti), and the price is right. There's almost always a line of people happily waiting to get in, bottles of wine in hand. ♦ Italian ♦ 275 Bleecker St (Jones-Cornelia Sts) No credit cards. 924.2707

31 Faicco's Pork Store Terrific Italian cheeses, cold cuts and homemade sausages. Italian bread. ♦ Closed M. 260 Bleecker St (Leroy-Morton Sts) 243.1974

Time was when the gay community centered itself solely around the Village. **Gay Liberation** got its start in 1968 at the **Stonewall** on Christopher St. But times have changed, and although the Village still has a large population of gay residents, it is no longer realistic to say the Christopher St area is a true reflection of New York's gay community. East Side, West Side, uptown and downtown—gay visibility is everywhere. We suggest the **Lesbian and Gay Community Services Center, Inc.** (208 W 13th St. 620.7310) as a first stop for gay visitors. Over 150 groups meet on a regular basis to discuss everything from politics to health and social services. The atmosphere is safe and nonthreatening, and the staff is available daily 9AM-11PM. Among the city's many bookstores, bars and restaurants, the Center suggests **Oscar Wilde Memorial Bookshop; A Different Light; Uncle Charlie's Downtown** (men's bar), 56 Greenwich Ave, 255.8787; **Duchess II** (women's bar), 70 Grove St, 242.1408; **Cubby Hole** (women's bar), 438 Hudson St, 243.9079; **Tracks** (disco for men and women), 531 W 19th St, 627.2333. Other helpful information is available through the **Gay and Lesbian Switchboard**, 777.1800, and several gay publications: *Sappho's Isle, Womanews, New York Native, Outweek*. All give up-to-date information and are available at most newsstands.

31 Zampagnaro's A wonderfully authentic mom-and-pop Italian grocery, complete with hanging provolones. ♦ 262 Bleecker St (6th Ave-7th Ave So) 929.8566

32 A. Zito & Sons Bakery The bread's crunchy crust and delicate inside texture lures such devoted customers as **Frank Sinatra**. I love to pick out my own loaf, just out of the oven. ♦ 259 Bleecker St (6th Ave-Cornelia St) 929.6139

32 Murray's Cheese Store The competitive prices of the large assortment of cheeses—of which 90 percent are imported—and superior service will keep you coming back. A small stock of groceries is also sold out of this tiny storefront. ♦ Closed Su. 42 Cornelia St (Bleecker St) 243.3289

33 Sabor $$ A Cuban restaurant that is un-even—sometimes good, sometimes not. Everything comes with the traditional rice, beans and fried plantains, none of which is as heavy as is typical. Excellent tropical mixed drinks and desserts. ♦ Cuban ♦ 20 Cornelia St (W 4th St) Reservations recommended. 243.9579

34 Cornelia Street Café $$ A charming atmo-sphere on a neat little Village side street. The food's okay but a little pricey considering its neighborhood appeal. ♦ Cafe/bistro ♦ 29 Cornelia St (Bleecker-W 3rd Sts) 989.9318

35 The Bagel $ This tiny restaurant and deli is known for its Village Breakfast—strawberry pancakes—as well as the standard deli fare. The Bagel also makes a great sandwich; try the pastrami or—my favorite—corned beef. ♦ American ♦ 170 W 4th St (Cornelia St) No credit cards. 255.0106

36 Pink Pussycat Boutique Take a peek at the incredible selection of erotic paraphernalia, even if you're too embarrassed to buy any-thing. ♦ 161 W 4th St (6th Ave-7th Ave So) 243.0077

37 St. Joseph's Church (1834, **John Doran**) The oldest Roman Catholic church building in Manhattan, this Greek Revival temple has a gallery inside as well as delicate crystal chandeliers and a gilded sanctuary that contrasts with the simplicity of the Greek Revival exterior. The outside wall on Washington Pl is made of Manhattan schist, which underlies the whole island. ♦ 371 6th Ave (W. Washington Pl)

38 Gay Street Thought to be named after a family who lived here in the mid- to late-18th century. A well-preserved group of Greek Re–

vival houses on the east side and Federal row houses on the west. No. 14 is the location of the basement apartment that was the setting for **Ruth McKenney**'s play, *My Sister Eileen*, which later was made into the musical *Wonderful Town*. ◆ Waverly-Christopher Sts

39 **Oscar Wilde Memorial Bookshop** Small shop offering a tasteful selection of books on gay and lesbian subject matter, including literary classics, legal guides, sociology and periodicals. ◆ 15 Christopher St (Waverly Pl) 255.8097

40 **158 Waverly Place** In 1948, while playing the role of Billie Dawn in *Born Yesterday,* **Judy Holliday** and her husband, **David Oppenheim**, moved into a large apartment on the 7th floor of this building. They lived here until 1952, when they moved into the Dakota on the West Side. ◆ Gay-Christopher Sts

40 **Pierre's** ★$$$ The bistro's cozy atmosphere is enhanced by wandering minstrels who entertain with classic French favorites. Try the salmon puff pastries (delicate morsels stuffed with spinach), and for dessert, the *tarte tatin* (apple pie baked with a caramel sauce and served with homemade whipped cream). The steak *pommes frites* are good as well. ◆ French ◆ 170 Waverly Pl (Christopher St) Reservations required. No credit cards. 929.7194

40 **Northern Dispensary** (1831, **Henry Bayard** and **John C. Tucker**) This basic brick, Georgian-vernacular, triangular building is in the odd position of having 2 sides on one street—Waverly Pl as it splits; and one side on 2 streets—where Grove and Christopher run together. It is the home of a public clinic established in 1827. According to records, **Edgar Allan Poe** was treated here for a head cold in 1837. ◆ 165 Waverly Pl (Grove-Christopher Sts) 242.5511

41 **Lion's Head** $$$ One of the major hangouts for local journalists, writers and community politicians. The bar is the main thing, but the food is perfectly acceptable. ◆ Continental ◆ 59 Christopher St (7th Ave So) 929.0670

42 **Three Lives & Company** The kind of bookstore you read about. This shop carries a wonderful selection (especially fiction and specialty books) and hosts Thursday night readings. The owners are knowledgeable and helpful. ◆ 154 W 10th St (6th Ave-7th Ave So) 741.2069

43 **New York Public Library, Jefferson Market Branch** (1877, **Frederick Clark Withers** and **Calvert Vaux**; remodeling 1967, **Giorgio Cavaglieri**) Vaux and Withers modeled this structure, built on the site of the old **Jefferson Market** and originally used as the **Third Judicial District Courthouse**, after **Mad King Ludwig II** of Bavaria's castle *Neuschwanstein*. It is the epitome of Victorian Gothic, with steeply sloping roofs, gables, pinnacles, sets of variously shaped arched windows and stone carvings all set off by a rather unusual clock tower that served as a fire lookout. After the occupants moved out in 1945, the building sat idle until citizens pressured the city government to find a new user and the public library agreed to move in. Hours may change because of recent budget cuts. ◆ M, Sa 10AM-6PM; Tu noon-6PM; W-Th noon-8PM. 425 6th Ave (W 10th St) 243.4334

44 **Balducci's** In Greenwich Village, the *ne plus ultra* grocer. From humble beginnings many years ago as a produce stand across the street

Greenwich Village

from its present site, this family-run store has become one of the most grand and best-stocked specialty shops in the city. Not only is there still gorgeous produce, but now also first-rate cheese, fish, cold cut, takeout and bakery departments. The shelves hold packaged products from all over the world, but concentrate on delicacies from Italy and France. ◆ 424 6th Ave (W 9th St) 673.2600

45 **Jefferson Market** There's one of just about everything you might want here—meats and fish are especially fine. The staff's extremely helpful; longtime customers are treated with neighborly respect. A considerably tamer version of Balducci's, just across the avenue. ◆ 455 6th Ave (W 10th St) 675.2277

45 **Patchin Place** (1848, **Aaron D. Patchin**) Like **Milligan Place** around the corner on 6th Ave, this cluster of charming small houses was built as rooming houses for waiters and other personnel from the now-departed **Brevoort Hotel** over on 5th Ave. It became famous in the 1920s as the home of poet **e.e. cummings**, among others. ◆ W 10th St (6th-Greenwich Aves)

They're all over New York, but rooftop water tanks seem more visible in the Village than anywhere else. Their average height above sea level is about the same as a 5-story building, and any building higher than that needs to pump water to its upper floors. The tanks are made of western yellow cedar or California redwood, and have a life expectancy of about 30 years. The 2in boards, which are as strong as 14in of concrete, are held together with steel bands around the outside, and the water inside swells the wood to a tight fit. The insulating properties of wood prevent freezing in winter and keep the water cool, if not cold, in summer.

46 Gran Caffé Degli Artisti ★$ Don't choose a window seat; instead, ask for a table in the back, where it's dark, cozy, candlelit and filled with funky antique furnishings. Skip the real food and go directly to the iced mochaccino and one of the decadent pastries or cakes. ♦ Cafe ♦ Closed Sa-Su. 46 Greenwich Ave (W 10th-W 11th Sts) 371.1823

47 El Charro Espanol $$ Though not authentic Mexican, or even Tex-Mex, the food is fresh, tasty, abundant and fairly priced at this cozy, casual spot. Ignore the Spanish side of the menu. ♦ Tex-Mex ♦ 4 Charles St (Greenwich Ave) Reservations recommended F-Su. 242.9547

48 Village Vanguard This world-famous basement jazz club features the renowned **Mel Lewis** and his 17-piece **Big Band** on Monday nights. Dixieland, blues, avant-garde, folk music is performed—even pop singers, comedians and poets have appeared here. ♦ Cover. Shows: 9:30, 11:30PM, 1AM. 178 7th Ave So (Perry St) Reservations required. 255.4037

Greenwich Village

49 Pleasure Chest Not as froofy-looking as the Pink Pussycat; perhaps this erotic emporium is for folks into more serious pleasures. ♦ 156 7th Ave So (Charles St) 242.2158. Also at: 302 E 52nd St. 371.4465

50 John Clancy's ★★$$$ The first New York restaurant to introduce the now-familiar method of mesquite-grilled seafood. This is the real thing—just the right amount of woody flavor; the delicacy of the fish shines through. Wonderful, rich desserts and a superb wine list. ♦ American ♦ 181 W 10th St (7th Ave So) Reservations required. 242.7350

51 Riviera Café $$ People-watching is the best thing on the menu here, which includes standards like burgers and salads. Sip some wine and watch most of Greenwich Village pass by your table. Indoor and outdoor dining. ♦ American ♦ 225 W 4th St (Christopher St-7th Ave So) 242.8732

52 La Metairie ★★$$$ A white picket fence and hand-painted duck sign welcome you to this minuscule French/American restaurant. Start with foie gras or carpaccio. Excellent filet mignon and grilled fish. ♦ French/American ♦ 189 W 10th (Bleecker St-7th Ave So) Reservations required. 989.0343

52 Kelter/Malce Antique quilts from the early 1800s, including a good selection of Amish and patchwork quilts, Beacon and Pendleton blankets, Navajo weavings, folk art and antique Christmas ornaments. ♦ Closed Su. 361 Bleecker St (Charles-W 10th Sts) 989.6760

53 Very Special Flowers You won't find the usual mums, gladioli or carnations here. Instead, VSF concentrates on complicated topiary, dried-flower arrangements and exotic bouquets made from flowers flown in daily from Holland and France. ♦ Closed Su. 204 W 10th St (Bleecker St) 206.7236

54 Patisserie J. Lanciani ★$ A pretty storefront cafe serving magnificent cakes, tarts, brownies, croissants. I always sit near a window. ♦ Cafe ♦ 271 W 4th St (Perry-W 11th Sts) 929.0739, 477.2788

55 Cottonwood Cafe $$ A low-down Texan joint in the heart of the West Village. The crisp-breaded chicken-fried steak with sides of fabulously lumpy mashed potatoes, cornmeal-dipped fried okra and obligatory cream gravy is enough to make the roughest ranchero coo with pleasure. The hefty beef ribs are the most authentic mesquite-smoked, Texas-style barbecued ribs in town. After 10PM, something called *original Texas* music—C&W with an overlay of Village artiness—is performed in the back room. Great nonclassic margaritas. Lone Star beer. Neighborhood crowd. ♦ Southern ♦ 415 Bleecker St (W 11th-Bank Sts) No credit cards. 924.6271

55 Bird Jungle This is the place to pick up a parrot or a mynah bird or any one of a dozen different varieties of feathered friends. The window action can be a bit frightening at times. ♦ 401 Bleecker St (W 11th St) 242.1757

56 Biography Bookshop The best selection anywhere. Feel free to browse. ♦ Closed M. 400 Bleecker St (W 11th St) 807.8655

57 Twigs, Inc. If you want your living room to look like an English garden, or have a passion for roses (more than 30 varieties flown in daily from France and Holland), peonies or wildflowers. A day's advance notice is usually sufficient for parties. ♦ Closed Su. 381 Bleecker St (Charles-Perry Sts) 620.8188

57 Pierre Deux Provençal furniture, china, clothing, fabrics and accessories. ♦ Closed Su. 367 Bleecker St (Charles St) 243.7740. Also at: 870 Madison Ave. 570.9343

58 Lucy Anna Folk Art & Antique Quilts

When **Karen Taber**'s grandmothers—Lucy and Anna—handed down their quilts to their granddaughter, they planted a seed of interest that has blossomed into this charming shop filled with antique quilts (lots of pastels) as well as new items—such as stuffed animals—made out of quilt scraps. ♦ 502 Hudson St (Christopher-W 10th Sts) 645.9463

59 Sazerac House ★$$ Better-than-average gumbo, jambalaya and other New Orleans fare. Brunch is the way to go here. Eggs are transformed into a delicious concoction called *Eggs Sardou*—poached eggs on toast, topped with hollandaise sauce and surrounded by artichoke hearts. This is the oldest structure on the street (1826) and was once part of a farm. ◆ Cajun/Creole ◆ 533 Hudson St (Charles St) Reservations recommended. 989.0313

59 Taylor's A snug gourmet takeout run by **Spartan** and **Cindi Taylor**. The onion-poppy hot dog buns—with Pommery mustard mixed into the dough—give you a good reason to eat hot dogs, and the triple-fudge brownies will throw off your calorie count for the week. ◆ 523 Hudson St (W 10th-Charles Sts) 645.8200

60 Different Light Books An excellent place to find literature on a wide variety of gay- and lesbian-related topics and issues. Probably the best bookstore of its kind in the city. ◆ 548 Hudson St (Charles-Perry Sts) 989.4850

61 Caribe $$ Yet another Island motif restaurant bar: Jamaican food and music in a junglelike setting. The food is pretty good—try the jerk chicken or pork—and the atmosphere, well, let's call it West Indian/West Village. Funky and fun. ◆ West Indian ◆ 117 Perry St (Greenwich St) 255.9191

62 Fishs Eddy This shop specializes in collecting and selling odd and interesting bits of glassware and porcelain, such as old dishes from railroad cars, and remnants from extinct social clubs. You won't find a full set of china, but you will find something just right for Aunt Betty. ◆ 551 Hudson St (Perry-11th Sts) 627.3956. Also at: 889 Broadway. 420.9020

62 White Horse Tavern $ Okay French fries, edible burgers. Among the folks who have frequented this famous bar was the poet **Dylan Thomas**, who, in a particularly depressive funk, literally drank himself to death in the corner. His supposed last words: *I've had 19 straight whiskeys. I believe that's the record.* ◆ American ◆ 567 Hudson St (W 11th St) 243.9260

62 Burgundy Wine Company Specialists in the finest wines of Burgundy and the Rhone. Ask for a mail-order catalog, an informative brochure filled with vignettes about wine merchant **Al Hotchkin**'s travels through the vineyards plus his thoughts on the wines he discovers. ◆ Closed Su. 323 W 11th St (Hudson-West Sts) 691.9092

63 Harlequin ★$$$ Paella is the house specialty in this rather elegant Spanish restaurant, but the fact is, if Spanish food is your favorite, you might feel underwhelmed. ◆ Spanish ◆ 569 Hudson St (W 11th St) 255.4950

63 Penguin Cafe $$ This comfortable place with ceiling-high windows, ideal for people-watching, serves decent food (burgers, chili, potpies, sandwiches) at decent prices. ◆ American ◆ 581 Hudson St (Bank St) 627.7277

Restaurants/Nightlife: Red
Shops/Parks: Green

Hotels: Blue
Sights/Culture: Black

64 Tortilla Flats A West Village dive that serves up cheap Tex-Mex eats and wild times. ◆ Tex-Mex ◆ 767 Washington St (W 12th St) 243.1053

65 The Black Sheep $$$ This is every tourist's idea of a Village restaurant—brick walls, bad paintings, comfortable and dark. The 6-course dinner with limited choices is a good value. Excellent wine list. ◆ French ◆ 342 W 11th St (Washington St) Reservations recommended. 741.9772

AAG

66 Westbeth (1900, **Cyrus Eidlitz**; renovated 1965, **Richard Meier Associates**) In its years as **Bell Telephone Laboratories**, this was where the transistor was invented and the first television pictures were transmitted. When Bell Labs moved to the suburbs, the building was turned into housing exclusively for artists, and includes the **Westbeth Theater** complex and the studios of the **Merce Cunningham Dance Company**. ◆ 463 West St (Bank St)

67 Gulf Coast ★$$ A popular spot for the after-work, briefcase-toting crowd, this Cajun joint is always jumping, particularly on weekend nights. Spicy appetizers at the bar (if you can get a seat) will tide you over until they shout that your table is ready—count on a 90-minute wait and be pleasantly surprised if it's less. ◆ Cajun ◆ 489 West St (W 12th St) 206.8790

68 Restaurant Florent ★★$$ A meat market diner-turned-hip-bistro, this is a welcome late-night spot for diners seeking a complete meal, not something off the snack menu. The meat entrees are, of course, the specialties of the house (and try the *boudin noir* appetizer if you're the red-blooded type), but the fish dishes are also fine. After midnight, you can order from the all-night breakfast menu. Part of the attraction of this well-turned-out establishment is the ongoing involvement of **Tibor Kalman's M & Co, A Design Group**, which is responsible for the graphic design and, to some extent, the layout of the restaurant itself. ◆ Continental ◆ 24hrs. 69 Gansevoort St (Greenwich-Washington Sts) 989.5779

69 Gansevoort Market This collection of old brick buildings houses the city's wholesale meat district. The action here intensifies in the early morning hours before the sun comes up, when people from restaurants all over New York converge to find the best meat to offer you for dinner. ♦ Gansevoort-W 14th Sts (9th Ave-Hudson River)

70 El Faro ★$$ A casual Spanish restaurant in an out-of-the-way spot. The rich and fragrant paella is a standard. ♦ Spanish ♦ 823 Greenwich St (Horatio St) 929.8210

71 Kaleidoscope Antiques Over 1200 new and antique cookie jars—Raggedy Ann and Andy, doughboys, clowns, cows, robots, slot machines and telephones—ranging in price from $35 to thousands. If you ask to see one on the top shelf, be prepared to watch the shopkeeper climb on and over whatever is in his way—it's kind of scary. ♦ 636 Hudson St (Horatio St) 989.1036

71 Myers of Keswick If you're an Anglophile you'll have fun perusing this English grocery

Greenwich Village

and its selection of typical Brit eats: Oxo, Bovril, Marmite, Lucozade, Smarties, and fresh pork pies and bangers. Also Kensington teapots and mugs and circular tea bags. ♦ 634 Hudson St (Jane-Horatio Sts) 691.4194

72 Peanut Butter & Jane A children's clothing store stocked with over 200 different brands, from basics to one-of-a-kinds by local artists. Toys and accessories as well. ♦ 617 Hudson St (W 12th-Jane Sts) 620.7952. Also at: 28 Duane St. 619.2324

73 La Ripaille ★★$$$ It is fairly successful at looking like a French farmhouse, and the provincial dishes are never less than good—sometimes quite good. A mite too pricey, however, for what it is. ♦ French ♦ Closed Su. 605 Hudson St (Bethune-W 12th Sts) Reservations recommended. 255.4406

74 Abingdon Square Named for **Charlotte Warren**, wife of the **Earl of Abingdon** and daughter of **Sir Peter Warren**, whose estate once covered this area. The statue at the uptown entrance, placed here in 1921, is a memorial to the American dead of WWI. ♦ 8th Ave (W 12th-Hudson Sts)

Restaurants/Nightlife: Red	Hotels: Blue
Shops/Parks: Green	**Sights/Culture: Black**

75 Foul Play Books of Mystery & Suspense This specialty shop with black walls and red neon has a wide selection of mystery, espionage, suspense and true crime books in both hardcover and paperback. Do a little detective work of your own and see if you can find the hidden door in the rear of the store. ♦ 302 W 12th St (8th Ave) 675.5115. Also at: 1465B 2nd Ave. 517.3222

76 Casa di Pré ★$ Often overlooked, but it serves honest, homey food cooked with a light hand. ♦ Italian ♦ Closed Su. 283 W 12th St (W 4th St) Reservations required for 3 or more. 243.7073

77 Corner Bistro $ If strolling around the Village has whetted your appetite for a fat, juicy burger, this neighborhood standby is the place to go. And you'll have plenty of time to check out the locals in this dark, cozy pub—the aloof service is usually extremely slow. ♦ American ♦ 331 W 4th St (12th-Jane Sts) No credit cards. 242.9502

78 Jane Street Seafood Cafe ★$$$ Fresh and simple seafood dishes, and some surprisingly well-executed, complex, original ones. But the service and the brick-walled setting are perhaps too nonchalant for the prices. I'm a big fan of the complimentary coleslaw. ♦ Seafood ♦ 31 8th Ave (Jane St) 243.9237

79 Nell's The doormen are less choosy these days, now that the club is less in vogue. But you might still spy hip literary types and the occasional celeb lounging on one of the cushy couches. The club's main claim to fame among younger patrons is that its owner, Nell, starred in *The Rocky Horror Picture Show*. ♦ Cover. 246 W 14th St (7th-8th Aves) 675.1567

79 Jerry Ohlinger's Movie Material Store Did you ever wish you had a poster advertising the Belgian version of *Some Like It Hot?* Or a photo of Godzilla? They've got it here. The collection includes innumerable posters and thousands of stills in both color and black-and-white, including some 10,000 from Disney films alone. ♦ 242 W 14th St (7th-8th Aves) 989.0869

·QUATORZE·

79 Quatorze ★★$$$ A charming bistro that is a reminder of the days a century ago when this neighborhood included New York's largest French community. The quality of the food and the attentive service would make a Parisian feel right at home. The restaurant has a devoted following and many admirers among those who yearn for simple, classic French dishes that are dependably well-cooked. I always ask for a table along the east wall. ♦ French ♦ 240 W 14th St (7th-8th Aves) Reservations recommended. 206.7006. Also at: 323 E 79th St. 535.1414

80 Integral Yoga Institute Presents all aspects of yoga teaching: meditation, breathing, relaxation, diet and nutrition, stress management, Hatha for pregnant women, video classes, chanting. The institute's store next door sells all kinds of macrobiotic essentials as well as natural cosmetics and remedies. Vitamins, minerals, herbs and homeopathic remedies are for sale across the street at the **Natural Apothecary** (No. 234). ◆ Closed Su. 227 W 13th St (7th-8th Aves) 929.0586

81 Café de Bruxelles ★$$$ A sophisticated bar scene is the best attraction at this lovely spot, which has also made a name for itself as the only Belgian restaurant downtown. Rich *waterzooi*, a Belgian bouillabaisse, is the ticket. ◆ Continental ◆ 118 Greenwich Ave (W 13th St) Reservations recommended. 206.1830

82 Ye Waverly Inn $$ Longtime Villagers don't seem to care that the quality of the food has declined badly. They still like the authentic Early American charm and low prices. ◆ American ◆ 16 Bank St (Waverly Pl) 929.4377

83 Chez Brigitte ★$$ Homey, simple, inexpensive French food cooked by a friendly French woman. Counter service, only. ◆ French ◆ Closed Su. 77 Greenwich Ave (W 11th St) No credit cards. 929.6736

84 St. Vincent's Hospital (1979, **Ferrez & Taylor**) The modern monstrosity that is the hospital's main building is proof that not every Village community protest is effective. But St. Vincent's has been serving the community well in every other way since it was founded by the **Sisters of Charity** in 1849. In the years since, it has become the largest Catholic hospital in the US. St. Vincent's has a Doctor Directory and a physician referral service (790.1111). ◆ 7th Ave So (W 11th-W 12th Sts)

ZINNO 🎹

85 Zinno $$$ A sleek ground-floor townhouse bar and restaurant—good pasta—offering chamber jazz. ◆ Italian ◆ Closed Su. 126 W 13th St (6th Ave-7th Ave So) 354.4444

85 La Tulipe ★★$$$$ Without a doubt, one of the most overpriced restaurants in New York. The food, service and atmosphere are all pleasant enough, but the high fixed price isn't. No luxury ingredients, no extravagances of any kind. The service and the chairs are uncomfortable. A nice bistro that is thought much too highly of, by itself as well as by others, although dessert is always good, especially the homemade ice cream. ◆ French ◆ Closed M. 104 W 13th St (6th Ave-7th Ave So) Jacket recommended. Reservations required. 691.8860

86 Village Community Church (1846) This abandoned gem is thought by architectural historians to be the best Greek Revival church in the city. The original design is attributed to **Samuel Thompson** and based on the **Theseum** in Athens. But the materials are the antithesis of the Doric model: the 6 huge columns and the pediment are of wood, and the walls are brick and stucco. ◆ 143 W 13th St (6th Ave-7th Ave So)

87 West 14th Street Best known as a magnet for bargain-hunters, it is also home to a number of noteworthy loft buildings. Walk on the north side of the street and look across at Nos. 138-146 (1899), an ostentatious confection that drew on the 1893 Chicago World's Fair for its inspiration; and Nos. 154-160 (1913), **Herman Lee Meader**'s colorful glass and tile design that is literally grounded in Art Nouveau and aspiring to Art Deco. ◆ 6th Ave-7th Ave So

87 Salvation Army Centennial Memorial Temple (1930, **Voorhees, Gmelin & Walker**) This is one of the best Art Deco ex-

travaganzas around, with an overblown entrance and unrestrained interiors that capture the exuberance and color of the era. The building houses the executive offices and programs of the Salvation Army. ◆ 120 W 14th St (6th Ave)

88 La Gauloise ★★$$$ One of the most charming bistros in town. The mirrors, brass rails, early 20th-century decorations and butcher-aproned waiters in black tie—all very professional—add a classy, romantic tone. The solid kitchen prepares all the expected classic Provençal dishes, featuring daily specials such as cassoulet, *choucroute, confit de canard* and bouillabaisse. ◆ French ◆ Closed Su. 502 6th Ave (W 13th St) Reservations required. 691.1363

89 Butterfield House (1962, **Mayer, Whittlesey & Glass**) An unusually sensitive apartment block. The fine 7-story, bay-windowed section on 12th St is an in-scale counterpoint to a series of row houses. Beyond an interior courtyard, the wing on 13th St is taller, adapting to the stronger, larger scale of that block. ◆ 37 W 12th St (5th-6th Aves)

90 Rose Cafe ★★$$$ Excellent New American cuisine with a touch of California: potato pancakes with caviar, Peking duck California-style, grilled scallops on top of fried spinach, seared tuna. ◆ American ◆ 24 5th Ave (W 9th St) 260.4118

In 1942, distressed by commercial publishers' lack of interest in her work, **Anaïs Nin** borrowed $175 and, with a friend, rented a loft at 144 MacDougal St, purchased a used printing press and went on to print 3 of her books. In 1944, in search of more professional surroundings, she moved to a larger space at 17 E 13th St.

New York City boasts 2700 traffic signals.

91 First Presbyterian Church (1846, **Joseph C. Wells**; south transept 1893, **McKim, Mead & White**) A fine Gothic Revival church with an imposing tower modeled after **Magdalen College** at Oxford. The McKim, Mead & White addition includes an outdoor pulpit overlooking the inviting garden. The **Church House**, which adjoins the church on the uptown side, was designed in 1960 by **Edgar Tafel** to perfectly match the 1846 building. A 3-year restoration of all the wood, stained glass and masonry is scheduled to be completed in the spring of 1991. ♦ 48 5th Ave (W 11th-W 12th Sts)

92 Forbes Building (1925, **Carrère & Hastings**) The heart of the Forbes publishing empire. What's best here is the **Forbes Magazine Galleries** on the main floor. The collection includes over 500 toy boats, displayed along with Art Deco fittings from the liner *Normandie* and models of the late **Malcolm Forbes**' private yachts. Beyond that display is a collection of 12,000 toy soldiers; and beyond that, 250 trophies awarded for every accomplishment from raising Leghorn

Greenwich Village

chickens to surviving a working lifetime in the corporate battlefields. American history is represented in a collection of **Presidential Papers**, historical documents and model rooms. But the best part, for many, is a display of 12 **Fabergé** Easter eggs, the world's largest private collection of these priceless objects created for the czars of Russia. Admission is limited to 900 tickets/day, and is reserved for group tours and advance reservations on Thursday. ♦ Free. Tu-W, F-Sa 10AM-4PM. 62 5th Ave (W 12th St) 206.5548

93 Parsons School of Design Parsons holds a unique place in American education. Here, art and industry were firmly linked for the first time on a large institutional level, even before **Gropius** and the **Bauhaus** school. Founded in 1896 by painter/art teacher **William Merritt Chase**, it was **Frank Alvah Parsons** whose leadership spurred the school to its current high position in the world of art and design education. Parsons became the school's president in 1910, implementing his vision of art, and directly influencing both industry and everyday life. Under his direction the school changed its name to the New York School of Fine and Applied Arts and added programs such as interior architecture and design, fashion design and illustration, and advertising art. In 1940, the name was changed to honor President Parsons. In 1970, Parsons School again took an innovative step in art education, joining with the **New School for Social Research** to broaden the scope of both institutions. Parsons moved to a site within the New School campus near Washington Sq in Greenwich Village. Here nearly 7000 full- and part-time students can utilize the city's vast cultural and professional resources. The Parsons staff is made up primarily of professionals working in New York's vibrant art and design industry. Parsons offers studies at its sister campuses at the Otis Art Institute of Parsons School of Design in Los Angeles, and at the American School in Paris. A summer study program in Tokyo is also available. In 1977, the school added a Garment District extension, the **David Schwartz Fashion Center**, at 40th St and 7th Ave. Work by Parson's students is shown March-June at the exhibition center at 2 W 13th Street and 66 5th Ave. ♦ 66 5th Ave (W 13th-W 14th Sts) 741.8900

93 East West Books Excellent source for books on Eastern philosophy, religion, cooking, medicine and New Age lifestyles. ♦ 78 5th Ave (W 13th-W 14th Sts) 243.5994

94 Kate's Paperie Stocks all sorts of *papier*, from gift wraps and marbleized papers to printmaking and handmade papers, paper quilts by **Carolyn Cole, Noguchi** paper lamps and Samurai-inspired dolls constructed with different textures of handmade grass papers. In addition, a nice selection of journals, photo albums and pens, and printing and engraving services. ♦ Closed Su. 8 W 13th St (5th-6th Aves) 633.0570

95 Cafe Loup $$ A comfortable standby for simple French cooking. Informal, friendly atmosphere. ♦ French ♦ 18 E 13th St (University Pl-5th Ave) Reservations recommended. 255.4746

96 Bowlmor Lanes The New Amsterdam Dutch introduced bowling to America, but their legacy seems to be unappreciated in Manhattan, where there are only 5 places to play the game. This one includes a bar and grill and a pro shop. ♦ 110 University Pl (E 12th-E 13th Sts) 255.8188

97 Asti $$ Amateur opera sung while you eat routine Southern Italian standards. As has been said, *The canto is better than the cannelloni*. Go for fun, not food. ♦ Italian ♦ Closed M. 13 E 12th St (University Pl-5th Ave) 741.9105

GOTHAM
Bar and Grill

98 Gotham Bar and Grill ★★★$$$$ Although it seemed destined to fail shortly after opening in 1984, chef **Alfred Portale** changed the fate of this breathtaking restaurant with his culinary talents. Now one of the most consistently successful venues in the neighborhood, this palatial Postmodern setting (winner of the **1984 Restaurant and Hotel Design Award**) makes you feel important for just being here. I recommend one of the inventive pastas to tantalize your palate before the main course. The kitchen doesn't falter in the basics either—the rack of lamb will truly melt in your mouth. The service *can* be haughty but is always completely professional. ◆ Continental ◆ 12 E 12th St (University Pl-5th Ave) Reservations required. 620.4020

99 Cedar Tavern $ A barnlike restaurant and bar that was a hangout for Abstract Expressionist artists in the 1950s. Now it's just a dark bar. Among its regulars were **Jackson Pollock, Roy Lichtenstein** and **Larry Rivers**. ◆ American ◆ 82 University Pl (E 11th St) 929.9089

99 Bradley's ★$$ Some of the most famous musicians in the progressive jazz world might show up to play a set in this Village hangout, which plays host to writers from the nearby *Village Voice*. Simple good cooking. ◆ American ◆ 70 University Pl (E 11th-E 12th Sts) 228.6440

100 Margo Feiden Galleries The specialty here is the work of caricaturist **Al Hirschfeld** (see page 141), who has been capturing the essence of famous faces for *The New York Times* since the 1920s. The list of subjects ranges from **Marlon Brando** to **Madonna, Thomas E. Dewey** to **Albert Einstein**. The trick is to find all the *Nina*'s in each drawing. Hirschfeld hides his daughter's name within folds of clothing, pompadours, wherever. One clue: the number of times *Nina* appears is indicated next to his sign-off. Original pen and ink drawings, limited editions, etchings and lithographs. ◆ M-F 10AM-6PM; Sa-Su 1-5PM. 75 University Pl (E 11th St) 677.5330

101 Forbidden Planet Headquarters for science fiction, horror and fantasy books, comics and related merchandise. Its only close competitor for such things is its own branch up on 59th St near 3rd Ave. ◆ 821 Broadway (E 12th St) 473.1576. Also at: 227 E 59th St. 751.4386

102 The Cast Iron Building (1868, **John Kellum**) This building was converted from the **James McCreery Dry Goods Store** into apartments by **Stephen B. Jacobs** in 1973. In a city known for outstanding cast-iron structures, this is a most representative example, sporting layers of Corinthian columns topped by arches. Unfortunately, the uppermost story added later is an insensitive mismatch. ◆ 67 E 11th St (Broadway)

103 M.M. Einhorn Maxwell Books This impessive collection of mostly rare and out-of-print books on cooking and related pleasures has won the favor of the city's gourmets. A mail-order catalog is available. ◆ By appointment. 50 E 10th St (Broadway) 477.5066

103 Il Cantinori ★★$$$ Country antiques from Italy set the stage for an authentic Tuscan meal. For a starter, try the assortment of grilled vegetables, and move on to the *tonno alla* pesto, a grilled tuna steak sliced and served with pesto vinaigrette and diced tomatoes. And for dessert? Apple tart, gelati of all kinds, tiramisu, chocolate double-layer cake. ◆ Italian ◆ 32 E 10th St (University Pl-Broadway) 673.6044

104 Robert Barth A women's specialty store featuring classic clothing and accessories by **Bettina Reidel, Patti Cappalli** and **Laise Adzer**. ◆ 21 E 10th St (University Pl-5th Ave) 677.1599

105 Knickerbocker Bar & Grill ★$$$ A casual Neo-Village bar and restaurant filled with fascinating 19th-century artifacts and posters. The classy menu offers good steakhouse fare, along with grilled fish and pasta dishes, in a subdued atmosphere. Live jazz, often featuring name performers, is also provided. ◆ American ◆ 33 University Pl (E 9th St) Reservations recommended. 228.8490

Greenwich Village

106 Marylou's ★★$$ Skip the banal appetizers and soups and go directly to the generous main courses, particularly the perfectly broiled fish. There are usually at least a half-dozen fresh choices, and all come with slightly crunchy sautéed julienne vegetables and either boiled new potatoes or a decent white-and-wild-rice mix. Desserts—among them a chocolate double-layer cake and a light rice pudding with rum-soaked raisins—are knockouts. In fact, given the graceful, traditional appointments—pleasant, wood-framed paintings, fireplaces, library walls—in the several dining rooms, the friendly service and fair prices, this is the best seafood restaurant in the Village, and one of the top in town. ◆ Seafood ◆ 21 W 9th St (5th-6th Aves) Reservations recommended. 533.0012

107 Eighth Street Since the 1960s, the stretch between 6th Ave and Broadway has been the shopping district for suburban raffish types who want that Village look, whatever that may be. The selection of stores—mostly shoes and accessories—has spilled over to Broadway, where secondhand reigns. ◆ Broadway-6th Ave

108 B. Dalton Bookseller The same generous variety from the 5th Ave store is famous for, but in smaller quantities. The same helpful service too. ◆ 396 6th Ave (W 8th St) 674.8780. Also at: 666 5th Ave. 247.1740

The New York City Council passed a bill requiring photographic records be made of any building about to be razed. Photos become part of the municipal archives. Councilman **Harry Stein**, sponsor of the bill, said his only regret was that no one had thought of the idea 150 years ago.

The average New York City pedestrian travels at a speed of about 300 feet per minute.

109 MacDougal Alley Like **Washington Mews**, this is another street of converted stables, with the advantage of trees but the same disadvantage of parked cars. No. 7, on the north side, was built in 1899 as a studio for a stained glass artisan. No. 17 ¹/₂ was converted to a home for **Gertrude Vanderbilt Whitney**, founder of the **Whitney Museum**, in 1934. No. 19, on the south side, was built in 1901 as an automobile stable, and the 1854 stable that is No. 21 was reconstructed in 1920 by architect **Raymond Hood**. ◆ MacDougal St (Washington Sq No-W 8th St)

110 New York Studio School Of Drawing, Painting & Sculpture The **Whitney Museum** was established here in 1931. Tradition was already evident on the block, which was the heart of the Village art scene at the time. It began with the conversion of a stable at 4 W 8th St by **John Taylor Johnston** as a gallery for his private art collection. His friends were so impressed that they got together and founded the **Metropolitan Museum of Art** in 1870. ◆ 8 W 8th St (5th-6th Aves)

111 Gate $ A Japanese restaurant serving mostly macrobiotic dishes—lots of sushi, soups and vegetables. Start with the *shumai* (steamed crabmeat dumplings). ◆ Japanese ◆ 7 W 8th St (5th Ave-MacDougal St) 674.2718

112 Washington Mews Some of these charming little buildings behind the townhouses on Washington Sq No were originally stables built in the early 1900s. But those on the south side of the alley, more uniform because they were all stuccoed at the same time, date from the '30s. Most are now used by NYU. Their size and quaintness contribute to the small-scale, congenial atmosphere of the neighborhood. ◆ Washington Sq No-E 8th St (University Pl-5th Ave)

113 Gaia ★$$ Environmentally correct seasonal cuisine: no chemical preservatives, pesticides or processed ingredients. ◆ American ◆ 19 Waverly Pl (Mercer-Greene Sts) 473.5261

114 Caffè Pane e Cioccolato ★$ Lighter fare for the aprés-park tour. Surprisingly good pastas and salads, and excellent cappuccino. ◆ Cafe ◆ 10 Waverly Pl (Mercer St) 473.3944

TO COMMEMORATE THE ONE HUNDREDTH ANNIVERSARY OF THE INAUGURATION OF GEORGE WASHINGTON AS FIRST PRESIDENT OF THE UNITED STATES

ERECTED BY THE PEOPLE OF THE CITY OF NEW YORK

Up these 110 steps to the top of the arch went dignitaries for its opening, including a photographer from Pach Brothers whose acrophobia delayed the opening ceremonies. In 1916 **Marcel Duchamp** *and several painters of the Ashcan School, including* **John Sloan**, *forced open the door to the stairs and climbed to the top of the arch to declare the Village the separate city of New Bohemia, to which the mayor responded by sending the militia to end the demonstration. It is rumored that during WWII a man secretly lived within the arch for 7 months and was discovered when he hung his wash out to dry.*

Joyce Gold, *From Trout Stream To Bohemia*

McKim, Mead & White

Memorial Arch, Washington Square

115 Bottom Line Cabaret A small cabaret-style nightclub with a superlative sound system, it was the model for Boston's **Paradise** and LA's **Roxy**. Best known as the launching pad for **Bruce Springsteen** and **Patti Smith**, among others, its days as an industry showcase are long gone. But the club still continues a remarkably consistent booking policy, which includes jazz groups, comedy, drama and assorted special presentations. Comfortable, clean and efficient, maybe even too much so. Bar menu. ◆ Cover, minimum. 15 W 4th St (Mercer St) 228.7880

116 Grey Art Gallery An offbeat art gallery in a renovated building, it offers changing high-quality art and photography shows. The backdrop for exhibitions is a grid of white-painted Doric columns ◆ Tu, Th-F 11AM-6:30PM; W 11AM-8:30PM; Sa 11AM-5PM. 33 Washington Pl (Washington Sq E) 998.6780

117 Washington Square This is the largest public space south of 14th St, and is a center of Village activity. Joggers, children, punks and grandes dames provide the local color; flea markets and fairs occupy the grounds on weekends. The area was a marsh, a potter's field, a venue for public hangings and a military parade ground before it was claimed as a public park in 1828. Elaborate, fashionable houses soon appeared around it, and NYU appropriated the east side in the late 1830s. The **Memorial Arch**, designed by **Stanford White** of **McKim, Mead & White**, was originally a wooden monument built in 1889 for the centennial celebration of **George Washington**'s inauguration. It became so well liked that private funds were raised to rebuild it permanently in stone. Another notable feature is the sculpture of Washington on the west pier, which was created by **Alexander Stirling Calder**, father of the late **Alexander Calder**. By the 1950s, the park had seriously decayed. The city transit authority was using the arch as a bus turnaround, and there was a proposal to run 5th Ave underneath it. The popular outrage that blocked the tunnel also put a halt to the buses and gave momentum to the movement to redesign the park—a community effort which was realized in the '60s. In recent years, the park has become haven to a variety of street types—performers, wanderers and drug-dealers—but the local community has made a concerted effort to keep the park safe. Weekend afternoons in warm weather still bring out a wild mix. ◆ W 4th St-Waverly Pl (University Pl-MacDougal St)

118 Washington Square North (1831) At one time there were 28 of these exemplary Greek Revival row houses—home to the cream of New York society when they were built, and later the center of an artistic community. The first 6 constructed, Nos. 21-26, by **Martin E. Thompson**, remain intact. Nos. 7-13 were gutted in the late '30s, and the facades alone are left, fronts for an apartment complex now owned by NYU. Of those demolished, No. 1 was at one time or another the home of **Edith Wharton, William Dean Howells** and **Henry**

James, who set his novel *Washington Square* at No. 18, his grandmother's house; No. 3 was where **John Dos Passos** wrote *Manhattan Transfer*; and No. 8 was once the official residence of the mayor. To the west of 5th Ave, the mock-Federal wing of the apartment tower at 2 5th Ave was a compromise by the builder, **Samuel Rudin**, in response to vociferous community objection to the original plan, which had the tower directly on the square. ◆ University Pl-MacDougal St

119 Washington Square Hotel $$ In 1961, this was called the **Hotel Earle** and was the first New York residence of **Bob Dylan**, who played bars and coffeehouses in the neighborhood. Today, its modest accommodations are popular with dollar-conscious graduate students and young Europeans. Ask for one of the renovated rooms (all 180 should be completed by the spring of '91) overlooking Washington Sq. No restaurant, porters or room service, but the location is perfect if you plan to spend a lot of time in the Village. ◆ 103 Waverly Pl (Washington Sq W) 777.9515

120 The Coach House ★$$$$ Although it has a reputation as one of the great American restaurants, it is no longer so great, and never was truly American, except in its eclecticism. The kitchen excels in a wide variety of dishes prepared with unimpeachably fresh ingredients—including a worthily famous black-bean soup, any poached fish, any roasted meat—but the cuisine is not as grand as the prices or the demeanor of the staff, which often treats unknown customers haughtily. ◆ Continental ◆ Closed M. 110 Waverly Pl (Washington Sq W) Jacket requested. Reservations required. 777.0303

121 New York University Fourteen schools, including the **Tisch School of the Arts** and the highly regarded **NYU School of Business and Public Administration**. Over 15,000 full-time students study at the Washington Sq campus of New York's largest private university. The campus extends beyond the classroom and dormitory buildings and into the converted lofts and Greek Revival row houses common in Greenwich Village. When the old University Heights campus was sold to the **City University of New York** in 1973, NYU's focus shifted here. Architects **Philip Johnson** and **Richard Foster** were commissioned to make a master plan that would unify the disjointed collection of buildings, and enable the campus to handle the increased activity. Their plan called for rebuilding some of the older structures, refacing the existing ones with red sandstone, and establishing design guidelines for future construction. Only 3 buildings were refaced before the plan was abandoned.

89

Within NYU:

Elmer Holmes Bobst Library (1973, **Philip Johnson** and **Richard Foster**) Designed as the focal point of the university, it is a stolid-looking cube, 150ft high, clad in Longmeadow redstone (in the tradition of Washington Sq), with a 12-story interior atrium around which the stacks and reading rooms are organized. Chevronlike stairways with gold anodized aluminum railings give scale to the atrium, and the design of the black, gray and white marble floor, influenced by **Palladio**'s piazza for **San Giorgio Maggiore**, adds to the decorative interior detailing that is the antithesis of the austere exterior. ♦ Washington Sq So at La Guardia Pl

122 Judson Memorial Baptist Church (1892, **McKim, Mead & White**) This Romanesque church was built as a bridge between the poor to the south of the square and the rich above it, and has always had a full program of social activities. The best part is inside, where you can appreciate the fine stained-glass windows by **John LaFarge**. The church was named for

Greenwich Village

Adinoram D. Judson, the first Baptist missionary to Burma. **Judson Hall** and the bell tower above it are now NYU dormitories. ♦ 55 Washington Sq So (Thompson-Sullivan Sts)

122 Hagop Kevorkian Center for Near Eastern Studies (1972, **Philip Johnson** and **Richard Foster**) This huge granite building fits snugly into its corner site and is highlighted by an interesting array of angled corner windows. Peer through the double glass doors on the Sullivan St entrance to see decorative elements taken from an 18th-century Damascene house. The **Metropolitan Museum** has a similar house from the same neighborhood. ♦ 50 Washington Sq So (Sullivan St) 998.8877

123 Provincetown Playhouse Provincetown, on Cape Cod, has 20th-century theatrical roots in **Eugene O'Neill** and the gay vanguard. O'Neill has been performed here too. ♦ Seats 248. 133 MacDougal St (W 4th St) 477.5048

123 La Lanterna di Vittorio ★★$ Although the least known of the Village's coffeehouses, it is one of my favorites. No sidewalk seating, but you can sit as long as you like at the marble tables inside. Order a cup of concentrated espresso or frothy cappuccino and a *Mount St. Helens*, a peak of crisp, bitter chocolate concealing stripes of chocolate mousse and sweetened coconut—an adult Mounds bar. ♦ Cafe ♦ 129 MacDougal St (W 3rd St) 777.9074

Caffè Reggio, at 119 MacDougal St, turns up in a number of films: *Next Stop, Greenwich Village; Serpico; The Godfather, Part II* and *The Next Man*.

In the 1790s, 22,000 victims of yellow fever were buried in Washington Square Park. In 1824, a huge celebration was held when 20 highwaymen were hanged from an elm in the park's northwest corner.

123 Blue Note Jazz Club Top jazz artists perform here nightly at 9 and 11:30PM, and on weekends for a jazz brunch and matinee at 3 and 5PM. A reasonably priced Continental menu is available, and there is a varying cover charge according to the performer. **Grover Washington Jr., Modern Jazz Quartet** and **Oscar Peterson** all make appearances. ♦ Cover, minimum. 131 W 3rd St (MacDougal St-6th Ave) Reservations recommended. 475.8592

124 Caffè Reggio ★$ Built around 1785, this was the first cafe in America. Fabulously dingy and dark, you may recognize it from *The Godfather II* and *Serpico*. ♦ Cafe ♦ 119 MacDougal St (W 3rd St) No credit cards. 475.9557

124 Players Theatre When the **Shakespeare Wright Company** first opened this theater in 1959, they mainly performed works by the Bard. Today, they rent out the space for a variety of performance venues: music, drama, comedy, one-person shows. ♦ Seats 248. 115 MacDougal St (W 3rd St) 254.5076

124 Minetta Tavern ★$ The caricatures and murals behind the old oak bar and elsewhere in this Italian restaurant will take you back to the Village of the 1930s. ♦ Italian ♦ 113 MacDougal St (Minetta Ln) 475.3850

125 La Bohème ★$$ This homey bistro is tucked away on tiny Minetta Ln, across from the **Waverly Cinema**. In the warmer months, the room opens onto a charming, quiet street, a rare situation in noisy Manhattan. Specialties from Provence enliven the menu—coal-oven pizza is a favored item. ♦ Italian ♦ Closed M. 24 Minetta Ln (6th Ave) 473.6447

125 Minetta Lane Theatre A newer Off Broadway theater presenting revues as well as new plays in a more comfortable setting than many. ♦ Seats 378. 18 Minetta Ln (Minetta St-6th Ave) 420.8000

125 1 Minetta Street **DeWitt Wallace** and his wife, **Lila Acheson**, published the first issue of the *Reader's Digest* from a basement apartment in 1922. ♦ 6th Ave

126 Speakeasy Of the city's 3 surviving folk music venues (Bitter End, Bottom Line), this is the one that feels like the way it used to be—not always a plus, but generally the mood is good. Go when there's a name act, like **Eric Andersen**. ♦ 107 MacDougal St (Bleecker St-Minetta Ln) 598.9670

127 Caffè Dante ★★$ You will hear Italian, or some dialect, spoken here, but the strong coffee and let-them-sit-as-long-as-they-want attitude is really what makes it seem so authentic. If you're not counting calories, I recommend the cheesecake. ♦ Cafe ♦ 79 MacDougal St (W. Houston-Bleecker Sts) No credit cards. 982.5275

127 Joe's ★★$$$ Though the clean, modern rooms belie its age, for more than 4 decades Joe's has been one of the neighborhood's better choices for zesty Italian cooking. ♦ Italian ♦ Closed Tu. 79 MacDougal St (W. Houston-Bleecker Sts) 473.8834

128 Da Silvano ★$$$ An uneven, too-pricey, but quite interesting menu drawing heavily on the central Italian kitchen. The charming, elegantly rustic rooms draw a handsome, affluent clientele. Service is correct. Well-selected Italian wine list. ♦ Italian ♦ 260 6th Ave (W. Houston St) Reservations recommended. 982.0090

128 Billy Tso's ★★ $ A restaurant *Chinois* par excellence. Squares of shrimp-stuffed eggplant shimmer with a fragrant black-bean-and-chive sauce; delicate fried potato strands and a plum-wine sauce top grilled quail; sake and ginger give new meaning to mussels. ♦ Euro-Chinese ♦ 248 6th Ave (W. Houston-Bleecker Sts) 353.2828

129 Film Forum Forced to leave the Watts St location, the Film Forum moved here in September 1990. The intriguing new space was designed by architects **Stephen Tilly** and **Jay Hibbs**. The agenda is the same: independent American and foreign films and retrospectives (the work of **Samuel Arkoff** and **Preston Sturges** for example). ♦ 209 W. Houston St (Varick St-6th Ave) 627.2035

130 Aggie's ★★$ It looks like an LA diner; the attitude is pure New York; the food is good home-cooking no matter where you're from. ♦ American ♦ 146 W. Houston St (MacDougal St) No credit cards. 673.8994

130 Raffetto's Fresh pasta made daily (you can see the alchemy going on next door) and cut into a variety of widths before your eyes. Also fresh ravioli and tortellini, and imported Italian products that comprise first-rate spaghetti helper. There's none better in Manhattan. ♦ Closed M, Su. 144 W. Houston St (Sullivan-MacDougal Sts) 777.1261

130 Chez Jacqueline ★$$ Order carefully and you can get a good meal in this popular bistro. Kidneys in cognac, cream and mustard sauce, and roasts of the day are safe main courses. The garlic-laden *brandade* (warm salt cod puree) or fatty *rillettes* are good starters. Skip dessert. ♦ French ♦ 72 MacDougal St (W. Houston St) Reservations required. 505.0727

131 MacDougal-Sullivan Gardens Historic District (1844–50) In 1920, in order to attract middle-class professionals, **Willian Sloane Coffin** (heir to the **W & J Sloane** furniture fortune) modernized these 24 houses on MacDougal and Sullivan Sts. Their gardens were combined to make a midblock private park. ♦ W. Houston-Bleecker Sts (Sullivan-MacDougal Sts)

132 Sullivan Street Playhouse It has long been home to the longest-running production in American history, *The Fantasticks*, which opened in May 1960. In honor of this feat, Sullivan St along this block has been dubbed *Fantasticks' Lane* by the city. ♦ Seats 153. 181 Sullivan St (W. Houston-Bleecker Sts) 674.3838

133 Le Figaro Café $ Not the Beat hangout it once was, and no more underground shows downstairs. Now it's a high-volume beanery serving the weekend blitz on Bleecker St. A little softer on Sunday, but still a teen dream. ♦ Cafe/bistro ♦ 168 Bleecker St (MacDougal St) No credit cards. 677.1100

134 Caffè Borgia ★$ An old-world coffeehouse authentic right up to the smoke-faded mural. A perfect place to sip a cappuccino and spend an afternoon with a good book. ♦ Cafe ♦ 185 Bleecker St (MacDougal St) 674.9589. Also: Caffé Borgia II, 161 Prince St. 677.1850

135 Collector's Stadium Once upon a time if you wanted baseball cards, you had to take a

rubbery piece of gum along with them. They're collector's items now, and serious collectors come here. ♦ 214 Sullivan St (Bleecker-W 3rd Sts) 353.1531

136 Comic Art Gallery If your mom threw away all your neat old comic books, you can replace them here from an extensive collection that also includes books about comic books. ♦ 227 Sullivan St (Bleecker-W 3rd Sts) 777.2770

137 Il Mulino ★★★$$$$ Behind the most unassuming facade is the best Italian restaurant in the Village; only the wait at dinnertime—even with reservations—brings it down a notch. Try it at lunch if you're impatient. Once seated, you'll be treated to crispy fried zucchini. Order any of the pastas, seafood (salmon sometimes comes with porcini mushrooms) and the house red. If you're still in the running after all that, go for the sinfully rich chocolate mousse (this wicked concoction is turned out daily), or if that seems too much, do as I do and order a poached pear topped with fresh cream. ♦ Italian ♦ Closed Su. 86 W 3rd St (Thompson-Sullivan Sts) Reservations required. 673.3783

Restaurants/Nightlife: Red **Hotels:** Blue
Shops/Parks: Green **Sights/Culture:** Black

138 Village Chess Shop You can play chess from noon to midnight with another expert like yourself, or buy unique chess sets made from materials ranging from nuts and bolts to ivory and onyx. ♦ 230 Thompson St (Bleecker-W 3rd Sts) 475.9580

138 Grand Ticino ★★$$ Down a few steps from the street, this dark little Italian restaurant will satisfy your romantic notions of an evening out in Greenwich Village—forest-green walls and burnished wood, muted wall sconces, linen tablecloths, waiters who are Italian and really do this for a career...aaahhh. And the Southern Italian cuisine won't disappoint either, though it's not the best in the area. Just the sweetest room. Yes, it's the place featured in *Moonstruck*. ♦ Italian ♦ Closed Su. 228 Thompson St (Bleecker-W 3rd Sts) 777.5922

138 El Rincon de España ★$$ Good Spanish fare if you stick to seafood. A best bet for paella, of which there are several versions. The huge portions are eminently shareable for a small surcharge. Go to a nearby coffeehouse for dessert. ♦ Spanish ♦ 226 Thompson St

Greenwich Village

(Bleecker-W 3rd Sts) 260.4950

138 Stella Dallas A good source of reasonably priced men's and women's Retro rags from the 1930s-50s, collected for this shop by a fashion stylist and a clothing designer. ♦ 218 Thompson St (Bleecker-W 3rd Sts) 674.0447

138 Il Ponte Vecchio ★★$$ One of the better neighborhood Italian restaurants. If the *agnoletti* (pasta stuffed with cheese or meat) is not on the menu, request it. ♦ Italian ♦ 206 Thompson St (Bleecker-W 3rd Sts) Reservations recommended. 228.7701

139 Nostalgia and All That Jazz An impressive selection of vintage records with an emphasis on jazz, as well as one of New York's best selections of early radio programs and film soundtracks. ♦ 217 Thompson St (Bleecker-W 3rd Sts) 420.1940

139 Bath House Here, in **Cindy Annchild**'s petite shop, you'll find all the essentials for a long, luxurious soak in the tub, including bath oil scented with herbs of love from Shakespaere's plays, Middle Eastern back washers made of woven rice fibers and pear-scented powder. She also stocks a good selection of essential oils that can be custom-mixed and used to scent your skin- and hair-care basics. ♦ 215 Thompson St (Bleecker-W 3rd Sts) 533.0690

140 Science Fiction Shop Although New York's sci-fi fans may miss the other-worldly atmosphere of the old shop on 8th Ave,

they're still hooked on the excellent stock of new, out-of-print and used books and periodicals sold here. ♦ 163 Bleecker St (Thompson-Sullivan Sts) 473.3010

140 Circle in the Square Theatre (Downtown) In 1951, a struggling young actress named **Geraldine Page** appeared here in *Summer and Smoke* by **Tennessee Williams**. The Circle has since introduced new playwrights such as **Leonard Melfi, Jules Feiffer, Lanford Wilson** and **Murray Schisgal**. The Circle company has moved uptown and now rents this theater to various producers. ♦ Seats 299. 159 Bleecker St (Thompson-Sullivan Sts) 254.6330. Also at: 1633 Broadway. 307.2700

141 Village Gate/Top of the Gate Once a commercial laundry, this vital establishment is run by owner **Art D'Lugoff**. Famous productions include *MacBird* and *Jacques Brel is Alive and Well and Living In Paris*. Big barnlike downstairs room hosts salsa night on Monday. More intimate upstairs cabaret often has performance revues or comedy shows. Call for show schedules. No cover at the street-level cafe. ♦ Cover, minimum. Seats: 450, 299. 160 Bleecker St (Thompson St) 475.5120, 473.7270

142 Peculier Pub Over 250 brands of beer from 35 countries are served here to students from almost as many American colleges. ♦ Closed Su. 145 Bleecker St (Thompson St-La Guardia Pl) 353.1327

142 Bitter End This small room has served as a springboard for numerous musical careers, but now features mostly once-famous folkies and/or young hopefuls. Rock, folk, country and occasionally comedy. Food and drink are served, but go for the show. ♦ Cover, minimum. 147 Bleecker St (La Guardia Pl-Thompson St) 673.7030

143 Ennio & Michael ★★$$$ A large, well-run, smartly designed and happily busy trattoria. Hearty food with a bit more refinement than is usually found in such places. Everything from antipasto through pasta is first-rate, and better cannoli cannot be found. ♦ Italian ♦ 539 La Guardia Pl (Bleecker St) 677.8577

144 University Village (1966, **I.M. Pei & Partners**) This high-rise housing complex is noteworthy in a city where high rises are the norm, because of the architect's deft handling of scale, a result of the well-articulated facade. The concrete framing and recessed glass clearly define each apartment unit and provide a straightforward, unadorned exterior pattern. Because of a pinwheel apartment plan, the inner corridors are short, and apartments are unusually spacious. Two towers are owned by NYU, the third is a co-op. A 36ft-high sculpture in the plaza between the towers is an enlargement of a cubist piece by **Picasso**. Pei & Partners used the same exterior treatment in the **Kip's Bay** housing project (2nd Ave at W 30th St). ♦ 100, 110 Bleecker St (La Guardia Pl); 505 La Guardia Pl (Bleecker St)

145 Tommy's Red Caddy ★★$$ Good Mexican food at good prices. This friendly place has one of the best lunch specials in town, and there's never a wait. Reasonable and simple. ♦ Tex-Mex ♦ 92 W. Houston St (La Guardia Pl) 777.0300

145 Time Landscape An environmental sculpture of a precolonial forest demonstrates what the area looked like in the 15th century. To gain access call 431.9563. ♦ W. Houston St at W. Broadway

146 Cable Building (1894, **McKim, Mead & White**) Once the headquarters and power-house of the Broadway Cable Traction Co, which operated streetcars propelled by under-ground cables in the 19th century. ♦ 611 Broadway (W. Houston St)

Within the Cable Building:

Angelika Film Center This 6-screen cin-ema shows big commerical hits as well as a selection of independent and foreign films. The cafe, a good spot for reading the paper or writing in a journal, serves snacks until mid-night. ♦ 995.2000

Bests

Merce Cunningham
Artistic Director, Merce Cunningham Dance Company

The sight—in early summer on a Sunday morning, the traffic sounds becoming muted—of 10,000 bicycles coming up 6th Ave, most of the riders wearing orange jackets, and some of them in tandem. Occasionally an oddity such as a unicycle or a 2-wheeled vehicle, the front one small, the back one enormous.

The **Greenmarket** at Union Square on any market day, but particularly in the late spring through fall when the fresh produce and flowers and people are at their best. Beware the pickpockets, the signs say.

This one doesn't repeat. The vision of **King Kong** strapped to the Empire State Building a few years ago, the huge balloon-animal wrapped around the tower, flattened by the wind, saddened by the experience.

The vision of a large cruise ship through the windows of **Westbeth**, making a stately, steady progress down the Hudson to the open sea, when I am teaching a class of dancers. The ship's rhythm and movement is a delicious addition, however brief, to the bustle of the class, particularly in late afternoon, with the rays of the polluted sunset over New Jersey.

Being in the theater, backstage or out front, just before the curtain goes up.

Nearly 50 percent of the households in Greenwich Village consist of one person, and about 30 percent of the residents are between 25 and 34 years old. The Village is a haven, providing over 500 places for people to eat and drink.

Music

Sweet Basil 88 7th Ave So (Grove-Bleecker Sts) 242.1785

Lone Star Cafe 61 5th Ave (13th St) 242.1664

Fat Tuesday's 190 3rd Ave (16th-17th Sts) 533.7902

Sweetwaters 170 Amsterdam Ave (67th-68th Sts) 873.4100

Village Gate 160 Bleecker St (Thompson St) 475.5120

Carnegie Hall 881 7th Ave (57th St) 247.7800

Avery Fisher Hall North side of Lincoln Center Plaza, 65th St at Broadway. 874.2424

The Chamber Music Society of Lincoln Center Alice Tully Hall, 65th at Broadway. 362.1900

92nd Street Y 1395 Lexington Ave (92nd St) 996.1100

The Ballroom 253 W 28th St (8th Ave) 244.2424

The Bottom Line 15 W 4th St (Mercer St) 228.6300

Dance

City Center 130 W 56th St (6th-7th Aves) 247.0430

Dance Theater Workshop 219 W 19th St (7th-8th Aves) 924.0077

Merce Cunningham Dance Studio 463 West St (Bank St) 691.9751

Kitchen Center for Video, Music, Dance, Performance and Film 512 W 19th St (10th-11th Aves) 255.5793

P.S. 122 150 1st Ave (9th St) 228.4249

New York State Theater South side of Lincoln Center Plaza, 150 W 65th St (Broadway) 870.5570

Metropolitan Opera House West side of Lincoln Center Plaza, 65th St at Broadway. 362.6000

Joyce Theater 175 8th Ave (19th St) 242.0800

Comedy

Catch a Rising Star 1487 1st Ave (77th-78th Sts) 794.1906

The Comic Strip 1568 2nd Ave (81st-82nd Sts) 861.9386

The Original New York Improvisation (aka The Improv) 358 W 44th St (8th-9th Aves) 765.8268

Caroline's Comedy Club Call for info, 620.5971

Dangerfield's 1118 1st Ave (61st-62nd Sts) 593.1650

Stand Up NY 236 W 78th St (Broadway) 595.0850

Chicago City Limits 351 E 74th St (1st-2nd Aves) 772.8707

In the 1820s a stagecoach ride from the Battery to Greenwich Village took one hour. By 1830, horse-drawn trolleys had reached 15th St.

East Village

The **East Village**, bounded by **Broadway**, the **East River**, **Houston** and **14th Sts**, was the grandest part of **Greenwich Village**. Governor Peter Stuyvesant's estate covered the area from the present 4th Ave to the East River and from 5th to 17th Sts. He was buried beneath his chapel, now the site of **St. Mark's-in-the-Bowery Church** (built in 1799), known as much for its ministry to the disadvantaged and its far-out religious services as for its historical significance.

In the 1830s, the houses of the **Astors**, **Vanderbilts** and **Delanos** lined Lafayette St from Great Jones St to Astor Pl. There is almost nothing left from those times except the **Old Merchants' House** on 4th St near Lafayette St and the remaining homes of **Colonnade Row** (also known as **LaGrange Terrace**), where **John Jacob Astor** and **Warren Delano**, FDR's grandfather, lived.

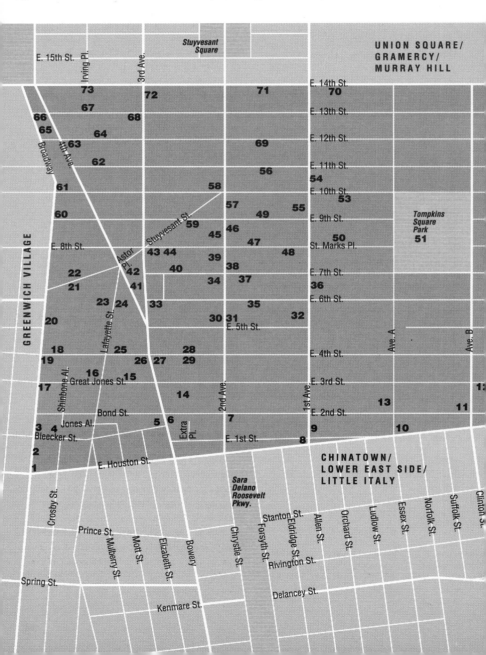

Astor Place had been the scene of the **Vauxhall Gardens**, where people went in the summer to enjoy music and theater. It was replaced by the popular **Astor Place Opera House**, which is remembered chiefly for the 1849 riot between rival claques (hands hired to applaud a certain performer or act) of the British actor **William Macready**, in which 34 people were killed (or 22, depending on which account you read) before the militia brought the crowd under control. Astor Pl was named for the first John Jacob Astor, who arrived from Germany in 1789 at the age of 21 with $25. Before his death at the age of 85, he had made a fortune in fur trading and Manhattan real estate.

The **Astor Library** was built here with a bequest from John Jacob Astor. The building is now the home base of the **New York Shakespeare Festival** at the **Public Theater**, a multimedia, multistage enterprise, where something exciting is always on the boards or on the screen. Another survivor from the 1850s is the Italianate **Cooper Union**, the country's first coeducational college, and the first open to all races and creeds.

Since it opened in the 1850s, everyone who counts has had a glass of the special dark ale at **McSorley's Old Ale House** on 7th St. **John Sloan** painted it, and **Brendan Behan** hung out in a corner near the pot-belly stove.

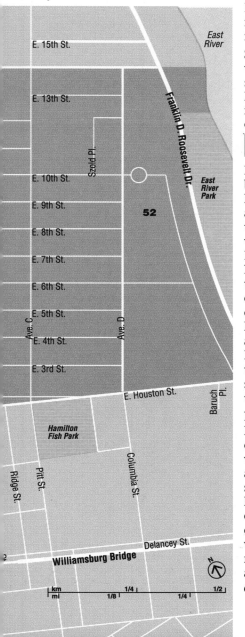

East Village

Little India No. 3, the stretch of 6th St between 1st and 2nd Aves, contains at least 20 Indian restaurants, with another half-dozen spilling over onto the avenues. It all started in 1968, when 5 brothers arrived here from India. They liked everything about New York except the distance they had to travel to find a good Indian meal. So one of them solved the problem by opening his own restaurant. Before long his brothers got into the business as well; others soon followed. (**Little India No. 1** is out in Queens, where the most recent immigrants have settled. **No. 2** is the stretch of Lexington Ave in the mid 20s.)

Near Astor Pl at 3rd Ave and 7th St is **Little Ukraine**—a world of Byzantine churches with onion domes, shops with Slavic music and painted eggs, and restaurants serving goulash and stuffed cabbage. Other ethnic groups have clung to enclaves here too. These days the East Village is an even crazier culture quilt. Although none of the old waves have been totally driven out, a new generation is replacing the old antimaterialist crowd—call it the *counterculture-gone-behind-the-cour*

Storefront art galleries (which turn over with startling rapidity), boutiques, clubs, restaurants and cafes have sprung up here as far east as Ave C, and particularly along the Ave A side of **Tompkins Square Park**, representing the cutting edge of what's *next* in downtown.

1 K-Paul's New York $$ If Cajun cuisine is your bag, this is the place. Although Paul has not cooked for 8 years, he trains the chefs and does show up at least twice a month. His blackened fish is still the best. Service is pleasant, the atmosphere relaxed. ♦ Cajun ♦ Closed M, Su. 622 Broadway (E. Houston St) Reservations required. 460.9633

2 Center for Book Arts Gallery, teaching and work space for the crafts of hand-producing and publishing books, including hand bookbinding, papermaking and letterpress printing. ♦ Gallery M-F 10AM-6PM; Sa noon-5PM. 626 Broadway (E. Houston-Bleecker Sts) 5th floor. 460.9768

2 New York Mercantile Exchange (1882, **Herman J. Schwartzmann**) A cast-iron jungle with bamboo stems, lilies and roses complemented with Oriental motifs. The Exchange, obviously no longer here, was once headquar-

East Village

ters for all the big butter-and-egg men and wholesale dealers in coffee, tea and spices. The ground floor is currently occupied by **Urban Outfitters,** clothier to many a university student. ♦ 628 Broadway (E. Houston-Bleecker Sts)

3 Blue Willow ★$$ A casual restaurant; one claim to fame is that the food is prepared without salt. But that's not all: almost no 2 chairs or tables match and the chinaware is eclectic too. If you're lucky, your dinner (I suggest the veal piccata showered with grated spinach) may be served on a plate in the famous blue willow pattern. ♦ Continental ♦ 644 Broadway (Bleecker St) 673.6480

4 Bayard Condict Building (1898, **Louis Sullivan**) The one and only Louis Sullivan building in New York is hidden among the industrial high rises on Bleecker St. The Bayard (formerly the **Condict Building**) was an anachronism even in 1898, when the Renaissance Revival that followed the 1893 Chicago World's Fair turned popular taste away from the elegant, quintessentially American style of Sullivan and the Chicago School. The intricate cornice filigree and soaring vertical lines of the terracotta-clad steel piers are Sullivan trademarks; the 6 angels at the roofline were applied under client duress. ♦ 65 Bleecker St (Crosby St)

5 Bouwerie Lane Theatre (1874, **Henry Engelbert**) When the lower end of the Bowery was a theater district, this fanciful cast-iron building was built as a bank. Today it is the home of the **Jean Cocteau Repertory**, an unusual company of resident actors that often performs several different works in the same

week. Its presentations are usually classical plays or plays by writers better known for other literary endeavors. ♦ Seats 140. 330 Bowery (Bond St) 677.0060

6 C.B.G.B. and OMFUG Long after everyone has forgotten what the initials of this Bowery dive stand for (Country, Bluegrass, Blues and Other Music for Uplifting Gourmandisers), they will remember it as the birthplace of punk rock. A long, dark bar illuminated by neon beer signs, it still plays host to an array of groups under a wide banner of styles. Uptowners used to go slumming here; now it attracts the suburban hard-core crowd and the nostalgic, but it still boasts one of the best rock PA systems in town. ♦ 315 Bowery (Bleecker St) 982.4052

7 Anthology Film Archives Located in the **Second Avenue Courthouse** building, the Archives is a center for the preservation and exhibition of film and video works. Students, scholars, museums and universities have access to the Archives' library. Daily screenings. Call for schedule. ♦ 32 2nd Ave (E 2nd St) 477.2714

8 Shrimpton & Gilligan Chris Isles and Angel Zimick design for women who enjoy witty clothing. Are you looking for a baseball cap that unbuttons on the top (so you can release tension), or a Daisy Mae-style midriff blouse? ♦ Closed Tu. 70 E 1st St (1st-2nd Aves) 254.1249

8 City Lore In a gentrified brownstone just off 1st Ave, a group of serious folklorists explore New York cultural traditions through photo and tape archives, oral histories, discussion groups, music and film festivals and concerts. ♦ Closed Sa-Su. 72 E 1st St (1st-2nd Aves) 529.1955

C A V E   C   A N E M

9 Cave Canem $$ Once a high-concept restaurant that set out to re-create authentic ancient Roman cuisine. The decadent, multi-level setting remains, but they now serve straightforward American fare. ♦ American ♦ 24 1st Ave (E 1st-E 2nd Sts) Reservations recommended. 529.9665

9 ARKA A general store for the Ukraninan community: tapes, records, books and newspapers, embroidery threads and fabrics, egg decorating kits. ♦ 26 1st Ave (E 1st-E 2nd Sts) 473.3550

10 The Spiral A live-music club with a circular theme (you'll know you're almost there when you spot the neon curlicue above the entrance) that prefers the offbeat (a jazz-infused funk band is cool) to the more conventional rock- and blues-type bands. Shows begin at 10PM. ♦ 244 E. Houston St (Ave A) 353.1740

10 Cafe News ★★$$ **Bernard Leroy**, co-owner of this organically correct restaurant, told *The New York Times*: *Everyday someone eats organic food, [he] stops polluting himself with unnecessary chemicals, additives, pesticides. He stops polluting the ocean, the earth, the air.* Do it for yourself *and* Mother Nature. ♦ Vegetarian ♦ 10 Ave A (E. Houston St) 979.8080

11 Gas Station Operated by **Post-Vanguard Inc.**, an organization praised for its willingness to take artistic risks, this formerly abandoned service station is one of the most active alternative performance spaces in the city. Call for information about readings, concerts, performances and exhibitions in every medium. ♦ Ave B at E 2nd St. 228.4587

12 Nuyorican Poet's Cafe $ A forum for young Puerto Rican poets in the 1970s. By the time it closed in 1982, one of the founding members, the late **Miguelo Pinero**, had achieved international acclaim as a playwright. Back in business in 1990, the place is packed with poets and an eclectic audience. ♦ Cafe ♦ 236 E 3rd St (Aves B-C) No phone

13 Two Boots ★$ The Italian roots of Louisiana cooking are uncovered here in this skylit East Village original. Try the shrimp *Mosca* (skillet-baked on a bed of spicy Cajun breadcrumbs), crabmeat minestrone or shrimp pizza. And if you can't make it in to admire the counterculture memorabilia embedded in the see-through plastic bar, or play the Cajun-flavored jukebox, you can still order the pizza for home delivery from **Two Boots to Go** across the street (505.5450). Beer and wine only. ♦ Cajun ♦ Closed M. 37 Ave A (E 2nd-E 3rd Sts) No credit cards. 505.2276

14 New York Marble Cemetery (early 1800s) Located on the inside portion of the block (enter from an alley on 2nd St), this is not only one of the first, but one of the very few cemeteries left in Manhattan. The burial vaults are underground, and the names of those interred are carved into marble tablets set into a perimeter wall that surrounds a small grassy area. Down the block (52-74 E 2nd St) is the **New York City Marble Cemetery**, started in 1831 along the same nonsectarian lines, but with above-ground vaults and handsome headstones. Genealogists can trace New York's early first families—the **Scribners, Varicks, Beekmans, Van Zandts, Hoyts**and one branch of the **Roosevelt** family—from tombstone information. Burial here is restricted to the descendants of the original vault owners, but no one has applied since 1917. ♦ E 2nd-E 3rd Sts (2nd Ave-Bowery)

15 Engine Company 33 (1898, **Ernest Flagg** and **W.B. Chambers**) The architects of the **US Naval Academy** and **Scribner's Book Store** designed this home for Engine Company 33, which was formed in 1865, the same year the professional fire department replaced volunteer companies. ♦ 44 Great Jones St (Bowery-Lafayette St)

15 Great Jones Cafe ★$ Blackened fish, fried okra, roadside bar atmosphere. Always lively and loud—and the eats are decent and reasonably priced. ♦ Cajun ♦ 54 Great Jones St (Bowery-Lafayette St) No credit cards. 674.9304

16 376-380 Lafayette Street (1888, **Henry Hardenbergh**) A richly ornamented yet somewhat uncomfortable warehouse most notable because it was designed by Hardenbergh several years after he did the **Dakota** apartments up on 72nd St. ♦ Great Jones St

17 Acme Bar & Grill ★$$ Carbo-loading at its finest. Cajun-style chicken, jambalaya, gumbo and the best mashed potatoes with cream gravy. A ledge along one entire wall is lined with every conceivable kind of hot sauce, if you dare. And there's a music room (separate cover charge) downstairs featuring R&B and blues. I stop in

here after a cassette binge at Tower Records. ♦ Southern ♦ 9 Great Jones St (Lafayette St-Broadway) No credit cards. 420.1934

18 Island Trading Company Check out the crocheted African hats by designer **Xenobia Bailey**; you may recognize them from Benetton billboards. You'll also find **Mary Benson**'s one-of-a-kind clothing for men and women, Jamaican hand-paintings and baby clothing from Australia. ♦ 15 E 4th St (Lafayette St-Broadway) 353.0297

TOWER RECORDS

19 Tower Records The ultimate complex for the listener. There's a main building on Broadway and 4th St for all the pop, jazz, R&B, dance, etc, a classical annex next door (on Lafayette St) and video and electronic annexes in between. If they don't have it, chances are it's going to be tough to find. ♦ 692 Broadway (E 4th St) 505.1500. Also at: 1961 Broadway. 799.2500

20 Bayamo ★$$ One of the better eateries on the lower Broadway strip, the menu here seems a little gimmicky, but it's consistently good. The inventive appetizers include fried or grilled chicken wings, fried wontons and sushi. Happy hours and late nights get a little crowded, and sometimes they go 6-deep at the bar, clamoring for silly drinks. If that's not your speed, maybe lunch or early evening is best. Note painter **Susan Rodin**'s wonderful party scene on the wall just as you enter. I always sit on the balcony. ♦ Cuban/Chinese ♦ 704 Broadway (Washington Pl- E 4th St) 475.5151

20 Shakespeare & Co. Not related to its Paris namesake, but still a favorite among New Yorkers. ♦ 716 Broadway (Washington Pl-E 4th St) 529.1330. Also at: 2259 Broadway. 580.7800

20 Unique Clothing Warehouse Truly an experience in creative clothing for men and women. Where cheap is, indeed, chic! ♦ 726 Broadway (Waverly Pl-Washington St) 674.1767

21 Astor Place Hairstylists Considering all there is to do in New York, it may seem strange that watching haircuts has become a spectator sport on Astor Pl, but look at the pictures in the window and on the walls and you'll understand why. One of the signs in the window says they also do regular haircuts, but don't count on it. ♦ 2 Astor Pl (4th Ave-Broadway) 475.9854

21 Astor Home Liquors Large selection, generally good prices, but less than thoroughly knowledgeable service. ♦ Closed Su. 12 Astor Pl (Lafayette St) 674.7500

22 Cooper Sq Books At 6000sq ft, this is one of the largest independent bookstores in the city. Big pickings in the philosophy, literature, travel and children's sections. ♦ 21 Astor Pl (Broadway) 533.2595

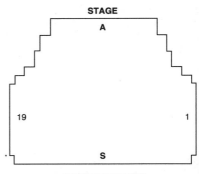

NEWMAN THEATER

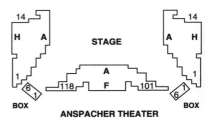

ANSPACHER THEATER

East Village

23 Indochine ★★$$$ French/Vietnamese cuisine with a trendy overtone, the food is consistently good (though not as good as either a true French or Vietnamese bistro). But the room is lovely, and the people-watching here lovelier still. There's a nameless, late-night bar downstairs, if you're so inclined. ♦ French/ Vietnamese ♦ 430 Lafayette St (Astor Pl-E 4th St) Reservations required. 505.5111

23 Astor Place Theatre Across the street from the more artistically ambitious **Public Theater**, this little Off Broadway venue has long runs (*The Foreigner*) and interesting musicals (*Tent Meeting, Middle of Nowhere*) that click with the theater crowd. ♦ Seats 299. 434 Lafayette (Astor Pl-E 4th Sts) 254.4370

23 Colonnade Row (1833, **Seth Greer**) Once the homes of the city's business and social leaders—the **Astors, Vanderbilts, Delanos**— only 4 of the original 9 houses remain. The streetfront Corinthian colonnade was used to give the row a sense of unity and solidity. Despite designation as a New York City Landmark, these unique and historic structures have fallen into disrepair. The block is also known as **LaGrange Terrace**. ♦ 428-434 Lafayette St (E 4th St)

24 Public Theater (South wing 1853, **Alexander Saeltzer**; center 1859, **Griffith Thomas**; north wing 1881, **Thomas Stent**; conversion to theater 1966, **Giorgio Cavaglieri**) The **New York Shakespeare Festival** (NYSF) was founded more than 30 years ago by that dynamic man of the theater **Joseph Papp**. Its landmark building in the East Village has 6 theaters. The collection of Romanesque Revival buildings was built for **John Jacob Astor** as New York City's first free library and served as the **Hebrew Immigrant Aid Sheltering Society**. It was on the verge of being demolished in the mid-1960s, when Papp came to the rescue. Today the NYSF not only manages continually to mount superb presentations, but always seems to find the money needed to avert financial crises. The run-on list of extraordinary shows that have originated here includes *Hair* by **Gerome Ragni** and **James Rado**, *That Championship Season* by **Jason Miller**, **Michael Bennett**'s *A Chorus Line* (which won 3 Pulitzers), **David Rabe**'s *Sticks and Bones*, **Caryl Churchill**'s *Serious Money* and **Rupert Holmes**' *The Mystery of Edwin Drood*. All went on to Broadway. About 25 theatrical productions are done each year; the lively **Festival Latino** is a regular summer event. Film performances were introduced in 1981.

Giorgio Cavaglieri—who also renovated the **Jefferson Market Courthouse**—did an admirable job salvaging much of the interior: many of the theater spaces are impressive, and the entrance and lobby still include the original Corinthian colonnade. **Quiktix**, $1/2$-price tickets for performances Tuesday-Sunday, available 2hr before curtain. ♦ Theaters: **Newman** (seats 299); **Anspacher** (seats 299); **Martinson** (seats 1650); **LuEster** (seats 135); **Susan Stein Shiva** (seats 100); **Little Theater** (seats 90). 425 Lafayette St (E 4th St-Astor Pl) 598.7150

24 **Cheyenne Social Club** ★$$ Owner **Jonathan Ressler** was so inspired after being at a real cowboy bar in Utah that for years he dreamed of reproducing the same in New York City. That dream has now come true: this *club* offers live entertainment, hardy food and its own special-brewed beer, and promises to appeal to anyone who's ever sung *Home on the Range*. ◆ American ◆ Closed M, Su. 417 Lafayette St (Astor Pl-E 4th Sts) 979.7550

25 **Old Merchants' House** This outstanding example of an 1830s Greek Revival townhouse remains intact with interiors and furnishings just the way they were when **Seabury Tredwell**, a wealthy merchant, and his family lived here, thanks to Tredwell's daughter, **Gertrude**. Having fallen in love with an unacceptable suitor whom she was forbidden to marry, Gertude chose not to marry at all and, after her father's death, resolved to maintain the family home just as her father would have liked. Paintings, furniture, china and books give an insight into their tasteful and conservative style. The hours that the house is open to the public may be expanded. Call for more information. ◆ Admission. Groups of over 20 by appointment M-F; individuals Su 1-4PM. Closed Aug. 29 E 4th St (Bowery-Lafayette St) 777.1089

26 **Marion's Continental Restaurant and Lounge** ★$$ This was the place to be in the '60s, when senators, presidents and movie stars were regulars. Marion's closed in the early '70s because the glamorous proprietor, **Marion Nagy**, wanted to spend more time with her family. In 1990, Marion's son and a business partner reopened the landmark with much of its signature decor intact: the corner banquette reserved for **John** and **Jackie Kennedy**, the tropical fish tank, the tile bar and the walls adorned with clown paintings, **Utrillo** reproductions and signed photographs of **Clark Gable** and **Frank Sinatra**. Vodka Gibsons (Marion's drink), Old Fashioneds and Manhattans are inexpensive. The quality of the food is not uniformly dependable, although the Caesar salad and the lamb shank with lentils are both good. ◆ Continental ◆ 354 Bowery (E 4th-Great Jones Sts) No credit cards. 475.7621

27 **Phebes Place** $ During the '60s this was a popular hangout among Off-Broadway playwrights **Sam Shepard, Robert Patrick** and **Leonard Melfi.** Today it continues to attract the East Village arts crowd as well as a lot of police officers. ◆ American/Mexican ◆ Closed Su. 361 Bowery (E 4th St) 473.9008

Inside the doorway of the **Public Theater** are 2 white rectangular columns on which is written, in Japanese and English, *May Peace Prevail on Earth.* The columns were sent to Joseph Papp by the Society of Prayer for World Peace, an organization that does not aim to convert lost souls, but is dedicated to planting as many peace poles as possible.

28 **Cucina di Pesce** ★$$ A more reasonably priced and consistently good seafood restaurant—with an Italian overtone—would be hard to find in Manhattan. Have the steaming hot and fragrant bouillabaisse. To accommodate the crowds, a new annex has been built across the street (No. 28). Ideally located next to the **La Mama** theater complex. ◆ Italian ◆ 87 E 4th St (2nd-3rd Aves) No credit cards. 260.6800

28 **Fourth Wall Theatre** Political theater often on the bill, both domestic and foreign. ◆ Seats 250. 79 E 4th St (2nd-3rd Aves) 254.5060

29 **La Mama E.T.C.** First called **Café La Mama**, this theater has been in the vanguard of the Off Broadway movement since 1962. Under the direction of **Ellen Stewart**, it has been instrumental in presenting international experimental theater artists to this country. Stewart nurtured playwrights **Sam Shepard, Lanford Wilson, Ed Bullins, Tom Eyen, Israel Horovitz** and **Elizabeth Swados**, among others. Directors **Tom O'Horgan, Marshall Mason, Wilford Leach, Andrei Serban** and **Peter Brook** have helped to stage many extraordinary productions here. ◆ Seats: 99, 99. 74A E 4th St (2nd-3rd Aves) 475.7710.

Also at: **The Annex** (seats 299) 66 E 4th St. 473.8745

30 **Sugar Reef** ★$$ Colorful decor, Island menu, active bar scene. Scenes come and go, but Sugar Reef seems to have found its niche, thanks to the consistently good food (accent on the West Indian) and interest- ing crowd. Chicken and shrimp dishes are particularly good, and they always get the mood music right. ◆ West Indian ◆ 93 2nd Ave (E 5th-E 6th Sts) 477.8427

31 **Civilization** A wonderful store that has cherry-picked jewelry, *objets d'art* and interior design pieces (columns, vases, dishes, etc), many by local artists and artisans. A small but good book and magazine selection too. ◆ 78 2nd Ave (E 5th-E 6th Sts) 254.3788

32 **Gaylord** ★★$$ The most comfortable and elegant of all the Indian restaurants, Gaylord has a clay oven on the premises, where excellent tandoori dishes are prepared and delivered sizzling and aromatic to your table. ◆ Indian ◆ 87 1st Ave (E 5th-E 6th Sts) Reservations recommended. 529.7990

33 **Manhattan Fruitier** Owner **Jehv Gold** puts together stupendous baskets filled with exotic seasonal fruits from all over the world. No matter what your needs are, he can supply the appropriate arrangement. Delivery in and around Manhattan. ◆ Closed Su. 210 E 6th St (2nd-3rd Aves) 260.2280

34 Kiev ★★$ A better buy, not to mention better borscht, would be hard to find. One of the best low-down restaurants in town. The constant traffic sometimes poses cleanliness problems and makes it difficult to get a table, but most of the food and all of the prices are wonderful. The fried cheese blintzes, fried or boiled cheese or potato *pirogen*, fried veal cutlets and all the soups are deeply satisfying. *An RSW recommendation.* ◆ Russian ◆ 24hrs. 117 2nd Ave (E 7th St) No credit cards. 674.4040

35 Back From Guatemala This appealing shop features the best merchandise from Central and South America and Asia, including scarves, exotic ethnic clothing and various crafts. For a twist on the same theme (and run by the same people), visit **Chrysalis** up the block at 340 E 6th St (533.8252), which

East Village

focuses on contemporary ethnic jewelry, accessories, stationery and gift items. ◆ 306 E 6th St (1st-2nd Aves) 260.7010

35 Anar Bagh $$ Appetizers are the most recommendable dishes on the menu, and there are enough of them to make a full meal for an insanely reasonable price. ◆ Indian ◆ 338 E 6th St (1st-2nd Aves) Reservations recommended. 529.1937

35 Mitali ★$$ The most popular restaurant on the block, in spite of its being a tad pricey. ◆ Indian ◆ 334 E 6th St (1st-2nd Aves) 533.2508

36 Miracle Grill ★$$ Grilled chicken on skewers with papaya-tomatillo salsa, New York steak with *chipotle* (smoked jalapeño pepper) butter, and vanilla-bean flan are just a few of the inventive specialties served at this tiny and casual restaurant. ◆ Southwestern ◆ 112 1st Ave (E 6th-E 7th Sts) No credit cards. 254.2353

37 Caffè della Pace $ A warm and unpretentious little cafe, a few steps up from the street —just when you need it. Good cappuccino and great tiramisu (literal translation—*pick-me-up*), which is too rich to describe. ◆ Cafe ◆ 48 E 7th St (1st-2nd Aves) No credit cards. 529.8024

37 Enelra Lots of expensive, sexy, imaginative (where else could you buy a bra with skulls painted on it?) lingerie. ◆ 48 1/2 E 7th St (1st-2nd Aves) 473.2454

38 Orpheum Theatre This refurbished theater has been around since 1908, when it housed many Yiddish theater hits. *Little Mary*

Sunshine had a long run here. In recent years, it's had long runs with *Little Shop of Horrors* and comedienne **Sandra Bernhard**'s one-woman show. ◆ Seats 347. 126 2nd Ave (E 7th-E 8th Sts) 477.2477

39 Gem Spa Smoke Shop An old-style newsstand that sells just about every relevant paper and periodical. While you're browsing—and that's allowed—slide up to the counter for a luscious egg cream, the quintessential New York drink. Nowadays they're served up by the current owners, who are East Indian. ◆ 24hrs. 131 2nd Ave (St. Mark's Pl)

39 B&H Dairy and Vegetarian Cuisine Restaurant $ No one is still around from the days when B&H stood for **Bergson and Heller**, and the clientele was the cast and crew of the Yiddish theater productions along 2nd Ave. And neither are the classic countermen who used to patrol the place. But then again, neither are the junkies who used to fall asleep in their Yankee bean soup. It's been refurbished several times (the vegetarian offerings are quite recent), but thank goodness they haven't messed with the challah recipe. The French toast is heavenly, and a bargain at twice the price. ◆ Dairy ◆ 127 2nd Ave (E 7th St-St. Mark's Pl) 505.8065

40 The Fragrance Shoppe Formerly a city fireman, owner **Michael DeMeo** and his congenial staff love to get to know their customers and share their knowledge of fragrance and bodycare products. They'll introduce you to the store's own line, which includes facial and skincare products, body oils and shampoos; help you to develop a signature scent using a selection of over 100 essential perfume oils; and show you the products they import from other companies, including Mason Pearson brushes from England. ◆ 21 E 7th St (2nd Ave-Bowery) 254.8950

40 St. George's Ukranian Catholic Church (1977, **Apollinaire Osadca**) An old-world cathedral with modern touches, this is the anchor of a Ukrainian neighborhood of more than 1500 people. ◆ 33 E 7th St (2nd Ave-Bowery)

40 McSorley's Old Ale House Not so long ago, this saloon, which has been here since 1854, had a men-only policy—it was among the first targets of the women's liberation movement in 1970. The current clientele, which includes women, is mostly college students, but except for that, McSorley's hasn't changed much since it was a gathering place for crusty old Irishmen who slept in Bowery hotels and spent all their waking hours here. ◆ 15 E 7th St (2nd Ave-Bowery) No credit cards. 473.9148

40 Surma A Ukrainian shop with a good selection of Slavic cards, books, videos and records, plus egg-decorating kits and honey and honey-based products—made by **Myron Surmach**, a 97-year-old beekeeper (and the father of the shop's proprietor). ◆ 11 E 7th St (2nd Ave-Bowery) 477.0729

41 Cooper Square The statue of **Peter Cooper** seated in this triangular park is by **Augustus Saint-Gaudens**, a former Cooper Union student. Its base is by **Stanford White**, who spent his boyhood in this neighborhood. Cooper was a self-made man who used the profits from a small grocery store to buy a glue factory up on 34th St. He then invented a new way to make better glue and became the biggest manufacturer of the stuff in the country. He invested the profits from that enterprise in Manhattan real estate and branched out to Baltimore, where he made a killing selling land. When iron ore was found on his property, he went into business making rails for the expanding railroads. He also went into partnership with **Cyrus Field** to develop the transatlantic telegraph cable, and with **Samuel F.B. Morse** to perfect his telegraph. Cooper had an inventive mind himself, and as a boy created an automatic fly swatter and a self-rocking cradle. ◆ E 7th St (Bowery-4th Ave)

The Cooper Union-Nicholas Ohotin

42 Cooper Union (1859, **Frederick A. Peterson**; reconstruction 1974, **John Hejduk**) This is still the tuition-free public college founded by multimillionaire **Peter Cooper** in 1859. The inventor and industrialist, so brilliant with problems of application in the country's young iron and rail industries, spent his entire life ashamed that he'd never learned to spell or read. The founding of Cooper Union was his attempt to help underprivileged young men and women get the education they deserved but couldn't afford. Cooper Union was the first coeducational college, the first open to all races and creeds and the first to offer free adult education courses, many at night, to accommodate those working in the daytime. Frederick A. Peterson used the rails Cooper produced in his iron works in Cooper Union's construction: a grid of T-shaped rails was used to transmit loads to the walls. This building is considered by some authorities to be the oldest extant building in America framed with steel beams, and was declared a National Landmark in 1962. Two other breakthroughs in the building were the use of an elevator and the placing of vents under each of the 2000 seats in the **Great Hall** auditorium—in the basement—through which fresh air was pumped. The Great Hall has, since the school's founding, been the scene of open expression on crucial issues of the day, from suffrage to civil rights. **Abraham Lincoln** delivered one of his most eloquent speeches here shortly before he was nominated as a presidential candidate. Both the NAACP and the American Red Cross were started in the building. Cooper Union still has a provocative lecture series called **Forum**, which is open to the public. When the building was gutted and renovated in 1974, pristine classrooms, offices and exhibition space were provided—all with a high-modern Corbusian vocabulary. **Augustus Saint-Gaudens, Adolph A. Weinman** and **Leo Friedlander** were graduates of the art school. More recent alumni include **Milton Glaser, Alex Katz** and **Seymour Chwast**. ◆ 7 E 7th St (3rd-4th Aves) 254.6300

East Village

43 St. Mark's Place In the 1960s, this extension of 8th St from the Bowery to Tompkins Square Park was the East Coast capital of hippiedom. The sidewalks were crowded with flower children and the smell of marijuana was everywhere. Among the shared interests of the street's denizens was the famous rock club, **The Electric Circus**, which was in a former Polish social club at No. 23. Then, in the '70s, the street became the punk boardwalk, and multicolored Mohawks filled the air. The street is considerably quieter these days—witness the corner of 2nd Ave, where the old **St. Mark's Cinema** has been converted into co-op apartments and the street-level retail stores have been taken over by **The Gap**—but the street's far from dead. ◆ Ave A-3rd Ave

44 St. Mark's Bookshop A popular bookstore and a good source for journals on African culture, feminist issues and socialism. ◆ 12 St. Marks Pl (2nd-3rd Aves) 260.7853

44 St. Mark's Sounds A true music-lover's store, it doesn't have the conveyor-belt feeling of **Tower Records**, and they sell and trade used records in excellent condition. A video annex is at 14 Stuyvesant St. ◆ 20 St. Mark's Pl (2nd-3rd Aves) 677.3444

There are currently 11,787 medallion cabbies on New York City's streets—the same number for the past 52 years.

Restaurants/Nightlife: Red   Hotels: Blue
Shops/Parks: Green   **Sights/Culture:** Black

44 Dojo ★$ The menu is a combination of Oriental and healthy (try the chicken sukiyaki salad or the incredibly inexpensive soy burger with tahini sauce). There's an outdoor porch for warm-weather dining, which is great for people-watching, not great when panhandlers and car exhaust mingle at your table. ♦ Oriental/Health food ♦ 24 St. Mark's Pl (2nd-3rd Aves) No credit cards. 674.9821

44 Khyber Pass ★$$ An authentic Afghan restaurant run by a former judge of the Supreme Court in Afghanistan. Sit back on a throw pillow and enjoy stuffed raviolis with lamb, tender, moist lamb kabobs, fresh salads with yogurt dressing and, for dessert, rice pudding topped with pistachios. ♦ Afghan ♦ 34 St. Marks Pl (2nd Ave-Bowery) 473.0989

45 Ottendorfer Library (1884, **William Schickel**) This terracotta beauty was funded by **Anna Ottendorfer**, founder of the German-language newspaper *New York Staats Zeitung*. Before becoming a branch of the New York Public Library, it was the **Freie Bibliothek und Lesehalle**, a German-language library and reading room. ♦ M noon-7PM; Tu-W, F noon-6PM; Th 10AM-6PM. 135 2nd Ave (St. Mark's Pl-E 9th St) 674.0947

East Village

46 Ukrainian $ Within the Ukranian National Home. Wonderful Ukrainian specialties like *pirogen*, blintzes and stuffed cabbage. The combination platter gives you a sampling of all 3. ♦ Ukrainian ♦ 140 2nd Ave (St. Mark's Pl) 529.5024

46 Veselka ★$ This bare-bones yet cozy establishment turns out an amazing array of Eastern European specialties—*pirogen*, *kielbasas*, blintzes, stuffed cabbage—at bargain-basement prices. ♦ Polish ♦ 144 2nd Ave (E 9th St) 228.9682

47 Café Orlin $ Neighborhood regulars congregate here for good coffee and desserts. During the warmer months, choose an outside table and watch the parade. ♦ Cafe ♦ 41 St. Mark's Pl (1st-2nd Aves) 777.1447

Among the many names given to this section is *Alphabet City*, coined by the late playwright **Miguel Pinero** It refers to the lettered streets, Aves A to D, east of 1st Ave. Their differences go beyond their names. All of the other north-south avenues above Houston St are 100ft wide. Ave A is 80ft, and Aves B and C are the same width as the city's east-west streets (60ft). The lettered streets were created in the 1811 grid plan to accommodate a bulge in the island at this point, but no one seriously thought they'd ever be built. Until the late 1820s, the area north of Houston St and east of 1st Ave was a salt marsh. Shipyards were common along the East River, as were the foundries that turned out most of the cast-iron building facades for a growing city. The 2 industries never got together, and when iron ships became the norm in the 1870s, the East River shipyards went out of business. At about the same time, cast-iron buildings went out of fashion and the foundries began locking their doors.

47 The Holiday Cocktail Lounge A funky old bar frequented by everyone from skinheads to ladies with crocheted vests and platinum-blond wigs. The amazingly low-priced drinks (for New York, anyway) are the main draw. ♦ 75 St. Mark's Pl (1st-2nd Aves) 777.9637

48 Theater 80 St. Mark's If nostalgic classics like *The Philadelphia Story* and *Bringing Up Baby* just don't make it on TV, come here. Serious film students as well as those longing for a taste of Old Hollywood frequent this tiny revival house. An East Village institution. Check the computer printout posted in the front window or call for the schedule. ♦ 80 St. Mark's Pl (1st-2nd Aves) 254.7400

49 Enchantments Local and visiting witches stop here regularly for the tools of their craft: herbs, oils, tarot cards, caldrons and ceremonial knives (used to cut air and create a sacred space) plus jewelry, books and calendars. ♦ 341 E 9th St (1st-2nd Aves) 228.4394

50 Mogador ★$$ Moroccan cuisine, done simply without fanfare. Lamb, beef and *merguez* (sausage) kabobs, couscous and a selection of appetizers are brought around to your table on an enormous tray. I hope you'll go the whole way and top off your meal with Turkish coffee—as delicious as it is muddy. They also serve a very good and reasonably priced brunch. ♦ Moroccan/Middle Eastern ♦ 101 St. Mark's Pl (Ave A-1st Ave) No credit cards. 677.2226

50 Empirial House Russian émigré **Eduard Erlikh**'s work as a costume designer is evident in his simultaneously dramatic and whimsical collections of women's clothing; recent creations have included the *Empire Lenin Dress*, with Lenin buttons and an empire waist, a cancan skirt adorned with bunches of cloth flowers at the waist and a hat decorated with chili peppers. ♦ Closed M. 119 St. Marks Pl (Ave A-1st Ave) 533.2895

51 Tompkins Square Park The original plan for this 16-acre park called for extending it all the way east to the river. It was to be a farmers' market, and part of the plan was to cut a canal through the middle to give easy access to Long Island farmers. It became a parade ground instead in the 1830s. In 1874 it was the site of America's first labor demonstration, when a carpenters' union clashed with club-wielding police. Among the injured was **Samuel Gompers**, who later became president of the **American Federation of Labor**. The little Greek temple near the center covers a drinking fountain placed there by a temperance organization in 1891. The park gained its modern-day notoriety during hippiedom, when it served as the grounds for *love-ins* and *be-ins*, and more recently when it was the site of violent confrontation over real-estate speculation in the area, and efforts to enforce a nighttime curfew. ♦ E 7th-E 10th Sts (Aves A-B)

Restaurants/Nightlife: Red   **Hotels:** Blue
Shops/Parks: Green   **Sights/Culture:** Black

52 Jacob Riis Houses Plaza (1966, **M. Paul Friedberg**) The large number of people who actually use this park is a tribute to Friedberg's careful and creative plan. Both adults and children find it a pleasant alternative to the streets, with its amphitheater, clever playground furniture and plenty of room in which to roam. ♦ E 6th-E 10th Sts (FDR Drive-Ave D)

RUSSIAN &TURKISH BATHS

53 10th Street Baths The last remaining bathhouse in a neighborhood that once was full of them. They still get their steam heat here the old-fashioned way: they heat up enormous boulders in the subbasement and when they're red-hot, throw water on them, releasing what they claim is true, penetrating wet heat—not mere steam heat. And if you've never had a *platza* rub, try it. Softened oak branches are tied together in the old Russian style to form a natural loofalike scrub, soapy and tingly and very refreshing. There's also a Turkish bath (sauna). There are cots upstairs if you're overwhelmed, and a small food and drink bar. ♦ Daily 9AM-10PM (coed: M-Tu, F-Sa; women: W; men: Th, Su). 268 E 10th St (Ave A-1st Ave) 473.8806

54 DeRobertis Pastry Shop ★$ If you can get past the display counters filled with traffic-stopping cheesecakes, pies, cakes and *biscotti*, you'll find a wonderfully tiled coffeehouse that hasn't changed a bit since they began making frothy cappuccino here back in 1904. ♦ Cafe/bakery ♦ 176 1st Ave (E 10th-E 11th Sts) 674.7137

55 Theater for the New City Now located in what used to be an indoor market, this offbeat, roots-in-the-1960s troupe has managed to keep its old ambience and point-of-view. Hit and miss. Contains 4 theaters, each seating between 60 and 100. ♦ 155 1st Ave (E 9th-E 10th Sts) 254.1109

56 Veniero's Pasticceria ★$ Mirrors, gold, chandeliers—hey, it's only a bakery and cafe! Let your eyes feast not on the fixtures but on the *biscotti*, the creamy pastries, the golden cheesecakes! These are the true bounty of Veniero's, which also supplies many of New York's Italian cafes with its baked goods. There's also a seating area, where cappuccino goes well with a *sfogliatelle*. ♦ Cafe/bakery ♦ 342 E 11th St (1st-2nd Aves) No credit cards. 674.7264

56 Balducci's Piccola Cucina An extension of the fine food emporium on 6th Ave, this *little kitchen* stocks European kitchenware, serving pieces and tabletop accesories. **Andrew Balducci** explains: *First we had the melon, then the prosciutto, now comes the plate.* ♦ Closed Su, Memorial Day-Labor Day. 334 E 11th St (1st-2nd Aves) 982.7471

57 Second Avenue Deli ★$$ Very famous, very popular and very good, for certain Jewish specialties. Actor **Yves Montand** makes a pastrami stop whenever he's in town; you might also try the superb chopped liver—passed out on bits of rye bread to the waiting crowds when lines get long on weekends—stuffed breast of veal, Rumanian tenderloin steak, boiled beef, stuffed derma or kasha *varnishkas*. I always ask to be seated in the **Molly Picon** room, with its wealth of Yiddish theater memorabilia. ♦ Jewish ♦ 156 2nd Ave (E 10th St) No credit cards. 677.0606

58 St. Mark's-in-the-Bowery Church (1799) Erected on the site of a garden chapel on **Peter Stuyvesant**'s estate, it has always been held in high regard as a neighborhood church, and the late-Georgian style encourages this congenial attitude. As the member-

ship grew, a Greek Revival steeple was added (1828, **Ithiel Towne**) to give the church a more urban image; a cast-iron Italianate portico was added to the entrance in 1854. This mélange does not mesh successfully, but it does reflect the parishioners' concerns during the church's early history. A fire nearly destroyed the building in 1978. Architect **Herman Hassinger** took charge of the restoration, which included rebuilding the steeple according to the original design. The interior was gutted and redesigned in a simple and straightforward manner, typical of the pre- and post-Revolutionary War period. The stained-glass windows on the ground floor, newly designed by Hassinger, use themes similar to the original windows. The churchyard where Peter and 6 generations of Stuyvesants are buried has been covered with cobblestones and is now used as a play yard. St. Mark's is also home to the **Poetry Project, Inc** (674.0910), **Danspace** (674.8112) and **Theater ReGenesis** (674.6377). ♦ 2nd Ave at E 10th St. 674.6377

59 Cloisters Café ★$$ A tiny restaurant serving gigantic salads and inventive entrees in a stained-glass-filled environment. In good weather, its garden is the most inviting spot in the neighborhood. ♦ American ♦ 238 E 9th St (2nd-3rd Aves) No credit cards. 777.9128

60 El Coyote ★★$$ Could be the city's best Tex-Mex. It is always busy and boisterous. The enchiladas are always wonderful, as are the margaritas. ♦ Tex-Mex ♦ 774 Broadway (E 9th St) 677.4291

61 Grace Church (1846, **James Renwick Jr.**) The fascinating spire atop this white marble church is sited at a bend of Broadway, providing a focal point for any southern approach. Renwick won the right to design the Episcopal church in a competition. He worked with an unfettered *Puginesque* vocabulary to produce a Gothic Revival structure that many consider to be the city's best. **Heins & La Farge** designed an enlargement for the chancel in 1900. Renwick's rectory, next door at 804 Broadway, is another marvel—a restrained foil for the more fanciful church. ◆ 800 Broadway (E 10th St)

62 The Ritz By attrition, the biggest downtown rock venue in New York. There are no seats, it gets very crowded, and it can be downright unpleasant in the summer. But some acts play just The Ritz, and if you have to see them, you have to see them here. ◆ Cover. 119 E 11th St (3rd-4th Aves) 541.8900

63 Utrecht Art & Drafting Supplies Excellent prices from this major manufacturer of professional art and drafting supplies. Mail-order catalogs available at the store or by calling 800/223.9132. ◆ Closed Su. 111 4th Ave (E 11th-E 12th Sts) 777.5353

East Village

64 Footlight Records Collectors of vintage LPs rejoice! The world's largest selection of film soundtracks and original Broadway cast albums. Top vocalists (**Sinatra, Crosby, Merman**). Jazz greats (**Django Reinhardt, Bix Beiderbecke**). Out-of-print records of all sorts. In most cases, you may listen before buying. ◆ 113 E 12th St (3rd-4th Aves) 533.1572

STRAND

65 Strand Bookstore The largest used bookstore in New York has a fanatical following hooked on its thousands of review copies of new books, its hundreds of coffee-table books and its tables full of mass market and trade paperbacks, all sold at a generous discount. Antiquarian books too. If you have to get lost somewhere in New York, this is the best possible place. ◆ 828 Broadway (E 12th St) 473.1452

66 The Cat Club Maybe the only place in town where you can catch a *Flashdance*-type performance. Sunday night *Swing Nights* are especially fun, featuring live big band jazz and often including a solo vocalist. ◆ Cover. 76 E 13th St (4th Ave-Broadway) 505.0090

67 Dullsville The owners of this shop—formerly named The Good, Bad and Ugly—travel to flea markets all over the country to accumulate an odd assortment of goods, including **Russell Wright** dinnerware, and the largest selection of Bakelite jewelry in New York City. ◆ Closed Su. 143 E 13th St (3rd-4th Aves) 505.2505

68 CSC Repertory Classics with a contemporary twist. New adaptations and translations of classic dramas, *recontextualized*, as they say. ◆ Seats 180. 136 E 13th St (3rd Ave) 677.4210

69 John's of Twelfth Street ★$$ Remember those little Italian restaurants lit by dripping candles stuck in wine bottles that used to turn up in the movies? John's could have been the model for all of them. It's one of the city's oldest and was once a favorite of **Arturo Toscanini**. The menu is traditional, the special salad outstanding. ◆ Italian ◆ 302 E 12th St (1st-2nd Aves) Reservations recommended. No credit cards. 475.9531

70 Immaculate Conception Church (1894, **Barney & Chapman**) Now a Roman Catholic church, this was originally an Episcopal mission of Grace Church, which included a hospital and social service facilities arranged in a cloisterlike setting punctuated by the elaborate tower. ◆ 414 E 14th St (Ave A-1st Ave)

71 Jewish Repertory Theatre Plays that relate to the Jewish experience are given standard-to-excellent treatment here. Revivals (of **Chekhov, Neil Simon**), originals (*Crossing Delancey* premiered here) and musicals. ◆ Seats 99. 344 E 14th St (1st-2nd Aves) 505.2667

71 Las Mañanitas ★$$ A restaurant in the basement floor of an old townhouse. The bill of fare, which includes all the Tex-Mex standards along with margaritas famous all over the neighborhood, is complemented by live music on Friday. ◆ Mexican ◆ 322 E 14th St (1st-2nd Aves) 475.2558

72 Kiehl's Since 1851 Located at the historical **Peter Stuyvesant Pear Tree Corner**, this vintage establishment produces handmade cosmetics and 118 essences (including 4 kinds of patchouli oil), using natural ingredients and extracts according to centuries-old formulations. **Ultra Facial Moisturizer** is a top seller. (This divine concoction absorbs immediately and doesn't clog a single pore!) The white-coated staff is extremely helpful and generous with samples. Kiehl's is in the process of expanding into the space next door, not only to provide more shelf space for its products, but to make room for a display of new and vintage motorcycles. An East Village *must.* ◆ Closed Su. 109 3rd Ave (E 13th-E 14th Sts) 475.3400

73 Palladium (redesigned 1985, principal designer, **Arata Isozaki**) Partners **Steve Rubell** and **Ian Schrager** (of **Studio 54** and **Morgan's** fame) had a great idea—to convert the old Academy of Music into a dance palace. They hired Arata Isozaki and **Eiko Ishioko** to revamp the interior, and commissioned artists like **Francesco Clemente** and **Keith Haring** to do their thing in individual rooms and spaces. These days, the clientele is mostly out-of-towners and the very young. Immense banks of video monitors pulsate over the vast dance floor. Look up: you might see yourself in living color. ◆ Cover. Closed M-W, Su. 126 E 14th St (3rd-4th Aves) 473.7171

It has taken the better part of a century, but the esteemed *Oxford English Dictionary* is finally going to accept *Big Apple* as a synonym for New York City. Although it was the focus of a media blitz to spur tourism during the 1970s, opinion differs as to exactly where the nickname comes from. One source claims it was originally *The Apple*, a term coined by jazz musicians in the 1930s, and that *Big* was added later, as in the *Big Cheese* or the *Big Time*. Another source cites a 1927 **Walter Winchell** article. All this is rubbish, according to etymologist **David Shulman**, who has pinned the first—and not exactly flattering—use of Big Apple to a 1909 collection of essays edited by **Edward S. Martin**. In his introduction, Martin wrote that the country at large feels the *big apple gets a disproportionate share of the national sap.*

Rick Cook
Concierge, The Stanhope Hotel

The **Metropolitan Museum**, late on Friday and Saturday nights, the steps out front—anytime—for the people!

The **Conservatory Garden** at 5th Ave and 105th St—lavish, beautiful, peaceful and inspiring.

The skyline of Manhattan viewed from the north end of the **Great Lawn** in Central Park.

Eating in our great restaurants and trying to keep in shape. My favorites: **Le Perigord, Le Bernardin, Andiamo!** and **Le Refuge**. I don't think it gets any better than this!

The **flea markets** around town on Sunday—Columbus Ave at 76th-77th Sts; 6th Ave in the 20s. There are bargains to be found, and too many choices.

JoAnne Akalaitis
Associate Director, Public Theater

The **Greenmarket**—it gets better and better every year.

Shakespeare in the Park—when twilight fades to dark. The warmth and glamour of the lit stage with the audience leaning forward, watching, listening.

The **Encore Bakery** on 2nd Ave between 8th and 9th Sts.

The early autumn—on a morning after a thunderstorm.

The **Strand Bookstore**.

And...numerous bars, restaurants, coffeeshops and backyards on the **Lower East Side**.

Horace Havemeyer III
Publisher, *Metropolis, The Architecture and Design Magazine of New York*

Favorite activities and places:

Having lunch on weekends in the winter in SoHo or Midtown before or after visiting galleries or museums. The **MoMA** dining rooms are great for their views.

Browsing in any good bookstore. **Rizzoli's** on 57th St is open at night so we can drop in, often after a concert. The **Doubleday** and **Brentano** bookstores on 5th Ave are also favorites.

Walking almost anywhere looking at buildings and their details. Especially:

Park Ave in the 60s, 70s and 80s. Looking at the detail in the pre-WWII buildings.

TriBeCa. Walk along Greenwich St and look in at **Duane Square**. Note the continuity between the area's industrial past and residential present.

Battery Park City. The best new city of the 1980s.

Along the waterfront looking at the rivers, river traffic and opposite shores, such as the **Finley Walk** along the East River between 72nd and 90th Sts. Going downtown from the East 80s, I always try to take the **East River Drive**.

Queen Anne-style Row Houses. My favorites are the row of 10 houses at 146-156 E 89th St, the **Henderson houses** on East End between 86th and 87th Sts, and those between Amsterdam and Columbus on 81st St.

Gramercy Park, its surrounding buildings and Park Ave in the low 20s.

Alan Siegel
Chairman of the Board and CEO, Siegel & Gale

Biking in **Central Park**.

Thanksgiving dinner at the **Four Seasons**.

Vito Giallo Antiques.

Lecture series at the **New York Public Library**.

Paul Taylor Dance Company.

Concerts at **Carnegie Hall**.

Vinnie's Pizzeria.

Madison Ave from 57th St to 96th St.

Radio City Music Hall.

The Museum of Modern Art.

Union Square/ Gramercy/Murray Hill

Union Square, the area that was formerly known as Stuyvesant, and **Murray Hill**, both residential neighborhods, were named for farms; while **Gramercy** was named for an early 19th-century housing development that lured the rich by offering them access to their own private park. Together they cover the blocks bounded by **14th** and **39th Sts, 6th Ave** and the **East River**. In recent years, publishers, advertising agencies and other companies running from high uptown rents have moved into these neighborhods, which had become residential after the commercial center of the city moved north in the 19th century. Almost none have tampered with the exteriors of the buildings, except to restore them. The result is a comfortable area with a newfound energy.

Gramercy Park, the centerpiece of the downtown portion, was established in the 1830s by a lawyer named **Samuel Ruggles**. To make one of his tracts more valuable, he gave up 42 potential building lots for a London-style park. Then he

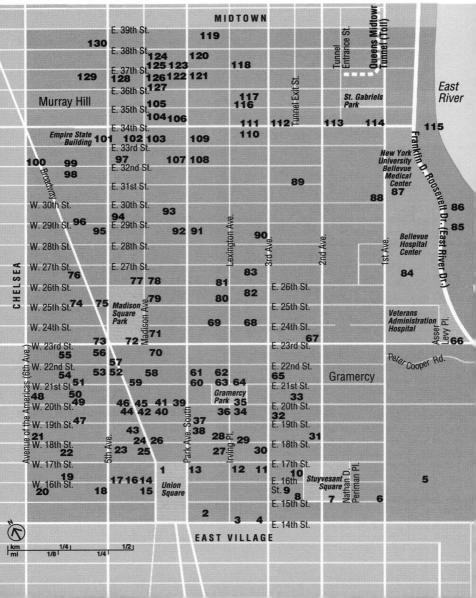

set aside more land for a wide avenue north of the park (which he named Lexington for the Revolutionary War battle) and for Irving Place south of it (which he named for his friend **Washington Irving**, the writer who created one of the symbols of New York, *Father Knickerbocker*).

The land that Ruggles owned was once part of a huge estate that belonged to **Peter Stuyvesant**, the last governor-general of New Netherlands, who retired there after the British took over. His original 1651 deed noted a valley created by a creek it called *Crommessie*, a combination of 2 Dutch words meaning crooked little knife (for the shape of a nearby brook). The name was altered to fall more easily off English-speaking tongues.

Stuyvesant's name lives on in the neighborhood east of Gramercy, and in another London-style park that straddles 2nd Ave. After the Stuyvesant family sold that part of the estate to the Delanceys in 1746, it was developed into a working farm known as Rose Hill. It is a quiet residential area today, but through the beginning of the 20th century, the notorious **Gas House Gang** ruled the neighborhood, averaging an estimated 30 holdups each and every night on 18th St alone.

The original Gas Housers' territory included another residential neighborhood called Murray Hill, which extends north from 34th to 39th Sts, and east from 6th Ave. The gang took its name from factories along the East River that turned out illuminating gas to light the city in the 18th century. The stretch between 23rd and 34th Sts is often called **Kips Bay**. The name comes from a farm established by **Jacobus Kip** in 1655.

By the end of the 19th century, when **J. Pierpont Morgan** moved to Kips Bay, a gentlemen's agreement had been established restricting Murray Hill's streets to private houses. Until the invasion of high-rise hotels and apartments in the 1920s, it was a neighborhood of elegant mansions, many of which are still standing.

Today, where gas storage tanks once sprouted east of Stuyvesant Square, thousands of people are housed in complexes like **Stuyvesant Town, Peter Cooper Village** (both attacked in the late 1940s for being grim, even fascist) and **Waterside** (built in 1974 on the East River between 25th and 30th Sts). Also visible from the FDR Drive is **Bellevue Hospital Center**, 26th to 30th Sts. Bellevue originated as a 6-bed infirmary on the site of the present City Hall in a building that it shared with a poorhouse and a jail.

---

1 Union Square In 1811, when the city fathers decreed that all of Manhattan's streets should follow a rigid grid pattern, Broadway was already in place, cutting an angle from southeast to northwest. Rather than change it, they turned it to the city's advantage by creating squares wherever Broadway crossed a north-south avenue. What may have inspired them was this existing square, which grew up around the meeting point of Broadway, the post road to Albany, and Boston Post Road, which later became 3rd Ave. In the years before the Civil War, it was the heart of a fashionable residential neighborhood, surrounded by prestigious stores and theaters. When fashion moved uptown, the square became a center for labor demonstrations and rallies. It was landscaped and altered in 1936, when it was also raised a few feet above ground level to allow for the subway station under it. The pavilion at the north end, sometimes used for summer concerts, was added at the same time. The city fathers' redesign also forced Broadway to make a left turn at 17th St, and share its right-of-way with Park Ave So before getting back on course at 14th St. The landscapers came back almost 50 years later to begin a multiphase renovation (phase 1 began in 1984) that will transform the area once again. (The park had become a gloomy hangout for drug pushers and derelicts.) Among their accomplishments to date is the replacement of the magnificent **Independence Flagstaff** at the center of the park, originally donated by **Tammany Hall** (see page 33). The face-lift also includes new Art Deco subway kiosks, which flank the equestrian statue of **George Washington**, the masterpiece of sculptor **John Quincy Adams Ward**, which was placed there in 1856. Ward's collaborator was **Henry Kirke Brown**, who did the figure of **Abraham Lincoln** at the other end of the park. Nearby is a representation of the **Marquis de Lafayette**, created in 1876 by **Frederic Auguste Bartholdi**, who gave us the *Statue of Liberty* 10 years later. ◆ E 14th-E 17th Sts (Park Ave So-University Pl)

Greenmarket

1 Union Square Greenmarket In 1976, as part of the effort to turn around Union Square, the **Manhattan Planning Office of the New York City Planning Department** urged the **Council on the Environment** to start a greenmarket in what was a parking lot. (A market was already in full swing at 59th St and 2nd Ave.) After a slow start—due to the community's well-founded negative feelings toward the illicit activities within the park—the turnaround came in 1984, when the **Parks Dept** rebuilt the park itself and the **New York City Dept of Transportation** rebuilt the public place just north of it. As many as 60 regional farmers and food producers participate in Manhattan's 25 greenmarkets. Baked goods, fish, cheese, eggs, honey, plants and flour, are sold, in addition to a huge variety of fruits and vegetables. I make a beeline for the fresh flowers. All perishables must be sold within 24 hours of harvesting. ♦ W, Sa 8AM-6PM. E 17th St at Broadway. 566.0990

Union Square/Gramercy/Murray Hill

2 Zeckendorf Plaza (1987, **Davis, Brody & Associates**) There are more than 670 cooperative apartments in this building, which covers the full block bounded by 14th and 15th Sts, Irving Pl and Union Sq E. Four illuminated pyramids sit atop the sprawling complex. Different sections are designated to represent lifestyles in various Manhattan neighborhoods, but life here is self-contained, with such amenities as a health club and shopping facilities. At 108 E 15th is the 225-seat **Gertrude and Irving Dimson Theater**, the permanent home of the multidimensional **Vineyard Theater Company**. The development is often cited as a key to the gentrification of the Union Square neighborhood. Only time will tell if it is up to the task.

3 Consolidated Edison Building (1915-29, **Henry J. Hardenbergh**; tower 1926, **Warren & Wetmore**) This massive structure has its critics, but everyone loves its clocktower, which is softly lit at night, as it should be, considering that its owner is the electric light company. The building, which fills nearly the whole block, replaced 2 structures that each had an impact on the city. **Tammany Hall**, which controlled City Hall for more than 100 years, was headquartered here in a large but unassuming brick building that had a large auditorium for public meetings, and a smaller one that became a profit center as **Tony Pastor's Music Hall**, which in 1881 was the birthplace of American vaudeville. It was next door to a jewel box of a building known as the **Academy**

Consolidated Edison Building

of Music, the predecessor of the Metropolitan Opera, which in its decline became the scene of anti-Tammany rallies. In its heyday, it was the anchor for a string of the city's best restaurants, hotels and theaters. ♦ 4 Irving Pl (E 14th St)

4 Con Edison Energy Museum The age of electricity, brought to New York in 1882 by **Thomas Edison**, is chronicled with exhibitions, artifacts and imaginative displays that extend to the present and into the future. A representation of today's New York at night is reached through a long passageway that is a tour of underground New York, complete with a passing subway. ♦ Free. Tu-Sa 10AM-4PM. 145 E 14th St (3rd Ave-Irving Pl) 460.6244

5 Stuyvesant Town (1947, **Irwin Clavan** and **Gilmore Clarke**) There are 8755 moderately-priced apartments in this complex, which looks forbidding from the street (when it was built, **Lewis Mumford** called it *police state architecture*). The inside is virtually free of cars. The tenants, many of whom are senior citizens, live a carefree existence, thanks to good security and careful maintenance provided by the landlord, the Metropolitan Life Insurance Company. In the blocks between 20th and 23rd Sts, the development becomes known as **Peter Cooper Village**, an upscale version of Stuyvesant Town, with larger apartments and higher rents. Peter Cooper people are also allowed air conditioners, forbidden below 20th St by the landlord, who pays the electric bills. ♦ E 14th-E 20th Sts (FDR Drive-1st Ave)

6 Stuyvesant High School (1906, C.B.J. Snyder) This exuberant French-style building houses one of the most prestigious public high schools in the country. Since the difficult-to-earn **Westinghouse** scholarships were first awarded, Stuyvesant students have routinely finished the competition among the top 10 from all over the US. Its graduates include Nobel laureates **Joshua Lederberg** and **Raoul Hoffman**. Although plans are in the works to move the school to a building in Battery Park City, the fate of this space is still undecided. ◆ 345 E 15th St (1st-2nd Aves)

7 Stuyvesant Square Created in 1836 at the edge of the **Gas House District** (one of the city's poorest neighborhoods), this 4-acre oasis, donated to the city by the Stuyvesant family, was the dividing line between rich and poor. In the center of the western half is a 1936 sculpture of **Peter Stuyvesant** by **Gertrude Vanderbilt Whitney**, founder of the Whitney Museum. ◆ E 15th-E 17th Sts (2nd Ave)

8 Friends Meeting House (1860, **Charles T. Bunting**) The simple, 2-story Greek Revival structure reflects the peaceful nature of the **Society of Friends**, which holds meetings here. ◆ 221 E 15th St (Rutherford Pl)

9 216 East 16th Street Part of a row of striking Italianate houses all built in the early 1850s, it is still a joy to behold. The lower stories are brownstone, but brick is used on the upper floors, which, along with its wonderful windows, makes it unusual. ◆ Rutherford Pl

10 St. George's Episcopal Church (1846, **Otto Blesch** and **Leopold Eidlitz**) It's easy to believe that this solid brownstone, vaguely Romanesque church was the church of financier **J.P. Morgan**. ◆ E 16th St at Rutherford Pl

10 St. George's Chapel (1911, **Matthew Lansing Emery** and **Henry George Emery**) A Romanesque companion in the shadow of the massive church—most certainly one of New York's overlooked treasures. ◆ Rutherford Pl (north of the church)

11 Tien Fu ★★$ A full range of Chinese specialties in a busy neighborhood restaurant. ◆ Chinese ◆ 180 3rd Ave (E 16th-E 17th Sts) 505.2000

12 Washington Irving High School (1912, **C.B.J. Snyder**) Originally a girls' technical high school, Washington Irving's curriculum expanded to include a full range of subjects for its female students when it moved here from Lafayette St. The huge bust of Irving at the 17th St corner was done in 1885 by **Friedrich Baer**. ◆ 40 Irving Pl (E 16th-E 17th Sts)

Under the 1988 *New York State Farmers Market Coupon Program*, specially printed coupons for buying fresh produce at designated markets are provided to low-income people in the *Women, Infants and Children* (WIC) and *Senior Citizens Nutrition* programs.

Restaurants/Nightlife: Red   **Hotels:** Blue
Shops/Parks: Green   **Sights/Culture:** Black

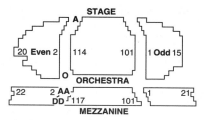

13 Roundabout Theatre (1928, **Thompson, Holmes & Converse**) Under the leadership of artistic director **Gene Feist**, the Roundabout has won recognition as one of the city's finest theatrical organizations. It remains committed to producing classics by the world's greatest playwrights at affordable prices—**Ibsen**'s *Ghosts*, **Pirandello**'s *Enrico 4*, **Carson McCullers**' *Member of the Wedding*. ◆ Seats 499. 100 E 17th St (Park Ave So) 420.1360

13 Guardian Life Insurance Company (1911, **D'Oench & Yost**) When this building was designed, there was a new architectural movement away from flat-topped buildings with cornices, which were beginning to get boring for many corporate clients. D'Oench & Yost responded by producing a 4-story mansard roof for the top of this lavish tower. Still not satisfied that it was unusual enough to become their signature, the clients added a huge

Union Square/Gramercy/Murray Hill

electric sign. It worked against them. Their name was **Germania Life**, which set them apart as pariahs when WWI broke out. They solved the problem by changing their name. The 1961 extension behind it, adding little more than space, was designed by **Skidmore, Owings & Merrill**. ◆ 201 Park Ave So (E 17th St)

14 Union Square Cafe ★★★$$$ Owner **Danny Meyer** is one of the brightest and most innovative among the new generation of restaurateurs. His young staff is welcoming, and the service is cordial yet professional. Food festivals, featuring produce from the nearby Union Sq Greenmarket, add to the Continental liveliness of this popular and attractive cafe. You can't go wrong with the generous tuna steak. *An RSW recommendation.* ◆ American ◆ Closed Su. 21 E 16th St (Union Sq W-5th Ave) 243.4020

14 Coffee Shop ★$$$ This imitation coffeeshop —lots of formica and tile—serves a mix of American and Brazilian fare: from a tuna-melt sandwich to coconut shrimp and marinated and broiled mahi-mahi. This hot (and noisy) spot is owned by the 3 former models who also run **Live Bait** on 23rd St. Go to be seen. ◆ American/Brazilian ◆ 29 Union Sq W (E 16th St) 243.7969

15 Richard Stoddard Performing Arts Books Mostly out-of-print books plus ephemera relating to the performing arts—playbills, autographs and periodicals. ◆ Closed W, Su. 18 E 16th St (Union Sq-5th Ave) Room 305. 645.9576

16 Revolution Books Before you start your revolution, stop here for inspiration from the masters of the art. ♦ 13 E 16th St (Union Sq W-5th Ave) 691.3345

16 Espace ★$$$ The work of downtown artists enlivens this otherwise Neoclassical French bistro, which features a rotating installation of painting and sculpture. Dishes such as salmon *grillé* with sorrel, mussels in saffron and roasted eggplant soup are accompanied by live music, suggesting a certain whimsy in this new restaurant. ♦ French ♦ 9 E 16th St (5th Ave) Reservations required. 463.7101

17 Chevignon This is Frenchman **Guy Azoulay**'s version of American sportswear based on his childhood images of America—Marlon Brando, rodeos, villains and Western heroes. ♦ 79 5th Ave (E 16th St) 691.3160

17 B. Shackman & Co. The original sign, which may have been placed here when the store opened in 1898, says Shackman specializes in favors and novelties. Its old-fashioned toys, Victorian cards, books and, yes, favors, make this a favorite stop for anyone with an ounce of nostalgia. ♦ Closed Su. 85 5th Ave (E 16th St) 989.5162

18 Paul Smith Rock stars and Wall Street bankers have been found here shopping for classic clothing with a twist. This is the eccen-

tric Englishman's only US outlet—he has 45 stores in Japan and 7 in London. Handsomely made suits, sports jackets and slacks, plus wacky play clothes like shirts dotted with espresso beans and a coat made with fabric that is imprinted with a photograph Smith took in India. ♦ Closed Su. 108 5th Ave (W 16th St) 627.9770

18 Emporio Armani If Emporio, rather than Giorgio, precedes Armani, it means that the merchandise (which includes men's and women's clothing, accessories, bath products and leather luggage) goes for about 50 percent less than Armani's signature collections. Check around for some Armani wit: wood sculptures of a bra, panties, a suitcase and ties; the eagle-shaped air-conditioner unit on the ceiling; and another eagle—this one with an antique manhole cover for an eye—worked into the 100-year-old chestnut floor. ♦ 110 5th Ave (W 16th St) 727.3240

18 Joan & David One of 2 boutiques in Manhattan—the other is at 816 Madison Ave—for exclusive lines of shoes, clothing and accessories from wife-and-husband team **Joan** and **David** Helpern. The high-tech interior was designed by London designer **Eva Jiricna**. A very friendly staff. ♦ 104 5th Ave (W 15th-W 16th Sts) 627.1780

19 17 West 16th Street (1846) **Margaret Sanger** established America's first birth control clinic in 1916 on Amboy St in the Brownsville section of Brooklyn. She moved

to this unusual Greek Revival house in 1923, and it was the headquarters for her Birth Control Clinical Research Bureau for the next 50 years. ♦ 5th-6th Aves

20 St. Francis Xavier Church (1882, P.C. Keely) This Baroque Roman Catholic monument to **St. Francis Xavier** would be right at home in the Jesuit missionary's native Spain. The interior is the sort of thing American tourists go out of their way to see in Europe. ♦ 30 W 16th St (5th-6th Aves)

21 Siegel-Cooper & Company (1896, DeLemos & Cordes) Originally **Siegel-Cooper Dry Goods Store**. In its heyday, this garish white brick and terra-cotta retail temple (fashioned under the influence of the Chicago World's Fair of 1893) lived up to its slogan *The Big Store—A City In Itself* with 15 1/2 acres of space, 17 elevators, a tropical garden and a smaller version of **Daniel Chester French**'s monument, *The Republic*, which had graced the Fair. The fountain at the base of the statue became a favorite rendezvous for New Yorkers, who used to say, *Meet me at the fountain*. The store was located in the fashionable shopping district called *Ladies' Mile*, but when **Macy's** and **B. Altman's** moved uptown, the store sold its inventory to **Gimbels**, and the statue to **Forest Lawn Cemetery** in Los Angeles. The building was converted into a military hospital during WWI, and in recent years has served as construction space for television scenery and garment manufacturing firms. ♦ 6th Ave (W 18th St)

22 Book-Friends Cafe An old-fashioned salon featuring books from the Victorian, Edwardian, Belle Epoque and Bloomsbury eras, and a cafe where you can discuss them. Go for afternoon tea or one of the *Conversations*, during which experts speak about things like Kiki's Paris, New York Literary Neighborhoods and Sylvia Beach and the Expatriates. ♦ 16 W 18th St (5th-6th Aves) 255.7407

22 Prix-Fixe ★★$$ Because chef **Terrance Brennan** shops prudently—bargains at the Fulton Fish Market, for example—he is able to turn out elegant cuisine at cut-rate prices. Especially good are salmon tournedo in a horseradish crust, and grilled chicken with basil mashed potatoes. ♦ American ♦ 18 W 18th St (5th-6th Aves) 675.6777

22 Academy Books and Records A good selection of out-of-print, used and rare books and records as well as used CDs. ♦ 10 W 18th St (5th-6th Aves) 242.4848

23 Barnes & Noble Bookstore Originally a purveyor of textbooks with branches at most major local colleges, this store has branched out all over town in recent years. There are 2 here, the main store on the SE corner and the **Sale Annex** across the street. You can still buy and sell textbooks here, but the selection of books and records beyond that is almost overwhelming, at prices that are surprisingly low. I usually head for an overlooked part of the annex—the corner in the back of the ground floor that sells used books, many of which are real treasures at affordable prices. ◆ 105 5th Ave (E 18th St) 807.0099

23 Daffy's Three floors of designer clothes for every age group at incredible discount prices. ◆ 111 5th Ave (E 18th St) 529.4477

24 America $$$ This was once the ultimate trendy restaurant. And though the luster is ever-so-slightly less luminous than it once was, it is still a great draw for the young crowd. Everything about it is big. It has 350 seats, and about as many things on the menu—many of them barely edible. But it isn't the food you come here for—it is the huge bar, where standing room is 3-deep. Almost everyone drinks Rolling Rock beer or large, sweet and powerful drinks with names like *Woo-Woo* and *Russian Quaaludes*. The appeal is the unrelenting noise and the sense of belonging that comes from elbowing through the mobs of people. Everyone here is the same age, went to the same school and has about the same number of pennies to jingle in the pocket of his or her designer jeans. The regulars love it, and so do out-of-town groupies. ◆ American ◆ 9 E 18th St (Broadway-5th Ave) 505.2110

25 Paragon For those who are *sportif*, this may be one of the best sportswear stops in the city. Its sales are spectacular. ◆ 867 Broadway (E 18th St) 255.8036

26 MacIntyre Building (1892, **R.H. Robertson**) This Romanesque office building has obviously seen better days, but it hasn't lost its pride. You can tell by the way those beasts at the corners are sticking their tongues out at you. ◆ 874 Broadway (E 18th St)

SAL ANTHONY'S

27 Sal Anthony's $$ A casual restaurant overlooking the street through a huge bay window above an outdoor cafe. The management claims it occupies a former apartment rented by **O. Henry**, which is not very likely, though the writer did live in the neighborhood and would have been pleased to work in such pleasant surroundings. ◆ Italian ◆ 55 Irving Pl (E 17th-E 18th Sts) Reservations required. 982.9030

28 Fresh Art All the requisites for an old-fashioned English garden—flowers, plants, planters and furniture—are available in this charming basement-level shop. ◆ Closed Su. 71 Irving Pl (E 18th-E 19th Sts) 995.5044

28 Friend of a Farmer ★$$ Country cooking and on-the-premises baking take you back to the days when your grandma's kitchen may have smelled just like this. If you bring her along, she'll undoubtedly ask for the recipe for

the daily special. The Long Island duckling and Cajun-style chicken are always good. ◆ American ◆ Closed M. 77 Irving Pl (E 18th-E 19th Sts) 477.2188

28 Choshi ★$$ The fresh and well-prepared sushi and sashimi are great buys at lunch. Indoor and outdoor dining. ◆ Japanese ◆ 77 Irving Pl (E 18th-E 19th Sts) 420.1419

29 Paul and Jimmy's ★$$$ A classic restaurant that still believes in hearty food served in an old-world manner. ◆ Italian ◆ 123 E 18th St (Irving Pl-Park Ave So) 475.9540

29 Pete's Tavern ★$$ There are several saloons in New York that claim to be the oldest in town, and this is one of them. Pete's also claims that **O. Henry** did some of his writing here in a corner booth. If the bar was as busy then as it is now, his powers of concentration must have been incredible. The menu, which runs from Italian specialties to hamburgers, isn't unusual, but the setting is unusually comfortable, and the sidewalk cafe is among the city's best. ◆ Italian/American ◆ 129 E 18th St (Irving Pl) 473.7676

30 Tuesday's $$ (1894, **Weber & Drosser**) Built in the days when this was a German neighborhood, it was originally called **Scheffel Hall** and housed a drinking and singing society. As **Joe King**'s rathskeller in

Union Square/Gramercy/Murray Hill

the years after WWI, it became a place for college students from all over the country to drink and sing, and a generation of them regularly lined up around the block for the pleasure. There are traces of them left in carved initials in the woodwork inside, but it has been modernized into a run-of-the-mill hangout for the quiche and salad set, who are treated to live jazz music with Saturday and Sunday brunch. ◆ American ◆ 190 3rd Ave (E 17th-E 18th Sts) 533.7900

30 Fat Tuesday's This basement room under the old rathskeller features top names from the jazz world, including frequent Monday night visits by **Les Paul**, the man who invented the new sounds. ◆ Shows: M-Th, Su 8, 10PM; F-Sa 8, 10PM, midnight. 190 3rd Ave (E 17th-E 18th Sts) 533.7902

31 Farnie's Second Avenue Steak Parlor ★$ If you're on a budget but feel like eating steak, look no further. A filet mignon with a salad and potato is well within reach. ◆ American ◆ 311 2nd Ave (E 18th St) 228.9280

32 Maryland Crab House $$ Crabs, including hardshells you crack with a mallet Baltimore-style, oysters and other fresh Southern seafood specialties, with friendly service. However, it doesn't compare to being in Maryland. ◆ Seafood ◆ 237 3rd Ave (E 19th-E 20th Sts) 598.4890

Restaurants/Nightlife: Red   **Hotels:** Blue
Shops/Parks: Green   **Sights/Culture:** Black

32 L'Affaire An inviting shop featuring couture lingerie and boudoir accessories, as well as unusual matching gifts for mothers and their infants. ♦ Closed Su. 228 3rd Ave (E 19th-E 20th Sts) 254.1922

33 Police Academy and Museum In spite of what you may have seen in the movies, this academy takes its job very seriously. The building has a swimming pool and a gymnasium, as well as a museum where you can find out how our police officers came to be called the finest, and study displays that help you understand what they've been through to earn the title. Call before visiting since they close when a meeting is called. ♦ Free. M-F 9AM-2PM. 235 E 20th St (2nd-3rd Aves) 477.9753

34 The Brotherhood Synagogue (1859, **King & Kellum**; remodeled 1975, **James Stewart Polshek**) This austere brownstone cube was originally designed as a Friends Meeting House, and was remodeled as a synagogue in 1975. ♦ 28 Gramercy Park So (3rd Ave-Irving Pl)

35 Gramercy Park/Gramercy Park Historic District Established by **Samuel Ruggles** in 1831, this former marshland became the model of a London square ringed by proper 19th-century Neoclassical townhouses. It is the sole surviving *private park* in New York

Union Square/Gramercy/Murray Hill

City—only nearby residents have a key to get in—but the perimeter is well worth a stroll. Many notables have lived here, including **James Harper**, the mayor of New York City in 1844, and **Samuel Tilden**, governor of New York State (1874–86), who was an unsuccessful presidential candidate. His home is now the **National Arts Club**. The statue in the park is of actor **Edwin Booth**, who lived at No. 16 Gramercy Park So until he had the building remodeled by **Stanford White** in 1888 for **The Players Club**. Nos. 34 and 36 on the east side are a pair of the city's earliest apartment buildings, designed in 1883 by **George DaConha** and in 1905 by **James Riles**, respectively. Note the magnificent ironwork on Nos. 3 and 4 Gramercy Park W, attributed to **Alexander Jackson Davis**, one of the city's more individualistic and energetic architects. The **Gramercy Park Historic District** extends in an irregular area out from the park, including all of the west and south frontages and part of the east, the park itself, and Irving Pl almost to 19th St on the west side and to 18th St on the east, as well as parts of 20th and 21st Sts west of the park. Of particular interest is the beautiful block between Irving Pl and 3rd Ave on 19th St (remodeled as a group by **Frederick J. Sterner**). ♦ E 20th-E 21st Sts (Lexington Ave)

36 National Arts Club (1845, **Calvert Vaux**) Since 1906, this building has housed the National Arts Club, but its colorful history began when politician **Samuel J. Tilden**, who gained fame by destroying the **Tweed Ring**, used the coup to become governor of New York. To protect himself in the topsy-turvy days of early unions and political machinery, Tilden installed steel doors at the front of this Victorian Gothic home and had a tunnel dug to 19th St as an escape route. ♦ 15 Gramercy Park So (Irving Pl)

36 The Hampden-Booth Theatre Library In 1888, founder **Edwin Booth** charged **The Players Club** with the task of creating *a library relating to the history of the American stage and the preservation of pictures, bills of the play, photographs and curiosities*. Small group tours and use of the library, which includes 4 major collections (from **Edwin Booth**, **Walter Hampden**, the **Union Square Theatre** and **William Henderson**) are granted by appointment only. ♦ 16 Gramercy Park So (Irving Pl) 228.7610

37 Cafe Iguana $$ They call it vacation cuisine; you may prefer to call it Tex-Mex. Either way, you'll find it an adventure in this modern, multilevel setting presided over by a crystal iguana suspended over the bar. ♦ Mexican ♦ 235 Park Ave So (E 19th St) 529.4770

38 Canastel's ★$$$ A popular restaurant featuring old-world specialties in a 1980s setting. ♦ Italian ♦ 229 Park Ave So (E 19th St) 677.9622

39 Positano ★★$$$ Another of the vaguely Italian restaurants that serve the fashionable and fashion-conscious crowd that fills the place to capacity every night. (Even the street outside is bumper-to-bumper with waiting limos.) The best elements of the place are the tasteful decoration (**Croxton Associates**) and the logo (**Milton Glaser**). ♦ Italian ♦ Closed Su. 250 Park Ave So (E 20th St) 777.6211

40 DARTS Unlimited Dart enthusiasts have been coming here for 21 years for their professional English darts (300 types), flights (over 1000 kinds) and the best-quality boards. Novices should request a copy of the *Rules and Regulations of the United States Darting Associatiion for English Darts*, which includes information about the history of darting, tips on good play and rules and standards. ♦ Closed M, Su. 30 E 20th St (Broadway-Park Ave So) 533.8684

Restaurants/Nightlife: Red
Shops/Parks: Green

Hotels: Blue
Sights/Culture: Black

40 Theodore Roosevelt Birthplace (1923, **Theodate Pope Riddle**) Teddy Roosevelt was born in 1858, and lived in a house on this site until he was a teenager. The original house was destroyed in 1916, but faithfully reconstructed 7 years later as a memorial to the 26th president. The National Historic Site incorporates 26 E 20th St, once the home of Roosevelt's uncle. The restoration contains 5 rooms of period furniture and an extensive collection of memorabilia, including teddy bears. ♦ Nominal admission; elders, children free. W-Su 9AM-5PM. 28 E 20th St (Park Ave So-Broadway) 260.1616

41 Lescale ★$$$ An authentic French bistro decorated with French movie posters. Steak, *pommes frites*, rabbit and lentil salad are favorites among the neighborhood *habituées*. Crème caramel is my choice from the dessert list. ♦ French ♦ Closed Su. 43 E 20th St (Park Ave So-Broadway) 477.1180

41 Robbin's ★$$ A state-of-the-art American bistro that boasts artwork by owner **Robbin Cullinen**'s pals and a reinterpretation of *simple—but never simple-minded* classics: garlicky chicken accompanied by mashed potatoes flavored with scallions and lots of butter; scallops with shiitake mushrooms, waffle potato chips and horseradish vinaigrette; and lemon tart. Don't miss the clock that tells time with moving colors. ♦ American ♦ 41 E 20th St (Park Ave So-Broadway) 260.6400

42 ABC Carpet (1882, **W. Wheeler Smith**) The original owner of this building was **W&J Sloane**, which moved uptown and became one of the city's leading furniture dealers. It specialized in carpets and rugs when it was here, and the tradition is continued by one of Sloane's former competitors, ABC, founded in 1897. One of New York's lowest-priced sources of fine carpets of every description; in this building you will find wall-to-wall carpeting, remnants and tile. Across the street, at No. 881, are 6 floors of merchandise, including antique and reproduction rugs and furniture, plus bed, bath, linen and lighting departments. ♦ 888 Broadway (E 19th St) 473.3000

43 Originally **Arnold Constable Dry Goods Store** (1869-77, **Griffith Thomas**) A glorious 2-story mansard roof tops this skillful marriage of Empire and Italianate styles. Note the rare combination of marble and cast-iron in the facade—the city's first use of cast-iron construction for retail space. ♦ 881-887 Broadway (E 19th St)

In Manhattan, there are gardens on roofs, gardens outside basement apartments and minigardens on miniterraces. How do the gardens grow? Expensively. And what do they grow? Almost anything. Apparently, even cash crops. Wild flowers have been tamed on tiny balconies, and families fed on vegetables nurtured in the alien soil bordered by sidewalks. **Ralph Caplan**, writer and design consultant

There are 26,575 lampposts in New York City.

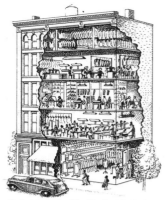

44 Saint Laurie Limited (1869, **James H. Giles**) This was originally part of the **Lord & Taylor** emporium and has been restored for a manufacturer of quality men's and women's suits, available here at wholesale prices. An on-site museum demonstrates how clothing is produced, with a tour of the workrooms and exhibitions of changing styles. Custom tailoring is also available at low prices, as is mail-order service. Worth a visit. ♦ 897 Broadway (E 19th-E 20th Sts) 473.0100

44 Manhattan Raceway Thirty-two lanes of slot-car racing on 4 championship tracks make for lots of laughter and excitement. Cars

and controllers for rent or purchase; demo cars available for test drives. Why not take a spin after seeing one of the 6 movies playing across the street at the Loews theater? ♦ 893 Broadway (E 19th-E 20th Sts) 473.5095, 800/852.RACE

45 Goelet Building (1887, **McKim, Mead & White**) Chicago architects developed steel-framed office buildings with highly ornamental exteriors, and in the 1880s, firms such as **McKim, Mead & White** began developing their own variations on the theme, which they called *New York Style*. This is a prime example of the art. ♦ 900 Broadway (E 20th St)

46 901 Broadway (1869, **James H. Giles**) Originally **Lord & Taylor Dry Goods Store**, a romantic cast-iron facade with echoes of Renaissance castle architecture remains as a monument to the glories of this formerly fashionable shopping neighborhood before Lord & Taylor moved uptown along with its neighbors **W&J Sloane** and **Arnold Constable**. Industrial tenants have occupied it ever since, and the remodeled mundane ground floor has no connection with the fanciful upper ones. ♦ E 20th St

47 Computer Center at SAM FLAX Known for its extensive stock of art materials, SF recently opened this state-of-the-art desktop publishing and computer graphics facility. Rent a workstation or drop off the job and one of the technicians will do it for you. ♦ 15 W 19th St (5th-6th Aves) 255.6246

47 Magickal Child Tucked away in the deep shade cast by high loft buildings, this is a perfect setting for a store specializing in swords, daggers, candlesticks and other supplies for your explorations into the occult. A free mail-order catalog is available. ♦ 35 W 19th St (5th-6th Aves) 242.7182

48 Church of the Holy Communion (1846, **Richard Upjohn**) In better days, this church had **John Jacob Astor** and **Cornelius Vanderbilt** among its parishioners. When the neighborhood died, the church died with it and, to add insult to injury, became the **Limelight** discothèque in 1982. ♦ 660 6th Ave (W 20th-W 21st Sts) 807.7850

49 Periyali ★$$$ The friendly staff is justly proud of the traditional Greek menu. Giant white beans with garlic sauce, charcoal-grilled octopus, *all* the phyllo pastries and fresh whole fish (flown in daily from Greece) are just a few options. For dessert, baklava, of course, and something wonderful called *diples* (thin strips of dough, deep-fried and dipped in honey). White stucco walls, wooden floors and soft Greek music complete the experience. ♦ Greek ♦ Closed Su. 35 W 20th St (5th-6th Aves) Reservations recommended. 463.7890

50 Chelsea Billiards Pool sharks rejoice! This state-of-the-art pool hall is the largest in the

US: 44 **Brunswick Gold Crown** pool tables, 4 tournament-size snooker tables. Call for information about the pool school. Open 24hrs. ♦ 54 W 21st St (5th-6th Aves) 989.0096

50 Putter's Paradise Manhattan's first, and only, miniature-golf course has a tropical theme. Obstacles include a shark fin, a seahorse and a revolving wooden banana. ♦ Closed M-Tu. 48 W 21st St (5th-6th Aves) 727.7888

51 Cadillac Bar ★$$ Don't let the name fool you. Don't even let the graffiti around the 100ft bar make you think the Cadillac is something it's not. The menu is pure Tex-Mex, in spite of the name and the Neo-New York decor. ♦ Tex-Mex ♦ Closed Su. 15 W 21st St (5th-6th Aves) 645.7220

52 Dot Zero The name of this store stands for the point of reference from which any map is made (for example, either pole is dot zero for a globe). Black, sleek and minimalistic, it's just what you'd expect a post year-2000 shop to be. Everything it sells, from clocks to scissors to marbles, is the epitome of high-tech design. This hip store is the brainchild of designers **Kevin Brynan** and **Harvey Bernstein**. ♦ 159 5th Ave (E 22nd St) 614.0540

53 Tropica Palm tree sponges, Venus Fly Traps, thongs adorned with clusters of plastic flowers, Balinese wood sculptures, crustacean napkin rings—if it's evocative of a tropical island you'll find it here. Pick up a macadamia-

nut cookie and a cup of Hawaiian coffee at the Kona Coffee Bar in the center of the shop, then close your eyes and dream about a trip to island paradise. ♦ Closed Su. 170 5th Ave (W 22nd St) 627.0808

54 Lola ★$$$ Lola and her co-owner, **Yvonne Bell**, are the guiding hands presiding over Manhattan's only West Indian/Caribbean restaurant. Simply decorated yet appealing, it serves spiced and curried authentic foods of the islands along with more familiar Italian fare, including such choices as deep-fried zucchini, squid and *osso buco*. The restaurant encourages grazing/tasting of several appetizers. I hope you won't bypass the *Lolita*, an intoxicating frozen combination of brandy, Triple Sec and lemon juice. ♦ West Indian/Caribbean ♦ 30 W 22nd St (5th-6th Aves) 675.6700

54 The Chocolate Gallery A rull range of supplies for cake bakers and candy makers, including the complete line from Wilton. A frequent stop for professionals. ♦ Closed M, Su. 34 W 22nd St (5th-6th Aves) 675.2253

55 Stern's Dry Goods Store (1878, **Henry Fernbach**) Possibly the most sensitive restoration of any cast-iron building in New York. ♦ 32-36 W 23rd St (5th-6th Aves)

56 Western Union Building (1884, **Henry J. Hardenbergh**) A reflection of the city's Dutch origins, created in the same year as Hardenbergh's **Dakota** apartment house up on Central Park. ♦ 186 5th Ave (W 23rd St)

57 Flatiron Building (1902, **David H. Burnham & Co.**) When Burnham (of Chicago World's Fair fame) filled the triangular site where Broadway crosses 5th Ave in a most reasonable but unconventional manner—with a triangular building—he raised many eyebrows and made history. This limestone-clad Renaissance *palazzo* skyscraper, 285ft high, is one of Burnham's best. At the juncture between traditionalism and modernism, the structure, with its articulated base and strong cornice, looks like an ocean liner in a column's clothing. Built as the Fuller Building, people soon dubbed it Flatiron for its shape, once they stopped calling it *Burnham's Folly.* ♦ 175 5th Ave (E 22nd-E 23rd Sts)

Within the Flatiron Building:

Scuba Network Fins, masks, snorkels and everything else you need to dive, including lessons that can lead to certification in as little as 2 weeks (if you have the time and the extra cash to pay for the rush service); it usually takes 5. ♦ Closed Su. 228.2080

58 Chefs, Cuisiniers Club ★★$$$ Backed by big wigs from **Aureole**, the **Water Club** and **Andiamo**, this watering hole for area chefs—a place where they can unwind and enjoy a good meal after their workday is over—opened in the fall of 1990 to hopeful preliminary reviews. The C.C. Club serves what the management calls Progressive American cuisine—it changes according to what is fresh and available on the market—and is open to the public. ♦ American ♦ Closed Su. 36 E 22nd St (Park Ave So-Broadway) 228.4399

58 Rascals ★$$ Featuring a simple but all-encompassing menu ranging from hamburgers to swordfish, this large restaurant also features dancing every night. ♦ American ♦ Closed Su. 12 E 22nd St (Park Ave So-Broadway) 420.1777

59 Stringfellows ★★$$ A well-designed Art Deco cocktail bar and restaurant. Disco dancing 11PM-4:30AM. ♦ American ♦ Closed M, Su. 35 E 21st St (Broadway) 254.2444

60 Calvary Church (1846, **James Renwick Jr.**) This Protestant Episcopal church by the architect of **St. Patrick's Cathedral** once had steeples that Renwick himself had removed in 1860 because, some critics said, they embarrassed him. If his exterior was less than perfect, he more than made up for it with the nave, which is exquisite. The Sunday school building on the uptown side, also a Renwick design, was added in 1867. The garden at the corner is lovingly tended and a welcome amenity. ♦ 273 Park Ave So (E 21st St)

61 Protestant Welfare Agencies Building (1894, **Robert W. Gibson** and **Edward J.N. Stent**) Originally the home of the Episcopal Church's missionary society. The sculpture over the entrance represents **St. Augustine** preaching to the barbarians in Britain, and the first Anglican bishop in the New World, **Samuel Seabury**, bringing Christianity to the native Americans. ♦ 281 Park Ave So (E 22nd St)

62 Umeda Learn to detect the subtleties of sake at this elegant bar. Fortunately, for novices, the menu offers a detailed explanation—origin, flavor, degree of dryness or sweetness—of more than 20 varieties of sake. ♦ 102 E 22nd St (Lexington-Park Aves) 505.1550

62 Russell Sage Foundation Building (1912, **Grosvenor Atterbury**) The foundation that set out to dispense $63 million for good works in 1906 did much of its own good work here before selling the building to Catholic Charities, who, in turn, sold it for development as apartments. ♦ 4 Lexington Ave (E 22nd St)

63 Gramercy Park Hotel $$ (1927, **Thompson & Churchill**) **Stanford White**'s last home, and a favorite of European travelers who fancy the relaxed Old World style and sensible prices. The choice rooms face the park (guests have access), which is ringed with historical landmarks and turn-of-the-century brownstones. Rooms vary in quality, so ask to see a few. ♦ 2 Lexington Ave (E 21st St) 475.4320, 800/221.4083; fax 505.0535

64 1 Lexington Avenue (1910, **Herbert Lucas**) The introduction of elevators and changed zoning laws allowed for bigger and better buildings, among them this apartment house. It replaced a mansion owned by **Cyrus W. Field**, who is remembered for connecting Europe and America by an underocean telegraph cable. The iron fence, designed by **Stanford White**, is all that is left of the original house. ♦ E 21st St

65 Rolf's Restaurant ★$$ Believe it or not, New York was once famous for its German restaurants. This is one of the few still operating. It

isn't a cavernous beer hall, but its walls and ceilings are covered with enough art, stained glass and wood carving to fill one. And the menu is just as good. Try the veal shank, shell steak or excellent potato pancakes. ♦ German ♦ 281 3rd Ave (E 22nd St) 473.8718

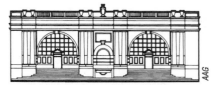

66 Public Baths, City of New York (1906, **Arnold W. Brunner** and **William Martin Aiken**) Right-thinking architects Brunner and Aiken finally used the overappropriated style of the Romans in its original manner—for baths (like *Caracalla*, or those of *Diocletian*). This pompous formal structure is now a public swimming pool open between Labor Day and the last day of school in June. ♦ E 23rd St at Asser Levy Pl (formerly Ave A)

67 School of Visual Arts Working professionals teach over 5500 students the fundamentals of illustration, photography, video, film, animation and other visual arts in buildings scattered throughout the neighborhood. Frequent exhibitions in the main building on 23rd St are open without charge. The luminary faculty includes **Milton Glaser, Eileen Hedy-Schultz, Ed Benguiat** and **Sal DeVito**. ♦ 209 E 23rd St (2nd-3rd Aves) 683.0600

68 H. Kauffman & Sons You can have your boots custom-made here, or choose from a huge selection of riding equipment that includes anything a horse or its owner could possibly need, even gifts for your horse-owning friends who think they have everything. ♦ 139 E 24th St (3rd-Lexington Aves) 684.6060

69 Samuel Weiser's Bookstore New and used New Age materials, including tarot cards, tapes, videos, crystals. ♦ 132 E 24th St (Lexington Ave-Park Ave So) 777.6363

69 Miller's Harness Company The flagship store of the largest supplier of riding apparel and equipment in the world has everything from derbies to chaps to videotapes on horsemanship. ♦ 117 E 24th St (Lexington Ave-Park Ave So) 673.1400

70 Live Bait $$ It's hard to tell who's better looking here, the staff or their pals who frequent this noisy hangout. They really pack them in after work, so be prepared to feel like a sardine as you down an oyster from a shot glass or a Corona straight from the bottle. The decor is like the inside of a fishing shack, and although a sign above the bar says, *If you want home cooking, stay home*, the cuisine is strictly Carolina homestyle. I like it—the waitresses are beautiful. ♦ Southeastern US ♦ 14 E 23rd St (Madison Ave) 353.2400

71 Metropolitan Life Insurance Company (main building 1893; tower 1909, **Napoleon LeBrun & Sons**; drastically altered 1961, **Lloyd Morgan**; north building at 24th St 1932, **Harvey Wiley Corbett** and **E. Everett Waid**) Before it was changed, the 700ft marble tower (adjacent to the main building) was decorated with 200 lion heads, ornamental columns and a copper roof. But its 4-sided clock, which at 26 1/2 feet is 4 1/2 feet taller than Big Ben, hasn't changed a bit in all those years. The north building, across 24th St, is surprisingly light for all its limestone mass. Note the sculptured quality of the polygonal setbacks, the vaulted entrances at each of the 4 corners and the Italian marble lobby. This block was the site of the Madison Square Presbyterian Church. Completed by **Stanford White** in 1906, it was his last, and many say his finest building. ♦ 1 Madison Ave (E 23rd-E 25th Sts)

72 Madison Square Even though this seems a quiet alcove in the midst of madness, imagine what it *was*—a swampy hunting ground, then a paupers' graveyard. The square dates from 1847, when it was a parade ground and only a small part of a proposed park that was laid out in the **Randell Plan** of 1811—the same plan that created the city's grid street pattern. Like other squares in this part of town, it was the focus of a fashionable residential district that flourished in pre-Civil War days. After the war, the fancy **Fifth Avenue Hotel**, the **Madison Square Theater** and the second home of **Madison Square Garden** all faced the square. This incarnation of the Garden will always be remembered because **Stanford White**, who designed the building, was shot and killed in its roof garden by **Harry Thaw**, the jealous husband who thought White was paying too much attention to his wife, **Evelyn Nesbit**. Today the square is ringed by heavy-duty public and commercial buildings, but manages to retain its air of quiet imperturbability. Stroll through and observe the statuary: *Chester A. Arthur* by **George Bissel**, 1898; *Admiral David Farragut* by **Augustus Saint-Gaudens**, 1880; *William H. Seward* by **Randolph Rogers**, 1876. Or find one of the private benches hidden along the square's fencing. ♦ E 23rd-E 26th Sts (Madison-5th Aves)

73 Fifth Avenue Building (1909, **Manyiche & Franke**) The center of America's wholesale toy business, which extends into several nearby buildings. Its 15 floors are a dreamland for children; who, alas, are not allowed to browse. But the lobby is open to the public and not to be missed. ♦ 200 5th Ave (E 23rd St)

74 Serbian Orthodox Cathedral of St. Sava (1855, **Richard Upjohn**) Originally a chapel connected with Trinity Church, it became a cathedral of the **Eastern Orthodox** faith in 1943. The beautiful altar and *reredos* inside are by **Frederick Clarke Withers**. The parish house was designed in 1860 by **Jacob Wrey Mould**. ♦ 15 W 25th St (Broadway-6th Ave)

75 M.K. ★$$$ This combination club/restaurant has the comfort of its clientele foremost in mind. After a dinner of say, pasta or grilled fish, wander onto any one of the 4 floors for a drink and conversation—the top floor has a library, pool table, a disco and vanity room. It's just like going to a fancy dinner party—except you have to settle a tab at the end of the evening. ♦ Continental ♦ Closed M-W, Su. 204 5th Ave (W 25th St) 779.1340

75 Worth Monument (1857, **James C. Batterson**) This richly ornamented obelisk in a plot separating Broadway and 5th Ave marks the grave of **Major General William Jenkins Worth**, for whom the street in Lower Manhattan and the city of Fort Worth TX, were named. After having fought the Seminoles in Florida, he went on to become a hero of the Mexican War in 1846. ♦ W 25th St at 5th Ave

New York City hosts the consulates or missions of 125 nations.

76 Ohashi Institute **Wataru Ohashi** believes it's our reaction to stress that causes physical, mental and emotional problems. With this in mind, he has developed a technique based on traditional *shiatsu* massage. After a session with the master himself, or with one of his superbly trained disciples, you'll feel both energized and at peace. ♦ Closed Su. 12 W 27th St (6th Ave-Broadway) 9th floor. 684.4190

77 50 Madison Avenue (1896, **Renwick, Aspinwall & Owen**) A perfectly harmonious adaptation of a Renaissance palace, this building was originally built as a home for the American Society for the Prevention of Cruelty to Animals. ♦ E 26th St

78 New York Life Insurance Company (1928, **Cass Gilbert**) A Gothic masterpiece by the architect of the Woolworth Building and New York's Federal Courthouse. The square tower topped by a gilded pyramid, a style Gilbert called *American Perpendicular*, is dramatically lighted at night. Its lobby is a panorama of detail, from polychromed coffered ceilings to bronze elevator doors, and ornate grills over the subway entrances. ♦ 45-55 Madison Ave (E 26th-E 27th Sts)

79 Appellate Division of the Supreme Court of the State of New York (1900, **James Brown Lord**) The busiest appellate court in the world, where 9 justices hear most appeals in civil and criminal cases arising in New York and surrounding counties. With few exceptions, their decisions are final. The building—murals, statuary and all—was finished at $5000 under budget with a final price tag of just under $644,000. It is one of the city's treasures. Stop in and be impressed. The building is open to the public weekdays, with access to the courtroom when the court is not sitting, from 9AM to 5PM. ♦ E 25th St at Madison Ave

80 69th Regiment Armory (1905, **Hunt & Hunt**) This is the armory of the infamous *Armory Show* that introduced Modern Art to New York in 1913—the most famous work in the show was **Marcel Duchamp**'s *Nude Descending a Staircase*. Note the gun bays overlooking Lexington Ave, and the expression on the Lexington Ave facade of the barrel-vaulted Drill Hall behind it. ♦ 68 Lexington Ave (E 25th-E 26th Sts)

Sido

81 Sido ★$$$ One of the best spots for Middle Eastern dishes. The menu lists all the standard fare and much that is unusual, including a very minty *tabouleh* salad and a spectacular dish of ground lamb baked in sesame sauce. The room is clean but unattractively kitsched up. In the evening, tables are often filled with expatriate Middle Easterners, and on Sunday, with their whole families. Take the house wine. Four kinds of halvah—plain, pistachio, almond and marble—are sold in the modestly stocked grocery store next door. ♦ Middle Eastern ♦ 84 Lexington Ave (E 26th St) Reservations recommended. 686.2031

82 La Colombe D'Or ★$$$ A small bistro that is always busy, with good reason. The food is well-prepared, the service efficient and the prices affordable. ♦ French ♦ Closed Su. 134 E 26th St (3rd-Lexington Aves) Reservations required. 689.0666

83 Per Bacco ★$$$ A well-established neighborhood restaurant with an extensive menu, friendly service and a relaxing setting. ♦ Ital-

Union Square/Gramercy/Murray Hill

ian ♦ Closed Su. 140 E 27th St (3rd-Lexington Aves) 532.8699

Little India, which runs up Lexington Ave from 24th to 30th Sts, is a center for Indian restaurants and specialty stores. You can buy a sari or a jar of hot mango chutney here, or you can relax in any of a dozen Indian and Pakistani restaurants that range from plain to fancy.

Restaurants/Nightlife: Red   **Hotels:** Blue
Shops/Parks: Green   **Sights/Culture:** Black

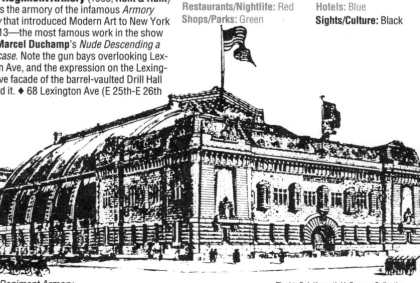

69th Regiment Armory

The Lt. Col. Kenneth H. Powers Collection

84 Bellevue Hospital Center (1939, **McKim, Mead & White**; additions 1974, **Katz, Weisman, Weber, Strauss; Joseph Blumenkranz; Pomerance & Brienes; Feld & Timoney**) Established in 1736, this municipal hospital cares for some 80,000 emergency cases per year. Its services are available to anyone, with no restrictions, including ability to pay. Bellevue was a pioneer in providing ambulance service, in performing appendectomies and Caesarean sections, and in the development of heart catheterization and microsurgery. For reasons unknown, it is often thought of as a solely psychiatric hospital. It began providing services for the mentally ill in 1939. ◆ E 26th-E 30th Sts (FDR Dr-1st Ave) 561.4141

85 Waterside (1974, **Davis, Brody & Associates**) There are 1600 apartments in these brown towers built on a platform over the East River. They are a world apart, reached by a footbridge across FDR Drive at E 25th St, or the riverfront esplanade from E 34th St. The river views here are spectacular. The complex overlooks a wide bay, the scene of Macy's annual 4th of July fireworks display. ◆ E 25th-E 30th Sts (East River-FDR Dr)

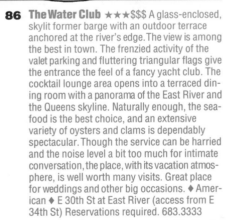

86 The Water Club ★★★$$$ A glass-enclosed, skylit former barge with an outdoor terrace anchored at the river's edge. The view is among the best in town. The frenzied activity of the valet parking and fluttering triangular flags give the entrance the feel of a fancy yacht club. The cocktail lounge area opens into a terraced dining room with a panorama of the East River and the Queens skyline. Naturally enough, the seafood is the best choice, and an extensive variety of oysters and clams is dependably spectacular. Though the service can be harried and the noise level a bit too much for intimate conversation, the place, with its vacation atmosphere, is well worth many visits. Great place for weddings and other big occasions. ◆ American ◆ E 30th St at East River (access from E 34th St) Reservations required. 683.3333

87 New York University/Bellevue Medical Center (1950, **Skidmore, Owings & Merrill**) A teaching hospital associated with NYU. ◆ E 30th-E 34th Sts (FDR Dr-1st Ave) 340.7300

88 Kips Bay Plaza (1960-1965, **I.M. Pei Associates** and **S.J. Kessler**) This pair of 21-story slabs facing an inner park were the first exposed concrete apartment houses in New York. The park is open only to the people who live in these apartments. ◆ E 30th-E 33rd Sts (1st-2nd Aves)

89 Marchi's ★$$$ Nothing much has changed since this restaurant opened in 1930. The menu is fixed, and the food keeps coming in a relentless procession, defying even the most indomitable diner to stagger through to the final stage of fruit, cookies and coffee. Prepare to spend the evening progressing through a meal that includes fish, meat, pasta, dessert and more—much, much more. Remember to tell your waiter, frequently, what a good time you are having. He will beam and bring some extra food. ◆ Italian ◆ Closed Su. 251 E 31st St (2nd-3rd Aves) Jacket required. 679.2494

90 Sumptuary Restaurant ★$$$ The word *sumptuary* actually has to do with regulating expenses, and the check here won't upset your budget. But *sumptuous* is a better word for this lavish setting and its creative menu, which is sometimes called California. There is a charming garden on the ground floor. ◆ American ◆ 400 3rd Ave (E 28th-E 29th Sts) 889.6056

91 Les Halles ★$$ The owners of **Park Bistro** set out to re-create the nameless hangouts that once surrounded the great wholesale food market in Paris, and succeeded quite well. Enter the dining room through the butcher shop and enjoy onion soup, garlicky sausage, steak with *pommes frites* or cassoulet. Expect to wait for your table—along with advertising and publishing execs who work nearby. ◆ French ◆ 411 Park Ave So (E 28th-E 29th Sts) 679.4111

92 Park Bistro ★★$$ Black-and-white photos of 1950s Paris line the walls in this friendly, French-style bistro. Chef **Jean-Michel Diot**'s specialties include a warm potato salad topped with goat cheese and served with a small green salad, fresh codfish with onion sauce and fried leeks and a scrumptious chocolate tart. ◆ French ◆ 414 Park Ave So (E 29th St) 689.1360

93 Martha Washington $ One of the last remaining women-only hotels in the city has an informal homelike atmosphere and a dining room. Rooms are small and not all have private baths, but they are cheerfully decorated and some have kitchenettes. Special rates for long-term stays. ◆ 30 E 30th St (Park Ave So-Madison Ave) 689.1900

94 Church of the Transfiguration, The Little Church Around the Corner (1849; Guild Hall, rectory and church 1861; Lich Gate 1896, **Frederick Clarke Withers**) When the actor **George Holland** died in 1870, a friend went to a nearby church to arrange for the funeral. *We don't accept actors here,* he was told, *but there's a little church around the corner that will.* They did, and the **Protestant Episcopal Church of the Transfiguration** got both a new name, and a new reputation among actors, some of whom, including **Edwin Booth, Gertrude Lawrence** and **Richard Mansfield**, are memorialized among the wealth of stained glass and other artifacts inside. During WWI and in the years following, it was the scene of more wedding ceremonies than any other church in the world. ◆ 1 E 29th St (Madison-5th Aves)

95 Marble Collegiate Church (1854, **Samuel A. Warner**) This Gothic Revival church is unchanged in any way from the day it was built. The clock is still wound by hand every 8 days, and the cane racks behind the pews are still waiting to receive your walking stick. It is a Dutch Reform church (the oldest denomination in the city) established here by **Peter Minuit** in 1628, and has served under the flags of Holland, England and the US. The most famous minister to use its pulpit is **Dr. Norman Vincent Peale**, author of *The Power of Positive Thinking*. ♦ 272 5th Ave (W 29th St)

96 The Olde Garden $$ Here's where you can still get the kind of food we ate before the gourmets took over—shrimp cocktail and fruit cup, veal cutlet Parmesan and hot turkey sandwiches. Before the restaurant was established in 1912, it was a stable, then an antique shop. ♦ American ♦ Closed Su. 15 W 29th St (5th-6th Aves) 532.8323

97 Grolier Once an exclusive hideaway for the bibliophiles of the Grolier Club, then a private home, this turn-of-the-century landmark building is now home to an elegant supper and nightclub. Although it bills itself as a private club—among the members are a fair share of Europeans, models and financial types—nonmembers are admitted (although they do have to pay an entrance fee) and can even make reservations. ♦ Closed Su. 29 E 32nd St (5th-Madison Aves) 679.2932

98 Kyoto Book Center One of several bookstores in the neighborhood serving the Korean community. Here, they also sell cosmetics. ♦ Closed Su. 22 W 32nd St (5th Ave-Broadway) 465.0923

99 M. Steuer Hosiery Co. A great source for discounted fitness attire—leotards and leggings by **Marika, Baryshnikov** and **Capezio**—hosiery and lingerie. ♦ Closed Su. 31 W 32nd St (5th Ave-Broadway) 563.0052

99 Stanford $ A small, newly renovated hotel that is convenient to Madison Square Garden and shopping. Color TV in each room. Limo service to the airports. ♦ 43 W 32nd St (5th-6th Aves) 563.1480

100 Greeley Square Alexander Doyle's statue of **Horace Greeley**, founder of the *New York Tribune*, was donated by members of the newspaper unions—which says something about Greeley's management style. The area around the square offers the best buys in cameras and related merchandise of any neighborhood north of the Caribbean. The building across 6th Ave, which will someday be the home of the Abraham & Straus department store, is where Gimbels kept its secrets safe from Macy's, which is only a block away on Herald Square. ♦ W 32nd-W 33rd Sts (6th Ave-Broadway)

101 The Empire State Building (1931, **Shreve, Lamb & Harmon Associates**) Yes, Virginia, this is the once-upon-a-time World's Tallest Building (if you count the twin towers of the World Trade Center as 2, it now ranks 4th), famous in fact and fiction, icon of New

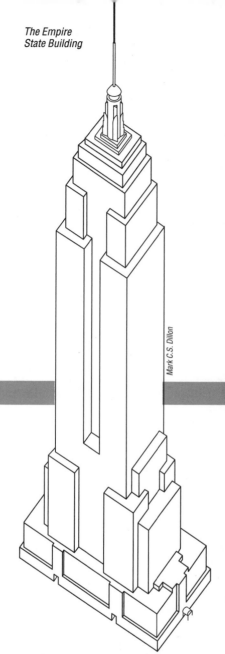

The Empire State Building

Mark C.S. Dillon

York City and the place from which to study the city first. It is an impressive collection of statistics: 1250ft to the top of the (unsuccessful) dirigible mooring mast, 102 floors, 1860 steps, 73 elevators, 60 miles of water pipes, 5 acres of windows, 365,000 tons of material—and it was under construction for only 19 months. Built during the Depression, it was known for many years as the *Empty State Building,* and the owners relied on income from the Observation Deck to pay their taxes. Oh yes, on a good day you can see for at least 50 miles.

The architects must be lauded for the way in which they handled the immense and potentially oppressive bulk of this building. The tower is balanced, set back from the street on a 5-story (street-scale) base. The subtly modulated shaft rises at a distance, terminating in a conservatively geometric crown. The limestone and granite cladding, with its steel mullions and flush windows, is restrained, with just a soupçon of an Art Deco air (compared to the exuberant ornamentalism of the Chrysler Building, for example). This is *dignity*. Belying the fears of the general public, the tower has not yet cracked or toppled, although it does sway quite a bit in high winds, and only once has a plane crashed into it (in 1945 a bomber broadsided the 79th floor). There have been a few suicides and a lot of birds have been knocked out of the sky during their migrating season.

The site, too, has a lively history. Between 1857 and 1893 it was the address of a pair of mansions belonging to members of the **Astor** family and the center of New York social life. In the early '90s a feud erupted, and **William Waldorf Astor**, who had the house on 33rd St, moved to Europe and replaced the house with a hotel—the Waldorf. His aunt across the garden, **Mrs. William Astor**, moved within the year, and had a connecting hotel completed by

Union Square/Gramercy/Murray Hill

1897. The **Waldorf** and **Astoria Hotels** immediately became a social center and operated as one hotel for many years, under the agreement that Mrs. Astor could have all connections between them closed off at any time. When the original structures were demolished in 1929, the Waldorf-Astoria moved uptown to Park Ave. ♦ 350 5th Ave (W 34th St)

Within the Empire State Building:

Empire State Observatories There is an open platform on all 4 sides of the 86th floor, well protected with heavy mesh and metal bars. A few steps above it is a glass-enclosed area with food service and a souvenir shop. An elevator takes you higher to the all-enclosed 102nd-floor lookout, where the view, amazingly, is slightly different. Tickets are available on the concourse, 1 level below the street. ♦ Admission. Daily 9:30AM-midnight. Enter on W 34th St. 736.3100 ext 55

Guinness World Records Exhibit Hall
Exhibitions, dioramas, videotapes, replicas and photographs document the achievements of humankind that possibly wouldn't have happened if there were no book called *The Guinness Book of World Records*. But achievements they are nonetheless, and this is their hall of fame. ♦ Admission. Daily 9AM-9PM. Concourse level. 947.2335

102 D. Sokolin Highly touted selection of wines and spirits. ♦ Closed Su. 178 Madison Ave (E 33rd St) 532.5893

103 Caffe Alpino $$$ Respectable Italian-American fare. Best for a bowl of steamed mussels and a plate of Southern Italian-style spaghetti. ♦ Italian ♦ Closed Su. 179 Madison Ave (E 33rd St) Reservations required. 684.1757

104 Complete Traveller Bookstore A small store with an amazingly large selection of books—including the full line of **ACCESS**® guides—enough to satisfy even the most jaded traveler. *An RSW recommendation.* ♦ 199 Madison Ave (E 35th St) 679.4339

105 Church of The Incarnation Episcopal (1864, **Emlen T. Littel**) A modest church that seems to be trying to hide the fact that it contains windows by **Louis Comfort Tiffany** and **John La Farge**, sculpture by **Daniel Chester French** and **Augustus Saint-Gaudens**, and a Gothic-style monument designed by **Henry Hobson Richardson**. Fortunately, the church provides a folder for a self-guided tour. ♦ 205 Madison Ave (E 35th St) 689.6350

106 Dolci On Park Caffe ★★$$ You can get a full meal here, but the best part is the desserts. Enjoy them, along with a cup of espresso, at one of the sidewalk tables. ♦ Italian ♦ Closed Su. 12 Park Ave (E 34th-E 35th Sts) 686.4331

107 2 Park Avenue (1927, **Ely Jacques Kahn**; **Leon Solon**, color consultant) A better-than-average office building that is particularly stunning at the top, where the basic structural pattern gives way to some jazzy, colorful Art Deco tile. ♦ E 32nd-E 33rd Sts

An American Place

107 An American Place ★★★$$$ Larry Forgione, the *wunderkind* of New American cooking, gives this cheery brasserie-style place culinary ooomph with a menu chock-full of homey, New Wave American dishes. I recommend the 3-fish terrine, roasted duck in cornmeal pancakes, and bread pudding with bourbon sauce. ♦ American ♦ Closed Su. 2 Park Ave (E 32nd-E 33rd Sts) 684.2122

108 1 Park Avenue (1925, **York & Sawyer**) When 4th Ave below 34th St had its designation upgraded to Park Ave South, this and 2 Park Ave across the street kept their original addresses. This site wasn't that upscale. In the previous century, it was the location of Peter Cooper's glue factory and later of barns for the livestock and horsecars of the New York and Harlem Railroad. ♦ E 32nd-E 33rd Sts

Getting to the top is the literal object of the annual *Empire State Building Run Up*, a marathon race of unusual proportions. Entrants must negotiate the building's 1575 steps. People from around the globe enter the event, held each February. Average winning time is 12 to 14 minutes, with winners and losers alike earning a splendid view from the 86th floor and an elevator ride down.

109 3 Park Avenue (1976, **Shreve, Lamb & Harmon Associates**) No. 3 Park Ave is a brick tower turned diagonally against its companions and the city. Compare this straight-up tower and its stylized mansard roof with the careful, soaring composition of the Empire State Building 2 blocks away—they were designed by the same firm. A plaque on the terrace wall at 33rd St marks this as the site of the **71st Regiment Armory** (1905, **Clinton & Russell**). ◆ E 33rd-E 34th Sts

110 Dumont Plaza Hotel $$$ Studios and 1- and 2-bedroom suites, each with its own kitchen. ◆ 150 E 34th St (3rd-Lexington Aves) 481.7600, 800/ME-SUITE; fax 889.8856

111 Astro Minerals Ltd. A collection of minerals and gems from 47 countries, ranging from amethyst crystals to zircons. A paradise for collectors, this is also a good source of fine jewelry at low prices. ◆ 155 E 34th St (3rd-Lexington Aves) 889.9000

112 Nicola Paone ★$$$$ The serious and traditional Northern Italian menu is enlivened by some imaginative offerings. Service is courtly and unusually helpful. The restaurant also has an enviable wine cellar—but only if you ask will you receive. You may have first heard of this restaurant on the radio—Paone does his own *singing* commercials—a tape is available for fans. ◆ Italian ◆ Closed Su. 207 E 34th St (2nd-3rd Aves) 889.3239

113 St. Vartan Cathedral (1967, **Steinman & Cain**) The cathedral of the Armenian Orthodox Church in America, with a Romanesque design inspired by churches in Asia Minor. ◆ 2nd Ave (E 34th-E 35th Sts)

114 El Parador ★★$$ Opened long before the current craze for Mexican food, it has remained popular with those who really know Mexican food as well as those who come just to have a good time. Expect to wait at the bar with a margarita so potent it will take the edge off any fidgeting or hunger pangs. Once you are seated, the wait will have been worthwhile. The host has a knack for making you feel like the most important person in his life. After a second margarita, you will believe him. ◆ Mexican ◆ 325 E 34th St (1st-2nd Aves) 679.6812

115 Island Helicopter Sightseeing A choice of 4 aerial tours of the city. ◆ Flights daily 9AM-6PM, Jan-Mar; 9AM-9PM, Apr-Dec. E 34th St at East River. 683.4575

116 Quark Gadgets galore from Swiss army knives, folding bicycles and talking translators to video camera tie clips and proton televisions. ◆ 537 3rd Avenue (E 35th St) 889.1808

117 Sniffen Court (ca 1850–60) This charming and unusually well-preserved mews of 10 carriage houses was built around the time of the Civil War and was designated a Historic District in 1966. ◆ 150-158 E 36th St (3rd-Lexington Aves)

118 Shelburne Murray Hill $$$ An all-suite hotel with kitchens. ◆ 303 Lexington Ave (E 37th St) 689.5200, 800/ME-SUITE; fax 779.7068

119 Doral Court Hotel $$$ Quiet, sunny rooms, an enthusiastic staff, a nearby fitness center (or have a bike brought to your room), and kitchenettes available upon request. **The Courtyard Cafe and Bar** is always a pleasure. A great bargain. ◆ 130 E 39th St (Lexington-Park Aves) 685.1100, 800/624.0607; fax 889.0287

119 Doral Tuscany Hotel $$$ The refrigerators in the rooms here are stocked with refreshments, and if you run out, room service will replenish them. Leave your shoes outside your door at night and they'll be shined by morning. And when you rise and shine, you can visit the hotel's squash club and sports training institute. ◆ 120 E 39th St (Lexington-Park Aves) 686.1600, 800/847.4078; fax 779.7822

Within the Doral Tuscany Hotel:

Time and Again $$ An extremely comfortable setting for a weekend breakfast or quiet

Union Square/Gramercy/Murray Hill

dinner. If you're in the mood for game, order the pheasant tureen. ◆ American/French ◆ 116 E 39th St (Park-Lexington Aves) 685.8887

120 Rossini's $$ A casual restaurant with a friendly setting. Hot antipasto is a specialty. Strolling tableside guitarists serenade diners nightly; an opera trio performs on Friday and Saturday. ◆ Italian ◆ Closed Su. 108 E 38th St (Lexington-Park Aves) Reservations required. 683.0135

120 Church of Our Savior (1959, **Paul C. Reilly**) This perfect example of Romanesque Gothic architecture was built at a time when architects were tossing off glass boxes with the excuse that there were no craftsmen left to do this kind of work. The interior of this Roman Catholic church proves there must have been at least a few in New York in the '50s. ◆ 59 Park Ave (E 38th St)

121 Sheraton Park Avenue $$$ Originally called the Russell, after **Judge Horace Russell**, who once had a home on this site. An oak-paneled lobby with book-lined shelves, spacious rooms—some with fireplaces—decorated with antiques, and the always attentive service make it seem like a private club or country home. An intimate bar, where a dramatic confrontation scene between **Paul Newman** and **Charlotte Rampling** was filmed for *The Verdict*, looks like all the movie's mellow Boston locales. ◆ 45 Park Ave (E 37th St) 685.7676, 800/325.3535; fax 889.3193

Restaurants/Nightlife: Red   **Hotels:** Blue
Shops/Parks: Green   **Sights/Culture:** Black

Within the Sheraton Park Avenue:

Judge's Chamber A wood-paneled cocktail lounge that features live jazz. ♦ 685.7676

122 Hotel Kitano $$$ A small hotel very popular with Japanese visitors, though the staff is also fluent in Chinese, Korean and Spanish. The lobby and guest rooms are American-style, except for a few authentic tatami suites with bedrolls and *furos* (hot tubs). The restaurant features one of the few Japanese breakfasts in Manhattan. ♦ 66 Park Ave (E 38th St) 685.0022; fax 532.5615

Within the Hotel Kitano:

Hakubai Restaurant ★★$$$ This is the only restaurant in town where you can get a traditional Japanese breakfast: a lacquer box holding cold noodles, smoked salmon, rice, salad and miso soup. At lunch, it fills up quickly with the publishing types who work in the area. The specialty here is *udon*—white noodles with vegetables and fish. ♦ 2nd floor. 686.3770

Union Square/Gramercy/Murray Hill

Doral ▥ Park Avenue

123 Doral Park Avenue Hotel $$$ An old-world-style hotel with modern touches, including access to a fitness center up the street on Park Ave. The rooms are well furnished, the atmosphere gracious and traditional. ♦ 70 Park Ave (E 38th St) 687.7050, 800/847.4135; fax 808.9029

Within the Doral Park Avenue Hotel:

Saturnia Restaurant ★$$$ A restaurant with a warm candlelit atmosphere. In season, it extends out to a sidewalk cafe. ♦ American ♦ 687.7050

124 Madison Towers Hotel $$ Completely modernized, this comfortable hotel has more than 200 rooms and meeting facilities. A small fee gives guests access to a sauna, health club and gym. Ask for a view of the Empire State Building. ♦ 22 E 38th St (Madison Ave) 685.3700, 800/225.4340; fax 689.0290

Within the Madison Towers Hotel:

The Whaler Bar High-beamed ceilings and a huge working fireplace make this a favorite midtown meeting place. Entertainment nightly. ♦ American ♦ 685.3700

To celebrate **King Kong**'s 50th birthday in 1981, a gigantic ape-shaped balloon was hung from the **Observatory** at the **Empire State Building**. The balloon version was approximately 80ft tall; the real King Kong measured only 18 inches.

MORGANS

125 Morgans $$$ A trendy hotel run by former discothèque owner **Ian Schrager** (who also refurbished the **Royalton** and, most recently, the **Paramount**), with rooms and furnishings created by designer **André Putman**. The hotel prides itself on getting you whatever you may want—if the urge for sushi strikes at midnight, no problem. All rooms have VCRs, stereos, blackout shades on the windows, refrigerators, and phones in the bed- and bathrooms. ♦ 237 Madison Ave (E 37th-E 38th Sts) 686.0300, 800/334.3408; fax 779.8352

126 Consulate General of The Polish People (1905, **C.P.H. Gilbet**) This opulent mansion was built for a Dutch sea captain. The equally decorative interiors are largely intact. ♦ 233 Madison Ave (E 37th St)

126 231 Madison Avenue (1852) This 45-room freestanding brownstone mansion, built for banker **Anson Phelps Stokes**, was bought by **J.P. Morgan** for his son in 1904. In 1944, it became the property of the Evangelical Lutheran Church, which is responsible for the sacrilegious brick addition on the 37th St side. It is being restored for incorporation into the **Morgan Library**. ♦ E 37th St

McKim, Mead & White

127 The Pierpont Morgan Library (1906, **C.F. McKim** of **McKim, Mead & White**; annex 1928, **Benjamin Wistar Morris**) J.P. Morgan began collecting books, manuscripts and drawings in earnest in 1890, and eventually had to construct this magnificent small palazzo to house his treasures. The building itself is a treasure, and the annex on the Madison Ave side complements it perfectly. Inside, the library and Morgan's office have been preserved exactly as they were when the financier died in 1913. The collection includes more than 1000 illuminated Medieval and Renaissance manuscripts, the finest in America. It also contains the country's best examples of fine bookbinding, from **Gutenberg** to modern times. And its collection of autographed manuscripts, both literary and musical, is considered one of the best in the world. Art historian **Kenneth Clark** summed it all up perfectly when he said: *...every object is a treasure, every item is perfect*. On your way out, visit the bookshop, where you'll find wonderful books, toys and cards. *An RSW must.* ♦ Voluntary contribution. Tu-Sa 10:30AM-5PM; Su 1-5PM. 29 E 36th St (Park-Madison Aves) 685.0610

Restaurants/Nightlife: Red	Hotels: Blue
Shops/Parks: Green	Sights/Culture: Black

128 Yarn Connection Phildar, Classic Elite, Filatura di Crosa plus the only NYC source of yarn from the Green Mountain Spinnery in Vermont and Twitchell in New Hampshire. There's always a cardboard box of odds-and-ends and great deals to dig through. Reasonably priced beginner to advanced classes. Yarn on cones for weavers and machine knitters is available next door at **Aberdeen**.
♦ Closed Su. 6 E 37th St (5th-Madison Aves) 684.5099

129 Goldberg's Marine Distributors Most of the stores on this block sell trimmings and ribbons, but if you need a stout coil of rope, Goldberg's has it. New York is America's biggest seaport, but it still comes as a surprise to find a place selling anchors, depth-finders, fishing equipment (including the tournament reels that are so much more expensive in Europe) and other gear for yacht enthusiasts and sailors. It is a perfect store for the shoes and foul-weather clothes and other outfits you need if you want to look like you belong to the yacht club set. ♦ Closed Su. 12 W 37th St (5th-6th Aves) 594.6065

Each John Doe burial in Potter's Field (on the Long Island Sound) costs New York City $300.

130 Lord & Taylor (1914, **Starrett & Van Vleck**) This store has made a specialty of stocking clothing by American designers, but it goes beyond fashion in its furniture and antiques departments, featuring sofas from **Henredon**, Chinese porcelain lamps, and reproductions of Louis XV tables. There is an occasional flash of innovation, particularly in avant-garde designs of the '30s and '40s by **Eileen Gray**. Its shoe department is legendary, as is the caring quality of its sales help, quite a rarity these days. Lord & Taylor is also justly famous for its annual Christmas window displays, without which the holidays in New York wouldn't be the same. The store was the first in the history of retailing to devote its window displays to anything but merchandise during the holiday season. The custom began during the unusually warm December of 1905 when customers didn't seem to feel Christmasy. Lord & Taylor got them into the proper mood by filling its windows with a snowstorm the likes of which New Yorkers hadn't seen since the *Blizzard of '88*. If you arrive 15 minutes before the store opens in the morning, Lord & Taylor provides seating, free coffee (there are also 3 restaurants within the store) and music just inside the front door.
♦ 424 5th Ave (W 38th-W 39th Sts) 391.3344

My No ★ Restaurants by George Lang

It is no secret that I spend quite a bit of my time thumbing my nose at the ever-growing crowd of pretentious foodies, ambitious chefs and tiresome critics.

You could say that I have given them some of the best jeers of my professional life.

The following is a mini-list of gastronomic outrages that irk me, and portions of prejudices I savor dearly.

I am tired of...

Restaurants so expensive that only tycoons with unlisted telephone companies can eat there.

Trendy places where the service is so slow that the chances are management may change between courses.

A wine list that is so recherché that the chardonnay comes from South Dakota and the sparkling wine from the shores of the Kashmiri lakes.

Menus, the size of a Japanese screen, that list as many items as a concise encyclopedia and tell more than I want to know about my prospective dinner: the number of rare fruit vinegars used in the salad, the temperature of the salade composé and the precise location where the lamb grazed during its short life.

Restaurants where the pepper mill is huge, the wine glasses are tiny, and the plates are so overheated that they'll cremate the sauce.

Dinner companions who are unable to choose between the frog legs carpaccio and the ravioli stuffed with plum-marinated plover brains—and agonize over the choice like a tragic Greek heroine faced with the choice of saving her spouse or her son.

Winecompoops who gargle with the finest Burgundies as if they were morning mouthwash.

Trendy chefs who invent garnishes that look like oddments in a long-forgotten drawer, invariably arranged in a kaleidoscopic, painfully symmetrical manner. (Didn't their mothers tell them not to play with their food?)

Personality chef-restaurateurs who give narcissism a bad name.

French-Japanese, Caribbean-Laotian-kosher and Mexican-Irish restaurants where the fodder creates traffic hazards for your palate.

Fish so undercooked that the waiter must have merely carried it through a hot kitchen.

Palate-teasing *degustation* dinners, which leave me so hungry with their minuscule portions that I would gladly continue with a plate of Surf & Turf.

High-action yuppeterias where the designers approximate the sound of a Balkan auction house by using as many hard surfaces as they can get their hands on.

Restaurant critics (bless their hearts, or whatever they carry around in their rib cages)—especially those who don't notice and judge *mother-love* foods (bread, butter, salad, coffee) and the quality of bar drinks (brands used, is the juice fresh?) and the rhythm of service, air circulation and housekeeping—and who don't report the cumulative effect of small pleasures that make me want to return.

Critics who act like prosecuting attorneys for whom the restaurateur is guilty until proved innocent.

And, finally, restaurant reviewers who write like someone trying to define the Taj Mahal by placing every square inch of its stones under a microscope.

Chelsea

Named for the estate **Captain Thomas Clarke** acquired in 1750, **Chelsea** was then bounded by **14th** and **25th Sts**, **8th Ave** and the **Hudson River**. Today, the area called Chelsea goes north to **34th St** and east to **6th Ave**, and is quite a mixed bag. **Clement Clarke Moore**, who had inherited his grandfather's land—and is best known as the author of the poem *A Visit from St. Nicholas*—laid out building lots in 1830 and at the time donated land to the **General Theological Seminary**. The surrounding area was a flourishing middle-class suburb that never quite made it as a desirable address. When the Hudson River Railroad opened on 11th Ave in 1851, it attracted breweries and slaughterhouses and the shanties and tenements of their workers. In the 1870s, those townhouse blocks that were left were invaded by the city's

first elevated railroad on 9th Ave.

Chelsea's decline continued, brightened briefly by a flurry of theatrical activity on 23rd St. But soon the theater world moved uptown, leaving behind the artists and writers (who eventually departed for the newer Bohemia in Greenwich Village).

The funky **Hotel Chelsea**, on 23rd St, was the focus of the theatrical and arts territory. In the '60s, Andy Warhol's superstars **Viva** and **Edie Sedgewick** lived there, and his film *Chelsea Girls* documented another chapter in the life of the old survivor.

The country's motion picture industry started in Chelsea in 1905, and for a decade flourished in the old lofts and theaters used for studios. **Adolph Zukor's Famous Players Studio**, which included **Mary Pickford** and **John Barrymore**, produced films here. But the **Astoria Studios** in Queens built a better facility, and eventually balmy Hollywood beckoned. The film business moved on.

In the 1930s, new industry found the area near the piers. The 11th Ave railroad was replaced by a less objectionable elevated, and the 9th Ave line shut down. The clean sweep of '50s and '60s urban renewal replaced slum housing with housing projects, and

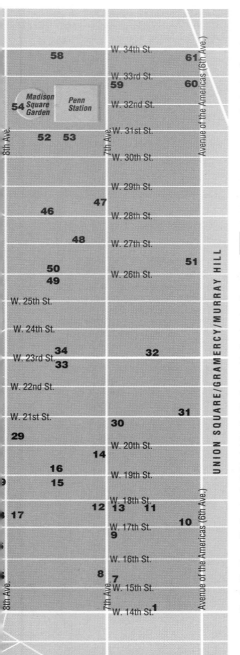

Chelsea

rehabilitation was started on desirable Federal and Greek Revival townhouses. Today Chelsea is a pastiche of these townhouses, housing projects, industrial buildings, tenements, secondhand office furniture stores and a remarkable number of churches.

As the gentry pursued their determined course uptown, so did fashionable stores. By the 1870s, 23rd St blossomed, and the blocks between 8th St and 23rd St were known as the *Ladies' Mile*. During the latter part of the century, giant dry goods stores of limestone and cast-iron lined 6th Ave (now Ave of the Americas) and Broadway. Many of the buildings that still stand, reminders of past retail glories, are used as loft and office space. By the early part of the 1900s, the fashion action had moved to 34th St, and by the '30s, 23rd St was a forgotten has-been.

Today the most interesting shops in Chelsea are those selling antiques on

9th Ave between 20th and 22nd Sts and the **Flower District** on the blocks between 27th and 30th Sts on Ave of the Americas. Daisies and orchids, rare palms and exotic bonsai overflow the wholesale and retail stores that supply the city with cut flowers and plants.

1 New York State Armory (1971, **Charles S. Kawecki**) The 42nd Infantry Division of the **New York National Guard** uses this building, obviously designed to make its members feel warlike, as its headquarters. ♦ 125 W 14th St (6th-7th Aves)

2 319 West 14th Street A 20-year-old **Orson Welles** and his first wife, **Virginia Nicholson**, lived in a basement apartment here between 1935 and 1937, during which time he directed the famous all-black *Macbeth* for Harlem's Negro Theater. The couple's next move was to a country house on the Hudson River. ♦ 8th-9th Aves

3 Old Homestead ★$$$ This is the oldest steakhouse in Manhattan, but the interior has been so gussied up that it seems to belong in the suburbs. They must be doing something right to have lasted all these years. The portions are large and the quality good. At the shop next door, fresh cuts of beef are for sale—1½in thick steaks—sauces and a variety of gourmet items, including the crème de la crème of chocolates—Valrhona from France and D'Orsay from Belgium. ♦ American ♦ 56 9th Ave (W 14th St) Reservations recommended. 242.9040

Chelsea

4 Basior-Schwartz Behind the beef carcasses hanging over the sidewalk is a shop selling gourmet foods to hotels, restaurants and the bargain-hungry public. ♦ 421 W 14th St (9th-10th Aves)

Frank's

4 Frank's ★★$$$ Frank's daytime clientele are the guys who work in the wholesale meat district, and they're hard to fool with anything less than the best steaks and chops in a plain wrapper. A find. ♦ American ♦ Closed Su. 431 W 14th St (9th-10th Aves) 243.1349

5 Port of New York Authority Commerce Building/Union Inland Terminal No. 1 (1932, **Abbott, Merckt & Co.**) The organization now known as the Port Authority of New York and New Jersey had its headquarters in this blockbuster before moving down to the World Trade Center. The top floors were designed for manufacturing, but the elevators can carry a 20-ton truck to any floor. ♦ 111 8th Ave (W 15th-W 16th Sts)

The New York World printed the first crossword puzzle in 1913. The first comic strip serial, The Yellow Kid, ran in an 1896 New York Journal.

6 Cajun $$ The honky-tonk atmosphere and live Dixieland music are fun on occasion; the hearty helpings of Creole-Cajun food generally provide good eating. ♦ Creole/Cajun ♦ 129 8th Ave (W 16th St) Reservations recommended for 5 or more. 691.6174

6 Miss Ruby's ★$$ The menu says they feature American eclectic cooking. If you've never heard the term, it's because not many restaurants are this ambitious. The bill of fare changes every month to reflect specialties of different regions of the US, though it might be better if they were to perfect one region and settle down like other folks. ♦ American ♦ 135 8th Ave (W 16th-W 17th Sts) 620.4055

7 Jensen-Lewis Two floors of creative, colorful merchandise (even bean-bag chairs), from sofas and beds to lamps and luggage. Especially known for the selection of director's chairs. ♦ 89 7th Ave (W 15th St) 929.4880

8 Blue Hen ★$$ A neighborhood favorite serving simple American food. Good choices are spicy cornmeal fried with goat cheese, chicken with dumplings and a rich seafood salad. ♦ American ♦ 78 7th Ave (W 15th-W 16th Sts) 645.3015

BARNEYS NEW YORK

9 Barneys New York A New York original. Name a famous designer for either men or women, and the nice person at the front desk will direct you to that designer's best work, from shoes to hats with every stop between. You can buy antiques, leather goods, jewelry, lingerie or children's clothes. Downstairs, you can get your hair cut (at **Roger Thompson**) and enjoy a fancy lunch, or cappuccino, surrounded by opulence. Barneys first opened here as a discount store for men and boys. But a 1986 expansion, especially the controversial annexation and modernization of townhouses behind the original store, has changed its character completely. A smaller, men's-only branch is at 225 Liberty St (2 World Financial Center) 945.1600. ♦ 7th Ave at W 17th St. 929.9000

10 da Umberto ★★$$$ This casual and restful trattoria concentrates on Tuscan dishes, especially wild game (hare, pheasant, venison). Ask to be seated in the skylit back room. ♦ Italian ♦ Closed Su. 107 W 17th St (6th-7th Aves) Reservations required. 989.0303

11 Two Worlds Gallery Direct importers of antiques and unique decorative objects. Paintings and custom artwork from well-known artists. ◆ M-Sa 10AM-6PM. 122 W 18th St (6th-7th Aves) 633.1668. Also at: 39 E 20th St. 473.9155

11 Movie Star News Millions of head shots, stills, lobby cards and press kits fill the filing cabinets in this garage space run by **Paula Klaw** and her family. They also stock movie posters and books on theater and film. A popular source for collectors, newspapers, magazines and television. ◆ Closed Su. 134 W 18th St (6th-7th Aves) 620.8160

11 Claiborne Gallery Leslie Cozart specializes in Mexican furniture, mostly from the 19th century, plus a line of iron furniture designed by her father, **Omer Claiborne.** ◆ Closed Su. 136 W 18th St (6th-7th Aves) 727.7219

11 Poster America Gallery The selection of vintage posters from 1870-1950, mostly original lithographs from Europe and the US, is among the best you'll find on either side of the Atlantic. In the 1880s, this space was used as a stable and a carriage house by the department stores along Ladies' Mile. ◆ Closed M. 138 W 18th St (6th-7th Aves) 206.0499

12 Citykids An eager, attentive staff helps you find what you need. Many of the clothes are designed just for this store. ◆ Closed Su. 130 7th Ave (W 17th-W 18th Sts) 620.0906

12 Books of Wonder If there are no children in your life, Books of Wonder will make you wish there were—or at least fondly remember when you were a child yourself. Authors and illustrators make frequent appearances here to read from their books and to sign your copies. These and other special events are described in the store's monthly newsletter. The Hudson St branch has a story hour on alternate Sundays. ◆ 132 7th Ave (W 18th St) 989.3270. Also at: 464 Hudson St. 645.8006

13 Le Madri ★★★$$$ Illustrious crowds flock to **Pino Luongo**'s tranquil restaurant, where a rotating cast of Italian women (*the mothers*) turns out specialties that remind you of grandma. I always order roasted vegetables for the whole table. You'll want to return again and again. ◆ Italian ◆ 168 W 18th St (7th Ave) Reservations required. 727.8022

14 Claire ★$$ Though often flawed by the intensity of the noise, this is a consistently reliable, reasonably priced seafood restaurant that will make you think you have just come in from a sunny Florida beach—the inventive decor is by set designer **Robin Wagner** (*Dream Girls*, *A Chorus Line*). The sometimes fierce and often intricate flavors are devised by its Thai chef. The choice of accompaniments is limited to one—white rice. There is usually only one vegetable to select as well. This lets the guests concentrate on the fish and shellfish. Try some key lime pie for dessert. ◆ Seafood ◆ 156 7th Ave (W 19th-W 20th Sts) 255.1955

15 The Billiard Club $ The lush Victorian decor of this vast (33 tables!) billiard emporium suggests formality, but fun (as in *good, clean*—no alcohol served) is your cue here. The light menu of sandwiches, salads and desserts can be enjoyed at small tables interspersed among the playing tables. The weekday lunch special includes nourishment for 2 and the use of a pool table for an hour. Call for reservations, fee schedule and party information. ◆ 220 W 19th St (7th-8th Aves) 206.POOL

16 Bessie Shonberg Theater Operated by **Dance Theater Workshop,** this theater (named after a dancer, choreographer and teacher) is one of the most active dance, mime and poetry houses in the city and offers young performing artists a variety of support services. Famous clown/dancer/mime **Bill Irwin** has often played here. DTW also runs the picture gallery in the lobby of the theater.

◆ Seats 160. 219 W 19th St (7th-8th Aves) 2nd floor. 924.0077

17 Cola's $ You must bring your own wine to accompany Cola's casual mix of Northern and Southern Italian cuisine, but hand-painted, antiqued walls lend a gentle ambience to the room, where a lively downtown crowd comes to take on the pasta. ◆ Italian ◆ 148 8th Ave (W 17th-W 18th Sts) No credit cards. 633.8020

17 Gascogne ★★$$ The restaurant's chef is **Pascal Coudoy**, the former chef of the Ambassador Grill. The decor is reminiscent of a French country restaurant with a backyard cafe. The menu, from the southwest of France, offers superb fish soup, foie gras, venison pâté in flaky pastry and an excellent cassoulet. Desserts are typical of Gascogne, such as prune ice cream or prune cake. ◆ French ◆ 158 8th Ave (W 17th-W 18th Sts) 675.6564

18 Chelsea Place $$ They bill this as the only speakeasy in America. You enter through the back door of an antique shop that leads to a crowded bar. The room behind it, which they call a garden because it has hanging plants, is quieter and more intimate. The upstairs bar offers jazz Thursday-Saturday evenings. ◆ Italian ◆ 147 8th Ave (W 17th-W 18th Sts) 924.8413

19 Man Ray ★$$ Guided by skilled chef **Matthew Tivy**, formerly at Canal Bar, this bistro serves a clientele who appreciate well-cooked, authentic French food. ◆ French ◆ 169 8th Ave (W 18th-W 19th Sts) 627.4220

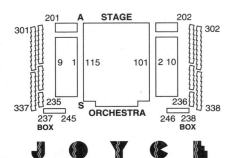

19 The Joyce Theater (Renovated 1981, **Hardy Holzman Pfeiffer Associates**) *By* dancers *for* dancers and the people who love dance. Elegant, intimate and deep in the heart of Chelsea. This building was once the decrepit and infamous **Elgin** movie house. The 1981 remodeling created the Joyce dance theater by complete replacement of the building's interior and re-Decoization of the exterior. It is named for the daughter of the principal donor. ◆ Seats 496. 175 8th Ave (W 18th-W 19th Sts) 242.0800

Chelsea

20 La Luncheonette $$$ The homey bar and open kitchen in the bistro style seem familiar enough, but the free-range chicken with mustard, the lamb sausage with apple *bé* cognac and the *gratinée trois poisson* (lobster, crab and sea scallops) are interesting turns on an honored cuisine. ◆ French ◆ 130 10th Ave (W 18th St) Reservations recommended. No credit cards. 675.0342

THE KITCHEN

21 The Kitchen This veteran institution for experimental performing and visual arts presents the works of young artists in dance, film, video, music and performance art. Programs are scheduled most evenings and some require that tickets be purchased in advance. Call for current performance schedule. ◆ 512 W 19th St (10th-11th Aves) 255.5793

The cast-iron pineapples in the **Cushman Row** are part of an iconography that began in New England in the days when merchant sea captains roamed the world in search of things to sell. After a voyage to the South Seas, it was customary for them to put pineapples outside their houses as a sign that they had returned and were receiving guests, who would be treated to exotic fruits and wild yarns. Eventually the pineapple became a symbol of hospitality, and was rendered in more permanent wood or iron.

22 Guardian Angel Church (1930, **John Van Pelt**) This little complex of Italian Romanesque buildings surrounds what is known as the **Shrine Church of the Sea**. The name reflects the one-time presence of the busiest piers in the Port of New York, a short walk to the west. The church's Renaissance interior is even more impressive than the red-brick-and-limestone facade. The priest in charge of this Roman Catholic church is designated **Chaplain of the Port**, with duties that include assigning chaplains to ships based here. ◆ 193 10th Ave (W 21st St)

23 West 21st Street Almost all the 19th-century houses on this block follow **Clement Clarke Moore**'s requirement of front gardens and street trees. In its earliest years as a residential community, all of Chelsea looked much like this. The building with the unusual peaked roof on the 9th Ave corner is the oldest house in the neighborhood. It was built in the 1820s by **James N. Wells**. ◆ 9th-10th Aves

24 Somethin' Else! There are dozens of antique shops scattered around this neighborhood, some authentic, some dubious, all of them browsers' delights. But this one is, indeed, something else. It's a collection of old toys, quilts, jewelry and an entire wall of crystal glasses. ◆ 182 9th Ave (W 21st St) 924.0006

25 Manhattan Doll House The largest collection of new and antique dolls, doll houses and doll accessories in the city—all for sale. ◆ Closed Su. 176 9th Ave (W 20th-W 21st Sts) 989.5220

26 General Theological Seminary (1883-1900, **Charles C. Haight**; Library 1960, **O'Connor & Kilham**) You're welcome to enter this oasis through the library building on 9th Ave during public hours or, in summer, to take the free *Grand Design* tour. Land for the Episcopal Seminary was donated by **Clement Clarke Moore** in 1830, on the condition that the seminary should always occupy the site. The **West Building**, built in 1835, is the oldest building on campus, as well as New York's oldest example of Gothic Revival architecture. It predates Haight's renovation, which includes all the other Gothic buildings. In the center is the **Chapel of the Good Shepherd**, with its outstanding bronze doors and 161ft-high square bell tower. **Hoffman Hall**, at the 10th Ave end, contains a Medieval-style dining hall complete with a barrel-vaulted ceiling walk-in fireplaces and a gallery for musicians. The other end is dominated by the new and very much out-of-place **St. Mark's Library**, containing, along with one of the world's largest collections of bibles in Latin, some 170,000 volumes. ◆ M-F noon-2:30PM; Sa 11AM-3PM; Su 2-4PM, closed when school is not in session. 175 9th Ave (W 20th St) 243.5150

Restaurants/Nightlife: Red
Shops/Parks: Green
Hotels: Blue
Sights/Culture: Black

27 406-24 West 20th Street (1837, Don Alonzo Cushman) An extremely well-preserved row of Greek Revival houses built by a dry goods merchant who developed much of Chelsea and built these as rental units. The attic windows are circled with wreaths, the doorways framed in brownstone. Even the newel posts, topped with cast-iron pineapples, are still intact. ♦ 9th-10th Aves

28 St. Peter's Episcopal Church (1838, Clement Clarke Moore and James W. Smith) This Episcopal church and its rectory and parish hall are outgrowths of Moore's plan to build them in the style of Greek temples. According to legend, the plan was changed when one of the vestrymen came back from England with tales of the Gothic buildings at Oxford. The congregation decided to switch styles, even though the foundations were already in place. The fence that surrounds this charming complex was brought here from Trinity Church on lower Broadway, where it had stood since 1790. Renovations are underway to replace the roof, repoint and preserve the masonry and repair or replace all of the woodwork in the tower and window and door openings. ♦ 346 W 20th St (8th-9th Aves)

29 Chelsea Foods Gorgeously designed modern store and cafe with many interesting, but expensive, prepared and packaged foods to go. I have a weakness for their brownies. ♦ Cafe/takeout ♦ 198 8th Ave (W 20th St) 691.3948

30 Meriken ★$$ New Wave Japanese served to a trendy crowd. Interesting Art Deco decor in celadon and pink. ♦ Japanese ♦ 189 W 21st St (7th Ave) Reservations recommended. 620.9684

31 Third Cemetery of the Spanish & Portuguese Synagogue (1829-51) Enclosed on 3 sides by painted brick loft buildings, this private hideaway is the third cemetery established by the first Jewish congregation in New York. The second cemetery is in Greenwich Village, the first on the Lower East Side. ♦ 98-110 W 21st St (6th-7th Aves)

32 165 West 23rd Street In 1896 *Red Badge of Courage* author **Stephen Crane** moved into a room on the 5th floor of this building. The struggling 24-year-old journalist made his living writing magazine and newspaper articles about poverty and vice in the city. ♦ 6th-7th Aves

From the end of the Civil War until Prohibition put an end to the fun in the 1920s, the stretch of 6th Ave from 24th to 30th Sts was known all over the country as **Satan's Circus**. It cut a swath through a neighborhood christened the **Tenderloin** by a police captain who, after being transferred there in 1876, said he was glad to be able to get a little tenderloin after years of chuck steak. The city's No. 1 tourist attraction at the time was the **Haymarket**, a saloon at 30th St and 6th Ave. The entertainment was called the *grande soirée dansant*, and it was well-known as the most risqué in town. For an extra fee, patrons were treated to a private demonstration of a new dance from Paris called the *cancan*.

33 Hotel Chelsea $$ (1884, Hubert, Pirrson & Co.) **Brendan Behan**, who lived here during his New York years, said that there was more space in the Hotel Chelsea than in the whole of Staten Island. It has housed more writers, poets and musicians than any hotel in the 5 boroughs of New York, Staten Island included. In the 1880s, Chelsea was the heart of the Theater District, attracting creative people as Greenwich Village would a decade later. In its early days the hotel was home to writers like **William Dean Howells** and **O. Henry**, and later to **Thomas Wolfe, Arthur Miller, Mary McCarthy, Vladimir Nabokov** and **Yevgeny Yevtushenko**. **Sarah Bernhardt** once lived

Chelsea

here, and this is where **Dylan Thomas** spent his last days. In the 1960s and '70s, it was a favorite stopping place for visiting rock stars (including the **Sex Pistols**), who shared the atmosphere with modern classical composers **George Kleinsinger** and **Virgil Thomson**. The Chelsea was originally an apartment building, the first in New York with a penthouse. When it was converted to a hotel in 1905, each of its 12 floors became a single suite. The lobby has been altered, but the stairway, best seen from the 2nd floor, is intact. ♦ 222 W 23rd St (7th-8th Aves) 243.3700; fax 243.3700 ext 2171

33 Manhattan Comics & Cards An extensive collection of new and old comic books and baseball cards. ♦ 228 W 23rd St (7th-8th Aves) 243.9349

33 Eze ★$$$ Owner/chef **Gina Zarrili**, who previously worked at the Quilted Giraffe, Chanterelle and Roxanne's, serves delicious Provençal cuisine in this charming dining room, reminiscent of a small restaurant on the Mediterranean. Among the appetizers are grilled quail with almonds and red peppers, and a fragrant mussel soup with saffron. The fish is wonderful, especially a rich seafood stew redolent of garlic. For dessert, there is walnut cake with ginger ice cream. In fair weather ask to sit in the garden. ♦ French ♦ 254 W 23rd St (7th-8th Aves) 691.1140

34 McBurney YMCA $ (1904, **Parish & Schroeder**) **Robert Ross McBurney**, one of the first social workers to deal with the problems of foreign-born New Yorkers, ran a Y at 23rd St and 4th Ave in the 1870s. This branch is its successor. It had its own electrical generator that ran all day charging storage batteries that provided power at night, when the noise of the machine might disturb sleeping guests. The building includes a track, a gymnasium and a rooftop sundeck. Maximum stay is 25 days. ♦ 215 W 23rd St (7th-8th Aves) 741.9226

34 Unity Book Center *For books that matter* is their tagline; topics include Marxism-Leninism, socialism, African-American literature and women's equality. ♦ Closed Su. 237 W 23rd St (7th-8th Aves) 242.2934

35 Penn Station South (1962, **Herman Jessor**) A 12-square-block complex of 2820 apartments built as middle-income housing by the **International Ladies' Garment Workers Union**. As you stroll by, look at the sidewalk on the uptown side of 24th St at 8th Ave, where autumn leaves have left a permanent impression. ♦ W 23rd-W 29th Sts (8th-9th Aves)

36 Luma ★★$$$ A new breed of restaurant for the health-conscious, and well-heeled, diners of the '90s. Try the barley risotto and the grilled vegetables with garlic-herb oil. Not an additive in sight! ♦ Vegetarian ♦ 200 9th Ave (W 22nd-W 23rd Sts) 633.8033

Chelsea

37 London Terrace Apartments (1930, **Farrar & Watmaugh**) This double row of buildings with a garden in the center contains 1670 apartments. It was built at the height of the Depression and stood virtually empty for several years. Its apartments went unrented despite lures like an Olympic-size swimming pool and doormen dressed as London bobbies. It is the second complex by that name on the site. The original, built in 1845, was a row of Greek Revival buildings with wide front lawns on 23rd St. Behind it, on 24th St, was a row of 2-story houses called Chelsea Cottages. The 1845 complex replaced **Clement Clarke Moore**'s house, which, though small, had been the only building on the block. ♦ W 23rd-W 24th Sts (9th-10th Aves)

38 Chateau Ruggero $$ The Franco-Italian name comes from the decor, which is French, and the current menu, which is Italian. The charming setting dates back to the London Terrace of the 1930s. ♦ Italian ♦ Closed Su. 461 W 23rd St (9th-10th Aves) 242.8641

39 Empire Diner ★$$ (Refurbished 1976, **Carl Laanes**) A 1930s-style diner that has all the trappings of the original, except the grease and the prices. It also has a bar. It may be the only diner in America whose late-night customers arrive in stretch limousines. Open 24hr, it is a favorite among patrons of discos and nightclubs, and among those who want to stay up all night and enjoy the best diner breakfast in town. In the summer I sit at one of the tables on the sidewalk for front-row viewing of the street action. ♦ American ♦ 210 10th Ave (W 22nd-W 23rd Sts) 243.2736

40 Chelsea Central ★★$$$ **Larry McIntyre** bills his charming and cozy old saloon—original tin ceilings, dark wood, old phone booths with folding doors—as an American bistro. And the food is terrific. Try the eggplant with mozzarella and roasted peppers, and a slice of chocolate amaretto cake. ♦ Continental ♦ 227 10th Ave (W 23rd-W 24th Sts) Reservations recommended. 620.0230

41 WPA Theater Under the impressive artistic direction of **Kyle Renick**, productions like *Steel Magnolias, Little Shop of Horrors* and *The Whales of August* have blossomed into memorable Off Broadway hits and feature films. ♦ Seats 122. 519 W 23rd St (10th-11th Aves) 691.2274

42 World Yacht Cruises ★★$$$ A fleet of 5 restaurant yachts that cruise the harbor year-round. Lunch cruises include light music. The food would make these restaurants impressive even if they were landlocked. Dinner includes music, dancing and the romance of the harbor. A wonderful place to get married—wedding vows may be exchanged as the boat passes the *Statue of Liberty*. ♦ Continental ♦ Daily Apr-Dec; Sa-Su Jan-Mar. Pier 62 (W 23rd St at Hudson River) Jacket and tie required for dinner. Reservations required. 929.7090

43 Starrett-Lehigh Building (1931, **Russell G. and Walter M. Cory** and **Yasuo Matsui**) A pacesetter in its day, this Art Deco collection of glass, concrete and brown brick with its rounded corners was built over the Lehigh Valley Railroad's yards, and had elevators powerful enough to lift fully loaded freight cars onto its upper warehouse floors. ♦ W 26th-W 27th Sts (11th-12th Aves)

44 Chelsea Stage A New York institution since 1922 (known as the **Hudson Guild Theatre** until June 1990), this theater produces 5 new plays a year, some of which find their way to Broadway. **Hugh Leonard**'s *Da*, first performed here in 1978, went on to become a movie, as did *On Golden Pond*, a 1979 Hudson Guild play. ♦ Seats 135. 441 W 26th St (9th-10th Aves) 760.9810, 645.4940

45 Church of the Holy Apostles (1848, **Minard Lafever**; transepts 1858, **Richard Upjohn**) The slate-roofed spire of this Episcopal church makes it a standout among the huge brick apartment houses all around it. It's an unusual feature of the view to the west from the Empire State Building Observatories. ♦ 300 9th Ave (W 27th-W 28th Sts)

46 The Ballroom ★★$$$ An authentic Spanish restaurant owned by well-regarded chef/showman **Felipe Rojas-Lombardi**. The best place to sit is at the long food bar, with its rows of hanging sausages, hams, dried cod and wondrous array of *tapas*—small morsels of traditional appetizers offered in 2-bite servings. Adjacent to the restaurant is a charming cabaret theater that showcases musicians and singers Tuesday-Saturday evenings and Sunday afternoons. Just one thing: call to check the cover policy before you reserve. ♦ Spanish ♦ 253 W 28th St (7th-8th Aves) Reservations required. 244.3005

47 Fur District Yes, that man you just passed did have a silver fox cape over his arm. No, he didn't steal it, and chances are no one will steal it from him. It's commonplace in the fur district for thousands of dollars worth of merchandise to be delivered in such a casual way. It's all in a day's work for the people who make and sell fur garments in this neighborhood. ♦ W 27th-W 30th Sts (6th-8th Aves)

48 Fashion Institute of Technology (1958–1977, **De Young & Moscowitz**) If there were a competition for the ugliest block in Manhattan, the center of this complex on 27th St would win easily. All the buildings are by the same firm, but obviously not by the same hand. The school, part of the **State University of New York**, was created by New York's garment industry to train young people in all aspects of the fashion business. ♦ W 27th St (7th-8th Aves)

49 Swedish Institute Clinic If you're seeking relief from arthritis, lower back pain, sciatica or simple chronic stress, a therapeutic massage may be what the doctor orders. If he or she does, bring your prescription here, where 7 half-hour healing treatments can be had for a reasonable rate. By appointment with a doctor's recommendation only. ♦ 226 W 26th St (7th-8th Aves) 924.0991

One out of every pair of New Yorkers is an immigrant or has one foreign-born parent.

50 221 West 26th Street This building was originally an armory. It was also once the **Famous Players Studio**, where, in 1915, **Adolph Zukor** paid **Mary Pickford** an unprecedented $2000/wk as one of his most famous players. Other film studios in the neighborhood were the Reliance, the Majestic and the Kalem Company. ♦ 7th-8th Aves

51 Flower District The best time to smell the flowers here is the early morning hours, when florists from all over the city arrive to refresh their stock. If you're in the market for a large plant or a small tree, you'll find it on the sidewalk soaking up the sun. ♦ 6th Ave (W 26th-W 29th Sts)

52 St. John the Baptist Church (1872, **Napoleon LeBrun**) This Roman Catholic church is noted for its white marble interior. ♦ 210 W 31st St (7th-8th Aves)

53 Schoepfer Studios Carrying on an 83-year-old family business started by his grandfather, taxidermist **Jim Schoepfer** stocks a zoo-full of animals, including zebras, armadillos, anteaters, birds and fish. Perhaps you recognize the crocodile from the film *Crocodile Dundee*? A sign on the door welcomes customers, not browsers; but, fortunately, there's a lot to see in the window display. ♦ Closed Sa-Su. 138 W 31st St (7th-8th Aves) 736.6939

Author **Edith Wharton** was born in 1862 at 14 W 23rd St.

Chocolate Egg Creams

According to one of the most widely believed accounts, chocolate egg creams were first served in the early 1900s in **Kaletsky's Candy Store** on Intervale Ave in the South Bronx.

Apparently, when mothers gave their children the 7 cents for Kaletsky's popular malteds they would also send along an egg for Mr. Kaletsky to throw into the drink. As it was, 7 cents was too steep for many of the kids, so, instead, the poorer children would order a 4-cent chocolate soda (seltzer water, a little bit of milk and chocolate syrup) into which they, too, would ask Mr. Kaletsky to break their eggs. So popular did the 4-cent drink, dubbed the *chocolate egg cream*, become, that by about 1918, Mr. Kaletsky, as well as other merchants, were including the beverage on their menus. The egg, it seems, disappeared during the Depression years.

Ask native New Yorkers about egg creams and you're bound to get a nostalgic reminiscence about afternoons whiled away at the neighborhood soda fountain. Ask 2 former *soda jerks* how to make an egg cream and you will probably instigate a heated debate about the order in which the ingredients are added, the proper method of squirting the seltzer into the glass and the proper amount of the ever-important chocolate syrup—some *experts* claim that it's not made anymore; others swear by Fox's U-Bet, which is sold in New York City grocery stores.

54 Madison Square Garden Center (1968, Charles Luckman Associates) America's premier entertainment facility hosts over 600 events and nearly 6 million spectators each year. Within the center are the 20,000-seat **Arena**, the 4600-plus-seat **Felt Forum** and the **Exposition Rotunda** with a 20-story office building. It is home to the **New York Knicks** and the **New York Rangers**. Throughout the year, the garden hosts exhibitions and trade shows, boxing, rodeos, dog, cat and horse shows, circuses, graduations, rock concerts, tennis, track and field, gymnastics and an occasional presidential convention. ◆ 7th Ave (W 31st-W 33rd Sts) 465.6741

Within Madison Square Garden Center:

Pennsylvania Station Make connections here for Long Island via the Long Island Railroad; for points north, south and west via Amtrak; or for southern Connecticut on the Metro-North line. ◆ W 31st-W 33rd Sts (7th-8th Aves)

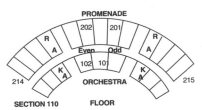

Main Floor Plan

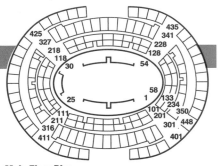

Felt Forum

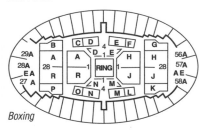

Boxing

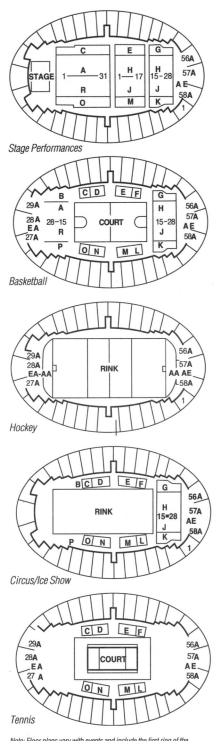

Stage Performances

Basketball

Hockey

Circus/Ice Show

Tennis

Note: Floor plans vary with events and include the first ring of the basic floor plan.

Restaurants/Nightlife: Red **Hotels:** Blue
Shops/Parks: Green **Sights/Culture:** Black

General Post Office

McKim, Mead & White

55 General Post Office (1913, **McKim, Mead & White**) Built to match the firm's original Penn Station across 8th Ave, the monumental stairway and the columned entrance topped with that famous inscription about rain, snow and the gloom of night made it the first attraction of visitors arriving by train. You'll find postal services available here at any hour of any day. ◆ W 31st-W 33rd Sts (8th-9th Aves)

56 Sky Rink (1970, **Davis, Brody & Associates**) Located on the 16th floor of a huge warehouse building, this Olympic-size ice-skating rink features figure skating sessions every day, as well as regular sessions for folks who prefer just going 'round and 'round. The public skating schedule varies; call for current hours. ◆ Fee; skate rental. 450 W 33rd St (10th Ave) 695.6555

57 Sloane House YMCA $ A co-ed, international young adult center with 1400 rooms for individuals and groups. ◆ 356 W 34th St (8th-9th Aves) 760.5850

58 1 Penn Plaza (1972, **Charles Luckman Associates**) This is the tallest of the complex of buildings that replaced the late, great Pennsylvania Station. ◆ W 34th St (7th-8th Aves) 239.7400

59 New York Penta Hotel $$ (1918, **McKim, Mead & White**) It used to be called the Hotel Pennsylvania because of its proximity to Pennsylvania Station. It is now the hotel closest to the Jacob K. Javits Convention Center. In the 1930s, it was a hot stop for the Big Bands: **Glenn Miller** immortalized its phone number with his *PEnnsylvania 6-5000*. All 1700 rooms have been renovated. ◆ W 33rd St at 7th Ave. 736.5000, 800/223.8585; fax 502.8798

60 A&S Plaza (1989, **RTKL Associates of Baltimore MD**) A taste of the suburbs in the city. Eight floors of shops plus a food court. **The Body Shop** (skincare products), **Accento** (handknit sweaters) and **Moose N' Around** (clothes and accessories adorned with favorite cartoon characters) are of particular interest, but 2 of the best reasons to visit this vertical mall are the clean bathrooms and the **Visitors Center** on the 7th floor; stop in if you need tourist brochures, transportation information or assistance making theater or restaurant reservations. ◆ W 33rd St at 6th Ave. 465.0500

61 Herald Center (1985, **Coeland, Novak, Israel & Simmon**) Though it was built before A&S Plaza, this shopping center, dubbed the *Tall Mall*, seems to have suffered in its shadow. Once home to 70 stores, at present most are closed except for the food court on the 8th floor and **Toys 'R Us** and **Kids 'R Us** (2nd and 3rd floors). The fate of the remaining space is undetermined. ◆ W 34th St at Broadway. 244.2555

On a clear day you can see... Manhattan!

When the streets get a little too littered, the air a bit too smoggy and the crowds just too intense, remember that everything looks better from a distance—and New York City's no exception. Unlike the aging actress whose left profile is better than her right, the **Big Apple** shines every which way, especially from:

Cadman Plaza ◆ At Furnam St, Downtown Brooklyn

Circle Line ◆ Pier 83. 42nd St at the Hudson River. 563.3200

Columbia Heights ◆ Pineapple St, Brooklyn Hts

Empire State Building Observatories ◆ 5th Ave at 34th St. 736.3100

Fort Tryon Park and the Cloisters ◆ Washington Hts

Liberty State Park ◆ So of the Holland Tunnel, New Jersey side

Promenade ◆ Brooklyn Hts

The Rainbow Room Restaurant ◆ 3 Mitchell Pl. 632.5000

River Cafe ◆ 1 Water St, Downtown Brooklyn. 718/522.5200

Riverside Church ◆ 120th St at Riverside Dr. 222.5900

Roosevelt Tramway ◆ 2nd Ave at 59th St

Staten Island Ferry ◆ Leaves from Battery Park. 806.6940

Statue of Liberty ◆ Liberty Island. 363.3200

The Terrace ◆ 400 W 119th St at Morningside Dr. 666.9490

Top of the Sixes Restaurant ◆ 666 5th Ave, 39th floor. 757.6662

Triborough Bridge ◆ Above Wards Island

Windows on the World Restaurant ◆ 1 World Trade Center, 107th floor. 938.1111

World Trade Center Observation Deck ◆ 2 World Trade Center, 107th floor. 466.7377

Theater/Garment

The **Theater District** and the **Garment Center** represent 2 of the most important factors in the New York economy: the tourist industry and the creation of American fashion, both of which New Yorkers take very seriously. For street theater, no part of town is more entertaining than the Garment Center, and without its creations, an evening at a Broadway theater just wouldn't be the same. It all happens on the blocks bounded by **34th** and **59th Sts**, **6th Ave** and the **Hudson River**.

Before 1900, the garment trade was centered below 14th St on the Lower East Side. By 1915, it had moved up along Broadway and 6th Ave as far as 30th St, replacing part of the rough-and-tumble neighborhood that had been known as the **Tenderloin**. The merchant princes who were establishing department stores along 5th Ave were annoyed to find garment workers mingling with their customers and formed a committee to put a stop to it. The committee's solution was the construction of Nos. 498 and 500 7th Ave at 37th St, a comfortable distance away. When the 2 loft buildings were finished in 1921, the name **Seventh**

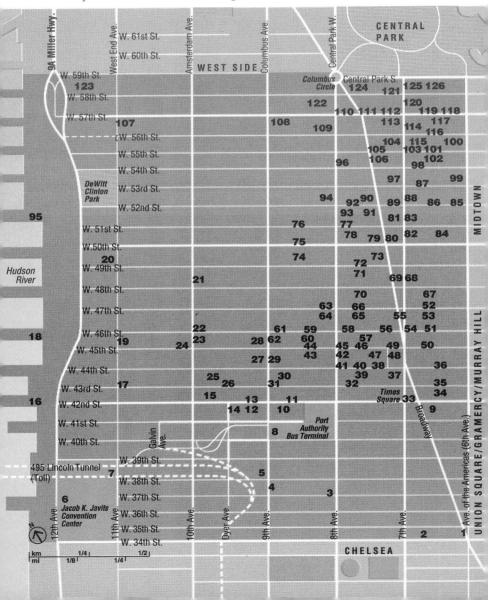

Ave was destined to become synonymous with the best in American fashion.

The Theater District has been at the center of the city since colonial times. When the Metropolitan Opera House arrived at 39th and Broadway in 1883, the **Floradora Girls** were already packing them in at the Casino Theater across the street. As the city's center moved uptown, the theaters moved along with it. When the first portion of **Macy's** was built at 34th St and Broadway in 1902, one of the buildings it replaced was Koster & Bial's Music Hall, where, in 1898, **Thomas Edison** first demonstrated moving pictures.

At the same time that the theatrical quarter leaped across 42nd St after the turn of the century, theater owners banded together in a syndicate to gain more control over the artists they booked. It gave them control over the competition as well, and any theatrical enterprise further downtown was effectively put down. The syndicate's mantle was picked up in 1916 by the 3 **Shubert** brothers when they began to build new theaters in the **Times Square** area, which the subway had put within easy reach of the entire city. Other entrepreneurs joined the rush, and their legacy is still with us.

In 1876, an elevated railroad was built along 9th Ave, and thousands of immigrants, chiefly from Ireland, moved into the nearby streets. There was work for them in sawmills along the Hudson River, as well as in warehouses, stone yards and stables. Well into the 20th century, long after gang wars in New York were declared officially over, merchants and property owners west of 8th Ave considered paying tribute to the **Hell's Kitchen Gang** a necessary fact of life. And though reformers thought they had put an end to the infamous Tenderloin, which they called **Satan's Circus**, it was with us until Prohibition closed down its major watering holes in 1920. The district, bounded by 5th and 7th Aves, and 23rd and 42nd Sts, had flourished as the city's center of vice for nearly 50 years.

The Times Square area is in the process of radical change again as developers are rushing to take advantage of construction incentives that are part of a long-heralded plan to clean up the area.

Theater/Garment

1 Herald Square During the 1880s and '90s, this was the heart of the **Tenderloin** district of dance halls, bordellos and cafes adjacent to **Hell's Kitchen**. New York City's theater and newspaper industries were once headquartered here. The square—which, like most of the squares in New York is anything but—was named for *The New York Herald*, which occupied a Venetian palazzo (1895-1921, **McKim, Mead & White**) on the north end. Greeley Square to the south is named for the founder of the *New-York Tribune*. Note the **Greenwich Savings Bank** by **York & Sawyer**—lots of columns inside and out. ◆ W 34th-W 35th Sts (6th Ave-Broadway)

2 Macy's (Broadway building 1901, **DeLemos & Cordes**; 7th Ave building 1931, **Robert D. Kohn**) Although it has always seemingly had more of everything than any other store (more than 400,000 items are displayed on its 9 floors), Macy's didn't have a compelling fashion image until 1974, when **Ed Finkelstein**, who had been president of Macy's in San Francisco, arrived in New York. Today, the store is both trendy and genuinely fashionable. There is a haven for children on the 5th floor, with a vast selection of imported and domestic clothing, a pet shop and even a place to relax over an ice-cream soda. The 9th-floor **Corner Shop** includes a dazzling array of linens and furniture in every style from Postmodern to fine antiques. Macy's **Cellar** turns shopping for the kitchen into a heady experience, and even includes fine food to go with the fine kitchenware (**Gene Hovis** creates down-home Southern specialties like buttermilk biscuits and buttermilk-fried chicken as well as a hearty Tuscan bean soup, macaroni and cheese, apple pie...). You can eat breakfast, lunch and dinner at Macy's, get a facial and a haircut, mail a letter, have your jewelry appraised, buy theater tickets and convert foreign currency into dollars. And if all that makes you tired, **Macy's Buy Appointment** will do your shopping for you. Store hours vary with special events and promotions. ◆ W 34th-W 35th Sts (Broadway-7th Ave) 695.4400

Restaurants/Nightlife: Red
Shops/Parks: Green

Hotels: Blue
Sights/Culture: Black

3 New York Astrology Center The country's largest source of astrology and spiritual books and healing and meditational tapes, plus greeting cards, incense and Tarot cards. The center also offers computerized and one-to-one horoscope interpretations. ◆ Closed Su. 545 8th Ave (W 37th St) 10th floor. 947.3609

4 Bellevues ★★$$ A modest bistro with an adventurous menu—skate in brown butter and sweet breads in Marsala—at a location that defies its name. ◆ French ◆ 496 9th Ave (W 37th-W 38th Sts) Reservations recommended. No credit cards. 967.7850

4 Hero Boy ★$ According to the **Manganaro** family, who established this enterprise as a satellite of their grocery store next door, the name of the hero sandwich, known as a *grinder,* a *po' boy* and a *submarine* in other cities, was coined here in 1940 by *Herald-Tribune* food writer **Clementine Paddleford,** who said you have to be a hero to finish one of these. The Manganaros claim to be the first to sell sandwiches by the foot. ◆ Italian ◆ Closed Su. 492 9th Ave (W 37th-W 38th Sts) 947.7325

4 Manganaro's ★$$ An Italian grocery store with a family-style restaurant in back that has been serving antipastos, pastas, meat dishes

Theater/Garment

and sandwiches since 1893. The store also sells imported delicacies by mail. ◆ Italian ◆ Closed Su. 488 9th Ave (W 37th-W 38th Sts) 563.5331, mail order 800/4.SALAMI

5 Supreme Macaroni Co. ★$$ Stepping innocently into this grocery store leads to a time before the words *gourmet* or *nouvelle cuisine* were ever uttered. In the back of the store is a restaurant that serves the best macaroni this side of Naples. The prices are moderate and the service straightforward. ◆ Italian ◆ Closed Su. 511 9th Ave (W 38th-W 39th Sts) Reservations required. No credit cards. 564.8074

6 Jacob K. Javits Convention Center (1986, **I.M. Pei & Partners**) This huge facility—amost entirely made of glass—covering 22 acres between 34th and 39th Sts, is the largest exposition hall under one roof in the Western hemisphere, and one of the biggest buildings in the world. It has 740,000sq ft of indoor exhibition space and another 50,000 outside. The lobby alone is big enough to contain Niagara Falls. It is more than 85 percent booked through the year 2000, and has events scheduled in the next century. When it was opened, it was called *the center at the center of the world.* Crosstown buses on 34th and 42nd Sts go right to its front door. Oddly

enough, the building appears opaque during the day, whereas at night, the interior lighting makes the structure glow. ◆ 655 W 34th St (11th-12th Aves) 216.2000

LEVEL THREE

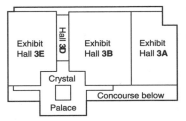

LEVEL ONE

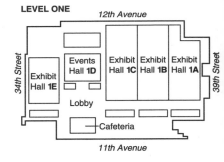

7 Lincoln Tunnel (1937, **Ole Singstad,** engineer; **Aymar Embury,** architect) The center tube, 8216ft long, was the original. It was joined by the 7482ft north tube in 1945, and the south tube, 8006ft long in 1957, making it the only 3-tube vehicular tunnel in the world. The tunnel, which is 97ft below the Hudson River, connects Manhattan with Weehawken NJ. More than 36 million vehicles use it every year. A toll is collected from eastbound cars. There is no tollbooth in the New Jersey-bound lanes. ◆ W 38th-W 41st Sts (10th-11th Aves) Manhattan to Weehawken NJ

New York City post offices once used underground pneumatic tubes to rush mail between branches at speeds 4 times faster than could be reached via the streets.

8 Port Authority Bus Terminal (1950; additions and expansion in 1963 and 1982, **Port Authority Design Staff**) This is the largest and busiest bus terminal in the world, serving all of New York's long-distance bus services and most of the commuter buses between New York and the New Jersey suburbs. A special section on the 42nd St side also serves all 3 airports. For people who prefer driving into Manhattan, but not through it, a rooftop parking garage connects directly by ramp to the Lincoln Tunnel, as do the terminal's 3 levels of bus platforms. As in any major transportation hub, exercise caution inside the terminal, which, especially in cold weather, affords temporary shelter to the homeless. Although the city is trying to deal with this problem, it is *essential* to be aware of your belongings at all times, and to avoid isolated areas, particularly the restrooms. ♦ 24hrs. W 40th-W 42nd Sts (8th-9th Aves) Bus information 564.8484

9 Hotalings News Agency The stand in New York City for out-of-town and international newspapers and magazines. ♦ 142 W 42nd St (6th-7th Aves) 840.1868

10 Group Health Insurance Building (1931, **Hood, Godley & Fouilhoux**) Better known as the original **McGraw-Hill Building**, this 35-story tower was commissioned when growth was expected in this area. Green and glorious, it still stands alone. The McGraw-Hill also has the distinction of being the only New York building mentioned in *The International Style*, the 1932 book by **Hitchcock** and **Johnson** that codified modern architecture. In fact, this tower is not strictly glass and steel esthetics, but an individual composition with Art Deco detailing. Eminent architectural historian **Vincent Scully** has called it *Proto-jukebox Modern*. ♦ 330 W 42nd St (8th-9th Aves)

11 Church of the Holy Cross (1870, **Henry Englebert**) Though this was built as the parish church of a poor neighborhood, it has several windows and mosaics designed by **Louis Comfort Tiffany**. **Father Francis P. Duffy**, chaplain of the famous Fighting 69th Division in WWI, fought from the pulpit of this church to break up the gangs of **Hell's Kitchen**. He served here until his death in 1932. ♦ 329 W 42nd St (8th-9th Aves) 246.4732

12 Chez Josephine ★★$$ The ebullient **Jean Claude Baker** launched this unique tribute to his late, adopted mother, cabaret legend **Josephine Baker**, in 1986, and has been gratifying critics and public alike ever since. The special decor, a tribute to the intimate Parisian nightclubs of the roaring '20s, only adds to the enjoyment of some of what I think is the best *boudin noir* in town, served with red cabbage. Also featured is lobster bisque, goat-cheese ravioli and rack of lamb. Bluesy lady pianists and a French tap dancer usually lend a musical note to the heady atmosphere. ♦ French ♦ Closed Su. 414 W 42nd St (9th Ave) Reservations recommended. 594.1925

13 West Bank Cafe ★$ The upstairs dining room features Thai dishes and seafood specials on tables covered with butcher paper; downstairs, enjoy musical comedy and original one-act plays in a cabaret setting. ♦ American/Thai ♦ 407 W 42nd St (9th Ave) Reservations recommended. 695.6909

13 Theatre Arts Bookshop New and used books, plays, magazines, autographed playbills and photographs. If you're new to the *biz*, there's a full selection of advise books like *How to Audition for Musical Theater* and *How to Sell Yourself as an Actor*. ♦ 405 W 42nd St (9th Ave) 564.0402

14 Theater Row Beginning with the former West Side Airlines Terminal, which now houses video recording studios and the National Spanish Television Network, this ambitious project begun in 1976 by **Playwrights Horizons** (No. 416) includes a dozen Off

Theater/Garment

Broadway theaters and a revitalized street scene that includes courtyards and **Richard Haas** wall paintings that give new life to the Lincoln Tunnel exit that cuts the block in half. Tickets for all theaters are available at Ticket Central located at Playwrights Horizons. ♦ Daily 1-8PM. 406 W 42nd St (9th Ave) 279.4200

15 Manhattan Plaza (1977, **David Todd & Associates**) These towers provide subsidized housing for performing artists, whose rent in the 1688 apartments is based on their income. Their presence pays dividends in the vitality they bring to the neighborhood. ♦ W 42nd-W 43rd Sts (9th-10th Aves)

Within the Manhattan Plaza:

Good & Plenty to Go A gourmet catering service and takeout designed by **Milton Glaser, Inc.** Fresh breads, including Swiss peasant, whole wheat (baked in a brick oven) and sourdough onion rolls; soups and salads; hot and cold pastas; sandwiches and pizza; and homestyle favorites like bourbon-baked ham, jambalaya, crabcakes and stuffed pork chops. A few small tables are placed outside during fair weather. ♦ Closed Su. 268.4385

LITTLE PIE COMPANY *OF THE BIG APPLE*

Little Pie Company The aromas are glorious and the pies are just like Mom's (maybe even better!). This small, bright shop offers 10 different all-natural pies—try the fresh fruit pies in summer, the sour cream apple or pumpkin in fall. Take home a 5-inch pie if you're all alone and can't resist the temptation. Little Pie also sells cakes, including old-fashioned chocolate and applesauce-carrot, which it will custom decorate upon request.
◆ 424 W 43rd St (9th-10th Aves) 736.4780

16 Circle Line There is simply no better way to orient yourself to Manhattan's wonders. This well-narrated tour heads down the Hudson River, past the *Statue of Liberty* and up the

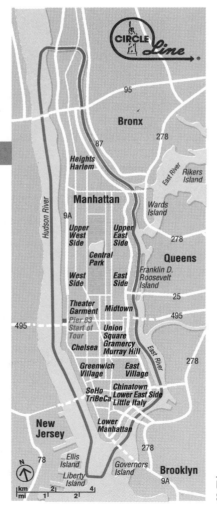

East River to the Harlem River, through Spuyten Duyvil and back down the Hudson. The 8 vessels are converted WWII landing craft or Coast Guard cutters. When you get on board, try to sit on the port side (left as you face forward). That way, all your views are of Manhattan. The schedule changes often; during the summer there are 12 cruises a day starting at 9:30AM. ◆ Fee. Closed Jan-Feb. Pier 83 (W 42nd St at Hudson River) 563.3200

17 Big City Diner $$ When **Chuck Hettinger** redesigned this faded diner from the '60s, transforming it into a restaurant, bar and disco, he called upon the World's Fair, the Jetsons and the Flintstones for inspiration. ◆ American ◆ 572 11th Ave (W 43rd St) 244.6033

18 Intrepid Sea Air Space Museum The veteran WWII and Vietnam War aircraft carrier *Intrepid* is now a technological and historical museum. Other than the **Air and Space Museum** in Washington DC, there is nothing like it anywhere for giving a picture of the past, present and future of warfare and technology in air, space or sea. The tamer **Pioneers Hall** shows mock-ups, antiques and film clips of flying machines from the turn of the century through the '30s. A present-day supercarrier comes alive in a vast museum showing the people, shops and aircraft that make up one of these floating cities, complete with a wide-screen movie that puts you on a flight deck as jets take off and land—clearly a promotional pitch for the Navy, but fascinating nonetheless. Future as well as contemporary insights into the exploration of the depths of the ocean and the far reaches of space are shown in **Technologies Hall**, along with the artifacts of 20th- and 21st-century warfare: jumbo jets, mammoth rockets and complex weaponry. On the *Intrepid's* 900ft flight deck are more real aircraft to be inspected. The newest acquisitions are the guided missile submarine *Growler* and the Vietnam-era destroyer *Edson*. Visitors can climb through the control bridges and command centers of the carrier, but spaces are cramped and there is often a wait. Dress warmly in winter months. ◆ Admission; under 6 and uniformed military free. W-Su 10AM-5PM. Last tickets sold at 4PM. Pier 86 (W 46th St at 12th Ave) 245.0072

19 Landmark Tavern ★$$ An old waterfront tavern cleaned up and refined for the comfort of modern-day theatergoers and those who seek out its authentic mid 19th-century rooms, where food is served from genuine antique sideboards. Some of the dishes could be better, and the better ones more consistent, but the hot, sweet raisin-cinnamon bread is lovable; the fish-and-chips, shepherd's pie, prime rib and hamburgers are recommendable. ◆ American ◆ 626 11th Ave (W 46th St) 757.8595

Restaurants/Nightlife: Red   **Hotels:** Blue
Shops/Parks: Green   **Sights/Culture:** Black

20 Munson Diner $ A silver-and-blue relic from 1908, open 24hr, serving good corned-beef hash. ♦ 600 W 49th St (11th Ave) 246.0964

21 Peruvian Restaurant ★$$ Ignore the flourescent lighting and formica tables, and concentrate instead on the best and most authentic Peruvian dishes in New York. Terrific sausages, baked fish with tomatoes and coriander, hearty stews and good potatoes. No wine. Pleasant service. ♦ Peruvian ♦ 688 10th Ave (W 48th-W 49th Sts) No credit cards. 581.5814

22 mud, sweat & tears A cheerful and neat pottery studio for beginning and expert potters. The facilities include 8 Brent & Amaco electric wheels, spacious table areas, basic handbuilding supplies, glazes, a kiln where firings are done frequently and a small retail area where the potters sell their wares. ♦ 654 10th Ave (W 46th St) 974.9121

23 Mike's American Bar and Grill ★$$ If you brave the unquestionably sleazy parade down this stretch of 10th Ave, you'll find a cheerful, intentionally down-at-the-heels joint. Go for the grilled specials, though some faithfuls claim Mike has the best enchiladas in Manhattan. ♦ American/Mexican ♦ 650 10th Ave (W 45th-W 46th Sts) 246.4115

24 Tenth Avenue Jukebox Café ★$$$ The menu is called *nouvelle American*, but the setting is 1940s American. And fun. ♦ American ♦ 637 10th Ave (W 45th St) 315.4690

25 The New Dramatists This company, which has free readings, was founded in 1949 by a group of Broadway's most important writers and producers in an effort to encourage new playwrights; alumni include **William Inge, John Guare** and **Emily Mann**. Formerly a Lutheran church, New Dramatists took occupancy of the building in 1968. ♦ Seats 90. 424 W 44th St (9th-10th Aves) 757.6960

25 The Actors Studio **Lee Strasberg** trained such stars as **Marlon Brando, Dustin Hoffman, Al Pacino** and **Shelley Winters** on this stage, once a Greek Orthodox church. Productions and readings are open to the public. ♦ Seats 125. 432 W 44th St (9th-10th Aves) 757.0870

26 Le Madeleine ★$$ A casual bistro, featuring salads, pastas, fish and light meats. In nice weather, the outdoor garden is open. ♦ French ♦ 403 W 43rd St (9th-10th Aves) 246.2993

26 Westside Arts Theater For more than 20 years the 2 theaters in this converted Episcopal church presented award-winning productions like *A Shayna Maidel* and *Extremities*. Its future is uncertain. ♦ Seats 210, 190. 407 W 43rd St (9th-10th Aves)

By 1643, 18 languages were spoken in New York City. More than 75 are spoken today.

27 Poseidon Greek Bakery Fans of Greek pastries have kept this tiny shop bustling for more than 50 years. You can have the phyllo specialties mailed anywhere in the US. ♦ Closed M. 629 9th Ave (W 44th-W 45th Sts) 757.6173

27 Rudy's Bar One of the area's few remaining neighborhood bars. Locals come for light snacks, conversation and good drinks. ♦ 627 9th Ave (W 44th-W 45th Sts) 974.9169

27 Film Center Cafe ★★$ The setting is diner deluxe—**Billie Holiday** and **Otis Redding** croon from the jukebox. Go for the meatloaf, Cajun chicken or any of the salads. ♦ American ♦ 635 9th Ave (W 44th-W 45th Sts) No credit cards. 262.2525

28 Bruno The King of Ravioli Established in 1888, the factory is closed to the public, but the neighboring retail shop sells a vast selection of fresh pastas and sauces: ravioli, manicotti, canelloni, lasagna, stuffed shells, gnocchi and cavatelli. ♦ Closed Su. 653 9th Ave (W 45th-W 46th Sts) 246.8456

29 Film Center Building (1929, **Buchman & Kahn**) The pink-and-black marble in the lobby and the pattern of the orange and blue tiles on the walls helped attract some 75 motion picture distributors, who made this building their headquarters. The stores on this block rent out moviemaking equipment. ♦ 630 9th Ave (W 44th-W 45th Sts) 757.6995

29 Jezebel ★★$$$ The nondescript entrance does not prepare you for the high-energy New Orleans bordello interior with, among other

Theater/Garment

delights, 2-story-high tropical trees, lawn swings, mirrored columns, Egyptian rugs on the walls and crystal chandeliers. I especially recommend the corn bread and deep-fried whole fish dishes. ♦ Soul food ♦ Closed Su. 630 9th Ave (W 45th St) Reservations required. 582.1045

30 The Original Improvisation This is the original, the place that has marked the start on the road to stardom for talents like **Richard Pryor, Robin Williams, Stiller & Meara** and **Rodney Dangerfield**. Light meals are served in casual surroundings. ♦ Cover, minimum. Shows: M-Th, Su continuous 9PM-closing; F 9PM, midnight; Sa 8, 10:30PM, 12:40AM. 358 W 44th St (8th-9th Aves) Reservations required. 765.8268

31 Thrift and New Shoppe A hodgepodge of stuff—bric-a-brac, American pottery and silver and gold jewelry—makes this antique shop fun. Treasures are waiting and the prices are reasonable. ♦ Closed Su. 602 9th Ave (W 43rd St) 265.3087

Macy's, which claims to be *The World's Largest Store*, boasts over 2 million sq ft of floor space and employs up to 10,000 salespeople.

Times Square
Carlos Diniz/Lee Harris Pomeroy

32 The New York Times (1913, **Ludlow & Peabody**) Less than 10 years after moving to Times Square, the *Times* had grown so much that this annex was built around the corner on 43rd St. Its size was doubled in 1924. The building was expanded again in 1945, and the original tower was eventually abandoned. Most copies of the newspaper are printed in a New Jersey plant, though a substantial number come off the presses in the basement here, and the activity on Saturday evenings on both the 43rd and 44th St sides, as delivery trucks head out with the Sunday edition, is intense. The newsroom, now computerized, is the largest in

Theater/Garment

the world. ♦ 229 W 43rd St (7th-8th Aves) 556.1234

33 Times Square Almost a year before *The New York Times* moved into what had been called **Longacre Square**, the mayor and the board of aldermen passed a resolution in April 1904, changing the name of the blocks bounded by 42nd and 47th Sts and Broadway and 7th Ave, to Times Square. It quickly became known as *The Crossroads of the World*, partly in deference to the *Times*, which certainly could claim that title. It is the heart of the Theater District and site of some of the most spectacular electric advertising signs ever created. The British novelist **G.K. Chesterton** said of them: *What a glorious garden of wonder this would be to anyone who was lucky enough to be unable to read.* It is one of a series of open spaces created as Broadway crosses the straight north-south avenues, in this case 7th Ave. Standing at the base of the old Times tower and looking uptown, Broadway comes into Times Square on your left, and leaves it behind you on your right, having cut across 7th Ave at the intersection of W 43rd St.

20 October 1896: *The New York Times* adopts the slogan, *All the News That's Fit to Print.*

33 1 Times Square (1904, **Eidlitz & MacKenzie**) When this building was under construction as headquarters for *The New York Times*, even the *Times'* archrival, the *Herald*, grudgingly ran a story under the headline *Deepest Hole in New York a Broadway Spectacle*, which said that the new *Times* tower was the most interesting engineering feat to be seen anywhere on Manhattan Island. The newspaper's pressroom was in the tower's basement, but because the building was being built over the city's biggest subway station, the basement had to be blasted out of solid rock 55ft down. The presses began printing the *Times* down there on 2 Jan 1905, after the new year had been welcomed with the dropping of a lighted ball down the flagpole up on the roof. The celebration has been repeated every year since, though the *Times* sold the building in 1966. The new owner, **Allied Chemical Co**, stripped it bare and refaced it with marble. (The ghost of the original lives on for the moment in a *trompe l'oeil* representation by **Richard Haas** [1979] on the tower of the Crossroads Building directly to the south). The building has since been sold again and is now an office building. ♦ W 42nd St (Broadway-6th Ave)

34 Shout! A 1960s-style rock 'n' roll dance club. It also has a 1959 Cadillac suspended over the stage. ♦ Cover. Closed M-Tu, Su. 124 W 43rd St (6th Ave-Broadway) 869.2088

35 The Town Hall (1921, **McKim, Mead & White**) This landmark is an elegant building with excellent acoustics. **Joan Sutherland** made her debut here. Today the hall is constantly in use for one cultural event or another. ♦ Seats 1498. 123 W 43rd St (6th Ave-Broadway) 840.2824

Backstage on Broadway hires theater professionals, including actors, directors and stage managers, to give 1hr lectures on how a Broadway show is put together. The lectures take place at Broadway theaters and often include backstage tours. Call 629.4284 for information.

Drawing by Al Hirschfeld
Courtesy Margo Felden Galleries, New York and Eastern Airlines

Sometimes it seems all New York is a stage. New ideas are born and grow old in the parks, garages, old libraries, churches and on college campuses. And, despite the ups and downs of the national economy and the vagaries of international politics, the performing arts continue to thrive.

Center Stage: Broadway

The name has become synonymous with theater in America, but *Broadway* has many other meanings as well. Geographically, it is the street that runs the entire length of Manhattan. Theatrically, it is the area around **Times Square**, where most of the commercial theaters are located. Legally, it is the place where only members of theatrical trade unions can work. But most importantly, Broadway symbolizes the whole complex of qualities associated with the glittering world of the theater: stars, polished performances, sophisticated plays and the *all-American musical*.

Broadway has been the heart of America's theater for over 100 years. The reasons are obvious. The audi-ence is here. The production money is here. The best actors, directors, playwrights, designers, choreographers and critics work here. To be accepted by Broadway is the ultimate recognition of their talent.

Drama: New Yorkers experienced their first real season in 1753 when the **Hallam Company** of London visited. A favorite theme of dramas of the period was the triumph of native honesty and worth over foreign affectation, as seen in plays such as **Royall Tyler**'s *The Contrast* (1787). By the 1830s, **Washington Irving** and **Walt Whitman**, in their roles as theater critics, advised that the stage offer more than just escape.

From 1850 to 1900, commercial houses featured melodramas, spectacle plays, comic operas, vaudeville and burlesques. The most popular play of the period was *Uncle Tom's Cabin*. It was during these years that the star system began, with **Joseph Jefferson** as *Rip Van Winkle*, **Edwin Booth** as *Hamlet* and **James O'Neill** (father of Eugene) as *The Count of Monte Cristo*. **John Drew, Maude Adams, Richard**

141

Mansfield and the Barrymores made their own names in various roles.

Around the time of WWI, producer Arthur Hopkins transformed Broadway by revitalizing the classics and by presenting the first modern war play, *What Price Glory?* Hopkins introduced Katharine Hepburn, Barbara Stanwyck and Clark Gable to the stage.

Homegrown drama received a welcome stimulus with the emergence of a group of New York City playwrights who were interested in social satire, dramatic realism and psychological expressionism. Eugene O'Neill, preoccupied with one's struggles with one's own psyche and with with the universe, expressed himself in such plays as *Beyond the Horizon, Anna Christie* and *Strange Interlude*. Later writers, influenced by O'Neill, went on to create a powerful stage legacy of their own: Elmer Rice, Clifford Odets, Arthur Miller and Tennessee Williams.

In the early '20s an extraordinarily successful organization, The Theatre Guild, brought the works of new

Theater/Garment

European dramatists like Tolstoy, Ibsen, Strindberg and Shaw to Broadway. Many of America's best-known actors appeared in their productions: Lynn Fontanne and Alfred Lunt, Edward G. Robinson, Helen Hayes and Ruth Gordon. Around this time, Brooks Atkinson became drama critic for *The New York Times*, and artist Al Hirschfeld began to capture the essence of the theater world with his caricatures, which still appear today.

In the '30s and '40s, The Group Theater, founded by Harold Clurman, explored and translated the theater of Stanislavski, while Lee Strasberg redefined his acting method and created The Actors Studio (see page 139 for famous graduates). The Mercury Theater, founded by Orson Welles and John Houseman, presented provocative works like Marc Blitzstein's *The Cradle Will Rock*. Dramas on Broadway at the time were *Abe Lincoln in Illinois* by Robert E. Sherwood, *The Little Foxes* by Lillian Hellman and *Our Town* by Thornton Wilder. Katharine Cornell became one of the most popular actresses in the American theater. Today, Zoe Caldwell and Ellen Burstyn, as well as the team of Jessica Tandy and Hume Cronyn continue in that tradition. In 1947, Elia Kazan directed 2 plays that exemplified American realism: *A Streetcar Named Desire* by Tennessee Williams and *Death of a Salesman* by Arthur Miller.

In the '60s, Edward Albee's *Who's Afraid of Virginia Woolf?* deeply impressed audiences, and Eugene Ionesco's *Rhinoceros* illustrated the *theater of the absurd*, which dramatized an illogical and incongruous world. Political assassinations, the Vietnam War and social problems of the '60s and '70s were reflected in plays like *Hair, The Great White Hope, Streamers* and *That Championship Season*. Many of these started Off Broadway, a trend that continues today. Many Broadway hits, such as *Fences* by August Wilson, also come from regional theaters. English productions are still popular today. The works of writers Peter Shaffer, Tom Stoppard, David Hare, Michael Frayn and director Peter Hall are among the favorite British imports.

Comedy: Stage comedy as we know it began in the mid 1800s with the debut of a satirical play called *A Glance at New York*. In 1926, *Abie's Irish Rose*, a romantic comedy, closed after a record-setting 4-year run. Fine examples of literary comedy in the '30s and '40s included Marc Connelly's *The Green Pastures* and Philip Barry's *The Philadelphia Story*. George S. Kaufman, a master of the wisecrack, wrote (alone and with Moss Hart) a series of zany comedies like *You Can't Take It With You* and *The Man Who Came To Dinner*. England's Noel Coward produced a string of frothy hits for the Broadway stage. The present-day king of comedy is Neil Simon, whose particular gift is creating hilarious situations with urbane one-liners. Harvey Fierstein, David Mamet and John Guare have also brought often-blistering comedies to Broadway in recent years.

Musical Comedy: The American musical has traveled a long way since *The Black Crook* was presented at Niblo's Garden in 1866. The opening performance lasted 5 $1/2$ hours, and the 100 undraped females and sexy songs proved irresistible to audiences.

Another genre of musical theater was the *minstrel show*, a revue with performers in blackface (later replaced by vaudeville). The first play to be called a *musical comedy* was *Evangeline* in 1874. During this time European operettas by Offenbach, Strauss and Gilbert and Sullivan dominated the scene. *H.M.S. Pinafore* was such wholesome entertainment that it finally brought women and children into the audience. The first great composer of operettas for the American stage was Victor Herbert; the last was Sigmund Romberg. Harrigan and Hart wrote hilarious farces about immigrant groups. Charles Hoyt's *A Trip to Chinatown* featured 2 hit songs: *After the Ball* and *The Bowery*. George Lederer introduced the *revue* in 1894 with his *Passing Show*, which opened up possibilities for comedians like **Weber and Fields** and stars like **Lillian Russell** and **Anna Held**. **Florenz Ziegfeld's** *Follies* and **Irving Berlin's** *Music Box Revues* were the rage.

Meanwhile, **George M. Cohan** romanticized the American identity in shows like *Little Johnny Jones*. In the '20s, **Rodgers and Hart, George and Ira Gershwin, Cole Porter** and **Oscar Hammerstein II** wrote some of the musical comedy stage's most beautiful songs. It was **Jerome Kern's** *Showboat*,

however, that first combined music and lyrics with the sophisticated adult libretto. All these musicians and lyricists worked in **Tin Pan Alley**, where sheet music was turned out by the pound. Political satire was introduced by the Gershwins in *Of Thee I Sing* and *Strike Up the Band*. In 1935, the folk opera *Porgy and Bess*, also by the Gershwins, brought musical theater to a new plateau.

The collaboration of **Rodgers** and **Hammerstein** started with the artistic triumph of *Oklahoma!* in the 1940s. This musical was brilliantly choreographed by **Agnes de Mille**. *Carousel, South Pacific, The King and I* and *The Sound of Music* also gave new meaning to the musical play. This tradition continued in the '50s and '60s with classics like *Guys and Dolls* by **Loesser**, *My Fair Lady* by **Lerner** and **Lowe**, *West Side Story* by **Bernstein** and **Sondheim** and *Fiddler on the Roof* by **Boch** and **Harnick**.

Musicals have dominated the Broadway stage over the last 3 decades. *Camelot, Funny Girl* and *Hello, Dolly!* opened a period of romanticism. In 1967, *Hair* represented the radical psychedelic movement of the Vietnam War years. In the mid 1970s, *A Chorus Line*, directed by **Michael Bennett**, dazzled audiences with the energy of its dance. Almost every major director of musicals in the last 10 years has been a choreographer. An exception is producer/director **Harold Prince**. In recent years, his productions of *Cabaret, Sweeney Todd* and *Evita* brought a fresh political and social viewpoint to musical theater. On the nostalgic side, *Ain't Misbehavin', 42nd Street* and *Anything Goes* provided grand entertainment. The English musical was the trend of the '80s: **Cameron Macintosh's** *Les Misérables* and fellow Brit **Andrew Lloyd Webber's** *Cats* and *The Phantom of the Opera* took the city by storm; Webber's 1990 *Aspects of Love* was less of a success. Macintosh's controversial *Miss Saigon* was the talk of the town in 1990.

Stage Left: Off and **Off Off Broadway:** As the whetstone for theatrical talent, the reservoir for Broadway and the mechanism for probing the desires of an ever-changing audience, Off and Off Off Broadway have thrived in New York since the 1950s. There are currently over 200 small theaters scattered throughout the city.

The **Provincetown Playhouse** and the **Washington Square Players** set the tone of the little theater movement in the '20s. Decades later, the **Circle in the Square** was the leader of the alternative dramatic scene in Greenwich Village. **Geraldine Page** appeared there in **Tennessee Williams'** *Summer and Smoke*. **Jason Robards** starred in **Eugene O'Neill's** *The Iceman Cometh*. The Circle also helped **George C. Scott, Colleen Dewhurst, Dustin Hoffman, Cicely Tyson** and **James Earl Jones** establish reputations.

Joseph Papp, head of the **New York Shakespeare Festival** at the **Public Theater**, is the most dynamic theater impresario in America today. With his multistage Public Theater on Astor Place, the outdoor Shakespeare Festival at the **Delacorte Theater** in Central Park and productions at **Lincoln Center's Beaumont Theater**, he has nurtured artists such as writers **Sam Shepard, David Rabe** and **Israel Horovitz**, and actors **Meryl Streep** and **Raul Julia**. Papp productions that have gone on to Broadway include *A Chorus Line*, *Plenty* and *The Mystery of Edwin Drood*.

As part of a revitalization of 42nd St, *Theater Row* was established several years ago between 9th and 10th Aves. Thanks to the vision of **Fred Papert**, this once run-down part of the Times Square area has been transformed into an attractive addition to Off Broadway. Tenants include the **Harold Clurman Theater**, the **South Street Theater** and **Playwrights Horizons**.

Off Off Broadway: As Off Broadway productions moved uptown, some artists felt the need to explore

subjects forbidden by the traditions of Broadway and Off Broadway, such as politics, profanity, nudity and sexuality—creating a marvelous spirit of experimentation. **The Living Theater**, founded by **Judith Malina** and **Julian Beck**, was the most controversial of the

politically oriented groups. Groups like **Mabou Mines, The Wooster Group** and the **Ridiculous Theatrical Company** are alive and well today.

The theater scene in all its colors is covered in newspapers like *The New York Times*, the *Village Voice* and *New York* magazine.

36 Café Un Deux Trois ★★$$$ The cafe covers the tables with paper cloths and supplies crayons for doodling. The gimmick seems unnecessary when the place provides satisfaction with its simple food: small steaks, heartrending French fries and fresh seasonal specials. ◆ French ◆ 123 W 44th St (6th-7th Aves) 354.4148

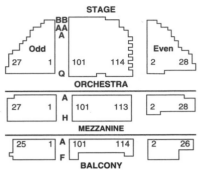

mezzanine **A** overhangs orchestra **J**
balcony **A** overhangs mezzanine **C**

36 Belasco (1907, **George Keister**) The eccentric **David Belasco,** whose preferred style of dress was a priest's frock, wrote and produced *Madame Butterfly* and *The Girl of the Golden West* here. Both were later adapted into operas by **Giacomo Puccini.** Belasco's ghost is said to continue to visit backstage. ◆ 111 W 44th St (6th-7th Aves) Telecharge 239.6200

36 Hotel Macklowe $$$ A handsome, new executive-style hotel with such businesslike

Theater/Garment

amenities as 2 dual-line speaker phones in each room, phone mail in 4 languages and television access to Macktel, an interactive communication system that allows guests to preview restaurant menus, order sporting event and theater tickets, and even check out. In addition, there is a restaurant and bar, a **Sewing Center** for last-minute seam repair and button replacement and a **Fitness Center** staffed with private trainers. The **Macklowe Conference Center** encompasses 38 meeting rooms and 3 boardrooms. At the 650-seat **Hudson Theatre,** a 1902 landmark next door, the hotel maintains a full-service auditorium and 35mm and 70mm screening facilities. One of the first events to take place in the refurbished theater was the 1990 World Chess Championship between **Gary Kasparov** and **Anatoly Karpov.** ◆ 145 W 44th St (6th Ave-Broadway) 768.4400, 800/MACKLOWE; fax 768.0847

37 Paramount Building (1926, **Rapp & Rapp**) The bank on the corner of 43rd St replaced the entrance to the famous **Paramount Theater.** The great glass globe on its pinnacle and the 4-sided clock make the building an attraction, as does its lavish lobby. Before the theater closed in 1964, its stage had been graced by such stars as **Mae West, Pola Negri, Tommy Dorsey, Bing Crosby** and, of course, **Frank Sinatra.** ◆ 1501 Broadway (W 43rd-W 44th Sts)

37 Sardi's ★$$$ On rare occasions a celebrity or 2 can be seen here, but these days there is more seeking than finding. Many of the big Broadway stars have moved on to other galaxies and other eateries, but their presence is still felt in the caricatures that decorate the walls of both floors. At the 2nd-floor bar, the drinks flow with reckless generosity—a compelling reason for it to have remained a favorite hangout for *New York Times* reporters, who search for inspiration among the clinking ice cubes. To encourage the creative process, the *Times* building has provided a back-door entrance that leads directly into Sardi's. I guess that management subscribes to the hallowed theory that serious drinking leads to serious thinking. ◆ Continental ◆ Closed Su. 234 W 44th St (Broadway-8th Ave) Jacket required. 221.8440

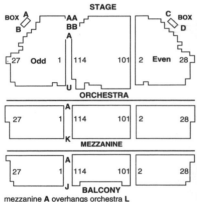

mezzanine **A** overhangs orchestra **L**
balcony **A** overhangs mezzanine **C**
center sections are numbered consecutively

38 Shubert (1913, **Henry B. Herts**) It will be hard to imagine anything but *A Chorus Line* here (after 6137 performances, the longest running musical on Broadway closed on 28 April 1990), but that's what they said about **Katharine Hepburn** in *The Philadelphia Story,* and **Barbra Streisand** in *I Can Get It For You Wholesale.* ◆ 221 W 44th St (Broadway-8th Ave) 246.5990; Telecharge 239.6200

38 Shubert Alley The stage doors of the Shubert Theater on 44th St and of the Booth on 45th open onto this space. So does the entrance to the offices of the **Shubert Organization,** making this a favorite spot for Broadway hopefuls to casually stroll up and down hoping to be noticed by the right people. A gift shop, **One Shubert Alley,** specializes in merchandise related to Broadway shows. ◆ W 44th-W 45th Sts (7th-8th Aves) 944.4133

Restaurants/Nightlife: Red   **Hotels:** Blue
Shops/Parks: Green   **Sights/Culture:** Black

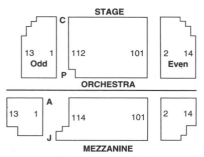

STAGE
ORCHESTRA

mezzanine A overhangs orchestra J

39 Helen Hayes (1912, Ingalls & Hoffman) In 1965, this theater, then known as the **Little Theatre**, became home to the *Merv Griffin* and *David Frost* shows. It reopened as a Broadway theater in 1974. In 1983, it was dedicated to Helen Hayes. ♦ 240 W 44th St (Broadway-8th Ave) 944.9450; Teletron 246.0102

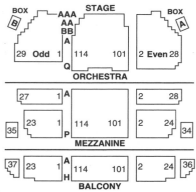

ORCHESTRA
MEZZANINE
BALCONY

mezzanine A overhangs orchestra G
balcony A overhangs mezzanine D
center sections are numbered consecutively

39 St. James (1927, Warren & Wetmore) Rodgers and Hammerstein's *Oklahoma!* was followed by **Ray Bolger** in *Where's Charley?* which in turn was followed by *The King and I*, *The Pajama Game* and others. ♦ 246 W 44th St (Broadway-8th Ave) 398.0280; Teletron 246.0102

D.W. Griffith's controversial landmark film, *The Birth of a Nation*, opened on 3 March 1915 at the Liberty Theater, 234 W 42nd St.

In December of 1988, an underground passageway was opened between the 42nd St subway station of the IND and the IRT's 5th Ave station. This passageway is unusual on many counts: it is not only well-lighted, its walls are adorned with photographic images of nearby street scenes that have been transferred to porcelain enamel panels.

Only a handful of all the semiactuated signals (those chest-high buttons that pedestrians can push to make the light change to green) installed on lightpoles around Manhattan actually work; most are located along 12th Ave.

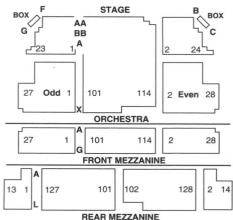

STAGE
ORCHESTRA
FRONT MEZZANINE
REAR MEZZANINE

orchestra is elevated beyond row J
front mezzanine A overhangs orchestra H
center sections are numbered consecutively

40 Majestic (1927, Herbert J. Krapp) *The Music Man*, *Carousel*, *A Little Night Music*, *The Wiz* and now *The Phantom of the Opera* have kept this theater living up to its name. ♦ 247 W 44th St (Broadway-8th Ave) 246.0730; Telecharge 239.6200

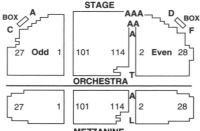

STAGE
ORCHESTRA
MEZZANINE

mezzanine A overhangs orchestra K
center sections are numbered consecutively

40 Broadhurst (1918, Herbert J. Krapp) Humphrey Bogart picked up his credentials as a tough guy when he appeared here with **Leslie Howard** in *The Petrified Forest*. ♦ 235 W 44th St (Broadway-8th Ave) 247.0472; Telecharge 239.6200

41 Mamma Leone's $$ The restaurant that was a landmark on 48th St from 1906, closed in 1987 to make way for a new building. It reopened here in 1988 with all its traditions intact. Among those traditions are waiters who ask for tips rather than work for them, and overcooked food. The management doesn't mind telling you that the restaurant caters to the tourist trade, which means they don't ever expect anyone to come here more than once. No one really wants to. ♦ Italian ♦ 261 W 44th St (7th-8th Aves) 586.5151

42 Milford Plaza $$ (1928, Schwartz & Gross) This hotel, originally known as the **Lincoln**, was built and first operated by the United Cigar Stores Co, which said it catered to the better element of the masses. Today it is a Best Western property advertising itself as the *Lulla-buy of Broadway*. Its 1300 rooms have all been modernized. ♦ 270 W 45th St (8th Ave) 869.3600, 800/221.2690; fax 914.1433

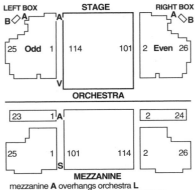

Your Gun and the incomparable **Zero Mostel** performing *If I Were a Rich Man* in *Fiddler on the Roof*. In October 1990, *Les Misérables* moved here from the Broadway theater. ◆ 249 W 45th St (Broadway-8th Ave) 239.6200; Telecharge 239.6200

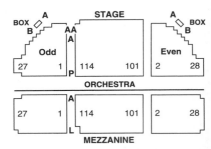

mezzanine **A** overhangs orchestra **J**

46 Music Box Composer **Irving Berlin** built this charming theater to accommodate his *Music Box Revue of 1921*. The first musical to win a Pulitzer Prize, **George Gershwin**'s *Of Thee I Sing*; **John Steinbeck**'s *Of Mice and Men*; **Kurt Weill**'s last musical, *Lost in the Stars*, and **Kim Stanley** in *Bus Stop* were all presented here. ◆ 239 W 45th St (Broadway-8th Ave) Telecharge 239.6200

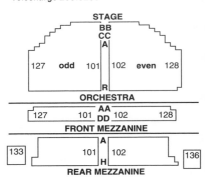

front mezzanine **A** overhangs orchestra **L**

47 Golden (1927, **Herbert J. Krapp**) One of the longest running shows in history, *Tobacco Road* (1933), played this house. *A Party with Comden and Green* (1958), *At the Drop of a Hat*, *Beyond the Fringe* and **Victor Borge** kept audiences laughing here. ◆ 252 W 45th St (Broadway-8th Ave) Telecharge 239.6200

Because of problems at the Chief Medical Examiner's office, an autopsy in New York City can take as long as 6 months.

America's first patent was issued in New York City on 31 July 1790. It was granted to a **Samuel Hopkins** for a process that involved the making and purifying of *potash*, an ingredient used in soap-making. The patent was signed by **President George Washington, Secretary of State Thomas Jefferson** and **Attorney General Edmund Randolf**.

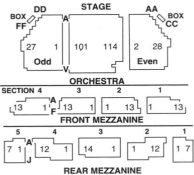

43 Martin Beck (1924, **G. Albert Lansburgh**) The famed **Theatre Guild Studio** used this house in the '30s. Great performances echo from the stage, including those of the **Lunts** in **Robert Sherwood**'s *Reunion in Vienna*, **Katharine Cornell** in *The Barretts of Wimpole Street* and **Ruth Gordon** in *Hotel Universe*. In the '50s, **Arthur Miller**'s *The Crucible* and **Tennessee Williams**' *Sweet Bird of Youth* played here. In 1965, **Peter Brook**'s incendiary production of *Marat/Sade* gave audiences a new look at documentary theater. **Liz Taylor** came out of Hollywood to make her Broadway debut in **Lillian Hellman**'s *The Little Foxes*. ◆ 302 W 45th St (8th-9th Aves) 246.6363; Teletron 246.0102

44 Triton Gallery Theater posters and show cards for current and past performaces on Broadway and elsewhere. Custom framing and mail-order

Theater/Garment

too. Ask for a catalog. ◆ M-Sa 10AM-6PM. 323 W 45th St (8th-9th Aves) 765.2472

45 Frankie and Johnnie's ★$$$ Popular, hectic and noisy old Broadway steakhouse with few discernible charms. ◆ Steakhouse ◆ Closed Su. 269 W 45th St (Broadway-8th Ave) Reservations required. 997.9494

45 Imperial (1923, **Herbert J. Krapp**) *Rosemarie* and *Oh, Kay!* set the tone for this theater. Hit musicals have always found a home here: *Babes in Toyland*, *Jubilee*, *Leave It to Me*, *Annie Get*

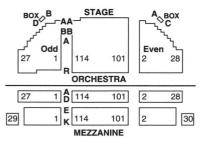

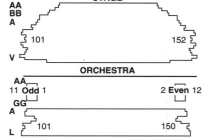

mezzanine A overhangs orchestra I
center sections are numbered consecutively

BALCONY AND MEZZANINE

47 Royale Mae West kept house here for 3 years as *Diamond Lil'*. It was used as a radio studio by CBS from 1936-40. **Laurence Olivier** dazzled audiences with his appearances in *The Entertainer* and *Becket*. *Grease*, Broadway's longest running musical at the time, settled here during its last years. ◆ 242 W 45th St (Broadway-8th Ave) Telecharge 239.6200

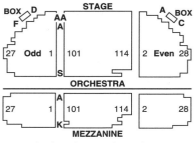

mezzanine A overhangs orchestra J

47 Plymouth (1917, **Herbert J. Krapp**) *Abe Lincoln in Illinois*, with **Raymond Massey**, opened not long after **John** and **Lionel Barrymore** appeared here together in *The Jest*. ◆ 236 W 45th St (Broadway-8th Ave) 730.1760; Telecharge 239.6200

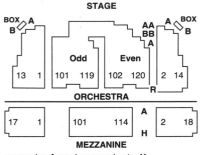

mezzanine A overhangs orchestra H

47 Booth (1913, **Henry B. Herts**) Though named for **Edwin Booth**, **Shirley Booth** made a name for herself here with **Sidney Blackmer** in *Come Back, Little Sheba*. ◆ 222 W 45th St (Broadway-8th Ave) 246.5969; Telecharge 239.6200

Restaurants/Nightlife: Red **Hotels:** Blue
Shops/Parks: Green **Sights/Culture:** Black

48 Minskoff (1973, **Kahn & Jacobs**) Debbie Reynolds opened this house with a revival of *Irene*. As a new theater, it has the best access for handicapped patrons. ◆ 1550 Broadway (W 45th St) 869.0550; Teletron 246.0102

49 Marriott Marquis $$$$ (1985, **John Portman**) This hotel boasts the world's tallest atrium, through which its glass-enclosed elevators zip up and down, serving 47 floors. It has a Broadway theater on the 3rd floor, New York's largest ballroom and its highest lobby (reached by a chain of escalators passing through floor after quiet floor of meeting rooms). The on-the-premises gym has nautilus, sauna, Jacuzzi and a trainer, if you need a push. Valet parking, concierge, 24hr room service and several restaurants and lounges. ◆ 1535 Broadway (W 45th St) 398.1900, 800/228.9290; fax 704.8930

Within the Mariott Marquis:

Marquis (1985, **John Portman**) New York's youngest Broadway theater, operated by the

Theater/Garment

famed **Nederlanders**. Many expected it to suffer from its somewhat untheatrical surroundings—and the bad press caused by the demolition of several old theaters to make way for it. The ill will seems to have been forgotten during the almost 4-year run of the Marquis' first production, *Me and My Girl*. ◆ 382.0100; Teletron 246.0102

The View ★$$$ Except for one at the old World's Fair site in Queens, this is New York's only revolving restaurant. It has a limited view, as do the revolving lounges above it, but when the turntable takes you past Rockefeller Center and the skyline to the east and uptown, you'll be glad you took a ride in that glass elevator. ◆ Continental ◆ Reservations recommended. 704.8900

50 Hamburger Harry's $ It's not just the 16 varieties of major league burgers they serve here, it's also the mesquite-grilled seafood and steaks that recommend this casual grill to New Yorkers in search of the rare and well-done. A Mexican accent adds color to the menu—my favorite, the *Ha-Ha Burger*, is freighted with chili, guacamole, *salsa verde* and cheddar cheese. ◆ American ◆ 145 W 45th St (6th-7th Aves) 840.2756. Also at: 157 Chambers St. 267.4446

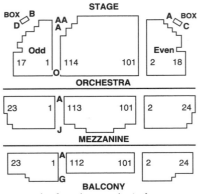

STAGE

BOX B
D

AA
A A

A BOX
C

Odd

Even

17 1 | 114 | 101 | 2 18

O

ORCHESTRA

23 1 | A 113 | 101 | 2 24

J

MEZZANINE

23 1 | A 112 | 101 | 2 24

G

BALCONY

mezzanine **A** overhangs orchestra **L**
balcony **A** overhangs mezzanine **C**

50 Lyceum (1903, **Herts & Tallant**) Producer **Daniel Frohman** built the Lyceum in 1903. Now a city landmark, it is the oldest New York theater still used for legitimate productions. It opened with *The Proud Prince*. In 1947, **Judy Holliday** and **Paul Douglas** wise-cracked through *Born Yesterday*. The **A.P.A.-Phoenix Repertory** made this home base for several seasons, and in 1980, *Morning's at Seven* by **Paul Osborn** was revived here. A lyric, Neo-Baroque structure with banded columns and undulating marquee, it was the first theater designed by Herts & Tallant, undisputed kings of theater architecture. Frohman was such a theater fan that he had his apartment above fitted with a trapdoor through which he could

Theater/Garment

see the stage. ♦ 149 W 45th St (6th-7th Aves) Telecharge 239.6200

Cabana Carioca

50 Cabana Carioca ★★$$$ Macho place for seriously large servings of Brazilian food. Don't miss the suckling pig, steak dishes and black beans. ♦ Brazilian ♦ 123 W 45th St (6th-7th Aves) 581.8088

50 47th Street Photo Old New York reigns supreme at this outpost of the famous 47th St branch. You'll find the same frenzied atmosphere and an equally frenzied, knowledgeable staff. ♦ Closed F afternoon-Sa, in observance of the Jewish sabbath. 115 W 45th St (6th Ave-Broadway) 398.1410. Also at: 64 W 47th St. 398.1410; 116 Nassau St. 608.6934

51 Actor's Equity Building This is the union for all American stage actors—from the virtually unknown to the most famous. It was founded in 1913 by 112 actors to protect the rights and establish good working conditions

for professional stage performers and stage managers. If you're into star gazing, keep your eyes peeled. ♦ 165 W 46th St (6th-7th Aves)

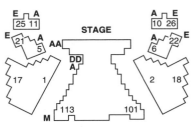

E A
25 11

STAGE

A E
10 26

E
21 A
5

AA

DD
A

A
6

E
22

E

17 1

2 18

113 101

M

51 American Place This theater was founded with the intention of providing a forum for living American playwrights. It opened originally at St. Clement's Church in 1964 with 2 memorable plays: **Robert Lowell**'s *Old Glory* and **William Alfred**'s *Hogan's Goat*. In 1971, a brand new theater with a modified thrust stage was built, adding another dimension to the quality productions. ♦ Seats 299, 74, 74. 111 W 46th St (6th-7th Aves) 840.3074

52 Dish of Salt $$$ A Chinese restaurant in a sophisticated 2-level, bamboo-decorated setting. The cocktail lounge offers equally sophisticated piano music. ♦ Cantonese ♦ Closed Su. 133 W 47th St (6th-7th Aves) 921.4242

53 Portland Square Hotel $ **James Cagney**, **Lila Lee** and **John Boles** once called it home. Today, it offers budget-priced, clean accommodations. ♦ 132 W 47th St (6th-7th Aves) 382.0600; fax 382.0684

54 I. Miller Building Almost hidden away behind advertising signs, on the facade of the building, are sculptures of great women of the theater: **Marilyn Miller, Rosa Ponsell, Ethel Barrymore** and **Mary Pickford**, none of whom would have thought of appearing on stage in anything but I. Miller shoes. The figures are by **A. Stirling Calder**, whose son, **Alexander Calder**, invented the mobile. The shoe store is gone, but the ladies are, for now at least, still here. ♦ W 46th St at NE corner of 7th Ave

55 Duffy Square **Father Francis P. Duffy**, who in WWI was chaplain of the Fighting 69th and served as pastor of nearby Holy Cross Church, is honored in this triangle with a 1937 sculpture by **Charles Keck** at 46th St. He shares the honor with a 1959 statue by **George Lober** of **George M. Cohan**, the actor/producer/writer who wrote *Give My Regards to Broadway*, among hundreds of other songs. ♦ W 46th-W 47th Sts (7th Ave-Broadway)

55 TKTS (1973, **Mayers & Schiff**) The **Theater Development Fund** offers tickets to Broadway and Off Broadway shows and Lincoln Center productions, beginning at 10AM for matinees and 3PM for evening performances, at half-price (plus a nominal fee) for performances on the day of sale. Tickets are not available for every show, but a board under the canopy tells you what is on sale. A better selection is sometimes available close to curtain time, when producers release unused house seats, and during bad weather, when fewer people venture out. ◆ W 47th St (7th Ave-Broadway) Cash or traveler's checks only, no credit cards or personal checks. 354.5800

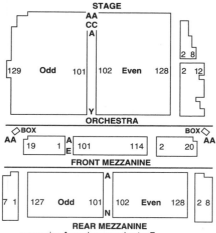

mezzanine **A** overhangs orchestra **F**
center section is numbered consecutively

56 Lunt-Fontanne (1910, **Carrère & Hastings**) **Mary Martin** and **Theodore Bikel** appeared here in *The Sound of Music*, and **Marlene Dietrich** appeared here alone not long afterward. ◆ 205 W 46th St (7th Ave-Broadway) 575.9200; Ticketron 246.0102

57 Richard Rodgers (1925, **Herbert J. Krapp**) **Gwen Verdon** appeared here in *Damn Yankees*, *Redhead* and *New Girl in Town*. It is also where **Olsen & Johnson** began the long-running *Hellzapoppin'*. Formerly the 46th Street Theater, it was dedicated to Richard Rodgers in March 1990. ◆ 226 W 46th St (Broadway-8th Ave) 221.1211; Ticketron 246.0102

58 Paramount Hotel $$ (1928, **Thomas W. Lamb**) This, the latest venture from hotelier **Ian Schraeger** and designer **Phillipe Starck**, was creating a stir months before its opening in August 1990. Slated as a more affordably priced Royalton, the 610-room hotel leaves some of the less young and trendy guests a bit mystified, though reports from guests are overwhelmingly positive—the staff gets an A+ for service. The focal point in the lobby, which is reminiscent of the set for a science-fiction movie, is a large gray staircase that looks as though it could lead up to a space ship, but only goes as far as the mezzanine, where food is served. Elevators are illuminated in different colors: purple and orange, for example, and the bathrooms in the small rooms contain some futuristic Starck designs like silver cone-shaped sinks and lamps reminiscent of stethoscopes. Amenities include a 24hr day-care center, fitness and business centers, 2 executive floors, VCRs and fresh flowers in every room. There is a **Dean & DeLuca** gourmet shop, a brasserie run by **Brian McNally** and a nightclub (where **Billy Rose's Diamond Horseshoe** used to be). Even if you prefer to put down your suitcases in a more conservative setting,

I hope you'll stop in for a peek; the newsstand sells international newspapers and magazines, postcards and gifts—all in black-and-white. ◆ 235 W 46th St (Broadway-8th Ave) 764.5500, 800/223.9868; fax 354.5237

59 Broadway Joe Steak House ★$$$ The steaks and chops are big and tender, the service casual. ◆ American ◆ 315 W 46th St (8th-9th Aves) 246.6513

59 Barbetta $$$ With the exception of its beautiful garden, where the outdoor setting for lunch and dinner almost justifies the mediocre quality of the food, people have been saying this long-established restaurant has lost its bloom. The wine list is extensive and knowledgeably assembled. Sip the wine and order the least complicated of the Northern Italian menu choices. Skip dessert. ◆ Italian ◆ Closed Su. 321 W 46th St (8th-9th Aves) 246.9171

60 Orso ★$$$ A Northern Italian bistro serving pastas, seafood, veal and wonderful pizzas. The handsome marble bar invites you to make yourself comfortable before or after the theater. Try the chicken-and-wild boar sausages with polenta, which arrive steaming hot on lively, hand-painted earthenware. ◆ Italian ◆ 322 W 46th St (8th-9th Aves) Reservations recommended. 489.7212

60 Joe Allen $$ Posters of failed Broadway shows, brick walls, a blackboard menu of simple food, handsome waiters, a stagestruck clientele and frequently the Broadway stars they idolize and emulate. For nourishment, try a salad, a hamburger, a bowl of chili or grilled

fish. ◆ American ◆ 326 W 46th St (8th-9th Aves) 581.6464

60 Le Rivage ★$$$ Continental specialties like filet mignon and poached salmon lyonnaise in a casual setting. ◆ French ◆ 340 W 46th St (8th-9th Aves) Reservations required. 765.7374

61 La Vielle Auberge ★★$$$ A casual old-world bistro. The roast veal is always good. ◆ French ◆ Closed Su. 347 W 46th St (8th-9th Aves) Reservations recommended. 247.4284

61 Lattanzi ★$$$ A taste of the Roman Jewish Quarter in a casual atmosphere. Baby artichokes sautéed in olive oil, grilled fish, homemade pastas—all made to order. ◆ Jewish/Italian ◆ Closed Su. 361 W 46th St (8th-9th Aves) 315.0980

61 Crepes Suzette ★$$$ Traditional bistro fare with homemade desserts. ◆ French ◆ 363 W 46th St (8th-9th Aves) 581.9717

61 Hour Glass Tavern $ Like it or not, the hourglass above the table will give you just 60 minutes to savor the reasonably priced, 3-course prix-fixe dinner. You can expect to see a lot of young Broadway hopefuls in a place like this. ◆ American ◆ 373 W 46th St (8th-9th Aves) No credit cards. 265.2060

62 Karen's Taste of the Tropics $ The tiniest and least expensive restaurant along this eating strip holds 3 tables—2 inside and one outside—and serves hot and spicy authentic Caribbean fare, including codfish patties, Jamaican beef patties and *roti*, a mixture of curried chicken, potato and meat wrapped in flatbread. If you're lucky, the owner, police officer **Karen O'Connor**, will be in when you visit; you'd be hard pressed to find a nicer, more interesting restaurateur. ◆ Caribbean ◆ 374 W 46th St (9th Ave) 586.7769

63 Trixies ★$$ This diner/restaurant, often compared to a 3-ring circus, was opened on New Year's Eve 1987 by a former Wall Street futures broker. The food is better than you might expect—fried chicken with pesto dip, blackened catfish, hickory-smoked ribs with cole slaw—and the nightly entertainment, sometimes scheduled, sometimes not, can be pretty zany. ◆ American ◆ Closed Su. 307 W 47th St (8th Ave) Reservations required. 582.5480

63 B. Smith's ★$$$ Featuring international cuisine creatively presented (shrimp scampi and sweet potato pecan pie are favorites), the fashionable decor reflects the style of the people who have made this one of the more popular restaurants in the Theater District. ◆ Continental ◆ 771 8th Ave (W 47th St) 247.2222

64 Acropolis $ Authentic specialties from Greece in a no-nonsense setting, at prices you'll agree are quite sensible. ◆ Greek ◆ 767 8th Ave (W 47th St) 581.2733

Theater/Garment

65 Pierre au Tunnel ★★$$$ Not only does this Theater District standby serve excellent bistro fare (ethnic specials like *tripes à la mode de Caën* and *tête de veau vinaigrette*), the solicitous staff make sure you're out in time for an 8 o'clock curtain. ◆ French ◆ Closed Su. 250 W 47th St (Broadway-8th Ave) Reservations recommended. 575.1220

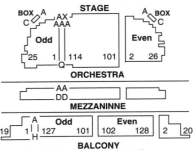

mezzanine **AA** overhangs orchestra **K**

65 Brooks Atkinson (1926, Herbert J. Krapp) The former Mansfield was renamed in 1960 in honor of the *Times* critic. The first in a series of **Neil Simon** comedy hits, *Come Blow Your*

Horn, opened here. **Charles Grodin** and **Ellen Burstyn** performed here for 3 years in *Same Time Next Year*. ◆ 256 W 47th St (Broadway-8th Ave) 719.4099; Teletron 246.0102

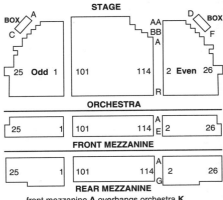

front mezzanine **A** overhangs orchestra **K** center sections are numbered consecutively

66 Barrymore (1928, Herbert J. Krapp) One of the great artists of her era, **Ethel Barrymore** opened the theater in 1928 in *Kingdom of God*. **Fred Astaire** danced his way to stardom in **Cole Porter**'s *The Gay Divorce* (filmed as *The Gay Divorcée*). **Walter Huston** introduced the haunting standard *September Song* in *Knickerbocker Holiday* here and one of America's great actors, **Marlon Brando**, first achieved prominence when he co-starred with **Jessica Tandy** in *A Streetcar Named Desire*. ◆ 243 W 47th St (Broadway-8th Ave) 246.0390; Telecharge 239.6200

67 Sam Ash Orchestral and rock 'n' roll musicians—from those struggling at the bottom of the heap to those celebrating at the top of the charts—come here for state-of-the-art supplies and musical equipment. I like to wander in just to see who's buying. ◆ Closed Su. 160 W 48th St (6th-7th Aves) 719.2661

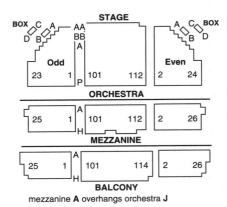

mezzanine **A** overhangs orchestra **J**

67 Cort Many fine plays have opened on this stage, including *The Swan, Merton of the Movies, Charley's Aunt* and *Lady Windermere's Fan*. But one of the most poignant was *The Diary of Anne Frank*, by famed Hollywood writers **Frances** and **Albert Hackett**, which won a Pulitzer in

1955. The theme of children under political oppression returned here in the '80s with *Sarafina*. In 1990, *The Grapes of Wrath* took the Tony for best play. ◆ 138 W 48th St (6th-7th Aves) Telecharge 239.6200

68 Drama Bookshop Established in 1923, it stocks the city's most comprehensive source of books on the dramatic arts aside from the Library of Performing Arts at Lincoln Center. Subject areas include domestic and foreign theater, performers, music, dance, makeup, lighting, props, staging, even puppetry and magic. ◆ 723 7th Ave (W 48th-W 49th Sts) 944.0595

69 Theatre Books Nice selection of new, used and out-of-print books on the theater and related areas. ◆ Closed Su. 1600 Broadway (W 48th-W 49th Sts) Room 1009. 757.2834

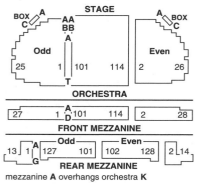

mezzanine **A** overhangs orchestra **K**
balcony **A** overhangs mezzanine **C**

70 Longacre (1913, **Henry B. Herts**) In the 1930s, **The Group Theater** premiered 3 **Clifford Odets** plays: *Waiting for Lefty*, *Paradise Lost* and *Till the Day I Die*. **Julie Harris** appeared in *The Lark* and *Little Moon of Alban*. In 1960, *theater of the absurd* invaded Broadway with the brilliant **Zero Mostel** in *Rhinoceros* by **Eugene Ionesco**. In 1980, *Children of a Lesser God* won a Tony. ◆ 220 W 48th St (Broadway-8th Ave) 246.5639; Telecharge 239.6200

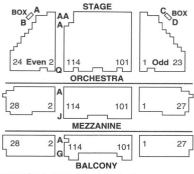

mezzanine **A** overhangs orchestra **K**

71 Eugene O'Neill (1925, **Herbert J. Krapp**) **Arthur Miller**'s first major success, *All My Sons*, opened here in 1947 with **Ed Begley** and **Arthur Kennedy**. The theater has more recently been associated with the works of

Neil Simon, who now owns it. ◆ 230 W 49th St (Broadway-8th Ave) 246.0220; Teletron 246.0102

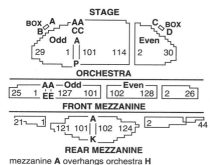

mezzanine **A** overhangs orchestra **H**

72 Ambassador (1921, **Herbert J. Krapp**) In 1939, **Imogene Coca**, **Alfred Drake** and **Danny Kaye** began their careers here in the *Strawhat Review*. ◆ 215 W 49th St (Broadway-8th Ave) 541.6490; Telecharge 239.6200

73 The Brill Building At the turn of the century, publishers of popular songs were all located on 28th St, west of Broadway. The noise of pianos and raspy-voiced song pluggers gave the name *Tin Pan Alley* to the street. When the action moved uptown, the publishers moved to this building and brought the name with them. The bust of the young man over the door is a memorial to the son of the building's original owner, who died just before construction began. ◆ 1619 Broadway (W 49th-W 50th Sts)

Within The Brill Building:

Colony Records A good source of recordings and sheet music for soundtracks, shows and jazz. Open until midnight every day. ◆ 265.2050

74 Worldwide Plaza (Apartment towers 1989, **Frank Williams**; office tower 1989, **Skidmore, Owings & Merrill**) Changes in zoning laws encouraged the construction of this mixed-use complex of residences and offices on the site of the second Madison Square Garden (1925-1966). Commercial occupants include Ogilvy & Mather and Polygram Records. ◆ W 49th-W 50th Sts (8th-9th Aves)

75 Chez Napoleon ★★$$$ A casual bistro hidden away at the edge of the Theater District. This tiny restaurant pays homage to **Napoleon** in its decor, and to Paris in its classic menu. ◆ French ◆ Closed Su. 365 W 50th St (8th-9th Aves) Reservations required. 265.6980

76 Café Des Sports ★$$$ A casual restaurant whose menu has a Gallic accent. It is one of New York's better-kept secrets because its regular customers like it the way it is. But you don't have to be a regular to find a warm welcome. ◆ French ◆ 329 W 51st St (8th-9th Aves) 974.9052

76 Rene Pujol ★★$$$ Enjoy a *choucroute* that is closer to the real thing than you'll find anywhere else in the city at this truly old-fashioned bistro complete with French country atmosphere and decor. Also recommended are the steak *aux poivres*, the cassoulet and, for dessert, crème brûlée. Good and reasonable wine list. ◆ French ◆ Closed Su. 321 W 51st St (8th-9th Aves) 246.3023

76 Tout Va Bien ★$$ Like the other comfortable restaurants in this neighborhood, this classic bistro has been serving a loyal following for decades. In summer, the charming little garden in back is open. ◆ French ◆ 311 W 51st St (8th-9th Aves) 265.0190

77 Les Pyrénèes ★★$$$ A casual country restaurant with a setting made cozier by its working fireplace. Fresh sea bass and roast veal with mustard sauce are winners. ◆ French ◆ 251 W 51st St (Broadway-8th Ave) 246.0044

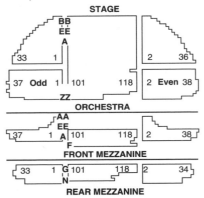

mezzanine A overhangs orchestra N

78 Gershwin (1972, **Ralph Alswang**) In its short history, such stars as **Tommy Tune, Alfred Drake, Bing Crosby, Frank Sinatra** and **Rudolf Nureyev** have appeared on this stage, formerly the Uris Theater, which was also the home of *Sweeney Todd.* ◆ 222 W 51st St (Broadway-8th Ave) 586.6510; Teletron 246.0102

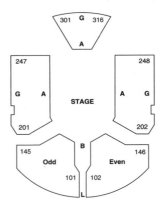

79 Circle in the Square In the past 3 decades, the Circle has produced more than 100 plays—many in the company's original house

in Greenwich Village—and has earned a national reputation for excellence. In 1972, directors **Theodore Mann** and **Paul Libin** built the present arena stage in response to what they saw as a need for classic theater on Broadway. In recent years, *Present Laughter* with **George C. Scott**, *The Caine Mutiny Court Martial* with **John Rubinstein** and *A Streetcar Named Desire* with **Blythe Danner** all achieved critical acclaim. ◆ 1633 Broadway (W 50th-51st Sts) 307.2700; Telecharge 239.6200

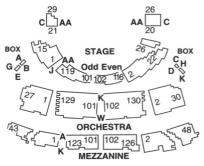

mezzanine A overhangs O at center of orchestra

80 Winter Garden (1910, **W.A. Swasey**) Al Jolson opened this beautiful theater in 1911. The **Shuberts** produced 12 annual editions of their revue *The Passing Show.* **Fanny Brice, Bob Hope** and **Josephine Baker** were featured in the *Ziegfeld Follies.* Other hit musicals *Plain and Fancy, West Side Story, Funny Girl* and those fabulous felines in *Cats.* ◆ 1634 Broadway (W 50th-W 51st Sts) 245.4878; Telecharge 239.6200

81 Sheraton City Squire $$$ A heated indoor swimming pool, a sun deck and a gym furnished with modern exercise equipment are features of this conveniently located hotel. Children stay here free if no extra bed is required. ◆ 790 7th Ave (W 51st St) 581.3300, 800/325.3535

82 Bellini ★$$$$ A first cousin of the famous **Harry's Bar** in Venice, this ultrachic cafe/restaurant attracts a dazzling crowd of the rich and famous. Mercifully, there are no gawkers pointing fingers and exclaiming over the illustrious company at the very closely placed next table. The mediocre food (although the calf's liver is perfection) and superb service keep them coming. Steer clear of the *Bellini*, a Venetian specialty made of champagne and pureed peaches. I always stick to champagne. ◆ Italian ◆ 777 7th Ave (W 51st St) Reservations required. 265.7770

82 Parc 51 $$$$ Some of the space of the old Taft Hotel has gotten a new lease on life in the form of this 178-room marble and crystal palace with 24hr room service, a concierge and access (for a fee) to a health club across the street. The larger-than-average rooms have TVs enclosed within hand-inlaid armoires (there are smaller TVs in the bathrooms). Large terry robes, hand cream, Crabtree and

Evelyn soaps, Dukar razors, bidets, powder rooms and valet parking are among the amenities. Another plus: this hotel *likes* children. ♦ Deluxe ♦ 152 W 51st St (7th Ave) 765.1900, 800/237.0990; fax 541.6604

83 Equitable Center (1985, **Edward Larrabee Barnes & Associates**) A huge mural created by **Roy Lichtenstein** for the building brings you in off the street, and when you get inside there are other works of art to be seen, the most striking of which are the murals in the corridor to your left that were painted in 1930 by **Thomas Hart Benton** and moved here from the New School for Social Research. Also off the Equitable's lobby is the **Whitney at Equitable Center**, a branch of the Whitney Museum of American Art with changing exhibitions), and **Treasury**, a jewel box of a gift shop whose profits are donated to the **Cathedral of St. John the Divine**. ♦ 787 7th Ave (W 51st-W 52nd Sts) 554.1975

Within the Equitable Center:

Le Bernardin ★★★★$$$$ When this brilliant seafood restaurant first exploded onto the scene in 1986, it was acclaimed by everyone who dined here. A few years later, it is still receiving rave reviews, and it is as difficult as ever to get a reservation. The dining room is distinguished—codfish sautéed with a ragout of wild mushrooms and topped with lobster dill sauce is a stand-out—and the prices breathtaking, but the experience justifies the tab, especially if someone else is paying. ♦ French ♦ Closed Su. 155 W 51st St. Reservations required. 489.1515

Palio ★★★$$$$ Named for a horse-racing festival in the town of Siena, Italy, it is well worth a visit, if only to see the stunning graphics by **Vignelli Assoc** and **SOM (Skidmore, Owings & Merrill Assoc)** and wraparound **Sandro Chia** mural that dominates the ground-floor bar. The restaurant itself is on the 2nd floor. From the crystal to the perfection of each rose petal, everything strives for, and achieves, the utmost opulence and luxury. It is a pity the food does not always soar to the same heights. The bar, however, is an experience. ♦ Italian ♦ Closed Su. 151 W 51st St. Jacket and tie required, even in the bar. Reservations required. 245.4850

Sam's ★$$$ *Sam* is **Mariel Hemingway**'s nickname, and this grand cafe/grill is her place, decorated to conjure up images of her (and grandfather **Papa Hemingway**'s) favorite haunts. A young clientele dines on Tex-Mex ravioli filled with corn, green peppers and gar-

lic; crabcakes; and hamburgers—all served by waiters in Western shirts and bolo ties. ♦ American ♦ Closed Su. 152 W 52nd St. Reservations required at lunch. 582.8700

84 La Cite $$$ Bored waiters serve mediocre food in the main restaurant, but excellent bistro-cum-cafe fare is available in the adjoining lunch brasserie. ♦ French ♦ 120 W 51st St (6th-7th Aves) 956.7100

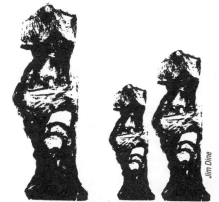

Jim Dine

85 Looking Toward the Avenue Installed in 1989, artist **Jim Dine**'s 3 enormous bronze Venuses (ranging in height from 14 to 23 feet) are a humanizing presence amid the impersonal towers that surround them. ♦ 1301 6th Ave (W 52nd-W 53rd Sts)

86 Ben Benson's Steakhouse ★★$$$ A classic New York restaurant in a relatively new

building. American antiques and prints help do the trick. The steaks are properly aged too. And the service is old-fashioned friendly. ♦ American ♦ 123 W 52nd St (6th-7th Aves) 581.8888

87 Remi ★★★$$$ Fresh antipastos, Venetian-style pastas and grilled meats and fish please both the dealmakers from nearby Time-Warner and Orion who lunch here, and the city's esteemed chefs, who reserve tables for their nights off. The desserts are worth the splurge; be sure to sample one of the 45 varieties of grappa. ♦ Italian ♦ 145 W 53rd St (6th-7th Aves) 581.4242

88 Sheraton Centre $$$ (1962, **Morris Lapidus & Associates**) An efficient modern hotel with excellent convention facilities for the mainly corporate clientele. Guests have use of the indoor swimming pool across the street at the **Sheraton City Squire**. Several restaurants and lounges and 24hr room service. ♦ 811 7th Ave (W 52nd-W 53rd Sts) 581.1000, 800/325.3535; fax 262.4410

Restaurants/Nightlife: Red   **Hotels:** Blue
Shops/Parks: Green   **Sights/Culture:** Black

89 Rosie O'Grady's ★$$$ A lively nouvelle Irish pub that would probably be more at home in O'Brien IA. It attracts a convivial crowd from the nearby hotels with entertainment and dancing every evening after 9:30. ♦ Irish ♦ 800 7th Ave (W 52nd St) 582.2975

90 Broadway (1924, **Eugene DeRosa**) **Ethel Merman** filled this theater with sound and ticket-holders as the star of *Gypsy*. This was also where **Barbra Streisand** performed as *Funny Girl*, and where **Yul Brynner** gave his final performance in *The King and I*. ♦ 1681 Broadway (W 52nd-W 53rd Sts) 247.3600; Telecharge 239.6200

91 Novotel $$$ (1984, **Gruzen & Partners**) Part of a respected French chain, the hotel begins on the 7th floor, and many of its 478 rooms and suites look down into the heart of Times Square. Room service until midnight, valet parking. ♦ 226 W 52nd St (Broadway) 315.0100, 800/221.4542; fax 765.5369

Within Novotel:

Cafe Nicole $$$ A restaurant and wine bar with a 7th floor view of the Theater District and featuring entertainment in the evening hours. Steamed salmon and roast duck are sure bets. ♦ French/American ♦ 315.0100

92 Roseland The legendary ballroom, which opened in 1919, still plays host to Big Bands and aspring Fred Astaires and Ginger Rodgers, although only 2 days a week now. ♦ Admission. Th, Sa 2:30PM-midnight. 239 W 52nd St (Broadway-8th Ave) 247.0200

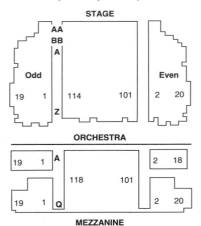

mezzanine **A** overhangs orchestra **K**

92 Virginia (1925, **Howard Crane**) Formerly called the **ANTA**, it was built in 1925 for the **Theatre Guild**. **Pat Hingle** and **Christopher Plummer** starred here in **Archibald MacLeish**'s *J.B.*, which won the Pulitzer Prize in 1959. **Sir Thomas More** was brilliantly played by **Paul Scofield** in **Robert Bolt**'s *A Man for All Seasons* in 1961. *No Place To Be Somebody* moved here from the **Public Theater** after its author, **Charles Gordone**, won the Pulitzer Prize in 1969. ♦ 245 W 52nd St (Broadway-8th Ave) 977.9370; Teletron 246.0102

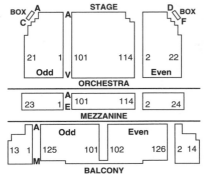

mezzanine **A** overhangs orchestra **K**

93 Neil Simon (1927, **Herbert J. Krapp**) **Fred** and **Adele Astaire** were in this theater's first production, **George** and **Ira Gershwin**'s *Funny Face*. A more recent hit was *Annie*, which arrived here exactly 50 years later. ♦ 250 W 52nd St (Broadway-8th Ave) 757.8646; Teletron 246.0102

93 Russian Samovar ★$$ Staples and specialties of Slavic cooking—*blini* with caviar, grilled fish and lamb—lead the menu here. A 4-course, prix-fixe dinner helps attract regulars, who enjoy the Russian decor and nightly piano/violin recitals. ♦ Russian ♦ 256 W 52nd St (Broadway-8th Ave) Reservations recommended. 757.0168

93 Gallaghers Steak House ★★$$$ The entrance to this vintage New York restaurant—a huge refrigerated locker (visible from the street) filled with steaks and baskets of strawberries—sets the stage for a restaurant that has hardly changed since it opened here in 1927. If you want to know what New York restaurants were like in the good old days, this is the place to do it. The front room with its huge bar can be noisy. It's quieter in back where most of the sound comes from sizzling steaks. ♦ American ♦ 228 W 52nd St (Broadway-8th Ave) 245.5336

94 Bangkok Cuisine ★★$$ The best dishes at this excellent Thai restaurant are the seafood soups spiced with pepper and lemon grass and the baked fish smothered with hot spices. Service is slow, so sip a cup of tea while waiting—it is flavorful and calming. Crowded in the early evening, but more peaceful later on. ♦ Thai ♦ 885 8th Ave (W 52nd-W 53rd Sts) 581.6370

95 Passenger Ship Terminal (1976, **Port Authority Design Staff**) The last of the great ocean liners, known as the *Cunard Queens*, the SS *France* and the USS *United States* used piers in this neighborhood. But before this terminal complex was finished, except for the *QE2* only cruise ships called here regularly. Most arrive Saturday morning and leave again the same afternoon. The facility is used at other times as exhibition space. ♦ 711 12th Ave (W 48th-W 55th Sts) 246.5451

96 Siam Inn ★$$ Spicy, authentic fare is offered in the humdrum dining room of this noisy and fashionable Thai restaurant. Fish and seafood dishes are best. The service isn't good. ♦ Thai ♦ 916 8th Ave (W 54th-W 55th Sts) 974.9583

96 Caramba! ★$$$ The slushy frozen margaritas alone may be worth a stop, but you also won't find better Tex/Mex (actually, this one is Arizona/Mex) in the neighborhood. Handy to theaters, Lincoln Center and Carnegie Hall, it attracts a crowd strong on the young, happy and stagestruck. The 2 brightly decorated white stucco and tile rooms turn over quickly, so don't worry, the long line you may see at the door moves fast. Don't miss the fried tortilla sprinkled with cinnamon sugar and heaped with vanilla ice cream. ♦ Tex/Mex ♦ 918 8th Ave (W 54th-W 55th Sts) 245.7910

97 Stage Delicatessen $$ Looking every bit the sellout that it is, this once-great spot for **Damon Runyon** Broadway characters is now in high disrepute among New Yorkers. Only the pastrami is still good, but the sandwiches are a mite skimpy and high-priced. ♦ Deli ♦ 834 7th Ave (W 53rd-W 54th Sts) No credit cards. 245.7850

98 RHIGA Royal Hotel $$$$ Every room is a suite in this new 54-story luxury hotel with great views and meeting facilities to accommodate up to 110. Amenites in each suite include Crabtree & Evelyn toiletries, VCRs, 2 independent phone lines and computer and facsimile ports. Chef **John Halligan**, from the St. James's Club in San Francisco, prepares Continental nouvelle cuisine in **The Halcyon**, and there is 24hr room service. ♦ 151 W 54th St (6th-7th Aves) 307.5000, 800/937.5454; fax 765.6530

99 New York Hilton $$$ (1963, **William B. Tabler**) The quintessential luxury convention hotel in town is a tower of over 2000 well-appointed rooms with services for businesspeople, such as quick checkout, a copy center, 24hr dictation, rental pocket beeper phones and a multilingual staff. **Executive Tower** rooms offer a refrigerator, radio alarm, electric shoe polisher and a free copy of *USA Today* with breakfast. A battery of restaurants and cocktail lounges includes a nightclub (**Pursuits**) and **Grill 53**, a fine restaurant with live entertainment in the evening hours. ♦ 1335 6th Ave (W 53rd-W 54th Sts) 586.7000, 800/HILTONS

100 Corrado ★★★$$$ The tortellini in Brodo are as good as they are in Bologna; the pasta is homemade; the sauces light and skillfully spiced; the desserts excellent, especially the flavorful ice creams. ♦ Italian ♦ 1373 6th Ave (W 55th-W 56th Sts) 333.3131

101 City Center of Music and Drama (1924, **H.P. Knowles**) This somewhat unlikely Moorish emporium was built as a Shriners' temple in 1924 and converted to City Center in 1943. It was the home of the **New York City Opera** and the **New York City Ballet** before they moved to Lincoln Center. City Center has been splendidly renovated and is now used exclusively for dance. With new raking and improved sightlines, audiences no longer have to strain their necks to see performances. ♦ Seats 2731. Box office noon-8PM. 131 W 55th St (6th-7th Aves) 581.7907

102 Castellano ★$$$ A re-creation of **Harry's Bar** in Venice, serving authentic Venetian cuisine. Ravioli with vegetables is a relatively simple dish made extraordinary by a just-right combination of flavors and textures. ♦ Italian ♦ 138 W 55th St (6th-7th Aves) Reservations required. 664.1975

103 Hotel Wellington $$ A 1930s gem often overlooked, even though it has 840 rooms, a coffeeshop, a restaurant and a cocktail lounge. ♦ 871 7th Ave (W 55th St) 247.3900, 800/652.1212; fax 581.1719

104 Carnegie Delicatessen ★★$$ The classic kosher-style deli and a legend in New York, serving sandwiches named after most of the other New York legends. The menu may seem a bit pricey at first—but then the sandwiches arrive, massive affairs that inevitably provide tasty leftovers to be carted home. Owner **Leo** died recently, but not before seeing the Carnegie immortalized in **Woody Allen**'s *Broadway Danny Rose*. Still a leader in the ongoing New York deli wars. One of my favorites. ♦ Deli ♦ 854 7th Ave (W 55th St) No credit cards. 757.2245

104 Omni Park Central $$$ (1927, **Groneburg & Leuchtag**) When the '20s roared, a lot of the sound and fury echoed through the halls of

Theater/Garment

the Park Central, which was a meeting place for bootleggers and small-time gangsters. The ghosts have all been exorcised, and the hotel has a new lease on life. On-site restaurant, lounge, pharmacy, newsstand and barbershop. ♦ 870 7th Ave (W 55th-W 56th Sts) 247.8000, 800/THE.OMNI; fax 484.3374

105 MONY Tower (1950, **Shreve, Lamb & Harmon**) When this building was built, the insurance company whose headquarters it is known as Mutual of New York. It has since become **MONY Financial Services**. The mast on top of the tower is all about change of another kind. If the light on top is green, look for fair weather. Orange means clouds are coming, and flashing orange signals rain. When it flashes white, expect snow. If the lights on the mast itself are rising, so will the temperature, and when they move from top to bottom, it is going to get cold. ♦ 1740 Broadway (W 55th-W 56th Sts)

106 Broadway Diner ★$$ An upscale diner with a wide variety of daily specials. Good salads, steaks and fresh fish. Lots of tables and a counter for a quick bite. ♦ American ♦ 1726 Broadway (W 55th St) 765.0909. Also at: 590 Lexington Ave. 486.8838

107 CBS Broadcast Center A TV production center and headquarters of **CBS News**. It was originally the headquarters of a dairy, and CBS old-timers still call it the *Cowbarn*. ♦ 524 W 57th St (10th-11th Aves) 975.4321

108 Parc Vendome Apartments (1931, **Henry Mandel**) This was one of the sites assembled for a second Metropolitan Opera House. The scheme died when opera patrons were told that a skyscraper would be built to help support it. *We don't need that kind of help*, they sniffed, and took their money elsewhere. The 570-unit apartment house contains a private dining room, a gymnasium and pool, a music room and terraced gardens. ♦ 340 W 57th St (9th-10th Aves) 247.6990

109 Hearst Magazine Building (1928, **Joseph Urban**) A bizarre concoction reminiscent of the Viennese Secession with strange obelisks standing on a heavy base and rising over the roof of the 6-story pile. Apparently, this was intended to be the plinth for another 7 stories; it would have remained a folly nonetheless. ♦ 959 8th Ave (W 56th-W 57th Sts) 262.5700

110 Coliseum Books A huge mix of both general interest and scholarly books: academic, trade and mass paperbacks; sports; how-to books; scholarly journals and oversize paper and hardcover remainders. Computer reference and a helpful staff. Another plus: late hours. ♦ 1771 Broadway (W 57th St) 757.8381

110 Biograph One of the few remaining revival movie houses in the city. Hopefully, the public will continue to fight vigorously each time at-

Theater/Garment

tempts are made to convert it into yet another mainstream cinema. ♦ 225 W 57th St (Broadway) 582.4582

111 Hard Rock Cafe ★★$$ Look for the tail end of a 1958 Cadillac that doubles as its marquee, or follow the young crowd that considers this branch of the Hard Rock that opened in London in 1971 a transcendental experience. If you're one of the unfortunate few without a Hard Rock sweatshirt, you can buy one in the gift shop next door. But then you won't see the guitar-shaped bar or the rock memorabilia that include dozens of gold records, **Prince**'s purple jacket and **Jimi Hendrix**'s guitar. And you'll miss the terrific hamburgers and the chance to pig out on the legendary desserts. ♦ American ♦ 221 W 57th St (7th Ave-Broadway) 489.6565

111 Art Students League (1892, **Henry J. Hardenbergh**) The 3 central panels on this French Renaissance palace represent the **Fine Arts Society**, the **Architectural League** and the **Art Students League**, all of whom originally shared this facility and made it the scene of nearly every important exhibition at the turn of the century. ♦ 215 W 57th St (7th Ave-Broadway) 247.4510

112 The Osborne (1885, **James E. Ware**) Except for the removal of its front porch and the addition of retail stores, this wonderful apartment building has hardly changed in 100 years. The lobby was designed by **Louis Comfort Tiffany**. ♦ 205 W 57th St (7th Ave)

113 Trattoria Dell'Arte ★★$$$ Here, opposite Carnegie Hall, in a colorful restaurant designed by **Milton Glaser**, presides the largest antipasto bar in the world, according to its proud management. A casual Italian menu features delicate, thin-crust pizza in the heart of New York's cultural center. In addition to other sources, Glaser drew inspiration from the noses of some 32 famous Italians—**Joe DiMaggio** and **Geraldine Ferraro** among them. ♦ Italian ♦ 200 W 57th St (7th Ave) Reservations recommended. 245.9800

Carnegie Hall Archives

114 Carnegie Hall (1891, **William B. Tuthill; William Morris Hunt** and **Dankmar Adler**, consultants; renovation 1986, **James Stewart Polshek and Partners**) Peter Ilyich Tchaikovsky conducted the **New York Philharmonic** in the opening concert here, and during the next 70 years the orchestra played under such greats as **Gustav Mahler, Bruno Walter, Arturo Toscanini, Leopold Stokowski** and **Leonard Bernstein**. Considered to have acoustics matched by few others in the world, the hall has attracted all of the 20th century's great musicians, and not just the classical variety. **W.C. Handy** brought his blues here in 1928, and was followed by **Count Basie, Duke Ellington, Benny Goodman** and others. In spite of it all, not one of Carnegie Hall's owners was ever able to make a profit, and in the 1960s, after Lincoln Center opened, it was announced the hall would be torn down. Violinist **Isaac Stern** and a group of concerned music lovers waged a successful campaign to save it. Their effort eventually resulted in a complete restoration that makes it as glorious visually as it is acoustically. The corridors are lined with scores and other memorabilia of the artists and composers who have added to Carnegie Hall's greatness. The space above the auditorium is made up of studios and apartments favored by musicians and artists. Part of the space is made up of the **Weill Recital Hall**, used by soloists and small chamber groups. In the spring of 1991, **Carnegie Hall Museum (James Stewart Polshek and Partners)** is scheduled to open at the Carnegie Hall Tower (**Cesar Pelli**), adjacent to the concert hall on 57th St. Tours of Carnegie Hall are given Tuesday and Thursday at 11:30AM, 2 and 3PM. ◆ Seats 2804. 154 W 57th St (7th Ave) 247.7800

115 Joseph Patelson Music House Musicians, from beginners to world-renowned maestros, have been coming to this former carriage house for their classical music needs (sheet music and books, orchestral and opera scores) ever since it opened in 1920. With the widest selection of music in the world, it's no surprise that Patelson's receives orders from as far away as Japan, Australia and Saudi Arabia. The knowledgable staff is always available to help; feel free to browse. Highly recommended. ◆ Closed Su. 160 W 56th St (6th-7th Aves) 582.5840

116 The Mysterious Bookshop If you want to know *whodunit*, the amazingly knowledgeable staff here won't spoil the fun by telling you, but they will guide you to the exact mystery book that will let you find out for yourself. There are thousands of such books, both new and out-of-print, in this 2-level shop. ◆ Closed Su. 129 W 56th St (6th-7th Aves) 765.0900

117 The Russian Tea Room ★★$$$ I think this may be the happiest place in town, with year-round Christmas decorations, paintings, samovars and bright colors trimmed with gleaming brass. The Tea Room also offers the exhilaration of celebrity-watching and mingling with beautifully dressed people. The dining experience often begins with caviar and ends with baklava, and includes other traditional Russian fare. In the Old Country they call it peasant food, but here it is served in a setting that would warm the heart of a czar. In

the '30s and '40s, the Tea Room had a cabaret, the **Casino Russe**; in the fall of 1990, a new cabaret opened above the restaurant, featuring performers like **Julie Wilson, David Staller** and **Andrea Marcovicci**. ◆ Russian ◆ 150 W 57th St (6th-7th Aves) Jacket, tie and reservations required. 265.0947

117 Parker Meridien $$$ Its main entrance is on 56th St, but they've included an attractive corridor leading to the other side, which gives it a more uptown address. When making a reservation, ask for an odd-numbered room above the 23rd floor, and you'll be rewarded with a wonderful view of Central Park. The 42-story hotel has 2 restaurants (**Le Patio** turns out a sumptuous buffet breakfast), a rooftop swimming pool with a jogging track, and racquetball and squash courts. The 24hr room service has a European flair, as does everything else about the Meridien. ◆ 118 W 57th St (6th-7th Aves) 245.5000, 800/543.4300; fax 307.1776

Within the Parker Meridien:

Maurice ★★★★$$$$ A supremely elegant room and exquisite flower arrangements set the mood for chef **Christian Delouvrier**'s cooking—roasted Maine lobster topped with a delicate vanilla wine sauce is a typically inventive combination. Wonderful wines and impeccable service. ◆ French ◆ Jacket and tie required. Reservations recommended. 245.7788

117 New York Delicatessen $$ (1938, **Ralph Bencker**) The building housing this 500-seat, 24hr restaurant featuring corned beef, blintzes

and the like is one of the few remaining of dozens like it that housed **Horn & Hardart** Automats a half-century ago. ◆ Deli ◆ 104 W 57th St (6th-7th Aves) 541.8320

117 Sidney Janis Gallery Long associated with gilt-edged modern art, the gallery covers the spectrum from Cubism to Abstract-Expressionism to Pop Art and the top young contemporary artists. Standbys include **Leger, Giacometti, Mondrian** and **Segal**. ◆ M-Sa 10AM-5:30PM. 110 W 57th St (6th-7th Aves) 586.0110

117 Poli Fabrics Fine fabrics at fair prices are well-labeled with the price, fiber content and, often, the name of a designer who has used it: **Carolyn Roehm** or **Ellen Tracy**, for example. ◆ Closed Su. 132 W 57th St (6th-7th Aves) 245.7750

118 Steinway Hall (1925, **Warren & Wetmore**) Look through the concave window into the showroom of this prestigious piano company, housed, appropriately, in a domed hall with a huge crystal chandelier. The 12-story building with a 3-story Greek temple on the roof also includes a recital salon. The relief of **Apollo** over the central arch is by **Leo Lentelli**. ◆ 109 W 57th St (6th-7th Aves) 246.1100

119 Salisbury Hotel $$ Most of the 320 large rooms have serving pantries and in-room safes. Straightforward American fare is served at the small and casual **Terrace Cafe**. ♦ 123 W 57th St (6th-7th Aves) 246.1300, 800/223.0680; fax 977.7752

119 Uncle Sam's Umbrella Shop This shop has been protecting New Yorkers from the elements for over 120 years with umbrellas in all different sizes, shapes and prices, and repairs while you wait. All of the umbrellas for the musical *My Fair Lady* were made here. ♦ Closed Su. 161 W 57th St (6th-7th Aves) 582.1977

120 Petrossian ★★★$$$$ In Paris, Petrossian is the leading source for caviar. It may also be true in New York, thanks to this lush marble and mink-trimmed room, where you can sample caviar in all its varieties as well as smoked salmon and *foie gras*, along with champagne or frosty vodka. Take-home delicacies are available in the adjoining retail shop. ♦ Continental ♦ 182 W 58th St (7th Ave) Jacket, tie and reservations required. 245.2214

120 Alwyn Court (1909, **Harde and Short**) The terracotta dragons and other decorations that

Theater/Garment

cover every inch of this apartment house are in the style of the great art patron of the Renaissance, **Francis I**. His symbol, a crowned salamander, is prominently displayed above the entrance at the 58th St corner. Almost no one ever passes by without stopping for a lingering look. ♦ 180 W 58th St (7th Ave)

121 Freed of London Best known to beginning and professional ballet dancers for their handmade shoes from England and Spain, Freeds also sells tap, ballroom and theatrical shoes plus dancewear. ♦ Closed Su. 922 7th Ave (W 58th St) 489.1055

122 Urban Grill $$ A simple coffeeshop where the eggs and sausage are just perfect for breakfast and the hamburgers and grilled chicken make a fine quick lunch or pretheater bite. ♦ Coffeeshop ♦ 330 W 58th St (8th-9th Aves) 586.3300

123 IRT Powerhouse (1904, **McKim, Mead & White**) The original subway line, called **Interboro Rapid Transit**, began running under Broadway in October 1904. It got its electric power from this building, which now generates electricity for Con Edison. ♦ W 58th-W 59th Sts (11th-12th Aves)

124 San Domenico ★★★$$$$ **Gianluigi Morini** and chef **Valentino Marcattilli** have brought their baby to New York from a suburb of Bologna, where they have been dazzling international food critics since 1970. A marble bar, a terracotta floor imported from Florence and smooth, ocher-tinted stucco walls applied by artisans from Rome put the diner firmly in a better world, where *uovo al tartufo* (spinach and ricotta topped with a soft egg ravioli and sprinkled with truffles) and other opulent splendors of Italian cuisine can temporarily create the illusion of perfection. Owned by **Anthony May**, who once owned Palio. ♦ Italian ♦ 240 Central Park So (7th Ave-Broadway) Reservations required. 265.5959

124 Gainsborough Studios (1908, **Charles W. Buckham**) One of the oldest apartment buildings in the city. It is worth passing by for a look at the frieze by **Isadore Konti** across the 2nd floor—a festival procession with a bust of Gainsborough at the center. One of the city's best facades. ♦ 222 Central Park So (7th Ave-Broadway)

125 The New York Athletic Club (1930, **York & Sawyer**) A 22-story building housing handball and squash courts and other exercise facilities, including a swimming pool. The club was founded in 1868 and has sent winning teams to many Olympic Games. There are guest rooms in the club, but visitors who want to begin their day running in Central Park are not permitted to go through the lobby in jogging outfits. ♦ 180 Central Park So (7th Ave) 247.5100

126 Essex House $$$$ (1930, **Frank Grad**) **Nikko Hotels**, which owns this property, is currently spending $70 million on renovations, which include increasing the size of the rooms, redecorating and adding a health club, French restaurant and cafe. The new, ultraluxurious Essex House is expected to open in mid 1991. Originally planned to be an apartment house named the Seville, the 43-story building's Art Deco details and artful use of setbacks make it one of Manhattan's more pleasing towers. ♦ 160 Central Park So (6th-7th Aves) 247.0300, 800/NIKKO.US

126 Hampshire House (1931, **Caughey & Evans**) A hotel converted to cooperative apartments, its peaked roof of copper turned a marvelous shade of green is one of the highlights of the skyline bordering Central Park. Its lobby is one of the joys of the neighborhood. When the cornerstone was put in place, it was filled with the best books and music of 1931. It will never have to be opened; the building itself does the job of explaining what 1931 was all about. ♦ 150 Central Park So (6th-7th Aves)

126 Ritz-Carlton $$$$ (Redesign by **Parrish-Hadley**, 1982) Until its refurbishing, which included the charming bow to another era of putting awnings over the windows, this was known as the **Navarro**. The new owner also owns the **Boston Ritz**, among other properties that follow the tradition of the great **Cezar Ritz**, who changed British tradition when he opened a hotel in London in 1898. The design of the hotel is in the style of English manor houses. Amenities include 24hr room service, robes, twice-daily housekeeping, turndown service, refrigerators upon request and no fewer than 3 phones in every room. ♦ Deluxe ♦ 112 Central Park So (6th-7th Aves) 757.1900, 800/223.7990; fax 757.9620

Within the Ritz-Carlton:

The Jockey Club ★$$$$ The British theme of the hotel is carried out in the hunt-club atmosphere of this room, which serves nouvelle French cuisine and has a comfortable bar. ♦ French ♦ Jacket and tie required in the evening. Reservations required. 757.1900

Bests

George Lang
Owner Café des Artistes, Consultant, Author

Remi I have rarely eaten Italian food as good as that served in this place, even in the Mother Country. Chef **Francesco Antonucci**'s dishes—like the roasted quail wrapped in bacon and served with warm lentil salad, fettuccine sautéed with miniature sea scallops in their shell with broccoli raab—remind me that a good chef is like a good fairy who dispenses happiness. Even the most knowledgeable Italian wine connoisseur will find surprises on the wine list, and what's more, they are so reasonably priced that while drinking, I don't have to shed a domestic tear into my imported wine.

Park Bistro When I stepped through the lace-lined door into the packed, noisy 65-seat restaurant with its plain wood floors, banquettes, posters and photos of the partners home territory, the accents of the waiters—for a moment I thought that my mind was playing tricks on me and I was in Paris. Even the dark red surfaces gave me a secret message; I found out later that one of the partners is from Bordeaux. Favorite dishes of mine include pizzette tartlettes baked with tomatoes and fresh sardines, fresh codfish served with lemon sauce and rice infused with the flavor of the verbena plant, and lamb shank braised for 7 hours with bits of dried apricots, currants, vegetables and wild mushrooms.

Chef's and Cuisinière's Club C.C.C. is truly directed toward the needs of fellow chefs—the 3 partners are friends from their days together at the **Culinary Institute of America**, and worked together at Côte Basque. You will eat some of the best foods anywhere in the unpretentious little dining room. At my last dinner, every dish was a winner, including super-crisp oysters fried in Japanese bread crumbs in an undercoat of rémoulade, a whole salmon cured in fennel marinade and dribbled with a mayonnaise made with cold-pressed olive oil with a canter of fresh fennel slaw, seared and braised fresh cod served with herb-roasted vegetables. The sweet-smelling desserts are not overly sweet—the tartlet containing caramelized banana slices with a streusel topping was a blissful ending to a dinner that was terrific by any standard. Wow!

Carmine's I think Carmine's reflects the post-Reagan era yearning for an America where the tables had 4 legs, the light source was not halogen and the pasta of choice was spaghetti. My recommendations, based on serious soul- and stomach-searching: fried calamari (for 2) or rigatoni with broccoli-and-fennel sausage. Chicken Contadina (a whole 4lb chicken cooked with quantities of sausage, potatoes, onions and peppers), a salad made with the maligned iceberg lettuce, pepperoni, olives and purple onion. Anything you order will be enough for 2 or more persons—more than half of each dish served here goes home in a doggy bag.

Brendan Gill
Writer, *The New Yorker*

Downstairs at *21*.

A midsummer night's sail from the **South Street Seaport Museum**.

Openings at the **Clocktower Gallery**, high above Broadway.

Sunday brunch at **Mortimer's**.

The latest theater piece at **LaMama E.T.C,** with Ellen Stewart presiding.

A ramble in the **Ramble**, in Central Park.

The **Big Apple Circus**.

The sound of brasses on Sunday morning at the **Cathedral of St. John the Divine**.

Crossing the windswept boardwalk of the **Brooklyn Bridge**.

The successful flagging down of a taxi at twilight on Park Ave.

Books & Company, a shop eager to serve customers even on Sunday.

Theater/Garment

Architectural exhibitions at the **Urban Center** in the historic **Villard Houses** on Madison Ave.

Ninth St, west of 5th Ave.

Lunch in the **Rose Room** of the **Algonquin**.

The **New York Society Library**.

The annual festival of the **Film Society of Lincoln Center**.

The **Café des Artistes**.

A big winter opening at the **Whitney Museum of American Art**.

Brandy at **Jim McMullen's**.

The delectable smell of **Bendel's**.

The pillared Palladian folly on W 57th St that leads one into the **Parker Meridien Hotel**.

Bradley's Bar, on University Pl.

Upstairs at *21*.

Sirio Maccioni
Owner and Manager, Le Cirque

Lutéce.

David Bouley.

Hotel Mayfair Regent.

Midtown

To most people, **Midtown** is the heart of Manhattan. They may disagree as to exactly what geographic area it encompasses (our answer is the neighborhood bounded by **40th** and **59th Sts**, **6th Ave** and the **East River**), but they will all agree that it has a concentration of important office complexes, handsome public buildings, grand hotels, tempting restaurants, glittering shops and high-rent residential enclaves.

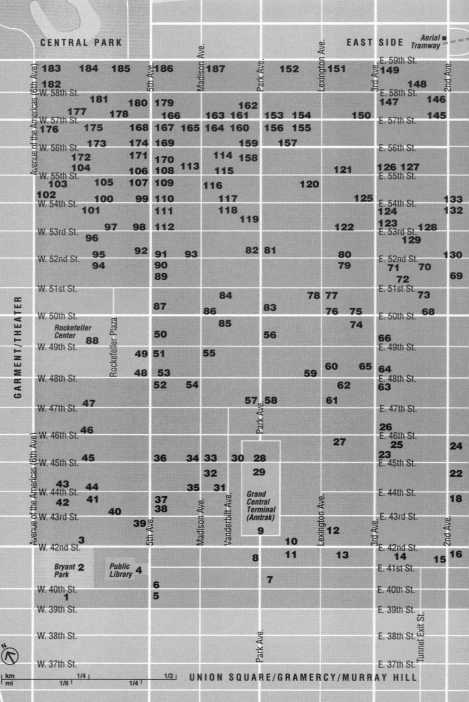

The neighborhood begins with a concentration of office buildings in what real-estate people call the **Grand Central Area**. It touches on **Rockefeller Center**. The headquarters of the **United Nations**, officially not a part of New York at all, is at its eastern edge.

It's a good bet that 90 percent of the people who jam Midtown's streets live elsewhere. In fact, those thousands who pour out of **Grand Central Terminal** every

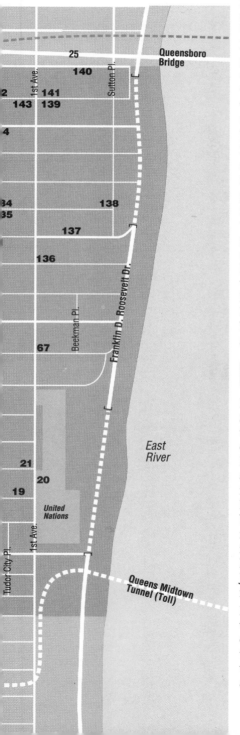

morning and rush to their offices without raising their eyes, and then hurry back in the afternoon without ever having *seen* New York, would be surprised to learn that Midtown is as wonderful a place to live in as it is to visit.

The possibilities include the huge **Tudor City** complex overlooking the UN. Or **Turtle Bay**, with blocks of brownstone houses in the 50s east of 3rd Ave. There are dozens of high-rise apartment buildings to consider too, many of them advertised as *pre-war*.

Beekman Place, 2 blocks of townhouses (49th to 51st Sts between 1st Ave and the river), is a hidden treasure. **Sutton Place**, a longer residential street above 50th St along the river, has the same high-privacy profile. It was part of a plan for English-style houses for the well-to-do developed by **Effingham B. Sutton** in 1875. **Morgans**, **Vanderbilts** and **Phippses**, among others, have lived here.

Midtown

But it wasn't always that way. When Sutton Place was built, it was in wild territory overlooking what was then called **Blackwell's Island** in the East River, where the city maintained an almshouse, workhouse, prison and insane asylum. Although there was a horsecar line running along 2nd Ave between Fulton and 129th Sts, Sutton's riverfront property was a long way from the mainstream. The neighborhood didn't become *acceptable* until **J.P. Morgan**'s daughter moved here in 1921.

Before then, society generally stayed west of Park Ave. In fact, in the 19th century they'd have hooted you out of the city if you mentioned that 4th Ave would one day be called Park. In 1832, a railroad line was built in the center of the dirt road, and steam trains huffed and puffed their way in and out of New York past squatters' shacks with goats in the front yards and pigs out back.

Little by little the tracks were roofed over, but it wasn't until the present Grand Central Terminal was designed in 1903 that anything was done about covering the railroad yards that had grown up between 42nd and 45th Sts, between Madison and Lexington Aves. When the UN moved into the area in 1947, the cattle pens disappeared and Midtown East became a neighborhood in its own right.

From the day it opened in 1837, the rich and famous began to penetrate 5th Ave. Railroad tycoon **Jay Gould** was one of the first. He built a mansion at 47th and 5th, and began taking important friends like **Russell Sage, Morton F. Plant** and **William H. Vanderbilt** to business dinners at the nearby **Windsor Hotel**.

By the late 1800s, W.H. Vanderbilt had built 3 mansions on the west side of 5th Ave at 51st St. His son, **William K. Vanderbilt**, built a 4th palace a few doors uptown. Another son, **Cornelius II**, tried to upstage them with an even grander house at 58th St. In their quest to outdo one another, they ended once and for all the idea of the traditional New York row house with a brownstone front. And who would have thought of living anywhere but on 5th Ave in the blocks between 40th and 59th Sts?

Mrs. Astor, that's who. When her husband's nephew, **William Waldorf Astor**, built a hotel next to her house on 5th Ave at 33rd St, she retaliated by tearing down the house and building another hotel next to his. Then she built a Renaissance palace for herself at 5th Ave and 65th St. After her inaugural ball there in 1896, *Millionaire's Row* packed in its limestone tents and began moving uptown.

Only a few reminders of the 19th-century mansions remain on 5th Ave, including the one that houses **Cartier** at 52nd St, which, according to one story, Morton F. Plant traded with **Pierre Cartier** for a string of pearls.

But many of the fine public buildings survive. Houses of worship include such landmarks as **St. Thomas Church, St. Patrick's Cathedral**, the Romanesque **St. Bartholomew's Church** and the vaguely Moorish **Central Synagogue** —the oldest building in New York City

in continuous use as a synagogue. Secular monuments also remain, such as the vast **New York Public Library** and, of course, Grand Central Terminal, which was saved after a long preservation battle.

Except for St. Bartholomew's Church, the **Waldorf-Astoria Hotel** and a few more holdouts, today Park Ave north of Grand Central Terminal is wall-to-wall office buildings, including important examples of the *glass box* genre built in the '50s: **Ludwig Mies van der Rohe** and **Philip Johnson's Seagram Building** and **Skidmore, Owings & Merrill's Lever House**.

Important office buildings and complexes on the other avenues range from the classic Rockefeller Center to the contemporary **Olympic Tower, Citicorp** and **IBM** buildings. Madison Ave above 50th St has seen an office-building boom, but it's 3rd Ave in the 20-block strip from 39th to 59th Sts that has had the real mega-office building explosion.

Unexpected pockets of distinctive apartment and townhouses continue to cling to the side streets of Midtown (54th St near the **Museum of Modern Art**, for example). In combination with small parks such as **Greenacre** and **Paley**, they bring greenery and human scale to what might seem at first glance to be a Midtown that is a solid concentration of high-rise towers and splendid public buildings.

1 American-Standard Building (1923, **Raymond Hood**) Originally known as the **American Radiator Building**, this was Raymond Hood's first major building in New York City (he had just won the **Chicago Tribune** commission). He went on to **McGraw-Hill**, the **Daily News** and **Rockefeller Center**. This 21-story midblock tower is a stylized variation of the Tribune design: Gothic details tempered by Art Deco lines. Hood used black brick so that the window holes would fade into the sculpted mass, and the gold ornamented top would be that much more spectacular. When lit, it has been compared to a glowing coal—appropriately enough for a manufacturer of heating equipment. The plumbing showroom in the lobby is not part of the original design. ♦ 40 W 40th St (5th-6th Aves)

2 Bryant Park (1934, **Lusby Simpson**; executed under the direction of **Robert Moses**) This is the only park in the city designed like a formal garden. It was named for the poet **William Cullen Bryant**, a prime mover in the campaign to establish Central Park and a champion of the Hudson River School of painters, which established the fashion for wild, naturalistic parks. Before it was a park, it was a potter's field, and in 1853 it was the site of America's first World's Fair, held in a magnificent domed pavilion of iron and glass known as the *Crystal Palace*. Among the wonders unveiled to the world there were **Elisha Graves Otis**' elevator, **Peter Cooper**'s steel wire and **Isaac Merrit Singer**'s sewing machine. The building stood here until 1858, when it burned to the ground in what an eyewitness called *a most beautiful fire*. After the ruins were cleared, the space was used as a parade ground for troops getting ready to defend the Union in the Civil War. And when the war was over, it was dedicated as a public park. But it was little more than a 2-block vacant lot until the public library was built and a terrace was added. The park was redesigned in 1934 as the result of a competition to aid unemployed architects. In the Depression years it was a gathering spot for the unemployed, and in the '60s it became a retail space for marijuana peddlers. In 1980, the Bryant Park Restoration Corporation (Hanna/Olin Ltd.) was born and began a massive restoration program that continues to this day. The program includes new landscaping and lighting, the restoration of monuments, footpaths and benches, the addition of food service and the renewal of public events within the park. As the program moves forward, the park becomes a safer, friendlier place to be. ♦ 6th Ave (W 40th-W 42nd Sts)

Within Bryant Park:

Music & Dance Tickets Booth Same-day $1/2$-price tickets for music and dance performances in all 5 boroughs. Also availabe are full-price advance tickets for TicketMaster sports and entertainment events. Cash or traveler's checks only. ♦ Tu, Th-F noon-2PM, 3-7PM; W, Sa 11AM-2PM, 3-7PM; Su noon-6PM. W 42nd St at 6th Ave. 382.2323

3 W.R. Grace Building (1974, **Skidmore, Owings & Merrill**) Some people actually like this sloping, ski-jump, wind-loading diagram, but it is generally considered a poor interruption of the street wall. Beyond that non-gesture, this building has a barren little plaza on the corner of 43rd St and 6th Ave—an alleged public amenity for which the developers were allowed extra floors. At the same time, SOM was building an identical structure for a different client on 57th St. ♦ 43 W 42nd St (5th-6th Aves)

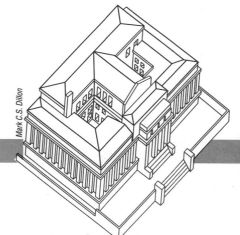

3 City University of New York Graduate Center (Recycled 1966, **Carl J. Petrilli**) This was originally **Aeolian Hall**, where **Paul Whiteman** premiered **George Gershwin**'s *Rhapsody in Blue* in 1924. The street-level arcade is used for exhibitions and occasional concerts, and also doubles, unfortunately, as a parking lot for officials of the school. ♦ 33 W 42nd St (5th-6th Aves) 642.1600

Mark C.S. Dillon

4 New York Public Library (1911, **Carrère & Hastings**) Before you do another thing, cross to the east side of 5th Ave and treat your soul to one of New York's greatest experiences, the sight of the front of the **New York Public Library's Central Research Building**. The lions, *Patience* and *Fortitude*, are familiar; they are the work of **Edward Clark Potter**. But there is more to see out here. Look at the bases of the 95ft-high, tapered steel flagposts (**Thomas Hastings**) up there on the terrace. And the lampposts. And the balustrades. And the urns. Look at the sculpture by **Paul Bartlett, George G. Barnard** and **John Donnelly** above you. And the fountains in front of you, both by **Frederick MacMonnies**; the one on your right represents Truth, the other Beauty. The library was built with the resources of 2 privately funded libraries, combined in 1895 with the infusion of a $2 million bequest by **Samuel J. Tilden**. **John Jacob Astor**'s library, the first general reference library in the New World, was enhanced by **James Lenox**'s collection of literature, history and theology. In 1891, **Andrew Carnegie** donated $52 million for the establishment of its 80 branches. This building is completely dedicated to research. None of its more than 6 million books or 17 million documents ever leave here. In fact, the original 4 floors of stacks beneath the building and behind the reading rooms have been supplemented by a new space underneath Bryant Park, which can hold up to 92mi of stacks. The main lobby, **Astor Hall**, contains the information desk, bookshop and an exhibition area. It is marble from floor to ceiling, lavishly decorated with carved garlands, ribbons and rosettes. The room directly behind Astor Hall is the **Gottesman Exhibition Hall**, whose ceiling is positively the most beautiful in the city of New York. The changing exhibitions here are built around special themes, such as children's books, bird prints and architectural history, and are usually based on the library's own impressive collection of rare books and prints. The **Third Floor Hall** and the rooms it serves are not only what this building is all about, but what make it such a pleasure to visit. Here the marble gives way to carved wood panels and richly decorated vaulted ceilings. The murals, by **Edward Lanning**, were executed as part of a WPA project. The library's art collection, including paintings by **Gilbert Stuart, Sir Joshua Reynolds** and **Rembrandt Peale**, is displayed in the **Edna B. Salomon Room**. Directly across the hall is **Room 315**, the **Catalogue Room**, where books are requested. (Make out a call slip and hand it to the librar-

Midtown

ian behind the central desk. You'll be given a number and told to wait in the main reading room until your number lights up, signaling that your book has been retrieved.) Room 315 leads into the **Main Reading Room**, 51ft high and 1 1/2 blocks long. The room is divided in half by the facilities for delivering books, but the ceiling soars above it all with its paintings of blue skies and white clouds and its carved scrolls, masks, flowers, dolphins, cherubs and satyrs. The building has been undergoing extensive restoration since 1963 by such design firms as **Davis, Brody & Associates**. The most recently completed room is the **Celeste Bartos Forum**, which opens directly onto the library's 42nd St entrance. It is used for lectures, concerts, films and special events. I recommend the free tours—Monday-Saturday at 11AM and 2PM—which meet at the front desk. ◆ Main Reading Room: M-W 10AM-8:45PM; Th-Sa 10AM-5:45PM. 5th Ave (W 40th-W 42nd Sts) 661.7220, 930.0800

New York is the only American city to house an American embassy, the **United States Mission**, located across the street from the United Nations.

5 New York Public Library, Mid-Manhattan Branch (Redesigned 1981, **Georgio Cavaglieri**) This was once **Arnold Constable**, the department store that provided trousseaus for fashionable brides in the 1890s. You can see their pictures in the library's collection of microfilm editions of old newspapers. Mid-Manhattan also has the largest circulating collection of any of the branch libraries. The ground floor includes a branch of the gift shop of the **Metropolitan Museum of Art**. Free tours—Monday, Wednesday and Friday at 2:30PM—meet at the ground floor information desk. ◆ M, W 9AM-9PM; Tu, Th 11AM-7PM; F-Sa 10AM-6PM. 455 5th Ave (W 40th St) 340.0849

6 Journey's End Hotel $$ 189 budget-priced rooms, including 10 rooms specially designed for disabled guests. Amenities include complimentary morning coffee and newspaper, in-room movies and laundry and dry-cleaning services. ◆ 3 E 40th St (5th Ave) 447.1500, 800/668.4200; fax 213.0972

7 101 Park Avenue (1983, **Eli Attia & Associates**) A speculative tower of black glass rises, angled and tucked, above a granite plaza on an awkward corner. Its slick outline and sheer height, which may be fun from the inside, are somewhat disturbing from the outside. ◆ E 40th St

8 Philip Morris Headquarters (1983, **Ulrich Franzen & Associates**) This light gray granite clad building is a glass box hiding behind a Postmodernist/historicist appliqué of Palladian patterns. The main facade, rather oddly, faces the Park Ave viaduct. In the enclosed garden and lobby of the building is an espresso bar, a gift shop featuring contemporary American Indian art, a chocolate shop, a magazine stand and the **Whitney Midtown**, a satellite exhibition space of the **Whitney Museum of Modern Art**. The vast high-ceilinged area is used for a permanent display of sculpture; a smaller, more intimate space houses changing exhibitions of 19th- and 20th-century American art, sometimes relating to the Midtown life around it (paintings by the **Ashcan School** depicting New York street life, for instance). Gallery talks take place Monday, Wednesday and Friday at 12:30PM. The site was originally the home of the Art Moderne **Airlines Building** (1940, **John B. Peterkin**). ◆ Museum free. General gallery: M-Sa 11AM-6PM. Exhibitions: M-Sa 7:30AM-9:30PM; Su 11AM-7PM. 120 Park Ave (E 41st-E 42nd Sts) 878.2550

9 Grand Central Terminal (1913, **Warren & Wetmore** and **Reed & Stem**) This extraordinary complex may appear slightly tarnished today, but it is a true jewel nonetheless (long awaited renovations are underway). Reed & Stem's designs for the new terminal to replace the New York Central and Hudson River Railroads' Grand Central Station were chosen in a competition that included submissions by **Daniel Burnham** and **McKim, Mead & White**; Warren & Wetmore were hired as associate architects

and were largely responsible for the design of the elaborate public structure. Reed & Stem, along with railroad engineer **William Wilgus**, was responsible for the still-efficient multilayered organization of the immense amount of traffic that flows through the terminal: trains (on 2 levels), subways, cars and people.

The main, southern facade of the terminal is dominated by a sculpture group of *Mercury*, *Hercules* and *Minerva* (*Glory of Commerce*, *Moral Energy* and *Mental Energy*) by **Jules Coutan**, and a clock 13ft in diameter. The bronze figure at the center of the facade is **Commodore Cornelius Vanderbilt**, founder of the railroad. The building's other major facade fronts Vanderbilt Ave and what was a genteel residential neighborhood to the west; the tenements to the east were disregarded. In building the terminal, 32mi of new tracks were laid, 18,000 tons of steel were used and 2.8 million cu yd of earth were excavated.

The inner workings of the terminal are organized around the impressive **Main Concourse**. When entered by way of the arcades from Lexington Ave, the sense of the soaring vault is particularly acute, but the space may be better appreciated as a whole from the marble stairs at the Vanderbilt Ave end. The hall is 160ft wide, 470ft long and 150ft high at its apogee—larger than the nave of **Notre Dame de Paris**. The ceiling, a plaster vault suspended from steel trusses, is decorated with a zodiac representing the winter sky—2500 stars that used to be lit, designed by **Paul Helleu**; it is, however, painted backwards—*as God would see it*, painter **Whitney Warren** is reported to have remarked. The floors are Tennessee marble; the trim is Italian Bottocino marble. The great arched windows are 60ft tall and 33ft wide; recently cleaned, they now let in massive amounts of light. You gotta look up!

Grand Central Terminal is the centerpiece of a gigantic real-estate development that included 8 hotels and 17 office buildings by 1934. When the railroad was forced to electrify, William Wilgus realized that if the trains were run underground and the tracks covered over, the air rights could be leased to developers. Thus Park Ave was born. Tours are conducted by the **Municipal Art Society** for a small fee. Meet at the Chemical Bank in the Main Concourse, Wednesday 12:30PM. ♦ E 42nd St at Park Ave

Within Grand Central Terminal:

The Café $ This restaurant and bar overlooking Grand Central's Main Concourse from the Vanderbilt Ave balcony is perfect for watching the activity in what was once called the *crossroads of a million private lives*. Stick to a niçoise salad or daily special. ♦ Continental ♦ 883.0009

Oyster Bar and Restaurant ★★$$$ It looks exactly like what it is—the basement of a railroad station with tables—and at the height of the lunch hour, the tiled, vaulted ceilings make it impossibly noisy. Nicely prepared, absolutely fresh seafood, including a large variety of oysters, is served in the main dining room, at a counter bar next to it (where I sit if I am by myself) and in a somewhat less hectic bar through swinging doors. Extensive, exclusively American wine list. ♦ Seafood ♦ Reservations recommended. 490.6650

10 **Grand Hyatt Hotel** $$$$ (1934, **Warren & Wetmore**; redone 1980, **Gruzen & Partners**) The old **Commodore Hotel** has been reclad

Midtown

and *atrium-ized*, and is now a bustling commercial hotel with glamorous dining and watering holes visible from the lobby, like the **Crystal Fountain** and **Sun Garden Restaurant**, which is cantilevered over 42nd St. The rooms are attractive, although some are small and the hotel is affiliated with 3 nearby health clubs, which can be used for a moderate fee. The hotel is the first cornerstone of what was developer **Donald Trump**'s *I'll Take Manhattan* empire. ♦ E 42nd-E 43rd Sts (Lexington-Park Aves) 883.1234, 800/228.9000; fax 697.3772

Within the Grand Hyatt Hotel:

Trumpets $$$$ Old friends and new acquaintances who once met under the clock in Grand Central Station now have a far more congenial rendezvous. The elegant dining room serves French food along with signature dishes of the new American cuisine repertoire in an attractive and unhurried setting. ♦ French ♦ Jacket required, tie requested. Reservations recommended. 883.1234

Restaurants/Nightlife: Red   **Hotels:** Blue
Shops/Parks: Green   **Sights/Culture:** Black

11 The Bowery Savings Bank (1923, **York & Sawyer**) Resembling a Roman basilica, the main banking room is 160ft long, 65ft high and definitely worth a visit. The walls are limestone and sandstone, and the mosaic floors are French and Italian marble. The bronze doors on the east and west sides once hung at the entrance. ◆ 110 E 42nd St (Lexington-Park Aves)

11 Chanin Building (1929, **Sloan & Robertson**) The headquarters of the Chanin real-estate empire is an Art Deco triumph. At the 3rd-floor level is an exuberant terracotta frieze; the detailing of the lobby is extraordinary, particularly the convector grilles and elevator doors. ◆ 122 E 42nd St (Lexington-Park Aves)

12 The Chrysler Building (1929, **William Van Alen**) This tower, which many consider the *best* of skyscrapers, is an Art Deco monument. Built for the **Chrysler Automobile Company**, many of the building's decorative elements are car-oriented: abstract friezes depicting automobiles, flared gargoyles at the 4th setback resembling 1929 radiator hood ornaments and the spire modeled after a radiator grille. The lobby, decorated with African marble and once used as a car showroom, is another Deco treasure. Use the Lexington Ave entrance and look up at the representation of the building

Bill Lacy

Midtown

on the ceiling of the lobby; then get a glimpse of an elevator cab. The lighting of the spire at night—with specially fitted lamps inside the triangular windows—was an idea of Van Alen's that was rediscovered and first implemented in 1981. The Chrysler Building was briefly the tallest building in the world until surpassed by the Empire State. ◆ 405 Lexington Ave (E 42nd St)

13 Mobil Building (1955, **Harrison & Abramovitz**) The self-cleaning stainless-steel skin on this monolith is .037in thick—self-cleaning because the creased panels create wind patterns that scour them. ◆ 150 E 42nd St (3rd-Lexington Aves)

14 New York Helmsley Hotel $$$ If you were looking for the **Harley Hotel**, this is it. **Harry Helmsley** is the present owner. He and his wife, **Leona**, have maintained the old-fashioned service—breakfast is delivered quickly, checkout is speedy and there is 24hr room service. There's also **Harry's New York Bar** for drinks with music in the lobby, and **Mindy's**

Restaurant for elegant dining. ◆ 212 E 42nd St (2nd-3rd Aves) 490.8900, 800/221.4982; fax 986.4792

14 Daily News Building (1930, **Howells & Hood**; 2nd Ave addition 1958, **Harrison & Abramovitz**) A clean, purely vertical, undecorated plastic mass from the pair who brought you the **Chicago Tribune Tower** (in all its Gothic wonder). This stringent composition even has a flat top—a bold step in 1930. The building tells its own story in the frieze over the entrance and in the lobby, where a globe is the center of an interplanetary geography lesson. The tale is that when the globe was first unveiled, it was spinning the wrong way. The 1958 addition is not up to the original. ◆ 220 E 42nd St (2nd-3rd Aves)

15 Extra! Extra! ★$$ The best fried calamari in New York comes with a choice of 3 sauces—try the Thai chili. The restaurant's **Babysitting Brunch** is a boon to haggard parents. On Sunday, one of the 3 levels is transformed into a play area for children, who are watched over by 2 college students. The whimsical interior by **Sam Lopata** (**Lox Around the Clock, Prunelle**) includes cartoon character cutouts, newsprint on the walls and splattered ink on the floor. ◆ American ◆ Closed Sa-Su. 767 2nd Ave (E 41st St) Reservations recommended. 490.2900

16 Hotel Tudor $$$ Scheduled to reopen in the spring of 1991, the renovated Hotel Tudor (once notorious for the smallest rooms in the city) will boast 320 expanded rooms, each with a new marble bathroom, a trouser press, a 2-line telephone and fax and PC ports. Within the hotel will be a restaurant, a bar and lounge, meeting rooms, conference and banquet facilities, a business center and a small health club facility. ◆ 304 E 42nd St (1st-2nd Aves) 986.8800, 800/TRI.TUDOR; fax 986.1758

17 Tudor City (1925, **Fred F. French Company** and **H. Douglas Ives**) This Gothically detailed development—on its own street that soars over 42nd—is comprised of 11 apartment buildings, a hotel, shops, a restaurant, a church and a park.

The complex's orientation toward the city seems ill-considered today, but when this enclave was planned, the East River shore below was a wasteland of breweries, slaughterhouses, glue factories and gasworks. At the turn of the century, the bluff, known as **Corcoran's Roost**, was the hideout of the infamous **Paddy Corcoran** and the **Rag Gang**. Now it provides a good vista of the UN. ◆ E 40th-E 43rd Sts (1st-2nd Aves)

17 Ford Foundation Building (1967, **Kevin Roche, John Dinkeloo & Associates**) This is probably the oldest and certainly the richest and least hermetic re-creation of a jungle in New York City. A small building with a rather typical entrance on 43rd St, it is fairly extroverted on the 42nd St side. It appears as if a container had been opened, leaving the black piers barely restraining an overflowing glass and Cor-ten steel box of offices that contains a luxuriant park inside a 12-story atrium. Although economically foolhardy and somewhat noisy, this building is handsome and very definitely not to be missed. ♦ 320 E 43rd St (1st-2nd Aves) 573.5000

18 Sichuan Pavilion ★★$$$ One of the most interesting Chinese menus around, but the quality of the ingredients and service has suffered since its auspicious opening as the first Chinese restaurant to receive mainland guidance. UN delegates crowd the handsome dining rooms and get preferential treatment at lunch, making dinner a better choice for the rest of us. ♦ Chinese ♦ 310 E 44th St (1st-2nd Aves) Reservations recommended. 972.7377

19 Unicef House At the **Danny Kaye Visitors Center** on the ground floor, visitors can watch *Within Our Reach*, a film about the challenges that face children all over the world, narrated by a larger-than-life parrot and a newscaster. An extensive collection of UNICEF cards and gifts is sold at the center's retail shop. ♦ 3 UN Plaza (1st-2nd Aves) 326.7706

19 1 United Nations Plaza (1976, **Kevin Roche, John Dinkeloo & Associates**) This combination office building, apartment house and hotel with its striking glass-curtain wall was so successful that it was duplicated in **2 UN Plaza**, adjoining it to the west, in 1980. ♦ UN Plaza (E 44th St at 1st Ave)

19 United Nations Plaza Hotel $$$ (1976, **Kevin Roche, John Dinkeloo & Associates**) Beginning on the 28th floor of 1 UN Plaza, this incredibly comfortable hotel includes a lounge and restaurant and a swimming pool and health club with a dazzling view. Complimentary limousine service to Wall Street, the Garment District and theaters. ♦ E 44th St (1st-2nd Aves) 355.3400, 800/228.9000; fax 702.5051

Within the United Nations Plaza Hotel:

Ambassador Grill Restaurant ★★$$$ A find. The dramatic mirrored room with its luxuriously comfortable upholstered banquettes is run by a brilliant team of chefs from Gascony. Working from an open kitchen, they serve forth the regional specialties: cassoulet and glorious sausages, casseroles dense with flavor and, best of all, fresh *foie gras* delicacies. Finish the meal with warm apple tart, prune ice cream and a glass of Armagnac. I recommend the weekend brunch, an event in itself. ♦ Continental ♦ Reservations recommended. 355.3400

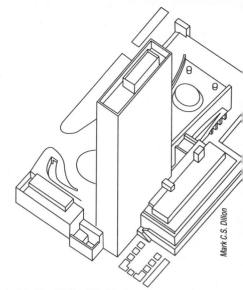

Mark C.S. Dillon

20 The United Nations (1952, designed by an international committee of 12 architects that included **Le Corbusier** (France), **Oscar Niemeyer** (Brazil) and **Sven Markelius** (Sweden); the committee was headed by American **Wallace K. Harrison**) The 39-story **Secretariat** was New York's first building with all-glass walls (these suspended between side slabs of Vermont marble), and is the only example that approaches the ideal of the tower-in-the-park urbanism of the '40s. (To make way for the UN building, the city diverted the traffic on 1st Ave into a tunnel under UN Plaza and created a small landscaped park, **Dag Hammarskjold Plaza**.) It is a remarkable sight seen broadside from 43rd St, where it was set

in deliberate opposition to the city grid. Measuring 544ft high and 72ft wide, this anonymously faced building houses the staff bureaucracy. The **General Assembly** meets in the solid, limestone-clad, flared white shape to the north under the dome. The complex, an enclave apart from the city and in formal contrast to it, has had tremendous influence on its surroundings as well as on the direction of architecture. The site—once the actual Turtle Bay where Saw Kill ran into the East River—was a rundown area with slaughterhouses, light industry and a railroad barge landing when **John D. Rockefeller Jr.** donated the money to purchase the land for this project.

Visitors enter through the north side of the **General Assembly Building** (45th St). Outside, flags of all member nations fly in alphabetical order, the same order in which delegates are seated in the General Assembly. More than 1 million visitors come here every year to see the physical presence of this forum of nations, but also in search of the elusive spirit of peace it symbolizes. Taking a tour (daily 9:15AM-4:45PM) is a good idea if you want to explore more than the grounds (don't miss the gardens) and the **Chagall** stained-glass windows in the lobby of the General Assembly Building, but don't expect to witness more than real estate, especially if the General Assembly isn't in session (regular sessions are from the 3rd Thursday in September through mid-December). Tours, conducted by young people from around the world, steer large groups through the elegant **Assembly Hall** (don't miss the **Léger** paintings on the walls); the Secretariat Building, where the staffs of member nations work; and the **Conference Building** that houses media, support systems and meeting rooms, including the **Security Council Chamber** (donated by Norway), the **Trusteeship Council Chamber** (donated by Denmark) and the **Economic and Social Council Chamber** (donated by Sweden). But you can find out more about how the UN actually functions by witnessing the public part of the UN's business as it takes place in the General Assembly and at meetings of the various councils. It is possible to obtain free tickets to these sessions at the **Information Desk** in the General Assembly lobby on a first-come, first-served basis. They are usually held at 10AM and 3PM. Call for information. ◆ E 45th St at 1st Ave. 963.7113

Within the United Nations:

Delegates' Dining Room ★$$ This delegates' dining room is open to the public during the week, serving a luncheon buffet and offering an à la carte menu. The view of the East River is the best of any restaurant in Manhattan. ◆ Continental ◆ Closed Sa-Su. UN Conference Building. Jacket required. Reservations recommended. 963.7625

Midtown

21 International Education Information Center An information center for foreign nationals interested in studying in the US, and for US nationals who wish to study abroad. Staffed primarily by volunteers, the center provides guidebooks, brochures, university catalogs, as well as materials describing scholarships, internships and teaching opportunities. ◆ 809 UN Plaza (E 45th-E 46th Sts) 984.5413

Palm

22 Palm and Palm Too ★★$$$$ Ranked as 2 of the city's best steakhouses. Serious carnivores don't seem to mind the close and chaotic premises, the long wait for a table or the surly, often rushed service. Caricatures of famous New York journalists are painted right on the walls, but you're more likely to recognize faces at the next table. The steaks and

lobsters are huge; the cottage-fried potatoes are addictive. ◆ Steakhouse ◆ Closed Su. Lunch reservations required at both restaurants. Palm: 837 2nd Ave (44th-45th Sts) 687.2953. Palm Too: 840 2nd Ave (E 44th-E 45th Sts) 697.5189

23 Pen & Pencil ★$$$ A steakhouse with a Continental accent, this gracious old-timer still has a capable kitchen. Getting genteelly shabby around the edges—and unfashionable —so it's a good place for a quiet little table in the corner. ◆ Steakhouse ◆ 205 E 45th St (2nd-3rd Aves) 682.8660

24 Captain's Table ★$$$ Superbly fresh fish in mostly Mediterranean preparations, both elegant and rustic. A not-very-prepossessing dining room, but concerned service. ◆ Seafood ◆ 860 2nd Ave (E 46th St) Reservations recommended. 697.9538

25 Sparks ★★$$$$ The main business at hand, beef, is not as consistently cooked to order as at the other great beef houses. But the wine list is among the best in the country. Not only is the selection extraordinary, but the prices are incredibly fair. A must stop for oenophiles. Best known for the murder of mobster **Paul Castellano** out front. ◆ Steakhouse ◆ Closed Su. 210 E 46th St (2nd-3rd Aves) Reservations required. 687.4855

26 Joe & Rose Restaurant ★$$$ A regular clientele of Midtown businesspeople makes this survivor of 3rd Ave demolition particularly busy at midday. Good meats, wonderfully greasy lyonnaise potatoes. Avoid the pasta. ◆ Italian ◆ Closed Sa-Su. 747 3rd Ave (E 46th-E 47th Sts) Reservations recommended. 980.3985

27 Christ Cella ★★$$$$ This is one of the oldest steakhouses in New York and has for years enjoyed a reputation among visiting salesmen as the best in town. (I bring my most carnivorous friends here.) You know the food must be good because Christ Cella is far from a triumph of the interior decorator's art. When you call for a reservation, ask to sit downstairs. It isn't any more elegant, but it's cozier. There are no printed menus, so feel free to ask the waiter about prices, which are high. The lobsters, steaks and chops will help you understand why those salesmen keep traveling back. Popular with the *power lunch* crowd. ◆ Steakhouse ◆ Closed Su. 160 E 46th St (3rd-Lexington Aves) Reservations required. 697.2479

27 Nanni ★$$$ If you are yearning for some genuine Northern Italian food and don't mind that the tables are a little close together, Nanni is the place for you. The pasta in all its multiplicity of forms is always superb, as are the *osso buco* and other veal specialties cooked under the direction of **Nanni** himself, who opened for business in this location more than 20 years ago. ◆ Italian ◆ Closed Su. 146 E 46th St (3rd-Lexington Aves) Reservations recommended. 599.9684

28 The Helmsley Building (1929, **Warren & Wetmore**) Originally the **New York Central Building**, then **New York General**. An example of creative, sensitive urban design, this fanciful tower was a lively addition to the architects' own **Grand Central Terminal** and the hotels that surrounded it. Built above 2 levels of railroad tracks, it essentially *floats* on its foundations—those inside feel nary a vibration. The gold-leafed building is worth a special viewing at night. Pause to appreciate the distinct separation of automobile and pedestrian traffic in the street-level arcades, and stop for a look at the wonderful rococo lobby. ♦ 230 Park Ave (E 45th-E 46th Sts)

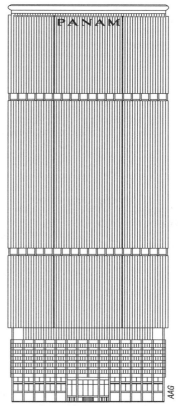

AAG

29 Pan Am Building (1963, **Emery Roth & Associates, Pietro Belluschi** and **Walter Gropius**) This 59-story monolith set indelicately between the **Helmsley Building** and **Grand Central Terminal** started as a purely speculative venture and became the largest commercial office building ever built—2.4 million sq ft. It was not well-received. Its siting is problematic, to say the least. But there is a positive, efficient connection with the terminal that forms an unintentionally ironic mating of the then-expanding airline and the failing railroad. Art in the lobby includes a mural by **Josef Albers** and a space sculpture by **Richard Lippold**. The shape of the tower is supposedly derived from an airplane wing section. There used to be a heliport on the roof, but one too many

helicopters had trouble. Bauhaus founder and High Modernist Gropius could have done better. ♦ 200 Park Ave (E 44th-E 45th Sts)

Within the Pan Am Building:

Trattoria ★$$ There are literally hundreds of Italian restaurants in New York better than this one. But, extending out onto the 45th St sidewalk from the Pan Am Building, it gets an A for location. Decent pastas and quite good gelati. ♦ Italian ♦ Closed Su. Lunch reservations required. 661.3090

30 Takesushi ★$$$ One of the best sushi bars, which is why there is always a long line at lunch. There is more tranquility after 5:30PM. The solicitous staff is more than willing to introduce you to the world of raw fish. ♦ Japanese ♦ Closed Su. 71 Vanderbilt Ave (E 45th St) Reservations recommended. 867.5120

31 The Yale Club (1913, **James Gamble Rogers**) In this neighborhood crowded with clubs waving the old school tie, this particular one boasts easy access to trains headed for New Haven for *Yalies* who get over-nostalgic. ♦ 50 Vanderbilt Ave (E 44th-E 45th Sts)

32 Orvis Fishing equipment and gear, a wide selection of books on topics like fly fishing, trout streams and duck decoys, as well as outdoor clothing and accessories that complement the country way of life. Enter on 45th St.

Midtown

♦ Closed Su. 355 Madison Ave (E 45th St) 697.3133

33 The Roosevelt Hotel $$ (1924, **George M. Post**) This old hotel was prestigious when railroads were the main form of transportation and the location near Grand Central was highly valued. It has soundproof rooms and a multilingual staff, and is popular with those doing business in the nearby mega-office district. In the hotel is a bar, a lobby lounge and **Crawdaddy**, well-known for its oyster bar, Creole cooking and New Orleans jazz. ♦ E 45th St at Madison Ave. 661.9600, 800/223.1870; fax 687.5064

New York City water, which comes from rainfall and snowmelt, almost always comes out on top in blind taste tests against bottled water or the water supplies of other cities. The city uses 1.5 billion gallons of water a day, flowing into New York from reservoirs and lakes as far as 125 miles away.

Restaurants/Nightlife: Red **Hotels:** Blue
Shops/Parks: Green **Sights/Culture:** Black

34 Paul Stuart Classic well-made clothing for the conservative gentleman: jackets and suits in herringbone, Shetland and tweed; handknit sweaters in alpaca, cashmere and Shetland wool; shirts of Sea Island cotton. Women have a tiny niche to themselves on the mezzanine level, where there are tailored skirted suits, Shetland sweaters and cotton shirts. If you're not the one shopping, a 17th-century Flemish tapestry and comfortable leather chairs make waiting for a friend quite pleasant. ♦ Closed Su. E 45th St at Madison Ave. 682.0320

35 Brooks Brothers The home of the Ivy League look—the natural-shoulder sack suit, worn with an oxford cloth shirt and silk rep tie—Brooks Brothers is an American establishment. The country's oldest menswear shop, founded in 1818, it continues to offer traditional, conservative clothing. Some wares have become classics, such as its trench coats, Shetland sweaters, oxford cloth shirts, and bathrobes of soft wool and cotton. For boys, there are shirts, slacks and sweaters. And for women, there is the feminine version of all the above. ♦ Closed Su. 346 Madison Ave (E 44th St) 682.8800

36 Fred F. French Building (1927, **Fred F. French Company** and **H. Douglas Ives**) The colorful glazed tiles in the tower call out to you from across the street. Answer the call; the lobby is a stunner. ♦ 551 5th Ave (E 45th St)

37 Chikubu ★★★$$$$ If you love Japanese food and can afford the high prices, sit at the counter and get the *omakase*—the chef will make the fabulous choices for you. ♦ Japanese ♦ 12 E 44th St (Madison-5th Aves) Reservations recommended. 818.0715

Midtown

37 J. Press They've been dressing the men of the Ivy League since 1902. Come here for the well-made classics and calico patchwork shorts and slacks. ♦ Closed Su. 16 E 44th St (Madison-5th Aves) 687.7642

38 Zen Oriental Book Store Most of the books and magazines are in Japanese. The ones in English cover Buddhism and Zen, Japanese language, history, society and literature, Japanese and Zen cooking, origami and bonsai. There's even a guide to job hunting in Japan. ♦ Closed Su. 521 5th Ave (E 43rd-E 44th Sts) 697.0840

39 Manufacturers Hanover Trust (1954, **Skidmore, Owings & Merrill**) This was the first bank to depart from the tradition of rock-solid architecture, and just to make sure potential customers would recognize it as a bank, they put the safe in the window. ♦ 510 5th Ave (W 43rd St) 997.0770

In 1982, Midtown real estate sold for $2000 a square ft

Restaurants/Nightlife: Red   **Hotels:** Blue
Shops/Parks: Green   **Sights/Culture:** Black

40 Century Association (1891, **McKim, Mead & White**) Palladian clubhouse for men of achievement in arts and letters (McKim and Mead were members). The large window above the entrance was originally a loggia. ♦ 7 W 43rd St (5th-6th Aves) 944.0090

41 General Society Library of Mechanics and Tradesmen Over 140,000 books of fiction, nonfiction and history. The comfortable, elegant surroundings are worth the low membership fee. Within this private library are the **Small Press Center**, a nonprofit facility exhibiting books by independent publishers, and the **John M. Mossman Collection of Locks**, where 375 different locks—antique padlocks, powder-proof key locks and friction locks—are on display. ♦ 20 W 44th St (5th-6th Aves)

42 Crossroads of Sport This is the oldest sporting gallery and shop in America, featuring books, rare artwork and prints, among other new and antique items with a hunting and fishing theme. ♦ Closed Sa-Su. 36 W 44th St (5th-6th Aves) 764.8877

42 Hotel Royalton $$$$ (1898, **Ehrick Rossiter**; altered 1988, **Gruzen, Samton, Steinglass**) The block-long lobby sets the stage for this dramatic space (cognac mahogany and green-gray slate) by French designer **Phillipe Starck**. The front desk and other hotel facilities are discreetly tucked away, as is the bar, patterned after **Hemingway**'s favorite at the Paris Ritz. The rooms, many with working fireplaces, are on the cutting edge of modern design and comfort. Daily newspaper delivery, concierge, fresh flowers at bedside and in the bath, **Kiehl** shampoos and bathcubes, valet parking. ♦ Deluxe ♦ 44 W 44th St (5th-6th Aves) 869.4400; fax 869.8965

Within Hotel Royalton:

Restaurant 44 ★★$$$ **Phillipe Starck**'s decor and the *Beautiful People* who inhabit it create a dramatic backdrop for the American nouvelle cuisine. Recommended are poached quail-egg salad with sautéed *pancetta* and *frisée* followed by crisp filet of grilled salmon flavored with cucumber and dates, or grilled lamb chops with potatoes and black-olive sauce. For dessert, try 3-chocolate terrine truffle with 3 chocolate sauces, or grappa tiramisu. ♦ American ♦ Reservations recommended. 944.8844

43 The Algonquin $$ (1902, **Goldwyn Starrett**) A gathering place for literary types even before the famous **Round Table** of such writers as **Alexander Woollcott**, **Robert Benchley** and **Dorothy Parker** began meeting regularly in the **Rose Room**. What the Round Table members had in common, besides their razor-sharp wit, was that they were contributors to *The New Yorker*, whose offices at 25 W 43rd St conveniently open into the hotel at 44th St. Few other nearby places are as comfortable as the hotel's lobby, where you can summon a cocktail with the ringing of a bell. Guests find all the comforts and friendliness of a country inn here. (Visiting writers favor **Room 306**; the suite's walls are adorned with *Playbill* magazine covers.) 1991 marks the completion of a 2-year effort to restore this landmark to its original splendor. ◆ 59 W 44th St (5th-6th Aves) 840.6800; fax 944.1419

Within The Algonquin:

Oak and Rose Rooms ★$$$ The dark paneling in the Oak Room contrasts with the brighter Rose Room. But the menu is the same in both, and the quality doesn't vary. The plate-size apple pancake topped with tart lingonberries is a perfect after-theater snack. After 8PM on weekdays, 6PM on Sunday, the Oak Room provides supper club entertainment. ◆ American ◆ Reservations recommended. 840.6800

43 **The New York Yacht Club** (1899, **Warren & Wetmore**) An unusually fanciful, sculptured piece of work. The highlight of the eccentric facade is sailing-ship sterns in the 3 window bays, complete with ocean waves and dolphins. The setback above the cornice used to be a pergola. This was the home of *The America's Cup* from 1857 to 1983. ◆ 37 W 44th St (5th-6th Aves) 382.1000

McKim, Mead & White

44 **Harvard Club** (1894, **McKim, Mead & White**) The interior of this Georgian-style building is much more impressive than its facade indicates. If you're not a Harvard alum, go around the block and see it through the magnificent window in back. ◆ 27 W 44th St (5th-6th Aves) 840.6600

45 **Train Shop** This block is well-known for its electronics stores, but this basement shop, along with **The Red Caboose** on the 4th floor at 16 W 45th St, makes it a major stop on the railroad lines that run in a child's imagination. ◆ Closed Su. 23 W 45th St (5th-6th Aves) 730.0409

46 **Wentworth** $ A modest, recently renovated Art Deco hotel with comfortable rooms that have color TVs, air conditioning and all the modern amenities. Guests get a convenience they wouldn't expect as well—the hotel's own **Jewelry Exchange** next door, where 60 dealers offer treasures like those sold on neighboring **Diamond Row** on 47th St. ◆ 59 W 46th St (5th-6th Aves) 719.2300; fax 768.3477

47 **47th Street Photo** This discount store offers greater bargains on cameras (including **Canon, Hasselblad, Nikon** and **Minox**) than any other discount camera shop. It also offers New York's best prices on computers, televisions, VCRs and other electronic appliances, as well as wristwatches and gold chains. As you enter and start the climb to its 2nd-floor location, a sign tells you to *Come Up to Keep the Prices Down*. The salesmen—from several generations of various Hasidic families—look harried. So do the customers. ◆ Closed F afternoon-Sa. 67 W 47th St (5th-6th Aves) 260.4410. Also at: 115 W 45th St. 398.1410; 116 Nassau St. 608.6934

47 **Gotham Book Mart & Gallery** The Gotham, founded by **Frances Steloff** in 1920, has long been a mecca for New York City's literati: **Theodore Dreiser, Eugene O'Neill, George Gershwin** and **Charlie Chaplin** all shopped here; **Tennessee Williams** worked as a clerk, but lasted only one day as he was not that good at his job. **Edmund Wilson** cashed his checks here; and when **Henry Miller** wrote to Miss Steloff of his financial hardship, she taped his letter to the wall and her customers provided what he needed (a small cart to carry his groceries, a shirt and socks) and what he wanted (lox). Today, this

New York equivalent to Paris' Shakespeare & Co. is a bibliophiles heaven: a messy hodge-podge of books, mostly literature (especially 20th century), poetry, drama, art and literary journals. Also small press, used and rare books. In the upstairs gallery, you'll find changing art exhibitions, including, my favorite, a summer show of vintage postcards from the extensive collection of the store's owner, **Andy Brown**. ◆ Closed Su. 41 W 47th St (5th-6th Aves) 719.4448

48 **Barnes & Noble Book Store** There are branches all over town, the largest of which is downtown. This one has 2 floors of books and games, plus a mezzanine full of records and tapes. Everything, including current bestsellers, is discounted. ◆ 600 5th Ave (W 48th St) 765.0590

49 **Goelet Building** (1932, **E.H. Faile & Co.**) Ignore the ground-floor shops of this crisp, early-Modern structure, but do stop in the elevator lobby. It's a highly ornamented, hidden Art Deco gem all the way to the paneling of the elevator cabs. Note the lighting in the pilasters and cornices. ◆ 608 5th Ave (W 49th St)

49 La Reserve ★★★$$$ A handsome, spacious restaurant, the right place for a romantic dinner. Since **Dominique Peyraudeau**, the former chef of **La Terrace**, took over the reins, the food—French classic—has taken on new dimensions. I hope you'll sample the delicate marinated onions and the scrumptious saddle of lamb. Among the desserts, the chocolate basket filled with a chocolate mousse and raspberries is a must. ◆ French ◆ 4 W 49th St (5th Ave) 247.2993

50 Saks Fifth Avenue Fashionable and always in good taste, Saks has another asset few other stores can offer: service. Great designer collections throughout the store can please any woman's sense of style, and the men's department is legendary. The selection for children is heaven-on-earth for grandparents, not to mention parents who enjoy seeing their children turned out in style. Food is available too, with a small luxury selection of candies, liquor cakes and chocolates, including beautiful truffles from Joseph Schmidt and decadent chocolate- and caramel-covered apples from Mrs. Prindables. Shopping in Saks is unadulterated joy for the fashion-conscious. Some regular customers have a very satisfying shopping experience by simply picking up the telephone. But when they do, they miss the serendipity that is at every turn in the store itself. ◆ 611 5th Ave (W 49th-W 50th Sts) 753.4000

51 Brentanos Bookstore (1913, **Ernest Flagg**) Formerly **Scribner Bookstore**, the entire 10-story French Renaissance-inspired composition is worth studying, but the 2-story wrought-iron and glass storefront takes the prize, along with the vaulted space inside. On the facade, medallions honor printers

Franklin, Caxton, Gutenberg and **Manutius**; also note the cherubs holding the former establishment's name. The 2-story, plaster-vaulted interior is equally impressive. ◆ 597 5th Ave (E 48th-E 49th Sts)

52 Chalet Suisse ★$$$ The ultimate civilized Swiss experience has been consistent for more than 50 years. Old-fashioned cooking, enchanting service by costumed waitresses, European-inn atmosphere. Good for everything from cheese or chocolate fondue to the earthy but elegant veal with *morilles*. ◆ Swiss ◆ Closed Sa-Su. 6 E 48th St (5th Ave) Jacket required. Reservations recommended. 355.0855

New York traffic engineers have not taken on the project of installing Walk/Don't Walk lights (aka *ped* lights) on Park Ave between 46th and 56th Sts because of what lies barely 8 inches below: the tunnels in and out of Grand Central Station.

Restaurants/Nightlife: Red   **Hotels:** Blue
Shops/Parks: Green   **Sights/Culture:** Black

53 Hatsuhana ★★★$$$ A big-league Japanese sushi bar that every aficionado in town rates No. 1 or 2. Sit at a table or at the counter where you can watch the slicing and forming action. Either way, sushi by the item adds up quickly; the prix-fixe lunch menu is a good buy. Tempura and some skewered grilled items are also available. ◆ Japanese ◆ Closed Su. 17 E 48th St (Madison-5th Aves) Reservations recommended. 355.3345

54 Crouch & Fitzgerald For luggage, handbags and business cases. An old New York institution. ◆ Closed Su. 400 Madison Ave (E 48th St) 755.5888

55 Richard Metz Golf Studio Learn the basics or just improve your swing with the help of a PGA pro and an instant replay television. Equipment and clothing are for sale. ◆ 425 Madison Ave (E 49th St) 759.6940

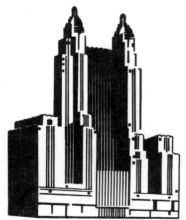

56 Waldorf-Astoria Hotel $$$ (1931, **Schultze & Weaver**) The Waldorf is a New York institution that has put up permanent guests such as the **Duchess of Windsor** and the American representative to the UN, and temporary guests such as **King Faisal** of Saudi Arabia and every US president since 1931. It takes up nearly the entire block between Park and Lexington Aves and 49th and 50th Sts, has almost 2000 spacious rooms and is like a mini city, now administered by the **Hilton** hotel chain. It is considered by many to be the best building on this stretch of Park Ave. The base is in proper relation to the surrounding buildings, while the unique twin towers are still noteworthy additions to the skyline. The hotel epitomized the good life of New York in the '30s, carrying on in the tradition of its fashionable predecessor at 34th St. (The hotel's tony guests often arrived underground in their private railway cars on a specially constructed spur off the tracks under Park Ave.) The luxurious Art Deco interiors have suffered some mistreatment and neglect over the years—the burled walnut elevator cabs, for example, were lined with brocade—but are being meticulously restored. Of particular interest are the **Louis Rigel** murals in the lobby and the *Wheel of Life* mosaic in the floor. The ornate gilded and marbled lobby teems with businesspeople and travelers from all over the world. A transportation desk handles logistical strategies, an international desk assists foreign guests, and the Waldorf's **Boutique Row** caters to the silk-stocking trade with shops such as **L'Bibi, S.T. Dupont** and **Sulka Men's Shop**. Decent fare can be had at the **Bull and Bear** and the pretty **Peacock Alley**. ◆ 301 Park Ave (E 49th-E 50th Sts) 355.3000, 800/445.8667; fax 758.9209

Within the Waldorf-Astoria Hotel:

Inagiku Japanese Restaurant ★$$$
When **Emperor Hirohito** stayed at the Waldorf, he was right at home here. Inagiku features sushi, sashimi, tempura and teriyaki in a setting that would be considered among the best in town in Tokyo. ◆ Japanese ◆ Jacket and reservations required. 355.0440

57 Manufacturers Hanover World Headquarters (1960, **Skidmore, Owings & Merrill**) This 53-story monster was built for **Union Carbide**, which has since moved to the suburbs. Railroad yards under the building made it necessary to begin the elevator shafts on the 2nd floor, which is why the ground-floor lobby looks forgotten. ◆ 270 Park Ave (E 47th-E 48th Sts)

58 ChemCort at Chemical Bank World Headquarters (Building 1962, **Emery Roth & Sons**; ChemCort addition 1982, **Haines Lundberg Waehler**) You don't have to be a banker to appreciate the soothing effect of the plants and miniwaterfalls in this greenhouse lobby. At the 48th St entrance is *Taxi,* a sculpture of a businessman hailing a taxi, by **J. Seward Johnson Jr**. ◆ 277 Park Ave (E 47th-E 48th Sts)

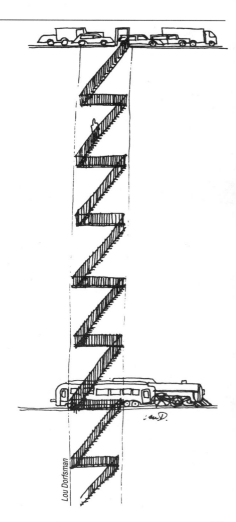

Level with the sidewalk on the 48th St side of the block-square Waldorf-Astoria, the hotel wall is punched full of entrances and exits—garage doors, restaurant doors, other doors. One unobtrusive, ordinary-size door (in bronze!) carries the identifying number 101-121.

About 20 years ago, an invitation to attend a party for **Andy Warhol** *at that address was mailed to me. (What the hell, another party at the Waldorf, I thought.)*

It subsequently turned out that this innocent door was the entrance to a scene out of Dante. Immediately upon opening 101-121, one is greeted with long flights of iron stairs set in the deepest stairwell I've ever seen. The stairs seem to go down into the bowels of the earth. And indeed they do. About 100 feet down, one enters an enormous space of crisscrossing railroad tracks of the New York Central Railroad. Dead trains are parked seemingly without plan or purpose. All of it in shades of dark gray, lots of black and very dingy lighting. A most fascinating environment. (A great set for a chase flick!)

This was the setting for the Andy Warhol party, with proper illumination added. The parked dining cars were used just for that...dining and drinking. A rock group filled the entire space with reverberating sound that bounded off the trains, tracks, walls, stairs and 30- to 40-foot ceiling.

Several hundred feet below the barn are train repair shops.

All this dusty, dirty mystery under the pristine Waldorf-Astoria Hotel!

Interesting sidebar. In the '30s and early '40s, **Franklin Delano Roosevelt***, when in New York, stayed at the Waldorf. His private presidential train would pull into this underground barn, and he would be transported in his wheelchair to a secret and very private elevator down there at the barn level that whisked him to his suite atop the hotel.*

Great place to visit (by appointment) and even better for a wild party!

Lou Dorfsman, Designer

59 Hotel Inter-Continental New York $$$ (1927, **Cross & Cross**) Once known as the **Barclay**, this was the most luxurious of the hotels built by the New York Central Railroad. Now part of the Inter-Continental chain, the hotel is as prestigious as ever, with special amenities to make life easier for visiting businesspeople (24hr room service, concierge, valet service and health spa). The Barclay name lives on in the **Barclay Restaurant** and in the gracious **Barclay Terrace** overlooking the lobby. The name of the clubby bar off the lobby was changed to **Bar One Eleven**. The Restaurant features American and Continental cuisine; the Terrace specializes in afternoon tea. Both recommend reservations. ◆ 111 E 48th St (Lexington-Park Aves) 755.5900, 800/33A.GAIN; fax 644.0079

60 New York Marriott East Side $$$ (1924, **Arthur Loomis Harmon**) Originally the **Shelton**, a club/hotel for men, this 34-story tower was the first major building to reflect the 1916 zoning regulations. Its set-back massing is admirable, and it became particularly famous as the winner of architectural awards and as the subject of many paintings by **Georgia O'Keeffe**. The hotel offers recently renovated, comfortable rooms of erratic sizes and shapes. They have character but are sometimes cramped. Each has a bathroom telephone, AM/FM alarm radio, scale, remote-control color TV and wall safe. Another personal touch—a babysitting service. Within are a coffee shop; **Shelton Grill** for more serious dining; and **Biff's Place** for live entertainment during the week. ◆ 525 Lexington Ave (E 48th-E 49th Sts) 755.4000, 800/223.0939; fax 751.3440

61 Hotel Lexington $$ The Lexington has a nightclub and 2 restaurants: **Beach & Bamboo**,

Midtown

for an odd mix of Oriental, Indian and American homestyle cuisine and **J. Sung's Dynasty**, with a Hunan and Manchurian menu. The Lexington was once home to the night club the **Hawaiian Room**, which was responsible for a national ukulele craze a few decades back. ◆ 511 Lexington Ave (E 48th St) 755.4400, 800/448.4471; fax 751.4091

61 Roger Smith Winthrop Hotel $$ A long-term renovation program is finally complete: all of the 183 rooms and suites have been re-decorated and the lobby has been redone with mahogany and free-form bronze sculptures by hotel president/artist **James Knowles**. All the rooms come with their own coffeemakers and most rooms on the **Concierge Floor** have granite bathrooms with Jacuzzis and hair dryers. ◆ 501 Lexington Ave (E 47th St) 755.1400, 800/455.0277; fax 319.9130

62 Helmsley Middletowne $$ Part of the Helmsley chain. An apartment hotel with junior and large suites, some with kitchenettes, terraces and fireplaces. ◆ 148 E 48th St (3rd-Lexington Aves) 755.3000; fax 832.0261

63 767 Third Avenue (1981, **Fox & Fowle**) This squeaky-clean curved tower is high-tech clothed in brick instead of aluminum, and wood instead of steel. The chessboard on the side wall of the building next door was provided by the developer, **Melvyn Kauffman**, so that people would have something to look at. A new move is made each week; ask the concierge at No. 767 for the bulletin and a short description of how to play the game. ◆ E 48th St

64 Lescaze Residence (1934) Glass blocks, stucco and industrial-pipe railings replaced the original brownstone front of this townhouse when modernist architect **Paul Lescaze** converted it to his combination office/residence. Lescaze is well-known as the co-designer of Philadelphia's extraordinary **PSFS Building** with **George Howe**. He also participated in the design of **1 New York Plaza** overlooking the harbor, and the **Municipal Courthouse** at 111 Centre St. ◆ 211 E 48th St (2nd-3rd Aves)

64 Turtle Bay Gardens (1870; remodeled 1920, **Clarence Dean**) When planning began for the UN complex just east of here, these blocks were slated for demolition. Cooler heads prevailed, and this little development was saved. The Gardens, not open to the public, were created for **Mrs. Walton Martin**, who bought a back-to-back row of 10 houses on each street, then ripped out all the walls and fences behind them to create a common garden. She left a 12ft strip down the middle for a path, at the center of which she installed a fountain copied from the **Villa Medici** in Rome. She redesigned the 20 houses so that their living rooms faced the private garden rather than the street and began attracting such tenants as **Tyrone Power, Leopold Stokowski** and **Katharine Hepburn**, who may still live here. ◆ 227-247 E 48th St and 226-246 E 49th St (2nd-3rd Aves)

65 780 Third Avenue (1983, **Skidmore, Owings & Merrill; Raul de Armas**, partner in charge) This skinny 50-story tower is clad in brick, but the cross patterns are the structure showing through—a sort of dressed **John Hancock Tower** (Chicago). A plaza on 3 sides is a relief in a crowded area. ◆ E 48th-E 49th Sts

66 Smith & Wollensky ★★$$$$ The meat palace most preferred by young corporate types. The steak won't disappoint you, and the restaurant's extraordinary American wine list won the 1988 *Wine Spectator* award. ◆ American ◆ 209 E 49th St (3rd Ave) Reservations recommended. 753.1530

67 Beekman Tower Hotel $$$ (1928, **John Mead Howells**) Originally called the **Panhellenic Hotel**, catering to women belonging to Greek-letter sororities, it is now an all-suite hotel catering to visitors looking for reasonably priced accommodations with fully equipped kitchens. For a wonderful view of the East River, have a drink in the **Top of the Tower**. ◆ 3 Mitchell Pl (E 49th St at 1st Ave) 355.7300, 800/ME.SUITE; fax 753.9366

Lutèce

68 Lutèce ★★★★$$$$ Consistently rated as the best French restaurant in the US since its opening in 1961. The Alsatian dishes—a fragrant onion tart, fresh trout in a heady cream sauce, *anything* with noodles—are especially wonderful. The man responsible is **André Soltner**, the owner and original chef, who can be seen at work in his kitchen and often chatting with diners. In spite of its awesome reputation, it is one of the friendliest restaurants in New York, and first-time diners are made to feel as welcome as celebrity regulars. ♦ French ♦ Closed Su. 249 E 50th St (2nd-3rd Aves) Reservations required, often weeks in advance. 752.2225

69 Artichoke Immaculate store with consistently fresh and delicious salads, as well as a small selection of meats, cheeses, packaged goods, breads, cakes and pastries. Prices are fair, and the knowledgeable service is a high point. ♦ Takeout ♦ Closed Su. 968 2nd Ave (E 51st-E 52nd Sts) 753.2030

70 242 East 52nd Street (1950, **Philip Johnson**) Along with the **Lescaze** house, a quintessentially modern composition in a row house lot. This one, commissioned by **John D. Rockefeller Jr.**, as a guesthouse for the **Museum of Modern Art**, was also used at one time by Philip Johnson as a New York City *pied-à-terre*. The base is Wrightian brick, the top Miesian steel and glass—the whole thing is almost Oriental in its simplicity and mystery. ♦ 2nd-3rd Aves

71 Bridge Kitchenware Corp. This is where the pros like **Craig Claiborne** and **Julia Child** pick up their copper pots, knife sets and pastry tubes. There is no better place for any staff more knowledgeable, in case you don't happen to be a pro yourself. I come here to stock up on oversize restaurant-weight dinner plates. ♦ Closed Su. 214 E 52nd St (2nd-3rd Aves) 688.4220

72 Greenacre Park (1971, **Sasaki, Dawson, DeMay Associates**) Another *vest pocket park*, this one is slightly larger and more elaborate than its cousin, **Paley Park**. It was a gift to the city by **Mrs. Jean Mauze**, daughter of **John D. Rockefeller Jr.** ♦ 217-221 E 51st St (2nd-3rd Aves)

73 Hotel Pickwick Arms $ Its 370 rooms have been redecorated; it has a roof garden, a cocktail lounge and a gourmet deli, not to mention a perfect location for midtowners. ♦ 230 E 51st St (2nd-3rd Aves) 355.0300

74 San Carlos Hotel $$ Comfortably furnished rooms, most with kitchenettes. The **Gin-Ray Restaurant** next to the hotel serves Japanese food and has a sushi bar. ♦ 150 E 50th St (3rd-Lexington Aves) 755.1800, 800/722.2010; fax 688.9778

75 Tatou ★$$$ Once an opera house and then the famous **Versailles** where **Edith Piaf** and **Judy Garland** performed, now a large supper club (although lunch is served Monday-Friday) designed to rekindle the spirit of 1850s New Orleans. A blues pianist provides the entertainment at dinner. For further merry-making, there is a disco and a private club upstairs. ♦ Creole ♦ Closed Su. 151 E 50th St (3rd-Lexington Aves) 753.1144

76 The Beverly $$ Most accommodations are suites or junior suites with kitchenettes in this homey and comfy, not-at-all chic hotel. **Kaufman Pharmacy** within the hotel is one of the few left in New York open 24 hours a day. Decent steak can be had at **Kenny's Steak and Seafood House**. ♦ 125 E 50th St (Lexington Ave) 753.2700, 800/223.0945; fax 753.2700

77 Loews Summit Hotel $$$ (1961, **Morris Lapidus** and **Harle & Liebman**) Plastic modern that is nonetheless cheery and comfortable. The Summit offers an in-hotel garage, barbershop, beauty salon for manicures, pedicures and waxing, pharmacy and jewelry shop. There is a coffeeshop, and the **Lexington Avenue Grill** for breakfast (an all-you-can-eat buffet lunch on weekends) and dinner. ♦ 569 Lexington Ave (E 51st St) 752.7000, 800/223.0888; fax 758.6311

78 General Electric Building (1931, **Cross & Cross**) This 51-story tower was designed to

Midtown

harmonize with the Byzantine lines of **St. Bartholomew's Church**, and is still best seen with the church at its feet. But it is a beauty from any angle, lavishly decorated with what possibly were intended to be stylized lightning bolts in honor of its first tenant, the **Radio Company of America**, which moved soon after to larger quarters in the new Rockefeller Center building—named **RCA** in its honor. ♦ 570 Lexington Ave (E 51st St)

79 Beijing Duck House ★$$ It is usually necessary to order Peking duck in advance, but not here. The duck is carved at your table, then rolled in a rice pancake with *hoisin* sauce, scallions and cucumbers. Since it is a whole duck, take a hungry friend along. ♦ Chinese ♦ 144 E 52nd St (3rd-Lexington Aves) Reservations required. 759.8260

79 Rand McNally Map and Travel Center A well-stocked book department plus travel videos, road maps, wall maps, globes, games for traveling, map puzzles, beachballs and pillows and geography games. Call 800/234.0679 for 24hr mail-order. ♦ Closed Su. 150 E 52nd St (3rd-Lexington Aves) 758.7488

80 Nippon ★★★$$$$ Reserve a formal *tatami* room, and experience the ultimate in Japanese elegance. Wonderful service. ◆ Japanese ◆ Closed Su. 155 E 52nd St (3rd-Lexington Aves) Reservations recommended. 758.0226

81 Seagram Building (1958, **Ludwig Mies van der Rohe** and **Philip Johnson**) The ultimate representation of pure Modernist reason, this classically proportioned and exquisitely detailed bronze, glass and steel box is the one they copied (see 6th Ave and other parts of Park Ave)—but it is still the best. The immutable object (ignore the back bit) is a vestigial column set back on a plaza that was an innovative relief when it was conceived. ◆ 375 Park Ave (E 52nd-E 53rd Sts)

Within the Seagram Building:

The Four Seasons ★★★$$$$ A city institution. A power center (especially middays in the **Bar Room Grill**, where the top echelon of New York's publishing world gathers to exchange notes and gossip). A major influence on American cooking, American restaurants and on New York (owned by **Thomas Margittai** and **Paul Kobi**). It is hard to fault the Four Seasons on anything. The food (lovingly created by chef **Hitsch Albin**) is incredibly good and original—classics include risotto with white truffles, medallion of venison with chestnut puree, chicken potpie. And then there is the **Picasso** stage backdrop in the hall, the **Philip Johnson** interior....Preferred

diner seating: the **Pool Room**, next to the fountain (where I always try to sit); the **Grill Room**, the east wall booths. Siberia: the **Grill Room Balcony**'s back tables. ◆ American ◆ Closed Su. 99 E 52nd St (Lexington-Park Aves) Jacket required. Reservations required well in advance. 754.9494

The Brasserie ★★$$ A pretty, upbeat restaurant with a matching menu—omelets, quiche, filet mignon, a fabulous onion soup and copies of the *Wall Street Journal* to peruse while you're waiting for your order. They take outgoing orders over the phone and by fax (for which they have a special menu of LeFax Picnique Boxes)—and guarantee no mistakes. ◆ French/American ◆ 24 hrs. 100 E 53rd St (Lexington-Park Aves) Reservations recommended. 751.4840; fax 308.3973

McKim, Mead & White

82 Racquet and Tennis Club (1918, **McKim, Mead & White**) A somewhat uninspired Florentine palazzo, it is an appropriate foil for the **Seagram Building** across the street. *Men only* partake in tennis, squash, racquets (an English game similar to squash but faster) and swimming. ◆ 370 Park Ave (E 52nd-E 53rd Sts) 753.9700

M. Shrewsbury

83 St. Bartholomew's Church (1919, **Bertram Goodhue**; Community House 1927, **Bertram Goodhue & Associates** and **Mayers, Murray & Philip**) This richly detailed Byzantine landmark with its charming little garden is the remaining bit of air and graciousness on Park Ave, and the object of a long-running battle between preservationists and church fathers, who want to sell off the **Community House** for commercial development. The portico was a **Vanderbilt**-financed, **Stanford White**-designed addition (1903) to a church by **James Renwick**. Goodhue inherited the portico and had to design the church—a confabulation handled with style. In the 1860s, the site was a **Schaefer** brewery. ◆ Park Ave (E 50th-E 51st Sts)

84 Sushisay ★$$ *Sushisay* means fresh sushi and that's what you'll get at this branch of the Tokyo original. White walls and shoji screens. Filled with Japanese businessmen at lunch. Good luck getting a seat at the sushi bar. ◆ Japanese ◆ Closed Su. 38 E 51st St (Park-Madison Aves) Reservations required. 755.1780

84 Tse Yang ★★★$$$ Like the original Tse Yang in Paris, this stateside outpost offers outstanding Peking cuisine and European-style service. The wine list is appropriate to its Gallic connection. I hope you'll sample the Peking hot-and-sour soup, orange beef (served cold) and the pickled cabbage—for dessert, caramelized apples for 2. ◆ French/Chinese ◆ 34 E 51st St (Park-Madison Aves) Jacket, tie and reservations required. 688.5447

Restaurants/Nightlife: Red   **Hotels:** Blue
Shops/Parks: Green   **Sights/Culture:** Black

McKim, Mead & White

85 Sky Books International Begun as a mail-order business by a former **RAF** flight instructor, this is the world's largest collection of books and magazines on military history and aviation. Upstairs on the 3rd floor is **Motobooks**, where you'll find even more male customers and new and used books on racing and rallying, motorcycles, trucks and buses, as well as repair manuals, videos and posters. ♦ Closed Su. 48 E 50th St (Park-Madison Aves) 688.5086

86 Gloucester House ★$$$ Seafood in infinite variety is served on scrubbed wooden tables in an austere setting. Though the restaurant is always filled and many customers are regulars, the one-time-only guest may find the dining experience often unforgivably flawed by superior waiters providing inferior service. ♦ Seafood ♦ Closed Su. 37 E 50th St (Madison Ave) Jacket, tie and reservations required. 755.7394

86 Helmsley Palace Hotel $$$ (1980, **Emery Roth & Sons**) *Queen* Leona **Helmsley** still stands guard over New York's tallest hotel, a 55-story glass tower that looms over the restored 100-year-old **Villard Houses**, parts of which are incorporated into the hotel's public rooms. It is an uneasy but interesting marriage. The bars and dining rooms in the old section are opulent, even excessively so, with the ornate woodwork, marble, frescoes and fireplaces from the Gilded Age all intact. The main dining room, **Le Trianon**, is tricked out as New York's answer to **Versailles**, but the **Gold Room**, with a vaulted ceiling and a harpist playing from a musician's balcony is, with all its ostentatiousness, a splendid spot for high tea (held every day of the year, including Christmas day, from 2-5PM). **Harry's New York Bar** is slickly contemporary, unlike the more atmospheric, paneled upstairs bar. Rooms are spacious, comfortably—if overly—decorated and thoughtfully appointed. Among other nice touches, there's 24hr room service. ♦ 455 Madison Ave (E 50th St) 888.7000, 800/221.4982; fax 355.0820

86 The Villard Houses (1884, **McKim, Mead & White**) This collection of 6 houses was designed to resemble a single Italian palazzo at the request of the original owner, publisher **Henry Villard**. They were later owned by the **Archdiocese of New York**, which sold them to **Harry Helmsley**. In a precedent-setting arrangement, Helmsley incorporated 2 of the landmark houses into his **Palace Hotel** (1980, **Emery Roth & Sons**) and restored the interiors to their turn-of-the-century Rococo splendor—although you might wonder if they ever looked as new as they do now. ♦ 451-455 Madison Ave (E 50th-E 51st Sts)

Within the Villard Houses:

Urban Center The Municipal Art Society, Parks Council, Architectural League of New

Midtown

York and the **New York Chapter of the American Institute of Architects** share the north wing, where they frequently host exhibitions that are open to the public. The **Information Exchange**, a service project of the Municipal Art Society that helps find answers to questions about New York City, *the built city*, is also here. The service will, for example, field questions about the history of **Central Park** or how to clean brownstones and repair old plasterwork. ♦ M-W, F-Sa 11AM-5PM. 935.3960

Urban Center Books As you would expect, the emphasis is on books, periodicals and journals about architecture, historic preservation and urban design. ♦ Closed Su. 935.3595

87 St. Patrick's Cathedral (1879, Archbishop's Residence and Rectory 1880; spires 1888, **James Renwick Jr.**; Lady Chapel 1906, **Charles T. Mathews**) Now dwarfed by its surroundings—particularly by **Rockefeller Center**—this church was too far *out of town* when first completed. The 11th largest church in the world, it is a finely detailed and well-proportioned but not very strict adaptation of its French Gothic predecessors. For example,

177

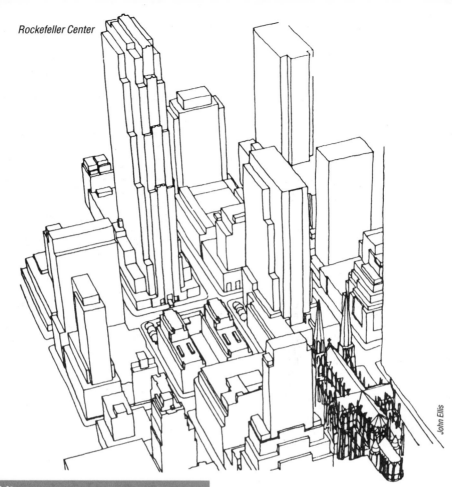

Rockefeller Center

John Ellis

there are no flying buttresses, but the pinnacles are there. The spires rise to 330ft; the rose window above the center portal is 26ft in diameter. More than half of the 70 stained-glass windows were made in Chartres and Nantes. Renwick also designed the high altar.
♦ 5th Ave (E 50th-E 51st Sts)

88 Rockefeller Center The largest privately owned business and entertainment complex in the world, with 19 buildings covering 22 acres. It all began when **John D. Rockefeller Jr.** secured leases on land in the area to provide a setting for the Metropolitan Opera House, which decided to move from the Garment Center in 1928. The Great Depression changed the Opera's plans and left the philanthropist with a long-term lease on 11.7 acres of Midtown Manhattan. He decided to develop it himself, and demolition of 228 buildings to make way for the project began in May 1931. The last of Rockefeller's original 14 buildings, the **Simon & Schuster Building** at 1230 6th Ave, was opened in April 1940. Construction started again in 1957, when **Marilyn Monroe** detonated the first charge of dynamite to be-

gin excavation for the **Time & Life Building**, designed by **Harrison & Abramovitz**, at 1271 6th Ave. Since then, the **Celanese Building** and the **McGraw-Hill** and **Exxon Buildings**, also by Harrison & Abramovitz, have been added along 6th Ave. The original complex was designed by a group called **Associated Architects**, a committee made up of **Reinhard & Hoffmeister, Corbett, Harrison and MacMurray**, and **Hood and Fouilhoux**. At its head, representing the Rockefeller interests, was **John R. Todd** of **Todd, Robertson & Todd Engineering Corp**. Their ideas included a north-south, midblock private street (**Rockefeller Plaza**) between 48th and 51st Sts, underground pedestrian and shopping passageways connecting all the buildings, and off-street freight delivery 30ft underground, capable of handling a thousand trucks a day. They seem to have thought of everything, including sloping the promenade downward from 5th Ave so that a stroller wandering in wouldn't be likely to turn around and go back uphill. The art that enhances the lobbies and exteriors is the work of 30 of the finest artists of the century. Unusual for an urban development, about one quarter of the available space has been left open, and much of it has been landscaped. Rockefeller Center's gardeners are kept busy with more than 20,000 flowering plants that are moved periodically. Some even push lawn mowers on rooftops, 2 acres of which are formal gardens. The crown jewel of Rockefeller Center is the 70-story **GE Building** (formerly the RCA Building). Todd told the architects that no desk anywhere in the building should be more than 30ft from a window. They obliged him by placing all the rentable space no farther than 28ft from natural light. A complete description of the buildings is in a printed step-by-step walking tour guide available free at the information desk in the lobby at 30 Rockefeller Plaza. A free exhibition chronicling the history of the center through photographs, models, an 11min video presentation and period memorabilia is located on the concourse level of 30 Rockefeller Plaza. ♦ W 48th-W 51st Sts (5th-6th Aves)

At Rockefeller Center:

Radio City Music Hall For more than 50 years, this Art Deco palace has maintained a tradition of spectacular entertainment. When it opened as a variety house operated by entrepreneur **Roxy Rothafel**, it was the largest theater in the world and included such features as a 50ft turntable on the 110ft stage, sections of which changed level, 75 rows of fly lines for scenery, a network of microphones, 6 motor-operated light bridges, a cyclorama 117ft by 75ft and a host of other controls and effects. The scale was overwhelming. *What are those mice doing on stage?* someone asked on opening night. *Those aren't mice, those are horses*, his neighbor replied.

The opening of the Music Hall in December 1932 drew celebrities like **Charlie Chaplin, Clark Gable, Amelia Earhart** and **Arturo Toscanini**. The premiere performance had 75 stellar acts, including such attractions as **Ray Bolger, The Wallendas** and the **Roxyettes** (later known as the **Rockettes**).

The hall was soon turned into a movie house with stage shows, featuring the Rockettes, the **Corps de Ballet**, the **Symphony Orchestra** and a variety of guest artists. The premiere feature film was **Frank Capra**'s *The Bitter Tea of General Yen* with **Barbara Stanwyck**. From 1933 until 1979, when it was *the* place to open a film, more than 650 features debuted at the Music Hall, including *King Kong, It Happened One Night, Jezebel, Top Hat, Snow White and the Seven Dwarfs, An American in Paris* and *Mister Roberts*. In 1979, a new format was introduced. Musical spectaculars, special film showings and pop personalities in concert are the current bill of fare, with an occasional one-shot—such as the **George Gershwin** classic, *Porgy and Bess*.

In 1979, Radio City Music Hall was awarded landmark status and completely restored. The public areas, designed largely by **Donald Deskey**, are grand: a plush foyer rises 50ft, overlooked by a sweeping stair and 3 mezza-

nine levels lined with gold mirrors and topped by a gold-leaf ceiling. The restrooms retain much of their fine Deco detailing—tilework, trim and fixtures—although most of the original art is gone. (A painting by **Stuart Davis** that was once in a men's room is now at the **Museum of Modern Art**.) The auditorium is all you ever dreamed a theater should be: a plaster vault of overlapping semicircles lit from the inside-edge in a rainbow of colors provides sunsets and sunrises as the lights go down and up. ♦ Seats 5882. Tours (depending on theater events): Admission. M-Sa 10:15AM-4:45PM; Su 11:15AM-4:45PM. W 50th St at 6th Ave. 247.4777

NBC Studio Tours A tour of the radio and television facilities of the **National Broadcasting Co**. Children under 6 not admitted. ♦ Admission. M-Sa 9:30AM-4:30PM. 30 Rockefeller Plaza. 664.4000

The Rink at Rockefeller Center This space is occupied by an outdoor restaurant in the summer. But every year in October it becomes an ice-skating rink, which stays slick and smooth right through April. ♦ Admission; skate rental. M-F 9AM-1PM, 1:30-5:30PM, 6-10PM; Sa-Su 9AM-noon, 12:30-3PM, 3:30-6PM, 6:30-10PM. Lower Plaza. 757.5730

Librairie de France and Librería Hispanica One of the best—albeit expensive—selections of books in French and in English about France. Also a smaller variety of Spanish books. ♦ Closed Su. 610 5th Ave (Channel Garden) 581.8810

Teuscher Chocolates of Switzerland Come here for some of the city's best (and

most expensive) chocolate bonbons. The window displays are stupendous and change with the season. ♦ 620 5th Ave (Channel Garden) 246.4416

Nikon House A showroom, photography gallery and repair center for Nikon cameras. Film is not sold. ♦ 620 5th Ave (Channel Garden)

Metropolitan Museum of Art Gift Shop At 3 floors and 6000sq ft, this is the largest of the museum's 9 outposts. The merchandise, for the most part inspired by the museum's permanent collections and special exhibitions, includes prints and posters, stationery, jewelry, tabletop accessories, sculpture reproductions and educational gifts for children. Especially popular are the Met's signature items, which include William, a reproduction of the 12th-dynasty Egyptian hippo (the Met's unofficial mascot), and Venus earrings, one black and one white teardrop, worn by the goddess of love in **Rubens'** *Venus Before the Mirror*. ♦ Closed Su. 610 5th Ave (Channel Garden) 332.1380

The Sea Grill ★★★$$$ Fresh seafood in a lush setting of cherrywood and rich fabrics. A favorite is the gingered red snapper with kumquats, pea pods and sweet peppers. Among the many gorgeous desserts: cappuccino flan with mocha sauce, golden-dusted Prometheus chocolate cake. I always request a window seat so I can watch the skaters in winter. ◆ Seafood ◆ Closed Su. 19 W 49th St (Rockefeller Plaza) Reservations required. 246.9201

American Festival Café ★★$$$ The menu is constantly changing in this festival of regional American cuisine. As part of its annual celebration of the wine harvest, **Barbara Ensrud**, the author of many books on food, including the outstanding *American Vineyards*, has designed a regional wine list and selected dishes for an accompanying menu. The wines and menu are served from 1 November through Thanksgiving; the selection of wines through the holidays. ◆ American ◆ 20 W 50th St (Rockefeller Plaza) Reservations required. 246.6699

RAINBOW.

The Rainbow Room ★★★★$$$$ When it reopened in 1987 after 2 years of restoration, *The New York Times* said the Rainbow Room is *exactly what you've always dreamed was on top of Rockefeller Center... a room that wants to be filled with people in formal dress and the sounds of Gershwin and Cole Porter.* The redesign (architecture, **Hardy, Holzman, Pfeiffer & Associates**; graphic design, **Milton Glaser**) was supervised by restaurateur **Joseph Baum**,

Midtown

whose other New York accomplishments have included **The Four Seasons**, **Windows on the World** and **Aurora**. Start with a Kir Royale (made at your table) and a cold seafood platter. Move on to grilled swordfish in red wine and marrow sauce, crisp, roast duckling with kumquats, or when in season, soft-shell crabs. Even without a view it would be a romantic place for dining and dancing, but as the song says, the great big city's a wondrous toy, and it's here glittering at your feet. A wonderful place for native New Yorkers as well as visitors; the later it gets the more *New York* it becomes. The view is at its best from the bar on the south side. ◆ Continental ◆ Closed Su. 30 Rockefeller Plaza (5th Ave) 65th floor. Jacket and tie required. Reservations required days in advance. 632.5100

New York Bound Bookshop Over 3000 books (new and out-of-print) on both the city and the state—from guidebooks to literature, architecture, city planning, performing arts and politics. Maps, photographs and prints as well. Linger awhile—they provide chairs for your comfort. ◆ Closed Su. 50 Rockefeller Plaza (W 50th-W 51st Sts) 245.8503

International Building North (1935, **Associated Architects**) This was originally planned to be **Deutsches Haus**, but the German government had other things on its mind in 1935, and negotiations got nowhere. The passport bureau is located on the mezzanine level. ◆ 630 5th Ave (W 50th-W 51st Sts)

89 Olympic Tower (1976, **Skidmore, Owings & Merrill**) A black glass box full of exclusive apartments. There is a hospitable interior arcade, complete with waterfall and a Japanese restaurant, **Shin-wa**, plus a foreign currency exchange office. Reflections of **St. Patrick's** are a nice bonus. ◆ 645 5th Ave (E 51st St)

Cartier

90 Cartier (1905, **Robert W. Gibson**; conversion 1917, **William Welles Bosworth**) Here are baubles for the body and the home, mostly at astronomical prices, but it is all so lovely to look at. The originator of the *tank watch* is always coming up with original designs, and there are all those rings of diamonds, emeralds and pearls. Don't miss **Les Musts**, the more affordable boutique collection of gifts, such as cigarette lighters. There are sterling silver, tableware, antiques and gift ideas galore. Once the residence of businessman **Morton F. Plant**, the Cartier

building is a Renaissance palazzo that is a rare survivor of the days when 5th Ave was lined with houses of people like **William Vanderbilt**, who lived diagonally across the street. Note the detailing of the entrance and centralized composition on 52nd St. ◆ Closed Su. 2 E 52nd St (5th Ave) 753.0111

90 Restaurant Dosanko $ An unusual fast-food chain, specializing in Japanese noodles served in broth with a variety of meat, fish, poultry and vegetable toppings, as well as good fried chicken. It's a perfect choice for inexpensive family meals. ◆ Japanese ◆ 10 E 52nd St (Madison-5th Aves) No credit cards. 759.6361

LA GRENOUILLE

91 La Grenouille ★★★$$$$ The budget for flowers is close to $100,000 a year, and worth every penny. There are mirrors sparkling everywhere, and the lighting is nearly perfect. The *Beautiful People* like to be seen here because it makes them look even more beautiful. But the food is an even better reason—grilled turbot with *beurre blanc* is particularly delicate and fragrant. The best time to go is at lunch, fashionably, at one. ◆ French ◆ Closed Su. 3 E 52nd St (5th Ave) Jacket and tie required. Reservations required days in advance. 752.1495

92 B. Dalton Bookseller The flagship store of the Dalton chain is organized by subject and arranged by author with hardcover, paperback and backlist included in each section. Authors are often doing something gimmicky like writing a book in the window. Computer software is downstairs. ◆ 666 5th Ave (W 52nd St) 247.1740. Also at: 396 6th Ave. 674.8780; 170 Broadway. 349.3560

93 Omni Berkshire Place $$$$ The old Berkshire has become one of the city's best personalized, European-style hotels. Many of its generously proportioned rooms have sitting areas. The lobby's gracious sunlit **Atrium** serves drinks and tea, and the **Rendez-Vous**, a pricey, popular bistro for new American and French nouvelle cuisine, can be hectic for lunch, but quiets down at dinnertime. ◆ 21 E 52nd St (Madison Ave) 753.5800, 800/843.6664; fax 308.9473

94 Traveller's Bookstore Owners **Candace Olmsted** and **Jane Grossman** don't stock every book in print on a certain destination. Instead, they read (and use, if possible) all of the available books and sell only the very best. *We really try to provide people with what they need*, Olmsted explains. Come here for guide books and related fiction and nonfiction, phrase books, practical maps from all over the world and sound advice from the congenial and knowledgeable staff. Extensive mail-order catalog available. *An RSW recommendation.* ◆ Closed Su. 22 W 52nd St (5th-6th Aves) 664.0995

94 Bombay Palace ★$$$ This is a very presentable Indian restaurant with pleasant service. The crisp and light Indian breads are delightful, the curries are mild, and the tandoori chicken is properly moist and tender. For dessert, try the mango ice cream or the Indian

rice pudding, if you don't mind the sweet taste of rosewater. ◆ Indian ◆ 30 W 52nd St (5th-6th Aves) 541.7777

95 21 Club ★★$$$$ During the 1920s, there was a speakeasy in every house on 52nd St between 5th and 6th Aves. This is the only survivor, and in 1967, it was purchased by **Marshall Cogan** (for $21 million) and in 1987 was renovated by **Charles Pfister** to cater to a younger clientele. The downstairs bar is as active as ever, and nothing was done to change the iron fence and jockeys that have been outside since this was a private mansion. It is still a gathering place for entertainers, politicians and society types, who don't seem to mind the wildly uneven menu and sky-high prices. The famous *21 Burger* is a truly amazing twist on an old standby. ◆ Continental ◆ 21 W 52nd St (5th-6th Aves) Jacket, tie and reservations required. 582.7200

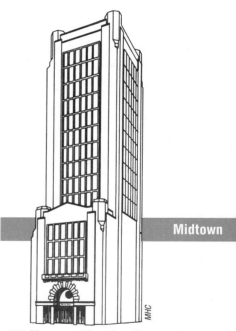

Midtown

MHC

95 Museum of Broadcasting (1990, **John Burgee Architects**) Scheduled opening: fall of 1991. Founded in 1965 by CBS Inc founder, the late **William S. Paley**. Only the winners will air here, like a **Hitchcock** retrospective or a tribute to **Henry Fonda**. You will also be able to select TV and radio programs of your choice from the museum's vast archives, and screen or listen for up to an hour at a time. A 1991 move from its longtime home next to Paley Park on 53rd St will more than double the museum's size and add 2 theaters, a screening room, a gallery space, an expanded library with computer access to catalogs and a museum shop. Docent-led tours will be held at 1:30PM on Tuesday. ◆ Voluntary contribution. Tu noon-8PM; W-Sa noon-5PM. 23 W 52nd St (5th-6th Aves) 752.7684, 752.4690

95 Hines Building (1986, Kevin Roche, John Dinkeloo & Associates) While designing this building, Kevin Roche was also working on plans for the new zoo in Central Park. The zoo has covered walkways supported by columns whose edges are sliced, in an effect called *chamfering*. He used the idea here and put the building on similar columns . In 1989, with the support of neighboring cultural institutions, including the American Craft Museum and the Museum of Broadcasting, the occupants established the ground-floor **Lobby Gallery**, a nonprofit exhibition space where approximately 10 shows a year are mounted. ◆ 31 W 52nd St (5th-6th Aves)

95 CBS Building (1965, Eero Saarinen & Associates) This is Saarinen's only high-rise building, although he didn't live to see its completion. A dark gray granite mass (known as **Black Rock**) removed from the street, its surface given depth by triangular columns. Its top the same as the bottom, this tower is the image of mystery (even the entrances are hard to identify)—the monolith from *2001* landed on 6th Ave. ◆ 51 W 52nd St (5th-6th Aves)

Within the CBS Building:

China Grill ★★$$$ Although not related to Wolfgang Puck's Santa Monica landmark, Chinois on Main, the cuisine—an amalgam of Oriental, French and California influences—is similarly inspired. No surprise when you realize that China Grill was opened by Chinois expatriots. A modern airy space, where the story of Marco Polo's journey to China is recounted on the floor and on the menu, and the food, as well as the people, is beautiful. ◆ Oriental/French/California ◆ Reservations required. 333.7788

Midtown

96 THE MoMA DESIGN STORE Merchandise inspired by the museums collections, including educational toys (Colorforms, kaleidoscopes, architectural blocks); furniture (designs by **Frank Lloyd Wright** and **Charles Eames**, plus a reproduction of the famous butterfly chair by **Antonio Bonet, Jorge Farrari** and **Juan Kurchen**; housewares and desk accessories. ◆ 44 W 53rd St (5th-6th Aves) 708.9669

96 American Craft Museum (1986, Fox & Fowle Architects) The appreciation of native American crafts has grown in recent years, partly due to an interest in things that are *not* machine-made and partly due to the pioneering of the **American Crafts Council** and its New York City museum. Go to see works in glass, fiber, wood, clay, metal and paper by America's most talented craftspeople, either from the museum's collection from 1900 to the present or from changing loan exhibitions. Sometimes the shows are amusing, sometimes serious, but the taste level is always high. ◆ Admission. Tu 10AM-8PM; W-Su 10AM-5PM. 40 W 53rd St (5th-6th Aves) 956.6047

96 New York Public Library, Donnell Library Center When he died in 1896, textile merchant **Ezekiel Donnell** left his estate to the New York Public Library to establish a place where young people could spend their evenings away from demoralizing influences. His legacy established this as the best collection of children's literature in the US. Each department has its own hours; call for specific times. ◆ Main floor: M noon-8PM; Tu, Th 9:30AM-8PM; W 9:30AM-6PM; F noon-6PM; Sa 10AM-5:30PM; Su 1-5PM. 20 W 53rd St (5th-6th Aves) 621.0618

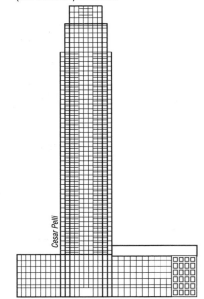

Cesar Pelli

97 Museum Tower (1983, Cesar Pelli & Associates) A prestigious apartment building built to raise funds for the support of the **Museum of Modern Art** next door. ◆ 15 W 53rd St (5th-6th Aves)

97 Museum of Modern Art (1939, Philip L. Goodwin and Edward Durell Stone; additions 1951 and 1964, Philip Johnson; Sculpture Garden 1953, Philip Johnson and Zion & Breen; expansion 1984, Cesar Pelli & Associates) When the Museum of Modern Art was founded in 1929, a few days after the big stock market crash, it was a novel idea, a museum no one in the US had thought of before. It was to be dedicated to the understanding and enjoyment of contemporary visual arts. Its 3 founding mothers, **Abby Aldrich Rockefeller** (wife of **John D. Jr.**), **Lillie P. Bliss** and **Mrs. Cornelius J. Sullivan**, were joined by other collectors and philanthropists in this venture. The collections have grown through the largesse of the early benefactors and others. Over the years, one of MoMA's most important contributions has been the embracing of disciplines that hadn't been considered worthy of museum status, such as architecture, film, photography and industrial design.

The original sleek white horizontal building

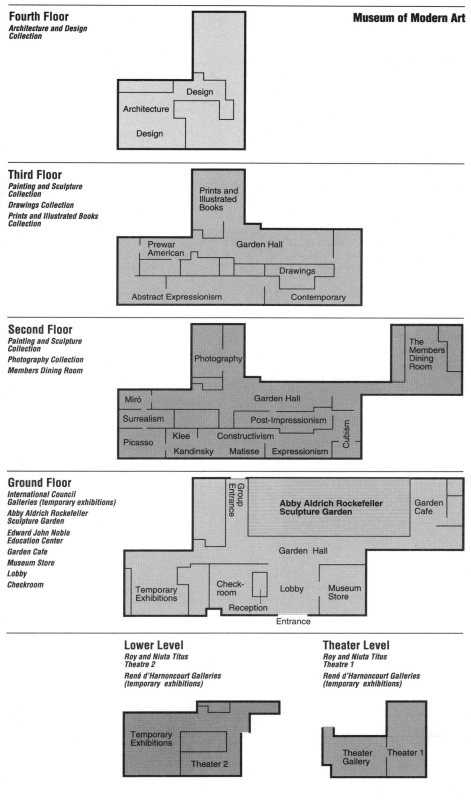

Fourth Floor
Architecture and Design Collection

Museum of Modern Art

Design

Architecture

Design

Third Floor
Painting and Sculpture Collection

Drawings Collection

Prints and Illustrated Books Collection

Prints and Illustrated Books

Prewar American

Garden Hall

Drawings

Abstract Expressionism

Contemporary

Second Floor
Painting and Sculpture Collection

Photography Collection

Members Dining Room

Photography

The Members Dining Room

Miró

Garden Hall

Surrealism

Post-Impressionism

Picasso

Klee

Constructivism

Cubism

Kandinsky

Matisse

Expressionism

Ground Floor
International Council Galleries (temporary exhibitions)

Abby Aldrich Rockefeller Sculpture Garden

Edward John Noble Education Center

Garden Cafe

Museum Store

Lobby

Checkroom

Group Entrance

Abby Aldrich Rockefeller Sculpture Garden

Garden Cafe

Garden Hall

Temporary Exhibitions

Check-room

Lobby

Museum Store

Reception

Entrance

Lower Level
Roy and Niuta Titus Theatre 2

René d'Harnoncourt Galleries (temporary exhibitions)

Temporary Exhibitions

Theater 2

Theater Level
Roy and Niuta Titus Theatre 1

René d'Harnoncourt Galleries (temporary exhibitions)

Theater Gallery

Theater 1

183

with its marble veneer and tile-and-glass facade was strictly International Style—a striking statement by an innovative institution, practicing what it preached in a row of brownstones. There was (briefly) a plan to cut a street through the 2 blocks from Rockefeller Center leading directly to the museum (the Rockefellers controlled the land in the vicinity). The first additions, black glass wings to the east and west, not only expanded the gallery space and improved the Sculpture Garden, but were an effective frame for the original front. The tower and addition by Cesar Pelli have replaced Philip Johnson's west wing; Pelli has also replaced the garden facade with a glassed-in **Garden Court** full of escalators. The somewhat banal condominium tower rising above the museum wing base is a source of income for the museum and a source of contention for those who appreciated a sunny garden and low-rise side streets. There are 11 shades of glass used in the cladding. The expansion doubled the space available for loan shows and for the permanent collection. These days, the former tend to be heavy on retrospectives of arrived figures in art and design with occasional historical or contemporary finds.

MoMA is strongest in art of the first half of the century—Impressionists, Cubists and Realists such as **Picasso, Matisse, Miró** and **Hopper**—but it also has good examples of post-WWII Abstract Expressionists through Conceptualists, such as **deKooning, Rothko, Lichtenstein, diSuvero** and **LeWitt**. The photography galleries are worth seeing, as are the galleries of architecture and design, where you will find 20th-century classics, such as **Thonet** bentwood chairs, **Tiffany** glass, **Bauhaus** textiles and **Marcel Breuer** furniture. Among the most im-

Midtown

portant paintings in the collection are **van Gogh**'s *Starry Night*, **Mondrian**'s *Broadway Boogie Woogie*, Matisse's *Dance*, Picasso's *Les Demoiselles d'Avignon*, **Andrew Wyeth**'s *Christina's World* and **Jackson Pollock**'s *One (Number 31, 1950)*.

The new MoMA reflects a philosophy put forth by the first director, **Alfred H. Barr Jr.**, back in 1929. While a professor at Wellesley College, Barr devised a theory of modern art, which included not only 20th-century painting and sculpture, but photography, film, theater, music, industrial design and architecture. His design for a museum of modern art reflected this concern.

The multidepartmental concept appeared radical for including practical as well as fine art. While at first the museum displayed only 19th-century painting, it began a slow and steady implementation of Barr's ideas. Today MoMA includes not only Barr's multidepartmental structure, but a publishing house, movie theater and film department.

With MoMA's renovation, each department has gained an area of its own. The lower level holds the **Roy and Niuta Titus Theaters**, showing off the **Department of Film**, the largest international collection of its kind. The ground floor leads to temporary exhibitions and the **Abby Aldrich Rockefeller Sculpture Garden**.

Stretching across MoMA's 2nd floor is the **Painting and Sculpture Collection**, with separate rooms allotted to Picasso and Matisse, among others.

The Drawing Collection on the 3rd floor has its own exhibition space. Acquisitions include **Max Pechstein**'s *Reclining Nude with Cat* and Picasso's 1913 *Head*. The **Prints & Illustrated Books** collection owns a 1968 etching by Picasso, the first of a series of 347 intaglio prints, and the only self-portrait of him as an old man. The **Architecture & Design Collection** on the 4th floor features 2 designs for houses by **Frank Lloyd Wright**, and a **Mindset Computer**.

Given MoMA's newfound spaciousness, the unrivaled multidepartmental museum has truly fulfilled Barr's dream. ♦ Admission; members and children under 16 accompanied by an adult free. M-Tu, F-Su 11AM-6PM; Th 11AM-9PM; voluntary contribution Th 5-9PM. 11 W 53rd St (5th-6th Aves) 708.9480; film schedule 708.9490

Within the Museum of Modern Art:

The Sculpture Garden One of the most pleasant outdoor spaces in the city, with sculpture by **Rodin, Renoir, Miró, Lipschitz** and **Picasso**, among others. Weather permitting, it's open the same hours as the museum. The **Garden Cafe** overlooks the garden and offers a variety of snacks and light meals. ♦ M-Tu, F-Su 11AM-6PM; Th 11AM-9PM. 708.9480

THE MoMA BOOKSTORE An extensive assortment of books, posters and cards relating to the museum's collection. ♦ 708.9700

Museum Bests

Richard Oldenburg
Director, The Museum of Modern Art

Bather by Cézanne

Starry Night by van Gogh

The Sleeping Gypsy by Rousseau

Dance and *The Red Studio* by Matisse

Four Seasons by Kandinsky

Les Demoiselles d'Avignon and *Girl Before a Mirror* by Picasso

Bird in Space by Brancusi

Broadway Boogie Woogie by Mondrian

The Birth of the World by Miró

One by Pollock

Australia by David Smith

Flag by Johns

Kastura by Stella

Twittering Machine by Klee

Bed by Rauschenberg
Cisitalia "202" GT CAR by Pinin Farina
Still Life with Watermelon by Penn
The Birth of a Nation by Griffith

98 St. Thomas Church (1914, **Cram Goodhue & Ferguson**) A picturesque French Gothic edifice on a tight corner. You have to wonder why a second tower wasn't included; the single one is rather awkward in an otherwise symmetrical composition. A dollar sign next to the *true lover's knot* over the **Bride's Door** is presumably a sculptor's comment on the social standing of the congregation. ♦ 1 W 53rd St (5th Ave)

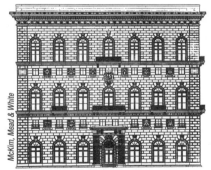

McKim, Mead & White

99 University Club (1899, **McKim, Mead & White**) Considered by many to be the finest work of **Charles Follen McKim**, it is an original composition with a bow to a half-dozen Italian palaces. When it was built, in the days before air conditioning, it had striped awnings in the windows, which made the pink marble exterior even more interesting. The interior is just as lavish. This club set the style for all the others that followed for decades. ♦ 1 W 54th St (5th Ave) 247.2100

Restaurants/Nightlife: Red   **Hotels:** Blue
Shops/Parks: Green   **Sights/Culture:** Black

100 Aquavit ★★★$$$ **Nelson Rockefeller** once lived in this townhouse, but he wouldn't recognize the 8-story atrium, complete with birch trees and a waterfall, that is now the main dining room of this modern restaurant. The potent liquor that is its namesake is one of the stars at the street-level bar, which offers light meals—including a wonderful *smorgasbord* platter that is so varied, and each morsel so sublime, it could be eaten forever and each time would seem new. The Swedish decor—contemporary and antique Scandinavian art and exquisite table settings—adds greatly to the pleasure of the fine food. *An RSW recommendation.* ♦ Scandinavian ♦ 13 W 54th St (5th-6th Aves) Reservations required. 307.7311

100 Rockefeller Apartments (1936, **Harrison & Fouilhoux**) When **John D. Rockefeller Jr.** was assembling the site for **Rockefeller Center**, he lived on this block. By the end of 1929, he owned 15 of the block's houses, having joined his neighbors, most of whom were members of his family, in protecting the street from commercial use. But he wasn't above a little commercialism himself, and had this building built a few months before he moved over to Park Ave. Its bay-windowed towers overlook the garden of the **Museum of Modern Art**, a site donated by Rockefeller through his wife, **Abby Aldrich Rockefeller**, who, with **Lillie T. Bliss** and **Mrs. Cornelius J. Sullivan**, was a founder of the museum. ♦ 17 W 54th St (5th-6th Aves)

101 Hotel Dorset $$$ An attractive, unassuming hotel with a very loyal following and a prime location—next door to the **Museum of Modern Art**. The bar and restaurant are jovial and

popular. ♦ 30 W 54th St (5th-6th Aves) 247.7300; fax 581.0153

Within the Hotel Dorset:

Dorset Room ★★$$$ One of this neighborhood's secrets. Bay scallops in cream sauce with white wine, escargot *saulieu* and wonderful cold appetizers are a few of the always delicious choices. The room is large, bright and comfortable. ♦ Continental ♦ Reservations required. 247.7300

102 Warwick Hotel $$$ A European-style hotel that was the stopping place for the **Beatles** when they looked for peace and quiet in New York. Amenities include babysitting and interpreting services. On the premises: a barbershop, beauty salon, bar and restaurant. ♦ 65 W 54th St (6th Ave) 247.2700, 800/522.5634; fax 957.8915

103 J.P. French Bakery Perhaps the best croissant in town, plus excellent French breads in several sizes—from *ficelle* (a thin baguette) to large, round loaves—all baked on the premises. ♦ 54 W 55th St (5th-6th Aves) 765.7575

103 La Bonne Soupe ★$$ Soups, omelets, a variety of chopped beef dishes and daily specials of provincial French food are good buys in a cute place with personable and efficient service. ♦ French ♦ 48 W 55th St (5th-6th Aves) 586.7650

104 La Caravelle ★★$$$$ Consistently rated as one of New York's best French restaurants since its opening in 1960, it's time to change this assessment. The standards have slipped alarmingly, and it no longer deserves the accolades it once wore with such distinction. The times have changed; La Caravelle should do so too. Stay tuned. ♦ French ♦ Closed Su. 33 W 55th St (5th-6th Aves) Jacket, tie and reservations required. 586.4252

104 Shoreham Hotel $$ A small hotel with only 75 rooms, each with its own serving pantry. ♦ 33 W 55th St (5th-6th Aves) 247.6700, 800/553.3347; fax 765.9741

104 La Fondue $$$ Swiss chocolate, cheese and filet mignon fondues, plus steaks, seafood and incredible desserts in the warm, casual atmosphere of a European cellar. ♦ Swiss ♦ 43 W 55th St (5th-6th Aves) 581.0820

105 Italian Pavilion Café ★★$$$ This restaurant began as the star attraction at the Italian Pavilion at the 1939-40 New York World's Fair. When the fair closed, it moved here, where it has been attracting a loyal following ever since. Garden dining is available. ♦ Italian ♦ Closed Su. 24 W 55th St (5th-6th Aves) Jacket and tie required. Reservations recommended. 753.7295

106 Fifth Avenue Presbyterian Church (1875, **Carl Pfeiffer**) When society moved uptown, this church, which had been at 19th

Midtown

St since 1855, moved with it. Future president **Theodore Roosevelt** was one of its original parishioners, along with the **Auchinclosses**, the **Livingstons** and the **Walcotts**. It was called the most influential congregation in New York. ♦ 7 W 55th St (5th Ave)

THE PENINSULA
NEW YORK

107 The Peninsula New York $$$$ (1905, **Hiss & Weeks**) For many years, as the **Gotham Hotel**, this was a favorite stopping place for movie stars. Then it briefly became **Maxim's**, and was completely restored in the Belle Epoque tradition of the original Maxim's in Paris. This latest incarnation reflects the *Peninsula* style. The 250 oversize rooms are outfitted with marble baths and Art Nouveau decor. The services range from newspaper delivery to 24hr room service, and the hotel includes 3 restaurants and a trilevel fitness center with a glass-enclosed rooftop swimming pool. ♦ 700 5th Ave (W 55th St) 247.2200, 800/262.9467; fax 903.3949

Within the Peninsula New York:

Adrienne

Adrienne ★$$$$ Overlooking 5th Ave, and introducing cuisine *du soleil*, a Mediterranean style that is basically French Provençal, but with a touch of Italian, Spanish, Greek and Moroccan influence. A typical choice is codfish with sweet onion juice and fried leeks. ♦ French ♦ Jacket and tie required at lunch and dinner. Reservations recommended. 247.2200

Penn-Top Bar and Terrace ★$$$ A glass-enclosed bar with a beautiful view of the Manhattan skyline. Lunch is served buffet-style on the terrace during the warmer months. ♦ Closed Su. 23rd floor

108 Christian Dior Boutique Reminiscent of Dior's Paris headquarters at 30 Avenue Montaigne, the luxurious 4500sq ft space is large enough to display **Gianfranco Ferre**'s complete haute couture and ready-to-wear collections. ♦ Closed Su. 703 5th Ave (E 55th St) 223.4646

108 Nat Sherman's Tobacconist to the stars, Nat Sherman has customers such as **Frank Sinatra**, **Milton Berle** and **Sylvester Stallone**. His specialty is the pure tobacco cigarette wrapped in brown or in such trendy colors as shocking pink, turquoise or scarlet. He also stocks cigars and **Dunhill** lighters. There is a humidor on the premises. ♦ 711 5th Ave (E 55th St) 751.9100

108 La Côte Basque ★★★$$$$ Considered by many as one of the top restaurants in New York. Chef/owner **Jean Jacques Rachou** provides food that is technically perfect and exquisitely served in a setting reminiscent of a French seaside village. The presentation of the lobster terrine, a combination of shellfish, green beans, tomato, shredded carrots and *celerie rémoulade*, is stunning and sure to please. A distinguished, cream-of-society clientele occupy their regular tables, but occasional guests are also treated graciously. An inspired choice for celebrating a special occasion if you can secure a reservation. ♦ French ♦ Closed Su. 5 E 55th St (Madison-5th Aves) Jacket and tie required. Reservations required days in advance. 688.6525

109 St. Regis Sheraton $$$$ (1904, **Trowbridge & Livingston**; renovation 1991, **Brennan, Beer Gorman**) When the St. Regis was built for **John Jacob Astor**, he said he wanted the finest hotel in the world, a place where guests would feel as comfortable as they did in a gracious private home. The exterior, with its stone garlands and flowers, its slate mansard roof, its bronze marquee and its brass kiosk for the doorman set the stage for the equally elegant interior. The lobby chandeliers are **Waterford** crystal; the floors and columns are of marble imported from France. The St. Regis was closed for renovations in 1988 and is scheduled to reopen in 1991. ♦ 5th Ave at E 55th St. 767.0525; fax 541.4736

110 Elizabeth Arden Salon The famous red door leads to a world apart, filled with designer fashions, lingerie and sportswear, and a salon that has made pampering a fine art. The salon includes exercise, massage, facials, hair styling and more, all calculated to make you look as terrific as you feel. ♦ Closed Su. 691 5th Ave (E 54th-E 55th Sts) 546.0200

110 Gucci Its stock is divided into 2 nearby shops. Shoes and leather goods for men and women are sold in the northernmost store (No. 689), and suits, topcoats, dresses, ties and scarves are found at the other (No. 685). The famed red and green stripe is omnipresent on handbags, boots and luggage. The sales staff ranges from very pleasant to downright snooty. ♦ Closed Su. 685 and 689 5th Ave (E 54th St) 826.2600

110 Bice ★★$$$ This Milanese trattoria is frequented by **Bill Blass, Calvin Klein, Oleg Cassini** and **Gianfranco Ferre.** The long, curved white marble bar, multilevel seating, bright lighting and exquisite flower arrangements create a luxurious setting. Among the more rewarding main courses are roast rack of veal with new potatoes, and grilled fish (salmon, swordfish or sole). Bice's Milan counterpart is every bit as elegant. ♦ Italian ♦ 7 E 54th St (Madison-5th Aves) Reservations required. 688.1999

111 Prunelle ★★$$$$ Designed by **Sam Lopata** (**Extra! Extra!, Lox Around the Clock**), this handsome Art Deco space has burled maple walls and luxurious fresh flower arrangements. The seafood is excellent, especially the salmon and the Dover sole. Prunelle also caters within a 50mi radius of New York. ♦ French ♦ 18 E 54th St (Madison-5th Aves) Jacket and tie required. Reservations recommended. 759.6410

111 Indonesian Pavilion (1900, **McKim, Mead & White**) One of the few remaining buildings from a time when 54th St east and west of 5th Ave was called *The Art Gallery of New York Streets.* It was built by **W.E.D. Stokes**, who sold it to **William H. Moore**, a founder of the **United States Steel** and **American Can Companies**. Note the massive balcony and strong cornices—evidence of Charles McKim's interest in Renaissance architecture. ♦ 4 E 54th St (5th Ave)

111 Fortunoff You would never expect to find a jewelry and silver discount store on 5th Ave, but here is one (complete with a glitzy facade) that offers 20-percent discounts on strings of

pearls, gold chains, hammered silver pitchers, urns, chalices, sterling silver and silver plate flatware by **Towle, Reed & Barton** and **Oneida**, and stainless steel flatware by **Fraser** and **Dansk**. Sales help is remarkably courteous. ♦ 681 5th Ave (E 53rd-E 54th Sts) 758.6660

112 Samuel Paley Plaza (1967, **Zion & Breen**, landscape architects; **Albert Preston Moore**, consulting architect) This park, named for the father of its benefactor, the late **William S. Paley** of CBS, is a spare, very welcome anomaly in the densest part of town. Good furniture and a wonderful waterfall (the perfect spot to steal a moment's peace). A counter sells light food and beverages. ♦ 3 E 53rd St (5th Ave)

112 Seryna ★★$$$ Lunch here is much too crowded; come for dinner and enjoy any of the excellent steak dishes. Good sushi and sashimi. ♦ Japanese ♦ Closed Su. 11 E 53rd St (Madison-5th Aves) Reservations recommended. 980.9393

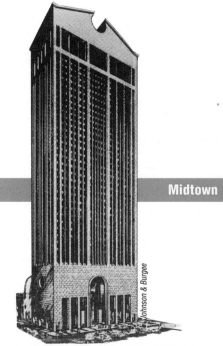

Midtown

Johnson & Burgee

113 AT&T Headquarters (1984, **Philip Johnson** and **John Burgee**) At the top, often referred to as *Chippendale* in style, an orbiculum pierces a pediment. The shaft is clad in pinkish granite. The base, an uninviting public arcade 60ft high and cross-vaulted, is filled with chairs that, for the most part, remain empty. In the center of this is **Evelyn Longworth**'s statue *The Spirit of Communication* (better known as *Golden Boy*), moved from the top of the company's downtown tower. All in all, this building is an ungracious gesture to the urban fabric of Manhattan. ♦ 550 Madison Ave (E 55th-E 56th Sts)

Within the AT&T Headquarters:

"the Quilted Giraffe"

The Quilted Giraffe ★★★★$$$$ Its nouvelle French cuisine is as unusual and playful as its name. The staging of dinner is in the hands of the innovator/trendsetter **Barry Wine**. The food is unique and brilliantly conceived and executed. You won't find anything on the menu here that you've ever had before—the slices of calf's liver are coated and sautéed with crushed pine nuts, pistachios and almonds; the rack of lamb is covered in a superb Chinese mustard sauce, and the veal scaloppine is served with soft polenta and truffles. The service is perfection, and its cost is included in the astronomical check. At lunch and on weekends the menu is more casual than in the evenings, though the standards of excellence are maintained. Stop by to read the menu in any case: note the outrageously priced portion of jelly beans! ♦ Continental ♦ Closed Su. Jacket, tie and reservations required. 593.1221

The AT&T Infoquest Center An exhibition space dedicated to science and technology. Discover the worlds of fiber optics, computers and robotics. An auditorium presentation has

Midtown

32 synchronized video screens. ♦ Free. Tu 10AM-9PM; W-Su 10AM-6PM. 605.5555

114 Mon Cher Ton Ton ★★★$$$$ Chef **Marc Meneau**, from the 3-star L'Esperance restaurant in Burgundy, flies in 4 days a month to supervise the kitchen staff. The menu includes a foie gras with fresh figs, exquisite fresh oysters in seawater aspic and Meneau's masterpiece, a boiled egg filled with cream and caviar served in a breadcrumb eggshell. The roster of fish and seafood dishes includes a braised salmon with champagne sauce, broiled rouget with celery sauce and a sparkling steamed bass. Meat dishes could include a duckling roasted to perfection with fresh peaches or a châteaubriand bedecked with tarragon sauce. The best dessert is a chocolate soufflé served with vanilla ice cream; rhubarb ice cream is luscious and delicately topped with exotic fresh fruits. ♦ French ♦ Closed Su. 68 E 56th St (Madison-Park Aves) 223.7575

115 Friars Club This is the private club for actors that invented the famous roasts, in which members poke fun at celebrity guests. ♦ 57 E 55th St (Park-Madison Aves) 751.7272

116 Morrell & Company, The Wine Emporium A playground for oenophiles, this large, well-organized store carries practically every label that is available and worthwhile, including many direct imports. Service is knowledgeable but occasionally impatient. ♦ Closed Su. 535 Madison Ave (E 54th-E 55th Sts) 688.9370

117 Le Cygne ★★★$$$$ The classic cuisine — superb fish and meat terrines, perfect oysters, tender *foie gras*—is masterfully produced, and the redone interior by **Voorsange & Mills Associates** is a masterwork of Postmodern design, at once stylish and timeless. In a few dishes, however, the seasoning could be more to the point, and both the upstairs and downstairs rooms are too crowded with tables and scurrying waiters. When they have time, the captains here are among the most considerate in town. ♦ French ♦ Closed Su. 55 E 54th St (Park-Madison Aves) Jacket, tie and reservations required. 759.5941

117 Bill's Gay Nineties ★$$$ A landmark that really is a holdover from the 1890s. Its sirloin steak special is named for **Diamond Jim Brady**, who would be right at home here. There is a pianist in the dining room, where American cuisine is served. ♦ American ♦ Closed Su. 57 E 54th St (Park-Madison Aves) 355.0243

117 Lello Ristorante $$$ Much of the food is quite good—a specialty is an excellent pasta and seafood cooked in a bag—but the prices are too high. ♦ Italian ♦ Closed Su. 65 E 54th St (Park-Madison Aves) Jacket required. Reservations recommended. 751.1555

118 Hotel Elysée $$$ **Tallulah Bankhead** used to be a regular here, as was **Tennessee Williams**. It retains its old-world atmosphere in spite of the modern buildings rising like weeds around it. Each of its 110 rooms has its own personality, and most go by names as well as numbers. Within the hotel, **Pisces** offers continental cuisine. **The Monkey Bar** is packed after work and again later in the evening, when the attraction is music and comedy. Refrigerators upon request. ♦ 60 E 54th St (Park-Madison Aves) 753.1066; fax 980.9278

119 Lever House (1952, **Skidmore, Owings & Merrill; Gordon Bunschaft**, partner in charge) The first glass wall on Park Ave, built when **Charles Luckman** was president of Lever Bros, has, after a long battle, been awarded landmark status and saved from possible destruction or disfigurement. This articulate building displays the tenets of orthodox, Corbusian Modernism: it is raised from the ground on columns; it has a roof garden; there is a free facade on the outside and free plan on the inside. With the **Seagram Building** across the way, this is a landmark corner that changed the face of the city. ♦ 390 Park Ave (E 53rd-E 54th Sts)

120 Central Synagogue (1872, **Henry Fernbach**) This Moorish Revival building is the oldest continuously used synagogue in the city. The onion domes on the 222ft towers and the brightly stenciled interior add a bit of fancy to the mottled brownstone facade. ♦ 652 Lexington Ave (E 55th St)

121 Enoteca Iperbole ★★$$$ The management calls this America's first wine library/restaurant. The setting is charming, the food is well-prepared, and there are more than 500 wines to choose from. ♦ Italian ♦ Closed Su. 137 E 55th St (3rd-Lexington Aves) Reservations recommended. 759.9720

121 Shun Lee Palace ★★$$$ The late **T.T. Wang**, founder of this fine restaurant, was the man who introduced America to a Chinese cuisine that goes beyond egg rolls and chow mein. The menu represents several regions of China, and the kitchen does justice to all of them. An interesting dish is the frog legs with black Chinese mushrooms and scallions in a ginger sauce with black beans. ♦ Chinese ♦ 155 E 55th St (3rd-Lexington Aves) Reservations required. 371.8844

122 Citicorp Center (1978, **Hugh Stubbins & Associates**) The rakish angle of its top was planned as a solar collector but is now nothing more than a vent for the cooling system, which provides a steamy effect for the night lighting. There is also a 400-ton, computer-operated **Tuned Mass Damper** (*earthquake machine* to most of us) up there under the roof. They don't expect an earthquake any time soon, but the building is cantilevered on 145ft columns that allow it to sway in the wind. Those 10-story-high stilts also make it possible for Citicorp Center to be the world's only skyscraper with skylights in the basement, where free concerts and other programs are given in the center of a gaggle of shops and restaurants. ♦ 153 E 53rd St (3rd-Lexington Aves) 559.1000

Within Citicorp Center:

St. Peter's Lutheran Church (1977, **Hugh Stubbins & Associates**; interior, **Massimo** and **Lella Vignelli**) St. Peter's is a major reason for the engineering and formal antics of Citicorp Center's design. The church refused to sell its air rights to Citicorp unless the bank agreed to build a new church clearly distinct from the tower. In contrast to the high-tech tower, the church is granite, with wooden furnishings and interior detailing. Within the church, the **Erol Beaker Chapel** was created by sculptor **Louise Nevelson**. Watch for jazz vespers at St. Peter's, known as the city's jazz ministry. Well worth a visit under any circumstances. ♦ E 54th St at Lexington Ave. 935.2200

Theatre at St. Peter's Church An excellent space in the basement of Citicorp Center. Two productions began here and went on to Broadway: *Tintypes* and *The Elephant Man*. ♦ Seats 165. 753.4318

The Market at Citicorp Center Accessible from the sunken plaza at the corner of 53rd St and Lexington Ave, this international bazaar offering 3 levels of dining and culinary and housewares shopping. There are tables where you can bring food from the shops and restaurants or just sit and read a newspaper. The slate floors and all-glass front add a homogeneity to this potpourri of individual shops. Semi-regular free entertainment enlivens the atrium: weeknight cabaret and pop concerts at 6PM, Saturday night jazz at 8PM, Sunday classical concerts at noon. There are also Saturday programs for kids at 11AM.

Alfredo's the Original of Rome specializes in pasta; **Auberge Suisse** has fondue, *raclette*

and Swiss wines; **Au bon Pain** has French bakery specialties; **Healthworks!** serves salads and other wholesome delights; **Charley O's** has turn-of-the century pub fare, including carved sandwiches and steaks. **The Market Coffee Shop** and **The Bear Cafe** both provide lighter dining. Other shops include **Famous Chocolate Chip Cookie**, **Chez Chocolate**, **Doubleday** books, **International Smoke Shop**, the **Market Card Shop**, **Pan American Phoenix** imported gifts, **Flowers by Konstantinos**.

Within the Market at Citicorp Center:

Conran's Conceived by **Terence Conran**, the founder of **Habitat**, an international chain of home furnishings shops started in England and now reaching to Japan, this US flagship store hosts a moderately priced collection of simple, cleanly designed contemporary home furnishings. ♦ 371.2225

In 1826, **Elisha Otis** demonstrated his *safety holster* (or elevator-breaking device) at America's first World's Fair, held at the Crystal Palace in New York City. His invention cleared the way for the construction of tall buildings.

Restaurants/Nightlife: Red   **Hotels:** Blue
Shops/Parks: Green   **Sights/Culture:** Black

Les Tournebroches $$ A good choice, if your eyes can handle the occasional smokiness from meat and fish deliciously grilling on the turning spit. Lovely table appointments, salads and vegetables. ◆ French ◆ Closed Su. Reservations required. 935.6029

Nyborg-Nelson ★★$ Scandinavian specialties, including packaged goods and prepared salads and fish. They'll assemble a lunch or supper for eating in the Citicorp atrium. ◆ Scandinavian ◆ 223.0700

123 Fisher & Levy **Chip Fisher** and **Doug Levy** are caterers who recently opened this decidedly upscale food store, where breakfasts as well as California-style pizzas are served—or delivered. Their lunches are available for delivery throughout Manhattan. Once you sample the pizza, you'll want all your friends to try it as well. No problem—Fisher & Levy will Federal Express pizza anywhere in the US (simply call 800/24.SLICE). ◆ Continental/Pizza ◆ Closed Su. 875 3rd Ave (E 53rd St) Concourse level. 832.3880

124 Toscana ★$$$$ Located in **Philip Johnson**'s *Lipstick Building*, the dramatic modern Italian decor (**Piero Sartaso**; graphics by **Massimo** and **Lella Vignelli**) is worth experiencing—as is the cuisine. Try the *ravioli a la fornariana* (a single ravioli stuffed with raw egg, asparagus and artichoke, served with raw vegetable sauce) and the Tuscan bean soup. Skip the desserts. ◆ Italian ◆ Closed Su. 200 E 54th St (3rd Ave) Reservations recommended. 371.8144

125 900 Third Avenue (1983, **Cesar Pelli & Associates** with **Rafael Vinoly**) The aluminum section at the base of this brick-clad tower

Midtown

and the silhouette of the greenhouse at the top are a reference across 54th St to the neighboring **Citicorp Center**. ◆ E 54th St

126 P.J. Clarke's ★$$ There are few better places to witness the slow pickling of Wall Street's younger and more rambunctious crowd during the cocktail hour. Mysteriously, the scrawny hamburgers are famous, although that's not the meat the young singles come here to get. ◆ American ◆ 915 3rd Ave (E 55th St) 759.1650

127 Michael's Pub ★$$$ Well-known jazz singers and instrumentalists, including **Mel Torme**, perform at **Gil Wiest**'s intimate restaurant nightly, but on Monday night when he's in town, **Woody Allen** puts in an appearance with his clarinet to play a few sets with the **Dixieland New Orleans Funeral and Ragtime Band**. ◆ American ◆ Closed Su. 211 E 55th St (2nd-3rd Aves) Jacket required. Reservations recommended. 758.2272

Restaurants/Nightlife: Red   Hotels: Blue
Shops/Parks: Green   Sights/Culture: Black

128 Tiny Doll House All the teeny, tiny furniture and accessories it takes to make a doll's home, including mini Degas paintings, handmade English chairs, chests and houses. If you think you can make something better yourself, all the supplies you need are here. ◆ Closed Su. 231 E 53rd St. (2nd-3rd Aves) 752.3082

128 Robert L. Brooks The source for an English suit of armor from 1640, a Scottish pistol from 1800 and swords from around the world. ◆ Closed Sa-Su. 235 E 53rd St (2nd-3rd Aves) 486.9829

128 Il Nido ★★$$$$ Excellent Italian food in a stylish yet comfortable atmosphere. Special care is taken with service: dishes are adorned with last-minute garnishes by an expert waiter at your table. ◆ Italian ◆ Closed Su. 251 E 53rd St (2nd-3rd Aves) Jacket, tie and reservations required. 753.8450

129 Quest Book Shop of the New York Theosophical Society The stated purpose of the society is: *To form a nucleus of the Universal Brotherhood of Humanity, without distinction of race, creed, sex, caste, or color. To encourage the study of Comparative Religion, Philosophy, and science. To investigate unexplained laws of Nature and the powers latent in man.* ◆ Closed Su. 240 E 53rd St (2nd-3rd Aves) 758.5521

130 Eamonn Doran $$ An Irish pub gone Continental. There is too much carpeting, comfort and Muzak for **James Joyce** fans, but rugby players and other assorted real and would-be Irish folk carouse here and take advantage of the extensive list of imported beers. The food is pleasant, but the brogues at the bar are even more so. ◆ Irish ◆ 998 2nd Ave (E 52nd St) Reservations required after 7PM. 752.8088

130 Taste of The Apple $ Executive chef **Alaine Sailhac** (formerly of the **21 Club**), said: *I spent 15 years eating hamburgers all over town, and the best is at Taste of The Apple.* **Mimi Sheraton** described them as *fresh and lusty.* ◆ American ◆ 1000 2nd Ave (E 52nd-E 53rd Sts) 751.1445. Also at: 283 Columbus Ave. 873.8892

131 Brazilian Pavillion ★★$$ You can argue as to whether or not it has the best Brazilian kitchen in town, but not about whether or not it is the most pleasant setting for this bold cuisine. It's light, modern and bright, and there's a fully garnished *fejoada* (a black-bean stew with pork) every night and at lunch on Wednesday and Sunday. ◆ Brazilian ◆ 316 E 53rd St (1st-2nd Aves) Reservations recommended. 758.8129

132 Chez Louis ★$$$ This bistro's specialty is roast chicken for 2 served with a delicious garlic-potato pie. For dessert, try the fresh fruit pie. ♦ French ♦ 1016 2nd Ave (E 53rd-E 54th Sts) Reservations recommended. 752.1400

133 Elmer's $$$ An informal pub and steakhouse (formerly the private **El Morocco**) caters to the **Vuitton** and gold-chain crowd. Its unique vulgarity and very good meat and potatoes make it quite popular and amusing. ♦ Steakhouse ♦ 1034 2nd Ave (E 54th St) Reservations recommended. 751.8020

133 Club El Morocco $$$ Yes, this is the place columnist **Earl Wilson** called the world's smartest and slickest nightclub back in the 1940s. It has come back in all its smart, slick glory. The famous zebra-striped banquettes are still here, along with the white palm trees and the stars that twinkle in the ceiling. ♦ Continental ♦ Admission. Closed M-W. 307 E 54th St (2nd Ave) Jacket and tie required. 750.1500

134 Cafe Europa & La Brioche $$ Buttery brioches stuffed with such things as curried beef and tarragon chicken are the specialties here, but the menu also includes chicken Kiev, beef Wellington and other choices. The wine garden in back adds a European atmosphere. ♦ French ♦ Closed Su. 347 E 54th St (1st-2nd Aves) 755.0160

135 54th Street Recreation Center (1906, **Werner & Windolph**) Turn-of-the-century enclosed public bathhouses that now offer an indoor running track, gymnasium facilities and an indoor swimming pool that is open all year. ♦ Closed Su. 348 E 54th St (1st-2nd Aves) 397.3154

136 Billy's $$ The sign outside says it was established in 1870, although a number of years ago it was moved panel-by-panel 4 blocks south of its original location. But it is still owned by the same family. The bill of fare is hamburgers, steaks, chops and other staples like french fries. ♦ American ♦ 948 1st Ave (E 52nd St) 355.8920

136 Le Perigord ★★$$$ UN ambassadors often frequent this cozy French restaurant. The decor is rather dull, but the extravagant flower arrangements add a sense of luxury. Excellent Dover sole. For dessert, the crepes-soufflés are a good bet. ♦ French ♦ Closed Su. 405 E 52nd St (1st Ave) Jacket, tie and reservations required. 755.6244

137 River House (1931, **Bottomley, Wagner & White**) This 26-story, twin-towered, limestone and gray brick cooperative has always been one of the most exclusive apartment buildings in the city—when there was a dock on the river, only the best yachts used it. The lower floors house the **River Club**, which includes squash and tennis courts, a pool and a ballroom. ♦ 435 E 53rd St (East River-1st Ave)

William H. Bonney, better known as **Billy the Kid**, was born in New York City in 1859.

138 Sutton Place and Sutton Place South This elegant end of York Ave was a run-down area until colonized by **Vanderbilts** and **Morgans** moving from 5th Ave in the early 1920s. The townhouses and elegant apartment buildings are by architects such as **Mott Schmidt, Rosario Candela, Delano & Aldrich** and **Cross & Cross**. Visit the park at the end of 55th St and the terrace on 57th St for views of the river and the **Queensboro Bridge**. Also peek in from 58th St, where **Riverview Terrace**, one of New York's last private streets, runs along the river lined with 5 ivy-covered brownstones. The secretary-general of the United Nations lives at Nos. 1-3. ♦ E 54th-E 59th Sts

139 March ★★★$$$ A romantic hideaway in a fin-de-siècle town house, decorated with elegant banquettes and a tapestry on the wall. The eclectic menu features such exciting appetizers as lobster and barley risotto or sweetbreads and pigs feet with morels. Among the best entrees are a spicy rack of lamb with herb crust and gnocchi, or a red snapper baked with red wine. Save room for desserts like light ginger custard with almond praline. Affordable wine list. ♦ Continental ♦ 408 E 58th St (1st Ave-Sutton Pl) Reservations recommended. 838.9393

Diamond Center Forty-seventh St between 5th and 6th Aves is the closest thing to a medieval bazaar that exists in Manhattan. Everyone on the street has the potential to be an independent businessman, living by an honor code unheard of in any other part of the business community. But unless you are a part of it, or are an expert, it may be best to do your jewelry buying elsewhere. The merchants in the hundreds of little

booths in every exchange on the street are more interested in wholesale business, even though their retail trade would make the average jeweler think the *Millennium* had come. The real business is conducted in upstairs offices, where a phone call to Amsterdam or Johannesburg can form a link in a deal worth many millions. In most cases, transactions take place among dealers right here, and a batch of stones may be sold and resold dozens of times without ever leaving 47th St. There is almost never a written record of a transaction until all the elements come together, and dealers routinely give brokers thousands of dollars worth of stones on consignment with nothing more to show for it than faith. Deals are always closed with a handshake and the Yiddish *mazel und brucha*—luck and blessing. With those words, a code is invoked and very rarely broken. The original Diamond Center in New York was on the Bowery in the Canal St area, but when Hitler moved into Holland and Belgium in the 1930s, merchants from Amsterdam and Antwerp began flocking to New York. The influx created a need for more space, and 47th St offered cheap rents and easy access to 5th Ave clients. The influential *Diamond Dealers Club*, the arbiter of the business, moved to the street in 1947, and the die was cast.

140 Sandros $$$ An authentic Roman trattoria serving delicious *Carciofi alla Guidia* (artichoke hearts crisply fried in olive oil) and *Porchetta alla Romana* (roast suckling pig). The interior, designed by architect **Philip George**, is spacious and colorful. ◆ Italian ◆ 420 E 59th St (York-1st Aves) Reservations recommended. 355.5150

141 Ararat Dardanelles ★$$$ This Armenian restaurant specializes in kabobs, at least one of which is made with yogurt, another staple in the Armenian kitchen. The menu includes moussaka and stuffed dolmas. A guitarist introduces you to Armenian songs Friday and Saturday evenings. ◆ Armenian ◆ 1076 1st Ave (E 58th-E 59th Sts) Reservations required. 752.2828

142 Café Nicholson ★$$ An intimate, romantic hideaway whose fanciful decor includes huge marble slabs, ornate handpainted 19th-century tiles and antique furniture, paintings and pottery. Dining here is a theatrical experience. Note: the eccentric owner opens the restaurant only when he feels like it, so be sure to confirm the reservation. On arrival, do not be surprised if the moment you are seated the first order of business is for you to decide whether you want the vanilla or chocolate soufflé. If you decide not to have either, there will be a decided chill in the atmosphere. Either way, the tip will be included in the bill. ◆ French ◆ Closed M, Su. 323 E 58th St (1st-2nd Aves) Reservations required. 355.6769

Midtown

143 Rosa Mexicano ★$$$ There are a few tortilla dishes on the menu, but the grilled meats and avocado-based appetizers are standouts. The frozen margaritas are wonderfully toxic. ◆ Mexican ◆ 1063 1st Ave (E 58th St) 753.7407

144 Mr. Chow of New York $$$ Although the duplex Art Deco room is spectacularly glamorous, mediocre food is served by the snobbiest group of waiters this side of Beverly Hills, where Mr. Chow's other American branch is located. The third Mr. Chow is in London, and all are patronized by an international crowd long on style but short on taste. ◆ Chinese ◆ 324 E 57th St (1st-2nd Aves) Reservations required. 751.9030

145 Iris Brown's Victorian Doll and Miniature Shop Brown specializes in miniature furniture and toys, dollhouses and Christmas ornaments of the Victorian era. ◆ Closed Su. 253 E 57th St (2nd-3rd Aves) 593.2882

145 Les Sans-Culottes $$$ Each meal opens with a basket overflowing with charcuterie. The main courses will make you wish you'd had a bit more restraint—the filet of sole is exceptionally light and the chicken cordon bleu well prepared. ◆ French ◆ 1085 2nd Ave (E 57th-E 58th Sts) Reservations recommended. 838.6660

146 Bruno ★$$$ As with many of the better Midtown Italian restaurants, most of the antipastos, pastas, vegetables and seafood are done to perfection, while prime quality meats can suffer from overthickened, undercooked wine-based sauces. A smart-looking modern room and gracious service make up for the lapses. ◆ Italian ◆ Closed Su. 240 E 58th St (2nd-3rd Aves) Jacket required. Reservations recommended. 688.4191

146 Tre Scalini $$$ Pasta, seafood, and pasta with seafood are the highlights of the house. Avoid the undercooked wine sauces on meats, relish the concerned service, and take note of some of the most heavily upholstered clientele around—they obviously eat well wherever they go. ◆ Italian ◆ 230 E 58th St (2nd-3rd Aves) Jacket, tie and reservations required. 688.6888

147 Dawat ★★$$$ There are entrees here from every region of India, mild to flamingly hot. Vegetarians are especially likely to find something to enjoy. ◆ Indian ◆ 210 E 58th St (2nd-3rd Aves) Reservations required. 355.7555

147 Girafe ★$$$ The oily deliciousness of much of the cooking is at odds with the *recherché* tone of the place and high civility of the staff. The contrast is what makes it all interesting. Try the veal in lemon with white wine sauce. ◆ Italian ◆ Closed Su. 208 E 58th St (2nd-3rd Aves) Jacket required. Reservations recommended. 752.3054

148 Felidia ★★$$$$ *Connoisseur* magazine said that this Italian restaurant serves the best martini in the world. This is just as well, because the food is erratic—sometimes great and at other times ho-hum. Despite its ranking among the top establishments serving the food of Trieste, critics note that a native of that city would not recognize many of the offerings on the menu. Nevertheless, the place is almost always full of people having a good time. ◆ Italian ◆ Closed Su. 243 E 58th St (2nd-3rd Aves) Jacket and reservations required. 758.1479

148 Silk Surplus Those in-the-know shop here and at the annex at No. 223 for generous discounts on **Scalamandre** and other luxurious fabrics used for upholstery, tablecloths, draperies, wallpapers and trimmings. ◆ Closed Su. 235 E 58th St (2nd-3rd Aves) 753.6511. Also at: 1147 Madison Ave. 794.9373

In 1939 the English historian **D.W. Brogan** said that New York is, above all, a harbour and a port. He was correct: nearly $1/3$ of all the foreign cargo that entered the US in 1950 came through New York.

Restaurants/Nightlife: Red **Hotels:** Blue
Shops/Parks: Green **Sights/Culture:** Black

148 La Camelia ★$$$ Northern and Southern Italian, cooked with an elegant hand, in a glamorous setting—plenty of marble, greenery, flowers, Italian charm. Piano bar in the evening. ◆ Italian ◆ Closed Su. 225 E 58th St (2nd-3rd Aves) Jacket and reservations required. 751.5488

149 Morton Books A small shop specializing in books and periodicals on architecture, gardening and interior design. ◆ Closed Su. 989 3rd Ave (E 59th St) 421.9025

150 Royal Athena Galleries Ancient, European, Oriental, pre-Columbian and tribal works of art. Each object is labeled and has a price tag, but the staff enjoys answering questions from browsers as well as from serious collectors. ◆ Closed Su. 153 E 57th St (3rd-Lexington Aves) 355.2034

150 Nesle, Inc. The wealth that was India's during the heyday of the maharajas is here in the form of extraordinary, lavish chandeliers, mirrors and thrones. **Albert Nesle** had combed the great houses of India, London and Paris to put together the greatest collection of chandeliers in the city, and has sold these glittering baubles to the White House, the State Department and restaurateur **Warner LeRoy**. ◆ Closed Sa-Su. 151 E 57th St (3rd-Lexington Aves) 755.0515

150 Hammacher Schlemmer Unintentionally one of the funniest stores in the city, it carries gadgetry to the limits of credibility with items such as a solar-powered ventilated golf cap, an electronic home casino and an interactive talking chess game. On the practical side, it was the first store to introduce the steam iron, electric razor and pressure cooker. The mail-order catalog is fun too. ◆ 147 E 57th St (3rd-Lexington Aves) 421.9000

151 Alexander's A department store that delivers fashionable clothes at moderate prices. Ready-to-wear apparel, accessories and gadgets from all parts of the world at discount prices. ◆ 731 Lexington Ave (E 59th St) 593.0880

152 Argosy Gallery There are few places in the US with a better selection of historical pictures: photographs, posters, playbills, maps, engravings, lithographs, etchings and woodcuts. ◆ Closed Su. 116 E 59th St (Lexington-Park Aves) 753.4455

152 New York Yankees Clubhouse Store Even if you can't make it out to the ballgame you can still pick up your Yankees paraphernalia. ◆ 110 E 59th St (Lexington-Park Aves) 758.7844

153 Ritz Tower (1925, **Emery Roth** and **Carrère & Hastings**) This 42-story tower was built as part of the **Hearst** apartment hotel chain. Its stepped spire is still a distinctive mark in the skyline. ◆ 465 Park Ave (E 57th St)

153 Mitsukoshi ★★★$$$$ Follow the lead of Japanese businessmen and come here for perfect sushi in a comfortable setting. ◆ Japanese ◆ Closed Su. 461 Park Ave (E 57th St) Reservations recommended. 935.6444

154 The Galleria (1975, **David Kenneth Specter, Philip Birnbaum and Associated Architects**) This midblock tower comprises luxury apartments above a health club, retail facilities and a public through-block arcade. At least here—unlike at **Olympic Tower**—the passerby knows there is something inside. Also worthwhile is the individualistic silhouette created by a multi-greenhouse quadriplex (considered Manhattan's most expensive apartment) custom-built for philanthropist **Stewart Mott**. He never lived here, however. Apparently Mott had such passion for fresh milk that he wanted to keep cows on the roof—the building's board turned him down. **RSW**: *It's one amazing place; the terrace views are among the city's most exquisite.* ◆ 117 E 57th St (Lexington-Park Aves)

154 Place des Antiquaires More than 50,000sq ft of galleries and exhibition halls on 2 basement levels of an office building. European paintings, Asian textiles, rare coins, antique scientific instruments, maps, prints and rare books. ◆ Closed Su. 125 E 57th St (Lexington Ave) 758.2900

155 Allerton Hotel for Women $ Homelike atmosphere and good location. Not all the

rooms have baths or air conditioning. Sunroof and restaurant. ◆ 130 E 57th St (Lexington Ave) 753.8841

156 Le Chantilly ★★$$$$ The vast room, bustling with service people who somehow never seem to be near your table when you need them, makes you feel as if you're dining on a deluxe ocean liner. A lot of affluent people seem to like that kind of thing. Technically, the classic cuisine is excellent—most noteworthy is the *confit de canard*. ◆ French ◆ Closed Su. 106 E 57th St (Lexington-Park Aves) Jacket and tie required. Reservations recommended. 751.2931

156 Universal Pictures Building (1947, **Kahn & Jacobs**) This is noteworthy as the first office building on this previously residential section of Park Ave, and as the first to be built to the *wedding cake* outline of the then-current zoning regulations. It is perhaps the best example of the pre glass-curtain wall type. Compare it to its 1972 counterpart across the street at **450 Park**. ◆ 445 Park Ave (E 56th-E 57th Sts)

157 **Lombardy** $$ (1927, **Henry Mandell**) A residential hotel with transient suites and studios, each with a different decor and all with serving pantries and refrigerators. The in-hotel **Laurent** serves classic French cuisine in a handsome setting. ♦ 111 E 56th St (Lexington-Park Aves) 753.8600

158 **Mercedes Benz Showroom** (1955, **Frank Lloyd Wright**; remodeled after the original design 1981) A curious exercise in glass, ramp, plants and fancy cars in a too-tight little space. ♦ 430 Park Ave (E 56th St)

159 **The Drake Swissôtel** $$$$ (1927, **Emery Roth**) In the 1960s, it was purchased by real estate entrepreneur **William Zeckendorf** and became the home of the city's first discothèque, **Shepheards**. In 1980, it was restored by the Swissôtel chain to its original elegance, and is more a setting for chamber music than rock. Amenities include refrigerators in every room, 24hr room service, concierge and parking facilities. ♦ 440 Park Ave (E 56th St) 421.0900, 800/DRAKENY; fax 371.4190

Within the Drake Swissôtel:

Restaurant Lafayette ★★★★$$$$ A splendid French restaurant that has received the highest accolades from the critics and all who dine in this gracious room. The food is extraordinary and a total delight, even for those who have tasted everything and eaten everywhere. Roasted lamb served with a po-

Midtown

tato-and-parmesan cake, and yellow pike simmered in celery juice are just 2 inventive concoctions. A winner that is setting exalted standards for hotel dining. ♦ Continental ♦ Closed Su. Jacket required at lunch; jacket and tie required at dinner. Reservations required. 832.1565

160 **Sherle Wagner International** Serves film stars, industrialists, kings and queens as the purveyor of the most luxurious bathtubs, toilets and sinks. There are tubs of rose quartz, counters of tiger's-eye, bidets of marble and gold-plated basins. ♦ Closed Sa-Su. 60 E 57th St (Park-Madison Aves) 758.3300

161 **Louis Vuitton** Luggage and leather accessories with the familiar **LV** signature. ♦ Closed Su. 51 E 57th St (Park-Madison Aves) 371.6111

161 **Regent of New York** (Scheduled opening, late 1991, **Pei Cobb Freed & Partners**) Construction is almost completed on this 46-story, world-class hotel on the former site of the **Blackstone Hotel** (Pei's first New York City building since the 1986 **Jacob K. Javits**

Center). The Regent (part of the Regent International Hotel chain) is being constructed of limestone and masonry, with dramatic setbacks marked by lanterns. When completed, each of the 400 rooms (designed by **Chhada Siembieda & Assoc.**) will be about 40 percent larger than the average New York hotel room, and have such amenities as a sunken bathtub, a dressing room, a VCR and a CD player, computer outlets and a fax machine. All rooms will have wonderful city views; some will face Central Park. On top of all this, the hotel will offer full secretarial services, a dining room, a bar and a lobby lounge, 24hr concierge, valet and room service, a health club and a multilingual staff. ♦ 57 E 57th St (Park-Madison Aves) No phone at press time

162 **Helene Arpels** A most expensive store for pampered feet that belong to people such as **Jacqueline de Ribes** and **Marie-Helene de Rothschild**. Shoes for both men and women can be custom-decorated with hand embroidery, bead appliqué, stone studding or exotic leathers. ♦ Closed Su. 470 Park Ave (E 57th-E 58th Sts) 755.1623

163 **Ronin Gallery** Japanese art, including woodblock prints, ivory *netsuke* and metalwork from the 17th-20th centuries. Free appraisals of Japanese art. ♦ M-Sa 10AM-6PM. 605 Madison Ave (E 57th-E 58th Sts) 688.0188

163 **Fuller Building** (1929, **Walker & Gillette**) The identification over the entrance of this black-and-white Art Deco tower (now home to many art galleries) is graced with a pair of figures by sculptor **Elie Nadelman**. ♦ 41 E 57th St (Madison Ave)

Within the Fuller Building:

Frank Caro Gallery Chinese, Indian and Southeast Asian sculpture, porcelains, paintings and bronzes and furniture from 3000 BC to the 18th century. ♦ Tu-Sa 10AM-5:30PM. 2nd floor. 753.2166

Kent Fine Art Don't let the bunker-like decor put you off—this is a serious enterprise with a program dedicated to the promotion of artists whose work lies in the tradition of the historical avant-garde, such as **Dennis Adams** and **Chris Burden**. They also mount scholarly and historical exhibitions, showing artists like **Frances Picabia** and **John Heartfield**. ♦ Tu-Sa 10AM-5:30PM. 3rd floor. 980.9696

Marisa del Re Gallery Contemporary American and European painting and some sculpture, including works by **Arman, Karel Appel, Arnaldo Pomodoro**. ♦ Tu-F 10AM-5:30PM; Sa 11AM-5PM. 4th floor. 688.1843

André Emmerich A gallery with staying power that represents distinguished American and European artists, including **Morris Louis, David Hockney, Beverly Pepper** and **Anthony Caro**. ♦ Tu-Sa 10AM-5:30PM. 5th, 6th floors. 752.0124

Susan Sheehan Gallery Nineteenth-century prints and drawings from American artists: **Mary Cassat, John Marin, Cy Twombly, Brice Marden**. ♦ Tu-Sa 10AM-5:30PM. 11th floor. 888.4220

164 Buccellati Silver The most opulent hand-crafted silver, including flatware, in New York. ♦ Closed Su. 46 E 57th St (Madison Ave) 308.2507

164 Guy Laroche The only place in town to buy the ready-to-wear collection of this French designer, which includes everything from silk camisoles to full-length ballgowns. ♦ Closed Su. 36 E 57th St (Madison-Park Aves) 759.2301

164 The Pace Gallery Among the heaviest of the city's heavy hitters, Pace represents a formidable roster of artists and artists' estates, including **Jim Dine, Chuck Close, Louise Nevelson, Mark Rothko** and **Lucas Samaras**. Housed in the same building are the gallery's many offspring—**Pace Prints, Pace Master Prints, Pace Primitive Art** and **Pace/MacGill**, for 20th-century photography. ♦ M-F 9:30AM-5:30PM; Sa 10AM-6PM. 32 E 57th St (Madison-Park Aves) 421.3292. Also at: 142 Greene St. 431.9224

165 IBM Building (1982, **Edward Larabee Barnes**) This 43-story green granite building rises dramatically over a high atrium containing tables and chairs for relaxing and lots of bamboo to take your mind off the traffic outside. That water rushing by outside the 56th St entrance is a horizontal fountain designed by **Michael Helzer**. ♦ 590 Madison Ave (E 56th-E 57th Sts)

165 Galeries Lafayette Once home to the famous New York Bonwit Teller, this 85,000sq ft space will be taken over by France's largest department store sometime in 1991. ♦ 4 E 57th St (5th Ave) No phone at press time

166 Laura Ashley Country styles and fabrics reminiscent of Edwardian England. ♦ Closed Su. 21 E 57th St (Madison-5th Aves) 752.7300. Also at: 4 Fulton St. 809.3555; 398 Columbus Ave. 496.5110; 714 Madison Ave (home furnishings only) 735.5000

166 James II Galleries Edwardian and Victorian jewelry, Spode pottery and ironstone, majolica, brass, silver plate, Art Nouveau and Art Deco silver. ♦ Closed Su. 15 E 57th St (Madison-5th Aves) 355.7040

166 Paul Drey Gallery Old Masters drawings, paintings and sculpture. ♦ By appointment only: M-F 9:30AM-5:30PM. 11 E 57th St (Madison-5th Aves) 4th floor. 753.2551

166 William H. Schab Gallery Master prints and drawings by such artists as **Delacroix, Dürer, Piranesi** and **Rembrandt**. ♦ Tu-Sa 9:30AM-5:30PM. 11 E 57th St (Madison-5th Aves) 5th floor. 758.0327

166 Hermès Saddlery, scarves and silk sweatshirts. A Parisian original. ♦ Closed Su. 11 E 57th St (Madison-5th Aves) Ground floor. 751.3181

166 Escada Future home to the women's clothing and accessory store based in Munich. Construction is underway, which includes adding a 6th floor. ♦ 11 E 57th St (5th Ave)

166 Burberrys Ltd. The Burberry raincoat has incomparable style, but the rest of the clothes for men and women, including hats, coats, jackets, trousers and skirts, do not—unless you like to look the way the British royal family does on a rainy day in Scotland. ♦ Closed Su. 9 E 57th St (5th Ave) 371.5010

166 Chanel A main-floor boutique and 2nd-floor showroom for the increasingly popular Chanel fashions. ♦ Closed Su. 5 E 57th St (5th Ave) 355.5050

167 Tiffany & Co. (1940, **Cross & Cross**) This store has become so famous for quality and style that many of its well-designed wares have become classic gifts: the all-purpose wineglass, the **Wedgwood** drabware, a sterling silver baby rattle in the shape of a dumbbell are all enhanced by the cachet of a gift in a Tiffany box. There is also extravagant jewelry by **Elsa Peretti** and **Paloma Picasso**, plus 3 floors of gems, silver, stationery, crystal, porcelain, clocks and watches at all prices. Salespeople are friendly and helpful. Tiffany windows are worth going out of your way to see—especially at Christmas. ♦ Closed Su. 727 5th Ave (E 56th-E 57th Sts) 755.8000

168 Grace Borgenicht Masters of 20th-century art and promising newcomers. ♦ M-F 10AM-5:30PM; Sa 11AM-5:30PM. 724 5th Ave (W 56th-W 57th Sts) 8th floor. 247.2111

168 The Crown Building (1922, **Warren & Wetmore**) This was once, at 26 stories, the tallest building on 5th Ave above 42nd St.

Originally called the **Heckscher Building**, it was built as a wholesale center for women's fashions. In 1929, the **Museum of Modern Art** opened its first gallery here. The gold leaf on its facade and tower is recent, as is the lighting of this entire intersection. ♦ 730 5th Ave (W 56th-W 57th Sts)

169 Trump Tower (1983, **Der Scutt** of **Swanke, Hayden, Connell & Partners**) Donald Trump, the developer whose name this building bears, currently lives here in a triplex. There are offices on the lower floors and a glitzy 6-story atrium with pricey boutiques and restaurants. ♦ Closed Su. 725 5th Ave (E 56th St) 832.2000

170 Steuben This is less a store than a museum for engraved sculptures featuring Chinese calligraphy, animals or even a forest of spreading pine. All are displayed in backlit glass cases in a gray-walled sanctuary. The State Department buys its gifts for heads of state here, and the hoi polloi find crystal in the shape of dolphins, elephants and hippopotamuses. ♦ Closed Su. 717 5th Ave (E 56th St) 752.1441, 800/223.1234

171 Harry Winston, Inc. The father of this world-famous seller of diamonds owned a little jewelry store on Columbus Ave, but Harry went into business for himself while he was still a teenager and eventually established what may be the most intimidating diamond salon in the city. It is the only store on 5th Ave that processes diamonds from rough stones to finished jewelry. ◆ Closed Sa-Su. 718 5th Ave (W 56th St) 245.2000

171 Fellissimo (1901, **Warren & Wetmore**) Located within a turn-of-the-century townhouse, this store is the first American outlet of one of the most successful retailers in Japan. It is scheduled to open in the fall of 1991, and will carry men's and women's clothing, accessories and gifts. ◆ 10 W 56th St (5th-6th Aves) No phone at press time

172 Darbar Indian Restaurant ★★★$$$ This is easily one of the best Indian restaurants in town, from every point of view. The decor is authentic and fascinatingly beautiful. If you want a quiet little table in the corner, there are several downstairs, separated by screens that give complete privacy. The staff is friendly and helpful, the kitchen thoroughly professional. To start, try the delightful *pakoras* (fried spinach fritters) and move on to the *josh vindaloo*, a lamb stew cooked with potatoes in a hot curry sauce. ◆ Indian ◆ 44

Midtown

W 56th St (5th-6th Aves) Reservations recommended. 432.7227

173 Kiiroi Hana ★★★$$$ Excellent Japanese restaurant with a simple but carefully selected menu of classic Japanese dishes. Sit at the sushi bar for fresh and beautifully arranged fish prepared by pleasant chefs. Good sake and excellent service. ◆ Japanese ◆ 23 W 56th St (5th-6th Aves) 582.7499

174 OMO Norma Kamali Kamali is the designer who put many American women into high-fashion sweatshirt dresses, blouses, slit skirts and cocoon wraps. The bottom floor of the store carries the mass market sweats, inexpensive cottons and knits. The upstairs floor has one-of-a-kind evening gowns, often with cleavage that plunges to the waist, loose or skin-tight dresses made of soft suede or lace and her famous, provocatively cut swimsuits. Now that her shop on Spring St has closed, home furnishings are sold here as well. ◆ Closed Su. 11 W 56th St (5th-6th Aves) 957.9797

174 Doubleday The largest of the 6 Manhattan Doubledays keeps a high profile of new releases in fiction and nonfiction, backlist books and trade and mass market paperbacks on 4 well-arranged floors. Especially good for cookbooks, art and applied art. ◆ 724 5th Ave (W 56th St) 397.0550. Also at: 777 3rd Ave. 888.5590

174 Virginia Zabriskie A quality gallery for American and European painting, sculpture and photography of the 20th century. Zabriskie represents the estates of modern masters like **Archipenko**, **Zorach** and **Kunioshi**. ◆ M-Sa 10AM-5:30PM. 724 5th Ave (W 56th St) 12th floor. 307.7430

175 Henri Bendel Its windows are among the most imaginative in New York, and shopping here is an experience no one should miss. The store is filled with unique merchandise, including tabletop wares by **Frank McIntosh**, and it is still fun to kick up your heels and announce you just got those stunning shoes at Bendels. When you do, be sure to say *Ben´-dls*, as the natives do. ◆ 10 W 57th St (5th-6th Aves) 247.1100

175 Blum Helman Gallery An unusually large space featuring contemporary American painting and sculpture. ◆ Tu-Sa 10AM-6PM. 20 W 57th St (5th-6th Aves) 2nd, 8th floors. 245.2888

175 Galerie Lelong Contemporary American and European paintings, drawings, graphics and sculpture, as well as books by important artists. ◆ Tu-Sa 10AM-5:30PM. 20 W 57th St (5th-6th Aves) 5th floor. 315.0470

175 Susan Bennis/Warren Edwards This collection of shoes for men and women is made of such exotic skins as baby crocodile, ostrich and emu. Styles include sexy hot-weather sandals, tasseled loafers, evening pumps of lace and peau de soie for women, patent leather for men, and boots in unusual materials and colors. ◆ Closed Su. 22 W 57th St (5th-6th Aves) 755.4197

175 Arras Gallery Modern painting and sculpture by European and American artists. ◆ Tu-Sa 10AM-6PM. 24 W 57th St (5th-6th Aves) Suite 301. 265.2222

175 Grand Central Art Galleries Begun by artists **John Singer Sargent, Walter Clark** and **Edmond Greacen** in 1922, the exhibitions include Realist portraits, still lifes, sculptures and the work of more than 100 artists. ◆ M-F 10AM-6PM; Sa 10AM-5PM. 24 W 57th St (5th-6th Aves) 2nd floor. 867.3344

175 Marian Goodman Gallery A longtime supporter of Arte Povera and other influential European movements, Goodman's stark but generous space is devoted to a host of weighty imported talents, including the German painter **Anselm Kiefer** and British sculptor **Tony Cragg**. Don't miss the gallery's new space, where **Multiples**, Goodman's print-publishing arm, displays its wares. ◆ M-Sa 10AM-6PM. 24 W 57th St (5th-6th Aves) 4th floor. 977.7160

Restaurants/Nightlife: Red
Shops/Parks: Green
Hotels: Blue
Sights/Culture: Black

175 Fischbach Gallery The works of contemporary American Realists. ♦ Tu-Sa 10AM-5:30PM. 24 W 57th St (5th-6th Aves) 8th floor. 757.0111

175 Galerie St. Etienne An import from Vienna, featuring Austrian and German Expressionists as well as European and American folk art. ♦ Tu-Sa 11AM-5PM. 24 W 57th St (5th-6th Aves) 8th floor. 245.6734

175 J.N. Bartfield Galleries & Books Nineteenth-century American and European art, including works by **Remington, Russell** and other masters of the American West. Elegantly bound antiquarian books by famous authors, such as **Shakespeare** and **Dickens**. ♦ M-F 10AM-5PM; Sa 10AM-2:30PM. 30 W 57th St (5th-6th Aves) 3rd floor. 245.8890

176 Marlborough Gallery One of New York's old-line establishments representing some of the most important names in European and American art, such as **Larry Rivers, Fernando Botero, Red Grooms** and **Magdalena Abakanowicz**. ♦ M-Sa 10AM-5:30PM. 40 W 57th St (5th-6th Aves) 2nd floor. 541.4900

176 Kennedy Galleries You'll find works by American artists from the 18th century on— **John Singleton Copley, Edward Hopper, Georgia O'Keeffe** and **John Marin**—at this gallery, founded in 1874. Wonderful catalogs. ♦ Tu-Sa 9:30AM-5:30PM. 40 W 57th St (5th-6th Aves) 5th floor. 541.9600

176 Frumkin/Adams Gallery A blue-ribbon stable of contemporary artists including **Jack Beal, Robert Arneson** and **Luis Cruz Azaceta**. ♦ Tu-Sa 10AM-6PM. 50 W 57th St (5th-6th Aves) 2nd floor. 757.6655

177 Hacker Art Books Features in- and out-of-print books and reprints, plus some excellent bargains on the literature of the visual arts. ♦ M-Sa 9AM-6PM. 45 W 57th St (5th-6th Aves) 688.7600

177 Hammer Galleries European and American paintings, including Impressionist works from the 19th century. ♦ M-F 9:30AM-5:30PM; Sa 10AM-5PM. 33 W 57th St (5th-6th Aves) 644.4400

177 Brewster Gallery Graphics by such important European artists as **Picasso, Miró** and **Chagall**. ♦ M-Sa 10:30AM-5:30PM. 41 W 57th St (5th-6th Aves) 2nd floor. 980.1975

177 Rizzoli Bookstore (ca 1905; restored 1985, **Hardy Holzman Pfeifer Associates**) The ultimate bookstore, it looks like the oak-paneled library of an opulent Italian villa, with classical music playing (records are for sale) and a hushed, unhurried atmosphere. Rizzoli is known for foreign-language, travel, art, architecture and design books. Outstanding foreign and domestic general interest and design periodical department, and a small gallery upstairs. All is well looked after by its president and publisher, **Gianfranco Monacelli**. ♦ 31 W 57th St (5th-6th Aves) 759.2424

177 Chickering Hall (1924, **Cross & Cross**) A recent restoration has emphasized the giant medals on the elevator tower above this 13-story Gothic building. They are reproductions of the *Legion d'Honneur* won by Chickering's pianos at the **Paris Exposition of 1867**. ♦ 29 W 57th St (5th-6th Aves)

178 9 West 57th Street (1974, **Skidmore, Owings & Merrill**) The best feature of this black glass swoop—kissing cousin to the **W.R. Grace Building** on 42nd St—is its address: the great big red **9** is by graphic designer **Ivan Chermayeff**. ♦ 5th-6th Aves

179 David McKee Gallery Once located in the old **Barbizon Hotel**, this small but very smart gallery boasts an impressive list of youngish artists like sculptor **Martin Puryear** and painters **Sean Scully** and **Jake Berthot**, as well as the estate of the influential **Philip Guston**. ♦ 745 5th Ave (E 57th-E 58th Sts) Tu-Sa 10AM-5:30PM. 688.5951

179 Bergdorf Goodman Men This store, according to Bergdorf's chairman, **Ira Neimark**, is *for the sort of men who dine at the best restaurants, stay at the best hotels, and join the best clubs*. What do these men wear? Shirts from **Turnbull & Asser** and **Charvet**, suits from **Brioni, Luciana Barbera** and **St. Andrews**; sportswear from **Willis & Geiger**. Additional boutiques within the store include the **London Tack Shop, W & H Gidden, Hermès, Lacoste** and **Kentshire Antiques**. ♦ Closed Su. 745 5th Ave (E 58th St) 753.7300

180 Bergdorf Goodman This is the most luxurious of the city's legendary stores. Although there is some moderately priced merchandise,

the idea that living well is the best revenge permeates the store, partly because of the architecture (high ceilings, delicate moldings, arched windows) and partly because of the wares. It was the first store to promote the designers of Milan with a vengeance. When it showed a spring collection by **Gianfranco Ferre** in which all the clothes were done in shades of white, cream and cocoa, the food served during the fashion show/cocktail party was in the same colors. Choose from impeccable clothes by **Donna Karan** and **Sonia Rykiel**. All the merchandise bears the stamp of luxury, whether it's the iridescent jewelry of **Ted Muehling**, the aromatic scents from London's **Penhaligon**, delicate candies from **Manon Chocolates** or glove-leather bags by **Paloma Picasso. Van Cleef & Arpels** has its inexpensive boutique in this store, meaning that you can find a bauble for a little less than a small fortune. The salespeople are helpful, low-key and candid. There is also a beauty salon (**Frederic Fekkai**) and a cafe. ♦ Closed Su. 754 5th Ave (W 57th-W 58th Sts) 753.7300

180 Van Cleef & Arpels When the late **Shah of Iran** needed a tiara made for his **Empress Farah**, he came here. The boutique department, where jewelry ranges from moderate to expensive, is actually in **Bergdorf's** main store next door, while gemstones that cost more are sold here. Jewelry can be custom-designed. Estate jewelry is also bought and sold. The guard is formidable, but the salespeople at least deign to acknowledge customers who make it past him. ♦ Closed Su. 744 5th Ave (W 57th St) 644.9500

181 Wyndham Hotel $$ A remarkably comfortable hotel that is a favorite with stars appearing on Broadway, many of whom, like **Peter Falk, Hume Cronyn** and the late **Ingrid Bergman**, could easily afford to stay at the Plaza. Some stars, planning for a long Broadway run, have been known to arrive with their own furniture. Their stay is made even homier by New York's best doorman, **Michael Ruiz**, who's been welcoming guests since the hotel's opening in 1961. ♦ 42 W 58th St (5th-6th Aves) 753.3500

182 The Manhattan Ocean Club ★★★$$$$ Excellent seafood, from *tonno con vitello* appetizer to blackened redfish (a specialty here), reflects an often overlooked fact—that New York is still a port, with access to the treasures of the sea. The owner's personal collection of more than a dozen **Picasso** ceramics is on display. ♦ Seafood ♦ 57 W 58th St (5th-

Midtown

6th Aves) Jacket, tie and reservations required. 371.7777

183 St. Moritz on the Park $$ (1931, **Emery Roth & Sons**) A strictly business hotel, no fancy stuff. The rooms are small but comfortable. Fax machine available. Room service 7AM-12:30AM, newsstand, gift shop. ♦ 50 Central Park So (6th Ave) 755.5800, 800/221.4774; fax 751.2952

Within St. Moritz on the Park:

Café de la Paix $$$ Possibly the best sidewalk cafe in New York, which is to be expected, considering the location. Have an anisette or orange cappuccino and soak up the atmosphere. ♦ Continental ♦ Reservations recommended. 755.5800

Rumpelmayer's $$ A perennial kiddie-pleaser: a counter and tables for Viennese pastries and ice cream concoctions, served in the company of a collection of stuffed animals. Anyone under 50 who had a middle- or upper-class childhood in Manhattan will tell you this is where you go for hot chocolate. A childhood must. ♦ Continental ♦ 755.5800

184 Mickey Mantle's ★★$ A great place to bring the kids. They can watch the day's big game or memorable moments in the world of sports on huge video screens, study the restaurant's collection of uniforms and memorabilia and, if they're lucky, catch sight of the man himself, who is often around to say *hi* and sign postcards. The food—gigantic burgers, ribs, hot-fudge sundaes—will please a not-too-finicky sports fan. ♦ American ♦ 42 Central Park So (5th-6th Aves) 688.7777

184 Park Lane Hotel $$$ (1971, **Emery Roth & Sons**) Though a relative newcomer to the block, the arches at the top of this 46-story tower add interest to the block. The always controversial **Harry** and **Leona Helmsley**, who own several hotels and a lot of real estate in Manhattan, picked this one as their own home address. Marble and chandeliers abound; the multilingual staff is alert and eager to please. ♦ 36 Central Park So (5th-6th Aves) 371.4000, 800/221.4982; fax 319.9065

185 The Plaza Hotel $$$$ (1907, **Henry J. Hardenbergh**; addition 1921, **Warren & Wetmore**) This stylish Edwardian/French pile is considered one of Hardenbergh's masterpieces (he also did the **Dakota** apartments). Its dignity on this unique site—one at which 2 sides of the building are equally exposed—has survived many years as the center of high social activity. The Plaza is a legend in its own time, a landmark that has hosted **Teddy Roosevelt**, the **Beatles**, and **F. Scott Fitzgerald** and his wife, **Zelda** (who, it is rumored, danced nude in the fountain out front). **Solomon R. Guggenheim** lived for years in the **State Suite** surrounded by fabulous paintings; it was **Frank Lloyd Wright**'s New York headquarters. It even had a book written about it. But would *Eloise*, the heroine, recognize the crowds that swirl around the lobby? Rooms vary wildly. Many of the lovely high-ceilinged ones are still in top condition, but some face air shafts. Request an outside room—or better still, a park view. The 24hr room service remains, and so do the flags outside representing countries of important foreign guests. Mega-developer **Donald Trump** bought the Plaza in 1988; his now ex-wife, **Ivana**, took charge of a major renovation and secured several of New York's top hotel personnel. The **Oak Bar and Restaurant** is still in its original (woody, elegant and comfortable) condition; the **Oyster Bar** still opens sparkling fresh clams and oysters to order; the venerable, paneled **Edwardian Room** is still a fashionable spot for dining and dancing. The fabled lobby **Palm Court** is fine and festive if you stick to the simple offerings. The lobby also includes an art gallery, a **Neuchatel** chocolate shop and **Maison Mendesolle** for fine clothing. ♦ W 59th St at 5th Ave. 759.3000, 800/228.3000; fax 759.3167

185 Grand Army Plaza One of the city's few formal pedestrian spaces, the plaza acts as both a forecourt to the **Plaza Hotel** and as an entrance terrace to **Central Park**. Although the wall of the square has been weakened by the **GM Building**, the center has held strong, solidly anchored by the circular *Pulitzer Memorial Fountain*. The memorial was built with funds provided in **Joseph Pulitzer**'s will, and was designed by **Carrère & Hastings**. The sculpture on top is by **Karl Bitter**, and the equestrian statue of **General William Tecumseh Sherman** (by **Augustus Saint-Gaudens**) was displayed at the World Exhibition in Paris in 1900. It was erected here in 1903. Tradition survives here in the horse-drawn carriages. They were the limousines of another era, and in the '30s, Hollywood loved to send romancing couples off in them for jaunts in Central Park. You can still take your romantic ride through the park in a carriage, many with top-hatted drivers, some glass-enclosed for cold weather. ♦ 5th Ave (W 58th-W 60th Sts)

186 F.A.O. Schwarz Because this is the best-stocked children's store in the US, some parents never bring their children here—the sight of so many toys can turn children into monsters of greed. The inexhaustible stock includes **Madame Alexander** dolls, **Steiff** stuffed animals, **LGB** electric trains, outdoor swings, magic tricks, video games and hundreds of other amusements. At Christmastime, you may have to wait on line just to go inside. ♦ 767 5th Ave (E 58th-E 59th Sts) 644.9400

186 General Motors Building (1968, **Edward Durell Stone, Emery Roth & Sons and Associated Architects**) This 50-story marble and glass monolith has never been acceptable as a replacement for the **Savoy Plaza Hotel**. Set back from the street wall behind its own sunken plaza, it makes little sense. ♦ 58th-59th Sts (Madison-5th Aves)

187 Baccarat The world-famous crystal, plus **Limoges** china and fine glassware and silver. ♦ Closed Su. 625 Madison Ave (E 58th-E 59th Sts) 826.4100

Barbara Cohen and Judith Stonehill
Co-owners, New York Bound Bookshop

Places for Book Lovers

Afternoon tea at **Anglers & Writers Cafe**, on Hudson St at St. Luke's Place. (Marianne Moore lived nearby and worked in the public library around the corner.)

The **New York Public Library**, with its extraordinary collection of over 6 million books spanning 88 miles of shelves. Wander upstairs...the Berg Collection's exhibits...the Rare Map Room, with the earliest maps of New York as well as the latest, among many rarities...the Great Hall (more than 2 city blocks long).

Gansevoort Street, where Herman Melville once worked as a customs officer and where you will find authentic French bistro food 24hr a day at **Florent**'s.

Walk down 44th St west of 5th Ave to the **General Society Library** to see the latest books at the Small Press Center, or to borrow a book from the library. Continue down 44th past the turn-of-the-century Harvard and New York Yacht clubs and the Bar Association to the fabled **Algonquin** for tea or a cocktail and a bit of reading.

A drink at the **White Horse Tavern** on Hudson St after work, to think of Dylan Thomas, Delmore Schwartz, Brendan Behan and other writers who drank hour after hour there.

The **Morgan Library**, with its priceless medieval and Renaissance manuscripts, rare editions and unique exhibitions on the book arts. Edith Wharton might have been at home in its old New York splendor.

Visit **Edgar Allan Poe**'s home, a clapboard cottage he rented in 1846, and where he wrote *Annabel Lee*. The house is located on the Grand Concourse in the Bronx, once a cherry orchard.

Midtown

A proper afternoon tea and a library of thousands of books on the British Commonwealth can be found at the **English Speaking Union** in its cozy townhouse. It is one of New York's best-kept secrets.

With breezes from the river and broad vistas, a walk along the grand **Battery** promenade evokes Melville and Whitman, especially after a summer evening reading held there by Symphony Space. (In the winter, we go uptown to Symphony Space on 95th St to hear actors read from literary works.)

Quiet places to read a book: the sculpture garden at the **Noguchi Museum**; the **Temple of Dundur Hall** at the Metropolitan Museum; the **Staten Island Ferry** during the quiet hours of the day.

There is always a surge of excitement coming to **Rockefeller Center**. One enters a vibrant world anchored by gray towers, international flags waving in the wind, fanciful gardens, golden sculptures, friezes, frescoes, murals, figure skaters whirling on clear ice and the world's most famous Christmas tree. For an equally grand ending to the day, have a drink 65 stories above in the **Rainbow Room** to watch the city slowly settle down for the night.

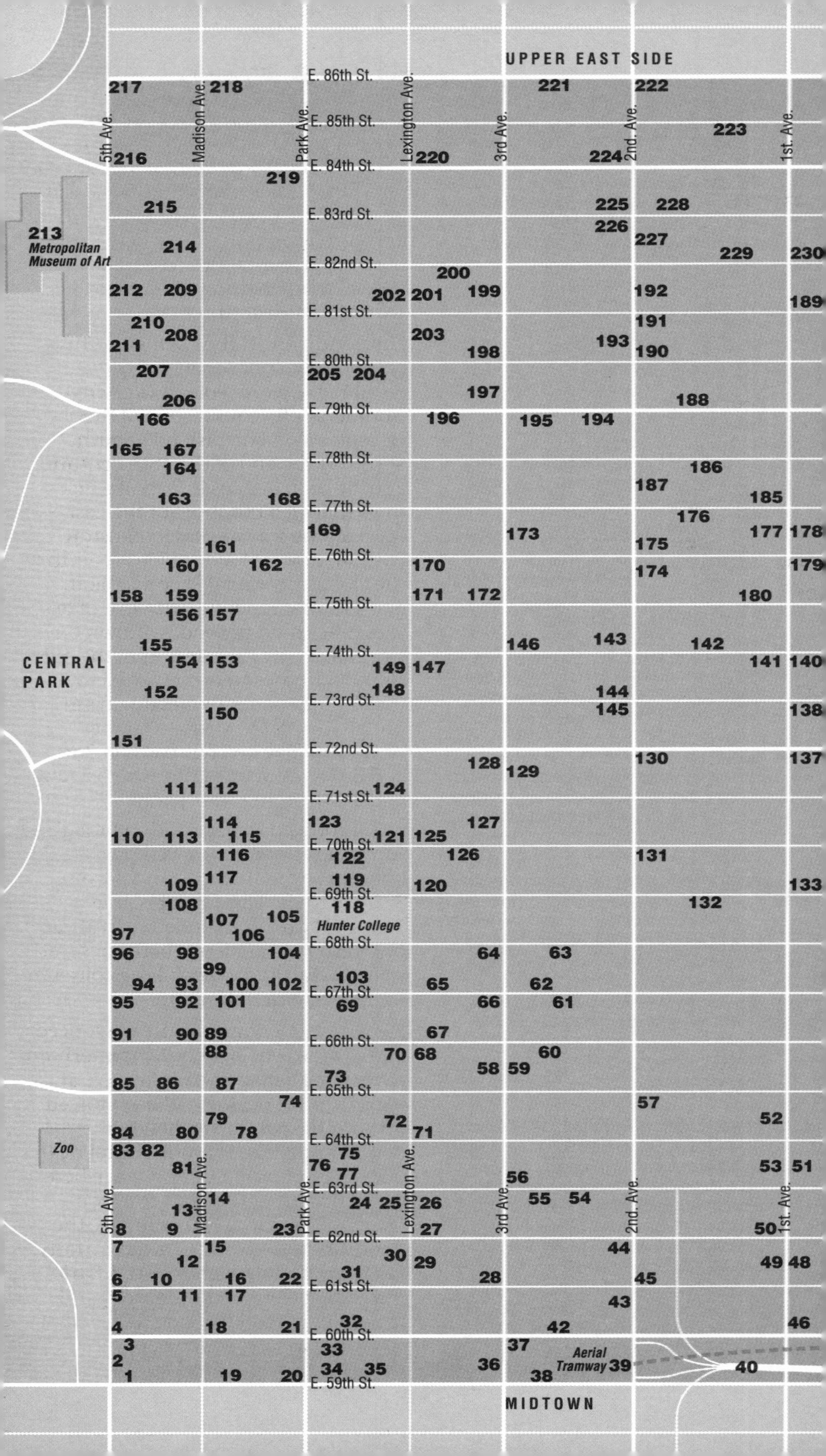

CENTRAL PARK

213
Metropolitan Museum of Art

Zoo

5th Ave.
Madison Ave.
Park Ave.
Lexington Ave.
3rd Ave.
2nd Ave.
1st Ave.

E. 86th St.
E. 85th St.
E. 84th St.
E. 83rd St.
E. 82nd St.
E. 81st St.
E. 80th St.
E. 79th St.
E. 78th St.
E. 77th St.
E. 76th St.
E. 75th St.
E. 74th St.
E. 73rd St.
E. 72nd St.
E. 71st St.
E. 70th St.
E. 69th St.
E. 68th St.
E. 67th St.
E. 66th St.
E. 65th St.
E. 64th St.
E. 63rd St.
E. 62nd St.
E. 61st St.
E. 60th St.
E. 59th St.

Hunter College

Aerial Tramway

217 218 221 222
216 223
219 220 224
215 225 228
214 226 227 229 230
212 209 200 202 201 199 192 189
210 208 203 198 191 193 190
211 207 205 204 197 188
206 196 195 194
166
165 167 186
164 187 185
163 168 176
169 173 177 178
161 170 175 179
160 162 171 172 174 180
158 159 156 157
155 146 143 142
154 153 149 147 141 140
152 148 144
150 145 138
151 128 129 130 137
111 112 124
110 113 114 115 123 121 125 127
116 122 126 131
109 117 119 120 133
108 118 132
97 107 105
96 98 99 106 64 63
94 93 100 102 103 65 62
95 92 101 69 66 61
91 90 89 67
88 70 68 58 59 60
85 86 87
74 57
84 80 79 73 52
83 82 78 72 71
81 75 53 51
13 14 76 77 56 55 54
8 9 23 24 25 26 50
7 15 30 27 44 49 48
12 31 29 28 45 43
6 10 16 22 32 42 46
5 11 17 33 37 39 40
4 18 21 34 35 36 38
3 2 19 20
1

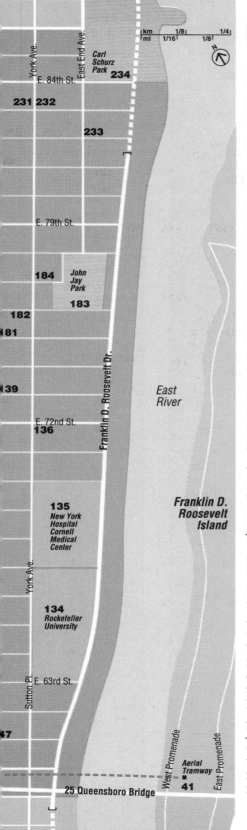

East Side

In the 1920s, *The New York Times* described the **East Side** as *a string of pearls: each pearl is a double block of millionaires, and Madison Avenue is the string.* Like everything else about New York, time has altered it. But there are few places in the city where the memory is as intact as in the blocks bounded by **59th** and **86th Sts**, **5th Ave** and the **East River**.

Until the close of the Civil War, this part of New York was where the fashionable gathered to escape city summers—the counterpart of the Hamptons on Long Island's South Shore. At the end of the 18th century, a string of mansions in parklike settings followed the shore of the East River all the way to Harlem. Boston Post Rd, now 3rd Ave, made access to the city below Canal St convenient, and summer residents with lots of leisure time could travel downtown on steamboats. By the late 1860s, the old summer houses were converted to year-round use for pioneering commuters, and a few years later, the coming of elevated railroads on 2nd and 3rd Aves opened the area to a new breed of working-class people.

The improved transportation brought summer fun-seekers as well. The area bounded by 66th and 75th Sts from 3rd Ave to the East River became **Jones's Wood**. It included such attractions as a beer garden, a bathhouse, an athletic club and a block-long coliseum for indoor entertainment.

High society became firmly ensconced in the area when **Caroline Schermerhorn Astor** built a mansion on 5th Ave at 65th St in 1896. (She had been forced uptown from 34th St when her nephew built the **Waldorf Hotel** next door to her house.) Her presence here was only part of the draw for people like the **Fiskes**, the **Havemeyers**, the **Armours** and jeweler **Charles Tiffany**. Just as important were **Central Park** (providing a buffer on the west) and the open railroad running down what is now **Park Ave**, which kept the riffraff in their place to the east.

Society had its heyday on the East Side between 1895 and the outbreak of WWI. The state of American architecture was unusually superb at the time, and the superrich had the financial resources to hire the best. Technology was very much in vogue at the time, and it was a rare 4-story house that didn't have at least one elevator. Nearly every house had an elaborate intercom system, and all had several dumbwaiters, usually electrically operated, to make life simpler for the servants.

But the showplace was the bathroom—no New York house had indoor plumbing until the **Croton Aqueduct** began operating in 1842. Until the turn of the century, the style had been to bathe in dark, wood-paneled rooms designed to conceal their use. As the East Side was developed after 1895, the style was changed. Elaborate ceramic fixtures, imported tiles, gold-plated plumbing and showers that sprayed water in several directions at once were promoted as absolute necessities.

Up until 1900 it was considered déclassé to live in the same house with other families (except servants, of course). But when the barrier fell, the *best of the best* apartment buildings appeared on the East Side, especially along Park Ave, which after 1915 became what one contemporary called *a mass production of millionaires*. The huge apartment houses created a kind of leveling effect among the wealthy, as well as a guarantee that this would remain *their* kind of neighborhood. They didn't even budge during the Great Depression of the 1930s, when armies of the unemployed took up residence across the way in Central Park.

The 1960s brought construction of uninspiring white and yellow brick apartment houses into the area, and many of the elegant town houses had been broken up into multiple-unit dwellings years before. Despite the turmoil, the neighborhood continues to be what it has been for nearly a century—New York City's elite enclave.

Mondrian

1 Mondrian ★★★$$$$ The soft lighting, warm wood paneling and soft leather seats make for an altogether delightful dining experience in the space that once housed the **Playboy Club**. Recommended are ragout of clams and pasta, corn chowder, braised red snapper in lemon vinaigrette, venison with black mushrooms and ganache cake. Named after Dutch artist Piet Mondrian, who worked in the neighborhood in the 1940s. ◆ French ◆ Closed Su. 7 E 59th St (Madison-5th Aves) Reservations recommended. 935.3434

2 Sherry-Netherland Hotel $$$$ (1927, **Schultze & Weaver**) Another of the grandes dames rimming Central Park, the Sherry was once the centerpiece of an elegant trio, sitting between the **Pierre** and the **Savoy-Plaza** (whose site now hosts the **General Motors** tower). Its high peaked roof sports gargoyles and chimneys like a Loire Valley confection. On the walls lining the entrance are panels rescued from a **Vanderbilt** mansion by

Richard Morris Hunt. The Sherry attracts bicoastal show biz people. Service is continental luxury class, the rooms are large, many with park views. ◆ Deluxe ◆ 781 5th Ave (E 59th St) 355.2800; fax 319.4306

3 The Harmonie Club (1906, **McKim, Mead & White**) In 1852, wealthy German Jews, excluded from most other men's clubs, formed this club they called *Harmonie Gesellschaft*. It was described at the time as *the most homelike of all clubs* because its members made it a practice to bring along their wives. ◆ 4 E 60th St (Madison-5th Aves)

3 Copacabana (1902, **R.C. Gildersleeve**) In the 1940s and '50s, you could be thrilled by the **Copa Girls** and entertained by personalities like **Sammy Davis Jr.** and **Jerry Vale**. Nightclub shows like those are a thing of the past, but the Copa is still a bright spot on Tuesday, when Latin music is the lure, and Friday and Saturday nights, when the Latin beat is augmented by an upstairs disco. The rest of the time it is used for private parties. ◆ Cover. Closed Su. 10 E 60th St (Madison Ave) 755.6010

In 1945, **Lena Horne** was the first black artist to perform in the **Copacabana**'s exclusive downstairs room—it wasn't until her second run there that blacks were admitted to the audience.

Metropolitan Club

4 Metropolitan Club (1894, McKim, Mead & White; addition 1912, **Ogden Codman**) An example of **Stanford White** in an enthusiastic mood. Note particularly the extravagant, colonnaded carriage entrance behind the gates of the chateau. I suggest you ignore all rules of etiquette and see if you can get a glimpse through a main-floor window: the Metropolitan was organized by **J.P. Morgan** for his friends who were not accepted at other clubs.
♦ 1 E 60th St (5th Ave)

5 The Pierre $$$$ (1930, **Schultze & Weaver**) Another of the grand old European-style hotels with many permanent guests and a loyal following of the rich and the powerful. A stretched mansard roof clothed in weathered bronze at the top of the tower gives the Pierre a distinctive silhouette; it and the **Sherry-Netherland** next door make a romantic couple. A wee bit intimidating perhaps, all those limos lined up in front and the miles of mural-lined lobby, but the Pierre offers the kind of luxury one could get used to: enormous rooms (good Central Park views from the upper floors) and vast bathrooms; 24hr room service; an attentive, multilingual staff; twice-daily maid service; complimentary shoe shine; even an unpacking service. And you don't have to go out to find a notary public, beauty salon or barber shop, or the **House of Bulgari** jewelers. Afternoon tea is served daily in the **Rotunda**; the **Café Pierre** serves lunch, dinner and supper; pianist nightly. ♦ Deluxe ♦ 2 E 61st St (5th Ave) 838.8000, 800/268.6282; fax 940.8109

6 800 Fifth Avenue (1978, **Ulrich Frazen & Associates**) Until her death in 1977, **Mrs. Marcellus Hartley Dodge**, a niece of **John D. Rockefeller Jr.** lived here with her famous collection of stray dogs in a 5-story brick mansion that was a mate to the nearby **Knickerbocker Club**. When she died, developers moved in, promising a tasteful building that would be a credit to the neighborhood. This 33-story building is how the promise was kept. The zoning law forced them to build a 3-story wall along 5th Ave. Unfortunately, it isn't high enough to hide the building behind it. ♦ E 61st St

7 The Knickerbocker Club (1914, **Delano & Aldrich**) In the 1860s, some members of the Union Club proposed that its membership be restricted to men descended from the Colonial families of New York, known as the **Knickerbockers**. When their suggestion was rejected, they started their own club. But one of its most influential founders was **August Belmont**, a German immigrant. ♦ 2 E 62nd St (5th Ave)

8 810 Fifth Avenue (1926, **J.E.R. Carpenter**) Famous former residents of this 13-story limestone apartment building include **William Randolph Hearst** and **Mrs. Hamilton Fish**, one of the last of the grandes dames of New York society. Before he moved to the White House in 1969, **Richard M. Nixon** lived here. His neighbor on the top floor was **Nelson Rockefeller**, who had New York's only fully equipped bomb shelter. ♦ E 62nd St

9 Arcadia ★★★★$$$$ Chef/owner **Anne Rosenzweig** is as impressive as ever. Signature dishes on her seasonal menu include

East Side

corncakes with crème fraîche and caviar, chimney-smoked lobster with tarragon butter and an irresistible chocolate bread pudding (swimming in a brandy custard sauce). The dining room's focal point—aside from the food—is the wraparound mural of the countryside as the seasons change. ♦ American ♦ Closed Su. 21 E 62nd St (Madison-5th Aves) Jacket, tie and reservations required. 223.2900

10 Maxim's ★★$$$$ The decor's a faithful homage to the *Belle Epoque* original; the food doesn't quite measure up. But for romance, Maxim's is hard to beat. Downstairs is **L'Omnibus de Maxim's**, more casual but just as elegant. ♦ Continental ♦ Maxim's: Closed M, Su. 21 E 61st St (Madison Ave) Jacket and tie required M-F; black tie required Sa. Reservations required. 751.5111. L'Omnibus de Maxim's: Reservations recommended. 980.6988

11 New York Women's Exchange Established in 1878 to help women support themselves without sacrificing their pride. It is an excellent source of handmade children's articles, lingerie and gifts. ♦ Closed Su. 660 Madison Ave (E 61st St) 753.2330

11 The Gazebo There are hundreds and hundreds of old and new quilts in this airy shop, which also features baskets, charming white wicker indoor and outdoor furniture, appliquéd and patchwork pillows and unusually wide (11ft) rag rugs. New quilts are produced to the Gazebo's specifications with American fabrics in Haiti. Both quilts and rugs can be custom-made. ♦ Closed Su afternoon. 660 Madison Ave (E 61st St) 832.7077

12 Fogal of Switzerland An impressive selection of fine hosiery. ♦ Closed Su. 680 Madison Ave (E 61st-E 62nd Sts) 759.9782. Also at: 510 Madison Ave. 355.3254

13 Addison on Madison Subdued yet interesting men's shirts of fine French cotton are offered in appealing gentle stripes and checks, with a few bolder stripes. Sleeves come short, regular and extra long. Collars come button-down, regular and white. Accessories include silk ties and crystal cuff links. ♦ Closed Su. 698 Madison Ave (E 62nd St) 308.2660. Also at: 725 5th Ave. 752.2300

13 Ca'Nova ★$$$ Mediterranean-influenced Italian food is prepared by an Egyptian-born, French-trained chef in a dining room reminiscent of a gentlemen's club. Friendly and relaxed. ♦ Italian ♦ 696 Madison Ave (E 62nd St) 838.3725

14 The Lowell Hotel $$$$ (1926, **Henry S. Churchill**) A small, charming hotel, where white-glove treatment is the norm. Many of the 61 rooms and suites have serving pantries and wood-burning fireplaces, and some can

East Side

accommodate formal board meetings. Room service meals arrive on a silver tray, or, if you prefer company, the 2nd-floor dining room is both cheerful and serene. One of New York City's very best. *An RSW recommendation.* ♦ 28 E 63rd St (Park-Madison Aves) 838.1400; fax 319.4230

Within the Lowell Hotel:

The Post House ★★$$$$ A classic New York steakhouse in a classic New York setting, possibly the most handsome in the city. And the atmosphere is ultracivilized. The *best* news is that after a bit of a slump, the kitchen is back in fine form. ♦ American ♦ Jacket, tie and reservations required. 935.2888

15 Julie: Artisans' Gallery Clothes conceived as art to wear: **Julie Hill**'s jackets of hand-painted silk, **Linda Mendelson**'s scarves and coats knitted in geometrical patterns, **Janet Lipkin**'s loom-knitted and hand-dyed garments and many other flights of fancy. Some seem more for display than to be worn. Not for the timid. ♦ Closed Su. 687 Madison Ave (E 62nd St) 688.2345

15 Georg Jensen/Royal Coppenhagen Silver, including flatware and exquisite jewelry: sleek, gleaming bangles and cuffs, Art Nouveau pins shaped like leaves and trimmed with precious stones. Also a good source for crystal glassware, and the entire collection of **Royal Copenhagen** china. ♦ Closed Su. 683 Madison Ave (E 61st St) 759.6457

15 Sherry Lehman One of the top wine merchants in America—certainly the most famous in New York. Courteous, expert advice; a handsome store for browsing. ♦ Closed Su. 679 Madison Ave (E 61st St) 838.7500

16 Mme. Romaine de Lyon ★★$$$ With more than 500 different kinds to choose from, it's safe to say that this is New York's ultimate place for an omelet. The setting is charming and comfortable, the staff is friendly and the kitchen has turned omelets into an art form. ♦ French ♦ 29 E 61st St (Park-Madison Aves) Reservations recommended. 759.5200

17 Aureole ★★★$$$$ A contrast to the quaint twig baskets scattered throughout the restaurant are the plaster reliefs of animals on the walls and ceiling, which, to say the least, are humorous. The roasted monkfish with a crisp potato tart is one of my favorite dishes. Treat yourself to Aureole's own chocolates and cookies. ♦ Continental ♦ Closed Su. 34 E 61st St (Park-Madison Aves) Reservations recommended. 319.1660

18 Bogner You expect slick, well-made active sportswear from this Austrian manufacturer of ski clothing. The surprise is the line of leisurewear for men and women—jackets, coats, sweaters, pants, skirts, shoes, bags—all in the same sensible, hardy mode. ♦ Closed Su. 655 Madison Ave (E 60th St) 752.2282

18 Boyd Chemists Legions of well-known women, including **Jackie Onassis** and **Cher**, have come here to choose from a vast international collection of makeup brushes, lip glosses, feather powder puffs, rouges, combs, hairbrushes and toothbrushes. While you're at it, pick up Boyd's mail-order catalog. ♦ Closed Su. 655 Madison Ave (E 60th St) 838.6558

18 Caviarteria A deceptively small store, considering the huge variety of caviar, pâtés, chocolates and other delicacies. The staff is very helpful—if you don't understand the mystique of caviar, don't be shy about asking. Also ask about mail-order service. Caviarteria is a direct importer and wholesaler, which keeps prices down. ♦ Closed Su. 29 E 60th St (Madison-Park Aves) 759.7410

19 Kaplan's $$ A large, clean, modern delicatessen, not big on atmosphere but with fair prices and better-than-average salads, sandwiches, soups and service. ♦ Deli ♦ 59 E 59th St (Park-Madison Aves) 755.5959

20 Christie's This is the New York headquarters of the famous London auction house specializing in Old Masters, Impressionists, 19th- and 20th-century European and American art. Tickets, available without charge a week or 2 before an auction, are often required. Previews of items to be auctioned are held 5 days prior to the auction itself, and catalogs are available. A series of free lectures on fine and decorative arts, called *Auction Talks*, is presented during the auction seasons. Call for schedule. ♦ M-Sa 10AM-5PM; Su 1-5PM. 502 Park Ave (E 59th St) 546.1000

20 Regine's ★$$$$ High-class disco and dinner setting for the nouveaux riches and the landed aristocracy. *Eleganza* and *ostentation* are the bywords here. (A charming smaller room, **Reginette**, is located at 69 E 59th St.) ♦ Continental ♦ Closed Su. 502 Park Ave (E 59th St) Jacket, tie and reservations required. 826.0990

21 The Grolier Club (1917, **Bertram G. Goodhue**) Named for the 16th-century bibliophile **Jean Grolier**, this Georgian structure houses a collection of fine bookbindings and a specialized library open to scholars and researchers. Regularly changing exhibitions display books, prints and rare manuscripts. ♦ Free. M-Sa 10AM-5PM. 47 E 60th St (Park-Madison Aves) 838.6690

21 Christ Church (1932, **Ralph Adams Cram**) An interesting limestone-and-brick Methodist church. One of the best ecclesiastical structures of the 1930s, designed to make you think it's hundreds of years old. ♦ 520 Park Ave (E 60th St)

22 The Regency $$$$ This elegant hotel is the scene of some of New York's most important power breakfasts, during which the city's movers and shakers get together to start their business day. Guests can take advantage of 24hr room service for their breakfast, but it isn't as exciting. They also have the advantage of a well-equipped fitness center and a large, multilingual staff. The hotel is furnished with French antiques, which gives it a feeling of luxury uncommon in newer buildings. ♦ 540 Park Ave (E 61st St) 759.4100, 800/223.0888; fax 826.5674

23 The Colony Club (1924, **Delano & Aldrich**) The building, which houses an exclusive club for society women, presents to the avenue a solid, Neo-Georgian, Federal red-brick face, settled on a limestone base. ♦ 564 Park Ave (E 62nd St)

24 Society of Illustrators (1875) A museum of American illustration featuring changing exhibitions of advertising art, book illustration, editorial art and other contemporary work. ♦ Free. M-F 10AM-5PM. 128 E 63rd St (Lexington-Park Aves) 838.2560

25 Saint-Remy Produits de Provence Pale, muted floral and paisley fabrics, mainly by the yard (but which can be ordered made up into napkins, table lamp shades and placemats), are sold here, along with fragrant spices, hand-painted pottery and baths oils. ♦ 818 Lexington Ave (E 62nd-E 63rd Sts) 759.8240

Guy Billout. Courtesy Milton Glaser

BARBIZON

26 The Barbizon Hotel $$$ (1927, **Murgatroyd & Ogden**) Its richly detailed brickwork and fine interiors have made this former residence for women—actresses **Candice Bergen, Gene Tierney** and **Grace Kelly** all stayed here at various times—one of the East Side's better-known buildings. Until 1981, when it was converted to a hotel open to both sexes, with interiors by **Milton Glaser**, its upper floors were off-limits to men. But the rooftop arcades framed skyline views that were made famous by photographer **Samuel Gottscho**. The view also inspired painter **Georgia O'Keeffe**.

East Side

Among its amenities are 12 tower suites, a multilingual staff, a cafe (**Café Barbizon**) and an oak-paneled meeting room with a pipe organ, stained-glass windows and a fireplace. The Morgan's Hotel Groups (**Morgan's, The Royalton, The Paramount**) purchased this fine old hotel in the fall of 1988. Their plans for its transformation are not yet public. ♦ 140 E 63rd St (Lexington Ave) 715.6900, 800/223.1020; fax 888.4276

27 Tender Buttons The home of millions and millions of buttons, new and antique, made of brass, stoneware, taqua nut, Lucite, wood, abalone, seashell, agate, plastic, silver—you name it. They come in every shape, from *Betty Boop* to ponies, butterflies, mice, cats and dogs. They are as practical as buttons for shirts or as esoteric as gold-colored filigree fasteners for antique Chinese robes. The supply is exhaustive, but endearingly and logically displayed. ♦ Closed Su. 143 E 62nd St (3rd-Lexington Aves) 758.7004

28 Trump Plaza (1987, **Philip Birnbaum & Associates**) You can easily pass this building by. It is another attempt to immortalize the name of developer **Donald Trump**. But don't pass up the waterfall or the open space to the left of the entrance that make it so pleasant. ◆ 167 E 61st St (3rd Ave)

28 Alo Alo ★★$$$ A large Italian restaurant with a circular bar, a noisy crowd of Upper East Siders and Europeans and an enchanting view of a neighboring vest-pocket park. The menu is large and offers some excellent appetizers, such as a thin, tender carpaccio with fresh Parmesan, well-seasoned salads and generous antipasto. The pasta is ordinary, but the simple meat dishes— breaded veal chop served with artichoke hearts, and calf's liver served with leeks and polenta—are perfectly cooked. For dessert, there are excellent fruit tarts, a rich chocolate cake and a sinful *St. Honoré.* ◆ Italian ◆ 1030 3rd Ave (E 61st St) 838.4343

29 New York Doll Hospital Even if your doll isn't sick, don't miss this experience. They buy and sell antique dolls and toys here, but what makes it so much fun is the collection of spare parts. ◆ Closed Su. 787 Lexington Ave (E 61st-E 62nd Sts) 2nd floor. 838.7527

29 Kamdin Designs In 6 to 12 months a custom-designed rug can be made. Bring in a wallpaper or fabric swatch, a picture or just an idea. Indian dhurries, Portugese needlepoint and Chinese petits points are for sale also. ◆ Closed Su. 791 Lexington Ave (E 61st St) 371.8833

30 Weyhe Art Books Strong selection of books on 20th-century art, and a good source for out-of-print art and architecture books. ◆ Closed Su. 794 Lexington Ave (E 61st St) 838.5466

31 Il Valletto ★$$$$ If **Nanni** (the owner) is around when you visit, let him order for you. If

East Side

he's not, here are some good choices: bruschetta, tender baked clams, eggplant Siciliana with light ricotta and spinach, linguini with delicate, tender clams in a light white sauce, a tender rollatine of beef. For dessert, try the baked pear with zabaglione or the fresh fruit salad. ◆ Italian ◆ Closed Su. 133 E 61st St (Park-Lexington Aves) 838.3939

32 Le Veau d'Or ★$$$ A great old bistro that longtime East Siders still flock to for well-prepared, basic French fare, unpretentious and efficient service and moderate prices. ◆ French ◆ Closed Su. 129 E 60th St (Lexington-Park Aves) 838.8133

33 Malvasia ★★★$$$$ Chic Italian restaurant with a simple, light and sunny decor. The menu, which tries to be trattoria but is much more elaborate, offers appetizers like squab salad, mozzarella *di bufala* with roasted peppers and prosciutto with figs. The pasta is light as air and served with a rich, pungent tomato sauce or with fresh sardines. Among the entrees are duck breast (cooked pink and served with dates and green olives), tender veal chops and grilled tuna with arugula. For dessert, the lemony cheesecake filled with tender morsels of preserved fruits is unbeatable. ◆ Italian ◆ Closed Su. 108 E 60th St (Lexington-Park Aves) 223.4790

34 The Lighthouse This is the headquarters of the **New York Association for The Blind**. The on-site gift shop, staffed by volunteers, sells items made by blind persons; all proceeds benefit the blind. ◆ Closed Sa-Su. 111 E 59th St (Lexington-Park Aves) 355.2200

35 Fiorucci Two flashing floors pulsing to rock music, filled with trendy Italian clothing for men and women. Even if New Wave isn't your style, it's worth a visit just to check out the amusing accessories and cards and the latest trends as worn by the salespeople and customers. ◆ 127 E 59th St (Lexington-Park Aves) 751.5638

bloomingdale's

36 Bloomingdale's No store promotes its products better or with more verve, imagination and sizzle. The store's buyers plumbed the heartland of China and came back with *Bloomie's*-inspired dishes, rugs and ashtrays the Chinese artisans would never have conceived of on their own. They went to India, Israel and the Philippines and brought back mirrored elephants, swimsuits and salty fish sauces. Bloomingdale's is show business. It caters to those who like to buy their clothes, food and sofas in an atmosphere that is a cross between a discothèque and a Middle Eastern suk. Music blares, ladies threaten to squirt perfume at you and television screens show endless tapes of designer fashion shows. Every object seems to catch your eye. For children, there are layettes, strollers, **Oshkosh** overalls and hand-knit sweaters. For women, there are slinky knits by **Missoni**, genteel but seductive knits by **Sonia Rykiel**, the American chic of **Ralph Lauren** and the luxe of **Yves Saint Laurent**. For men, there are clothes by **Cacharel, Ralph Lauren** and **Calvin Klein**. There are sexy outfits for discomaniacs, ski outfits for the *sportif* and a very thorough lingerie department with at least 40 different styles of bikinis. The **Main Course** is a cornucopia of kitchenware and gadgets. **Descamps** has a boutique in the linen department. There is a shop devoted solely to **Petrossian** caviar. Special shopping services are extensive; the store once delivered an entire household of brand-new furniture to the home of a Russian diplomat's wife when the couple left New York. ◆ 1000 3rd Ave (E 59th St) 705.2000

Within Bloomingdale's:

Le Train Bleu ★$$$ Well-designed to re-create the dining car on the famous **Orient Express**, the view from the windows of the train is a spectacular one of the **Queensboro Bridge**. The food is of indeterminate origin and dubious merit, but the restaurant itself is comfortable and a welcome resting ground for Bloomingdale's shoppers emotionally and financially drained from the effort of handing over credit cards at too fast a pace. ◆ Continental ◆ Closed Su. 6th floor. Reservations recommended. 705.2100

37 Yellowfingers ★★$$ A perfect place to recover after a splurge at **Bloomingdale's**. The open kitchen turns out generous salads, sandwiches (all served on *focaccia*—a thick bread baked with roasted peppers) and a hearty entree called *fa'vecchai*, a pizzalike bread baked with toppings—grilled mushrooms, braised onions, olives and eggplant. ◆ American/Italian ◆ 200 E 60th St (3rd Ave) 751.8615

Upstairs from Yellowfingers:

Contrapunto ★★$$ *Arigosta* (fresh pasta squares filled with lobster, scallops, fresh fennel and leeks in a lemon-cream sauce) and delicate angel hair pasta with littleneck clams are just 2 of my favorite choices. ◆ American/Italian ◆ 751.8616

37 Arizona 206 ★★$$$ Authentically en-sconced in lots of adobe, bare wood and desert flowers, this cavelike place serves up imaginative Southwest fare, such as squab in a cactus-pear sauce. To the left is the **Café**, a more casual restaurant with an inventive tasting-menu—depending on the size of your party, up to 12 different dishes served family-style. ◆ Southwestern ◆ 206 E 60th St (2nd-3rd Aves) 838.0440

37 Jane's Bar & Grill ★$$$ Restaurateurs **Jane Epstein** and **Richard Lavin** (**Lavin's, Sofi**) have given us a neighborhood restaurant that offers good food in a relaxed, welcoming atmosphere. **Bob Patino**'s charming 1950s interior is a perfect foil for the homey and inventive American menu—grilled fish with seasonal vegetables, and veal chop surrounded by perfectly crisped straw potatoes are just 2 choices. ◆ American ◆ Closed Su. 208 E 60th St (2nd-3rd Aves) Reservations recommended. 935.3353

38 Forbidden Planet This is a satellite of the store on 12th St and Broadway, specializing in science fiction and comic books and all the merchandise that goes with them. In addition, both stores also stock an impressive collection of detective fiction, from current titles in paperback to out-of-print and rare collector's items. ◆ 227 E 59th St (2nd-3rd Aves) 751.4386. Also at: 821 Broadway. 473.1576

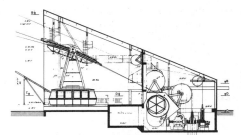

39 Roosevelt Island Tramway Station (1976, **Prentice & Chan, Ohlhausen**) The Swiss-made tram, more at home on a snow-covered mountain, takes you across the East River's West Channel at 16 mph, and provides wonderful views of the East Side and the Queensboro Bridge. Until October 1989, when the subway finally opened (after 25 years of planning and construction), the tram was the only access to or from Roosevelt Island, except for a short automobile bridge on the Queens side. ◆ Nominal fee. M-Th, Su 6AM-2AM; F-Sa 6AM-3:30AM. 2nd Ave (E 59th-E 60th Sts) 753.6626

40 Queensboro Bridge (1909, **Palmer & Hornbostel; Gustav Lindenthal**, engineer) The distinctive triple span of this bridge is the image of a machine, an intricate web of steel that speaks of power, if not finesse. Under the Manhattan ramp are great vaulted spaces now used for storage and parking; there are continual plans afoot to restore them to their original use as a farmers' market. ◆ E 59th St at 2nd Ave, Manhattan to Queens Plaza, Queens

41 Roosevelt Island Separated from Manhattan by 300 yards and more than a few decibels, but politically, it is very much a part of it. The community, built in the 1970s, is acces-

sible from Manhattan by tramway, subway and a small bridge from 36th Ave, Queens. The master plan for a series of U-shaped housing projects opening toward the river was designed by **Philip Johnson** and **John Burgee**. Only the southern section was built, and it's taller and denser than they recommended. Until the 1970s, when rental agents needed a name change, it was known as *Welfare Island* because of its many hospitals and sanitariums. Before 1921, it was **Blackwell's Island**, named for the family that farmed it for 2 centuries. A prison was built in 1828, and over the next several years, a workhouse, an almshouse and an insane asylum were added. A century later those institutions were swept away and hospitals substituted. The present city has reminders of each of the island's former lives. The ruin at the southern end was the **Smallpox Hospital**, designed in 1856 by the architect of **St. Patrick's Cathedral**, **James Renwick Jr**. Just above it are the remains of the 1859 **City Hospital**, and under the Queensboro Bridge is **Goldwater Memorial Hospital**, designed with short wings to give its chronically ill patients sunshine and river views. Not far from the tramway station is the **Blackwell Farmhouse** (1796–1804). Nearby are **Eastwood Apartments** (1976, **Sert, Jackson & Associates**), built for low- and middle-income tenants. On the Manhattan side are **Rivercross Apartments** (1975, **Johansen & Bhavnani**), for people who can afford to pay more. There are 2 more luxury complexes, **Westview** (1976, Sert, Jackson & Associates) and **Island House** (1975, Johansen & Bhavnani), which has a glassed-in swimming pool overlooking Manhattan. Cars are not allowed on the island except in the garage complex known as **Motorgate** (1974, **Kallman & McKinnell**). There are no sanitation trucks, either. Garbage is removed through vacuum tubes to the **AVAC** (Automated Vacuum Collection)—where it is sorted, sanitized and packed for removal. Near this monument to a *Brave New World* is the **Chapel of the Good Shepherd** (1889, **Frederick Clarke Withers**; restoration 1976, **Giorgio Cavaglieri**), now used as a recreation center. Landmarks at the northern end include the **Octagon Tower** (1839, **Alexander Jackson Davis**), all that's left of the **New York City Lunatic Asylum**, and a 50ft stone lighthouse designed in 1872 by James Renwick Jr. According to an inscription on the lighthouse, it was built by **John McCarthy**, an asylum inmate who busied himself by building a fort on the spot to defend himself against the British, but was persuaded to replace it with a more attractive lighthouse instead. The hospital at the uptown end of the island is the **Bird S. Coler Hospital for the Chronically Ill** (1952). A complex of 1104 apartments, **Northtown II**,

East Side

was completed by **Starrett Housing** in 1989. Currently, plans are underway for 15-acre **Octagon Park**, just south of the Coler Hospital, and **Southtown**, a complex of 2000 mixed-income apartments. Transportation on Roosevelt Island is provided by bus, but I think the best way to enjoy it is by walking on its riverside promenades (1975, **Zion & Breen**). ♦ East River (Manhattan to Queens)

42 Serendipity ★$$ It's an ice-cream parlor and informal restaurant named after *The Three Princes of Serendip*, **Horace Walpole**'s retelling of a Persian myth, and it will, as they say, delight children from 8 to 80. The overdone Victorianesque decorations, the decadent desserts—including the famed frozen hot chocolate—and the fine, simple food—from shepherd's pie to chicken barbecue casserole—have made it a prime attraction since its opening in 1954. The novelty boutique keeps you busy while you wait for a table. ♦ American ♦ 225 E 60th St (2nd-3rd Aves) 838.3531

42 Jean Pierre Inc. French and Italian suits for men in classic fabrics—small checks, pinstripes and subtly woven patterns—and a slightly relaxed European cut. There are also coats and separates for women. **Paul Anka** buys his clothes here; **Faye Dunaway** and **Yoko Ono** favor Jean Pierre's cashmere sweaters. ♦ Closed Su. 237 E 60th St (2nd-3rd Aves) 838.8680

42 Betsey Johnson Johnson has been ahead of her time for more than 2 decades. Her fashion statement is fun, sexy and wonderfully excessive. ♦ 251 E 60th St (2nd Ave) 319.7699. Also at: 248 Columbus Ave. 362.3364; 130 Thompson St. 420.0169

43 Joia As antique clothes from the 1930s and '40s become more scarce, this shop is carrying fewer Oriental robes and more **Clarice Cliff** china. Although the stock is mostly clothes for men and women, the treasure here is the jewelry. ♦ Closed Su. 1151 2nd Ave (E 60th St) 754.9017

43 A. Peter Pushbottom For devotees of classic preppie sweaters, this shop has them in spades: crewnecks, V-necks and turtlenecks, cable-stitched and plain in literally dozens of colors, from peach to plum, black to white. Most are cotton, but there are some Shetlands and worsteds. ♦ Closed Su. 1157 2nd Ave (E 60th-E 61st Sts) 759.1336

44 Pushbottom for Kids Outfits for children by this famous purveyor of quality sweaters. The little fashion plate in your family will turn everyone's head in one of Pushbottom's crocheted bow ties. ♦ Closed Su. 252 E 62nd St (2nd-3rd Aves) 888.3336

45 Darrow's Fun Antiques A place for grownups to become children: toy soldiers, cigar store Indians, antique windup monkeys, dogs, bears, movie star memorabilia and even the occasional funhouse mirror. ♦ Closed Su. 309 E 61st St (1st-2nd Aves) 838.0730

46 Magique Home of Chippendale's You think clubs with male go-go dancers are only in the suburbs? Not so. At Chippendale's, chiseled hunks titillate Manhattan's women at 8PM. There's also a large, circular disco with high-tech black, glittery walls and floor. Disco and New Wave music. ♦ Cover. Shows: W-Sa 8PM. 1110 1st Ave (E 61st St) 935.6060

47 Abigail Adams Smith Museum (1799) The daughter of **John Quincy Adams**, for whom this house/museum is named, never even slept here. But she and her husband, **Colonel William Smith**, did own the land it is built on. They bought 23 choice acres on the bank of the East River in 1786 with the idea of building a country estate called **Mt. Vernon** (Col. Smith served under **George Washington**). Because of financial reverses, they sold the estate in 1799. The stone stable that is now the museum was remodeled as an inn in the 1820s, then used as a private dwelling until the neighborhood fell on hard times. The **Colonial Dames of America** rescued it in

1924, furnished it in the style of the Federal period, planted an 18th-century garden and opened the house as a museum. Colonial Dames members, well-versed in the contents of the house (but not necessarily about antiques or the history of the period), show visitors the 9 rooms filled with delicate **Aubusson** rugs, graceful **Sheraton** chests, a framed letter from George Washington, a mannequin wearing a simple summer dress that Abagail had made for herself (she had indeed fallen on hard times) and unexpected touches such as a cardroom set up with a game of loo. ♦ Admission. M-F noon-4PM; Su 1-5PM. 421 E 61st St (York-1st Aves) 838.6878

48 Dangerfield's A club showcasing new and established comic talent, owned and operated by the well-known comedian **Rodney Dangerfield**. A typical Las Vegas/Atlantic City atmosphere, catering to suburbanites, known as the *bridge-and-tunnel* crowd. ♦ Cover, minimum. Shows: M-Th, Su 8:45PM; F 9, 11:30PM; Sa 8, 10:30PM, 12:30AM. 1118 1st Ave (E 61st-E 62nd Sts) 593.1650

49 Adam's Apple $$$ This cramped restaurant and deafening disco features dining on 2 levels, and 3 dance floors, 2 of which are suspended in midair. The place is filled with plants that create an ersatz Garden of Eden. The crowd is mostly snakes looking for an Eve for the evening. A holdover from the 1970s singles scene that dominated this neighborhood. ♦ Continental ♦ 1117 1st Ave (E 61st St) 371.8650

50 Il Vagabondo ★$$ A noisy, good-humored neighborhood trattoria with robust Italian cooking, mostly in the Southern style, and the city's only indoor boccie court—perfect for working off rich, homemade gnocchi. (Other specials include tuna steak, a fragrant veal stew and filet of sole.) Boccie, a type of bowling, has been a favorite Italian sport since the days of the Roman Empire. If you ask to be seated in the room with the court, you can watch the neighborhood players throw the boule while you dine. Unique, worth a visit. ♦ Italian ♦ 351 E 62nd St (1st-2nd Aves) 832.9221

50 Carol Rollo/Riding High Bold, luxurious—and expensive—clothing. For men and women, including designs from **Jean Paul Gaultier, Chlöe** and **Sitbon**. ♦ Closed Su. 1147 1st Ave (E 62nd St) 832.7927

51 T.G.I. Friday's $$ A casual, comfortable place to enjoy a hamburger, a salad and a couple of beers. If it looks familiar, it's because Friday's has been cloned in dozens of American cities. For what it's worth, this is the original. The full name, in case you didn't already know, is **Thank God It's Friday's**. ♦ American ♦ 1152 1st Ave (E 63rd St) 832.8512

52 Auntie Yuan ★★$$$ Just what you'd expect from a beautiful East Side dining room: fragrant, well-prepared cooking, and a discriminating audience to appreciate it. This auntie happens to be Chinese, coming up with such triumphs as feather-light duckskin pancakes or rich black mussels in oyster sauce, served by savvy waiters who know their stuff. ♦ Chinese ♦ 1191 1st Ave (E 64th St) Reservations required. 744.4040

53 Manhattan Café ★$$$ This is the place to get late-night traditional steakhouse fare in a comfortable, posh setting. Decent veal and pasta dishes, just for the record. ♦ American ♦ 1161 1st Ave (E 64th St) Reservations recommended. 888.6556

54 Bravo Gianni ★★$$$ An elegant place—gray suede walls, velvet banquettes and lots of smoked mirrors—but you may be treated a bit cavalierly unless you're one of the regulars. ♦ Italian ♦ 230 E 63rd St (2nd-3rd Aves) Reservations required. 752.7272

55 John Clancy's East ★★$$$$ John Clancy's downtown was so popular, they decided to open a counterpart on the East Side. The decor of this location is more sophisticated, but the food remains the same—mesquite-grilling is *the* thing at both restaurants. Although the fancier dishes may sound tempting, I tend to stick to those more simply prepared. The desserts are not to be missed! ♦ Seafood ♦ 206 E 63rd St (2nd-3rd Aves) Reservations required. 752.6666. Also at: 181 W 10th St. 242.7350

East Side

56 Henry Lehr This is the place if you want to look like the *au courant* leggy young girls of Paris, since it stocks only the most trendy casual separates from France: jumpsuits, jeans in their most hip variations (which could be baggy, skintight, ending at the knee, the calf or the ankle), sweatshirts and jackets. ♦ 1079 3rd Ave (E 63rd-E 64th Sts) 753.2720

57 Silver Star $$ A glorified diner that attracts a curious mix: everyone from local moviegoers to celebs in the mood for a hearty bite. The spaghetti with meatballs is a triumph of engineering; the meatballs are the size of tennis balls. Excellent baklava. ♦ American/Greek ♦ 24hrs. 1236 2nd Ave (E 65th St) 249.4250

Restaurants/Nightlife: Red   **Hotels:** Blue
Shops/Parks: Green   **Sights/Culture:** Black

A man born in New York 40 years ago finds nothing, absolutely nothing, of the New York he knew. If he chances to stumble upon a few old houses not yet leveled, he is fortunate. But the landmarks, the objects that marked the city to him, as a city, are gone.
Harper's Monthly, 1856

58 The Sign of The Dove ★★$$$$ The garden setting is a knockout, the furnishings are real antiques, and the dining experience is memorable. In its early years, it was regarded as a tourist attraction and nothing more. The atmosphere hasn't changed, but the kitchen now turns out quite good food. Try the shellfish stew with saffron. Cafe menu available after 5PM. Very romantic. ♦ American ♦ Closed M. 1110 3rd Ave (E 65th St) Jacket required. Reservations recommended. 861.8080

58 Ecce Panis (translation: *Behold, the bread*) True connoisseurs of good fresh bread—crispy outside, chewy inside and deeply flavored—come here for their daily fix. A sampling of the day's bounty—sourdough, rye, whole-wheat currant—sits in a basket on the counter. Good pastries too. ♦ 1120 3rd Ave (E 65th-E 66th Sts) 535.2099

59 David K ★★$$$$ The most expensive Chinese restaurant in the country, which probably means the world. The setting, overlooking the garden of **Manhattan House**, is elegant. ♦ Chinese ♦ 1115 3rd Ave (E 65th-E 66th Sts) Jacket and tie requested. Reservations recommended. 371.9090

60 Manhattan House (1950, **Skidmore, Owings & Merrill** and **Mayer & Whittlesey**) A larger-than-average full-block apartment house, and a better one than most that came after it. The bulk is broken up by the 5-bay

East Side

massing, and the skin was given a lively texture with varied window arrangements and a sprouting of balconies (contrast with **Imperial House** at 150 E 69th St). From 1896 to 1949, this was the site of the 3rd Ave carbarns, where an elaborate Second Empire-style shed by **Henry Hardenbergh** used to house horse-drawn and then electric streetcars. ♦ 200 E 66th St (2nd-3rd Aves)

61 Solow Houses (1983, **Attia & Perkins**) Developer **Sheldon Solow**, who built the innovative office building at 9 W 57th St, created these 11 houses, the first new townhouse row in the city since the turn of the century. The granite facade, which binds them together between flat and slightly bowed fronts, barely articulates each individual house. The front is fortresslike, hiding luxurious interiors. ♦ 222-242 E 67th St (2nd-3rd Aves)

To summon help, a subway motorman will blast his horn in a pattern of *long-short, long-short.*

62 Le Comptoir $$ A new bistro owned jointly by the owners of **La Goulue** and **Le Relais**. The menu, as close as can be to true French bistro fare, includes frisée with *lardons*, onion soup, duck confit with lentils, roasted rabbit, steak au poivre, *pommes frites* and pâtés. Desserts are simple: fruit tarts and ice creams. ♦ French ♦ 227 E 67th St (2nd-3rd Aves) 794.4950

63 Neikrug Photographica Contemporary and vintage photos, daguerreotypes, stereos and hardware. ♦ 224 E 68th St (2nd-3rd Aves) 288.7741

64 Fortune Garden ★$$ Although the kitchen has hosted Chinese master chefs from Shanghai and Canton, the cooking is more dependable than sparkling. ♦ Chinese ♦ 1160 3rd Ave (E 68th St) Reservations recommended. 744.1212

65 Park East Synagogue (1890, **Schneider & Herter**) A Moorish extravaganza with a more sedate Victorian interior. ♦ 163 E 67th St (3rd-Lexington Aves)

66 Janovic Plaza One of several outlets of the most thorough paint store in the city. It offers not only 8000 colors and finishes but also fabrics from design houses like **Country Gear, Jack Prince** and **Schumacher**, pure cotton towels and made-to-order custom curtains, bedspreads, comforter covers, draperies, Roman shades, canopies and shower curtains. ♦ 1150 3rd Ave (E 67th St) 772.1400

67 131-135 East 66th Street (1905, **Charles Adams Platt**) Two apartment blocks most noted for dignified grandeur and Mannerist porticoes. ♦ 3rd-Lexington Aves

68 Church of St. Vincent Ferrer (1923, **Bertram G. Goodhue**) When New York's Roman Catholic elite make wedding plans, **St. Patrick's Cathedral** is their first choice. If the cathedral is booked, this is where they turn. ♦ Lexington Ave (E 65th-E 66th Sts)

69 Seventh Regiment Armory (1880, **Charles W. Clinton**) A crenelated, almost cartoon fort in a very proper neighborhood. The interiors were furnished and detailed by **Louis Comfort Tiffany**. The hall is immense: 187ft by 290ft. It is the site of the **Winter Antiques Fair** and other mass events. From 1986-89 this was the setting for *Tamara*, **John Krizanc**'s participatory hit play (in which audience members follow any one of several actors around the armory). ♦ E 66th-E 67th Sts (Lexington-Park Aves) 744.8180

70 Cosmopolitan Club (1932, **Thomas Harlan Ellett**) The cast-iron balconies give a New Orleans flavor to this Greek Revival headquarters of a prestigious women's club that attracts members interested in the arts and sciences. ♦ 122 E 66th St (Lexington-Park Aves)

70 126 East 66th Street (1895, **W.J. Wallace** and **S.E. Sage**) A carriage house in Romanesque style built for **H.O. Havemeyer**, the sugar magnate, who lived at 1 E 66th St. Apparently it was too far from his house, because he sold it before it was finished to **Oliver H. Payne**, brother-in-law of **William C. Whitney**. It is still owned by **John Hay Whitney**. ♦ Lexington-Park Aves

70 The Forgotten Woman This unfortunately named store actually offers handsome designer clothing for the large woman, sizes 14 to 24. There are tailored suits, pure cashmere sweaters, cocktail dresses and leather skirts. Large teenagers can find preppy-look pleated skirts, casual jackets and Shetland sweaters. Service is exceptionally good. ♦ 888 Lexington Ave (E 66th St) 535.8848

70 Ashanti Sophisticated dresses of pure cotton, silk and wool for the large woman, sizes 14 to 24. Also accessories such as scarves and wrap belts. ♦ Closed Su. 872 Lexington Ave (E 65th St) 535.0740

71 Renny Renny Reynolds, one of the city's top florists and party designers, also stocks a staggering array of plants and flowers—wild country flowers, graceful lilies, numerous species of orchids—and the crystal and bamboo vases to hold them. He has designed parties for celebrities from **David Letterman** to **Calvin Klein**. For the premiere of **Paul Mazursky**'s movie, *Tempest*, Reynolds turned a Chinese junk into a Greek cargo vessel, complete with live goats, Greek food and a Greek band. ♦ Closed Su. 159 E 64th St (3rd-Lexington Aves) 288.7000

71 Bonsai Designs Experts will sell you a bonsai and teach you the art of maintaining it. If your efforts go awry (as mine invariably have), they'll diagnose the problem and prescribe a cure. The largest producer and retailer of bonsai in the East. ♦ Closed Su. 855 Lexington Ave (E 64th-E 65th Sts) 570.9160

72 Cherchez An upscale home and gift store worth a visit just for the smells. It is filled with dried flowers and herbs, scented papers, sachets and handmade potpourri. It is also a source of antique clothing and specialty gift items. **Barbara Milo Ohrback**, the owner, is the author of several books, including *The Scented Room*, *Antiques at Home*, *Bouquet of Flowers* and *Token of Friendship*. ♦ Closed Su. 862 Lexington Ave (E 65th St) 737.8313

72 Ségires à Solanée Classic Provençal designs—hand-painted wood furniture, iron furniture, faience from Moustiers-Sainte-Marie, linen placemats and napkins—abound in **Goergette Buckner**'s sunny shop. ♦ Closed Su. 866 Lexington Ave (E 65th St) 439.6109

72 The Elder Craftsmen Shop Men and women 55 years old and over make wooden toys, dollhouses, crib quilts, hand-knit sweaters, picture frames and hand-smocked dresses that are sold by volunteers of all ages in this tiny, cheerful store. ♦ Closed Su. 846 Lexington Ave (E 64th St) 535.8030

Restaurants/Nightlife: Red
Shops/Parks: Green
Hotels: Blue
Sights/Culture: Black

73 China House Gallery/China Institute in America (1905, **Charles A. Platt**) A gift of publisher **Henry R. Luce**, the son of missionaries to China, reflecting his lifelong interest in Sino-American cultural and political exchange. Along with changing exhibitions on Chinese fine arts and folk traditions, the institute conducts educational programs. ♦ Voluntary contribution. Closed Su. 125 E 65th St (Lexington-Park Aves) 744.8181

74 Mayfair Regent Hotel $$$$ (1925, **J.E.R. Carpenter**) Originally an apartment house, it was converted to a small European-style hotel in 1934—one of the few in the city with 24hr

manned elevator service. The lobby exudes an air of mellow marble, antique mahogany and old money. Most of the recently renovated, elegantly decorated rooms are large enough to include a sitting area, a working fireplace and a butler's pantry. Guests are offered a choice of soaps; terry robes; and an umbrella on rainy days. The Mayfair, run by the celebrated **International Regent** chain with **Dario Mariotti** as general manager, is possibly the finest hotel of its size in the city. *Highly recommended by RSW.* ♦ Deluxe ♦ 610 Park Ave (E 65th St) 288.0800, 800/545.4000; fax 737.0538

An estimated 1020 million riders use the New York City subways each year.

The thick-walled limestone-and-granite mansion at 11 E 73rd St was built for **Joseph Pulitzer**, who was suffering from an agonizing sensitivity to sound and a longing for absolute quiet.

Within the Mayfair Regent Hotel:

Le Cirque ★★★★$$$$ A favorite of actors, high-fashion models, as well as other representatives of the rich and powerful who fill it regularly. **Sirio Maccione**, owner and ringmaster, is the city's best host, and regulars to his bustling, posh establishment get royal treatment—whether titled or not—though unknowns are treated well too. Chef **Daniel Boulud** produces both standard haute cuisine and many original dishes. For the choicest morsels, concentrate on the specials rather than the printed menu. Pasta primavera, first popularized here, is never on the menu or an announced special, but is ordered by regulars in the know. Heavenly desserts include chocolate mousse cake and crème brûlée. Power tables: the front banquettes or, my first choice, the bar tables. ♦ French ♦ Closed Su. 58 E 65th St (Park-Madison Aves) Reservations required days in advance. 794.9292

75 Edward Durell Stone House (1956, **Edward Durell Stone**) The concrete grillwork covering the facade of the late architect's home is similar to the screen he used in his design for the **American Embassy** in New Delhi 2 years earlier. ♦ 130 E 64th St (Lexington-Park Aves)

75 112 East 64th Street (1959, **Philip Johnson & Associates**) The **Asia Society**, for which this was designed by Philip Johnson, has since moved to Park Ave. The classic Miesian darkglass box with its unclassic decorative white frame now houses the offices of

East Side

the **Russell Sage Foundation** and the **Robert Sterling Clarke Foundation**. It is an admirable example of glass used on a domestic scale. ♦ Lexington-Park Aves

76 Central Presbyterian Church (1922, **Henry C. Pelton** and **Allen & Collens**) John D. Rockefeller Jr., who taught Bible classes here, matched every contribution, dollar-for-dollar, to build this former Baptist church. In 1930, the congregation moved to **Riverside Church**, also largely funded by Rockefeller. ♦ 593 Park Ave (E 64th St)

77 101 East 63rd Street (Remodeled 1970, **Paul Rudolph**) The tripartite composition of this carriage house's dark glass front is a reflection of its interior. ♦ Lexington-Park Aves

78 Hotel Plaza Athénée $$$$ (1927, **George F. Pelham**) Formerly the **Alrae Apartments**, this intimate, ultraclassy hotel is modeled after the famous Paris original. Its relatively small size (160 spacious rooms and suites) and residential location attract guests, like the

Princess of Wales, in search of serenity rather than the hustle of Midtown. The lobby is a combination of French period furnishings, Italian marble floors and hand-painted mural tapestry walls. Amenities include 24hr concierge and room service, kitchenettes, **Porthault** robes, **Lanvin** toiletries, in-room safes (the hotel itself is extremely secure, with only one entrance) and fax machines upon request. The 4 duplex penthouse suite includes a terrace and solarium. ♦ Deluxe ♦ 37 E 64th St (Park-Madison Aves) 734.9100; fax 772.0958

Within the Hotel Plaza Athénée :

Le Regence ★★★★$$$$ Run by the expert **Rostang** family and guided by resident chef **Jean Robert De Cavel**, Le Regence continues to excel in all categories. The service is impeccable and the food top flight. At lunch, choose from the extensive à la carte menu—lamb chops, veal, anything from the sea. At dinner, go à la carte as well, or order either one of 2 elaborate prix-fixe meals. Duck liver salad, Mediterranean seafood soup and Dover sole are frequent offerings. The pumpkin cheesecake is light and fragrant. There is also a private dining room available for parties up to 25. ♦ French ♦ Jacket, tie and reservations required. 606.4647/8

79 Walter Steiger A women's shoe salon featuring the newest silhouettes from Europe by one of the leading designers. ♦ Closed Su. 739 Madison Ave (E 64th St) 570.1212

80 Chase Manhattan Bank (1932, **Morrel Smith**) A brick wall to the left of this Georgian bank conceals a colonial garden, a rarity on this busy street. ♦ 726 Madison Ave (E 64th St)

80 Wildenstein & Co. (1932, **Horace Trumbauer**) Known for the depth of its collections of old and contemporary paintings and *objets d'art*. Exhibitions often rival museum shows. ♦ Closed Sa-Su. 19 E 64th St (Madison-5th Aves) 879.0500

81 The Coach Store The well-known maker of soft leather handbags and briefcases offers its full line here. ♦ Closed Su. 710 Madison Ave (E 63rd-E 64th Sts) 319.1772. Also at: 193 Front St. 947.1727

81 Le Relais ★★$$$ Another one of those East Side places where models, soap opera players and other chic and beautiful trendies wile away evenings drinking white wine and Perrier, eating French food and looking at each other. It's fun to observe the outdoor cafe scene in the warmer months. ♦ French ♦ 712 Madison Ave (E 63rd St) Reservations recommended. 751.5108

81 Laura Ashley Home Furnishings Ashley is the Welsh designer who put nosegays and sprigs of flowers on pure cotton, and created an empire by whipping up the fabric into sweet Victorian dresses, petticoats, nightgowns, peasant skirts and little girls' dresses. Here her signature prints are available on furniture, in fabric by the roll, in wallpaper and in accessories for the home, such as picture frames and diaries. ♦ Closed Su. 714 Madison Ave (E 63rd-E 64th Sts) 735.5000. Also at: 21 E 57th St. 752.7300; 398 Columbus Ave. 496.5110; 4 Fulton St. 809.3555

81 M.J. Knoud Saddlery Manhattan's finest source of hunting and polo gear. There are hacking jackets from **Heythrop of England**, wool vests with brass buttons, handsome rubberized cotton riding raincoats, jodhpurs, britches and silk hats. ♦ Closed Su. 716 Madison Ave (E 63rd-E 64th Sts) 838.1434

82 Emilio Pucci (1882, **Theodore Weston**; facade 1920, **Mott B. Schmidt**) A boutique for the Italian designer in a house that was once owned by **Consuela Vanderbilt Smith**, daughter of **William K. Vanderbilt**. ♦ Closed Su. 24 E 64th St (Madison-5th Aves) 752.4777

83 Berwind Mansion (1896, **N.C. Mellon**) This Venetian Renaissance mansion was the home of **Edwin J. Berwind**, the largest owner of coal mines and the sole supplier of coal for America's warships. Today the building contains cooperative apartments. ♦ 2 E 64th St (5th Ave)

83 820 Fifth Avenue (1916, **Starrett & Van Vleck**) This is one of the earliest luxury apartment buildings on 5th Ave. Among its first tenants was New York's **Governor Al Smith**. ♦ E 64th St

84 India House (1903, **Warren & Wetmore**) An unusually wide (65ft) mansion that would be right at home on the streets of Paris. It was built for banker **Marshall Orme Wilson**, whose wife was **Carrie Astor**, daughter of *the* **Mrs. Astor**, who lived around the corner. It is now the property of the government of India. ♦ 3 E 64th St (5th Ave)

85 Temple Emanu-El (1929, **Robert D. Kohn, Charles Butler** and **Clarence Stein**) This impressive gray limestone edifice on the site of a mansion belonging to **Caroline Schermerhorn Astor** is the temple of the oldest Reform congregation in New York. Resembling only the nave of a cathedral, the structure has masonry-bearing walls. In style, it is Romanesque with Eastern influences; these are repeated on the interior with Byzantine ornaments. The hall is 77ft wide, 150ft long and 403ft high; it seats 2500— more than **St. Patrick's Cathedral**. ♦ 1 E 65th St (5th Ave)

86 Rita Ford Music Boxes An enchanting store brimming with music boxes, old and new, inexpensive and costly. The helpful salespeople will play any of them for you: tiny carousels that light up and whose horses ride up and down, feathered birds in cages and Pierrots who jump up and down on a stage. ♦ Closed Su. 19 E 65th St (Madison-5th Aves) 535.6717

3.1 percent of the US population lives in New York City.

86 Cambridge Chemists Any top-of-the-line European product can be found here, including **Cyclax of London, Innoxa, Roc** and **Vichy**. ♦ Closed Su. 21 E 65th St (Madison Ave) 734.5678

86 LS Collection Elegant housewares: leather desk accessories by **Arte Cuoio**, sterling silver desk accessories and vases from **Zucchi & Pampaloni** and perfume bottles from Canadian sculptor **Max Leser**. ♦ Closed Su. 765 Madison Ave (E 65th St) 472.3355

87 American Federation of the Arts (1910, **Trowbridge & Livingston**; interior 1960, **Edward Durell Stone**) The AFA is an organization that provides traveling exhibitions for small museums around the country. The interior of the building, now devoted to office space, is richly detailed. The walls are French limestone, the ceilings sculpted in plaster. Some rooms have oak-paneled walls. It was originally the home of stockbroker **Benson B. Sloan**. ♦ 41 E 65th St (Park-Madison Aves)

87 Sarah Delano Roosevelt Memorial House (1908, **Charles A. Platt**) A pair of houses commissioned by **Sarah Delano Roosevelt** when her son, **Franklin**, was married. One was for herself, the other for the newlyweds. The houses are identical, with a common entrance. Several of their rooms were connected by folding doors to make them larger when necessary, as well as to give interior access between the 2 houses. It was in the 4th-floor front bedroom of the house on the right that Roosevelt went through his long recovery from polio in 1921-22. The future president's mother wanted him to go to their estate in Hyde Park NY, but his wife, **Eleanor**, convinced him to stay in the city. She felt he had a future in politics and needed to be closer to the centers of power, even though bedridden.

Her decision doomed her to live under the thumb of her mother-in-law, not one of her favorite people. The buildings are now a community center for **Hunter College** students. ♦ 45-47 E 65th St (Park-Madison Aves)

88 Charles Jourdan Status shoes and woven leather handbags. ♦ Closed Su. 769 Madison Ave (E 66th St) 628.0133

89 45 East 66th Street (1900, **Harde & Short**) Lacy pastry exuberance at an even higher level than the **Alwyn Court Apartments** by the same firm. Note the Elizabethan and Flemish Gothic detailing and the sensuous curve of the round tower on the corner. ♦ Madison Ave

90 North Beach Leather Whether they prefer trendy or classic styles, male and female leather aficionados will find all manner of leather jeans, jackets, shirts, overblouses, coats, bras, bikini pants and dresses—some punched out, others adorned with feathers, beads or studs. ♦ 772 Madison Ave (E 66th St) 772.0707

91 The Lotos Club (1900, **Richard H. Hunt**) Once the home of **William J. Schieffelin**, head of a wholesale drug firm and a crusader for civil rights at the turn of the century. The rusticated limestone base supports a red-brick midsection and a double-story mansard roof. It is a vigorous Second Empire composite on the verge of being excessive. Now headquarters of the Lotos Club, an organization of artists, musicians, actors and journalists. ♦ 5 E 66th St (Madison-5th Aves)

92 Sonia Rykiel Rykiel's fashions are expensive but timeless. The colors, cut and workmanship make them seem like an investment, and Rykiel's followers say her clothes make them feel special. ♦ Closed Su. 792 Madison Ave (E 66th-E 67th Sts) 744.0880

93 Ronaldo Maia Ltd. Maia's party designs—tables are wrapped with rose moiré and ceilings are turned into topiaries—are much sought-after. He is the author of *Decorating with Flowers*. ♦ Closed Su. 27 E 67th St (Madison Ave) 288.1049

94 13 and 15 East 67th Street A curious pair, particularly in contrast to the Modernist red-granite face at No. 17. No. 13 (1921, **Henry Allan Jacobs**) is an Italian Renaissance concoction that was built for theatrical producer **Martin Beck**. No. 15 (1904, **Ernest Flagg**), now the **Regency Whist Club**, was the **Cortland Field Bishop House**. Concocted of stone and restrained ironwork, this rather Parisian house was designed by the man who did **Scribner's Bookstore**. ♦ Madison-5th Aves

95 4 East 67th Street (1902, **John H. Duncan**) An ornate Beaux-Arts mansion, built for banker **Henri P. Wertheim**. It is now the residence of the **Consul General of Japan**. ♦ Madison-5th Aves

East Side

96 6, 8 and 10 East 68th Street (1900, **John H. Duncan**; facade 1919, **Harry Allen Jacobs**) These 3 houses were bought by financier **Otto Kuhn**, of **Kuhn, Loeb & Co**, in 1916, and altered with a French Renaissance limestone facade. He refurbished the interiors and sold them to, among others, banker **Edward W. Harriman**. ♦ Madison-5th Aves

97 9 East 68th Street (1906, **Heins & LaFarge**) Formerly the **George T. Bliss House**, now the **Center for Marital Therapy**. Four giant columns hold up nothing but that little balcony and a brave front to the world. Remarkably out of scale, the house is noteworthy because it is engaging and not overly pretentious. ♦ Madison-5th Aves

98 Joseph Tricot The latest knits from London—some crude, some romantic, all representing the world of street chic. Also hats and leather bags. ♦ Closed Su. 804 Madison Ave (E 68th St) 570.0077

98 Ylang Ylang Garish or gorgeous, the costume jewelry sold here is certainly not made for the *Cracker Jack* set. Materials like stainless steel, rhinestones and small rocks are mixed and matched in necklaces, bracelets and earrings, creating the ultimate in showy accessories. ♦ Closed Su. 806 Madison Ave (E 68th St) 879.7028

98 Billy Martin's Western Wear Yes, it's the same **Billy Martin** who used to pace the dugout at Yankee Stadium. A one-stop source of cowboy boots, fancy belts and other expensive duds to make you look at home on the range. ♦ 812 Madison Ave (E 68th St) 861.3100

99 Montenapoleone Fabulously silky and embroidered Italian and French lingerie. ♦ Closed Su. 789 Madison Ave (E 67th St) 535.2660

99 Frette A sleek Italian shop featuring extravagant linens for bed and table, including pique bedspreads, linen sheets and damask tablecloths. ♦ Closed Su. 799 Madison Ave (E 67th St) 988.5221

99 Cerutti This may be the most useful children's clothing store in the city, due to its broad and well-chosen range. There are the practical, the perky and the extravagant (hand-knit sweaters and leggings sets from Italy). Little boys will find navy blue blazers, and little girls handmade, lavishly smocked dresses. ♦ Closed Su. 807 Madison Ave (E 67th-E 68th Sts) 737.7540

99 Emanuel Ungaro Here is the city's largest grouping of the designer's *prêt-à-porter* collection for women, including his opulently printed, jewel-toned fabrics—paisleys, stripes, florals and checks—in surprising combinations as weightless dresses, separates and evening gowns. The shop also sells such accessories as boots, shoes, belts and shawls. ♦ Closed Su. 803 Madison Ave (E 67th-E 68th Sts) 249.4090

100 45 East 67th Street (1913, **Walter B. Chambers**) Until 1973, this house was owned by **Gloria Vanderbilt**. It is now the property of the government of Peru. ♦ Park-Madison Aves

101 Koos Van Den Akker Along with the elaborate feminine skirts, jackets and blouses of patchwork and collage for which he is known, Koos also offers an exclusive special collection of handmade sweaters, along with such one-of-a-kind extravaganzas as a wedding dress with a lace top and a voluminous *Scarlett O'Hara* skirt of appliquéd silk and net. Sometimes he comes up with an unadorned silk or jersey dress for those not enamored of pattern-on-pattern. ♦ Closed Su. 34 E 67th St (Madison-Park Aves) 249.5432

102 660 Park Avenue (1927, **York & Sawyer**) **Philip Sawyer** carved a reputation for himself as a designer of banks, but his work on the rustication of this handsome apartment building is worthy of any of them. ◆ E 67th St

103 115 East 67th Street (1932, **Andrew J. Thomas**) A happy place with owls, squirrels and other small animals in the decorative panels and huge arched entry. ◆ Lexington-Park Aves

104 Council on Foreign Relations (1920, **Delano & Aldrich**) Built by **Harold I. Pratt**, son of **Charles Pratt**, a partner of **John D. Rockefeller Jr.** and founder of Brooklyn's **Pratt Institute**. The present owner is an organization that promotes interest in foreign relations and publishes the influential magazine, *Foreign Affairs*. ◆ 58 E 68th St (Park Ave)

105 680-690 Park Avenue A lively but not exceptional collection of brick and limestone Neo-Georgian buildings. This ensemble is special because it is the only full block of townhouses surviving on Park Ave. No. 680: **Center for Inter-American Relations**, formerly the **Soviet Delegation to the UN**, originally the **Percy Pyne House** (1909, **McKim, Mead & White**); No. 684: **Spanish Institute**, the house of Pyne's son-in-law, **Oliver D. Filey**, and built in Pyne's garden (1926, McKim, Mead & White); No. 686: **Institute Italiana di Cultura**, formerly **William Sloane House** (1918, **Delano & Aldrich**); No. 690: **Italian Consulate**, originally the **Henry P. Davidson House** (1917, **Walker & Gillette**). ◆ E 68th-E 69th Sts

105 Americas Society (1909, **McKim, Mead & White**) In the late 1940s and early '50s, this was the **Soviet Delegation to the United Nations**, which made this corner the scene of almost continuous anti-Communist demonstrations. Before the Russians arrived, it was the home of banker **Percy Rivington Pyne**. The building now houses a gallery specializing in Central and South and North American art. ◆ Closed Su. 680 Park Ave (E 68th St) 249.8950

106 45 East 68th Street (1912, **C.P.H. Gilbet**) In the 1950s and '60s, **Richard Kollmar** and his wife, **Dorothy Kilgallen**, used a 4th-floor studio in this house to broadcast their popular radio program, *Breakfast with Dorothy and Dick*. After their divorce, Kollmar's second wife, fashion designer **Anne Fogarty**, used the room as her studio. ◆ Park-Madison Aves

106 Automation House (1914, **Trowbridge & Livingston**; remodeled 1970, **Oppenheimer, Brady & Lehrecke**) An unfortunate renovation has reduced the appearance of this Georgian building. It was built for the grandson of **William Clark**, who developed 6-cord cotton sewing thread, sold under the name **O.N.T.** (Our New Thread). ◆ 49 E 68th St (Park-Madison Aves)

107 Giorgio Armani Boutique The Italian designer's total avant-garde ready-to-wear and couture lines for men and women are now under one roof. ◆ Closed Su. 815 Madison Ave (E 68th St) 988.9191

107 Valentino In a hushed and lavish setting, you can see the ready-to-wear collection of Valentino, including classic pants, beautifully shaped jackets and luxurious dresses for day and night. Fabrics are intensely sensuous—linens are weightless, cottons silken. Prices are out of this world. ◆ Closed Su. 825 Madison Ave (E 68th St) 772.6969

108 D. Porthault This shop can weave tablecloths that will go the entire length of a ballroom, sheets to fit the beds of private airplanes and duvet covers of fine linen. **Queen Elizabeth II** has slept on Porthault's sheets. Wealthy children wear its overalls of the silkiest cotton. ◆ Closed Su. 18 E 69th St (Madison Ave) 688.1660

109 The Westbury Hotel $$$$ There is a Westbury in London with an American flavor, but its American counterpart is decidedly British. Amenities include 24hr room service, in-room safes, PC and fax ports, same-day valet service and a multilingual staff. The Chippendale furniture and 17th-century Belgian tapestries in the lobby are genuine. All of its large 235 rooms and suites have been recently redecorated. ◆ 15 E 69th St (Madison Ave) 535.2000, 800/321.1569; fax 535.5058

Within the Westbury Hotel:

The Polo Lounge ★★★$$$ The atmosphere is appropriately clublike—plush leather chairs, banquette seating, dark mahogany walls with equestrian prints, brass sconces. I suggest the sautéed slice of fresh foie gras served with artichoke bottoms and a vinegar sauce—a memorable appetizer. The balance of the menu, American with French touches, has greatly improved. Service is polite and attentive. ◆ American/French ◆ Jacket required. Reservations recommended. 535.9141/2

East Side

109 The Pillowry **Marjorie Lawrence** sells kilims and Oriental rugs and makes pillows from antique rugs and textiles collected from all over the world. ◆ Closed Sa-Su. 19 E 69th St (Madison Ave) 3rd floor. 628.3844

109 Kenzo The first major Japanese designer to work in Paris combines the simple designs of his native country with the frills of his adopted one. ◆ Closed Su. 824 Madison Ave (E 69th-E 70th Sts) 737.8640

109 Missoni A whole store for the Missoni signature Italian knits on what is becoming *European Designers' Row*. The recognizable blend of subtle color combinations and patterns is worked up in all kinds of dashing sportswear for men and women. I have a weakness for the sweaters. ◆ Closed Su. 836 Madison Ave (E 69th St) 517.9339

109 Minna Rosenblatt An enchanting collection of **Tiffany** lamps and other glass antiques. ◆ Closed Su. 844 Madison Ave (E 69th-E 70th Sts) 288.0250

110 The Frick Collection (1914, **Carrère & Hastings**; renovation 1935, **John Russell Pope**; east wing addition and garden 1977, **John Barrington Bayley** and **Harry Van Dyke**; **Russell Page**, landscape architect) **Henry Clay Frick**, chairman of the Carnegie Steel Corp, wanted a place to display his art. He bought this site when the old Lenox Library was torn down and had an Italianate house built—one of the last great mansions on 5th Ave—with apartments for the family and reception rooms for the art. The architects were chosen on the recommendation of Frick's art advisor/dealer, **Lord Duveen**. In his will, Frick decreed that his wife could continue living there until her death, at which time it would be renovated and expanded as a museum. Duveen again chose the architect, John Russell Pope, who designed the **National Gallery** in Washington DC. He is responsible for the unique character of the museum, especially the glass-covered courtyard, a rewarding retreat from city anxieties if ever there was one. The Frick is everyone's favorite art museum. Visiting here is like being asked into the sumptuous private home of a collector who bought only the crème de la crème of the Old Masters, and then hung them along with fine furniture, porcelains and bronzes in the most restful, well-lit rooms. Treasures here include **Rembrandt**'s *The Polish Rider*, **Van Eyck**'s *Virgin and Child with Saints, and Donor*,

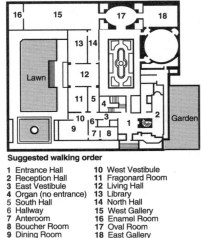

Suggested walking order

1	Entrance Hall	10	West Vestibule
2	Reception Hall	11	Fragonard Room
3	East Vestibule	12	Living Hall
4	Organ (no entrance)	13	Library
5	South Hall	14	North Hall
6	Hallway	15	West Gallery
7	Anteroom	16	Enamel Room
8	Boucher Room	17	Oval Room
9	Dining Room	18	East Gallery

East Side

Bellini's *Saint Francis in Ecstasy*, **Titian**'s *Man in a Red Cap*, **El Greco**'s *Saint Jerome*, **Piero della Francesca**'s *Saint Simon the Apostle* and a whole room of **Fragonard**. There are free lectures on the collection and the artists in it on selected afternoons, and chamber concerts on occasional Sundays. (Call or write for ticket information.) Absolutely worth a visit. ◆ Admission. Tu-Sa 10AM-6PM; Su 1-6PM. 1 E 70th St (5th Ave) 288.0700

111 Barbara Mathes Early to current 20th-century American paintings, drawings, sculpture. ◆ By appointment only. 19 E 71st St (Madison Ave) 3rd floor. 737.6066

111 Le Chocolatier Manon Fresh and lush caramels, truffles, marzipan and pralines displayed and packaged with seductive elegance. ◆ Closed Su. 872 Madison Ave (E 71st St) 288.8088

111 Pierre Deux The French family **Demery** has spent 300 years creating richly colored paisley and floral fabrics that are quintessentially Provençal. They sell their best designs—the **Souleiaido** line—to Pierre Deux. Fabric is sold by the yard or made up into tablecloths, napkins, placemats, quilts, pillows, scarves, shawls, neckties, shirts for men and dresses for women and little girls. ◆ Closed Su. 870 Madison Ave (E 71st St) 570.9343. Also at: 369 Bleecker St. 243.7740

112 St. James Protestant Episcopal Church (1884, **R.H. Robertson**; rebuilt 1924, **Ralph Adams Cram**; steeple 1950, **Richard Kimball**) This Episcopal church was established on the East Side before the invasion of the millionaires, but its future was solidly secured when people with names like **Schermerhorn, Rhinelander** and **Astor** became members of its vestry. ◆ Madison Ave at E 71st St

112 Polo-Ralph Lauren (1898, **Kimball & Thompson**) If you like the Polo look, you'll love the wonderland **Ralph Lauren** created here. The French Renaissance building was commissioned by **Gertrude Rhinelander Waldo**, a descendant of one of New York's most influential families. She lived here for a few months, but preferred to live across the street with her sister. She offered it to her son, but he preferred to live elsewhere too, and the house stood empty until it was sold in a foreclosure in 1920. Before Lauren moved in, it was the **Philips Auction Gallery**. Worth a visit even if you don't buy anything. ◆ Closed Su. 867 Madison Ave (E 72nd St) 606.2100

113 Knoedler Gallery (1910, **Thornton Chad**) The oldest New York-based art gallery, founded in 1846, Knoedler handles contemporary greats like **Richard Diebenkorn, Nancy Graves, Robert Motherwell, Frank Stella** and **Robert Rauschenberg**. Always worth checking out the current exhibition. ♦ M-F 9:30AM-5:30PM; Sa 10AM-5:30PM. 19 E 70th St (Madison-5th Aves) 794.0550

113 Hirschl & Adler Top-quality shows of 18th-, 19th- and 20th-century American and European art. Also American prints and contemporary paintings and sculpture. ♦ Tu-F 9:30AM-5:15PM; Sa 9:30AM-4:45PM. 21 E 70th St (Madison-5th Aves) 535.8810

114 Hirschl & Adler Modern American and European paintings, drawings, prints and sculpture from the mid 1950s through the present. ♦ M by appointment; Tu-F 9:30AM-5:30PM; Sa 9:30AM-5PM. 851 Madison Ave (E 70th-E 71st Sts) 2nd floor. 744.6700

114 Hirschl & Adler Folk American folk art, mostly from the 19th century. Weather vanes, quilts, furniture. ♦ Tu-F 9:30AM-5:30PM; Sa 9:45AM-4:45PM. 851 Madison Ave (E 70th-E 71st Sts) 2nd floor. 988.3655

114 Yves Saint Laurent-Rive Gauche Neighboring stores combine to offer the entire Saint Laurent line for men and women. Together they have the city's largest variety of his collections, including hats, umbrellas, shirts, slacks, dresses, suits and ball gowns. ♦ Closed Su. 855-859 Madison Ave (E 70th-E 71st Sts) 988.3821

115 45 East 70th Street (1929, **Aymar Embury II**) A nondescript townhouse, originally the home of investment banker **Arthur S. Lehman**. His wife was the former **Adele Lewisohn**, a philanthropist and championship tennis player. It is now the home of **Joseph** and **Estée Lauder**. ♦ Park-Madison Aves

116 La Goulue $$$ In summer, one of the prettiest outdoor cafes in town, certainly uptown. The handsome inside bistro, with a dark wood and polished brass turn-of-the-century Paris feel and a menu of cliché French dishes, can get noisy. Stick to the simplest dishes. ♦ French ♦ 28 E 70th St (Madison Ave) Reservations required. 988.8169

116 46 East 70th Street (1912, **Frederick Sterner**) This ornate Neo-Jacobean house was built for **Stephen C. Clark**, whose family owned the **Singer Sewing Machine Co.** Parts of his extensive art collection are in the **Metropolitan Museum of Art.** Among his other interests was baseball—he was founder of the **Baseball Hall of Fame** at Cooperstown NY. It is now the **Lowell Thomas Building of the Explorers Club.** ♦ Park-Madison Aves

117 Pratesi One of the more sybaritic bed- and-bath shops in town, Pratesi sells sheets of linen, silk and Egyptian cotton, as well as comforters filled with goose down or cashmere and covered in silk. Upstairs there are terry cloth robes, and towels to match the printed sheets. ♦ Closed Su. 829 Madison Ave (E 69th St) 288.2315

117 Madison Avenue Bookstore It looks deceptively small, but the 2 no-nonsense floors are packed with a wide range of literary criticism, art, current fiction and cookbooks. It stocks the full line of every major publisher, including a lot of first novels. Service is a strong point: mailing, delivery, special orders, out-of-print searches and, a real plus as far as I'm concerned, fancy gift-wrapping. ♦ Closed Su. 833 Madison Ave (E 69th St) 535.6130

117 Maraolo Italian-made shoes for men, women and children at reasonable prices, considering the location and the quality. ♦ 835 Madison Ave (E 69th-E 70th Sts) 628.5080. Also at: 782 Lexington Ave. 832.8182; 1321 3rd Ave. 535.6225

117 Thomas K. Woodard The city's premier shop for high-quality antique and early 20th-century quilts, ranging in size from crib to king. Designs include *sunbonnet, postage stamps* and *drunkard's path.* There are also baskets, spongeware, painted furniture, rag and hooked rugs. ♦ Closed Su. 835 Madison Ave (E 69th St) 2nd floor. 988.2906

118 Hunter College (Park Ave building 1940, **Shreve, Lamb & Harmon** with **Harrison & Fouilhoux**; Lexington Ave buildings 1986, **Ulrich Franzen & Associates**) One of the schools of the **City University of New York**, Hunter was founded in 1870 as a school for training teachers. Today the school emphasizes such practical disciplines as science, premed and nursing, as well as education. It also offers bachelor's degrees in the arts, humanities and social sciences. The **Hunter College Theater** (570.5825), in the main building is used for speakers, political forums,

music and dance programs. The diverse collection of buildings are standard modern, with an uneasy relationship to the surrounding streets. Shreve, Lamb & Harmon set their 16-story glass box away from Park Ave, but Franzen put his buildings up against, and even over, Lexington Ave. ♦ E 67th-E 69th Sts (Lexington-Park Aves) 772.4000

119 The Union Club (1932, **Delano & Aldrich**) Limestone and granite in a conservative and rather dry palazzo composition (compare **University** or **Metropolitan** clubs) looks the way you would expect the oldest men's club in New York City to look. ♦ 101 E 69th St (Park Ave)

120 S. Wyler The shop celebrated its 100th birthday in 1990. An excellent source of 18th- and 19th-century English sterling silver and Victorian and old Sheffield plate. Antique porcelain too. ♦ Closed Su. 941 Lexington Ave (E 69th St) 879.9848

121 Visiting Nurse Service of New York
(1921, **Walker & Gillette**) A Tudor Revival
mansion that was once home to **Thomas W.
Lamont**, chairman of **J.P. Morgan & Co.**
◆ 107 E 70th St (Lexington-Park Aves)

121 123 East 70th Street (1903, **Trowbridge &
Livingston**) **Samuel Trowbridge**, designer of
the **B. Altman** department store (which closed
in 1989), the **St. Regis Hotel** and other Beaux-
Arts gems, built this house for himself.
◆ Lexington-Park Aves

121 Paul Mellon House (1965, **H. Page Cross**)
A French Provincial townhouse, right at home
in New York, built for the industrialist and art
collector. ◆ 125 E 70th St (Lexington-Park
Aves)

122 124 East 70th Street (1941, **William
Lescaze**) Built for financier **Edward A.
Norman**, this International-style house was
cited by the **Museum of Modern Art** for its
innovative design. ◆ Lexington-Park Aves

123 The Asia Society (1981, **Edward Larrabee
Barnes**) This permanent collection of Asian
art was assembled by **John D. Rockefeller III**
between 1951 and 1979. It is known for its
outstanding Southeast Asian and Indian
sculpture, Chinese ceramics and bronzes, and
Japanese ceramics and wood sculptures.
Other galleries in this slick, extravagant building show changing exhibitions ranging from

East Side

Chinese snuff bottles to Islamic books from
the collection of **Prince Salruddin Aga Kahn**.
The Asia Society also sponsors lectures here
on Asian arts and adventures, as well as films
and performances. A large bookstore is well-
stocked with books and periodicals and prints
from or about Asia. ◆ Galleries: admission.
Tu-Sa 11AM-6PM; Su noon-5PM. Tours: free.
Tu-Sa 12:30PM. 725 Park Ave (E 70th St)
288.6400

124 131 East 71st Street (1867; facade 1910,
Ogden Codman Jr. and **Elsie de Wolfe**) Elsie
de Wolfe, America's first interior decorator,
lived here and used the house as a showcase
for her talents. ◆ Lexington-Park Aves

125 La Petite Ferme ★★$$$ One of those
places I would go to all the time for simply
cooked, fresh French food, if only the prices
were more reasonable. ◆ French ◆ Closed Su.
973 Lexington Ave (E 70th-E 71st Sts) Reser-
vations required. 249.3272

125 San Francisco Designer **Howard Partman**,
also the store's owner, sells conservative
women's suiting in lush fabrics, contempo-
rary sportswear, along with trench coats for
both men and women. ◆ Closed Su. 975
Lexington Ave (E 70th St) 472.8740

126 The Lenox School (1907, **Edward P.
Casey**) This Tudor house, built for **Stephen H.
Brown**, governor of the **New York Stock Ex-
change**, was considered one of the area's
showplaces before being converted to a
school in 1932. ◆ 154 E 70th St (3rd-Lexing-
ton Aves)

127 Gracious Home The ultimate neighbor-
hood hardware store: televisions, woks, umbrellas,
dishwashers, typewriters, radiator covers,
Mason jars and all the expected basics. Gra-
cious Home will also custom-order radiator
enclosures. At the store across the street (No.
1217), you will find a complete bath shop—
everything from sinks and faucets to shower
curtains and bath mats—decorative hard-
ware, moldings, wallpaper, bedding and gift
items. ◆ 1220 3rd Ave (E 70th St) 517.6300

128 Fay & Allen's Café $$ Light snacks and
sandwiches in a relaxed setting. ◆ Cafe
◆ 1240 3rd Ave (E 71st-E 72nd Sts) 794.1359

129 Grace's Marketplace An uptown version
of **Balducci's** gourmet food store in Greenwich Village, and an East Side answer to the
West Side's **Zabar's**. ◆ 1237 3rd Ave (E 71st
St) 737.0600

130 Cafe Greco $$ This lively, flower-filled res-
taurant orients its cuisine around the Mediter-
ranean. Spanish, Italian, French and Moroc-
can dishes all find their way onto the table.
◆ Continental ◆ 1390 2nd Ave (E 71st-E 72nd
Sts) 737.4300

131 Beach Café $$ Totally acceptable ham-
burger-omelet-salad fare. The lack of decora-
tion and the old mosaic tile floor make it seem
more down-to-earth and less pretentious than
other such spots in the neighborhood. And it
is. ◆ American ◆ 1326 2nd Ave (E 70th St)
988.7299

132 First Reformed Hungarian Church
(1915, **Emery Roth**) The Hungarian-born architect gave us a taste of the Old Country with
this ornamented white stucco church topped
by an 80ft, conical-roofed bell tower. ◆ 344 E
69th St (1st-2nd Aves)

133 Fins on First ★$ A small, inviting seafood
restaurant with the feel of a clean, bright fish
shop. Excellent chunky seafood chowder,
crisp calamari, tasty pasta topped with seafood and light fried sole. Summer dining in the
yard out back. ◆ Seafood ◆ 1288 1st Ave (E
69th St) 876.3467

134 Rockefeller University A collection of
buildings that constitutes what was originally
known as the **Rockefeller Institute for Medical Research**. The site, which was a summer
estate of the **Schermerhorn** family, was
acquired in 1901; the first building, **Founder's**

Hall, opened in 1903 as a laboratory. Most striking are the gray hemisphere of **Caspary Auditorium** (1957) and the **President's House** (1958), both by **Harrison & Abramovitz**. It's worth a visit. Ask the guard for permission to enter, and while you're there, stroll toward the river for a look at the gardens. ♦ E 64th-E 68th Sts (FDR Dr-York Ave)

135 New York Hospital/Cornell University Medical College (1932, **Coolidge, Shepley, Bullfinch and Abbott**) What appears to be a singular, almost solid, well-balanced mass is actually 15 buildings. Lumpishness is avoided by the strong vertical lines and the Gothic arches. The site is reported to have been the location of *Smuggler's Cave*—the hiding place of famous smuggler **David Provoost**, cousin of the first Protestant Episcopal Bishop of New York City. The first small-pox vaccination was given here in 1799, by **Dr. Valentine Seaman**. ♦ 525 E 68th St (FDR Dr-York Ave) 746.1701

136 Sotheby's The London-based Sotheby's is the largest and oldest fine-arts auctioneer in the world. With its original Madison Ave headquarters closed, it has relocated here in a larger but less personal shop, where there is a full round of important sales, exhibitions and free seminars. Admission to some auctions is by ticket only, but all viewings are open to the public. ♦ M-F 9:30AM-5PM; Sa 10AM-5PM; Su 1-5PM. 1334 York Ave (E 72nd St) 606.7000

137 Adam's Rib $$$ Famous for prime rib, which comes in a scaled-down version in case you're not that hungry. ♦ American ♦ 1340 1st Ave (E 72nd St) 535.2112

138 Petaluma ★★$$$ Fallen from the graces of the chic and trendy, this eclectic cafe still attracts a decent following. Singles flock to the bar, while folks of all shapes and sizes dine in this vast, pastel-colored Postmodern space. The food is passable—go for the view. But don't skip the chocolate cake if you're a confirmed chocoholic. ♦ Italian ♦ 1356 1st Ave (E 73rd St) Reservations recommended. 772.8800

139 Marlo Flowers, Ltd. Everything from tiny bouquets to dinner for 10,000. Romantic, totally artistic approach to compositional floristry. ♦ Closed Sa-Su. 421 E 73rd St (York-1st Aves) 628.2246

140 First Wok $$ Like all the other outlets in the First Wok chain, a boon to its neighborhood. Fresh ingredients are cooked skillfully and delivered to the table promptly by a polite staff. Nothing fancy, just good eats at a modest price. ♦ Chinese ♦ 1384 1st Ave (E 74th St) 535.8598

141 Café Crocodile ★$$ The fresh, home-cooked taste of everything—be it of Greek, French, Italian or North African ancestry—is the main appeal. The cook/owner is an amateur in the best sense of the word—a cook who cooks for the love of it, and it shows.

Upstairs dining room for private parties of 16 to 24. ♦ Mediterranean ♦ Closed Su. 354 E 74th St (1st-2nd Aves) Reservations recommended. 249.6619

142 Jan Hus Church (1914) A Presbyterian church founded by the Czech community, whose presence in this area led it to be known as *Little Bohemia* in the 1920s and '30s. The parsonage is furnished to resemble a Czechoslovakian peasant's house. ♦ 351 E 74th St (1st-2nd Aves)

Within Jan Hus Church:

Chicago City Limits Established in New York in 1980, this is one of the oldest, and probably the only self-sustaining, comedy improvisation groups in the city. It was formed in Chicago in 1977 by **George Todisco** and actors participating in workshops at that city's reknowned **Second City**. **Paul Zuckerman** and **Eddie Ellner** are standards. ♦ Shows: W-Th 8:30PM; F-Sa 8, 10:30PM. 772.8707

143 Little Mushroom Cafe $$ Thai specialties as well as Italian dishes like linguini with salmon. Top Thai choices: crispy duck or the aromatic *pad Thai* (sautéed noodles with either chicken or shrimp, peanuts, bean curd, bean sprouts and egg). ♦ Thai/Italian ♦ 1439 2nd Ave (E 75th St) Reservations recommended. 988.9006. Also at: 183 W 10th St. 242.1058

143 Pamir ★$$$ The latest in ethnic invasions presents exotic Afghani cuisine. Lots of skewered meats—lamb and chicken—are served with moist rice pilaf and side dishes of yogurt and sautéed eggplant. Save room for desserts like *gosh-e-feel* (elephant's ear) and unusual twists on baklava. ♦ Afghani ♦ Closed M. 1437 2nd Ave (E 74th-E 75th Sts) Reservations recommended. 734.3791

East Side

144 Camelback & Central ★$$ The prices are fair, the fish is fresh and they know how to roast a chicken, grill a chop, cook vegetables and mix a mean drink at this stylish neighborhood spot. Friendly service. ♦ American ♦ 1403 2nd Ave (E 73rd St) 249.8380

145 Fu's ★★$$$ Hostess **Gloria Chu** presides over this upscale Chinese restaurant. I always count on her to guide me through the extensive menu, although you can't go wrong ordering the Grand Marnier shrimp, the lemon chicken or the crabs in black-bean sauce. ♦ Chinese ♦ 1395 2nd Ave (E 72nd-E 73rd Sts) Reservations recommended. 517.9670

146 J.G. Mellon's ★$ Burgers, chili, salads and steaks—a real neighborhood hangout. Unpretentious and friendly. ♦ American ♦ 1291 3rd Ave (E 74th St) No credit cards. 650.1310. Also at: 340 Amsterdam Ave. 877.2220

Restaurants/Nightlife: Red   **Hotels:** Blue
Shops/Parks: Green   **Sights/Culture:** Black

146 Mezzaluna ★$$ A tiny restaurant that is quite popular among East Siders who like to be seen in all the right places. Pizzas baked in wood-burning ovens are featured at lunch and after 10PM. ♦ Italian ♦ 1295 3rd Ave (E 74th-E 75th Sts) 535.9600

147 Paraclete Bookstore specializing in theological works. ♦ Closed M, Su. 146 E 74th St (Lexington Ave) 535.4050

148 American Scandinavian Foundation (1903, **McKim, Mead & White**) This Colonial Revival house was designed by **Stanford White** for his friend, **Charles Dana Gibson**, the illustrator who created the famous *Gibson Girl*. One of Gibson's models was the 15-year-old **Evelyn Nesbit**, whom he painted in profile with her hair forming a question mark. It was one of his most famous works, known as *The Eternal Question*. Young Miss Nesbit became even more famous when, in 1906, her husband, **Harry K. Thaw**, shot White dead in a fit of jealousy on the roof of the old Madison Square Garden. ♦ 127 E 73rd St (Lexington-Park Aves) 879.9779

149 Vivolo ★$$$ One of the city's most popular Italian restaurants, and that is the problem. Crowded and noisy, the cafe's system is overtaxed and the ambience suffers. With all the rush, there doesn't seem to be time to create dishes that are better than merely ordinary. Fine if you're in the neighborhood. ♦ Italian ♦ Closed Su. 140 E 74th St (Lexington Ave) Reservations recommended. 737.3533. Also at: 222 E 58th St. 308.0112

150 Au Chat Botté Expensive charm pervades here, offering baby furniture, including cribs, changing tables, chairs, chests of drawers, clothes racks and bumper guards as well as children's clothes. ♦ Closed Su. 903 Madison Ave (E 72nd St) 772.7402

East Side

151 Lycée Français The French school now occupies 2 French Renaissance mansions: No. 7 (1899, **Flagg & Chambers**) was the **Oliver Gould Jennings House**; No. 9 (1896, **Carrère & Hastings**) was the **Henry T. Sloane House**. ♦ 7-9 E 72nd St (Madison-5th Aves)

152 La Maison du Chocolat From the acclaimed Parisian chocolatier, **Robert Linxe**, comes a shop for the true connoisseur. If the prices make you flinch, remember these are among the best chocolates in the world. ♦ 25 E 73rd St (5th Ave) 744.7117

153 Fraser-Morris Delicacies There are dozens of gourmet food stores in New York, but this is the original. It is still the best source for cheeses, quiches and imported treats. The bakery is excellent. ♦ 931 Madison Ave (E 74th) 288.2727. Also at: 1264 3rd Ave. 288.7717

154 Petit Bateau French children's clothing from a variety of designers, including **Petit Bateau, Dan Jean** and **Tartine et Chocolat**. Pure cotton footsies, T-shirts, nightgowns and pants in mushrooms, dolphin, polka dot and stripe patterns plus classic sweaters, snowsuits, dresses, pants and rompers. ♦ Closed Su. 930 Madison Ave (E 74th St) 288.1444

155 Coco Pazzo ★★★$$$ **Pino Luongo** has done it again! After **Le Madri**, he has just opened a family-style Italian restaurant. Though it may seem premature for us to be rating the restaurant, judging from the homemade spaghetti with a rich ragout sauce and the illustrious crowds that are already flocking here, it holds great promise. ♦ Italian ♦ 23 E 74th St (5th-6th Aves) 794.0205

156 The Chocolate Soup Charming children's clothes and accessories crammed into a minuscule store directly across the street from the **Whitney**. The most renowned item is the **Danish Souperbag**, an imported schoolbag that's as popular with adults (I own 3) as with their children. Great sales. ♦ 946 Madison Ave (E 74th-E 75th Sts) 861.2210

156 D.F. Sanders An uptown branch of the well-stocked SoHo high-tech housewares store is bringing its industrial look to the Silk-Stocking District. ♦ 952 Madison Ave (E 75th St) 879.6161. Also at: 386 W. Broadway. 925.9040

157 Books & Co. General bookstore with the focus on literature, literary periodicals and the complete works of many major writers. The leather sofa in the philosophy section is a welcome retreat for weary shoppers and museumgoers. Autographed books, literary events. ♦ 939 Madison Ave (E 74th St) 737.1450

157 Whitney Museum of American Art (1966, **Marcel Breuer** with **Hamilton Smith**) **Gertrude Vanderbilt Whitney**, a sculptor herself, founded this museum in 1931 to support young artists and increase awareness of American art. The nucleus of its collection was 600 of the works she owned by **Thomas Hart Benton, George Bellows, Maurice Prendergast, Edward Hopper, John Sloan** and other American artists of the era. The present building is the museum's third home.

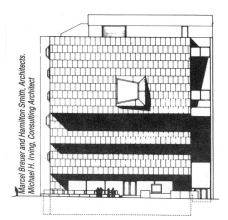

Marcel Breuer and Hamilton Smith, Architects.
Michael H. Irving, Consulting Architect

Like the **Guggenheim**, the Whitney is more sculpture than building. A dark rectilinear Brutalist mass steps out toward the street, almost threatening those who want to enter. Only the drawbridge entrance seems protective. The museum, perched on the corner, is isolated from its surroundings by sidewalls. You can peer down into the sunken sculpture garden and see through to parts of the lobby. But otherwise, the interior's workings are a mystery, guarded by angled trapezoidal windows that refuse to look you in the eye. (A proposed addition by **Michael Graves** has been held up by opposition from the Whitney's neighbors, who don't look forward to more such bulk.) The vast gallery spaces are surprisingly flexible, and can be quite appropriate for a variety of types of art—an important quality for a museum dedicated to temporary exhibitions of contemporary art. The permanent collection, which has been increased to 8000 pieces through gifts and acquisitions, includes **Calder, Nevelson, O'Keeffe, Rauschenberg, Reinhardt** and **Johns**, among others, and a portion of it is always on display. Special exhibitions often concentrate on the output of a single artist. It could be video artist of the '80s **Nam Jun Paik**, or Realist of the '30s Edward Hopper. The Whitney's regular invitational **Biennial**, which critics often pan, is a mixed bag of what's going on across the country. The museum has an aggressively independent series for American film and video artists, and makes adventurous forays into the performing arts. For information on these and gallery lectures, check the information desk. A restaurant overlooking the sculpture garden is a pleasant place for refreshments and light meals. The museum and its branches, including one at **Champion International Corp** in Stamford CT, owe much of their spirit and point of view to former director **Thomas Armstrong III**. (**David Ross** was appointed director in early 1991.) (The Whitney also maintains smaller exhibition spaces at the **Philip Morris Building**, Park Ave at 42nd St, at **Equitable Center**, 7th Ave at 51st St and at **Federal Reserve Plaza**, 37 Maiden Ln at Nassau St.) ◆ Admission. Tu 1-8PM; W-Sa 11AM-5PM; Su noon-6PM; free Tu 6-8PM. Madison Ave at E 75th St. 570.3676

158 Harkness House (1905, **Hale & Rogers**) Built for **Edward S. Harkness**, son of a **Standard Oil Co** founder. It is now headquarters of the **Commonwealth Fund**, a philanthropic foundation. ◆ 1 E 75th St (5th Ave)

159 Delorenzo Furniture of the Art Deco era may include pieces by such designers as **Emile Rouhlmann, Jean Dunand** and **Pierre Chareau.** ◆ Closed Su. 958 Madison Ave (E 75th St) 249.7575

159 Givenchy For women who want their haute couture brought to their doorstep, this boutique sends fitters from the **House of Givenchy** in Paris to New York each spring and fall to measure their local clients from stem to stern. Their clothes can be picked up on either side of the Atlantic. For others, there are blouses, skirts, sweaters, coats, suits, ball gowns and hats from both ready-to-wear and couture-adaptations, which feature the same styles as in the couture collection in less expensive fabrics. ◆ Closed Sa-Su. 21 E 75th St (Madison Ave) 772.1322

160 The Surrey $$$$ A small apartment-hotel in the Manhattan East group in a fashionable 70s block. The large rooms are tastefully decorated, and room service is from **Les Pleiades**, a French restaurant favored by the staff of the nearby **Whitney Museum** and other artwork movers and shakers. ◆ 20 E 76th St (Madison Ave) 288.3700, 800/637.8483; fax 628.1549

161 Carlyle Hotel $$$$ (1929, **Bien & Prince**) **John F. Kennedy** used to stay here, and the jet set still does. At 38 stories, the Carlyle soars above the East Side. Decorous charm and easy elegance pervade the premises; it is always at the top of someone's list of *Best New York City Hotels*, and one of the few hotels tolerated by those who are used to the grand European style. For them, the Tower apart-

East Side

ments seem to fill the bill for short stays or as permanent residences. From the custom-blended soap to the Chinese-red lacquered **Gallery**, it's a class act. Pianist **Bobby Short** has made the **Café Carlyle** famous, but his frequent substitutes are popular too. **Bemelmans Bar**, named for illustrator **Ludwig Bemelmans** who painted the murals here, features jazz singer/pianist **Barbara Carroll**, but the music is more for background than in Café Carlyle, where the audience maintains complete silence. Bemelmans is the more relaxed and less expensive of the pair. The Gallery is recommended for people-watching at tea time. The **Carlyle Restaurant** serves an elegant dinner. ◆ Deluxe ◆ 35 E 76th St (Madison Ave) 744.1600, 800/227.5737; fax 717.4682

Restaurants/Nightlife: Red   **Hotels:** Blue
Shops/Parks: Green   **Sights/Culture:** Black

221

162 William Secord Gallery William Secord, former director of the **Dog Museum** (now located in St. Louis), operates this gallery devoted to man's best friend. Exhibitions may also include cats and other barnyard animals. ♦ Tu-Sa 10AM-5PM. 52 E 76th St (Park-Madison Aves) 3rd floor. 249.0075

163 The Mark $$$$ An elegant and intimate luxury hotel boasting 18th-century Piranesi prints, feather pillows, VCRs, marble bathrooms, terry-cloth robes, heated towel racks and a good restaurant. Most of the 186 rooms have their own kitchen. ♦ 25 E 77th St (Madison Ave) 744.4300, 800/843.6275; fax 744.2749

Within The Mark:

Mark's ★$$$ A spacious, tranquil, softly lit dining room attended by a gracious staff. Recommended are sirloin steak with 3 peppers, roasted red snapper, farfalle with chanterelles and mixed vegetables and a lobster baked potato. ♦ French ♦ Reservations recommended. 879.1864

164 Sant Umbroeus ★★★$$$$ Elegant Italian fare followed by the best cappuccino and espresso around. Fusilli with onions and vegetables is a particularly well turned-out first course. Wonderful pastries—chestnut cake, chocolate mousse. ♦ Italian ♦ 1000 Madison Ave (E 77th-E 78th Sts) Reservations recommended. 570.2211

165 James B. Duke House (1912, **Horace Trumbauer**) A copy of an 18th-century chateau in Bordeaux, this mansion was built for the founder of the **American Tobacco Co**. It was given to New York University in 1959 by Duke's widow and her daughter, **Doris** (who, along with **Barbara Hutton**, was known as a *poor little rich girl* in the 1930s), and is now **NYU's Institute of Fine Arts**. Many of the

East Side

original furnishings are still here, including a **Gainsborough** portrait in the main hall. ♦ 1 E 78th St (5th Ave)

165 French Embassy (1906, **McKim, Mead & White**) This Italian Renaissance mansion, built for financier **Payne Whitney**, is typical of upper 5th Ave at the turn of the century before the arrival of massive apartment houses. ♦ 972 5th Ave (E 78th-E 79th Sts)

166 Acquavella One of the uptown heavy hitters showing 19th- and 20th-century European Masters and post-war American and European artists. ♦ M-F 10AM-5PM. 18 E 79th St (Madison Ave) 734.6300

166 Salander-O'Reilly Galleries Twentieth-century Modernist American painters of the **Stieglitz** group (**Alfred Maurer, Arthur Dove, Stuart Davis**) as well as bold, contemporary ones (**Susan Roth, Dan Christensen, John Greifen**). ♦ M-Sa 9:30AM-5:30PM. 20 E 79th St (Madison-5th Aves) 879.6606

167 Forum Twentieth-century figurative American paintings and sculpture. ♦ Tu-Sa 10AM-5:30PM. 1018 Madison Ave (E 78th St) 5th floor. 772.7666

167 Wittenborn Art Books Wide selection of art books; especially noted for scholarly works. ♦ Closed Su. 1018 Madison Ave (E 78th St) 2nd floor. 288.1558

167 Stuyvesant Fish House (1898, **McKim, Mead & White**) This Renaissance palace was once the scene of the city's most lavish parties. It was owned by **Stuyvesant Fish**, who was president of the Illinois Central Railroad. He and his wife, **Marion**, were prominent social leaders. ♦ 25 E 78th St (Madison Ave)

168 870 Park Avenue (1976, **Robert A.M. Stern** and **John S. Hagmann**) A total remodeling of an 1898 townhouse; the tripartite division of the facade alludes to that tradition and the scale of the surrounding buildings. In terms of styling, this is the next step after Modernism—see the **Lescaze Residence** and 112 E 64th St—and it holds its own. ♦ E 77th St

169 Lenox Hill Hospital (Uris Pavilion 1975, **Rogers, Butler, Burgun & Bradbury**) A hodgepodge of conflicting buildings covering a square block, providing yet another good reason to protect your health so you won't have to spend any time here. ♦ E 76th-E 77th Sts (Lexington-Park Aves) 439.2345

170 St. Jean Baptiste Church (1913, **Nicholas Serracino**) This Roman Catholic church was founded by French Canadians in the area. It is a little overwrought, but charming. Among its best features is the French-style organ, one of the finest in any New York church. ♦ Lexington Ave at E 76th St. 288.5082

171 Mortimer's ★★$$$ The neighborhood watering hole of one of the wealthiest neighborhoods in the world. Nothing pretentious, just a tavern with simple food that is good, but not so good that it distracts from conversation. The bar is kept busy by captains of industry, fashionable ladies—many with well-known wardrobes—and as gossip columnist **Suzy** would say (and often does about the crowd here), *others too rich and famous to mention*. Always crowded evenings and for Sunday brunch. ♦ Continental ♦ 1057 Lexington Ave (E 75th St) Reservations required for 5 or more. 517.6400

172 Bonté There is hardly a pastry or cake that you won't find divine, but the specialty is extravagantly decorated cakes with exquisite marzipan and spun-sugar work. One of the 2 or 3 best bakers, and definitely the best éclairs, in Manhattan. ♦ Closed Su. 1316 3rd Ave (E 75th St) 535.2360

173 Jim McMullen's ★★$$$ A handsome, modern tavern and an enduring singles—and networking—spectacle. More a place to experience than for dining. The simply grilled fish, meat and poultry are all fresh and adequately prepared, but one doesn't come for gastronomic satisfaction. Sustenance, a good time and a good social and/or business contact usually seem quite enough. **Dustin Hoffman** waited tables here at the beginning of the film *Tootsie*. ♦ American ♦ 1341 3rd Ave (E 76th-E 77th Sts) 861.4700

173 **J. McLaughlin** This is the store for sophisticated preppies. For men, it has tweed jackets, Shetland sweaters, oxford cloth shirts and trench coats. For women, there is the demure look of shirts with Peter Pan collars, box-pleated skirts and cashmere cardigans. ♦ 1343 3rd Ave (E 76th-E 77th Sts) 879.9565. Also at: 976 2nd Ave. 308.4100; 1311 Madison Ave. 369.4830; 7 W 57th St. 755.7732

174 **Bobby Dazzler** Casual European sportswear and separates for men, including double-pleated trousers, Shetland sweaters and pure cotton shirts in subtle checks, stripes and plaids. ♦ 1450 2nd Ave (E 75th-E 76 Sts) 628.2287

174 **Galleria Hugo** **Hugo Ramirez** is the master of restoration of 19th-century antique lighting. His work (all done by hand) can be found in Gracie Mansion, city museums and historic homes around the country. ♦ By appointment only. 304 E 76th St (1st-2nd Aves) 288.8444

175 **Il Monello** ★★$$$ The in-depth Italian wine list is not only laudable, but applaudable. The food is for those who like show biz at the table. The decor is of a type sometimes called *Bronx Renaissance*. Try the *saltimbocca* (veal sautéed in wine, with Italian prosciutto and sage). ♦ Italian ♦ Closed Su. 1460 2nd Ave (E 76th-E 77th Sts) Jacket and reservations required. 535.9310

176 **Lion's Rock** $$$ A piece of the 19th-century park known as **Jones's Wood** still exists in the back garden of this restaurant. It is an outcropping of red granite, with a spring-fed miniwaterfall that was once a favorite picnic spot. In winter, the view of the rock is glorious from within the restaurant. ♦ American ♦ 316 E 77th St (1st-2nd Aves) Reservations recommended. 988.3610

177 **American Trash** Unless you've just turned legal drinking age and don't mind waiting forever to get in, go somewhere else for a drink. ♦ 1471 1st Ave (E 76th-E 77th Sts) No credit cards. 988.9008

178 **Et Cetera** $$ Although the oversized neon sign in the window and the Miami motif are a bit much, the crowd, food, service and jukebox are all quite decent. ♦ Mexican ♦ 1470 1st Ave (E 76th-E 77th Sts) 382.0122

179 **Café San Martin** $$$ About as good as Spanish food gets in Manhattan, which isn't stupendous. Open hospitality and live piano attract a following. ♦ Spanish ♦ 1458 1st Ave (E 76th St) Reservations recommended. 288.0470

179 **Voulez Vous** ★$$ A glass-fronted French bistro with tinted mirrors, comfortable seating and a handsome bar where you can sample wine while waiting for your table. Excellent brunch on Sunday with cheese soufflés, couscous salad and steak tartare. Dinners include traditional fare like steak *pommes frites*, stews, baked fish and, for dessert, excellent crème brûlée and flaky homemade fruit tarts. ♦ French ♦ 1462 1st Ave (E 76th St) 249.1776

180 **Vasata** $$ A bistro straight from the streets of Prague, serving thick schnitzels in a comfortable setting with gaily colored pottery, and beamed ceilings. ♦ Czechoslovakian ♦ Closed M. 339 E 75th St (1st-2nd Aves) 988.7166

181 **The Red Tulip** ★$$ Pleasant, if you can deal with the nearly relentless live Hungarian—and otherwise—folk music. The bright dining room in back of the more dimly lit bar is gaily decorated with old hand-painted pottery, wooden shelves and cabinets. Booths around the sides of the room provide some romantic privacy with high-backed natural-wood banquettes. All the food is amply portioned, of fresh ingredients and with lots of cooked-in depth of flavor: rich goulash soup, sour cream and double-smoked bacon, Hungarian sausage, braised veal shank with vegetables, stuffed cabbage and delicate *spaetzle* (noodles). I recommend you sample the dessert pancakes—slightly heavy, but delectable. Extremely good value. ♦ Hungarian ♦ Closed M-Tu. 439 E 75th St (York-1st Aves) Reservations recommended. 734.4893

East Side

182 **Frederic York Avenue Patisserie** The inventive chef **Frederic Piepenburg** fills his shop with an interesting array of pastries, including oregano croissants, pâté-filled brioches and reduced-calorie apple tarts. ♦ 1431 York Ave (E 76th St) 628.5576

183 **John Jay Park** A neighborhood park with an outdoor public pool open from the end of the school year until Labor Day. Bring a padlock. ♦ E 77th St at FDR Dr

184 **Cherokee Apartments** (1909, **Henry Atterbury Smith**) Built as model housing for the working class, these apartments are distinguished by the amount of light and air admitted by large casements and balconies—an unusual commodity in the days of *dumbbell* tenements. Walk through the vaulted tunnels into the central courtyards and study the detailing on the sheltered stairs at each corner that allow tenants to walk up in style. ♦ E 77th-E 78th Sts (York Ave-Cherokee Pl)

MARUZZELLA

185 Maruzzella ★$$ Enter this cheery pizzeria, and you'll feel like you're in Italy, in some out-of-the-way spot known only to the locals. The simple stucco interior and wood-burning oven add to the charm. Start with the heady *ricotta di bufala* cheese with strips of roasted bell pepper, then move on to the pastas. Chef **Giovanni Pinato** does wonders with ravioli stuffed with spinach and cheese. Of course, there are the pizzas—perfect crusts topped with creamy mozzarella, sausages, vegetables, ham. And the calzone. For dessert, tiramisu. ◆ Italian ◆ 1479 1st Ave (E 77th St) 988.8877

185 Catch a Rising Star Your chance to pick a comer at this famed training ground for new talent. Comedians **David Brenner, Robin Williams, Andy Kaufman, Richard Newman** and singer **Pat Benatar** all got their start at this tiny comedy club/cabaret. ◆ Cover, minimum. Shows: M-Th, Su continuous 9PM-closing; F 8:30, 11PM; Sa 7:30, 10PM, 12:30AM. 1487 1st Ave (E 77th St) 794.1906

186 Rigo Hungarian Pastry The strudels, cakes, tortes and other attractions here are legendary. ◆ 318 E 78th St (1st-2nd Aves) 988.0052

187 Caffe Bianco ★$$ The entrees are fine—pastas, salads, chicken dishes—but the desserts, especially the Valencia orange cake, and cappuccinos are sublime! And the pretty decor is as authentic as it gets this side of the Atlantic. ◆ Italian ◆ 1486 2nd Ave (E 77th-E 78th Sts) No credit cards. 988.2655

187 Lusardi ★★$$$ One of several informal, clublike uptown trattorias that attract a sleek, affluent crowd. The food at this one, however, is more reliable than at others, and the service more concerned. ◆ Italian ◆ 1494 2nd Ave (E 78th St) Reservations recommended. 249.2020

East Side

188 Quatorze Bis ★★★$$$ **Peter Meltzer** and **Mark DiGuilio** have taken their love of French bistro food uptown. The new place is a touch more elegant than the original downtown, but serves the same excellent bistro food. Here you should sample the best *choucroute garnie* in town (sauerkraut with smoky sausages, ham and pork chops) or the excellent sautéed *boudin blanc* (a white veal sausage served with a strong Dijon mustard). Roast chicken

also tastes quite interesting, simply roasted with herbs. ◆ French ◆ 323 E 79th St (1st-2nd Aves) 535.1414. Also at: 240 14th St. 106.7006

189 Dieci Ristorante ★$$$ A cozy, slightly clubby meeting place for the neighborhood clientele. The Italian menu offers classic entrees like grilled swordfish with anchovies and veal chops topped with tomatoes and arugula. Desserts include zabaglione with whatever fruit is in season and traditional cheesecake. ◆ Italian ◆ Closed Su. 1568 1st Ave (E 81st St) 628.6565

190 Pig Heaven ★$$ The theme is *pig*—on the walls, menus, you name it. But the food is fairly typical Chinese, not restricted to pork dishes as you might have thought. The prices are higher than standard Chinese fare, presumably for the pleasure of dining in this silly and fun pig-infested place. Not the place to bring an important client, but the in-crowd does enjoy the barnyard effect. ◆ Chinese ◆ 1540 2nd Ave (E 80th-E 81st Sts) Reservations recommended. 744.4333

190 Paprikas Weiss Paprika is among the hundreds of imported spices you'll find here, but the store is named for its founder, a Hungarian immigrant who first sold spices from a pushcart. The store sells prepared foods, imported ingredients for Hungarian cooking, and gourmet cooking utensils as well as fresh condiments. Everything they sell is available by mail. Ask for the catalog. ◆ Closed Su. 1546 2nd Ave (E 80th-E 81st Sts) 288.6117

190 Divino Ristorante ★$$ Service and pasta are high points of this unpretentious favorite of Italian expatriates. Best second course is the breaded veal chop Milanese. Try also the more casual **Café Divino** (1544 2nd Ave, 517.9269) and the homey **Gastronomia Divino** (1542 2nd Ave, 861.1533), a trattoria that also offers a takeout menu. All 3 serve wonderful cappuccino. ◆ Italian ◆ 1556 2nd Ave (E 80th-E 81st Sts) Reservations required. 861.1096

190 Istanbul Cuisine $ A small Turkish restaurant with no decor to speak of, but excellent kabobs and rich honey-soaked desserts. Also good are the stuffed grape leaves, eggplant dishes and the broiled fish. Authentic and cheap. ◆ Turkish ◆ 303 E 80th St (1st-2nd Aves) 744.6903

191 Diva $$ A charmingly decorated long and narrow room serving simple and honestly cooked Italian-style dishes. Appetizers and pastas are particularly successful. Not called Diva for nothing: late in the evening, patrons and waiters often sing at the piano in the center of the room. ◆ Italian ◆ Closed F. 306 E 81st St (1st-2nd Aves) 650.1928

192 The Comic Strip A showcase club for stand-up comics and singers. **Eddie Murphy, Jerry Steinfeld** and **Paul Reiser** started here, and sometimes a big name will drop by. ◆ Cover, minimum. Shows: M-Th, Su 9PM; F 9, 11PM; Sa 8:30, 11PM. 1568 2nd Ave (E 81st-E 82nd Sts) 861.9386

193 Sistina ★★$$$ The attractive clientele makes up for the minimal but subtly pretty decor, which has become so typical of East Side restaurants. Even if you speak fluent Italian, the menu is annoyingly difficult to decipher. But if you can figure out what to order, the food is quite good. Share the *rigatoni ai quattro formaggi* (pasta with 4 cheeses) as an appetizer, then try the excellent *Sisto IV* (grilled herbed chicken) as your main dish. ♦ Italian ♦ 1555 2nd Ave (E 80th-E 81st Sts) Reservations required. 861.7660

194 Border Café $$ This is the original Border Café (its larger offspring is further uptown). Fajitas, nachos, chilis, chicken wings and, of course, frozen margaritas are the main draw here. The kitchen closes at midnight. ♦ Southwestern ♦ 244 E 79th St (2nd-3rd Aves) Reservations recommended. 535.4347. Also at: 2637 Broadway. 749.8888

195 New York Public Library, Yorkville Branch (1902, *Mames Brown Lord*) This rather academic Neoclassical building is the earliest of what are known as the *Carnegie Libraries*. There are 65 of these small branch libraries throughout the city, established by a donation from **Andrew Carnegie**. Later ones, similar in style, were designed by Lord and other distinguished architects such as **McKim, Mead & White, Carrère & Hastings** and **Babb, Cook & Willard**. ♦ M noon-8PM; Tu 10AM-6PM; W-Th noon-6PM; Sa 10AM-5PM. 222 E 79th St (2nd-3rd Aves) 744.5824

196 The Living Room A supper club frequented by young Upper East Siders who start the evening at the Victorian-style bar, eat upstairs in a dining room decorated with equestrian prints and Persian rugs and return downstairs around 11PM when the louder music beckons. ♦ Continental ♦ 154 E 79th St (3rd-Lexington Aves) 772.8488

197 Parma $$$ This plain-looking room was the first of the *in* uptown Italian trattorias. Others, newer, have surpassed it in popularity, but even so, the kitchen maintains its standards. The pastas are generally well prepared, the Italian-style vegetables—fully cooked and at room temperature—are brightly flavored. Have a grappa instead of dessert. ♦ Italian ♦ 1404 3rd Ave (E 79th St) Reservations recommended. 535.3520

197 Sam's Cafe $$$ A busy cafe with 2 large rooms. The front room is for the young crowd, while the back hosts a more mature clientele. Sam serves a good hamburger and some tasty sandwiches and salads. On the dinner menu, the sautéed foie gras with wild mushrooms is fairly good, as are the escargots. Among the main courses the grilled fish is the best choice. The desserts—including homemade fruit tarts—are better here than in some of the more elegant restaurants. ♦ Cafe ♦ 1406 3rd Ave (E 80th St) 988.5300

198 Tirami su ★$$ A fashionable Italian cafe filled with a crowd that is determined to have a good time, but really does care about the food. Excellent homemade pastas with strong zesty sauces, boutique pizzas with classic and unusual toppings, some acceptable salads and real Italian desserts served with excellent espresso. ♦ Italian ♦ 1410 3rd Ave (E 80th St) 988.9780

198 Anatolia ★★★$$$ One of the few Turkish restaurants in the city. Start with stuffed baby eggplant with garlic, onion and tomatoes, or air-dried beef cured with a touch of cumin, garlic and red pepper. My favorite main courses are the skewers of boned quail wrapped in leaves and the broiled *kafta*. Desserts are typical Middle Eastern, except for the puddings, which are made on the premises, and excellent Turkish coffee, which is served on brass trays. ♦ Turkish ♦ 1422 3rd Ave (E 80th-E 81st Sts) 517.6262

199 La Metairie ★$$$ An expensive bistro with an authentic country French decor and a fireplace. The unmistakably French menu includes a correct cassoulet, a tender steak *aux poivres* with thin *frites*, a well-spiced rare rack of lamb and the traditional coq au vin. For dessert, there are excellent fruit tarts and crème caramel. ♦ French ♦ 1442 3rd Ave (E 82nd St) 988.1800

200 Garasole ★$$$ Conservative East Siders dine at this dependable, noisy Italian restaurant located on the ground floor of a brownstone. Poultry and game dishes, like chicken sautéed with lemon, and grilled organic cornish hens with peppercorns, are best. ♦ Italian ♦ 151 E 82nd St (3rd-Lexington Aves) Dinner reservations required. 772.6690

200 Le Refuge ★★$$$ Bare wooden tables, kitchen towels for napkins, American stone-

East Side

ware and etched stemware provide a mood of romantic, rustic elegance. The ever changing menu is prepared with carefully chosen fresh ingredients and cooked with a sure and brilliant seasoning hand. Fish dishes are particularly delectable, and some consider the bouillabaisse the best in town. ♦ French ♦ 166 E 82nd St (3rd-Lexington Aves) Reservations recommended. No credit cards. 861.4505

201 Big City Kite Co., Inc. You'll find over 150 different kinds of kites here. They come in a variety of shapes, including tigers, teddy bears, sailboats, sharks, dragons and bats. There are octopus kites for toddlers, stunt kites for experienced fliers, and for most first-timers, a 6ft Delta. The proprietors, whose stock is about as ambitious as you'd care to get, can arrange parties for kite-flying lessons and shows. They will also guide you to nearby kite flights. ♦ Closed Su. 1201 Lexington Ave (E 81st-E 82nd Sts) 472.2623

Restaurants/Nightlife: Red   **Hotels:** Blue
Shops/Parks: Green   **Sights/Culture:** Black

202 Rosenthal Wine Merchant Unique wine finds from California and Europe (specializing in Burgundies). ♦ Closed Su. 1200 Lexington Ave (E 81st-E 82nd Sts) 249.6650

202 Jenny B. Goode A remarkably successful store with an odd but somehow appealing mixture of leather handbags, imported teapots, open stock of the French **Gien** and **D'Auteuil** porcelains, glassware and toys. ♦ Closed Su. 1194 Lexington Ave (E 81st-E 82nd Sts) 794.2492. Also at: 11 E 10th St. 505.7666

203 Johnny Jupiter A whimsical mixture of antiques and period kitsch, including **Steiff** stuffed animals for  children, and expensive dolls for adults or collectors. ♦ Closed Su. 1185 Lexington Ave (E 80th-E 81st Sts) 744.0818

204 Junior League of The City of New York (1928, **Mott B. Schmidt**) This sophisticated Regency-style mansion, one of a trio of perfect neighbors, was built for **Vincent Astor**. The other 2 are Schmidt's Georgian house for **Clarence Dillon** (1930) at 124 E 80th St, and the Federal-style **George Whitney House** (1930) at 120 E 80th St, by **Cross & Cross**. ♦ 130 E 80th St (Lexington-Park Aves)

205 Lewis Spencer Morris House (1923, **Cross & Cross**) The original owner, a direct descendant of a signer of the Declaration of Independence, significantly chose the Federal style for this townhouse. ♦ 116 E 80th St (Lexington-Park Aves)

206 Hanae Mori (1969; renovations, **Hans Hollein**) A striking balance of stucco front and off-center chrome cylinder, this slightly mysterious storefront is Hollein's first work in

East Side

Manhattan. Inside is the retail outlet for Mori's sophisticated Japanese-influenced women's clothing. ♦ Closed Su. 27 E 79th St (Madison-5th Aves) 472.2352

207 The Gibbon ★★$$$ I think this must be one of the oddest restaurants ever created: French and Japanese at the same time. The food, served in a tranquil setting, is beautifully prepared and extremely fresh. The Japanese appetizers are outstanding. ♦ French/Japanese ♦ Closed Su. 24 E 80th St (Madison-5th Aves) Jacket, tie and reservations required. 861.4001

208 E.A.T. ★★$$$ All the breads are made with a sourdough starter, including the famous *ficelle*, a crusty 22in long loaf with a diameter that is barely larger than a silver dollar's. The prices are stunning, but so is the quality of most of the cheeses, breads, salads, pastries, cakes, etc. Everyone gets the same, rather arrogant, service. Owned by **Eli Zabar**. ♦ American ♦ 1064 Madison Ave (E 80th-E 81st Sts) 772.0022

209 Frank E. Campbell Funeral Chapel Possibly the most prestigious funeral chapel in the world. In this building, the world has said farewell to **Elizabeth Arden, James Cagney, Jack Dempsey, Tommy Dorsey, Judy Garland, Howard Johnson, Robert F. Kennedy, John Lennon, J.C. Penney, Damon Runyon, Arturo Toscanini, Mae West** and **Tennessee Williams**, to name-drop just a few. ♦ 1076 Madison Ave (E 81st St) 288.3500

209 Burlington Book Shop Jane Trichter runs this neighborly bookstore, a fixture in the neighborhood for the last 50 years. Upstairs is the out-of-print department. Downstairs is **Burlington Antique Toys**, a dusty basement shop full of antique and vintage racing cars, tin soldiers, wooden boats and more. ♦ 1082 Madison Ave (E 81st-E 82nd Sts) 288.7420

210 Parioli Romanissimo ★★★$$$$ One of the most refined Italian kitchens in town, located in a charming townhouse. The delicate egg pasta is seriously divine, the fish entrees impeccable. Because it is run like a private club for favored patrons, it is often difficult to get a reservation. ♦ Italian ♦ Closed Su. 24 E 81st St (Madison-5th Ave) Jacket, tie and reservations required. 288.2391

211 The Stanhope Hotel $$$$ (1926, **Rosario Candela**) Strategically located across the street from the **Metropolitan Museum** and **Central Park**, the Stanhope has been freshened up without great disturbance to its gentility. The rooms (nearly all suites), decorated in the French style, have such amenities as in-room safes and multiple telephones. Room service and valet service are available 24hrs a day, and limousine service is provided to Lincoln Center and the Theater District. Rooms facing the museum and the park are particularly choice. **Le Salon** and the **Dining Room** are favorite escapes from museum overload. **Gerard's** is for those in need of stronger medicine. ♦ 995 5th Ave (E 81st St) 288.5800, 800/828.1123; fax 517.0088

212 998 Fifth Avenue (1912, **McKim, Mead & White**) This apartment building in the guise of an Italian Renaissance palazzo was built when the bulk of society lived in mansions up and down the avenue. The largest apartment here has 25 rooms; it was originally leased by **Murray Guggenheim**. ♦ E 81st St

212 1001 Fifth Avenue (1978, **Philip Birnbaum**; facade, **Philip Johnson/John Burgee**) An average apartment tower has been upgraded with a limestone facade. Half-round ornamental molding relates horizontally to the neighboring 998 5th Ave, while the mullions struggle for a vertical emphasis, pointing at the mansard-shaped cut-out roof. The distinctive silhouette is best admired from across the park. Up close, its one-dimensional character takes precedence; from the back you can see the struts bracing the facade like stage jacks bracing a scenery flat. ♦ E 81st-E 82nd Sts

213 Metropolitan Museum of Art (1880, **Calvert Vaux** and **Jacob Wrey Mould**; southwest wing 1888, **Theodore Weston**; north wing 1894, **Arthur Tuckerman**; central facade 1902, **Richard Morris Hunt, Richard Howland Hunt** and **George B. Post**; 5th Ave wings 1906, **McKim, Mead & White**; stairs, pool, Lehman Wing and Great Hall renovations 1970, **Kevin Roche, John Dinkeloo & Associates**; later additions, 1975-87, Kevin Roche, John Dinkeloo & Associates) Ten years after the first section was finished at the edge of Central Park, **Frederick Law Olmsted**, the park's designer, said he regretted having allowed it to be built there. He should see it now. The Met has grown to 1.4 million sq ft of floor space (more than 32 acres), with some 3.3 million works of art, making it the largest art museum in the Western Hemisphere. It seems to be expanding, building and getting better every day (much of this growth must be credited to director **Phillipe de Montebello**). A visit is essential!

Founded in 1870 by a group of art-collecting financiers and industrialists who were on the art committee of New York's **Union League Club**, the Metropolitan's original collection was a group of 174 paintings, mostly Dutch and Flemish, and a gift of antiquities from **General di Cesnola**, former US consul to Cyprus.

The newest additions, including the **Lila Acheson Wallace Wing** (20th-century art) with its beautiful roof garden, provide a dramatic contrast of high-tech glass curtain walls to the solid limestone Beaux-Arts front. Like an irresistible force meeting an immovable object, the result is fascinating. The new interiors are spectacular too, contrasting but not fighting with **Richard Morris Hunt**'s equally spectacular **Great Hall**, just inside the main entrance.

The list of benefactors who have swelled the museum's holdings over the years reads like a *Who's Who* of the city's First Families—**Morgan, Rockefeller, Altman, Marquand, Hearn, Bache, Lehman**. The push to house the collection in style has produced the **Sackler Wing** (1979) for the **Raymond R. Sackler Far East Art** collection; the entire Egyptian **Temple of Dendur** (1978), given to the people of the US for their support in saving monuments threatened by the construction of the Aswan High Dam; **Egyptian Galleries** (1983) for the Met's world-class permanent collection; the impressive **Michael C. Rockefeller Wing** (1982) for the art of Africa, the Americas and the Pacific Islands; the **Douglas Dillon Galleries of Chinese Painting** (1983) and **Astor Chinese Garden Court** (1980), with a reception hall from the home of a 16th-century scholar; an expanded and dramatically redesigned **American Wing** (1980); and the **Lehman Wing** (1975), displaying its collection of paintings, drawings and

decorative objects in rooms re-created from the original Lehman townhouse on W 54th St.

The permanent collection (about a third of which can be displayed at any one time) is expanding in every department. The museum already has the most comprehensive collection of American art in the world, and excels in Egyptian, Greek and Roman, and European art, including arms and armor, ranging from medieval to 20th-century. The list of priceless art and artifacts within these walls is almost too incredible to comprehend.

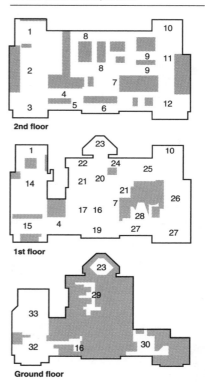

2nd floor

1st floor

Ground floor

1 Wallace Wing: 20th-century Art, 2 19th-century European Painting and Sculpture, 3 Islamic Art, 4 Greek and Roman Art, 5 Ancient Near Eastern Art, 6 Asian Art, 7 Gift Shop, 8 European Paintings, 9 Musical Instruments, 10 American Wing, 11 Japanese Galleries, 12 Chinese Paintings/Garden Court, 13 Ancient China, 14 Rockefeller Wing: Art of Africa/Americas/Pacific Islands, 15 Restaurant, 16 Library, 17 16th-century Spanish Patio, 18 Main Entrance, 19 Great Hall, 20 Medieval Art, 21 European Sculpture/Decorative Arts, 22 French Period Rooms, 23 Lehman Collection, 24 English Period Rooms, 25 American Wing Garden Court, 26 Sackler Wing/Temple of Dendur, 27 Egyptian Art, 28 Rogers Auditorium, 29 European Decorative Arts, 30 Costume Institute, 31 81st St Entrance, 32 Uris Center, 33 Garage

McKim, Mead & White

The **Costume Institute**, which has 35,000 articles of clothing in its collection, displays them in stylish theme exhibitions dreamed up by curator **Jean Druesedow**. And there are always special temporary blockbuster exhibitions you won't want to miss.

The **Information Desk** in the center of the Great Hall has floor plans and a helpful staff to direct you. They also have information about concerts and lectures in the museum's **Grace Rainey Rogers Auditorium**, and will help you arrange for a staff-guided tour, available in several languages. At the north end of the Great Hall, tape-recorded tours of most of the exhibitions are available for rental. Just off the Great Hall is the justly famous book and gift shop. In addition to art books, it offers postcards, slides, prints and high-quality reproductions of the art and artifacts in the Met's collection, including jewelry, sculpture, ceramics and fabric designs turned into scarves, blouses, neckties and desk accessories. It is also a source of unique toys and diversions for children.

The **Museum Restaurant** is a hectic, cafeteria-style arrangement with tables around a pool. A little-known resource is weekend brunch in the adjoing **Dining Room**, which, during the week, is only open to sponsors and patrons.

The museum's recently instituted Friday and Saturday evening hours have added a touch of civility and grace to the hectic city scene. Many of the museum's employees take advantage of the tranquil twilight hours, when beginning at 5PM, a string quartet serenades them from the Great Hall balcony, where a bar and candlelit tables are set up for their relaxation. Evening educational offerings—art lectures and documetaries—coincide with the concerts in the Grace Rainey Rogers Auditorium. ♦ Admission. Tu-Th, Su 9:30AM-5:15PM; F-Sa 9:30AM-8:45PM. 5th Ave at E 82nd St. 535.7710

East Side

214 **Diletto** Parisian Art Deco jewelry and Art Nouveau lapel pins—jetted, enameled and studded with ritzy rhinestones for that genuine heirloom look. ♦ Closed Su. 1100 Madison Ave (E 83rd St) 628.6415

214 **William Greenberg Jr., Inc.** Towering chocolate cakes decorated with whipped cream and chocolate wafers must be ordered months ahead. All the other buttery American-style goods go fast. ♦ Closed Su. 1100 Madison Ave (E 82nd-E 83rd Sts) 744.0304. Also at: 1377 3rd Ave. 861.1340; 912 7th Ave. 307.5930

215 **Eeyore's** Children of all ages will love browsing through this extensive selection of books while their elders get expert help with gift choices. ♦ 25 E 83rd St (Madison Ave) 988.3404. Also at: 2212 Broadway. 362.0634

216 **3 East 84th Street** (1928, **Raymond Hood**) A jewel of a small apartment house in gray stone, with Art Deco details designed by Raymond Hood—before **Rockefeller Center**. ♦ Madison-5th Aves

217 **The YIVO Institute for Jewish Research** (1914, **Carrère & Hastings**) The explorations of this organization (**Yidisher Visnschaftlekher Institut**) cover all aspects of Jewish life. It has the world's largest collections of books, letters and manuscripts in Yiddish, some dating back to 1600. Changing lobby displays reflect the institute's work, and its extensive library is open for browsing. ♦ M-Tu, Th-F 9:30AM-5:30PM. 1048 5th Ave (E 86th St) 535.6700

218 **Summer House** ★$$$ A charming setting with somewhat amateurish entrees, but excellent home-baked desserts. ♦ American ♦ 50 E 86th St (Park-Madison Aves) Reservations recommended. 249.6300

219 **Church of St. Ignatius Loyola** (1898, **Ditmars & Schickel**) An overscaled Vignoia facade on Park Ave. Its flat limestone late-Renaissance style looks very comfortable here—and it is a welcome change from all that Gothic. ♦ 980 Park Ave (E 84th St)

220 **Trastevere 84** ★★$$$ Smaller, quieter, less well turned-out version of **Trastevere**, but a good option when the other is crowded. ♦ Italian ♦ Closed F. 155 E 84th St (Lexington Ave) Reservations required. 744.0210

221 **Cafe Geiger** ★$$ This cozy place serves full meals such as *bauernwurst* with sauerkraut, and schnitzels. But the real reason for dropping in here are the strudels, tortes, cakes and other dessert specialties set before your eyes as soon as you enter. ♦ German ♦ 206 E 86th St (2nd-3rd Aves) 734.4428

221 **Kleine Konditorei** ★$$$ Sauerbraten, Wiener schnitzel, roast goose and *natur schnitzel* are all specialties here, along with potato pancakes and pastries. Not for the diet-conscious. ♦ German ♦ 234 E 86th St (2nd-3rd Aves) 737.7130

221 **Ideal** $ The sign outside is almost bigger than this little lunch counter/restaurant. The portions are huge, the prices amazingly low. ♦ German ♦ 238 E 86th St (2nd-3rd Aves) 535.0950

221 **Elk Candy Company** Search for the moist chocolate-covered marzipan behind the sweet disorder of owner **Albert Hadener**'s East Side institution. ♦ 240 E 86th St (2nd-3rd Aves) 650.1177

222 **Estia** ★★$$$ Fresh and always satisfying Greek food in a typical, noisy trattoria setting. Tuesday through Sunday, at about 8:30PM, the live music starts; by about 10, when the instrumentalists are joined by singers, conversation becomes impossible. The Greek antipasto for 2 is the best introduction to a hearty meal. I also suggest fried zucchini with a wondrous almond-garlic sauce for dipping. The standard specialties are all first-rate, which is why Greeks throng here. ♦ Greek ♦ Closed M. 308 E 86th St (1st-2nd Aves) Reservations required on weekends. 628.9100

222 Schaller & Weber This incredible store is filled from floor to ceiling with cold cuts. They are piled on counters, packed into display cases, and hung from the walls and ceilings. ◆ Closed Su. 1654 2nd Ave (E 85th-E 86th Sts) 879.3047

223 Paola ★$$$ A delightful Northern Italian restaurant with excellent pasta, especially the tortellini, good hearty soups, good veal dishes and creamy cheesecake for dessert. The room is noisy but the atmosphere is pleasant and intimate. ◆ Italian ◆ 347 E 85th St (1st-2nd Aves) 794.1890

224 Elio's ★★$$$ Serious Wall Streeters and bankers mix easily with media types and celebs at this *in* neighborhood eatery, a spin-off of the ever popular **Elaine's**. It's always crowded, always noisy and the food is always just okay. Stick with the specials, which seem to steal the kitchen's attention away from the regular menu. ◆ Italian ◆ 1621 2nd Ave (E 84th-E 85th Sts) Reservations recommended. 772.2242

225 Vico ★★$$$ A plain storefront restaurant that has been officially discovered: translated, this means delicious, moderately priced food and a long wait for tables. ◆ Italian ◆ 1603 2nd Ave (E 83rd-E 84th Sts) Reservations required. No credit cards. 772.7441

226 Erminia ★★$$$ Crowning achievements are Tuscan grilled lamb or pasta in lush sauces. The romantic candlelit atmosphere makes Erminia a popular place—reserve your table a couple of days in advance. ◆ Italian ◆ Closed Su. 250 E 83rd St (2nd-3rd Aves) Reservations required. 879.4284

227 Mocca Hungarian $$ Treat yourself to hearty Hungarian home-cooking that will please your purse as well as your palate. The portions are more than generous and the prices are impossibly low. As expected, the Wiener schnitzel and strudel are most satisfying. ◆ Hungarian ◆ 1588 2nd Ave (E 82nd-E 83rd Sts) No credit cards. 734.6470

228 Trastevere ★★$$$ Whenever you open a space that's small enough to legitimately exclude almost everyone from tasting your hearty Italian cooking, everyone and his cousin want to come. So call way ahead, then expect an affluent, casual crowd of heavy-duty garlic eaters, lots of noise, confusion and—despite it all—good humor. ◆ Italian ◆ 309 E 83rd St (1st-2nd Aves) Reservations required. 734.6343

229 AccScentiques Decorative and fragrant accents for the home—tapestry and moiré pillows, hand-painted boxes and mirrors, a bamboo desk and chair, sachets, dried flowers and potpourri—are squeezed into this petite boutique. ◆ Closed M-Tu. 351 E 82nd St (1st-2nd Aves) 288.3289

230 Primavera ★★$$$$ One of the great watering holes for the older, distinguished smart set—people whose money is so quiet, you can hear a diamond drop. They find honest food here, but nothing extraordinary. ◆ Italian ◆ 1578 1st Ave (E 82nd St) Jacket, tie and reservations required. 861.8608

231 Wilkinson's 1573 Seafood Café ★★$$ The interior is relaxed and intimate, with pastel-colored murals adorning the bare-brick walls. Warmed oysters in orange butter, sea bass and Chinese chicken in raspberry vinegar are just a few winning dishes. A little gem of a restaurant. ◆ Seafood ◆ 1573 York Ave (E 83rd St) 535.5454

232 Bistro Bamboche ★$$$ Just a smidgen of a place, where stylish French food is prepared to order by 2 siblings straight from Gdansk, Poland. I hope you'll save room for the heavenly dessert soufflés. ◆ French ◆ Closed Su. 1582 York Ave (E 83rd-E 84th Sts) Reservations recommended. 249.4002

233 Sirabella ★★$$ This neighborhood Italian restaurant is always packed because of its authentic homecooking, especially the fresh pasta made-in-*case*. On cold winter nights the rich textured soups are a must, as is the crisp calamari. The osso buco is delectable, and even the vegetables, the cooked escarole, for example, are redolent of garlic and olive oil. Desserts are overly sweet Italian concoctions, but the espresso is superb. ◆ Italian ◆ 72 East End Ave (82nd-83rd Sts) 988.6557

234 Carl Schurz Park (Remodeled 1938, **Harvey Stevenson** and **Cameron Clark**) The park, on land acquired by the city in 1891, was named in 1911 for **Carl Schurz**, a German immigrant who served as a general during the Civil War, was a senator from Missouri and secretary of the interior under **President Rutherford B. Hayes**, and went on to become editor of the *New*

East Side

York Evening Post and *Harper's Weekly*. The park is a delightful edge to the neighborhood of Yorkville. It is not very large, but its distinct sections and the varied topography make a walk here rewarding. The promenade along the East River above FDR Dr is named for **John Finley**, a former editor of *The New York Times* and an enthusiastic walker. **Gracie Mansion**, the residence of the mayor of New York City, occupies the center of the north end of the park.

Across the river is Astoria, Queens; spanning the river are the **Triborough Bridge** and **Hell Gate** railroad trestle; **Wards Island, Randalls Island**; the yellow building is **Manhattan State Mental Hospital** and the little island that looks like an elephant's head is known as **Mill Rock**. The lighthouse seen at the end of **Roosevelt Island** was designed by **James Renwick Jr**. This point of the river is a treacherous confluence of currents from the Harlem River, Long Island Sound and the harbor—hence the name Hell Gate. ◆ East End Ave (E 84th-E 90th Sts)

Upper East Side

The **Upper East Side** (bounded by 86th and 110th Sts, 5th Ave and the **East River**) has a heavy concentration of townhouses, deluxe apartment buildings, residential hotels and recycled mansions, interspersed with churches, clubs, museums, boutiques, restaurants and gourmet takeout stores.

Most of the great mansions of Park and 5th Aves and the cross streets between were built between 1900 and 1920, when the Classical tradition was in flower, so they all exhibit Neo-Georgian, Neo-Federal, Neo-French or Neo-Italian Renaissance styling. The original owners were **Whitneys, Astors, Straights, Dillons, Dukes, Mellons, Pulitzers** and **Harknesses**. It was an era of lavish balls and of *the 400* (so named because **Mrs. William Astor** could accommodate only 400 of her closest friends comfortably at one time).

Construction of apartment houses and hotels followed the mansions in a wave that began in 1881 and ended in 1932. The churches were almost all erected between 1890 and 1920. Although there are still isolated blocks of row houses from the late 1860s to 1880s, as well as a few Colonial relics and some contemporary buildings, the look, especially in the western part of the district, is

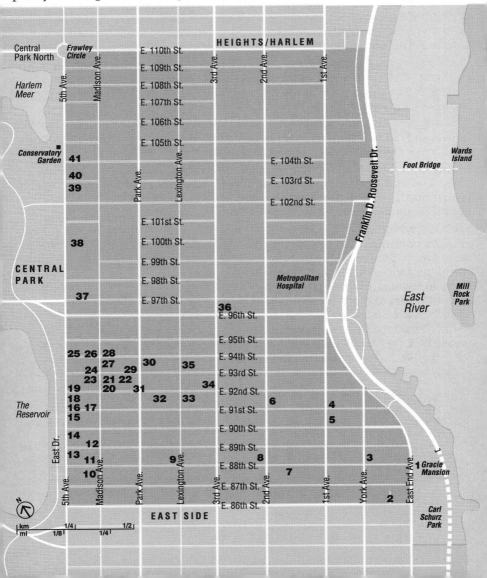

generally more uniform than elsewhere in the city. The reason for the relatively late start in populating this area is that, except for the German village of **Yorkville**, it was all open country. At the time work started on **Central Park** in 1857, it was still full of farms and squatters' shanties, and pigs grubbed on 5th Ave. Even after the park opened in 1863, steam trains chugging along the cut in Park Ave made this an undesirable residential neighborhood. But in 1907, when the **New York Central Railroad** electrified the trains and covered the Park Ave tracks, the Upper East Side took off as a place for the well-to-do to live.

Fifth Ave facing Central Park is New York City's *street of parades,* and the most elegant of the avenues. A few new buildings have been slipped into the unbroken front that progressed up 5th Ave north of Grand Army Plaza. *Museum Mile* begins at the heroic **Metropolitan Museum** on the park side of 5th Ave, and ends with the **Museum of the City of New York** at 103rd St. In between there are the **International Center of Photography**, the **Cooper-Hewitt**, the **Solomon R. Guggenheim** and the **Jewish Museums**. The vertical palace on 92nd St that was the former home of **Marjorie Merriwether Post** is only one of the numerous outstanding apartment buildings and houses in the neighborhood.

Among the many churches on the Upper East Side are the **Episcopal Church of the Holy Trinity** and **St. Christopher Home and Parsonage** at E 88th St, which form a Neo-Gothic grouping around a courtyard built on land donated by **Serena Rhinelander** that had been in her family since 1798.

Madison Ave has become largely a street of important art galleries, jewelry, antique and clothing stores and restaurants. Although the Saturday afternoon stroll is still a diversion for East Siders, Madison Ave seems tame compared to the newer SoHo galleries and boutiques and the funky Columbus Ave shops.

Park Ave, with its landscaped center island and legions of dignified apartment houses and old mansions (most of which are now occupied by foreign cultural missions or clubs), is still an address to conjure with.

Lexington Ave is a Madison Ave without the cachet—and often the quality. Third, 2nd and 1st Aves are lined with shops, restaurants and singles bars and, farther north, more high-rise *people boxes*. The side streets are a mix of tenements—some gentrified, some not—and modest townhouses.

Yorkville, which extends from the East River to Lexington Ave and from 77th to 96th Sts, continued to receive immigrants from Germany over the first half of this century. But the ethnic heart is shrinking. Once 86th St was filled with German restaurants, beer gardens and grocery, pastry and dry goods stores.

Upper East Side

Now there are inexpensive chain stores and fried chicken and pizza parlors. A few of the old restaurants, groceries and record stores remain. **Gracie Mansion** (in the park at 88th St) has been the official residence of New York City mayors since the 1942 term of **Fiorello La Guardia**.

---

1 Gracie Mansion (1799; addition 1966, **Mott B. Schmidt**) The site was known to the Dutch as **Hoek Van Hoorm**; when the British captured it during the Revolutionary War, the shelling destroyed the farmhouse that was there. The kernel of the present house was built by Scottish-born merchant **Archibald Gracie** as a country retreat. It was acquired by the city in 1887 and, among its many uses, served as the first home of the **Museum of the City of New York**, a refreshment stand and a storehouse. In 1942, at the urging of Parks Commissioner **Robert Moses, Fiorello La Guardia** accepted it as the mayor's official residence. The 98 men who preceded him in the office had lived in their own homes. Currently the home of **Mayor David Dinkins**, who stirred up quite a bit of controversy when word got out that he had purchased a headboard that cost taxpayers a purported $11,000-plus! The **Gracie Mansion Conservancy** has restored the mansion to something better than its former glory, and conducts tours and special programs there. ♦ Voluntary contribution. Tours (by appointment only) W 10, 11AM, 1, 2PM, Mar-Nov. East End Ave (E 88th St) Reservations required. 570.4751

2 Henderson Place (1882, **Lamb & Rich**) These 24 Queen Anne houses were commissioned by **John C. Henderson** (a fur importer and hat manufacturer) and designed as a self-contained community with river views. Symmetrical compositions tie the numerous pieces together below an enthusiastic profusion of turrets, parapets and dormers. There are rumors in the neighborhood that some of these houses are haunted. The ghosts may be looking for the 8 houses from the group that were demolished to allow for a yellow apartment block. ♦ East End Ave (E 86th-E 87th Sts)

3 Indian City ★$ With the generic, yet pleasant, decor, you won't know you're about to eat Indian food until you see the menu. But the dishes are authentic and well-prepared. Stick with the non-spicy entrees; the legendary chicken *vindaloo* can be better had elsewhere. ♦ Indian ♦ 1690 York Ave (E 88th-E 89th Sts) 535.6900

4 Second Story Once you're approved by the haughty doorman, enter the *South Hamptonese* palace of prep, and dance to your heart's content. The 1960s rock and the massive beer consumption are de rigueur. ♦ Cover. Closed M, Su. 415 E 91st St (York-1st Aves) 410.1360

5 Thai Express ★$ The room is long, narrow and tiny. But the price is right, and the beef *sate* (a heavily curried stick of beef) ranks with the best. ♦ Thai ♦ 1750 1st Ave (E 90th-E 91st Sts) No credit cards. 831.3813

5 El Pollo ★★$ This tiny storefront lacks atmosphere, but you can't beat the South American barbecued chicken served with a side order of fried plantains. Wash it down with **Inca Kola**. Top it all off with an exotic pudding made of raisins, cinnamon and *quinoa* (a 5000-year-old nutty grain that

Upper East Side

tastes a bit like brown rice). ♦ Peruvian ♦ 1746 1st Ave (E 90th-E 91st Sts) No credit cards. 996.7810

6 Ruby's River Road Cafe ★★$$ Some people might be turned off by the idea, but Ruby's patrons seem to love downing a shot or 2 of Jell-O! The normally benign wiggly matter is spiked with vodka and either Triple Sec or strawberry schnapps. After a couple of the above, you'll be ready to dive into a bowl of gumbo. ♦ American ♦ 1754 2nd Ave (E 91st-E 92nd Sts) 348.2328

St. Patrick's Day is the holiday of choice for New York's more than 300,000 citizens of Irish descent. The city's traffic department traditionally prepares 5th Ave for the day's annual parade by painting a 42-block-long stripe down the avenue. The feat requires 40 gallons of kelly-green paint.

7 Church of the Holy Trinity (1897, **Barney & Chapman**) The picturesque gold-brown-red Victorian church modestly slipped into this side street encloses a charming garden. The sleek tower with its fanciful Gothic crown is rather nice too. ♦ 316 E 88th St (1st-2nd Aves) 289.4100

Elaine's

8 Elaine's ★★$$$ If you absolutely must see **Woody** and **Mia** eating steamed mussels together, you will most likely accomplish that mission here. It's a kind of club for media celebrities, gossips and so-called literati, but not for food. Try to sit near **Elaine**—all the action revolves around her. ♦ Italian ♦ 1703 2nd Ave (E 88th-E 89th Sts) Reservations required. 534.8103

9 Dumas Not only great pastries and cakes, but many pastry-based savories, fresh or frozen and ready for reheating. Vies with **Bonté** as best French baker, but each has its own strengths. ♦ Closed Su. 1330 Lexington Ave (E 88th St) 369.3900

10 Petite Pleasures For the woman who's under 5'4", this shop has a collection of sophisticated perfect-for-the-office trousers, dresses, jackets and suits cut proportionally for the small figure. Sizes range from 0 to 8, with a size 0 blouse measuring only 13in at the shoulders. ♦ Closed Su. 1192 Madison Ave (E 87th St) 369.3437

11 Soldier Shop Books, miniature soldiers and medals. ♦ Closed Su. 1222 Madison Ave (E 88th-E 89th Sts) 535.6788

12 Personal Pursuit The young students from the prestigious private schools in the neighborhood are a captive audience for the personalized toys and toychests, desk accessories, mirrors and frames. ♦ Closed Su. 1242 Madison Ave (E 89th St) 722.3222

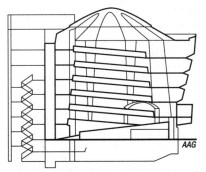

AAG

13 Solomon R. Guggenheim Museum (1959, **Frank Lloyd Wright**; addition 1968, **Taliesin Associates**; annex, projected completion 1992, **Gwathmey Siegel & Associates Architects**) Closed for renovations until 1992. **Solomon Guggenheim** wanted a museum that would *foster an appreciation of art by ac-*

quainting museum visitors with significant painting and sculpture of our time. The repository he founded has remained a testament to his personal taste. Guggenheim collected Old Masters at first, but in the 1920s he began acquiring the avant-garde work of painters like **Delaunay**, **Kandinsky** and **Léger**. Soon his apartment at the Plaza was bursting at the seams (the Old Masters were relegated to his wife's bedroom), and he began to look for other quarters for his burgeoning collection. During 2 sojourns in rented space, his new museum began to buy more of everything by both established and new talent. Finally, the need for a permanent home was realized in a Frank Lloyd Wright-designed building.

The museum, Wright's only New York building, is one of the architect's fantasies, first dreamed of in the mid 1940s. It is an extraordinary structure: a massive concrete spiral sits atop one end of a low horizontal base, expanding as it ascends, dominating not only its plinth and a counterweight block of offices at the other end, but the site itself and the blocks around it. Some feel it should be freestanding in Central Park across the street.

The display of art as we know it was clearly not Wright's real concern. The essence of architecture for the sake of architecture, the Guggenheim is a building that everyone seems to have an opinion about. Wright personally handled all the details, down to the 5th Ave sidewalk. The first addition is not up to snuff. Taliesin, Wright's successors and keepers-of-the-flame, never had the touch of the Master.

Construction of the the second addition, an annex located behind the current structure, began in May 1990 and will, upon completion, double the museum's gallery space. ♦ 5th Ave at E 89th St. 360.3500

14 National Academy of Design (Remodeled 1915, **Ogden Codman Jr.**) Since its founding in 1825 by **Samuel F.B. Morse**, painter and inventor of the telegraph, the National Academy has been an artist-run museum, school of fine arts and honorary organization of artists. Headquartered in an early 1900s Beaux-Arts townhouse around the corner from its **School of Fine Arts**, the academy is the second-oldest museum school in the country. In addition to an annual exhibition (alternately open to member artists and all artists), the academy presents special exhibitions of art and architecture. Painters, sculptors, watercolorists, graphic artists and architects number among its members today. ♦ Admission. Tu noon-8PM; W-Su noon-5PM; free Tu 5-8PM. 1083 5th Ave (E 89th St) 369.4880

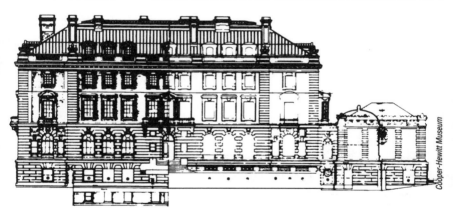

Cooper-Hewitt Museum

15 The Cooper-Hewitt (1903, Babb, Cook & Willard, renovated 1977, **Hardy Holzman Pfeiffer Associates**) What better setting for the **Smithsonian Institution's National Museum of Design** than this splendidly decorative mansion? It was built on the northern fringe of the well-heeled stretch of 5th Ave mansions for industrialist **Andrew Carnegie**, who requested *the most modest, plainest and most roomy house in New York City*. The rather standard Renaissance-Georgian mix of red brick and limestone trim on a rusticated base is most noteworthy for the fact that it is freestanding in quite an expansive garden. The richly ornamented rooms of the sumptuous mansion sometimes compete with the exhibitions; the conservatory is particularly pleasant. Also notice the very low door to what was once the library at the west end—Carnegie was a short man, and this was his private room. The permanent collection of the Cooper-Hewitt—based on the collections of the Cooper and Hewitt families and now under the stewardship of museum director **Diane Pilgrim**—encompasses textiles dating back 3000 years, jewelry, furniture, wallpaper, metal-, glass- and earthenware. It also includes the single largest group of architectural drawings in this country. The library is a design student's reference paradise of picture collections, auction catalogs and 17th- and 18th-century architecture books. Lectures, symposia, summer concerts and classes for school groups take place on a regular basis. A small shop sells design objects, catalogs, postcards and museum publications. ♦ Admission. Tu 10AM-9PM; W-Sa 10AM-5PM; Su noon-5PM; free Tu 5-9PM. 2 E 91st St (5th Ave) 860.6868

16 The Convent of the Sacred Heart (1918, **C.P.H. Gilbert** and **J. Armstrong Stenhouse**) This extravagant Italian palazzo was one of the largest private houses built in New York City, and the last on *Millionaire's Row*. It was the home of **Otto Kahn**, banker, philanthropist and art patron. Now it's a private school for girls. ◆ 1 E 91st St (5th Ave)

17 Mrs. James A. Burden House (1902, **Warren & Wetmore**) When Vanderbilt heiress **Adele Sloane** married **James A. Burden**, heir to a steel fortune, they moved into this free-standing mansion. The spiral staircase under a stained-glass skylight is one of the city's grandest, and was called the *stairway to heaven.* ◆ 7 E 91st St (Madison-5th Aves)

17 Mrs. John Henry Hammond House (1906, **Carrère & Hastings**) When Hammond saw the plans for this house, he said this gift from his wife's family made him feel *like a kept man.* He moved in anyway, along with a staff of 16 full-time servants. The couple's musicales were legendary. **Benny Goodman** came here frequently in the 1930s to play **Mozart**'s clarinet works. ◆ 9 E 91st St (Madison-5th Aves)

18 1107 5th Ave (1925, **Rouse & Goldstone**) A perfectly ordinary apartment building except for a few anomalies on the facade—evidence of an era past. When it was built, **Marjorie Merriwether Post** (at the time married to stockbroker **E.F. Hutton**) commissioned a 54-room complex for herself. The Palladian window near the top center of the facade opened onto the main foyer of this apartment. ◆ E 92nd St

19 Jewish Museum (1908, **C.P.H. Gilbert**; annex 1963, **Samuel Glazer**; annex 1993, **Kevin Roche**) In November 1990, the Jewish Museum closed for a 2-year renovation and expansion that will double the museum's exhibition space and provide classrooms and improved public amenities such as a cafe and an enlarged book and gift shop. Until renovations are complete (1993), the museum, which holds the country's largest collection of Judaica, will carry on its exhibition and educational

programs at the **New-York Historical Society** (170 Central Park West, 399.3344). This French Renaissance mansion was the home of financier **Felix M. Warburg.** ◆ 1109 5th Ave (E 92nd St) 860.1889

20 Island ★$$$ This is the sort of place you expect to find on the West Side: plenty of young people wolfing down quite good if slightly overpriced pasta and grilled dishes. ◆ Continental ◆ 1305 Madison Ave (E 92nd St) Reservations recommended. 996.1200

20 Busby's $$$ Young chef **Jonathon Eisman** runs this all-American, California-influenced restaurant. The imaginative menu features appetizers such as roasted goat cheese wrapped in grilled eggplant. Among my favorite entrees are broiled salmon with lemon grass and sautéed liver with cassis. ◆ 45 E 92nd St (Madison Ave) 360.7373

20 Wales Hotel $$ A small, moderately priced European-style hotel that is ideally located if you plan to spend a lot of time on Museum Mile or in Central Park. Ask for a large, bright room or you may end up with the opposite. ◆ 1295 Madison Ave (E 92nd-E 93rd Sts) 876.6000

20 Sarabeth's Kitchen ★★$$$ Many a New Yorker has stood on line for a weekend brunch of Sarabeth's gourmet comfort foods—homemade waffles and pancakes crowned with fresh fruit, hot porridge and warm-from-the-oven muffins. On your way out, pick up homemade brownies and cookies and, for your deserving pooch, Sarabeth's new gourmet doggie biscuits. ◆ American ◆ 1295 Madison Ave (E 92nd-E 93rd Sts) 410.7335. Also at: 423 Amsterdam Ave. 496.6280

21 Corner Bookstore A wide selection of books, over a third for children, in an atmosphere conducive to browsing. Heavy on literature, art and architecture. ◆ 1313 Madison Ave (E 93rd St) 831.3554

22 Smithers Alcoholism Center (1932, **Walker & Gillette**) This former home of showman **Billy Rose** was the last of the large, great mansions to be built in New York. It is in the delicate style of the 18th-century Scottish brothers, **Lambert** and **Nicholas Adam**, who created most of the best houses in Edinburgh and London.◆ 56 E 93rd St (Park-Madison Aves)

22 60 East 93rd Street (1930, **John Russell Pope**) After **Mrs. William K. Vanderbilt** divorced her husband, she leased an apartment on Park Ave, only to discover that her ex-husband had one in the same building. She broke the lease and built this beautiful French Renaissance mansion. ◆ Park-Madison Aves

23 Bistro du Nord ★$$$ Hearty meals and warm service are the specialties of this cozy little bistro. ◆ French ◆ 1312 Madison Ave (E 93rd St) Reservations recommended. 289.0997

24 Military Bookman Specializing in used and out-of-print books on just about every aspect of the armed forces of the world. ◆ Closed M, Su. 29 E 93rd St (Madison-5th Aves) 348.1280

24 The Wicker Garden and Wicker Garden's Baby Adjacent wickeries specializing, on the left, in wicker furniture, new and antique, quilts and handpainted furniture; on the right, in white wicker cribs, bassinets and highchairs, along with pure cotton clothes for newborns to 10 year olds. ◆ Closed Su. 1318-20 Madison Ave (E 93rd-E 94th Sts) 348.1166

25 International Center of Photography (1914, **Delano & Aldrich**) The only museum in New York City—and perhaps the world—devoted entirely to photography. The ICP is an ebullient and hospitable home for practitioners of the art, where the best and the brightest are given shows and encouragement. Every inch of the Georgian townhouse it occupies is used in the service of photography: 4 galleries for revolving shows; workshops and photo labs; a screening room; and a gallery for the permanent collection, which includes 20th-century photographers **W. Eugene Smith** and **Henri Cartier-Bresson**, among others. A gift shop sells books, catalogs, posters and, of course, picture postcards. The center maintains additional gallery space at 1133 6th Ave. ◆ Admission. Tu noon-8PM; W-F noon-5PM; Sa-Su 11AM-6PM; free Tu 5-8PM. 1130 5th Ave (E 94th St) 860.1777

26 Saranac ★$$ A small American restaurant with the feel of an Adirondack lodge. The reasonable prices belie its *Bonfire of the Vanities* location. Well-prepared steaks, hamburgers and grilled fish. ◆ American ◆ 1350 Madison Ave (E 94th-E 95th Sts) 289.9600

27 Dollhouse Antics All the necessary Lilliputian accessories for dollhouse decorating: playpens, paint easels, overstuffed sofas, sterling silver knives and forks, copper pots and pans, and hundreds of other minute items. Houses can be custom-ordered and even wired for electricity. ◆ Closed Su. 1343 Madison Ave (E 94th St) 876.2288

28 Squadron A and Eighth Regiment Armory/Hunter High School (Armory 1895, **John Rochester Thomas**; school 1971, **Morris Ketchum Jr. & Associates**) When the armory—a distinctly businesslike fortress—was on the verge of being torn down altogether, community protest saved at least the facade on Madison Ave. The school's architects did a marvelous task of using it as both a backdrop to the playground and as a formal inspiration for the new building. ◆ E 94th-E 95th Sts (Park-Madison Aves)

29 Synod of Bishops of the Russian Orthodox Church Outside Russia (1917; addition 1928, **Delano & Aldrich**) Built for **Francis F. Palmer** and renovated in 1928 for banker **George F. Baker**, this unusually large Georgian mansion has remained virtually unchanged, except for the introduction of exquisite Russian icons. A small cathedral occupies the former ballroom. ◆ 1180 Park Ave (E 93rd St)

30 1185 Park Avenue (1929, **Schwartz & Gross**) This is the only East Side version of the full-block courtyard apartment house typified by the **Belnord, Astor Court** and **Apthorp** across town. The Gothicized entrance adds needed levity to an otherwise traditional composition. ◆ E 93rd-E 94th Sts

31 Night Presence IV The intentionally rusty steel sculpture is by the late artist **Louise Nevelson**. The view down the avenue from here is picture-perfect. ◆ Park Ave at E 92nd St

32 120 and 122 East 92nd Street (1850) Because fire laws made them illegal in the 1860s, there are very few wooden houses in Manhattan. This pair (and the frame houses at 160 E 92nd St and 128 E 93rd St) are a reminder of what this whole neighborhood was like in the mid-19th century. ◆ Lexington-Park Aves

33 92nd Street Y This branch of the **Young Men's/Women's Hebrew Association** is one of the city's cultural landmarks. Under music director **Gerard Schwartz**, its **Kaufman Concert Hall** has become New York's best place to hear chamber music and recitals. Such groups as the **Guarneri, Cleveland** and **Tokyo Quartets** are regulars here. The renowned **Poetry Center** has offered readings by every major poet in the world since its founding in 1939, and the tradition continues with such writers as **Saul Bellow, Joseph Brodsky** and **Isaac Bashevis Singer**. The **American Jewish Theater** also presents its works here. The Y

sponsors lectures, seminars and workshops, even unusual tours of the city's neighborhoods. ◆ Seats 916 (Kaufman Concert Hall) 1395 Lexington Ave (E 92nd St) 427.6000

34 Yura and Company One of the neighborhood's best gourmet takeouts and catering kitchens. Excellent bouillabaisse and decadent desserts. ◆ 1650 3rd Ave (E 92nd St) 860.8060

35 Kitchen Arts & Letters More than 2200 cookbooks are on display. You'll also find paintings and photographs of food, wonderful old wine labels, reproduction tin biscuit boxes and other culinary memorabilia. *An RSW recommendation.* ◆ Closed Su. 1435 Lexington Ave (E 93rd St) 876.5550

Restaurants/Nightlife: Red	Hotels: Blue
Shops/Parks: Green	Sights/Culture: Black

235

36 Islamic Cultural Center (1991, **Skidmore, Owings & Merrill**) A computer was used to ensure that this mosque faces *Mecca*, as Islamic law requires. It is New York's first major mosque, and is intended as the spiritual home of the city's 400,000 Moslems and to serve diplomats from Islamic countries. ♦ 3rd Ave at E 96th St

37 Russian Orthodox Cathedral of St. Nicholas (1901-2) This church is unusual because set above the polychromatic Victorian body, there are 5 onion domes. ♦ 15 E 97th St (Madison-5th Aves)

38 Mount Sinai Hospital (1904, **Arnold Brunner**; Klingenstein Pavilion 1952, **Kahn & Jacobs**; Annenberg Building 1974, **Skidmore, Owings & Merrill**; additions, in progress, **Pei Cobb Freed & Partners**) In 1986, work began on an extensive construction project, which when completed, in 1992, will include 3 new hospital towers in one grand pavilion called the **New North Pavilion**. These new facilities replace 10 older buildings—some dating as far back as 1904—all of which have been demolished. Also of architectural interest is the **Anneburg Building**, a 436ft Cor-Ten steel box that gets its color from a coating of rust that protects the steel from further corrosion. ♦ E 98th-E 101st Sts (Madison-5th Aves)

39 New York Academy of Medicine (1926, **York & Sawyer**) A charming combination of Byzantine and Romanesque architecture, it contains one of the most important medical libraries in the country. The collection includes 4000 cookbooks, a gift of **Dr. Margaret Barclay Wilson**, who believed good nutrition was the key to good health. ♦ M noon-5PM; Tu-Sa 9AM-5PM. 2 E 103rd St (5th Ave) 876.8200

40 Museum of the City of New York (1932, **Joseph Freedlander**) The story of New York City is told through historical paintings, **Currier & Ives** prints, period rooms, costumes, **Duncan Phyfe** furniture, **Tiffany** silver, ship models and wonderful toys and dolls, all handsomely displayed in a roomy Neo-Georgian building. The structure, red brick with white trim, was built for the museum as a repository for its collection after it moved from **Gracie Mansion**. Puppet shows for children, concerts and lectures for adults. ♦ Free. Tu-Sa 10AM-5PM; Su 1-5PM. 1220 5th Ave (E 103rd-E 104th Sts) 534.1672

41 El Museo del Barrio A culture center and showcase for the historic and contemporary arts of Latin America (especially Puerto Rico) that began as a neighborhood museum in an East Harlem classroom. Video, painting, sculpture, photography, theater and film are featured. Permanent collections include pre-Columbian art and *Santos de Palo*, the hand-carved wooden saints that are one of the culture's most important art forms. ♦ Voluntary contribution. W-Su 11AM-5PM. 1 E 104th St (5th Ave) 831.7272

41 AMAS Music Theater This organization (AMAS means *you love* in Latin), guided by **Rosetta LeNoire**, is dedicated to the development of black musical theater, with an emphasis on biographies of famed artists such as **Scott Joplin, Ethel Waters** and **Eubie Blake**. *Bubblin' Brown Sugar* started here. ♦ Seats 99. 1 E 104th St (5th Ave) 369.8000

George Page
Host, PBS *Nature* series

The **Hudson River**. One of the world's greatest and most beautiful estuaries—a natural wonder and a highway of American history. Take the **Dayliner cruise** to **Bear Mountain State Park** or, better still, rent a yacht for the trip. The **Circle Line cruise** around Manhattan is also recommended and only takes 3 hours.

The **Metropolitan Museum**. Simply the world's most glorious museum.

The **Palm Court**, the **Oak Room** and the **Oak Bar, Plaza Hotel**. All retain an ageless elegance and gentility that is quintessential old New York.

July and August. Under no circumstances should you visit New York in July and August unless you enjoy walking around in the world's largest steambath.

Lutèce. Splurge. It's still the best restaurant in New York, if not the world.

Robert A.M. Stern
Robert A.M. Stern Architects

W 67th St between Central Park W and Columbus Ave. Elegant studio buildings, containing dramatic double-height rooms, that make the block in some ways more like Paris than Paris.

The **Sheep's Meadow** in Central Park. New York's great front lawn, framed by the fantastic manmade mountain range of Midtown's skyscrapers.

The **Promenade** along Brooklyn Heights. A brilliant urban sleight of hand, overwhelming the sight and sound of the Brooklyn-Queens Expwy with breathtaking views of the harbor and Lower Manhattan.

The soaring lobby of the main branch of the **Brooklyn Public Library**, where Classicism and Modernism join forces to form grand public space.

As the crowds gather for an evening's theatergoing, the main plaza at **Lincoln Center** becomes an outdoor stage.

John D. Rockefeller's bedroom and dressing room can be seen at the **Museum of the City of New York**. They were taken from his mansion at 5th Ave and 54th St when it was demolished in 1937.

New York City in Fact

Art and Architecture

On Broadway: A Journey Uptown Over Time **David W. Dunlap** (1990, Rizzoli)

New York Architecture 1970-1990 **Heinrich Klotz** (1989, Rizzoli)

Manhattan Architecture **Richard Berenholtz** and **Donald Martin Reynolds** (1988, Prentice Hall Press)

AIA Guide to New York City **Norval White** and **Elliot Willensky** (1988, Harcourt Brace Jovanovich)

The City That Never Was: 200 Years of Fantastic and Fascinating Plans that Might Have Changed the Face of NYC **Rebecca Reed Shanor** (1988, Viking Press)

The Landmarks of New York **Barbaralee Diamonstein** (1988, Harry N. Abrams)

Nightmares in the Sky **Stephen King** and **f-stop Fitzgerald** (1988, Viking Penguin Inc.)

The Building of Manhattan **Donald Mackay** (1987, Harper & Row)

Lost New York: Pictorial Record of Vanished NYC **Nathan Silver** (1982, American Legacy Press)

The City Observed: New York. A Guide to the Architecture of Manhattan **Paul Goldberger** (1979, Random House)

The Columbia Historical Portrait of New York **John A. Kouwenhoven** (1972, Harper & Row)

Guidebooks

Ethnic New York: A Complete Guide to the Many Faces and Cultures of New York **Mark Leeds** (1991, Passport Books)

New York City Yesterday & Today: 30 Timeless Walking Adventures **Judith H. Browning** (1990, Corsair Publications)

Where to Find It, Buy It, Eat It and Save Time and Money in New York **Gerry Frank** (1990, Gerry's Frankly Speaking)

The Streets Where They Lived: A Walking Guide to the Residences of Famous New Yorkers **Stephen W. Plumb** (1989, Marlor Press)

The Best Guided Walking Tours of NYC **Leslie Gourse** (1989, The Globe Pequot Press)

Literary Neighborhoods of New York **Marcia Leisner** (1989, Starrhill Press)

Manhattan's Outdoor Sculpture **Margot Gayle** and **Michele Cohen** (1988, Prentice Hall Press)

From Windmills To The World Trade Center: A Walking Guide to Lower Manhattan History **Joyce Gold** (1988, Old Warren Press)

From Trout Stream To Bohemia: A Walking Guide to Greenwich Village History **Joyce Gold** (1988, Old Warren Press)

New York, A Guide to the Metropolis. Walking Tours of Architecture and History **Gerard R. Wolfe** (1988, McGraw-Hill)

Permanent New Yorkers: A Biographical Guide to the Cemeteries **Judi Culbertson** and **Tom Randall** (1987, Chelsea Green Publishers)

Other

Zagat New York Restaurant Survey (1991, Zagat Survey)

The Best Guided Walking Tours of NYC **Leslie Gourse** (1989, The Globe Pequot Press)

Movie Lover's Guide to New York **Richard Alleman** (1988, Harper & Row)

Under the Sidewalks of New York: The Story of the World's Great Subway Station **Brian J. Cudahy** (1988, The Stephen Greene Press/ Pelham Books)

The New York Theatre Sourcebook **Chuck Lawliss** (1981, Simon & Schuster)

The Street Book—An Encyclopedia of Manhattan's Street Names and Their Origins **Henry Moscow** (1978, Fordham University Press)

...and Fiction

New York Observed: Artists and Writers Look at the City, 1650 to the Present, edited by **Barbara Cohen, Seymour Chwast** and **Steven Heller** (1988, Harry N. Abrams)

Time and Again **Jack Finney** (1970, Simon & Schuster)

Catcher in the Rye **J.D. Salinger**, originally published 1951 (1964, Bantam Books)

A Tree Grows in Brooklyn **Betty Smith**, originally published 1943 (1968, Harper & Row)

Diedrick Knickerbocker's History of New York **Washington Irving**, originally published 1940 (1981, Sleepy Hollow)

This Side of Paradise **F. Scott Fitzgerald** (1920, Charles Scribner's Sons)

The Age of Innocence **Edith Wharton**, originally published 1920 (1968, Charles Scribner's Sons)

The House of Mirth **Edith Wharton** (1905, Charles Scribner's Sons)

Upper East Side

Washington Square **Henry James**, originally published 1880 (1990, New American Library)

Children's Books

From The Mixed up Files of Mrs. Basil E. Frankweiler **E.L. Konigsburg** (1967, Atheneum Childrens Book)

Harriet the Spy **Louise Fitzhugh** (1964, Harper & Row Junior Books)

The Cricket in Times Square **George Selden** (1960, Farrar, Straus & Gironx)

Eloise **Kay Thompson** (1955, Simon & Schuster)

Stuart Little **E.B. White** (1945, Harper & Row Junior Books)

The Little Red Lighthouse and the Great Gray Bridge **Hildegarde H. Swift** (1942, Harcourt Brace Jovanovich)

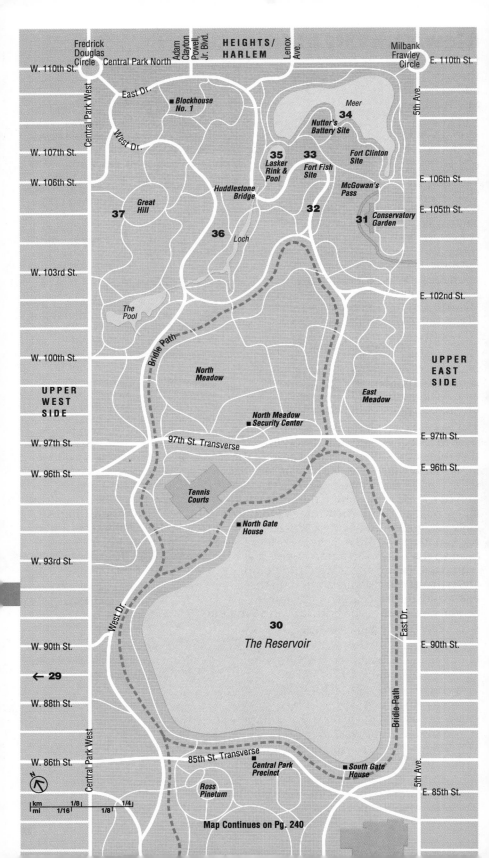

Map Continues on Pg. 240

Central Park

This different and many smiling presence, is how **Henry James** once referred to **Central Park**. It is unlike any other urban park in the US. Over 14 million people wander through it every year, 250 species of birds are regularly sighted in its treetops, and its 843 acres are completely man-made. Its boundaries are **59th** and **110th Sts**, **5th Ave** and **Central Park West**, an extension of 8th Ave.

Not long after work began to clear the site on 12 August 1857, a friend suggested to journalist **Frederick Law Olmsted**, whose avocation was landscaping, that he should compete for the job of superintendent of the new Central Park. He quickly found backers in newspaper editors **Horace Greeley** and **William Cullen Bryant**, and when writer **Washington Irving** added his name to the list, Olmsted got the job. Later that same year, the Parks Commission announced a design competition for the new park, and Olmsted's friend, architect **Calvert Vaux**, suggested they join forces. Olmsted wasn't interested at first—he was concerned that the commissioners might consider his participation a conflict of interest—but when his superiors convinced him otherwise, he accepted Vaux's proposal, and the 2 men went to work. Olmsted would later become known as the nation's foremost landscape architect. His legacy includes Yosemite National Park in California, Fairmont Park in Philadelphia, the Capitol grounds in Washington DC, George W. Vanderbilt's estate in Asheville NC and the grounds of the 1893 World's Columbian Exposition in Chicago.

On 28 April 1858, after Olmsted and Vaux submitted what they called their **Greensward** plan, Olmsted wrote: *Every foot of the Park's surface, every tree and bush, as well as every arch, roadway and walk, has been placed where it is with a purpose.* In the years since, buildings have been added, monuments put in place and playgrounds, roads, even parking lots have been constructed. But the original purpose is still well served.

The groundswell for the park had begun in 1844 when William Cullen Bryant warned that commerce was devouring Manhattan inch by inch. He pointed out that there were still unoccupied parts of the island, but that *while we are discussing the subject, the advancing population of the city is sweeping over them and covering them from our reach.* By the mayoral election of 1851, Bryant and others had moved the cause forward to the point where it was the only issue both candidates could agree on. The winner of the race, **Ambrose C. Kingsland**, immediately recommended buying a 153-acre tract known as **Jones's Wood** between the East River and 3rd Ave, from 66th to 75th Sts. His proposal was attacked from all sides: park supporters argued it was too small; influential businessmen objected to giving up the waterfront property to any purpose but commerce. In 1853, the state legislature authorized the city to buy the larger and much more central present site. The price tag was $5 million.

It was no bargain. The place was a swampy pesthole filled with pig farms and squatters' shacks. It was used as a garbage dump and was a prime location for bone-boiling plants. After surveying it, Olmsted called it a *pestilential spot where miasmatic odors taint every breath of air.* He succeeded in turning it into what New Yorkers today proudly call the *lungs of the city*.

Actual work began in 1857, and by the time it was considered finished 16 years later, nearly 5 million cubic yards of stone and dirt had been rearranged and nearly 5 million trees planted. Before construction started, there were 42 species of trees growing on the site, and by the time it was completed, 402 kinds of deciduous trees were thriving there, along with 230 species of evergreens and 815 varieties of shrubs. There were also 58mi of pedestrian walks, $6^1/2$mi of roads, and a bridle path $4^1/2$mi long. One hundred and six acres were covered by a reservoir and another 22 acres by a sprawling lake. A series of smaller lakes and

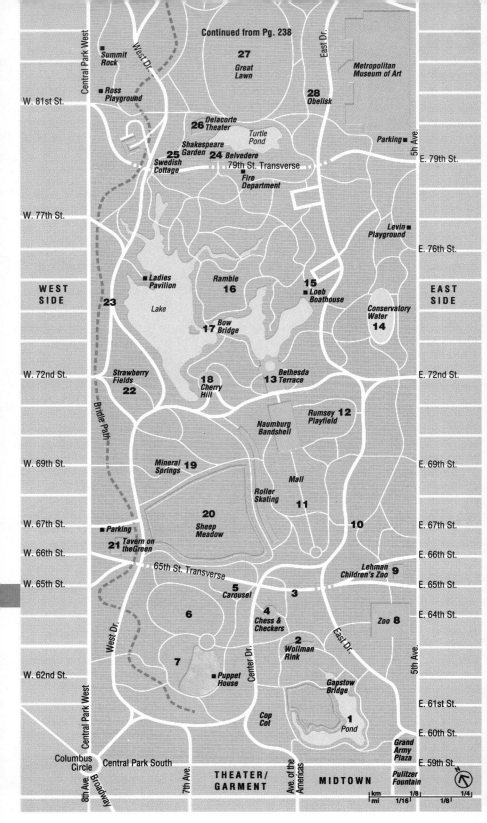

Continued from Pg. 238

27
Great
Lawn

Metropolitan
Museum of Art

28 Obelisk

Summit
Rock

West Dr.

Central Park West

East Dr.

W. 81st St.

Ross
Playground

26 Delacorte
Theater

Turtle
Pond

Parking ■

5th Ave.

E. 79th St.

Shakespeare
Garden

25
Swedish
Cottage

24 Belvedere
79th St. Transverse

Fire
Department

W. 77th St.

Levin ■
Playground

E. 76th St.

WEST
SIDE

Ladies
Pavilion

Ramble
16

15
■ Loeb
Boathouse

EAST
SIDE

23

Lake

Conservatory
Water
14

17 Bow
Bridge

W. 72nd St.

Strawberry
Fields
22

18
Cherry
Hill

13 Bethesda
Terrace

E. 72nd St.

Bridle Path

Rumsey 12
Playfield

Naumburg
Bandshell

W. 69th St.

Mineral
Springs 19

Mall

E. 69th St.

Roller
Skating

11

W. 67th St.

■ Parking

20
Sheep
Meadow

10

E. 67th St.

21 Tavern on
theGreen

W. 66th St.

E. 66th St.

65th St. Transverse

Lehman 9
Children's Zoo

W. 65th St.

5
Carousel

3

E. 65th St.

West Dr.

6

4
Chess &
Checkers

Zoo 8

E. 64th St.

Center Dr.

2
Wollman
Rink

East Dr.

5th Ave.

7

Puppet
House

Gapstow
Bridge

W. 62nd St.

E. 61st St.

Cop
Cot

1
Pond

E. 60th St.

Central Park West

8th Ave.

Broadway

Columbus
Circle

Central Park South

7th Ave.

THEATER/
GARMENT

Ave. of the Americas

MIDTOWN

Grand
Army
Plaza

E. 59th St.

Pulitzer
Fountain

N

km   1/8   1/4
mi   1/16   1/8

ponds were created as well, and some 62mi of pipe installed to carry off unwanted water. In those days, earthmovers were gangs of men with picks and shovels and teams of horses pulling wagonloads of dirt.

Olmsted was single-minded about what he wanted, and as superintendent of construction, he usually got his way. He was firmly against buildings not related to the park itself. *Reservoirs and museums are not part of the Park, but deductions from it*, he said. The original Croton Receiving Reservoir, which he replaced with a more natural-looking version, wasn't removed to create the **Great Lawn** until 1929, and the **Metropolitan Museum of Art** hasn't stopped deducting from the park since Calvert Vaux designed the original building in 1880. Olmsted was also testy about monuments: *The Park is not a place for sepulchral memorials. The beautiful cemeteries in the vicinity of the city offer abundant opportunities to commemorate the virtues of those who are passing away*. Today there are more than 80 monuments in Central Park. Frederick Law Olmsted may well be turning over in his grave.

But it could have been worse. In 1918, someone in all seriousness suggested digging trenches in the **North Meadow** to give us an idea of what the *doughboys* were going through *over there*. A year later, plans were submitted for an airport near **Tavern on the Green**, which was a sheepfold back then. There have been several proposals to use some of the space for housing projects, and plans for underground parking garages have been coming and going since the 1920s. Fortunately, Central Park is alive and well in spite of countless schemes to improve it. The **Parks Dept** and the **Central Park Conservancy** have been working for a decade or more to restore the park to what it once was. The result is that one of the best things about New York is getting better every day.

We want a ground to which people may easily go after their day's work is done, and where they may stroll for an hour, seeing, hearing, and feeling nothing of the bustle and jar of the streets, where they shall, in effect, find the city put far away from them. We want the greatest possible contrast with the streets and the shops and the rooms of the town which will be consistent with convenience and the preservation of good order and neatness. We want, especially, the greatest possible contrast with the restraining and confining conditions which compel us to walk circumspectly, watchfully, jealously, which compel us to look closely upon others without sympathy. Practically, what we want is a simple, broad, open space of clean greensward, with sufficient play of surface and a sufficient number of trees about it to supply a variety of light and shade. This we want as a central feature. We want depth of wood enough about it not only for comfort in hot weather, but to completely shut out the city from our landscapes.

Frederick Law Olmsted, *Public Parks and the Enlargement of Towns*, 1870

1 The Pond If you have your camera with you, the reflection of the nearby buildings, especially the Plaza Hotel, in this crescent-shaped haven for ducks and other waterfowl may be among the best pictures you'll take home. The view is from the **Gapstow Bridge**, which crosses the northern end. The Pond was created to reflect the rocks in what is now a bird sanctuary on its western shore. From the time the park opened until 1924, swan boats like the ones still used in the Boston Garden dodged real swans here. The Pond was reduced to about half its original size in 1951 when the Wollman Memorial Skating Rink was built. ♦ 60th-67th Sts (5th Ave)

2 Wollman Memorial Skating Rink The original rink lasted less than 30 years, and when the city attempted to rebuild it, the project became mired in so much red tape that it began to look as though it might take another 30 years to replace it. In 1986, real-estate and casino millionaire **Donald Trump** took it upon himself to do the job—without the regulations the city imposes on itself—and finished it in record time. Trump often appears here himself on winter weekends to accept the warm thanks of the skaters. Though an encroachment on the park, it is a hugely popular one, and space on the ice is usually at a premium. Ice-skating, early September to late April; roller-skating at other times. ♦ Admission; skate rental. 59th St at 6th Ave. 517.4800

Restaurants/Nightlife: Red   **Hotels:** Blue
Shops/Parks: Green   **Sights/Culture:** Black

Glenn Wolff

3 The Dairy When this Gothic building was built in 1870, fresh milk was a relative luxury. The park's planners, following European models, added milkmaids and a herd of cows to enhance the sylvan setting, and to provide children with a healthy treat. After the turn of the century, the cows were sent off to the country, the milkmaids retired and the building became a storehouse. In 1981, it was restored and its wooden porch replaced and painted in Victorian colors. It is now the park's **Visitor Center**, with an information desk, exhibitions and a sales desk. Weekend walking tours, led by the Urban Park Rangers, usually begin here. ◆ 65th St (W of the Zoo) Tour information 397.3080; special events 360.1333

4 The Chess & Checkers House A gift of financier **Bernard Baruch** in 1952, this mecca for checkers-playing retirees sits on top of a rock known as the *Kinderberg* (Children's Mountain). It was named for a rustic summerhouse that once stood here as a retreat for children. ◆ 64th St (W of the Dairy)

5 The Carousel There has been a merry-go-round here since 1871. The original was powered by real horses that walked a treadmill in an underground pit. The present one, built in 1908 at Coney Island, was moved here in 1951. Its 58 horses were hand-carved by **Stein & Goldstein**, considered the best woodcarvers of their day. Don't just stand there. Climb up and go for the ride of your life.

Central Park

◆ Nominal admission. 65th St at Center Dr. 879.0244

6 Heckscher Playground The original park plan didn't include sports facilities, but this was one of 3 loosely connected areas for children who had secured the proper permits to play games like baseball and croquet. In the 1920s, adults wanted to get into the game and pressured the city to build them 5 softball diamonds with backstops and bleachers. At about the same time, the former meadow was converted into an asphalt-covered playground to give the kids something to do while the adults were running bases. It was the first formal playground in the park. The softball fields are available by permit only, and are used by teams from corporations, Broadway shows and other groups. Call 427.6100 to see who's playing today; for a permit for your own team, call 408.0209. ◆ 60th-65th Sts (Center-West Drs)

7 Umpire Rock Central Park is laced with rocky outcrops like this one, left behind some 20,000 years ago by the **Laurentian Glacier**. The boulder on top is called an *erratic*, which was carried down with the ice from the Far North. The tracks on the face of the rock, called *striations*, were formed by the scraping of large stones embedded in the glacier as it moved southeast across Manhattan. Most of the rocky outcrops in the park are a type of mica-rich shale called *Manhattan Schist*. 400 million years ago, they formed the base of a mountain chain about as high as the present-day Rocky Mountains. The rocks were already here when the park was built, of course, but Olmsted exposed many that had previously been below the surface. Most experts agree that the *erratic* on Umpire Rock was moved here by Olmsted's construction crews. But many of the *erratics* in the park were left where the glacier had deposited them. ◆ 62nd St (overlooking ballfields)

8 The Arsenal (1848, **Martin E. Thompson**) The 10 acres of land around this building was a park before Central Park was even a dream. The Arsenal's original use as a storehouse for arms and ammunition accounts for the iconography of cannons and rifles around the 5th Ave entrance. It became the citywide headquarters of the Parks and Recreation Dept in 1934, following use as a police precinct, a weather bureau, a menagerie and the first home of the American Museum of Natural History. A 3rd-floor gallery contains, among other exhibits, the original Greensward plan, whose results are all around you. ◆ M-F 9AM-4:30PM. 64th St at 5th Ave. 360.8111

8 The Zoo (1988, **Kevin Roche, John Dinkeloo Associates**) After 4 years of construction and $35 million of expense, this new home for 450 animals representing more than 100 different species, reopened in 1988. The zoo it replaced had elephants, antelopes and other animals too large for such cramped quarters, and they have been given to other zoos with more hospitable facilities. The bears and sea lions have been given new, more natural homes here, and 2 flocks of penguins cavort under a simulated ice pack in a pool with glass walls that allow you to watch their underwater antics. Monkeys swing in trees in a reproduction of an African environment, bats fly through their own naturalistic cave and alligators swim in the most comfortable swamp north of the Okefenokee. The 5½-acre complex, encompassing 3 different climatic zones, is administered by the **New York Zoological Society**. A cafeteria and a gift shop at the southern edge are accessible without entering the grounds. ◆ Admission. M, W-F 10AM-5PM, Tu 10AM-8PM, Sa-Su 10AM-5:30PM, May-Sep; M-F 10AM-5PM, Sa-Su 10AM-5:30PM, Apr, Oct; daily 10AM-4:30PM, Nov-Mar. 63rd-65th Sts (5th Ave) 861.6030

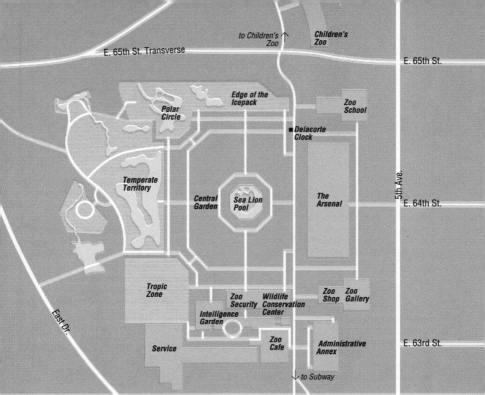

Central Park Zoo

9 **The Children's Zoo** Walk into the jaws of Jonah's whale, or tour Noah's Ark and the junior-sized castle. Visit nose-to-nose with *Stardust*, the llama, and at a safer distance with *Godzilla*, a 3-foot iguana. The bronze animals of the beautiful **Delacorte Clock** parade every half-hour to seasonal music. ♦ Nominal admission. Daily 10AM-4:30PM. 65th St at 5th Ave. 408.0271

10 **Balto** One of the most popular monuments in the park, this 1925 bronze portrait by **Frederick G.R. Roth** represents the husky who led his team of dogs from Anchorage to Nome (1000mi) to deliver serum to stem a diphtheria epidemic. ♦ 66th St at East Dr

11 **The Mall** This formal promenade was largely the work of **Ignaz Anton Pilat**, a plant expert who worked with Olmsted and Vaux on the overall design of the park. He deviated from the romantic naturalism of the plan by planting a double row of elm trees along the length of the Mall, but in the process gave us a reminder of what country roads and New England villages were like a century ago. The promenade was placed on a NW angle to provide a sightline directly to a high outcropping above 79th St known as **Vista Rock**. Vaux designed a miniature castle for the top of the rock to create an impression of greater distance. The bandshell in the NE corner was designed in 1923 by **William G. Tachau** and donated by **Elkan Naumburg**, who presented concerts here for many years. It replaced an 1862 cast-iron band-stand that included a sky-blue cupola dotted with gold-leaf stars. The current bandshell is still used for dance, music and opera performances, as well as special events. ♦ 66th-72nd Sts (Center-Terrace Drs) 860.1355

12 **The Naumburg Bandshell** This is a vital summertime center for jazz, folk dance and theatrical performances. ♦ 70th St (the Mall) 360.2756

12 **Rumsey Playground** A 1938 sculpture of *Mother Goose* by **Frederick G.R. Roth** and **Walter Beretta** provides a welcome to this walk-up playground with a wisteria-covered

Central Park

pergola at its western edge. Its location at the top of a hill and a less-than-inviting design make it unattractive to parents of small children. A recent decline in the number of children living near the park has reduced the use of all the park's playgrounds. This one is used primarily as an athletic field for nearby private schools. It was built on the site of the Central Park Casino, a cottage originally designed as a ladies' house of refreshment. In the 1920s, it was turned into a restaurant, designed by **Joseph Urban**, which became the most popular place in town for the likes of **Gentleman Jimmy Walker**, whose basic rule of life was that the only real sin was to go to bed on the same day that you got up. ♦ 71st St at East Dr

als, there is also an authentic Venetian gondola that holds 6 people. The Venetians gave a gondola to the park in 1862, but for lack of a gondolier, it rotted away. This one, a more recent gift, includes the services of an expert to pole it around the Lake. Bicycle rentals are also available, call 861.4137 for information. ◆ Rowboat rentals: M-F 11:30AM-5PM; Sa-Su 11:30AM-6PM. Gondola rides: fee. M-F 5-10PM; Sa-Su 3-10PM, Mar-Oct. Reservation required. 74th St at East Dr. 517.2233

Within Loeb Boathouse:

Boathouse Cafe ★★★$$ Light fare in one of New York's best settings. In good weather you can sit on the outdoor terrace with a peaceful view of the Lake. But I think the view from inside is just as good, and it's unusually pleasant (and uncrowded) on rainy days, when the landscape outside becomes dramatic. ◆ American ◆ Mar-Nov

13 Bethesda Terrace This terrace between the Lake and the Mall has always been considered the heart of Central Park. It was named for a pool in Jerusalem that the Gospel of St. John tells us was given healing powers by the annual visitation of an angel. The *Angel of the Waters*, Emma Stebbins' statue on top of the magnificent fountain, recreates the event. It was unveiled in 1873, but Bethesda Terrace itself had opened in 1861. The basic design is the work of **Calvert Vaux**. But the arcade ceiling, the tile floors, and the elaborate friezes and other ornamentation are by **Jacob Wrey Mould**, whose early background was in Islamic architecture—which explains why the terrace is so much like a courtyard in a Spanish palace. ◆ 72nd St at Terrace Dr

13 Sweet Feast Cafe Live jazz or classical music in the magical outdoor setting of Bethesda Terrace. Enjoy a healthy gourmet snack; or just sit and soak up the music. ◆ Weather permitting Sa-Su 11AM-dusk, Apr-Oct. 72nd St at Terrace Dr. 227.5789

14 Conservatory Water The name for this pond comes from a conservatory that was

never built. The space is occupied by the Kerbs Memorial Model Boathouse, designed by **Aymar Embury II** in 1954. It houses model yachts that race on the pond every Saturday. At the north end is **José de Creeff**'s fanciful *Alice in Wonderland* group, given to the park in 1960 by publisher **George Delacorte**. And at the western edge is **George Lober**'s 1956 bronze statue of **Hans Christian Andersen**, a gift of the Danish people. A storyteller appears here every Saturday at 11AM. There is a small snack bar with outdoor tables overlooking the water on the east side. ◆ 72nd St at 5th Ave

15 Loeb Boathouse Built in 1954, this is the third boathouse on the Lake. It was tucked away here in the NE corner so it wouldn't spoil lake views. Besides rowboat and bicycle rent-

16 The Ramble This section of the park was conceived as a wild garden preserve for native plants. It was also intended as a foreground for Vista Rock as seen from the Mall. It has seen better days, but it is still a wild place, with a brook meandering through and tumbling over several small waterfalls, and a perfect place for birdwatching. One of the winding paths led to a man-made cave at the edge of the lake, but the cave was walled up in the 1920s. There are few better places to get away from it all. But because this little forest can be relatively deserted, it may be best to share its pleasures with a friend. ◆ 74th-79th Sts (East-West Drs)

17 Bow Bridge Calvert Vaux designed most of the park's bridges, and no 2 are alike. This one, crossing the narrowest part of the Lake, is considered one of the most beautiful. When the cast-iron bridge was put in place, it was supposedly set on cannonballs to allow for expansion caused by temperature changes. But when it was restored in 1974, no cannonballs were found. ◆ 74th St (the Ramble-Cherry Hill)

18 Cherry Hill Designed as a vantage point with a view of the Mall, the Lake, Bethesda Terrace and the Ramble, it also provided a turnaround for carriages, and a fountain for watering the horses. It was converted into a parking lot in 1934, but restored with 8500 new trees and shrubs and 23,000sq ft of new sod in 1981. ◆ Terrace Dr (west of Bethesda Terrace)

19 Bowling Green Lawn bowling and croquet were brought here in the 1920s. The folks who play here take their games very seriously, which explains why the greens are so well-maintained. You can get a permit to join them by calling 360.8133. ◆ 70th St at West Dr

19 Mineral Springs The concession stand overlooking Sheep Meadow also houses a comfort station. It replaced the Mineral Springs Pavilion, built in 1868 by a mineral water company that used it to dispense some 30 varieties of water. ◆ 70th St at West Dr

20 Sheep Meadow The original park design called for a meadow here to enhance the view from the gentle hill to the north. Today the hill is largely covered with asphalt, and the meadow, which was resodded in 1980 after concerts and other crowd-pleasing events had reduced it to hardpan, is encircled with a chain-link fence. But the view from the hill with the city skyline in the background is in some ways more breathtaking than the park's architects ever envisioned. ♦ 67th-70th Sts (West Dr)

Glenn Wolff

TAVERN ON THE GREEN

21 Tavern on the Green ★★$$$ (1870, **Jacob Wrey Mould**) This building, added over Olmsted's strenuous objection by parks commissioners controlled by **Boss Tweed** and **Tammany Hall**, was originally the Sheepfold, which housed the herd of Southdown sheep that grazed on the nearby meadow. In 1934, the sheep were exiled to Brooklyn's Prospect Park, and the building was converted into a restaurant. It was reconverted in 1976 by **Paul K.Y. Chen** and **Warner LeRoy** along the lines of LeRoy's late lamented Maxwell's Plum—which closed in 1988. The outdoor garden is a wonderful place to spend a summer evening in, and is spectacularly lit by twinkling lights in the trees from November to May. But at any time of year, the **Crystal Room**, dripping with chandeliers, is an unforgettable experience, especially for Sunday brunch. If you're lucky enough to be here when snow is falling outside, you'll never want to go home. ♦ American ♦ 67th St at Central Park West. Reservations recommended. 873.3200

22 Strawberry Fields A teardrop-shaped memorial grove, rehabilitated and maintained with funds provided by **Yoko Ono** in memory of her late husband, **John Lennon**. The former Beatle was assassinated in front of the Dakota apartment house, which overlooks this tranquil spot. ♦ 72nd St at Central Park West

23 Winter Drive Evergreens were originally planted in all parts of the park to provide color in the winter months, but the heaviest concentration is here, where 19th-century gay blades entered for ice-skating. When the ice on the Lake was hard enough, a red ball was hoisted on the flagpole above Belvedere Castle, and horsecars on Broadway carried the message downtown by displaying special flags. The parks commissioners estimated that as many as 80,000 people a day crowded the 20-acre frozen lake in the 1850s. The Arthur Ross Pinetum, added in 1971 at the north end of the Great Lawn, enhances the original plantings with unusual species of conifers from all over the world. ♦ West Dr (77th-100th Sts)

If you get lost in the park, find the nearest lamppost. The first 2 numbers signify the nearest numbered (east-west) street.

24 Belvedere Castle A scaled-down version of a Scottish castle was placed here to become part of the view. Its interior is just as impressive. The building houses a National Weather Service station and the **Central Park Learning Center**. ♦ Closed M. 79th St at West Dr. 772.0210

25 Shakespeare Garden A series of pathways, pools and cascades among trees and plants mentioned in the works of William Shakespeare. ♦ 80th St at West Dr

On 22 June 1901, Central Park visitors discovered that the benches along the Mall had been replaced with green rocking chairs. When they sat in them, they were approached by uniformed attendants who demanded a nickel for the use of a chair with arms, and 3 cents for one without. Most paid without a whimper, but those who complained were told that the chairs were the property of **Oscar F. Spate**, who had secured a Tammany Hall franchise for them. The chairs had cost him $1.50 each, and he said he could make a profit of about $250/day on them. But he said his plan went beyond the profit motive because it would keep dirty loungers out of the parks. He claimed he had invested $30,000 in his enterprise, but reporters noted that his cost had been only $9000. Spate simply said, *There's always expenses in a thing like this, you know.* But just as New Yorkers' objections began to cool, the city was hit with a heat wave. Thousands looked for relief in the parks. But the only places to sit in the shade were Spate's 5-cent rockers. It led to a riot when a man in Madison Square refused to pay, and onlookers ran the collectors out of the park. The next day, the mob marched on Central Park and be-

Central Park

gan smashing the chairs or carrying them off to furnish their own apartments. The rioting continued for almost a week until the Parks Commission ruled Spate's franchise invalid. Spate sued and lost. The Commission then appropriated $20,000 to replace the benches that had been removed, and used some of the money to buy Spate's stock of rocking chairs. When the chairs reappeared, each had a sign that said: *For the Exclusive Use of Women and Children,* followed by large letters spelling out the word *free.*

In its influence as an educator, as a place of agreeable resort, as a source of scientific interest, and in its effect upon the health, happiness, and comfort of our people may be found its chief value. **Frederick Law Olmsted,** *Report of the Commissioners of Central Park,* 1870

25 Swedish Cottage Moved here from Philadelphia after the 1876 Centennial Exposition, this building was used as a comfort station until Swedish-Americans mounted a protest. After many years as a laboratory, it was converted into a marionette theater in 1973. ♦ Admission. General public: Sa noon, 3PM; school groups: Tu-F 10:30AM, noon. 79th St at West Dr. Reservations required. 988.9093

26 Delacorte Theatre A 1960 addition to the park provides a modern home for **Joseph Papp**'s New York Shakespeare Festival. Free performances are given Tuesday-Sunday evenings at 8PM from late June until early September. Obtaining one of the 2000 tickets (which are given out to the general public only on the day of the performance) is a time-consuming process that begins early in the day when would-be audience members queue up for several hours in order to receive line numbers, which are handed out after the first 200 people have arrived. Holders of line numbers are then required to stay in line until about 6:15PM, when the numbers are exchanged for actual tickets. Although it is possible to obtain a line number for members of your party who are not present, no one can obtain an admission ticket for someone else. With good friends and a picnic, it can be a pleasant, albeit time-consuming, experience. ♦ 80th St at West Dr. 861.PAPP

27 The Great Lawn At 15 acres, this is the largest field in the park. It was formerly a rectangular reservoir that was drained just in time to provide a location for a Depression-inspired collection of squatters' shacks known as a *Hooverville*. By 1936 it was cleared again, and the oval-shaped lawn, with Belvedere Lake at the south end and 2 playgrounds to the north, was fenced off to create a cooling patch of green. It didn't stay that way long. It is now surrounded by ball fields with their backstops where the lawn should be, and overuse has almost completely eliminated the grass. In 1980, **Elton John** drew 300,000 people here for a concert; **Simon & Garfunkel** attracted

500,000 a year later; and in 1982, an anti-nuclear rally brought out 750,000. There are fewer such gatherings these days, but the New York Philharmonic and the Metropolitan Opera give several free performances here each summer, each of which attracts about 100,000 people. ♦ 80th-85th Sts (East-West Drs)

28 Cleopatra's Needle The Khedive of Egypt gave this obelisk to New York in 1881 and presented its mate to **Queen Victoria**, who had it placed on the Thames Embankment in London. When the 200-ton granite shaft was delivered to New York, it was placed in a special cradle and rolled here from the Hudson River on cannonballs. Because it had stood for many centuries in front of a temple built by Cleopatra, New Yorkers immediately dubbed it Cleopatra's Needle. It was, however, built by Egypt's **King Thotmes III** in 1600 BC. The hieroglyphics on its sides had survived for 3500 years, but air pollution here has rendered them unreadable in fewer than 100. Movie producer **Cecil B. De Mille** thoughtfully provided us with plaques translating the tales they told of Thotmes III, Rameses II and Osorkon I. ♦ 82nd St at East Dr

29 Claremont Stables Though not actually in the park, the stables are very much a part of it. Riders experienced with English saddle rent horses here and enjoy Central Park from its bridal path. ♦ 175 W 89th St (Columbus-Amsterdam Aves) Reservations required. 724.5100

30 The Reservoir Designed as part of the Croton Water System, this still-active receiving reservoir, covering nearly 107 acres, is better known for the soft-surface track that encircles it, providing a perfect amenity for serious runners. Once around is 1.58mi. ♦ 5th Ave-Central Park West (86th-96th Sts)

31 Conservatory Garden A park nursery was replaced in 1899 by a glass conservatory, which was removed in 1934 to create this series of gardens. It remains one of Central Park's best kept secrets, even though its presence is announced by an elaborate iron gate that once stood in front of the **Cornelius Vanderbilt II** mansion. The roofs of the buildings set into the hillside overlook 3 formal gardens, one of which is planted with seasonal flowers, another with perennials and a third with grass surrounded by yew hedges and flowering trees and featuring a wisteria-covered pergola. Each is enhanced by a fountain. ♦ 105th St at 5th Ave. 860.1330

32 The Mount When **General Washington**'s army was retreating through Manhattan in 1776, the British were held at bay here from a small fortress overlooking McGowan's Pass. The Mount was named for a tavern on top of the hill, which in 1846 became, of all things, a convent. The sisters moved out when the park was created, and the building was converted back into a tavern. It was one of the city's better restaurants in the late 19th century, but was demolished on orders of **Mayor John Purroy Mitchel** in 1917. ♦ 105th St at 5th Ave

33 The Forts During the War of 1812, 3 forts were built on the future park site to fend off an anticipated British attack. None was actually used, but their now-barren sites are marked with plaques and waiting for a history buff to recreate them. A little farther to the north, an 1814 blockhouse, the oldest structure in the park, is also waiting for renovation. These days, its thick walls, laced with gunports, look into groves of trees. But when they were placed there, men inside could spot an enemy miles away. None ever came, and few people climb the hill to see the site today. ♦ 106th-108th Sts (East Dr)

34 Harlem Meer The park's original northern boundary was at 106th St until 1863, when it was extended another 4 blocks northward, at which time this lake was created. It uses the Dutch word for *lake*, although it hardly qualified for a lake or a meer for a long time. In 1941, the Parks Dept altered its shoreline to eliminate the natural coves and inlets the original designers had placed there, and the whole thing was rimmed and lined with concrete. Fortunately, this once beautiful corner of the park, desperately in need of loving care, is being rebuilt. Work is underway (proposed completion 1991) to restore the 11-acre lake to its natural appearance; rebuild the boathouse and create a discovery center for children; and build a playground along 5th Ave and an esplanade for small concerts at 110th St. ♦ 110th St at 5th Ave

35 Lasker Pool Built in 1964, this shallow swimming pool doubles as an ice-skating rink in the winter months (10AM-10PM). It gets considerably less traffic than the downtown Wollman Rink, even though it costs less to use. It was built at the mouth of the stream that feeds Harlem Meer. ♦ Jul-Sep. 110th St at Lenox Ave

36 The Loch A natural pond undisturbed by the original designers that has been left alone to the point of being silted almost out of existence. A brook leading from the north end forms a small waterfall near the Huddleston Bridge, which carries the East Dr over it. ♦ 103rd-105th Sts (East Dr)

37 Great Hill The mansion of the **Bogardus** family that once stood on the crest of this 134ft hill was home to **Frederick Law Olmsted** during the park's construction. He considered replacing it with a lookout tower because of the view, not only of the park, but of the Hudson River to the west. The view is gone. So is the charm of Great Hill, which, although recently resodded and replanted, remains capped with asphalt. ♦ 103rd St at Central Park West

---

The first **New York City Marathon** took place in 1970, when 127 runners circled Central Park 4 times. The meager $1000 budget left no room for extravagance: to save money, post-race sodas were purchased in the Village and lugged uptown, where soda was more expensive.

The **New York City Marathon**, as we know it today, was born out of a misunderstanding. In 1976 the City Council was looking for a way to promote the bicentennial. **Ted Corbitt**, former Olympic runner and race organizer, seeing an opportunity to promote the marathon, which for the past 6 years had been a poorly attended event consisting of 4-plus loops around Central Park (26.2mi), suggested that the best racers from each of the 5 boroughs run. Council members, who somehow thought Corbitt meant that the participants would run through the streets of each of the 5 boroughs, absolutely loved the idea and urged the race organizers to make it happen, which they reluctantly did. Today, the marathon is the largest in the world with over 23,000 runners and 2.5 million spectators.

Beverly Sills
Diva, Former Director of the New York City Opera

The **New York City Opera**.

The best restaurants in the world, and I should know.

The greatest theater district in the world.

Brooklyn, where I was born.

Rita Di Renzo
Concierge Manager/Tower Manager, UN Plaza Hotel

Sichuan Pavilion, 44th St between 1st and 2nd Aves. Best Chinese food in the area, true to the Szechuan tradition.

Gospel music on Sunday mornings at the **New Canaan Church** in Harlem, followed by a wonderful lunch/brunch at **Sylvia's** on Broadway in Harlem. Sylvia's home-cooking is worth the trip. Meeting Sylvia is even better.

All prejudice aside—sunrise from one of the rooms at the **UN Plaza Hotel** is worth the price of a one-night stay.

Springtime in the **United Nations Park**. The rose garden in June conjures up enough serenity to make one understand the meaning of peace.

Walter Cronkite
Newscaster Emeritus, CBS Evening News

Museum of Broadcasting.

South Street Seaport Museum.

Staten Island Ferry. Best $1.00 ride in the city. Magnificent view of Lower Manhattan.

Cable ride from Manhattan to **Roosevelt Island**. Exciting view of the East River.

Ellis Island. Where freedom began for many Americans.

Brooklyn Botanic Garden. Where bonsai and horticultural beauty abound.

Gracie Mansion.

Clarke's Bar. A saloon at the corner of 55th St and 3rd Ave in the best tradition of the old New York City saloons before they tore down the *el*.

Zabar's, the deli supreme. However, almost any deli in New York should be visited for its odors and sights.

City Hall. A magnificent example of Federal architecture.

The **John Finley Walk** along the East River near **Gracie Square**, where you can watch the ships coming down the river.

Museum of Holography.

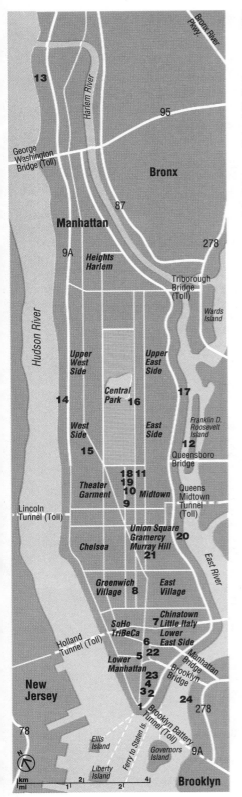

Places Lost & Found

1 Battery Park

Lost: A Civil War prison camp; the Castle Clinton as a fortification and later an aquarium.

Found: One of the greatest promenades on the New York City waterfront. Ferry rides to the *Statue of Liberty*. Castle Clinton Fort with its fascinating exhibits.

2 Jeannette Park
(alias Vietnam Veterans Memorial)

Lost: The plaza's first name, Jeannette Park, named after the ship that carried an ill-fated expedition to the North Pole, where all hands went down. Also lost—the famous L train.

Found: All Wall Streeters' lunch room and the future home of New York's Vietnam Veterans Memorial.

3 Bowling Green

Here is where **Peter Minuit** supposedly bought Manhattan for a pile of trinkets.

Lost: A field where Colonial gentlemen played bowles and which was leased to citizens for the annual fee of one peppercorn. Rebellious New Yorkers tore down the original statue of **George III**, dragged it through the streets and melted it into bullets.

Found: A period-piece restoration of the city's oldest public park and a foreground for the Custom House.

4 Wall Street

Lost: The wall was intended to defend the city from marauding Indians and Englishmen. Unfortunately, the protection was symbolic, since the settlers regularly dismantled the wall to heat or shore up their homes.

Found: The Grand Canyon of high finance.

5 City Hall Park and Square

Lost: This park has seen many faces. It served as an Old Negro Burial Ground, a parade ground, a training yard, a poorhouse, a prison and even the site of public executions—the apple trees were converted to gallows. It later was the site of the Croton Fountain and a post office.

Found: A delightful green retreat with the Delacorte Fountain that serves as an important ceremonial space for the city.

6 Canal Street

Lost: A real canal, 40ft wide, flanked by trees and a promenade. Even then, environmentalists opposed the canal because it bred mosquitoes and ruined a good fishing spot and ice-skating rink.

Found: New York City's biggest floating flea market. Here you will discover that every square foot of the sidewalk is a counter and everything is for sale.

Places Found

7 Orchard Street
Lost: The beautiful orchards from which it derives its name.

Found: A vestige of the old Lower East Side—a bargain hunter's paradise!

8 Washington Square
Lost: Layered under the current design are colonists' favorite duck-hunting grounds, a paupers' graveyard and the scene of militia parades. The square's darker days included a place of execution from the *Hanging Elm*, said to be the oldest tree in the city. The arch, originally wooden, was designed by **Stanford White** to commemorate the centennial of **George Washington**'s inauguration as president. It was so successful that it was re-created in marble.

Found: The living room of Greenwich Village. Here, everyone is a performer.

9 Bryant Park/New York Public Library
Lost: The Croton Reservoir, the city's first great reservoir, and the glorious Crystal Palace.

Found: A bit of classical Europe in Manhattan and, around the corner on 5th Ave, the Spanish Steps. This is where you go to watch the world parade goby.

10 Rockefeller Center
Lost: New York City's first botanical garden, later rented to farmers, and a plethora of speakeasies.

Found: The heart of Manhattan, a city within a city—one of the most important and most successful urban spaces of the century. The Channel Gardens: one side represents France, the other England, ergo its name; a wonderful place to sit and wait for a friend. The golden statue of Prometheus, which oversees the ice skaters and diners al fresco. This is where New York City puts out its Christmas tree.

11 Paley Park
Lost: An old stock club and not much else.

Found: An oasis. This exquisite little park, with a cascading water wall to drown out the city sounds, is the father of the *vest pocket park*—the most elegant spot to have a hot dog and relax.

12 Roosevelt Island
Lost: Called *Hog Island*, it served as a convenient spot to lodge the sick, insane and criminal elements of society. Later known as *Blackwell's Island*, the site housed a prison; here the legendary sex goddess **Mae West** demanded silk undies from her jailers and got them. Later it became a poorhouse as well as a laboratory for medical research. The name was then changed to *Welfare Island*.

Found: A dynamic place where you can take a soaring aerial tram ride high above towering skyscrapers to visit a unique experiment in community-oriented urban design that embodies new housing concepts for the future (only a 3 1/2 min tram ride from Midtown).

13 Cloisters Gardens
Located on a hill in Fort Tryon Park, the Cloisters Garden is a fabulous re-creation of a medieval garden..

14 79th Street Boat Basin
The variety of pleasure boats and unusual houseboats makes this a real fantasy trip; the surreal fountain only enhances the experience.

15 Lincoln Center
This cluster of cultural places may be of mixed merit, but the experience is a knockout, and other cities have followed with their own art centers.

16 The Metropolitan Museum of Art
One of the grandest, most popular amphitheaters, where people can sit on the steps and watch the world go by!

17 Carl Schurz Park
(alias East River Park) A promenade park along the East River near the mayor's house, with views, winding walks and surprise gardens

18 Museum of Modern Art Sculpture Garden
An elegantly designed garden by **Philip Johnson** that utilizes natural backdrops for great works of art.

19 666 5th Avenue
A tantalizing water wall by **Isamu Noguchi** forms the terminus of this shopping arcade.

20 Water Club
A public park with an elegant restaurant that functions as yet another link for the waterfront promenade spreading from the northern tip to the southern tip of Manhattan. Interestingly enough, the entire park is built over a wharf.

21 Gramercy Park
A unique 19th-century treasure, the park is owned by the residents of the buildings facing it. You need a key to enter.

22 Police Plaza and Duane Street
The plaza is a bridge. A piece of Europe in downtown Manhattan. Al fresco dining at the summer food festivals, pastry delights from **Ferrara's** or **Umberto's**.

23 Chase Manhattan Bank Plaza
Dubuffet's striking black-and-white sculpture, *Group of 4 Trees*, and **Isamu Noguchi**'s abstract stone and water garden.

24 Brooklyn Promenade and River Cafe
If you're in Brooklyn, this is the best view of Manhattan. If you're not, this may *still* be the best view of Manhattan.

M. Paul Friedberg

West Side

When Bloomingdale Road—its Dutch name (*Bloemendael*) now anglicized—linked up with Broadway, the **West Side** became even more accessible. But it got a later start than the East Side and never became as acceptable to the fast-moving social set.

In the early part of this century, many of the Lower East Side immigrants, especially Eastern European Jews, moved north of Midtown, on the West Side. Their children, in turn, left the conservative environment for the free-wheeling life of Greenwich Village or the East Side. Today, young people are moving back to restore homes and raise their children in the less restricted cultural and

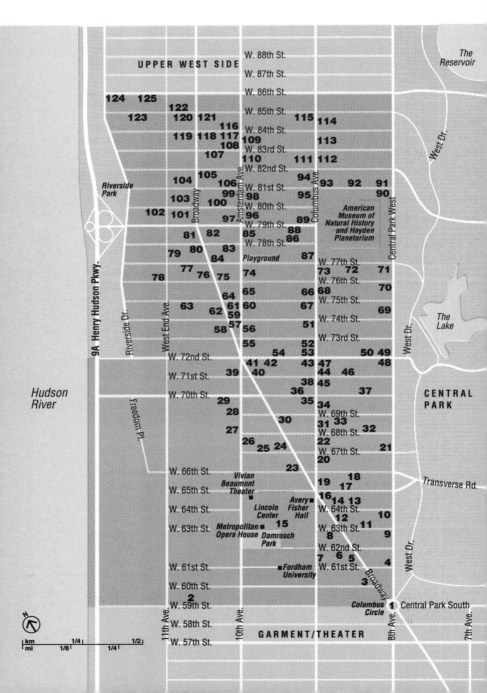

men and women. In addition to a popular sports/fitness center, it has a family and youth services department. ♦ 5 W 63rd St (Central Park West-Broadway) 787.4400

12 Fiorello's ★$$ Its location across from Lincoln Center has, no doubt, been the main reason the tables here continue to fill. The lighter offerings—pasta, salads—are quite good as a post-performance snack. More substantial dishes are less successful. ♦ Italian ♦ 1900 Broadway (W 63rd St) Reservations required. 595.5330

13 The Ginger Man ★$$ A city institution, the pubby atmosphere is conducive to good conversation, good people-watching and good drinking, especially after a Lincoln Center performance. Keep it simple—burgers, salads. Or come early for breakfast, a simple à la carte menu; waffles on the weekend. Don't miss the original 50ft mock-up of the *Statue of Liberty* on the roof. ♦ Continental ♦ 51 W 64th St (Broadway) Reservations recommended. 399.2358

14 The Saloon $$ Service in the cavernous room and street cafe is as erratic as the food on the enormous snack and dinner menu. But the crew of roller skate-shod waiters is amusing if not always efficient, and the outdoor tables are a great vantage point for people-watching. **The Saloon Grill** next door serves the same food in a slightly calmer atmosphere. (I like to sit on the upper level.) ♦ Continental ♦ 1920 Broadway (W 64th St) Reservations recommended. 874.1500

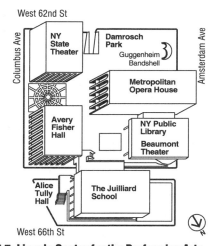

West 62nd St

15 Lincoln Center for the Performing Arts (1962-68, individual architects; master plan and coordination, **Wallace K. Harrison**) **Robert Moses**, planner and New York powerbroker, initiated the idea of a center for the city's major performing arts institutions in the 1950s, and this conglomeration of travertine halls came slowly into existence. Massed on a plaza above the street, they have been called an **Acropolis**, but the arrangement around the fountain is actually a static version

of **Michelangelo's Capitoline Hill** in Rome. Although the main theaters all take their formal cues from images of Classical architecture, they never really come together as a whole, and remain, at best, individual *tours de trite*.

At Lincoln Center:

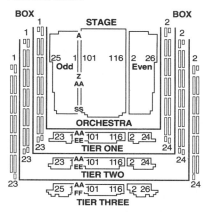

Center sections are numbered consecutively

Avery Fisher Hall (1966, **Max Abramovitz**) Opposite the State Theater. Originally **Philharmonic Hall**, this theater has been reconstructed several times in attempts to improve the acoustics. The final gutting and rebuilding of the interior in 1976 by **Johnson/Burgee** and acoustical consultant **Cyril Harris** resulted in better sound and a sleek auditorium with much light-wood paneling. The stabile in the foyer is by **Richard Lippold**. The **New York Philharmonic** is in residence here from September through May. Music director **Zubin Mehta** is the latest in an illustrious line that had included the late **Leonard Bernstein, Arturo Toscanini** and **Leopold Stokowski**. The inexpensive, informal *Mostly Mozart* concerts are held September through May. The Philharmonic's *Young People's Concerts* have been letting kids in on the motives behind the music since 1898; performances happen 4 times a year—don't miss the regularly scheduled open rehearsals. Films from around the world are shown here every September at the

New York Film Festival. ♦ Seats 2742. Broadway at 65th St. 580.8700. Film Society 877.1800

Metropolitan Opera House (1966, **Wallace K. Harrison**) The plaza's magnificent centerpiece, and home to the **Metropolitan Opera Company**, opened in 1966 with **Samuel Barber**'s *Cleopatra*. Behind the thin, 10-story colonnade and sheer glass walls, 2 wonderful colorful murals by **Marc Chagall** beam out onto the plaza. The interior is filled with a red-carpeted lobby, a dramatic staircase lit by exquisite Austrian crystal chandeliers and an

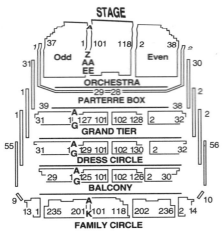

STAGE

Odd Z AA EE ... Even

ORCHESTRA

PARTERRE BOX 29=28

GRAND TIER

DRESS CIRCLE

BALCONY

FAMILY CIRCLE

Center sections are numbered consecutively

equally plush auditorium. There are 7 rehearsal halls in the building. The opera season, from mid September to April, leaves the stage available for visiting performers and companies, including the **American Ballet Theater**, during the rest of the year. ♦ Seats 3800. Broadway at W 65th St. 362.6000

Metropolitan Opera Shop Imaginative opera- and music-related gifts and clothing, most of them exclusive to this shop. Hard-to-find books, records, posters and libretti, with proceeds going to the Metropolitan Opera. ♦ Next to the Met box office. 580.4090

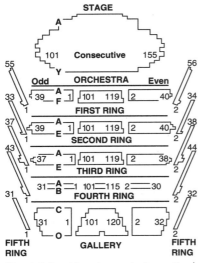

STAGE

Consecutive

ORCHESTRA Odd Even

FIRST RING

SECOND RING

THIRD RING

FOURTH RING

FIFTH RING   GALLERY   FIFTH RING

Rings 1, 2, 3 and 4 overhang orchestra row S

New York State Theater (1964, **Philip Johnson** and **Richard Foster**) On the plaza's south side. At the culmination of a series of increasingly grand entrance spaces is a striking 4-story foyer with balconies at every level, a pair of sculptures by **Elie Nadelman** and a gold-leaf ceiling. The rich red and gold auditorium was designed for both ballet and musical

theater. From 1964-69, under the artistic directorship of **Richard Rodgers**, revivals of musical classics were staged here. Now it is home to the New York City Ballet and the **New York City Opera**. In March 1989, conductor **Christopher Keene** took over the opera company's direction from former opera star **Beverly Sills**, who assumed the position in 1979. The ballet's season is usually November through February, and April through July. It's *Nutcracker* season from December 1 to 31. The City Opera performs from July through November. Note the diamond-shaped floodlights surrounding the building. ♦ Seats 2806. 150 W 65th St (Broadway) 870.5570

Adagio Buffet Have dinner overlooking the fountain before the performance. Open from 5-8PM. ♦ Closed M, Su. Avery Fisher Hall, courtyard side. 874.7000

Panevino Pleasant lunches, dinners, pastry and coffee, or just drinks. During the summer, the cafe spills out onto the plaza. ♦ Avery Fisher Hall, lobby. 874.7000

Guggenheim Bandshell (1969, **The Eggars Partnership**) South of the Met, within **Damrosch Park**. A beautiful space for free concerts. ♦ Seats 2500. SW corner of Lincoln Center. 877.2011

Vivian Beaumont Theater (1965, **Eero Saarinen & Associates**) North of the Met, behind a tree-studded plaza and reflecting pool (sculpture by **Henry Moore**). Recently reconstructed from a thrust to a proscenium stage, this theater has been plagued by trouble since the **Repertory Company of Lincoln Center** opened here in 1962 under the direction of **Robert Whitehead** and **Elia Kazan** with **Arthur Miller**'s apologia *After the Fall*. After several mediocre productions, there was a change of leadership. The new team, **Jules Irving** and **Herbert Blau** of the **Actor's Workshop** in San Francisco, had trouble adjusting to the thrust stage for the first few seasons, but produced some fine plays like **Bertolt Brecht**'s *Galileo*, **Heinar Kipphardt**'s *In the Matter of J. Robert Oppenheimer* and a revival of **Tennessee Williams**' *A Streetcar Named Desire*. The theater, however, was losing money, and after 8 years, impresario **Joseph Papp** took over. His **New York Shakespeare Festival at Lincoln Center** presented many innovative productions here and at the **Mitzi E. Newhouse**, including **David Rabe**'s *Streamers*, Brecht's *Threepenny Opera*, **Miguel Pinero**'s *Short Eyes* and **Anton Chekov**'s *The Cherry Orchard* (directed by **André Serban**). After continued deficits and power struggles, however, Papp left in 1977. The Beaumont was dark for 3 years, until director **Richmond Crinkley** formed a sextet of famous entertainment-world personalities to chart a new course for the theater, including playwright/actor/director **Woody Allen**, opera director **Sarah Caldwell**, playwright **Edward Albee**, director **Robin Phillips**, director **Ellis Rabb** and director **Liviu Ciulei**. **Gregory Mosher** is the Beaumont's current, and extremely successful, director. ◆ Seats 1100. 150 W 65th St (Broadway) 239.6277

Mitzi E. Newhouse Theater (1965, **Eero Saarinen & Associates**) Directly below the Beaumont, this smaller theater is for experimental and workshop productions, like **Mike Nichols'** controversial *Waiting for Godot* starring **Steve Martin, Robin Williams** and **Bill Irwin**. ◆ Seats 290. 150 W 65th St (Broadway) 787.6868

Juilliard School of Music (1968, **Pietro Belluschi** with **Eduardo Catalano** and **Westerman & Miller**) Across a large terrace/bridge over 66th St. Founded in 1905 by **Augustus D. Juilliard**, this is one of the nation's most acclaimed performing arts schools. Juilliard limits its enrollment to less than 1000; acceptance in itself is a career achievement for gifted students of music, dance and drama. The building is a Brutalist contrast to the center's Classicism. ◆ Theaters: **Juilliard Theater** (seats 933); **Drama Theater** (seats 206); **C. Michael Paul Hall** (seats 278) 144 W 66th St (Broadway) 799.5000

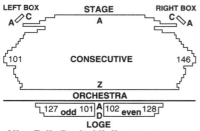

Alice Tully Recital Hall (1969, **Pietro Belluschi**) South of Juilliard, entered from Broadway, Alice Tully is the most intimate and best of the auditoriums at Lincoln Center. Designed for chamber music and recitals, it is the home of the **Chamber Music Society of Lincoln Center** from October through May. Students of the Juilliard School perform here too. ◆ Seats 1026. 1941 Broadway (W 66th St) 362.1911

New York Public Library, Library and Museum of the Performing Arts (1965, **Skidmore, Owings & Merrill**) The 2 galleries at this popular branch of the **New York Public Library** show costume and set designs, music scores and other tools and tricks of the trade, as well as art. The 212-seat **Bruno Walter Auditorium** presents showcase productions and music recitals. In addition to the most extensive collection of books on the performing arts in the city, the library is equiped with state-of-the-art audio equipment and a vast collection of recordings. ◆ M, Th noon-8PM; Tu-W, F noon-6PM; Sa 10AM-6PM. Lincoln Center Plaza, 111 Amsterdam Ave (W 65th St) 870.1630

Lincoln Center Guided Tours You not only see the physical plant and hear the legends and history, but you also get a peek at whatever else is going on: a rehearsal of the Philharmonic, auditions for the Met. Another plus: the expertise and enthusiasm of the tour guides, who are often performers themselves. Tours, which last about 1hr, are offered daily; call ahead as the schedule varies. ◆ Fee. Main Concourse (accessible through the lobby of the Met) 877.1800

Performing Arts Gift Shop Records, music boxes, jewelry, clothing and toys, all tuned into the performing arts. Many items, like the composer signature mugs and a belt with a music staff brass buckle, are designed for and sold exclusively at Lincoln Center. ◆ Main Concourse. 580.4356

Lincoln Center Poster Gallery This is the sales outlet for specially commissioned Lincoln Center prints and posters by such artists as **Josef Albers, Marc Chagall, Robert Indiana** and **Andy Warhol**. ◆ Closed Su. Main Concourse. 580.4673

Lincoln Center North (1990, **Davis Brody and Assoc.**) Tenants on the first 10 floors of this recently completed tower will include the Riverside branch of the **New York Public Library**, a theater for the **Film Society of Lincoln Center** and Lincoln Center Inc offices. Floors 12-29 are dormitories for students at Juilliard and the School of American Ballet. In order to finance construction of this building, Lincoln Center Inc sold $60 million worth of air rights to the **Stillman Group**, the developers of the neighboring condominiums at 3 Lincoln Plaza. ◆ W 65th St-Amsterdam Ave

16 Sfuzzi ★★$$$ Dramatic decor and fun food are served up in this liveliest addition to the Lincoln Center area. The bar is packed before and after the theater with smart young trendy

types sipping frozen *Sfuzzis*—a special combination of fresh peach nectar, champagne and peach schnapps, which comes in small, medium and ridiculous sizes. Or sit in the elevated dining area and try one of the inventive pastas, salads or pizzas on the menu. The stars come out at night, from **Madonna** to **Placido Domingo**. *An RSW recommendation.* ◆ Italian ◆ 58 W 65th St (Central Park West-Broadway) Reservations recommended. 873.3700

Restaurants/Nightlife: Red   **Hotels:** Blue
Shops/Parks: Green   **Sights/Culture:** Black

America's first streetcar was made in New York in 1932.

17 Shun Lee ★$$$ Long a favorite of the Lincoln Center crowd, the kitchen covers many regional Chinese cuisines and does them justice. The vast dining room is comfortable and gracious, though not as fancy as the prices. ◆ Chinese ◆ 43 W 65th St (Central Park West-Broadway) Reservations required. 595.8895

18 First Battery Armory, New York National Guard (1901, **Horgan & Slattery**; alterations 1978, **Kohn Pederson Fox**) Now **ABC** television studios hide behind this fun fortress facade. ◆ 56 W 66th St (Central Park West-Broadway)

19 Museum of American Folk Art/Eva and Morris Feld Gallery at Lincoln Square The best of American folk art, from the 18th century to the present: paintings, sculpture, textiles, furniture and decorative arts. The museum holds regular lectures and workshops, and has an adjacent gift shop. ◆ Voluntary contribution. Daily 9AM-9PM. 2 Lincoln Sq (Columbus Ave between W 65th-W 66th Sts) 496.2966

20 American Broadcasting Company Facilities (ABC) (1979, **Kohn Pederson Fox**) Two relatively new buildings fail to intrude on this quiet, low-scale street: 30 W 67th, the technical center, is set back respectfully; limestone, tan brick and glass are in harmony with the surroundings. The local television studios at 7 Lincoln Sq could have been a blank brick box, but the architects have used a lot of glass: the lobby is inviting. Try to see the atrium at night with its flying staircase on the top 3 floors. ◆ 30 W 67th St and 7 Lincoln Sq (Central Park West-Broadway)

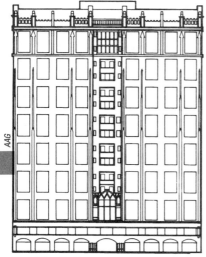

AAG

21 Hotel des Artistes (1913, **George Mort Pollard**) An early studio building designed specifically for artists—duplexes with double-height main spaces—this overscaled Elizabethan building is now one of the more lavish co-ops around. It has always attracted noteworthy tenants, among them **Isadora Duncan**,

Alexander Woollcott, Norman Rockwell, Noel Coward and **Howard Chandler Christy**. ◆ 1 W 67th St (Central Park West-Columbus Ave) 362.6700

Within the Hotel des Artistes:

Café des Artistes ★★★★$$$$ The West Side's most charming and romantic restaurant is entered through the hotel lobby. By day, light streams through the leaded-glass windows (come for the famous weekend brunch); the original 1934 murals of ethereal female nudes by **Howard Chandler Christy** are an inspiration. Owner **George Lang** updates the menu and wine list daily as well as seasonally; his renowned asparagus festival occurs every May and June. I hope you won't leave without sampling sweets beyond your wildest dreams on the **Great Dessert Plate**. Open late for after-theater supper. ◆ French ◆ Jacket and tie required after 5PM. Reservations required. 877.3500

22 Cameos ★$$ Another solution to Lincoln Center area dining—not stupendous, but certainly more than merely acceptable. Try the grilled chicken, salmon scallops or the succulent crabcakes. At lunchtime, the pretty room fills with sunlight. ◆ Continental ◆ 169 Columbus Ave (W 67th-W 68th Sts) 2nd floor. Reservations recommended. 874.2280

22 67 Wine & Spirits Service could sometimes be more personal, but it's hard to find a wider selection of fine wines and spirits at decent prices. ◆ Closed Su. 179 Columbus Ave (W 68th St) 724.6767

23 Tower Records and Tower Video Sister stores to the larger downtown branch; together the West Side's most complete resource for audio and video home entertainment.·◆ Records: 1965 Broadway (W 66th St) 799.2500. Video: 1977 Broadway (W 67th St) 496.2500

24 Andiamo! ★★$$$$ This dramatic room with a soaring skylight is adorned with the owner's collection of modern art. But don't let the flash put you off—the kitchen is refreshingly on target, with inventive risotto specials and a knack for perfectly grilled meats. Entered through the street-level **Café Bel Canto**, a casual spot owned by the same developer/restaurateur, Andiamo is a welcome alternative to the generally disappointing dining near

Lincoln Center. No smoking. ♦ Italian ♦ 1991 Broadway (W 67th-W 68th Sts) Reservations recommended. 362.3315

24 Café Bel Canto ★$ A 3-story, plant-filled atrium serviced by a personable staff. Good pasta specials and sandwiches, but if you just want to hang out, you don't have to order a thing. ♦ Italian ♦ 1991 Broadway (W 67th-W 68th Sts) 362.4642

25 Merkin Concert Hall Concert series, including ensemble programs, contemporary and chamber music. Located in the **Abraham Goodman House.** ♦ Seats 457. 129 W 67th St (Broadway-Amsterdam Ave) 362.8719

26 The Good Earth A health food supermarket, where you can get everything from all-natural allergy pills to free-range chicken. ♦ 167 Amsterdam Ave (W 68th St) 496.1616

27 Sweetwater's One of the few remaining cabaret rooms in town, with occasional forays into R&B and jazz. Consistently solid bookings, some big-name singers and groups, and an audience that knows talent. ♦ Cover. 170 Amsterdam Ave (W 68th St) Reservations recommended. 873.4100

28 Lincoln Square Synagogue (1970, **Hausman & Rosenberg**) A mannered, curved building with fins and rectangular block attached, all clad in travertine, *à la* neighboring Lincoln Center. One of Manhattan's most popular Orthodox synagogues. ♦ 200 Amsterdam Ave (W 69th St) 874.6100

29 Cafe Luxembourg ★★$$$ A people-watcher's Art Deco brasserie, affiliated with TriBeCa's trendy **Odeon.** The zinc-topped bar draws a stylish, international crowd, and the menu is a mélange of French, Italian and regional American offerings. Order the duck cassoulet or any salad. ♦ French ♦ 200 W 70th St (Amsterdam-West End Aves) Reservations recommended. 873.7411

30 Christ and St. Stephen's Church (1880, **William H. Day**; alterations 1897, **J.D. Fouquet**) This is a charming country church holding up well in the big city. ♦ 120 W 69th St (Columbus Ave-Broadway) 787.2755

31 La Boîte en Bois ★★$$$ A charming French bistro a few steps downstairs but far from the madding crowd on Columbus Ave. Country atmosphere and Provençale accented menu. Pretheater dinner 5:30-6:30PM. ♦ French ♦ 75 W 68th St (Central Park West-Columbus Ave) Reservations recommended. No credit cards. 874.2705

32 19 West 68th Street In 1953, at 22 years old, **James Dean** moved into his first New York apartment on the top floor of this building. One year later he moved to California to

work on his first movie, *East of Eden.* ♦ Central Park West-Columbus Ave

33 Santa Fe ★$$ The refurbished old townhouse dining room is painted a flattering, soft desert tone, and fitted with fine detailing and Southwestern arts and crafts. Though a pleasure to sit in, the mostly Mexican food—with some original American dishes—is bland. ♦ Mexican ♦ 72 W 69th St (Central Park West-Columbus Ave) Reservations recommended. 724.0822

34 Columbus $$ Where the Brat Pack kicks back. American regional dishes, pub fare (soup, salad, omelets, burgers) and a relaxed atmosphere mask serious celebrity-spotting. Owned by **Mikhail Baryshnikov, Regis Philbin** and company. ♦ American ♦ 201 Columbus Ave (W 69th St) 799.8090

35 Rikyu ★$$ Predates the trendy invasion of Columbus Ave, and is still popular with the locals and the Lincoln Center crowd. Competition from the neighboring sushi bars keeps the prices reasonable. Good sushi and traditional dishes. ♦ Japanese ♦ 210 Columbus Ave (W 69th St) 799.7847

35 Soutine A small bake shop with the feel of a French *boulangerie.* ♦ 106 W 70th St (Columbus Ave) 496.1450

36 Ying ★$$ Pretty flowers and food, but not quite up to Chinatown standards. Unusual salads and tasty chicken dishes. Service is pleasant. ♦ Chinese ♦ 117 W 70th St (Columbus Ave-Broadway) 724.2031

37 Body Design by Gilda Stylish workout attire for women designed by **Gilda Marx,** one of the original promoters of aerobic dance, is sold in this small studio. Well-choreographed aerobics classes, many taught by young dancers, are offered all day long. ♦ 55 W 70th (Columbus Ave) 799.8540

38 Dapy *Objet d'pop art,* or designer bric-a-brac? Your call. ♦ 232 Columbus Ave (W 70th-W 71st Sts) 877.4710. Also at: 431 W. Broadway. 925.5082

38 Victor's ★$$$ Cuban cuisine at its best if you are fond of simple fare like black beans and rice. Sit at the enclosed terrace and enjoy

Columbus Ave movement while sampling plantain and chicken stews. After the theater, try the Cuban sandwiches (*Cubano*): saffron bread filled with ham, roast pork, pickles and a touch of mayonnaise. Coffee here is almost as rich as the espresso served in Little Havana in Miami. ♦ Cuban ♦ 240 Columbus Ave (W 71st St) 595.8599

39 Applause Theater Books For thespians, a good place to find an obscure play or movie scenario. There are books on other performing arts too. ♦ 211 W 71st St (Broadway-West End Ave) 496.7511

40 The Dorilton (1902, **Janes & Leo**) When this Beaux-Arts masterpiece was completed in 1902, critic **Montgomery Schuyler** was so displeased with its design that he wrote the following in *Architectural Record: The incendiary qualities of the edifice may be referred, first to violence of color, then to violence of scale, then to violence of 'thingness', to the multiplicity and importunity of the details.* When the Landmarks Preservation Commision granted it landmark status in 1974, they described it as *exceptionally handsome.* ◆ 171 W 71st St (Broadway)

41 Sherman Square Another one of those places where Broadway crosses the city grid to form a bow tie, not a square. Sherman Sq is occupied by an **IRT Subway Control House** (1904, **Heins & LaFarge**). This is one of 2 surviving ornate entrances to the original IRT subway line (the other is at the **Battery Park Control House** in Lower Manhattan). Note the stylish detailing of the Neo-Dutch, somewhat Baroque shed. Directly to the north, the other half of the tie is **Verdi Square**, where a patch of trees surrounds a statue of composer **Giuseppe Verdi** with characters from 4 of his operas (1906, **Pasquale Civiletti**; a gift from the Italian community). ◆ W 72nd St (Broadway at Amsterdam Ave)

41 Gray's Papaya $ An international cast of characters frequents this round-the-clock takeout that boasts hot dogs that are *tastier than filet mignon*, and a papaya drink that is *a definite aid to digestion.* ◆ Hot dogs ◆ 2090 Broadway (W 72nd St) 799.0243

42 Acker-Merrall-Condit Old established liquor merchants with a reputation for good service. Experts on Burgundy. Nice store design too. Late-night hours—until 11:30PM—are handy when a last-minute gift is needed. ◆ Closed Su. 160 W 72nd St (Columbus Ave-Broadway) 787.1700

42 Fine & Schapiro ★$$ Classic kosher delicatessen. The food makes one nostalgic for the days before cholesterol-counts. (As a concession, there's a salt-free corner on the menu.) Their hot dogs may cost more than the street-corner version, but they're theologically correct. ◆ Jewish deli ◆ 138 W 72nd St (Columbus Ave-Broadway) 877.2874

West Side

BETSEY JOHNSON.

43 Betsey Johnson The West Side branch of this trendy boutique, full of the designer's whimsical and colorful outfits and accouterments. ◆ 248 Columbus Ave (W 71st-W 72nd Sts) 362.3364. Also at: 130 Thompson St. 420.0169; 251 E 60th St. 319.7699

In 1884 the *New York Daily Graphic* reported that the Dakota is *one of the most perfect apartment houses in the world.* No wonder **Lauren Bacall, Judy Holliday, Roberta Flack** and **Gilda Radner**, among many others, have called it home.

43 To Boot West Side landmark specializing in cowboy boots, but now also stocking the best in men's and women's footwear—casual, business and formal. Also handwoven ties and scarves. ◆ 256 Columbus Ave (W 71st-W 72nd Sts) 724.8249

44 Shu Uemura Ultraminimalist Japanese skincare boutique situated on 3 levels—sleek, sleeker, sleekest. Worth a look for the decor. ◆ 241 Columbus Ave (W 71st St) 724.0684

45 La Kasbah $$$ A fairly good Moroccan restaurant with semiauthentic decor. The service is slow and indifferent, but the couscous is excellent, the falafel is fresh and the kabobs are spicy and tender. Desserts are heavy and overly sweetened with honey, but the coffee is wonderfully aromatic—just the way they like it at the sidewalk cafes in Fez. ◆ Moroccan ◆ Closed F. 70 W 71st St (Central Park West-Columbus Ave) 769.1690

46 Los Panchos $$ Nice outdoor dining area in summer is a reason to go, not the hit-or-miss food. ◆ Tex-Mex ◆ 71 W 71st St (Columbus Ave) 874.7336

46 Café La Fortuna ★$ A mainstay of the neighborhood for years—**John Lennon's** former hangout—this pleasant, unassuming cafe serves excellent Italian coffees and a mouth-watering array of traditional pastries and other sweets. The garden in the rear is an ideal respite from summer's heat—the favorite seasonal drink: unparalleled iced cappuccino laced with homemade chocolate or coffee ice. ◆ Cafe ◆ 69 W 71st St (Columbus Ave) No credit cards. 724.5846

CHARIVARI

47 Charivari 72 An intriguing mix of clothes for men and women, ranging from leather coats by **Claude Montana**, and hand-knit sweaters to evening dresses—all expensive. ◆ 58 W 72nd St (Columbus Ave) 787.7272

48 Sidewalkers ★$$$ As close as you'll find to a Chesapeake Bay shorefront crab shack, except it's located at the rear of an old residential hotel lobby. ◆ Seafood ◆ Closed Su. 12 W 72nd St (Central Park West-Columbus Ave) 799.6070

49 Dakota Apartments (1884, **Henry J. Hardenbergh**) One of the first luxury apartment houses in the city (along with the **Osborne** on W 57th St and **34 Gramercy Park East**), the building was christened when someone remarked to its owner, **Edward Clark**, president of the Singer Sewing Company, that it was so far out of town, *it might as well be in Dakota Territory.* Clark, not without

a sense of humor, went on to instruct the architect, Henry Hardenbergh, to embellish the building with symbols of the Wild West: arrowheads, sheaves of wheat and ears of corn appear in bas-relief on the building's interior and exterior facades. Hardenbergh later designed the **Plaza Hotel**. The same skill is evident here, but the style is very different. This is a highly original masonry mass with echoes of the Romanesque and German Renaissance. Victorian details and miscellaneous pieces sprout at every turn—turrets, gables, oriels, dormers, pinnacles—but all are under control. The top 3 floors were once servants' quarters, a playroom and a gymnasium for children; they are now some of the most prized apartments in Manhattan. The building has gained notoriety not only as the setting for the film *Rosemary's Baby*, but as the home of **Boris Karloff, Judy Garland, Lauren Bacall, Leonard Bernstein, Rex Reed, Roberta Flack, Yoko Ono** and **John Lennon, Kim Basinger** and **Chris Whittle**. ♦ 1 W 72nd St (Central Park West)

50 Dallas Barbecue ★★$$ The barbecued ribs and chicken are well-seasoned, tender, juicy and handily inexpensive. However, for many the most wonderful thing at this large, informal, spaciously arranged multilevel room—well-populated with locals—is the *huge* loaf of addictive, fabulously greasy onion rings. ♦ Barbecue ♦ 27 W 72nd St (Central Park West-Columbus Ave) 873.2004

51 Tommy Hilfiger Men's sportswear by the self-promoting designer. ♦ 282 and 284 Columbus Ave (W 73rd-W 74th Sts) 769.4910

51 Last Wound-Up All windup toys, for the lawn, the floor, the countertop and the bathtub. Also a selection of music boxes, new and antique. One of my favorite stores. ♦ 290 Columbus Ave (W 73rd-W 74th Sts) 787.3388

52 Cavaliere ★★$$$ Slightly pricey but satisfactory Italian restaurant with a Nouvelle overtone. Best bets are the tuna with watercress, mushrooms and scallions, and the monkfish with sun-dried tomatoes, leeks, lemon and white wine. Pretheater prix-fixe dinner served all night. ♦ Italian ♦ 108 W 73rd St (Columbus-Amsterdam Aves) Reservations recommended. 799.8282

52 Silver Palate Kitchens Inc. This premium catering, takeout and specialty food company was purchased from the originators, **Julee Rosso** and **Sheila Lukins**, by a New Jersey food manufacturer in 1988. Quality and service remain high. ♦ 274 Columbus Ave (W 72nd-W 73rd Sts) 799.6340

53 Blades West Rent a pair of in-line skates (aka *Rollerblades*) and protective gear, then set off for a day of *blading* in the park. The blades, as well as ice skates, skateboards, snowboards, helmets and accessories, are also for sale. ♦ 105 W 72nd St (Columbus Ave) 787.3911

54 Eclair $$ Open since 1939, this cafe is the last remnant of the time when W 72nd St was home to a wave of Middle European immigrants and was known as **Little Vienna**. The restaurant is not what it used to be, but a midafternoon *kaffee und kuchen* (try the *Schwarzwalder* kirsch torte or Linzer torte) is optimal. ♦ Cafe ♦ 141 W 72nd St (Columbus Ave-Broadway) No credit cards. 873.7700

55 Genoa ★★$$ Don't let the standard Italian restaurant interior stop you: Genoa's pasta is fresh and authentic. Bowls of imported grated sardo cheese on each table lead the way for carefully prepared entrees: sautéed shrimp *fra diavolo*, or *simone* (ziti and vegetables in marinara sauce). Dishes range from the simple to the spicy, and all succeed. Reservations are not accepted, so be prepared for a wait in line. ♦ Italian ♦ Closed M. 271 Amsterdam Ave (W 72nd-W 73rd Sts) 787.1094

55 Star Magic Crystals, New Age-inspired accessories and trinkets for the astral traveler. ♦ 275 Amsterdam Ave (W 73rd St) 769.2020. Also at: 743 Broadway. 228.7770

56 Vinnie's Pizza ★$ Deserves its first-rate reputation—the thin-crust pizza is loaded with cheese and superfresh toppings. The parlor

itself wouldn't win any prizes, so be sure to get your pie to go. ♦ Pizza ♦ 285 Amsterdam Ave (W 73rd-W 74th Sts) 874.4382

57 Apple Bank (1928) A Florentine palace seems like an appropriate model for a bank. This one, by the masters **York & Sawyer** (who also designed the **Federal Reserve Bank of New York**), skillfully contains a proper rectangular banking hall within the trapezoidal building necessary on the site—the additional triangular wedge inside is filled by alcoves and mezzanines behind the arches. ♦ 2100 Broadway (W 73rd-W 74th Sts) 573.6551

58 Ansonia Hotel (1904, **Graves & Duboy**) The grande dame of the Belle Epoque apartment buildings in New York. (As with the **Hotel des Artistes**, this was never a hotel at all; the appellation is from the French *hôtel de ville*.) This lyric masterpiece, bristling with ornament, balconies, towers and dormers is the *Queen of Broadway*. The thick walls and floors required for fireproofing have made the 16-story building a favorite of musicians. Among those who have lived here are: **Enrico Caruso, Arturo Toscanini, Lily Pons, Igor Stravinsky** and **Ezio Pinza**; also **Florenz Ziegfeld, Sol Hurok, Theodore Dreiser** and **George Herman (Babe) Ruth**. ♦ 2109 Broadway (W 73rd-W 74th Sts) 724.2600

59 Coastal ★★$$$ Fresh ingredients and a certain degree of inventiveness in the kitchen keep Coastal a cut above its similarly noisy and crowded neighbors. Good appetizers (order the grilled vegetables), interestingly sauced fish, homemade ice creams. ♦ American ♦ Closed Su. 300 Amsterdam Ave (W 74th St) Reservations accepted for more than 4. 769.3988

60 Freddy and Pepe's Gourmet Pizza ★$ A good pizza base under a myriad of toppings make for a filling meal at this terrific pizza place. Try the unusual seafood smorgasbord pie. ♦ Pizza ♦ 303 Amsterdam Ave (W 74th-W 75th Sts) No credit cards. 799.2378

61 Beacon Theatre Special films, dance groups, foreign performing arts groups, as well as mainstream soul and rock artists appear here. Some say the magnificent interior by **Walter Ahlschlager** is second only to **Radio City**'s. ♦ Seats 2700. 2124 Broadway (W 75th St) 496.7070

61 China Club A fun dance bar featuring sounds from Motown to **Prince**. Live music every night. Young, energetic crowd. ♦ Cover. 2130 Broadway (W 75th St) 877.1166

62 Fairway Residents swear by this all-purpose market, which has the best produce, freshest cheese and zaniest service. Best times to shop: early morning or after 8PM. ♦ 2127 Broadway (W 74th-W 75th Sts) 595.1888

West Side

62 Citarella Fish Retail fish store and raw seafood bar, ideal for a quick stand-up snack before a show at the **Beacon Theater**. The elaborate fish-sculpture displays add a new dimension to window dressing. ♦ 2135 Broadway (W 74th St) 874.0383

63 254 West 75th Street (1885) This house, distinguished by 3 arches and excellent brick-stone-and-ironwork, stands out among the many fine houses in this area. ♦ Amsterdam-West End Aves

64 Ernie's $$$ Table-hopping is the key word here; if you don't know anybody, it can get really lonely. The angel hair pasta and grilled baby chicken are good enough to eat; the rest of the menu is just an excuse to congregate beneath the high ceilings of this spacious, Postmodern watering hole. ♦ Italian ♦ 2150 Broadway (W 75th St) 496.1588

65 Bennie's $ The perfect place to pick up an inexpensive lunch to bring to nearby Central Park. ♦ Lebanese ♦ 321¹/₂ Amsterdam Ave (W 75th-W 76th Sts) 874.3032

66 Mughali $$ If I feel hungry for Indian food that is not too spicy or far out, this is the place. The *tandoori* is best, and there is always a good mango chutney served with the curry, which is on the mild side. Desserts are dull and plain, except for the rice pudding with rosewater, which is recommended. Amiable service and pleasant decor. ♦ Indian ♦ 320 Columbus Ave (W 75th St) 724.6363

67 Pappardella $$$ Very acceptable pastas and *secondi* with a Florentine accent. Try a thin-crusted pizza with a glass of Chianti, and relish the escape from the bustle of Columbus Ave. ♦ Italian ♦ 316 Columbus Ave (W 75th St) 595.7996

68 Memphis ★★$$$ Southern and Cajun-style cuisine, and as consistently reliable a place as you'll find serving below-Mason-Dixon fare in the 5 boroughs. Its nondescript, slate-gray entrance is easy to overlook, not so the eats. ♦ American ♦ 329 Columbus Ave (W 75th-W 76th Sts) 496.1840

68 Putumayo Fashions from developing countries around the world—Thailand, Peru, Guatemala—in vivid, eye-appealing colors. Create complete outfits of woven skirts and crisp linen blouses and shirts, or use one piece, like the classic llama sweaters, to match any kind of wardrobe. ♦ 339 Columbus Ave (W 76th St) 595.3441. Also at: 857 Lexington Ave. 734.3111; 147 Spring St. 966.4458

69 San Remo (1930, **Emory Roth**) In contrast to the streamlined **Century** and **Majestic** apartments by **Irwin Chanin**, Roth's twin towers are capped with Roman temples surmounted by finials. ♦ 145-146 Central Park West (W 74th-W 75th Sts)

Jack Dempsey's 14-room apartment at 145 Central Park West included a huge kitchen where the fighter practiced his favorite hobby—cooking.

70 Central Park West/76th Street Historic District (Designated 1973) This district comprises the blocks on Central Park West between W 75th and W 77th Sts, and about half of 76th St. It includes a variety of row houses built at the turn of the century; the Neo-Grecian Nos. 21-31 (**George M. Walgrove**) were the earliest, and the Baroque Nos. 8-10 (**John H. Duncan**) the most recent. Of interest as well are the **Kenilworth** (151 Central Park West, 1908, **Townsend, Steinle & Haskell**)—an apartment building noteworthy for its convex mansard roof and highly ornamented limestone—and the Oxfordish **Universalist Church of New York** (W 76th St at Central Park West, 1898, **William A. Potter**). Also included in the designated area is 44 W 77th St (1909, **Harde & Short**), a Gothic-style building designed as artists' studios; much of the ornament was removed in 1944. ♦ Central Park West (W 75th-W 77th Sts)

71 New-York Historical Society (Central portion 1908, **York & Sawyer**; north and south wings 1938, **Walker and Gillette**) Although the society is housed in a dry, Neoclassical French building with unimaginative additions, the collection itself is rich with Americana. Wall-to-wall silver, rare maps, antique toys, splendid carriages, portraits by **Gilbert Stuart** and **Benjamin West**, watercolors by **John James Audubon** and landscapes by again-popular **Frederic Church** and the rest of the **Hudson River** boys. The society also has stunning 17th-, 18th- and 19th-century furniture arranged in chronological order. Changing shows touch on cast-iron stoves or American bands or early women's magazines, and are truly entertaining. Until 1993, the society will be the temporary home for the exhibitions, educational programs and gift shop of the **Jewish Museum**, whose permanent space on 5th Ave at 92nd St is undergoing renovation. The library here is one of the major reference libraries of American history in this country. If you're wondering about the hyphen in *New-York Historical Society*: it's a point of pride for the museum: when it was founded in 1804, everybody spelled New-York that way. *An RSW recommendation.* ♦ Admission. Tu-Sa 10AM-5PM; voluntary contribution Tu. 170 Central Park West (W 76th-W 77th Sts) 873.3400

72 Scarletta ★★$$$ A lovely Northern Italian restaurant with a large dinner menu and fast and efficient service. Excellent pastas and antipastos, especially the prosciutto. Try the specials of the day, which are often Italian dishes that one can usually find only in Italian homes. Desserts are of the rich Italian variey. Good espresso. ♦ Italian ♦ 50 W 77th St (Central Park West-Columbus Ave) 769.9191

73 Isabella $$ Typical West Side Italian restaurant with a simple, pleasant decor and an inviting sidewalk cafe. The menu sports good pasta and grilled dishes, such as veal chops and chicken. Salads are ordinary and desserts should be avoided. The espresso, however, is good. Jammed with a young crowd in the spring and summer. ♦ American ♦ 359 Columbus Ave (W 77th St) 724.2100

73 Kenneth Cole Shoes by the self-promoting designer. Copies of his print ads, which address the political and social issues of the moment—one even suggests that customers buy one less pair of shoes and, instead, donate the money to AIDS research—are displayed along the right-hand wall as you enter. ♦ 353 Columbus Ave (W 76th-W 77th Sts) 873.2061

74 Alcala ★★$$$ When I enter this Spanish restaurant, I always stop at the bar, where the tapas are as authentic as they can be outside of Spain. The menu here is traditional. The shrimps in garlic sauce are fresh and well-spiced and the grilled sardines are also good. Among the main courses, the suckling pig is delicate and succulent and scores higher than the salted cod with garlic confit. For those with a sweet tooth, the Catalan cream is excellent. ♦ Spanish ♦ 349 Amsterdam Ave (W 76th-W 77th Sts) 769.9600

75 The Alameda $$ An adaptation of **Diego Rivera**'s famous *Alameda* mural greets diners, who enjoy traditional Mexican dishes. Look for the ghost eagle in the mirror of the Victorian bar. ♦ Mexican ♦ 2160 Broadway (W 76th St) 873.1500

75 Promenade Theatre Now the home of the **Second Stage Company**, which features revivals of out-of-town, early and lesser-known plays by established playwrights, often with big-name stars returning to the boards to hone their craft. ♦ Seats 399. 2162 Broadway (W 76th-W 77th Sts) 580.1313

76 Pizza Joint ★$ Terrific pie with all the fixin's. ♦ Pizza ♦ 2165 Broadway (W 77th St) No credit cards. 724.2010. Also at: 70 W 71st St. 799.2222

77 Caffè e Trattoria Bernini ★$$ Lovely and unpretentious trattoria with a Northern Italian

accent. Call ahead to find out if you need to BYOB. ♦ Italian ♦ 250 W 77th St (Broadway-West End Ave) Reservations recommended. No credit cards. 496.6674

Between March and August of 1946, 26 sessions of the **United Nations Security Council** were held in the Hunter College gymnasium in the Bronx. Other locations used included a building on the East River and another in Lake Success in Long Island.

Restaurants/Nightlife: Red   **Hotels:** Blue
Shops/Parks: Green   **Sights/Culture:** Black

78 343-357 West End Avenue (1891, **Lamb & Rich**) This complete block-front on West End and around both corners is a lively, well-ordered collection typical of Victorian townhouses, and the only West Side block without high rises between West End Ave and Riverside Dr. (Rumor has it that **Mayor Jimmy Walker**'s mistress lived at 76th and Broadway; supposedly the block was zoned to protect his river view.) The variety of shapes and materials—gables, bays and dormers; limestone, red and tan brick—is clearly under control, resulting in a stylish, humorous energy with no dissonance. ◆ W 76th-W 77th Sts

79 West End Collegiate Church and School (1893, **Robert W. Gibson**) The school, which was established by the Dutch in 1637, built itself a copy of the market building in Haarlem, Holland. This is a particularly good example of Dutch detailing; note the stepped gables and the use of long bricks. ◆ 370 West End Ave (W 77th St) 787.1566

80 La Caridad $ An inexpensive Cuban/Chinese beanery that's been discovered. That means factor in waiting time. Still, the best of its kind. ◆ Cuban/Chinese ◆ 2199 Broadway (W 78th St) No credit cards. 874.2780

81 Apthorp Apartments (1908, **Clinton & Russell**) This is the best of the 3 big West Side courtyard buildings (the **Belnord** on 86th St, and **Astor Court** on Broadway between 89th and 90th Sts are the others). The ornate ironwork here is especially wonderful. It was built by **William Waldorf Astor**, who owned much of the land in the area, and was named for the man who had owned the site in 1763. ◆ 2101-2119 Broadway (W 78th-W 79th Sts)

82 Eeyore's Children browse happily through the extensive selection of books while adults get expert help with gift choices. Story hour on Sunday; call for details. ◆ 2212 Broadway (W 78th-W 79th Sts) 362.0634. Also at: 25 E 83rd St. 988.3404

West Side

83 Stand-Up NY Comedy club for up-and-coming as well as established merchants of the one-liner. ◆ Cover, minimum. Shows: M-Th, Su 9PM; F 9, 11:30PM; Sa 8, 10:15PM, 12:30AM. 236 W 78th St (Amsterdam Ave-Broadway) Reservations required. 595.0850

84 Sports $$ A blackboard lists the sporting events of the day, viewable on any number of TV screens. If you're shut out of table space, there are always the bleachers in the back. Eat if you must. ◆ American ◆ 2182 Broadway (W 77th-W 78th Sts) 874.7208

85 Aris Mixon & Co. This store holds a wonderful mix of antique and vintage stemware, jewelry, turn-of-the-century prints, collectible salt and pepper shakers, ceramics and handmade toys. At Christmas, it becomes a wonderland of ornaments and small gifts. ◆ 381 Amsterdam Ave (W 78th-W 79th Sts) 724.6904

86 21-131 West 78th Street (1886) Built by **Raphael Gustavino**, an Italian mason famous for his vaults (see the **Oyster Bar** at **Grand Central Terminal**), these 6 red and white houses are unified by their symmetrical arrangement and cheery details. ◆ Columbus-Amsterdam Aves

87 Museum Cafe ★$$ A perfect stop for a quick lunch or dinner just across the street from the **American Museum of Natural History**. The interior is a dull, restful pink with wood trimmings; try to eat in the enclosed sidewalk cafe. The restaurant stays open all night on Thanksgiving Eve—the **Macy's Day Parade** floats are inflated out front. Stick to the Grecian chicken salad or the gargantuan bowls of pasta. ◆ American ◆ 366 Columbus Ave (W 77th St) 799.0150

87 Les Delices Guy Pascal $ A small French-style cafe serving breakfast and dessert pastries, sandwiches, quiches and pâtés, salads and hot and cold beverages. A civilized place to stop before or after a visit to the museum. ◆ 370 Columbus Ave (W 77th-W 78th Sts) 874.5400

87 Mythology An irresistible store with a selection of antique tin toys, artists' books, masks, fantastic robots, postcards from the 1940s and eye-fooling, joke-inspiring fake food. Furniture and other pieces by local artists and craftspeople. ◆ 370 Columbus Ave (W 77th-W 78th Sts) 874.0774

88 Bag One Gallery Limited-edition graphics by **John Lennon**. Named after the interviews that John and Yoko gave from the inside of a black bag. ◆ By appointment only. 110 W 79th St (Columbus-Amsterdam Aves) 595.5537

89 Only Hearts Silky lingerie, sweet-smelling sachets, jewelry, books about hearts and kissing and heart-shaped waffle irons and fly swatters are sold in this pretty shop for the shameless romantic. ◆ 386 Columbus Ave (W 79th St) 724.5608

89 Laura Ashley It's as if **Louisa May Alcott** had gone into retailing a century later. Floral patterns, frilly trim and classic understatement. Home furnishings and fashions. ◆ 398 Columbus Ave (W 79th St) 496.5110

The ornate iron gates and vast interior courtyard of the **Apthorp Apartments** at 2207 Broadway have turned up in a number of movies: *Heartburn, Network, Eyewitness, The Cotton Club, The Changeling* and *The Money Pit*, to name a few.

AAG

90 American Museum of Natural History

(Original wing 1872, **Calvert Vaux** and **Jacob Wrey Mould**; body 1899, **J.C. Cady & Co.** and **Cady, Berg & See**; Columbus Ave wing 1908, **Charles Volz**; other additions 1924, 1926, 1933, **Trowbridge & Livingston**) One of the memorable New York experiences for families is a day spent with the dinosaurs and wild elephants, the *Star of India* sapphire and the cross section of a 1300-year-old sequoia. During 1991, to the despair of many regular visitors, the dinosaurs will be removed for restoration, in phases, as part of a 5-year remodeling project. Although museum officials promise bigger and better skeletons, New Yorkers who grew up visiting the dinosaurs feel as though they are losing their old friends. For now, most of the other exhibitions, including the musty dioramas, will be left alone. The museum officials know that there would be an angry protest meeting if anyone suggested a replacement for the obviously fake 90ft fiberglass blue whale that hangs in the **Hall of Ocean Life**. It's all part of the old-fashioned charm of this gigantic storehouse of nature's mysteries, one of the largest of its kind in the world (more than 34 million artifacts and specimens). It's not all animal, vegetable or mineral, either. The museum is strong on archaeology and anthropology as well. There's a **People Center**, where you can learn about different cultures and see live dance, music and crafts programs, and permanent and special exhibitions about everything from the home life of North American Indians to the discovery of an Aztec temple. Especially intriguing for children is the **Discovery Room**, where they can touch and smell the wonders of nature. (Special shows Saturday with magicians, puppets and storytellers.)

Built in the middle of a landscape of goats and squatters, the original building can now be glimpsed only from Columbus Ave. The body of the museum, an example of Romanesque Revival at its grandest, can best be admired from 77th St. The building itself is nothing if not a piecemeal reflection of changing tastes in style. In between the turreted extensions, a massive carriage entrance passes under a sweeping flight of stairs: the heavy red-brown brick and granite add to the Medieval aura and positive strength typified by the 7-arch colonnade. That welcoming entrance is now ignored, and the main facade of the museum has been shifted to the **Theodore Roosevelt**

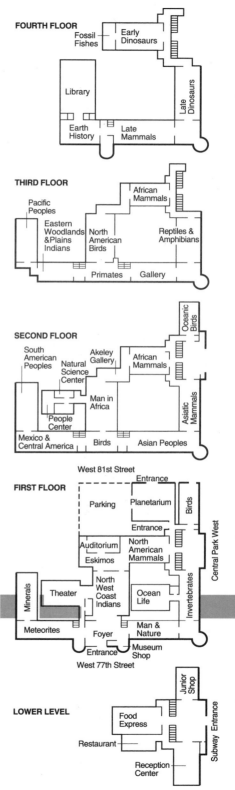

FOURTH FLOOR
Fossil Fishes — Early Dinosaurs — Late Dinosaurs — Library — Earth History — Late Mammals

THIRD FLOOR
Pacific Peoples — Eastern Woodlands & Plains Indians — North American Birds — African Mammals — Reptiles & Amphibians — Primates — Gallery

SECOND FLOOR
South American Peoples — Natural Science Center — Akeley Gallery — African Mammals — Oceanic Birds — Man in Africa — People Center — Asiatic Mammals — Mexico & Central America — Birds — Asian Peoples

FIRST FLOOR
West 81st Street — Entrance — Parking — Planetarium — Birds — Entrance — Auditorium — North American Mammals — Eskimos — North West Coast Indians — Minerals — Theater — Ocean Life — Invertebrates — Central Park West — Meteorites — Foyer — Man & Nature — Entrance — Museum Shop — West 77th Street

LOWER LEVEL
Food Express — Restaurant — Junior Shop — Subway Entrance — Reception Center

263

Memorial facing Central Park West—a rather pompous Beaux-Arts triumphal arch and terrace designed by **John Russell Pope** in 1936. On top of the 4 giant Ionic columns are statues of explorers **Boone, Audubon, Lewis and Clark** (these and the attic frieze are by **James Earle Fraser**; the animal relief is by **James L. Clark**). Behind this facade is an equally intimidating **Memorial Hall**.

The museum has an ongoing program of lectures, films, plays and concerts. Free **Museum Highlights Tours** assemble at the 2nd-floor information desk. Two gift shops, one just for children, offer Mexican and Indian crafts, microscopes, puppets, books, petrified wood and other surprises. **Museum Shop, Whale's Lair** (bar), Hall of Ocean Life, 1st floor; **Junior Shop**, basement; **American Museum Restaurant** and **Food Express** (cafeteria) lower level. Limited paid parking in museum lot, W 81st St. ♦ Suggested admission. M-Tu, Th, Su 10AM-5:45PM; W, F-Sa 10AM-9PM; free F-Sa 5-9PM. Central Park West at 79th St. 769.5000

Within the American Museum of Natural History:

Nature Max Theater Shows super-spectacular films daily on a 4-story-high screen that puts you right into the action. Call for schedule. ♦ Admission. 769.5000

AAG

Hayden Planetarium Sits on the north side of the museum. The copper dome on the brick box outside is an obvious reflection of the spaces inside, which house astronomy exhibitions such as the **Hall of the Sun**, the **Laserium** and **Astronomia**. The **Sky Theater** auditorium is 75ft in diameter and 48ft to the top of the dome, and hosts the famous **Sky**

West Side

Shows that keep you in touch with what the heavens are up to. Imbedded into the concrete in front of the planetarium is **Michele Oka Doner**'s *Celestial Plaza*, a sculpture comprised of 300 cast bronze pieces that represent astronomical Bodies. Changing shows that last 1hr. Admission charge covers museum admission. Call for schedule. ♦ Admission. Central Park West (81st St) 769.5920

91 The Beresford (1929, **Emery Roth**) On a street of twin-towered landmarks, this deluxe apartment building distinguishes itself by having 3 rather squat Baroque turrets that give it a double silhouette from 2 directions. Famous

residents have included poet **Sara Teasdale**, underworld crime leader **Meyer Lansky, Margaret Mead** and **Rock Hudson**. Tennis great **John McEnroe** and newscaster **Peter Jennings** are among the current residents. ♦ 211 Central Park West (W 81st St)

92 Excelsior $ In a classy block across the street from the grounds of the **American Museum of Natural History**, a budget hotel that is attractive and well-maintained. ♦ 45 W 81st St (Central Park West-Columbus Ave) 362.9200, 800/368.4575; fax 721.2994

93 Charivari Workshop The latest inspirations from designers like **Matsuda, Paul Smith** and **Katharine Hamnett**. ♦ 441 Columbus Ave (W 81st-W 82nd Sts) 496.8700

93 Maxilla & Mandible When they say you can find anything in this city, they mean it—this shop specializes in selling all types of bones. Definitely worth a visit. ♦ 453 Columbus Ave (W 81st-W 82nd Sts) 724.6173

94 Greenstones & Cie European clothing for children, including brightly colored, French sportswear from **Petit Boy** and **Maugin** and dressy duds from Italy's **Mona Lisa**. Happily, nothing is so extravagant that it's unwearable. ♦ 442 Columbus Ave (W 81st-W 82nd Sts) 580.4322. Also at: 1184 Madison Ave. 427.1665

94 Penny Whistle Toys The **Pustefix** teddy bear out front is forever blowing bubbles to get your attention. If he could talk, he'd tell you all about the quality classics inside: board games, stuffed animals, dolls, cars, indoor gyms, table soccer games, rattles for infants and—surprise!—no electronic video games! Owned by **Meredith Brokaw**—yes, she's related to Tom. ♦ 448 Columbus Ave (W 81st-W 82nd Sts) 873.9090. Also at: 1283 Madison Ave. 369.3868; 132 Spring St. 925.2088

94 Endicott Booksellers Soft music plays as you browse leisurely among library shelves of university and small press books, a full literature section, recent fiction and nonfiction and a backlist of authors in paperback. Seating is provided for casual perusing. Readings by neighborhood authors. ♦ 450 Columbus Ave (W 81st-W 82nd Sts) 787.6300

94 Boutique Descamps A French company devoted to the luxury of bed and bath: plush toweling and robes, cotton sheets in delicate prints, down comforters and pillows. ♦ 454 Columbus Ave (W 82nd St) 769.9260. Also at: 723 Madison Ave. 355.2522

95 Street Life This shop caters to the young and hip and not-over-*twentysomething*-female who aspires to **Yohji** and **Matsuda**—

someday. In the meantime, perhaps a more affordable statement. ♦ 422 Columbus Ave (W 80th-W 81st Sts) 769.8858. Also at: 470 Broadway. 219.3764

95 Pizzeria Uno $ Deep-dish pizza, Chicago-style, or maybe Sicily was first. No matter. What counts here is that it's decent and quite reasonable. Pizzeria Uno is one of the very few places near the **American Museum of Natural History** where people with small children can manage. The express lunch is ready in 5 minutes flat. ♦ Pizza ♦ 432 Columbus Ave (W 81st St) 595.4700

96 Roman Ruins Two friendly *empresses*, **Ivette** and **Madeline**, rule over this gallery/store devoted to art and decoration related to ancient Rome and Greece: architectural and sculptural reproductions, wrought-iron chairs, hand painted jewelry and other unique items. ♦ 417 Amsterdan Ave (W 80th St) 496.7390

96 sabrina monet European Cafe $$ This calm cafe is named after the owners' 2 daughters, **Sabrina** and **Audrey Monet,** who were named after, respectively, the film starring **Audrey Hepburn** and the actress herself. Fresh-baked goods, soups, salads and light entrees. Interesting quotes from known and unknown sources and changing art exhibitions share wall space. ♦ Cafe ♦ 413 Amsterdam Ave (W 80th St) 873.5500. Also at: 1286 Madison Ave. 534.7733

97 Charivari Sport For the gentleman and lady at leisure. ♦ 201 W 79th St (Amsterdam Ave) 799.8650

97 Dublin House Tap Room At night, the area's younger, newer residents take over this former workingman's retreat, and the place gets very lively indeed. The brilliant neon harp over the door beckons you to have a lager, and the separate back room makes you wish you'd invited the whole team. ♦ 225 W 79th St (Amsterdam Ave-Broadway) 874.9528

97 Baci ★★$$$ Zippy Sicilian fare served in an upbeat, handsome room. The fresh pastas includes fettuccine with sardines and fennel, and linguine *Trapanese*, rich with black olives and olive paste. Chicken and veal dishes are prepared with a light, well-seasoned touch. I suggest you save room for the wickedly rich, homemade tiramisu. ♦ Italian ♦ 412 Amsterdam Ave (W 79th-W 80th Sts) No credit cards. 496.1550

97 Au Rivage ★$$ A new bistro, which, like all the others that have recently opened on the West Side, has a basic menu of steak, broiled or baked fish, roast chicken and several excellent pasta dishes. The service is quick and the atmosphere of the restaurant is welcoming. However, go elsewhere if you have to end your dinner on a sweet note. ♦ French ♦ 408 Amsterdam Ave (W 79th-W 80th Sts) 787.6900

Sarabeth's Kitchen

98 Sarabeth's Kitchen ★★$$$ One of the better—and busier—brunch spots, and often worth the wait. Better still at breakfast during the week. Pancakes and waffles served with fresh fruit are delicious, and in winter, Sarabeth's hot porridge is a cure. Dinner is also served, but the menu is ambitious in a way that's anything but homey. ♦ American ♦ 423 Amsterdam Ave (W 80th-W 81st Sts) 496.6280. Also at: 1295 Madison Ave. 410.7355

99 Amsterdams Bar and Rotisserie ★$ The bar crowd is noisy and young, and the roast chicken with French fries and generous salads better than average. Take a table in the back, keep it simple and skip dessert. ♦ American ♦ 428 Amsterdam Ave (W 80th-W 81st Sts) 874.1377. Also at: 454 Broadway. 925.6166

100 VideoTown Laundrette Come here to make copies, rent videos or a mailbox, send or receive a fax, soak up some rays in the tanning salon and, oh yes, do your laundry. While you're waiting for the clothes to dry you can munch on the popcorn and candy for sale at the counter, sit out back on the patio and read a book or watch music videos. ♦ 217 W 80th St (Broadway) 721.1706

100 Gryphon Book Shop Used and rare books at decent prices. General humanities plus theater, performing arts and children's books, especially the *Oz* books by **L. Frank Baum**. An annex is located around the corner at 246 W 80th St. ♦ 2246 Broadway (W 80th-W 81st Sts) 362.0706

West Side

101 H&H Bagels West They never stop baking here—60,000 bagels a day, shipped nationwide and to London! Stop in for one fresh from the oven 24hrs a day. While you're at it, check out the section of kosher and non-kosher products. One of the last Manhattan bastions of the *baker's dozen* (buy 12, get 13). ♦ 2239 Broadway (W 80th St) 595.8000, 800/NY.BAGEL. Also at: 1551 2nd Ave. 734.7441

Restaurants/Nightlife: Red   **Hotels:** Blue
Shops/Parks: Green   **Sights/Culture:** Black

102 411 West End Avenue (1936, **George F. Pelham II**) Basic yellow brick, but with streamlined details and Art Deco massing at the top. Of special note are the steel drapes on the facade. ◆ W 80th St

103 Zabar's Cafe ★$ The West Side's finest cappuccino in the neighborhood's most undistinguished interior. Try a warm knish or a pastry with your coffee for a superlative afternoon delight. I often stop in here for a restorative espresso after a whirlwind trip through Zabar's. ◆ Cafe/takeout ◆ 2245 Broadway (W 80th St) 787.2000

103 Zabar's A 3-star food bazaar—like no other in the world. Though it grew from a small Jewish appetizing store to become this giant grocery and housewares store—with cookware, appliances and packaged, prepared and fresh foods from all over the world—it retains a distinctly New York character. On weekends, a line forms for the Western Nova Salmon—if you're lucky, the counter help will pass you a slice to nosh on. Prices are usually better than the competition. ◆ 2245 Broadway (W 80th St) 787.2000

103 Shakespeare & Co. Large store with a huge selection of quality and hard-to-find paperbacks. In the rear are children's and cookbook sections, and upstairs gift books and a wing for the performing arts. ◆ 2259 Broadway (W 81st St) 580.7800

104 Teachers Too $$ Originally an annex of the now defunct **Teachers**, it features the same pub menu, same good spinach salad and more or less the same crowd. ◆ American ◆ 2271 Broadway (W 81st-W 82nd Sts) 362.4900

105 Marvin Gardens $$ Good salads, lively bar scene, less crowded than **Teachers Too** across the street, where the food is better. ◆ American ◆ 2274 Broadway (W 81st-W 82nd Sts) 799.0578

105 The Yarn Co. One of the best sources of yarn and expert knitting instruction in the city. Also one of the most pleasant yarn shops, with a big wooden farm table and chairs in the center of the room and an abundant stock of high-quality yarns—from **Rowan, Tahki Imports, Missoni** and others—lining the walls. Also available are needlepoint supplies, a finishing and lining service and custom-designed sweaters for those who don't knit. ◆ 2274 Broadway (W 81st-W 82nd Sts) 2nd floor. 787.7878

Restaurants/Nightlife: Red   **Hotels:** Blue
Shops/Parks: Green   **Sights/Culture:** Black

106 Yellow Rose Café ★$$$ The hearty Texas fare appeals to the *more is more* crowd. Best bet is the distinguished barbecue, framed by fresh cornbread and mounds of chunky mashed potatoes drenched in gravy. ◆ American ◆ 450 Amsterdam Ave (W 81st-W 82nd Sts) 595.8760

107 Children's Museum of Manhattan An educational playground of interactive exhibitions and activity centers—all built around the museum's theme of self-discovery. On the 1st floor, a 4-minute film, which takes place on the ceiling of the **Brainatarium**, explains basic functions of the brain and the 5 senses and introduces viewers to the **Magical Patterns**, an exhibition where children discover patterns in art, culture and nature, and are given the chance to create their own. On the 2nd floor is the **Time Warner Center for Media**, where children can produce their own videotapes, newscasts and public affairs programs. Exhibition interpreters are always on hand to provide assistance, and entertainers are stationed at key points to provide further understanding through song, dance or puppetry. There is an art studio where classes in book- and papermaking and other studio arts are held, and a theater where performances are given by theater groups, dancers, musicians, puppeteers and storytellers as well as children participating in the museum's education and video programs and workshops. ◆ Admission. Tu-F 2-5PM; Sa-Su 10AM-5PM. 212 W 83rd St (Amsterdam Ave-Broadway) 721.1223

108 The Raccoon Lodge West Siders come here for the pool table, friendly atmosphere and great jukebox. And the drinks are cheap! ◆ 480 Amsterdam Ave (W 83rd St) 874.9984. Also at: 59 Warren St. 766.9656

108 Cafe Lalo $ A dessert-only cafe with brick walls, a wooden floor and long French-style windows that open onto the street. Although it is quite pleasant to linger over a cappuccino during the day, it can get crowded and loud at night. ◆ Cafe ◆ 201 W 83rd St (Amsterdam Ave) 496.6031

109 Good Enough to Eat ★★$$ Breakfast and weekend brunch are the best bets at this tiny Vermont-style outpost. Prepare to wait in line for pecan-flecked waffles, cinnamon-swirl French toast or the Lumberjack breakfast—as big as it sounds. Lunches and dinners are prepared with a homemade, if less inventive, touch. ◆ American ◆ 483 Amsterdam Ave (W 83rd-W 84th Sts) Dinner reservations recommended. 496.0163

110 Avventura A small shop that carries exquisite vases, china and crystal in singular, sculptural shapes and patterns. Beautifully and simply displayed and lit, the pieces are cool to the eye and tempting to touch. Don't bring the kids. ♦ Closed F afternoon-Sa. 463 Amsterdam Ave (W 82nd-W 83rd Sts) 769.2510

110 Bath Island An oasis for stressed out New Yorkers in search of biodegradable beauty and bath products: bubble bath, shampoo, essential perfume oils (the most potent form of fragrance and the base of all perfumes), skincare products, cotton kimonos, loofah sponges and, perhaps best of all, great service from 2 of the friendliest merchants around, **Janet Loeffler** and **Sebastian Rafala**. You can't miss the store; every morning they scent the sidewalk with hot sudsy water and one of the 75 available perfume oils. ♦ 469 Amsterdam Ave (W 82nd-W 83rd Sts) 787.9415

111 Poiret ★★$$$ Designer **Nancy Mah** has re-created the style of turn-of-the-century French designer **Paul Poiret**. The bistro's white walls are stenciled with green branches and red roses, Poiret's trademark. The long list of daily specials gives you much to choose from, but don't leave without sampling the chocolate-mousse cake. ♦ French ♦ 474 Columbus Ave (W 82nd-W 83rd Sts) Reservations recommended. 724.6880

112 Fujiyama Mama ★$$$ Best to sit at the sashimi counter and get friendly with the chef at this high-tech Japanese restaurant where rock music is played much too loud and waitresses wear traditional kimonos. The menu has some interesting offerings, especially the *yakitori* or broiled dishes. ♦ Japanese ♦ 467 Columbus Ave (W 82nd-W 83rd Sts) Reservations required. 769.1144

113 Handblock For those who like the exotic look of handblocked fabrics, this is an oasis. The owners have asked their suppliers in India to make traditional patterns as well as totally untraditional ones, such as checks and Provençal-inspired florals, and to whip them up into pillowcases, duvet covers, table cloths, placemats and pillow shams. ♦ 487 Columbus Ave (W 83rd-W 84th Sts) 799.4342

113 The Hero's Journey Although this shop carries all the latest crystals, New Age books, trinkets and paraphernalia some might feel that spiritualism and commercialism just aren't meant to mix the way they do here. ♦ 489 Columbus Ave (W 83rd-W 84th Sts) 874.4630

114 Lucy's $$ A crowded, noisy, kitschy place up front, where the bar is long and the space for patrons narrow. They fill it regularly, holding their blue and pink drinks aloft like riders on a jerky subway. Squeeze into the back, where a Tex-Mex dining room features the same kind of whimsy, but delivers professional, reliable food. The staff is personable and attractive,

but if you find yourself waiting in line, there are other choices nearby. ♦ American ♦ 503 Columbus Ave (W 84th-W 85th Sts) 787.3009

115 Down Quilt Shop Reasonably priced antique quilts as well as less interesting new quilts. Down comforters too. ♦ 518 Columbus Ave (W 85th St) 496.8980

116 Shoofly You may want to only admire, not buy, the adorable children's shoes and accessories here, as many cost more than parents spend on themselves. The European shoes are displayed on low shelves that children can reach (gulp!), and the hats, either from Europe or made by local artisans, are each hung on a different-shaped hook, ranging from a dinosaur to a crab to a corn cob. An old pipe is made to look like a tree, the floor is painted to resemble moss and a low table and chairs made out of a tree stump and branches is set up for kids who are tired of shopping (you should be so lucky). Styles range from classic to zany. Larger sizes for older kids and moms are sold in the adjoining space. ♦ 506 Amsterdam Ave (W 84th-W 85th Sts) 580.4390

116 Harriet's Kitchen $ Excellent chicken soup and straightforward family fare—roast chicken, green beans and carrots, fudge layer cake—from this unpretentious takeout that opens its doors at 4:30PM, the hour tired parents decide they're not in the mood to cook. ♦ Takeout ♦ 502 Amsterdam Ave (W 84th-W 85th Sts) 721.0045

117 Chez David $ Kosher pizza place with ecumenical clientele. Freshly prepared falafel and Middle Eastern specialties. ♦ Kosher ♦ 494 Amsterdam Ave (W 84th St) 874.4974

117 206 West 84th Street Edgar Allan Poe finished writing *The Raven* in December of 1844 while he and his wife were boarders at **Patrick** and **Mary Brennan**'s farmhouse at this site. ♦ Amsterdam Ave

118 Loew's 84th Street Showplace Once a grand movie palace, the **Loew's 84th Street**, now a suburban-styled, multiscreened venture tucked rather discreetly onto a row of newly opened retail shops on the ground floor of the **Bromley**. If you remember the old

place, you shrug; if you want to see a movie, you go anyway—they're showing 'em all. The site of former **Mayor Koch**'s failed attempt at a boycott of the $7 movie ticket, the price has since climbed even higher. ♦ 2310 Broadway (W 84th St) 877.3600

119 Charivari (the women's store) Taken together, the 4 Charivari stores offer the West Side's best clothes shopping. This branch features sophisticated business and evening wear for women who are not daunted by top designer names, or by their price tags. ♦ 2307 Broadway (W 83rd-W 84th Sts) 873.1424

120 Charivari (the men's store) Likewise.
♦ 2339 Broadway (W 84th St) 873.7242

121 Patzo $$ A 2-level Italian restaurant where the pizza is better than usual. The crust is thin and well-baked and the list of toppings will make you dizzy. Good pasta is also available. Crowded on the weekends; peaceful at lunchtime during the week. ♦ Italian ♦ 2330 Broadway (W 85th St) 496.9240

122 520 West End Avenue (1892, Clarence F. True) Neighborhood residents vehemently defended their many-gabled *castle* when, in 1987, a misled developer proposed building an apartment house on this site. ♦ W 85th St

123 The Red House (1904, Harde & Short) In this 6-story apartment building, an Elizabethan manor has been crossed with a red brick row house. Note the dragon and crown near the top. ♦ 350 W 85th St (West End Ave-Riverside Dr)

124 The Clarendon (1903, Charles Birge) William Randolph Hearst moved his family into a 30-room apartment on the top 3 floors of this building in 1908. In 1913, when the landlord refused to ask the residents on the other 9 floors to leave so that Hearst, his family and his art collection could spread out, Hearst simply purchased the building and forced them out himself. Faced with financial woes, he sold the property in 1938. ♦ 137 Riverside Dr (W 86th St)

125 La Mirabelle ★$$ Good, solid French bistro with a fresh, inviting decor, efficient service and food that is a notch above the ordinary. Good choices are escargots, soft-shell crabs cooked with lots of garlic and tomatoes, rack of lamb that is nicely pink and spicy and the best steak *pommes frites* on the West Side. Desserts are nothing to write home about. ♦ French ♦ 333 W 86th St (West End Ave-Riverside Dr) 496.0458

Bookstores

There is a marvelous abundance of bookstores in New York City. Just take a look at the 8-plus pages of listings in the *Yellow Pages*. Following are some of our favorites. (Many of these bookstores are mentioned elsewhere in the book. Check the index for page numbers.)

General Interest
Books & Co. ♦ 939 Madison Ave. 737.1450
Burlington Bookshop ♦ 1082 Madison Ave. 288.7420
Canterbury ♦ 1045 Lexington Ave. 737.7525
Coliseum Books ♦ 1771 Broadway. 757.8381
Gotham Book Mart and Gallery ♦ 41 W 47th St. 719.4448
Madison Avenue Bookstore ♦ 833 Madison Ave. 535.6130
St. Mark's Books ♦ 13 St. Mark's Pl. 260.7853
Shakespeare & Co. ♦ 716 Broadway. 529.1330; 2259 Broadway. 580.7800
Tower Books ♦ 383 Lafayette St. 228.5100

Art and Architecture
Asia Society ♦ 725 Park Ave. 288.6400

Hacker Art Books ♦ 45 W 57th St. 688.7600
Morton Books ♦ 989 3rd Ave. 421.9025
Untitled ♦ 680 Broadway. 254.1360; 159 Prince St. 982.2088
Urban Center Books ♦ 457 Madison Ave (within Villard Houses) 935.3595
Wittenborn Art Books ♦ 1018 Madison Ave. 288.1558

Specialty
A Photographer's Place ♦ 133 Mercer St. 431.9358
Applause ♦ 211 W 71st St. 496.7511
Biography Bookstore ♦ 400 Bleecker St. 807.8655

Books of Wonder ♦ 132 7th Ave So. 989.3270; 464 Hudson St. 645.8006
The Drama Bookshop ♦ 723 7th Ave So. 944.0595
East West Books ♦ 78 5th Ave. 243.5994; 568 Columbus Ave. 787.7552
Eeyore's Books for Children ♦ 2212 Broadway. 362.0634; 25 E 83rd St. 988.3404
Forbidden Planet ♦ 227 E 59th St. 751.4386; 821 Broadway. 473.1576
Judith's Room ♦ 681 Washington St. 727.7330
Joseph Patelson Music House ♦ 160 W 56th St. 582.5840
Kitchen Arts & Letters ♦ 1435 Lexington Ave. 876.5550
Liberation Bookshop ♦ 421 Lenox Ave. 281.4615
New York Bound Bookshop ♦ 50 Rockefeller Plaza. 245.8503
Oscar Wilde Memorial Bookshop ♦ 15 Christopher St. 255.8097
Paraclete ♦ 146 E 74th St. 535.4050
Revolution Books ♦ 13 E 16th St. 691.3345
Three Lives & Company ♦ 154 W 10th St. 741.2069
Traveller's Bookstore ♦ 22 W 52nd St. 541.7777

Secondhand and Out-of-Print
Academy Books and Records ♦ 10 W 18th St. 242.4848
Argosy Bookstore ♦ 116 E 59th St. 753.4455
Gotham Book Mart and Gallery ♦ 42 W 47th St. 719.4448
Gryphon Bookshop ♦ 2246 Broadway. 362.0706
Strand Bookstore ♦ 828 Broadway. 473.1452

Foreign Language
Fuchs (German) ♦ 1841 Broadway. 757.6075
Kinokuniya Bookstore (Japanese) ♦ 10 W 49th St. 765.1461
Librarie de France ♦ 610 5th Ave. 581.8810
Libreria Hispanica ♦ 115 5th Ave. 673.7400
Vanni (Italian) ♦ 30 W 12th St. 675.6336

George Lois
Lois GGK

My idea of blowing a Saturday afternoon is doing *The Dirty Dozen*, a hit and run look at 12 of the greatest galleries in the world that deal in much of the kind of art that excites me.

My starting point is **Michael Ward** at 9 E 93rd, who continually surprises with brilliant shows of scholarship and artifacts, including Celtic art, Medieval art and African weaponry.

Quickly to **Barry Friedman** at 84th St and Madison, a great young dealer specializing in late 19th-century and early 20th-century decorative arts.

If you're looking for original Bauhaus for your house, he's your man.

Then the beginning of a trek down Madison to **Mert Simpson**, probably the world's greatest dealer in tribal art to study his selection of masterpieces of African, Oceanic and Northwest Coast Indian art.

A few blocks down to a second Tribal arts dealer, **Leloup**, and then to **DeLorenzo**, where you lose your heart to the most sensational Art Deco furniture ever collected in one gallery. The Ruhlmanns, Dunands and Chareau's can make (and have made) a grown man cry.

Next door and up the stairs to **Jordan Volpe**, the best dealers in the world for the American Arts and Crafts Movement.

A block south is **Galerie Metropol**, which singlehandedly reintroduced the arts of the Wiener Werkstätte to America.

At 70th St, **Hirschl & Adler Folk** (early American Folk art), **Hirschl & Adler Modern**, and across the street **Hirschl & Adler**, the leading specialists in American art.

Two blocks south on E 68th St is **Primavera**, a miniature version of DeLorenzo but also a treasure house for Art Deco jewelry.

Continuing south to 61st St is the **Macklowe Gallery**, loaded with Art Nouveau and Art Deco.

The whole trek to me is even more exciting than the Cooper-Hewitt, Guggenheim, Metropolitan, Whitney, Museum of Modern Art 2-mile art museum safari!

Marcia Tucker
Director, The New Museum of Contemporary Art

Studio Museum in Harlem. Sunday afternoon openings; among the most exciting shows in town, and a wonderful event as well (plus a fabulous gift shop).

Manhattan's **Circle Line Cruises**. For New Yorkers who have never seen their own town from a tourist's point of view. Bring a picnic and marvel at where and how we live.

A cappuccino at **Caffè Dante**, on MacDougal St. The closest you can get to Italy in the Village.

A Sunday visit to the Lower East Side, particularly the shops on Orchard St. Unbelievable bargains, great

knishes at **Yona Schimmel**'s on Houston St, on your way there or back.

Radio City Music Hall's Easter and Christmas shows. The best kitsch anywhere in the world, destined to make you weep for the good old days.

Taking any 6-year-old girl to the **Plaza** for tea. Makes you see the world somewhat differently—a little better and brighter.

The **Cowgirl Hall of Fame**. Ranks tops among eating and drinking establishments for the name alone, but the rest lives up to it. The decor provides instant respite from city overload.

Marcelle Cattan
Chef/Concierge, Beverly Hotel

A **World Yacht** dinner with a splendid view of the New York City skyline.

Sunset cocktails at **Windows on the World**.

Gourmet food shopping at **Grace's Market** (72nd St at 3rd Ave).

Bargain hunting on Sunday on **Orchard St**.

Browsing or shopping at **Bloomingdale's**.

Viewing ice skaters at **Rockefeller Center** at Christmastime.

A visit to the **Metropolitan Museum of Art**.

Summer concerts at **Lincoln Center**.

Just absorbing New York City around you!

Martin Anker
Concierge, Ritz-Carlton Hotel

As a concierge in New York City I always try to look at my city from a visitor's point of view. How would a visitor like to spend a perfect day in Manhattan? One recent itinerary included places that I like to visit frequently: for breakfast, I enjoyed the casual atmosphere at **Aggie's**, a funky restaurant/diner on W. Houston St. Afterward I took a cab down to the **World Financial Center**, and spent some time relaxing under those majestic palm trees. It is definitely one of my favorite places to unwind. From the 21st century to the past: a wonderful trip to newly renovated **Ellis Island**, a landmark in recent American history. This great

museum and exhibition is a real must for any visitor to Manhattan. For lunch, I went to one of my favorite bistros, the **Bridge Cafe** near South Street Seaport, on Water St. They have a wonderfully eclectic menu and a great regional American wine list. In the afternoon I headed to the **American Craft Museum** on W 53rd St, which is not only a beautifully designed building, but always has very interesting exhibitions. Dinner was a real treat: I never tire of the excellent Northern Italian cuisine at **Lusardi's**, a great restaurant on 2nd Ave. The food and the service are far superior to many short-lived new and trendy restaurants. A nightcap at **Top of the Tower** on Beekman Place convinced me once again that Manhattan is one exciting city!

Upper West Side

Although it is still in transition, the **Upper West Side** (the neighborhood west of **Central Park** to the **Hudson River**, from **86th St** to **Cathedral Pkwy-110th St**) is undergoing the same kind of gentrifying process that has taken place farther south. The commercial zone is extending up Broadway and Amsterdam and Columbus Aves, and the residential zone that surrounds **Columbia University** is moving down those same streets. While Central Park blocks (the numbered streets between Columbus Ave and Central Park West) contain brownstones and apartments that are in excellent condition as far north as 95th St, even the blocks of tenements and middle-income apartments between Amsterdam Ave and Broadway, in disrepair for years, have become desirable residences—if only for their proximity to the burgeoning shopping and dining strips. The residential West End Ave and Riverside Dr remain staunchly unchanged, except perhaps for the parade of new windows in the grand old high rises, most of which have been converted to co-ops as far north as Duke Ellington Blvd (106th St).

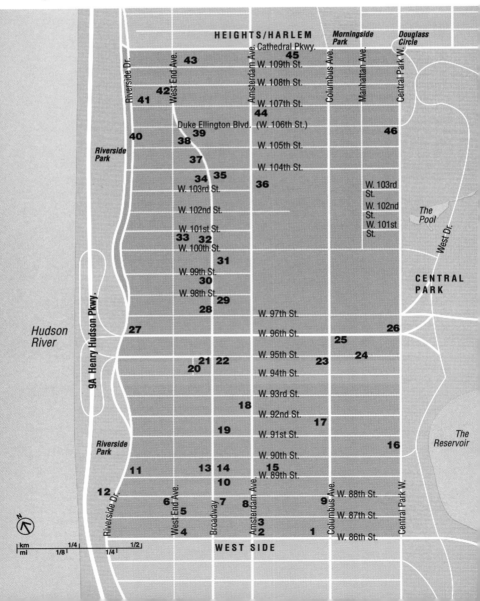

Recently erected high rises and salvaged storefronts have restored some order to the chaos along the major avenues. Where only a few years ago it seemed to be a fading reminder of the Old World, the West Side north of 86th St is now a thriving cosmopolitan mix that feels like the best of both worlds. Fronted by sidewalk cafes and attractive retail stores, these new developments are graceful and stabilizing newcomers to a rapidly changing upper Broadway. Columbus Ave buzzes with life spilling in and out of its restaurants, bars, antique shops and clothing stores. Even the area from 96th to 110th Sts is sprucing up, particularly east of Broadway, where what was once considered part of Harlem has been given a name of its own—**Manhattan Valley**—and has been annexed to the Upper West Side.

And although there's more of Central Park to enjoy in this area, along the Hudson River north of 72nd St is **Riverside Park**, a 50-block oasis designed by **Frederick Law Olmsted**.

1 **West Side Comics** Large selection of comics and comic book art. ◆ 107 W 86th St (Columbus-Amsterdam Aves) 724.0432

2 **West Park Presbyterian Church** (1890, **Henry F. Kilburn**) Originally the **Park Presbyterian Church**. The rough-hewn red sandstone of this Richardsonian Romanesque mass is enlivened by the lightness of the almost Byzantine details of the capitals and doorways, and the fineness of the colonettes in the tower. The church's boldness is emphasized by the asymmetrical massing —the single tower holds the corner between 2 strong facades. ◆ Amsterdam Ave at W 86th St

3 **Popover Café** ★$ The most easygoing of the local sandwich/salad spots. Best bets are the popovers with strawberry jam, perhaps with a steaming bowl of homemade soup. Keep it simple. ◆ American ◆ 551 Amsterdam Ave (W 86th-W 87th Sts) 595.8555

3 **Barney Greengrass (The Sturgeon King)** ★$$ Folksier than **Zabar's**, though not as complete, this Jewish appetizing store has good roots: opened in 1908, in its present location since 1929, and run by son **Moe** and grandson **Gary Greengrass**. There's a small dining room attached to the takeout store. Though the staff is generally quite rude, I think it's worth a visit for the vintage New York ambience. ◆ Deli ◆ 541 Amsterdam Ave (W 86th-W 87th Sts) 724.4707

4 **Church of St. Paul and St. Andrew** (1897, **R.H. Robertson**) This is not your average-style Revival church, but has overtones of the manners of **Boulee**, particularly in the octagonal tower. Note the angels in the spandrels. ◆ West End Ave at W 86th St

5 **Murder Ink** Just the way you picture it: cozy and English, with fat fuzzy cats and a clutter of new and out-of-print mysteries, references and periodicals. ◆ 271 W 87th St (Broadway-West End Ave) No credit cards. 362.8905

6 **565 West End Avenue** (1937, **H.I. Feldman**) This is a Neo-Renaissance building in Art Deco fabric—brick instead of stone, corner windows instead of quoins. At the bottom, banded brick represents the shadow of a traditional plinth, and the cornice is stainless steel. ◆ W 87th St

7 **Boulevard** $$ Pleasant restaurant with an American menu and the feel of a French outdoor cafe. Excellent hamburgers, well-done pastas and not-so-good grilled chicken. Service is slow, but when the weather is good does it really matter? ◆ American ◆ 2398 Broadway (W 88th St) 874.7400

8 **The Cat Store** Feline beauties on every surface imaginable: jewelry, stationery, cookie molds, books, clocks, sweaters, chairs and the floor near the door—where **Honey** likes to lounge. ◆ 562 Amsterdam Ave (W 87th-W 88th Sts) 595.8728

8 **Ozu** $ Simple Japanese decor. Solid macrobiotic fare. ◆ Macrobiotic ◆ 566 Amsterdam Ave (W 87th-W 88th Sts) 787.8316

9 **Grossinger's Uptown Bake Shop** An old-fashioned bakery selling Jewish comfort food: *babka, ruggalah,* coffeecake, cheesecake. ◆ 570 Columbus Ave (W 87th St) 874.6996

9 **East West Books** A New Age bookstore and home to the **Himalayan Institute of New York**, which offers instruction in many areas, including yoga, meditation, relaxation and breathing, homeopathy and stress management. ◆ 568 Columbus Ave (W 87th St) 787.7552

Restaurants/Nightlife: Red   **Hotels:** Blue
Shops/Parks: Green   **Sights/Culture:** Black

10 Westside Judaica Religious articles and a large stock of fiction and nonfiction covering all aspects of the Jewish experience. Cassette tapes, videos and holiday decorations for children's parties. ♦ Closed F afternoon-Sa. 2404 Broadway (W 88th St) 362.7846

11 Yeshiva Chofetz Chaim (1901, Herts & Tallant) This house was built for **Isaac L. Rice**, who named it *Villa Julia* for his wife, the founder of the now defunct **Society for the Suppression of Unnecessary Noise**. This and the former **Schinasi Residence** (351 Riverside Dr) are the only 2 mansions left from the days when Riverside Dr was lined with them. Note the slightly askew *porte-cochère* (a porch large enough for wheeled vehicles to pass through). These architects also did the **Lyceum Theater**. ♦ 346 W 89th St (Riverside Dr) 362.1435

12 Riverside Park (1873-1910, Frederick Law Olmsted; additions 1888, Calvert Vaux, Samuel Parsons Jr.; 1937, Clinton F. Lloyd) A welcome strip of greenery between the city and the river, that stretches for 3 miles (blessedly covering a rail line below), where there's space for jogging, tennis and baseball; when there's snow, people actually sleigh ride. Not a monument in itself, as is Central Park, this piece of land is spattered with a few little memorials—most notably the **Soldiers' and Sailors' Monument** (1902, Stoughton & Stoughton and Paul E.M. Duboy) at 89th St, modeled after the **Choragic Monument of Lysicrates** in Athens; the **Firemen's Memorial** at 100th St (1913, Attilio Piccirilli, sculptor; H. Van Buren Magonigle, architect), graced by statues of *Courage* and *Duty*; and the easy-to-overlook but not-to-be-forgotten **Carrère Memorial** (1916), a small terrace and plaque at 99th St honoring a great architect (**John Merven Carrère**), designed by his partner **Thomas Hastings**. Carrère died in an automobile accident in 1911. ♦ Riverside Dr-Hudson River (W 72nd-W 145th Sts)

13 Docks Oyster Bar and Seafood Grill ★★$$ This lively neighborhood haunt

features fresh seafood in a perky black-and-white tiled dining room. The catch of the day varies, but fried oysters coated in cornmeal are a sure bet anytime, and the French-fried yams an inspiration. One wishes the kitchen were a bit more consistent and the service less slow. ♦ Seafood ♦ 2427 Broadway (W 89th-W 90th Sts) Reservations required. 724.5588

13 Murray's Sturgeon The ultimate Jewish appetizing store has maintained its reputation for high quality herring, lox, whitefish and all things *dairy* through more than half a century and the neighborhood's many vicissitudes. ♦ 2429 Broadway (W 89th-W 90th Sts) 724.2650

14 The Armadillo $$ It's worth a visit just to see the neon cactus that winds its way up the main pillar. The menu is a curious mix of Southern, Southwestern and Mexican cooking. A typical meal might be Southern-fried chicken accompanied by a fiery Mexican martini. I suggest the chili. ♦ Mexican/American ♦ 2420 Broadway (W 89th St) 496.1066

15 Claremont Riding Academy (1982, Frank A. Rooke) A multistory stable, it's the only one left in Manhattan for riding horses. The bridle paths are a few blocks away in **Central Park**. Lessons available. ♦ 175 W 89th St (Columbus-Amsterdam Aves) Reservations required. 724.5100

16 The Eldorado (1931, Margon & Holder) The northernmost of the twin-towered silhouettes on Central Park West, this apartment building is characterized by its Art Deco detailing. ♦ 300 Central Park West (W 90th-W 91st Sts)

17 Trinity School and Trinity House (Main building 1894, Charles C. Haight; east building 1892, William A. Potter; apartment tower and school addition 1969, Brown, Guenther, Battaglia, Seckler) Straight, wonderful Romanesque Revival, now locked to an intricate 1960s tower. Much better than average. ♦ 100 W 92nd St and 139 W 91st St (Columbus-Amsterdam Aves)

18 Les Friandises ★★$$ Trained at world-famous **Le Nôtre**, owner/pâtissiere **Jean Kahn** turns out an impressive variety of elegant cakes and pastries. Her sumptuous breakfast treats with a cup of strong French coffee are worth a detour. ♦ Cafe ♦ 664 Amsterdam Ave (W 92nd-W 93rd Sts) 316.1515

18 Mi Tierra ★★$ The first Mexican restaurant on the Upper West Side (opened in 1963), still one of the best, and definitely the best buy. No high-design interior, no funny drinks, just authentic cuisine from the Yucatan and Venezuela (try the *pernil*—roast leg of pork with sautéed onions). The standard Mexican fare is consistently good. The only phone is the pay phone at the bar. ♦ Mexican ♦ 668 Amsterdam Ave (W 92nd-W 93rd Sts)

19 Pumpkin Eater $$ Although its detractors have referred to it as *Chez Bland*, this small restaurant proves that food can be healthful and taste good too! ♦ Vegetarian ♦ 2452 Broadway (W 91st-W 92nd Sts) 877.0132

19 Carmine's $$ Come hungry and bring a friend with whom you can share the huge portions. ♦ Italian ♦ 2450 Broadway (W 91st St) 362.2200

20 Pomander Walk (1922, **King & Campbell**) A surprising little enclave, this double row of mock-Tudor townhouses was named after a play that was produced in London and played on Broadway in 1911. The houses, originally built for members of the acting profession, were meant to look like the stage set for the New York production. Tenants have included **Rosalind Russell, Humphrey Bogart** and **Lillian** and **Dorothy Gish**. ♦ W 94th-W 95th Sts (Broadway-West End Ave)

21 Symphony Space Constructed during the first decade of this century, this building began as the **Crystal Carnival Skating Rink** and was converted into a movie house in the 1920s. Under the guidance of artistic directors **Isaiah Sheffer** and **Allan Miller**, it has become a performing arts center that has contributed to a cultural renaissance on the Upper West Side. Marathon musical events such as *Wall to Wall Bach*, a free birthday salute to composer **John Cage** and a glorious **Aaron Copeland** celebration are some items from the bill of fare. Notable supporters include violinists **Itzak Perlman** and **Pinchas Zuckerman**, jazz pianist **Billy Taylor**, John Cage, actor **Fritz Weaver** and actresses **Estelle Parsons** and **Claire Bloom**. Although the block that includes Symphony Space is rumored to be slated for demolition, they're still trotting across the boards with their usual eclectic program. ♦ Seats 884. 2537 Broadway (W 94th-W 95th Sts) 864.5400

22 Key West Diner $$ Finally, upper Broadway has its own *Miami Vice* lookalike. But don't let the salmon-and-turquoise interior fool you—this is an honest-to-goodness diner in the best sense of the term. Omelets with home fries and giant bagels are generous and fresh, as is the light challah French toast. ♦ Diner ♦ 2532 Broadway (W 94th-W 95th Sts) 932.0068

Appointed in 1911, **Samuel Battle** was New York's first black police officer. He was promoted to lieutenant and later became a member of the Parole Commission.

Restaurants/Nightlife: Red **Hotels:** Blue
Shops/Parks: Green **Sights/Culture:** Black

23 West Side Storey ★$$ A cozy neighborhood place to relax and enjoy good service and even better food. The Thai entrees on the varied menu are especially well-prepared. ♦ International ♦ 700 Columbus Ave (W 95th St) No credit cards. 749.1900

24 West 95th Street These blocks of diverse row houses represent one aspect of the **Upper West Side Urban Renewal** effort. Between the housing projects on the avenues, side streets such as this one, which provide a unique and charming character, are being restored. ♦ Central Park West-Amsterdam Ave

25 Down Generation The large inventory of down-filled outerwear—in sizes to outfit the entire family—stuffed into this shop barely leaves enough room for trying the garments on. The reasonable prices make the bother worthwhile. ♦ 725 Columbus Ave (W 95th-W 96th Sts) 663.3112

26 First Church of Christ, Scientist (1903, **Carrère & Hastings**) This is, surprisingly, not particularly Beaux-Arts, but more in the style of the English Renaissance, with a touch of Hawksmoor in the energetic facade and steeple. The marble interiors are quite impressive. Carrère and Hastings also designed the **New York Public Library** and the **Frick Residence**. ♦ 1 W 96th St (Central Park West)

27 The Cliff Dwellers' Apartments (1914, **Herman Lee Leader**) The facade is decorated with a frieze of mountain lions, snakes and buffalo skulls—symbols of the Arizona cliff dwellers. An unusual example of Art Deco interest in prehistoric art and culture. ♦ 243 Riverside Dr (W 96th St)

28 J's ★$$$ Jazz singer **Judy Barnett** opened this neighborhood restaurant/club because

Upper West Side

she wanted a place *devoid of trendiness, with good food and no cover*. Jazz and a full menu—pastas, salads, grilled meats and fish—every night (the kitchen closes at 11:30PM Sunday-Thursday and 12:30AM Friday and Saturday). A favorite after-hours haunt for late workers and insomniacs. ♦ Continental ♦ 2581 Broadway (W 97th-W 98th Sts) 666.3600

29 **The Hunan Balcony** $$ Dependably fresh ingredients, low prices, clean, bright surroundings—and when they say *spicy*, they mean it. It's hard to ask for more from a neighborhood spot. ◆ Chinese ◆ 2596 Broadway (W 98th St) Reservations recommended. 865.0400

30 **Health Nuts** Natural vitamins, grains, nuts, herbs, honeys and breads. ◆ 2611 Broadway (W 99th St) 678.0054

31 **Bahama Mama** ★$$ Festive, multicolored Caribbean motif greets you one flight up. And just in case you don't know where you are, order one of the many rum-based concoctions and enjoy the lofty view of Broadway. The Island-inspired menu is also full of fun and tasty dishes like coconut shrimp-and-conch fritters served with hearts of palm salad, or, my favorite, Trinidad Pepper Pot, a hearty meat stew with a memorable zing. Order too many of the ridiculously named cocktails and you're likely to try the curried goat. Friendly and informal service tends to be slow, but no one seems in a great rush to leave. ◆ Caribbean ◆ 2628 Broadway (W 99th-W 100th Sts) Reservations recommended. 866.7760

32 **Border Café** ★$$ The first-rate guacamole and the fried jicama sticks are perfect companions to the enormous frozen margaritas and impressive selection of beers. Live music—lots of R&B—on Thursday and Saturday evenings. ◆ Southwestern ◆ 2637 Broadway (W 100th St) Reservations recommended. 749.8888. Also at: 244 E 79th St. 535.4347

33 **838 West End Avenue** (1914, **George and Edward Blum**) Covered with terracotta decoration, both geometric patterns and stylized natural forms. ◆ W 101st St

34 **Broadway Barber Shop** The gilt lettering on the windows is fading, but all the other fixtures seem to be intact in this quaint barbershop, which opened in 1907. *It's the oldest barber shop in New York*, a heavily accented barber calls out as he circles a supine head in his chair. *Number one! It's in* GQ *this month*. Good shave; great photo opportunity. ◆ 2713 Broadway (W 103rd-W 104th Sts) 666.3042

35 **Evita Argentine** ★$$ Meat lovers crowd in for the excellent broiled and BBQ beef and sausages. Vegetable lovers go away hungry. ◆ Argentinean ◆ 2720 Broadway (W 104th St) No credit cards. 678.0932

Upper West Side

36 **New York International AYH-Hostels** $ (1883, **Richard Morris Hunt**) Unlike many other hostels, no work is required in exchange for the clean, safe and inexpensive accommodations; there is no curfew and the hostel stays open all day long. Like other hostels, all guests must be members of American Youth Hostels (nonmembers can join on the spot) and must bring a sleeping bag or rent sheets. Not open to New York City residents. The building itself, once a home operated by the **Association for the Relief of Respectable Aged Indigent Females**, is a Designated Landmark of the City of New York. Hunt also designed the facade of the Great Hall of the Metropolitan Museum of Art and the base of the *Statue of Liberty*. ◆ 891 Amsterdam Ave (W 103rd-W 104th Sts) 932.2300

37 **Positively 104th Street Cafe** ★★$$ Specialty foods like roast duckling and grilled Norwegian salmon with arugula-pecan pesto, served in a cozy Art Deco setting. ◆ American ◆ 2725 Broadway (W 104th-W 105th Sts) Reservations recommended. 316.0372

37 **Au Petit Beurre** ★$ A pleasant, airy resting spot that calls itself a French cafe, but shows signs of student-inspired whole earth consciousness. Good cappuccino and excellent homemade muffins. Neighborhood clientele —the old and the new. ◆ Cafe ◆ 2737 Broadway (W 105th St) 663.7010

38 **Birdland** ★$$ Jazz/supper club featuring the likes of pianist **Henry Butler, Mark Morganelli and the Jazz Forum All-Stars** and the **Harper Brothers**. ◆ American ◆ 2745 Broadway (W 105th St) Reservations required. 749.2228

39 **Avalon Repertory Theater** Built in the 1930s, the building served as a Hatian social club, a baseball aficionados club and a warehouse before being renovated in 1989 by a group of up-and-coming actors *dedicated to works of great language, ideas and social relevance*. Recent performances have included plays by **George Bernard Shaw, Lanford Wilson** and **Horton Foote**. ◆ 2744 Broadway (W 105th-W 106th Sts) 2nd floor. 316.2668

40 **Riverside Drive/West 105th Street Historic District** (Designated 1973) Riverside Dr between 105th and 106th Sts (plus some of W 105th St), has an excellent collection of turn-of-the-century French Beaux-Arts townhouses. Of special interest is No. 331 (1902, **Janes & Leo**), formerly **Marion Davies**' residence, now part of the **New York Buddhist Church** and **American Buddhist Academy**. ◆ W 105th-W 106 Sts

41 **Nicholas Roerich Museum** Roerich was well-known in his native Russia and throughout the world as an artist, philosopher, archaeologist and founder of an educational institution to promote world peace through the arts. This beautiful old townhouse, one unit of his **Master Institute**, overflows with his landscapes, books and pamphlets on art, culture and philosophy. Lectures and concerts. ◆ Free. Tu-Su 2-5PM. 319 W 107th St (Broadway-Riverside Dr) 864.7752

The running track at 72nd St in Riverside Park is 1/8 mile around.

42 107 West ★★$$ A mostly young upscale crowd keeps this 3-room establishment bustling. Spicy Cajun specialties are best (blackened everything), especially fresh salmon in season. Good wine list. ◆ American ◆ 2787 Broadway (W 107th-W 108th Sts) 864.1555

43 Santerello ★★★$$$ One of the pioneer Italian establishments on the Upper West Side, this intimate, side-street venue continues to serve excellent Northern Italian fare. Try the daily fish specials or the especially flavorful chicken in a pungent Gorgonzola sauce. ◆ Italian ◆ 239 W 109th St (Broadway-Amsterdam Ave) 749.7044

44 Asmara ★$ Hard to find, hard to figure out, hard to forget: Asmara is an African restaurant named after a city that prospered under Italian colonial rule. Thus, curries spiced with cardamom, raw beef spiced with *berbere* (hot red pepper), and lamb sautéed in spiced butter— all served with *injera*, a soft bread that also substitutes for eating utensils—share menu space with *Spaghetti alla Asmara*, which resembles *alla Arrabbiata*, only with chunks of braised meat added to the hot-and-spicy sauce. The uninitiated may want to try the Combination Grand Special, chef **Mebrak**'s sampler du jour. Rewarding for the curious; an adventure for most. ◆ African ◆ 951 Amsterdam Ave (W 106th-W 107th Sts) 662.1065

45 Cathedral Parkway Houses (1975, **Davis, Brody & Associates** and **Roger Glasgow**) These 2 massive towers were carefully articulated in an attempt to accommodate them to the much smaller scale of the neighborhood. ◆ 125 W 109th St (Columbus-Amsterdam Aves)

46 Towers Nursing Home (1887, **Charles C. Haight**) Typically Victorian with its squat towers and conical roofs, this was originally the **New York Cancer Hospital**, the first in the nation devoted to the care of cancer patients. Haight was also architect of the main buildings of the **General Theological Seminary** and **Trinity School**. ◆ 2 W 106th St (Central Park West-Columbus Ave)

Bests

Jimmy Breslin
Writer, *New York Newsday*

Rao's in the rain, looking up the steps at the sidewalk. 114th and Pleasant Ave, probably Manhattan's oldest restaurant.

Cafe 2000 on 101st Ave and 103rd St in Ozone Park, Queens, where you sit at table over espresso in the morning and watch old women come down stone steps of a great old church while bells toll. Europe in Queens.

Pell Stand Doyers St. Doyers is narrow and bends. At the bend, at the angle, more were killed at that spot in Chinese Tong Wars than ever were killed on any one street in New York.

Meat market by the **Howard Beach Station** of the *A* train. Women sit on stools and talk in the morning while the butchers work and the women sit facing the counter and watch like hawks while talking.

Walking into the **Laurent Bar** on 56th St between Park and Lex. It is the greatest entrance to a bar in the world. Through drapes and at the top of a few steps and straight ahead is deep polished wood and gleaming bottles and white starch of napkins and light glares off glasses and the hand cannot wait to hold one.

Walk in **Rockaway** at dusk from 116th St to the end of **Riis Park** and back with the sky rose on purple and the waves spitting white into the cold air.

Sit at night on **Shore Rd** and watch the *Queen Elizabeth II* slide under the Verrazano Bridge. The ship at first seems to be part of another shore. Then you see it moving so quickly.

Don Peppe Vesuvio Restaurant, Lefferts Blvd and South Conduit Ave in Richmond Hill, Queens. Look into the kitchen as the waiters and chefs scream at each other. A fight, at first. Then you hear that the bitterness is over a horse that lost at Aqueduct, right around the corner. Then the waiters bring out tubs of mussels and clams. One of the world's great restaurants. Caters to racetrack people with taste.

Coming from Queens to Manhattan at night over the **Queensboro Bridge**. Perhaps the world's greatest sight.

Living anywhere on the water in Brooklyn Heights, Williamsburg, Long Island City or up on the hill in Maspeth and Middle Village in Queens and looking over at Manhattan. The people in Manhattan can only see Queens with its Pepsi-Cola signs. The smart people live in Queens and get a view that is unique in the world, even to photos, for the most sophisticated camera people don't know where these neighborhoods are and they can't take the pictures.

The **May Wave** in the **Ramble** at **Central Park** and in the **Bird Sanctuary** at **Jamaica Bay**. The flocks come north again and on 10 May the same birds are in the same places. For decades the same type of bird is in the same spot, in the Ramble or at the bird sanctuary. So many types that even the best books cannot have them all cataloged. They are en route to Canada and as far as the North Pole.

Third Ave and 42nd St and all the sidewalks in every direction at 5PM at night. Crowds going home. Crowds of such size that it is hard to think that one place can hold them. Nature's finest sight is still a crowded street.

Bar of **Dimitri's** restaurant on Columbus Ave and 67th St in the evening when the opera crowd comes in. It is like being in Europe.

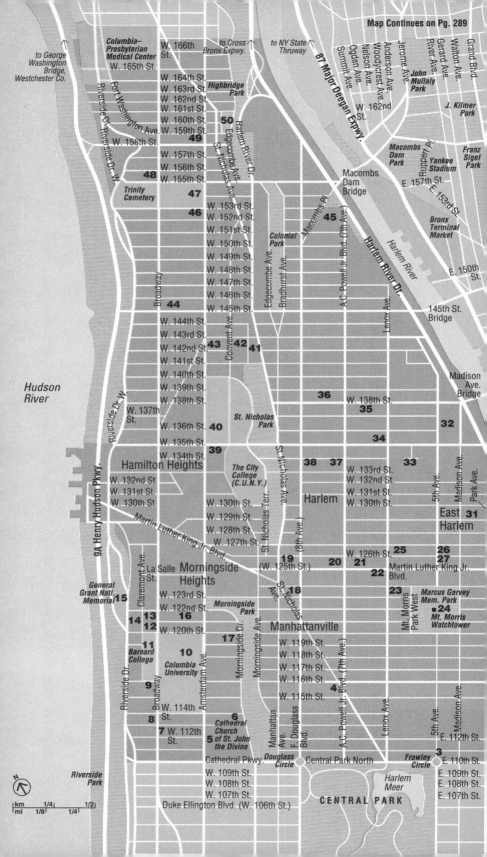

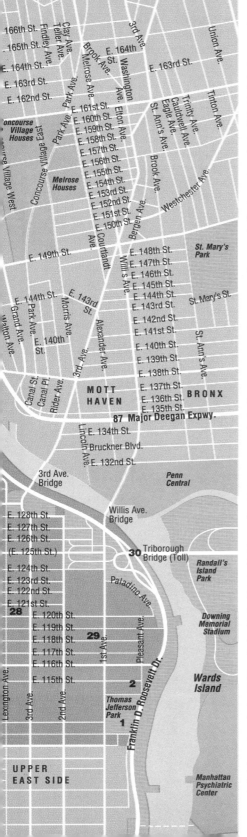

Heights/ Harlem

North of Cathedral Pkwy (110th St), the geographical peaks and valleys of the **Heights** and **Harlem** more or less define neighborhood boundaries all the way up to **Spuyten-Duyvil**, where the Hudson and East rivers join at 225th St.

Morningside Heights, the hilly terrain between Cathedral Pkwy and 125th St, is dominated by educational giants. **Union Theological Seminary**, **Jewish Theological Seminary**, **Columbia University** and **Barnard College** form the cornerstone of this outstanding academic community.

Two other structures of importance stand out in the landscape: the massive work-in-progress of the **Cathedral Church of St. John the Divine**, and the **Riverside Church**, an important religious and cultural center in its own right. While you're in the neighborhood, don't forget **Grant's Tomb**, high above the river.

This area of Manhattan was largely undeveloped until the opening of **Morningside Park** in 1887 and of **Riverside Dr** in 1891. World-renowned scholars began to settle in shortly thereafter. Broadway is the main drag here, just as it is on the Upper West Side. But it is less prettied up, although major property owner Columbia University has been bringing in more chic—and consequently more expensive—stores and restaurants.

Hamilton Heights, from 125th St north to **Trinity Cemetery** (155th St at Riverside Dr), is a former factory and ferry-landing town named for **Alexander Hamilton**, who had a country estate built here in 1802.

Heights/Harlem

There are other 19th-century buildings, but most of the development occurred after 1904, when the Broadway IRT subway opened. It has remained a primarily residential area. Today, some of the most desirable residences are the turn-of-the-century row houses in the

Hamilton Heights Historic District. City College of New York (CCNY), the northernmost Manhattan outpost of the **City University of New York (CUNY)** system, moved into the former campus of **Manhattanville College** (now located in Riverdale) in 1950.

Harlem, to the east, which becomes **East Harlem** east of 5th Ave, is Manhattan's black ghetto, where immigrants from the Caribbean and Africa, and economic refugees from the American states live, often in inadequate surroundings. Those of Hispanic origin, mostly from Puerto Rico, have settled in East Harlem, renaming it *El Barrio* (*the neighborhood* in Spanish), while the later wave of Dominicans and Cubans have settled along upper Broadway (Broadway in the 140s is known as *Little Dominica*), and on the east side of Broadway as far north as **Inwood** (207th St). The 2 Harlems are older than most black urban communities in this country, and larger—6sq mi, from 110th St north to the Harlem River, and bounded on the east by the East River. Unlike many other ghettos in the US, housing stock was excellent, and although much of it has deteriorated, it is still worth renovating—which is what increasing numbers of middle-class families are doing.

This section of the island was wooded hills and valleys inhabited by Indians when the Dutch started the settlement of *Nieuw Haarlem* in 1658. Black slaves owned by the West India Co helped build a road, later called Broadway, and the *Haarlem* outpost grew. In the early 19th century, affluent Manhattanites, including **James Roosevelt**, built estates and plantations here. It was also a haven for the poor. Irish immigrants were among those who built shantytowns on the East River, where they raised free-roaming hogs, geese, sheep and goats.

Harlem began to develop as a suburb for the well-to-do when the **New York and Harlem Railroad** started service from Lower Manhattan in 1837. More lines followed, and as handsome brownstones, schools and stores went up, immigrant families who had achieved some degree of success, many of them German Jews, moved up from the Lower East Side.

The announcement that work was starting on the IRT Lenox subway line touched off another round of development. This time the boom went bust. When the subway was completed in 1905, most of the buildings were still empty. Blacks began renting, often at inflated rates, as they were squeezed out of other parts of the city by commercial development. Eventually the only whites who remained were poor and lived on the fringes. Harlem became *the* black community in the US. Subsequent waves of blacks that poured in were often in need of jobs and lacked skills and education. East Harlem never had the middle- and upper-class population of **West Harlem**.

Although many blacks in Harlem were existing at poverty level in the '20s and '30s, black culture blossomed in the dance, drama and music that originated here. Speakeasies flourished in the area during Prohibition, and the smart set came uptown to the **Sugar Cane Club** and the **Cotton Club** (now a private club) to hear **Count Basie, Duke Ellington** and other popular jazz legends. **Lena Horne** got her start here.

In the 1950s, urban renewal made a dent in the declining housing stock by clearing blocks of slums and replacing them with housing developments. Gentrification began in Harlem in earnest in the '70s, and continues today, as middle-class families move into **Striver's Row** in the **St. Nicholas District** and to the **Mount Morris Park Historic District,** where the brownstones are among the city's finest.

Washington Heights, starting at Trinity Cemetery and going north to Dyckman St, was once an Irish neighborhood. In addition to the descendants of the Irish, there is now an ethnic mix of blacks, Puerto Ricans and other Latins, Greeks and Armenians—welfare—as well as working-class.

Audubon Terrace, a turn-of-the-century Beaux-Arts museum complex, seems out of place at 155th and Broadway, where it is surrounded by housing projects and tenements. But the complex is easy to reach by subway and worth a visit. North and east of Audubon Terrace is the **Jumel Terrace Historic District**.

Another important Heights landmark is **Fort Tryon Park** (pronounced *try-on*), the site of **Fort Tryon**, the northernmost defense of **Fort Washington**. Its crowning jewel is the **Cloisters**, which houses the medieval collection of the **Metropolitan Museum of Art**. Just south of the Cloisters is a little-known shrine, the **St. Frances Cabrini Chapel**. Here, under the altar in a crystal casket, lies the body of **Mother Cabrini**, the patron saint of all immigrants; above her neck is a wax mask, because her head is in Rome. (It seems that shortly after her death in 1917, a lock of her hair restored an infant's eyesight. That infant is now a priest in Texas.)

Inwood Hill Park, where Indian cave dwellers lived, ends the island with a rural flourish. There are playing fields and open park land with views over the Hudson and the **George Washington Bridge**, and as far as the **Tappan Zee Bridge**; these also give access to the water's edge. And there is a wilderness of hackberry bushes, maples, Chinese white ash and Oriental pine trees, from which you can see the end of the island, and where you can wander trails and imagine what it was like when the **Algonquin Indians** had a whole forest paradise to themselves.

1 Thomas Jefferson Public Pool Outdoor public pool open the last Saturday in June until Labor Day. Call for schedule and bring a padlock. ♦ E 111th St at 1st Ave. 397.3112

2 Rao V ★★★$$$ Judging from the limousines parked outside, you'd think this was the most exclusive Italian restaurant in Manhattan, and in some ways it is. Even with hard-to-come-by reservations, you might get squeezed out by **Sinatra** and his entourage. But take your chances, because this unassuming little bistro, run by the **Rao** family, is first-rate all the way. ♦ Italian ♦ Closed Sa-Su. 455 E 114th St (Pleasant Ave) Reservations required days in advance. No credit cards. 534.9625

3 Arthur A. Schomburg Plaza (1975, **Gruzen & Partners** and **Castro-Blanco, Piscioneri & Feder**) These 35-story octagonal apartment towers are distinguished markers at the corner of Central Park. The pairing of the balconies creates an original rhythm in moderating the scale; the multilevel deck is an inviting open space. ♦ E 110th-E 111th Sts (Madison-5th Aves)

4 New York Public Library, 115th Street Branch (1908, **McKim, Mead & White**) A Renaissance composition in limestone—as to be expected from this firm—and one of the finest of the branch libraries. ♦ M, Th 1-6PM; Tu 11AM-7PM; W 10AM-6PM. 203 W 115th St (Adam Clayton Powell Jr.-Frederick Douglass Blvds) 666.9393

5 The Cathedral Church of St. John the Divine This edifice was begun in 1892 under the sponsorship of **Bishop Henry Codman**

Heights/Harlem

Potter to designs by **Heins & LaFarge**. It's a giant, slightly rough Byzantine church with Romanesque influences. By 1911, the apse, choir and crossing were done, the architects and the bishop were dead, and fashions had changed. Gothic enthusiast **Ralph Adams Cram** of **Cram & Ferguson** drew up new plans to complete the church. The nave and western

Restaurants/Nightlife: Red   Hotels: Blue
Shops/Parks: Green   Sights/Culture: Black

facade are, therefore, fine French Gothic. Work was discontinued in 1941, but resumed within the last decade in an effort to complete the cathedral, particularly the towers. There is a stone yard in operation next to the church, where 2 dozen artisans—many of them neighborhood youths—apprenticed under a master mason from England, are carving blocks in a centuries-old tradition.

When St. John's is finished (a project that will carry over into the next century), it will be the largest cathedral in the world. The nave is 601ft long and 146ft wide; when completed, the transepts will be just as wide and span 320ft. The floor area is greater than **Chartres** and **Notre Dame** together. The towers will be 300ft high. Although not entirely complete, 4 of the 5 portals have been fitted with Burmese teak doors; the bronze door of the central portal was cast in Paris by **M. Barbedienne**, who cast the *Statue of Liberty*.

The interior is spectacular. There are 7 apsidal chapels in a variety of styles by a collection of prominent architects—the finest is that of **St. Ambrose**, a Renaissance-inspired composition by **Carrère & Hastings**. The 8 granite columns that ring the sanctuary are 55ft high and weigh 130 tons each. The dome over the crossing, intended to be temporary, was erected in 1909. Master woodworker **George Nakashima**'s massive heart-shaped **Altar for Peace**, cut from a 125ft English walnut tree from Long Island and finished with his trademark rosewood inlays, is the sight of monthly meditations for peace. The church hosts an impressive schedule of concerts, art exhibitions, lectures and theater and dance events. ◆ Amsterdam Ave at W112th St. 316.7540; box office 662.2133

6 St. Luke's Hospital (1896, Ernest Flagg) At least the central entrance pavilion and east wing remain of Flagg's Classical/Baroque composition that includes a little something extra.

Charming, dignified, slightly busy, it was certainly original. ◆ Morningside Dr (W 113th-W 114th Sts)

7 Symposium $ A popular and comfortable spot for Greek specialties like moussaka, spinach pie and *exohiko* (lamb, feta cheese, artichoke hearts and peas all wrapped up in a phyllo dough). The atmosphere and food are strictly authentic. During spring and summer, the garden is available for dining. ◆ Greek ◆ 544 W 113th St (Amsterdam Ave) 865.1011

8 West End Gate Cafe $$ A Columbia University hangout that draws in the rest of the community for its many entertainment programs: comedy shows every night; jazz on Tuesday and Wednesday; music brunches followed by children's theater every Saturday; and Sunday morning chess tournaments. The basic American food is secondary. ◆ American ◆ 2911 Broadway (W 113th-W 114th Sts) 662.8830

8 Papyrus Booksellers The paperbacks here are geared to Columbia students. Fine periodical section with a leaning toward politics and the arts. ◆ 2915 Broadway (W 114th St) 222.3350

9 Bookforum A bookstore located near Columbia naturally stocks a lot of scholarly paperbacks and books used in courses. This one also focuses on newly released hardcovers. You'll find older ones marked down on the tables outside. ◆ 2955 Broadway (W 116th St) 749.5535

10 Columbia University (Original design and early buildings 1897, **McKim, Mead & White**) This historic Ivy League school, founded in 1754, has an enrollment of more than 18,000. Now subdued compared to it in the politically outspoken 1960s, the student body has settled down to its studies in Columbia's 3 undergraduate schools: **Columbia College, School of General Studies** and **School of Engineering and Applied Science**. On the site of the

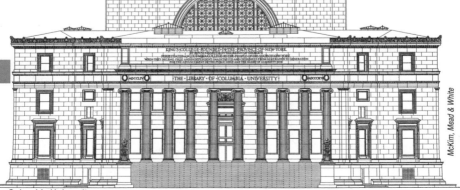

Columbia University

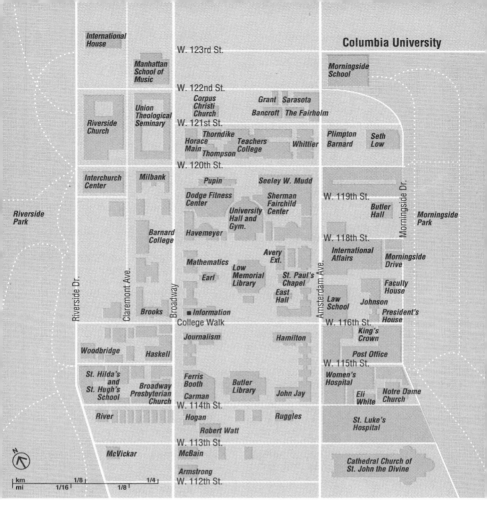

International House

Manhattan School of Music

Morningside School

W. 123rd St.

W. 122nd St.

Corpus Christi Church

Grant Sarasota

Bancroft The Fairholm

Union Theological Seminary

W. 121st St.

Riverside Church

Thorndike

Horace Teachers
Main College
Thompson

Whittier

Plimpton Seth
Barnard Low

W. 120th St.

Interchurch Center

Milbank

Pupin

Seeley W. Mudd

Riverside Park

Dodge Fitness Center

Sherman Fairchild Center

W. 119th St.

Morningside Dr.

Butler Hall

Morningside Park

University Hall and Gym.

Barnard College

Havemeyer

W. 118th St.

Claremont Ave.

Avery Ext.

International Affairs

Morningside Drive

Mathematics

Low Memorial Library

St. Paul's Chapel

Faculty House

Earl

Amsterdam Ave.

East Hall

Law School

Johnson

President's House

Brooks

Broadway

■ Information

College Walk

W. 116th St.

King's Crown

Journalism

Hamilton

Post Office

Woodbridge

Haskell

W. 115th St.

St. Hilda's and St. Hugh's School

Broadway Presbyterian Church

Ferris Booth

Butler Library

Women's Hospital

Eli Notre Dame
White Church

Carman

John Jay

W. 114th St.

River

Hogan

Ruggles

St. Luke's Hospital

Robert Watt

W. 113th St.

McVickar

McBain

Cathedral Church of St. John the Divine

Armstrong

W. 112th St.

N

km 1/8
mi 1/16 1/8 1/4
1/8

Bloomingdale Insane Asylum (of which East Hall is a remnant), the urban campus (the third one Columbia has occupied) was planned by **Charles Follen McKim** in a grand Beaux-Arts tradition. Although only a segment of his plan was completed, most of its elements can be discerned. The Italian Renaissance-inspired institutional buildings—in red brick with limestone trim and copper roofs—are arranged around a central quad on a terrace 2 stories above the street. There were to be 6 smaller side courts like the one between **Avery** and **Fayerweather Hall**s (somewhat changed now due to the extension of **Avery Library**).

MM&W's dominant central element is the magnificent **Low Library** (1897), a monumental pantheon named after Columbia president **Seth Low** (who was also mayor of New York City from 1902–3). Now no longer used as a library, Low remains the administrative and ceremonial center of the university. The statue of the *Alma Mater* on the front steps—made famous during the riots of 1968—is by **Daniel Chester French** (1903).

Other noteworthy buildings on the Columbia campus include **Butler Library** (1934, **James Gamble Rogers**), a colonnaded box facing Low's rotunda; the **Sherman Fairchild Center for the Life Sciences** (1977, **Mitchell/ Giurgola**), an interesting contextual essay in which a glass-and-metal building has been hidden behind a screen of quarry tile that resembles the ground pavers; the **Law School** and **School of International Affairs** extension (1963 and 1971, **Harrison & Abramovitz**), a great white mass beyond a block-long bridge that spans Amsterdam Ave; and the charming,

Heights/Harlem

modest Byzantine/Renaissance **St. Paul's Chapel** (1907, **Howells & Stokes**)—the interiors here are lovely, vaulted and light. The **Center for Engineering and Physical Science Research** (**Hellmuth, Obata and Kassabaum**) is scheduled for an early 1992 completion. Tours of the campus, which originate at 201 **Dodge Hall** (854.2845), are given according to public interest and the availability of guides. Call in advance. Main entrance at W 116th St. ♦ W 114th-W 120th Sts (Amsterdam Ave-Broadway) 854.1754

11 Barnard College The 2200-student women's school, an undergraduate college of **Columbia University**, offers bachelor's degrees in 27 majors, with emphasis on liberal arts. Across Broadway from the elegant expanse of Columbia, the Barnard campus appears crowded, but somehow more lively. The older buildings at the north end of campus—**Millbank** (1890), **Brinkerhoff** (1896) and **Fiske** (1897) **Halls**—were designed by **Lamb & Rich** in a sort of New England academic style. More interesting is the heart of the campus today: the limestone counterpoints of **MacIntosh Center** and **Altschul Hall**, both by Philadelphia architect **Vincent G. Kling** (1969). In 1989, 400 students moved into **Centennial Hall**, a 17-story tower at the southern end of campus, designed by **James Stewart Polshek & Partners**. ♦ W 116th-W 120th Sts (Broadway-Claremont Ave) 854.5262

12 Union Theological Seminary Bookstore Any and all in-print books that concern theology, as well as periodicals. ♦ Closed Sa-Su. 3041 Broadway (W 120th St) 662.7100

13 Union Theological Seminary (1910, **Allen & Collens**; alterations 1952, **Collens, Willis & Beckonert**) In a landscape studded with institutions, this is one of the few that truly manages to keep the city at bay. It is an example of collegiate Gothic borrowed from Oxbridge and, in that tradition, has a secluded interior courtyard. ♦ W 120th-W 122nd Sts (Broadway-Claremont Ave)

14 Riverside Church (1930, **Allen & Collens and Henry C. Pelton, Burnham Hoyt**; south wing 1960, **Collens, Willis & Beckonert**) Funded by **John D. Rockefeller Jr.**, this is a steel frame in a thin, institutional Gothic skin. The fine nave is almost overpowered by the tower, which rises 21 stories. The 74-bell carillon is the largest in the world. Visit the

Observation Deck in the tower, not only to look at the bells on the way up but for a splendid view of the Hudson, Riverside Park and the surrounding institutions. Forty-five-minute guided tours are offered Sunday at 12:30 or 1PM, after services. ♦ M-Sa 9AM-4PM; Su 12:30-4PM. Carillon bell concerts: Su noon, 3PM. Riverside Dr (W 120th-W 122nd Sts) 222.5900

Within Riverside Church:

Theater at Riverside Church For more than a decade, dancers and choreographers tested their mettle on this tiny stage as part of the **Riverside Dance Festival**. These days, the church no longer sponsors performances, but still opens its doors to theater, music, video and dance productions. ♦ Seats 275. 864.2929

15 Grant's Tomb/General Grant National Memorial (1897, **John H. Duncan**) Now's *our* chance to pose the infamous college exam question: who is buried in Grant's Tomb? A massive granite mausoleum set on a hill overlooking the river, the tomb dominates its surroundings. It is an impressive sequence: along the terrace, up the stairs, through the colonnade and bronze doors, and you find yourself under a high dome looking down on the identical black marble sarcophagi of the general and his wife in the center of a rotunda—an open crypt similar to **Napoleon's** tomb at the **Hôtel des Invalides** in Paris. It is surrounded by bronze busts of the general's comrades-in-arms and by allegorical figures between the arches representing scenes from his life. Photographs in 2 flanking rooms fill in with more realistic details. More fun, however, are the benches on the outside (1973, **Pedro Silva, Cityarts Workshop**), where the bright mosaic decorations were done by the community residents. A daytime trip only, as Grant's Tomb at night attracts denizens of the underground economy. Oh, yes, the answer: **Ulysses S. Grant** and his wife, **Julia**. ♦ Free. W-Su 9AM-5PM. Riverside Dr at W 122nd St. 666.1640

16 Teachers College, Bancroft Hall (1911, **Emery Roth**) A stew of abstracted details—basically Beaux-Arts Renaissance, but with a touch of Spanish and a pinch of Art Nouveau—enliven the facade of this apartment house. ♦ 509 W 121st St (Amsterdam Ave-Broadway)

17 The Terrace ★★★$$$$ The views alone—skyscrapers to the south and the glittering **George Washington Bridge** to the northwest—would make a trip to this unusual location worthwhile. But serendipitously, from soup to dessert, a thoroughly delightful meal can also be found here. Sometimes the chef's original ideas are high-reaching, but his technical mastery pulls him through. I recommend his warm lobster salad, homemade pasta and chocolate mousse. ♦ French ♦ Closed Su. 400 W 119th St (Morningside Dr) Jacket and reservations required. 666.9490

18 28th Precinct Station House (1974, **Lehrecke & Tonetti**) A particularly good job on a difficult triangular site, this station evidences a subtle sensibility in terms of material and massing, not unlike the work of the late, great **Louis I. Kahn**. ♦ 2271 Frederick Douglass Blvd (W 122nd-W 123rd Sts)

19 Frank Silvera Writers' Workshop Founded in 1973 by **Garland Lee Thompson**, this workshop is a memorial to the late **Frank Silvera**, who was active in nurturing black writers. Productions include *No Left Turn* by **Buriel Clay II** and *Inacent Black and Five Brothers* by **Marcus Hemphill**. Monday evening readings and critiques of new plays as well as seminars on play- and screenwriting are scheduled. ♦ Seats 125. 317 W 125th St (St. Nicholas Ave) 3rd floor. 662.8463

20 The Apollo (1914, **George Keister**) This former vaudeville house became the entertainment center of the black community in the '30s, and by the '50s it had become the venue for black popular music. A decade later, however, the Apollo fell on hard times as big-name acts began playing larger downtown venues. It wasn't until the early '80s, when it was rescued by **Inner City Broadcasting**, that the faded theater was given a much-needed facelift and turned into a center for black television productions as well as live entertainment. Now it's the showplace it used to be. Wednesday amateur nights are always fun and packed with budding talents. ♦ Seats 1500. 253 W 125th St (Adam Clayton Powell Jr.-Frederick Douglass Blvds) 749.5838

21 New York State Office Building (1973, **Ifill-Johnson-Hanchard**) An overbearing monument of glass and concrete on a vast, unpopulated site. More a political gesture than a necessary building. ♦ 163 W 125th St (Adam Clayton Powell Jr. Blvd)

22 Studio Museum in Harlem A small, black fine arts museum that features changing exhibitions of black art and culture from Africa, the Caribbean and America. Its year-round education programs, including the well-known *Vital Expression in American Art*, offers lectures, concerts and poetry readings. ♦ Admission. W-F 10AM-5PM; Sa-Su 1-6PM. 144 W 125th St (Lenox Ave-Adam Clayton Powell Jr. Blvd) 864.4500

23 Mount Morris Park Historical District (Designated 1971) The character of this district, with its distinct Victorian charms, was established during the speculative boom at the end of the 19th century, when it was first urbanized by descendants of Dutch, Irish and English immigrants. After 1900, it became a primarily German-Jewish neighborhood. Of the houses, the block on Lenox Ave between 120th and 121st Sts (1888, **Demeuron & Smith**) is particularly captivating. The **Mount Morris Bank and Safety Deposit Vaults** at 81-85 E 125th St was originally the **Morris Apartments** (1889, **Lamb & Rich**), distinguished by Richardsonian

Romanesque arches and stained glass. There is also a fine collection of religious buildings. The Neoclassical **Mount Olivet Baptist Church**, 201 Lenox Ave (1907, **Arnold Brunner**), was originally **Temple Israel**, one of the most prestigious synagogues in the city. **St. Martin's Episcopal Church**, Lenox Ave at 122nd St (1888, **William A. Potter**), a bulky, asymmetrical Romanesque composition, has a carillon of 40 bells, second in size only to that of Riverside Church. The **Bethel Gospel Pentecostal Assembly**, 36 W 123rd St, used to be the **Harlem Club** (1889, Lamb & Rich), and the **Greater Bethel AME Church** next door was originally the **Harlem Free Library** (1892, Lamb & Rich). The **Ethiopian Hebrew Congregation** meets in what was once the **Dwight Residence**, 1 W 123rd St (1890, **Frank H. Smith**), a Renaissance mansion with an unusual round- and flat-bayed front that is a strong addition to the block of fine brownstones on W 123rd St. ♦ W 119th-W 124th Sts (Mt Morris Park W-Lenox Ave)

24 Marcus Garvey Memorial Park Originally **Mount Morris Park** (land purchased by the city in 1839), this craggy square was renamed in 1973. Garvey was a brilliant orator, the founder of the **Universal Negro Improvement Association** and of the now defunct newspaper, *Negro World*. The highland in the center supports the only fire watchtower (1856, **Julius Kroehl**) surviving in the city. Its steel frame and sweeping spiral stairs, once practical innovations, are now nostalgic. ♦ 120th-124th Sts (Madison Ave-Mt Morris Park W)

25 Sylvia's ★★$$ The most renowned soul-food restaurant in Harlem has expanded into a second dining room and, during the warmer months, into an open patio next door. Southern-fried and smothered chicken (my favorite) are stand-outs, as are the dumplings, *candied sweets* (yams) and dessert puddings. Lunch-eonettelike atmosphere. ♦ Southern ♦ 328 Lenox Ave (W 126th-W 127th Sts) 996.0660

26 National Black Theater Courses, readings, performance workshops and productions. ♦ Seats 99. 2035 5th Ave (E 126th-E 127th Sts) 427.5615

Billie Holiday called her home at 108 W 139th St *a combination YMCA, boardinghouse for broke musicians, soup kitchen for anyone with a hard luck story, community center and after-hours joint where a couple of bucks would get you a shot of whiskey and the most fabulous fried chicken.*

27 La Famille ★$$$ Tucked into a brownstone, this is a lovely place for dinner near the **Apollo**. Home-cooked soul food, especially the short ribs of beef, is highly recommended, and the service couldn't be friendlier or more accommodating. Live jazz on weekends, sometimes during the week as well. ♦ Southern ♦ 2017 5th Ave (E 124th-E 125th Sts) Reservations required. 534.9909

28 Harlem Courthouse (1891, **Thom & Wilson**) A Romanesque pile in a variety of brick and stone. With its gables, archways and corner tower, this dignified and delicate mass represents the American tradition of great *country* courthouses. ♦ 170 E 121st St (3rd-Lexington Aves)

29 Patsy's Pizzeria ★$ It's still worth a side trip to East Harlem for one of the best slices— and pies—in the city. Thin crust, perfect balance, a treat for countertop connoisseurs. ♦ Pizza ♦ Closed M. 2287 1st Ave (E 118th St) 534.9783

30 Triborough Bridge A lift span connects Manhattan and Randalls Island, a fixed roadway springs from Randalls Island to the Bronx, and a suspension span crosses the Hell Gate. The impressive connector-collection was designed by **Othmar Ammann** and **Aymar Embury II** in 1936. ♦ Harlem River Dr at E 125th St, Manhattan to Grand Central Expwy, Queens to Bruckner Expwy, Bronx

31 All Saints Church (1894, **Renwick, Aspinwall & Russell**; rectory 1889, **Renwick, Aspinwall & Russell**; school 1904, **W.W. Renwick**) A fine group of buildings in the Gothic tradition of firm founder **James Renwick Jr.** that is arguably more pleasing than his own **St. Patrick's**. Especially worthwhile is the harmony of the terracotta tracery and buff, honey and brown brick. ♦ E 129th St at Madison Ave

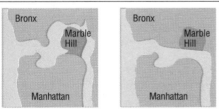

This small area, known as **Marble Hill**, is actually part of Manhattan. It was originally a peninsula at the northern tip of the island. The **Spuyten-Duyvil Creek** (Dutch for Spout-Devil), which separated Marble Hill from the mainland (the Bronx), was too narrow for ships.

Heights/Harlem

In 1895, the creek was filled (with dirt from the excavation of Grand Central Station), then the channel at the apex of the Harlem River was straightened and deepened. The latter action pushed Marble Hill up into the Bronx. This created a bit of an uproar as the residents were not thrilled about losing their status as Manhattanites. They quickly drafted a successful petition to remain part of the island politically, if not physically.

32 Riverbend Houses (1967, **Davis, Brody & Associates**) A complex of 625 apartments for moderate-income families, these buildings are respectful of context and in their use of material, while assembled with great style and imagination. They are landmarks in the recent tradition of publicly subsidized housing. ♦ 5th Ave (E 135th-E 138th Sts)

33 Hansborough Public Pool Indoor public pool open year-round to members (anyone who has paid the minimal yearly fee). Call for schedule of children's swimming hours and arts and crafts programs. Bring a padlock. ♦ Closed Su. 34 W 134th St (5th-Lenox Aves) 397.3134

34 Schomburg Center for Research in Black Culture Primarily a research center with the largest library of black and African culture in the US, collected by Puerto Rican black **Arthur Schomburg** (1874-1938). Occasionally shows by African and black American artists. ♦ Free. M-W noon-8PM; Th-Sa 10AM-6PM. 515 Lenox Ave (W 135th St) 862.4000

35 Abyssinian Baptist Church (1923, **Charles W. Bolton**) A bluestone Gothic Tudor building renowned for its late pastor, US Congressman **Adam Clayton Powell Jr.** Founded in 1808, it is New York's oldest black church. ♦ 132 W 138th St (Lenox Ave-Adam Clayton Powell Jr. Blvd)

36 St. Nicholas Historic District/King Model Houses (Designated 1967) In an unusual and highly successful 1891 venture, speculative builder **David King** chose 3 different architects to design the row housing on these 3 blocks. Nos. 202-250 W 138th St and Nos. 2350-2354 Adam Clayton Powell Jr. Blvd are by **James Brown Lord**, all in simple Georgian red brick on a brownstone base. Nos. 203-271 W 138th St, Nos. 2360-2390 Adam Clayton Powell Jr. Blvd and Nos. 202-272 W 139th St are by **Bruce Price** and **Clarence S. Luce**. Nos. 203-267 W 139th St and Nos. 1380-2390 Adam Clayton Powell Jr. Blvd are the finest—elegantly detailed, Renaissance-inspired simplicity by **McKim, Mead & White**. The harmony of the ensemble, achieved through similarity of scale and sensitivity, despite the variety of styles and materials, is extraordinary. This came to be known as *Striver's Row*, the home of the area's young and professionally ambitious. ♦ W 138th-W 139th Sts (Adam Clayton Powell Jr.-Frederick Douglass Blvds)

37 Jamaican Hot Pot ★★$ Yvonne Richards and **Gary Walters** turn out fabulous Jamaican specialties—fried chicken and oxtail stew are just 2 winning dishes. Locals love this place. ♦ Jamaican ♦ 2260 Adam Clayton Powell Jr. Blvd (W 133rd St) 491.5270

38 P.S. 92 (1965, **Percival Goodman**) Elegantly articulated and warmly detailed. ♦ 222 W 134th St (Adam Clayton Powell Jr.-Frederick Douglass Blvds)

39 135th Street Gatehouse, Croton Aqueduct (1890) This brownstone-and-granite watchtower, a Roman echo, was the end of the aqueduct over High Bridge. From here, water was taken in pipes to 119th St, by an aqueduct under Amsterdam Ave to 113th St, and then by pipe again to the city. Finely crafted gatehouses still stand at 119th and 113th Sts. ◆ Convent Ave

40 City University of New York, City College (1905, **George B. Post**) Nearly 12,000 students—75 percent minority—attend classes at this 34-acre campus. Bachelor's and master's degrees are offered in liberal arts, education, engineering, architecture and nursing. The science programs are also noteworthy. The campus is an ornately costumed, energetic collection of white-trimmed, Neo-Gothic buildings built with Manhattan schist excavated during the construction of the IRT subway. The old campus is especially wonderful in contrast to the more recent buildings that have grown up around it. The Romanesque south campus used to be **Manhattanville College of the Sacred Heart**, originally an academy and convent. ◆ W 130th-W 140th Sts (St. Nicholas Terr-Amsterdam Ave) 690.6741

Within City College:

Aaron Davis Hall at City College In the **Leonard Davis Performing Arts Center**. A multiarts theater hosting, among others, the **Dance Theater of Harlem** and the **Negro Ensemble Co**. ◆ Seats 750, 300, 75. W 135th St at Convent Ave. 690.4100

41 Harlem School of the Arts (1977, **Ulrich Franzen & Associates**) In 1965, soprano **Dorothy Maynor** began teaching piano in the basement of the **St. James Presbyterian Church Community Center**. From that modest beginning, HSA has grown to 1300 students (from 4 year olds to senior citizens, with the majority falling between the ages of 4 and 18), and has gained national prominence as a performing arts school. Several former students and teachers now have active Broadway careers. With world-famous mezzo-soprano **Betty Allen** as executive director, the school now teaches musical instrument study (piano, orchestral string, percussion),

ballet and modern dance, visual and dramatic arts. (The orchestral string department is especially noteworthy; the 23-member **Suzuki Ensemble**, made up of 8- to 17-year-olds, is known throughout the city.) Through the *Opportunities for Learning in the Arts* program, students from other schools are brought in to take classes during the day. The *Community and Culture in Harlem* program hosts concerts, art exhibitions and readings. The school's award-winning building is a complex marriage of classrooms, practice studios, 3 large dance studios, auditoriums, offices and an enclosed garden. An adjacent building holds the 200-seat **Harlem School of the Arts Theater**. ◆ 645 St. Nicholas Ave (W 141st St) 926.4100; theater 491.5977

42 Hamilton Heights Historic District (Designated 1974) The area of Hamilton Heights was once the country estate of **Alexander Hamilton**, whose house, the **Grange**, stands at Convent Ave and 141st St next to **St. Luke's**. The district has a generally high-quality collection of row houses dating from the turn of the century that exhibit a mixture of styles and wealth of ornament. W 144th St is exemplary; the row at Nos. 413-423 (1898, **T.H. Dum**) has Venetian Gothic, Italian and French Renaissance elements. Because there is very little through traffic, the neighborhood has always been slightly secluded and desirable. It is occupied primarily by faculty from nearby **City College**. ◆ W 141st-W 145th Sts (Hamilton Terr-Convent Ave)

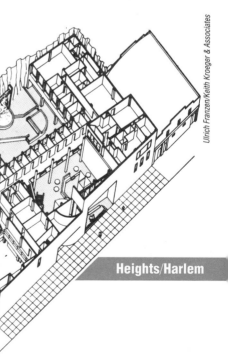

Ulrich Franzen/Keith Kroeger & Associates

Harlem School of the Arts

42 Aunt Len's Doll and Toy Museum Over 5000 dolls and toys, collected by a former school teacher, **Mrs. Lennon Holder Hoyte**, fill up this typical Hamilton Terrace row house. Call before visiting. ♦ 6 Hamilton Terr (W 141st St) 281.4143

43 Our Lady of Lourdes Church (1904, **O'Reilly Brothers**) A scavenger's monument, this church is, quite literally, composed of pieces from 3 other buildings: the Ruskinian Gothic, gray and white marble and bluestone facade on 142nd St is from the old **National Academy of Design** (1865, **P.B. Wight**) that stood at 23rd St at Park Ave So; the apse and part of the east wall were once the Madison Ave end of **St. Patrick's Cathedral**—removed for the construction of the Lady Chapel; the pedestals flanking the steps are from **A.T. Stewart**'s palatial department store (1867, **John Kellum**), once on 34th St at 5th Ave. ♦ 467 W 142nd St (Convent-Amsterdam Aves)

44 Copeland's ★$$ Southern style goes Continental. Louisiana gumbo, barbecued jumbo shrimp and live dinner music. No sneakers or sports clothes after 4PM. ♦ Southern/Continental ♦ 547 W 145th St (Amsterdam Ave-Broadway) Reservations recommended. 234.2357

45 Harlem River Houses (1937, **Archibald Manning Brown** with **Charles F. Fuller, Horace Ginsbern, Frank J. Forster, Will Rice Amon, Richard W. Buckley** and **John L. Wilson; Michael Rapuano**, landscape architect) Nine acres of public housing developed by the **Federal Administration of Public Works**, this is an exemplary complex. An energetic variety of building shapes are arranged in 3 groups around a central plaza and landscaped courts, becoming less formal nearer the river. The sculpture inside the 151st St entrance is by **Paul Manship**, who also did the *Prometheus* at **Rockefeller Center**. ♦ E 151st-E 153rd Sts (Harlem River Dr-Macomb Pl)

46 Originally the 32nd Precinct Station House (1872, **N.D. Bush**) This is a Victorian charmer with a cast-iron crest and mansard roof. ♦ 1854 Amsterdam Ave (W 152nd St)

47 Trinity Cemetery (Boundary walls and gates, 1876; gatehouse and keeper's lodge 1883, **Vaux & Radford**; grounds 1881, **Vaux & Co.**) This hilly cemetery used to be a part of the estate of American naturalist **J.J. Audubon**, who is among those buried here. Others include many members of families that

made New York: **Schermerhorns, Astors, Bleeckers, Van Burens.** At Christmastime, the grave of **Clement Moore** draws special attention—he wrote *A Visit from St. Nicholas* (*Twas the night before Christmas and all through the house....*). ♦ Daily 8AM-dusk. W 153rd-W 155th Sts (Amsterdam Ave-Riverside Dr) 602.0787

At Trinity Cemetery:

Chapel of the Intercession (1914, **Cram, Goodhue & Ferguson**) This is essentially a large country church set in the middle of rural **Trinity Cemetery**. The cloister at the 155th St entrance is particularly nice, and the richly detailed interior is marvelous, highlighted by an altar inlaid with stones from the Holy Land and sites of early Christian worship. The ashes of architect **Bertram Goodhue** are entombed in a memorial in the north transept. ♦ Broadway at W 155th St

48 Audubon Terrace This Classical cultural collection was first planned in 1908, and bankrolled by poet and scholar **Archer M. Huntington**. The master plan was by **Charles Pratt Huntington**, his nephew, who also designed 5 of the buildings: the **Museum of the American Indian, Heye Foundation** (1916); the **American Geographic Society** (1916); the **Hispanic Society of America** (north building 1916; south building 1910–26); the **American Numismatic Society** (1908); and the **Church of Our Lady of Esperanza** (1912). The 2 buildings of the **American Academy and Institute of Arts and Letters** are by **William M. Kendall** (administration building 1923) and **Cass Gilbert** (auditorium and gallery 1930). Such a concentration was a striking idea, but unfortunately, I think, did not have a brilliant execution. The Beaux-Arts exercise here is unwieldy, despite the comfortably small scale. The green-and-gold interior of the church is rather nice; the stained glass, skylight and lamps were gifts of the king of Spain, who also knighted the architect. ♦ Broadway (W 155th-W 156th Sts)

At Audubon Terrace:

National Museum of the American Indian (Smithsonian Institution) It is worth coming all the way uptown to see one of the largest collections of American Indian artifacts in the world, but not enough people do. Started from the private collection of **George G. Heye**, the material displayed runs the gamut from prehistoric to contemporary illustrations of the esthetic contributions and daily lives of the Indians in North, Central and South Americas. It's a dazzling array of Iroquois masks, Apache playing cards, Mexican play figurines, **William Penn**'s Wampum belts, personal possessions of **Geronimo** and **Sitting Bull** and shrunken human figures from the Jivaro Indians of Ecuador. The presentations run from excellent to jumbled, so if the often sketchy labels whet your appetite for more information, try the **Museum Shop**. There's an exhaustive stock of books on Indian cultures. Also high-quality jewelry, rugs, paintings, *molas* and other Indian crafts at fair prices. ♦ Admission. Tu-Sa 10AM-5PM; Su 1-5PM. 3753 Broadway (W 155th St) 283.2420

Hispanic Society of America The museum of the Hispanic Society is in a lavishly appointed building lined with the paintings of Old Masters—**El Greco, Goya, Velázquez**—

archaeological finds, ceramics and other decorative arts of the Iberian peninsula. A library in the building across the terrace is an important research center. ♦ Free. Tu-Sa 10AM-4:30PM; Su 1-4PM. 613 W 155th St (Broadway) 926.2234

American Numismatic Society Downstairs are rotating examples of the world's coinage—past and present—and a display of medals and decorations. On the 2nd floor is the most comprehensive numismatic library in America. For collectors, a **Public Inquiry Counter** is staffed by a curator to answer questions. Write or call in advance to get help with investigating a specific type of coinage in the collection. ♦ Free. Tu-Su 9AM-4:30PM. Broadway at W 155th St. 234.3130

American Academy and Institute of Arts and Letters Regular exhibitions of the work of members and nonmembers of this honor society for American writers, artists and composers. Call for schedule. ♦ Free. 633 W 155th St (Broadway-Riverside Dr) 368.5900

49 Wilson's Bakery & Restaurant ★★$$ A Harlem institution. The bakery next door insures the freshest baked goods at the restaurant table—the perfect complement to the outstanding baked ribs. ♦ Bakery/Southern ♦ 1980 Amsterdam Ave (W 158th St) 923.9821

50 Morris-Jumel Mansion (1765; portico, 1810) This house was built by **Roger Morris** as a summer residence on an estate that stretched from river to river. During the Revolution, **Washington** *did* sleep here and, in fact, he used it as a headquarters briefly, until New York City was taken over by the British. After being used as a tavern, it was bought and remodeled by French merchant **Stephen Jumel**. It is a typical Federal wood house; note the conceit of the quoins—a stone form mimicked in wood.

The elegant home has been decorated in excellent Georgian, Federal and French Empire-style furnishings, silver and china. All the draperies were woven and donated by master fabric maker **Franco Scalamandre** using period patterns. Some of **Napoleon**'s furniture is here, as are a trunk and desk-table that belonged to **Aaron Burr**. Tours of the mansion are conducted by the **Daughters of the American Revolution**. Lectures and concerts are held here as well. Picnickers are welcome to use the Colonial herb and rose gardens. Around the mansion is the **Jumel Terrace Historic District** (designated 1970), a charming neighborhood of well-kept 19th-century row houses. ♦ Admission. M by appointment; Tu-Su 10AM-4PM. 1765 Jumel Terr (Edgecombe Ave at W 160th St) 923.8008

51 Columbia-Presbyterian Medical Center An enormous hospital complex, still growing and adding on. The hospital enjoys the reputation of being a topnotch teaching facility (**Columbia University**) and working hospital, and it has stabilized the neighborhood it serves. ♦ 622 W 168th St (Broadway-Riverside Dr) 305.2500

52 High Bridge (1839-48, **John B. Jervis**) Originally an aqueduct as well, this is the oldest bridge extant connecting Manhattan to the mainland. Jervis also designed the **Highbridge Tower** (1872), which was used to equalize pressure in the Croton Aqueduct. ♦ Highbridge Park at W 174th St, Manhattan to W 170th St at University Ave, Bronx

53 Bloch & Falk These kosher butchers and caterers prepare cold cuts and condiments to suit the tastes of the German-Jewish community of Washington Heights, as well as the new black and Hispanic middle class. ♦ 4100 Broadway (W 173rd St) 927.5010

54 The United Church (1930, **Thomas W. Lamb**) Originally **Loew's 175th Street Theater**, this Miami-Egyptian concoction is movie palace architecture at the height of its glory. It's one of the few remaining movie palaces in Manhattan *not* to suffer from the sixplex syndrome, but the stage has been given over to **Reverend Ike**, the positive-thinking preacher. ♦ 4140 Broadway (W 175th St) 568.6700

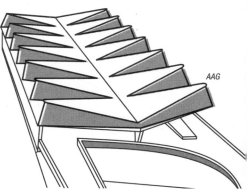

AAG

55 George Washington Bridge Bus Station (1963, **Port of New York Authority** and architect/engineer **Pier Luigi Nervi**) This concrete butterfly is a noteworthy attempt at celebrating the bus station in the shadow of a grand bridge. ♦ W 178th St (Broadway-Fort Washington Ave) Bus information 564.1114

Heights/Harlem

All that remains of Revolutionary War-era **Fort Washington** is the outline of the foundation, marked by paving stones, in **Bennett Park**. Here at Ft. Washington Ave, between 183rd and 185th Sts, is the highest point in Manhattan, 267.75 feet above sea level.

At 280ft above sea level, 184th St at Ft. Washington Ave is the highest point in the city.

Restaurants/Nightlife: Red   **Hotels:** Blue
Shops/Parks: Green   **Sights/Culture:** Black

56 George Washington Bridge (1931, **Othmar Amman**) In 1947, **Le Corbusier**, French architect and master of Modernism, called this spectacularly sited and magnificently elegant suspension bridge with its 3500ft span *the most beautiful bridge in the world...it gleams like a reversed arch. It is blessed.* If the original plans had been completed, architectural consultant **Cass Gilbert** would have encased the towers in stone. It took 4 years to build the George Washington; in 1962, it was expanded to become the world's first 14-lane suspension bridge. Its roadway peaks at 212ft above the water and its towers rise 604ft. Today the CMI Engineering landmark is the world's busiest bridge, with 100 million vehicles traveling across it yearly. For pedestrians, there is a good view of the bridge from 181st St, west of Fort Washington. But the real heart-thumper is a walk across the bridge itself. ♦ W 178th St at Hudson River, Manhattan to Fort Lee NJ

57 Little Red Lighthouse (1921) Now overshadowed by the eastern tower of the **George Washington Bridge**, this was built to steer barges away from **Jeffrey's Hook**. Because navigation lights were put on the bridge, the lighthouse was put up for auction in 1951, but was saved by the community's affection. It is the subject of a well-known children's book by **Hildegarde Hoyt Swift** entitled *The Little Red Lighthouse and the Great Gray Bridge.* ♦ Fort Washington Park (Washington Bridge)

58 Yeshiva University Yeshiva, the oldest Jewish studies center in the country, celebrated its centennial in 1986. The independent university offers both undergraduate and graduate degrees in programs ranging from Hebraic Studies to biomedicine, law to rabbinics. Also part of the university are the **Albert Einstein College of Medicine**, Bronx; **Brookdale Center-Cardozo School of Law**, Greenwich Village; **Stern College for Women** and **Teachers Institute for Women**, Midtown. The main building of its Washington Heights campus (1928, **Charles B. Meyers Associates**) is characterized by a fanciful, romantic composition of institutional underpinnings overlaid with a Middle Eastern collection of turrets, towers and tracery, minarets, arches and balconies—all in an unusual orange, with marble and granite striping. The light in the auditorium is especially extraordinary, with mirrored chandeliers and orange and yellow windows. ♦ W 186th St at Amsterdam Ave. 960.5400

Heights/Harlem

59 Fort Tryon Park (Landscaping, **Frederick Law Olmsted Jr.**) This 62-acre park, with its sweeping views of the Hudson River, is beyond exquisite. Originally the **C.K.G. Billings** estate (whose entrance was the triple-arched driveway from Riverside Dr), the land was bought by **John D. Rockefeller Jr.** in 1909 and given to the city in 1930. (As part of the gift, the city had to agree to close off the ends of several streets above 60th St to create the site for **Rockefeller University**.) There are still signs of **Fort Tryon**, a Revolutionary War bulwark. Don't miss the magnificent flower gardens. ♦ W 192nd-Dyckman Sts (Broadway-Riverside Dr)

Within Fort Tryon Park:

1 Gothic Chapel	13 Late-Gothic Hall
2 Early Gothic Hall	14 Campin Room
3 Chapter House from Pontaut	15 Tapestry Hall
4 Langnon Chapel	16 Boppard Room
5 West Terrace	17 Hall of the Unicorn Tapestries
6 Ramparts	18 Heroes Tapestry Room
7 St. Guilhem Cloister	
8 Romanesque Hall	19 Cuxa Cloister
9 Fuentaduena Chapel	20 Gothic Hall
10 Books and Reproductions	21 Glass Gallery
11 Entrance Hall	22 Treasury
12 Froville Arcade	23 Trie Cloister
	24 Bonnefont Cloister

The Cloisters (1934–38, **Charles Collens**; altered for the addition of the Fuentaduena Chapel 1962, **Brown, Lawford & Forbes**) Both the building and the contents of this branch of the **Metropolitan Museum of Art** were a gift of the munificent **John D. Rockefeller Jr.** Arranged among cloisters and other architectural elements from monasteries in southern France and Spain, this is very much a medieval ensemble, incorporating both Gothic and Romanesque elements dating from the 12th to 15th centuries. It was built to house the Met's Medieval collection. (Thoughtfully, Rockefeller protected the view by also buying the land on the Palisades opposite and restricting development.) The best way to see the pastiche of architectural and art fragments is in chronological sequence—past romantic gardens, ancient stained-glass windows, altar pieces, sculpture and tapestries along the way. You will pass through the **Treasury**, where precious enamels, Roman

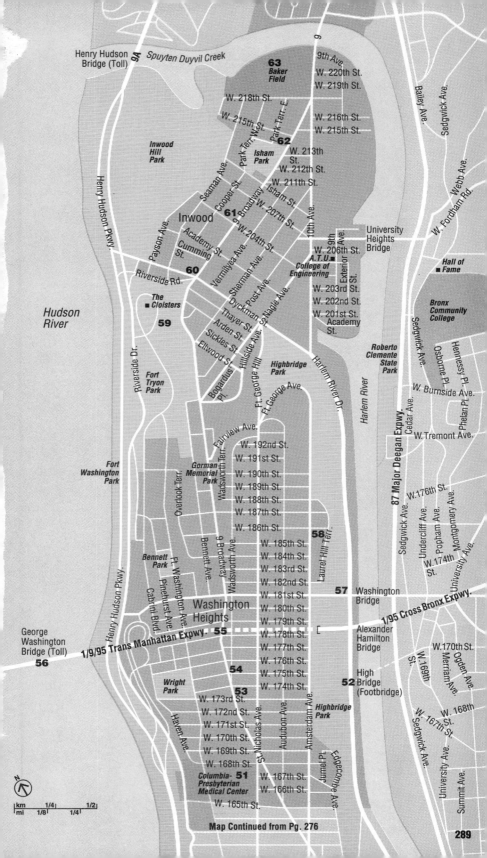

Henry Hudson Bridge (Toll)
9A
Spuyten Duyvil Creek
9

63
Baker Field

9th Ave.
W. 220th St.
W. 219th St.

W. 218th St.
W. 216th St.
W. 215th St.
W. 215th St.

Park Terr. E.
Park Terr. W.
Seaman Ave.

62
Isham St.
Isham Park
W. 213th
W. 212th St.
W. 211th St.
W. 207th St.
Broadway
Isham St.
10th Ave.

Inwood Hill Park

Cooper St.
Vermilyea Ave.

61
W. 204th St.

Inwood

Academy St.
Cumming St.
Sherman Ave.
Post Ave.
Nagle Ave.
9th Ave.

W. 206th St.
A.T.U.
College of Engineering
Exterior St.

University Heights Bridge

Bailey Ave.
Sedgwick Ave.
W. Fordham Rd.
Webb Ave.

Payson Ave.

60
Riverside Rd.
W. 203rd St.
W. 202nd St.
W. 201st St.
Academy St.

Hall of Fame

Bronx Community College

The Cloisters

59

Hudson River

Dyckman St.
Thayer St.
Arden St.
Sickles St.
Eltwood St.
Bogardus Pl.
Hillside Ave.
Ft. George Hill

Harlem River Dr.

Sedgwick Ave.
W. Burnside Ave.

Hennessy Pl.
Osborne Pl.
Phelan Pl.
Cedar Ave.

Riverside Dr.

Fort Tryon Park

Highbridge Park
Ft. George Ave.

Roberto Clemente State Park

Harlem River

W. Tremont Ave.

Fairview Ave.

Fort Washington Park

Wadsworth Terr.
Gorman Memorial Park
W. 192nd St.
W. 191st St.
W. 190th St.
W. 189th St.
W. 188th St.
W. 187th St.
W. 186th St.

87 Major Deegan Expwy.

W.176th St.
Sedgwick Ave.
Undercliff Ave.
Popham Ave.
Montgomery Ave.
University Ave.

Overlook Terr.

Bennett Park
9 Broadway
Bennett Ave.
Wadsworth Ave.

W. 185th St.
W. 184th St.
W. 183rd St.
W. 182nd St.
W. 181st St.
W. 180th St.
W. 179th St.
W. 178th St.
W. 177th St.
W. 176th St.
W. 175th St.
W. 174th St.

58
Laurel Hill Terr.

W.174th St.

57 Washington Bridge

1/95 Cross Bronx Expwy.

Ft. Washington Ave.
Pinehurst Ave.
Cabrini Blvd.

Washington Heights

Alexander Hamilton Bridge

George Washington Bridge (Toll)

56

Henry Hudson Pkwy.

1/9/95 Trans Manhattan Expwy. **55**

54
53
Wright Park
W. 173rd St.
W. 172nd St.
W. 171st St.
W. 170th St.
W. 169th St.
W. 168th St.

St. Nicholas Ave.
Audubon Ave.
Amsterdam Ave.

52 High Bridge (Footbridge)

Highbridge Park
Jumel Pl.
Edgecombe Ave.

W.170th St.
Ogden Ave.
Merriam Ave.
W. 169th St.
W. 168th
Sedgwick Ave.

Haven Ave.

Columbia-Presbyterian Medical Center **51**

W. 167th St.
W. 166th St.
W. 165th St.

University Ave.
Summit Ave.

N

km 1/4   1/2
mi 1/8   1/4

Map Continued from Pg. 276

289

manuscripts and ivories are on display, and then come to the *pièce de résistance*—the celebrated **Unicorn Tapestries** from the late 15th and early 16th centuries. Recorded medieval music sets the mood. Special programs, including gallery talks, musical performances and demonstrations, are scheduled on Saturday at noon and 2PM. Two special places to relax: the herb garden, with a view of the Palisades as **Henry Hudson** might have seen it—thoughtfully, Rockefeller protected the view by also buying the land on the Palisades opposite and restricting development—and the cafe next door, where a hot chocolate in the winter or an iced tea in the summer is the perfect way to *take five*. **RSW**: *An absolute must!* ♦ Voluntary contribution. Tu-Su 9:30AM-4:45PM. Free tours Tu-Sa 3PM. W 193rd St at Fort Washington Ave. 923.3700

60 International Gourmet and Gift Center China, cutlery, crystal, appliances, food and cosmetics imported mainly from Germany. This well-stocked store is one of the last outposts of the German-Jewish community of Washington Heights that was once referred to as *The Fourth Reich*. ♦ Closed F afternoon, Sa. 4797 Broadway (Dyckman-Academy Sts) 569.2611

61 Dyckman House (1783) The only 18th-century Dutch farmhouse in Manhattan survives despite the inroads of 20th-century apartment houses and supermarkets. The house, given to the city as a museum in 1915, has been restored and filled with original Dutch and English family furnishings, and gets high marks for authenticity and charm. An herb garden, smokehouse and reproduction of a Revolutionary hut are further reminders of life on a farm in the colonies. Worth a visit. ♦ Free. Tu-Su 11AM-5PM. 4881 Broadway (W 204th St) 304.9422

62 Carrot Top Pastries Owner **Renee Allen Mancino** bakes the single best carrot cake in New York, as well as delicious pecan, sweet-potato and pumpkin pies, according to the devoted customers—who include **Stevie Wonder** and **Richard Pryor**—at her 2 cafes. The outlet near **Columbia-Presbyterian Medical Center** has a small seating area. Special orders accepted. ♦ 5025 Broadway (W 214th St) 927.3999. Also at: 3931 Broadway (W 164th St) 569.1532

63 Baker Field Athletic Complex/ Lawrence Wein Stadium Columbia University's uptown athletic facility features Manhattan's only college football stadium and the country's *losingest* college football team

Heights/Harlem

(8 out of 9 in 1990, for example). The views from **Wein Stadium** (**Inwood Hill Park** is just to the west, **Spuyten-Duyvil** just beyond the northern end zone) are a welcome distraction. There's a soccer field closer to Broadway, and that team fares much better. Call for schedule. ♦ W 218th St (Broadway-Seaman Ave) 942.0431

Bests

Sam Hall Kaplan
Los Angeles-based Design Critic and Author

Things a person born and bred in New York but moved to LA likes to do when he returns to New York:

On separate weekdays, visit the **Met**, the **Whitney**, the **Guggenheim**, the **Cooper-Hewitt** and **MoMA**.

At dusk, check out the old neighborhood, walking down **Broadway** from about 96th St to **Lincoln Center**, catch a concert, then after, stroll up **Columbus Ave** and have a late snack at a sidewalk café.

Any day, anytime, sit on the edge of the **Pulitzer Fountain** at 59th St and 5th Ave and watch the crowds go by, then join them in any direction.

On an early Saturday, wander from **Greenwich Village**, through **Washington Square Park**, **SoHo**, **Little Italy**, **Chinatown**, to the **South Street Seaport** and back again, but on different streets, noshing all the way.

On Sunday, have brunch at the **Russian Tea Room** or **Tavern on the Green**, then rent or borrow a bicycle to work off the calories exploring **Central Park**.

Later, especially if it is warm, pedal or walk to the East Side and **Carl Schurz Park**, catch a breeze and watch the boats chug by, or to the West Side and **Riverside Park** at the 79th St boat basin.

Or spend Sunday at the **Cloisters**, bicycling or busing there.

Anne Rosenzweig
Chef/Owner, Arcadia; Vice Chairperson, 21 Club

An unusual perspective of Manhattan begins with an early-morning breakfast at **Sylvia's** (salmon cakes, grits, deep-fried slab bacon and biscuits). This is the perfect start to a walking day. Then a stroll through the marvelous but crumbling architecture of Harlem, especially around **Mt. Morris Park**. Then to **La Marqueta**, the Spanish market under the train tracks at Park Ave and 116th St. Wonderful and unearthly smells and sights—fresh baby goats, huge aloe vera plants (which soothe kitchen burns and cuts), all sorts of tropical fruits and botanicals, pigs' snouts, love elixirs mixed to order, etc....Then down to the **Conservatory Gardens** at 5th Ave and 105th St. Every season the gardens are completely transformed. In spring, huge lilac bushes create an intoxicating aroma under which one can read the Sunday papers. During the summer, they are the setting of some of the most beautiful weddings in New York.

Sitting in the upper decks of **Shea Stadium** on a hot, hot summer night just to catch a good breeze.

The perfect $4^1/_2$ min New York lunch: papaya drink and extra-crispy hot dog at **Papaya King**.

All the museums on upper 5th Ave on a Tuesday evening, when they're all free.

On the rare occasions when the city is under a deep, fresh blanket of snow—cross-country skiing in **Central Park** and getting hot roasted chestnuts afterward.

The Indian restaurants on 6th St in summer—eating outside in back with a gang of friends on picnic tables for the cheapest sums possible.

Buying bags of flattened fortune cookies at one of the many bakeries in **Chinatown**—they're the ones that didn't make it.

Jazz cruises at night up the **Hudson River** and being able to see the skyline at twilight.

André Emmerich
Owner, André Emmerich Gallery

Lunch uptown at **Les Plèiades**, watching the passing parade of half of the art world.

Lunch midtown in the **Grill Room** of the **Four Seasons** with its unequaled spa cuisine and sparkling fellow guests.

Early, pretheater dinner at **Le Bernardin**—the best food in the world that stays safely within Pritikin limits.

Sunday night dinner at **Elaine's**, the most relaxing setting for the tensest people in the world—New York's intelligentsia.

Shopping the gentleman's quarter-mile along Madison Ave from **Chipp, Brooks Brothers, Paul Stuart, Orvis, Tripler** and on, ending at **Saks Fifth Avenue** on 49th St.

The antique furniture shops around Broadway below 13th St.

The revived **Brooklyn Museum**—as the French guide books say, well worth the *detour* to see its spectacular exhibitions.

A harbor cruise on a party boat, especially when the ship sails close to the floodlit *Statue of Liberty*, still the grandest public sculpture in the world.

Finally, New York at sunset seen from my apartment, 380ft above the avenue right behind the **Guggenheim**.

The newly installed galleries of ancient Greek and Roman art at the **Metropolitan Museum**.

The drive into Manhattan from the north along the **Henry Hudson Pkwy**.

Edward Kosner
Editor and Publisher, *New York Magazine*

Lunch in the **Grill Room** of the **Four Seasons**.

Chili and a bacon-cheeseburger in the back room of **P.J. Clarke's**.

The **Carousel** in **Central Park**.

The **Cloisters**.

The **Century Association clubhouse**.

The **Café des Artistes**.

The gallery with the fountain at the **Frick Collection**.

Fifth Ave from 12th St to Washington Square.

The promenade at **Battery Park City**.

Le Cirque at lunch.

The view of **Midtown Manhattan** from the riverside in Long Island City.

The **Metropolitan Opera** in top form.

The **Oak Bar** at the **Plaza** at dusk on a winter evening.

Madison Square Garden when the Knicks are hot.

Alexandra Penney
Editor-in-Chief, *Self* Magazine

The **Four Seasons**. Best place to take a European.

Little Italy. Nonduplicable delights for your kitchen.

Hayden Planetarium. When the gridlock gets to you.

San Domenico restaurant (Central Park So). When you want to feel you're in the most sophisticated city in the world.

Flea Market at 6th Ave and 26th St. At 8 on Sunday morning—best way to buy Christmas presents.

Florent. For 7AM breakfast to get energized.

Strand Bookstore. A place to hang out and find great book deals.

Il Cantinori restaurant. You can't ever tire of it!

Grand Central Station. The most delicious soft ice in the world (by the baggage stand).

Drinks under the blue whale in the **American Museum of Natural History**.

Renting a rowboat in **Central Park**.

Charles Gwathmey
Architect

A helicopter ride crossing Manhattan from river to river, from the George Washington Bridge to the Verrazano-Narrows Bridge. A boat ride around Manhattan. A run around **Central Park**, the only major outdoor space in the city.

A walk through SoHo and TriBeCa, Wall Street and Lower Manhattan, Madison and 5th Aves from 90th St down to 42nd St.

The **Frick Collection** and the **Cloisters** are still the most civilized museums.

Stay at **Morgans** hotel, eat inexpensively at **Vico** and **Due** (Italian), **Odeon** and **Luxemburg** (Continental) and **Phoenix Gardens** (Chinese), breakfast at **E.A.T,**

and dine at **Bernardin** for an elegant, expensive, great meal.

A visit to the **International Design Center** (IDC/NY) to see the furniture showrooms and the architecture, and when in Queens, a visit to the **American Museum of the Moving Image**. Finally, see Frank Lloyd Wright's **Guggenheim Museum**.

Boroughs

Manhattanites refer to **Brooklyn, Queens**, the **Bronx** and **Staten Island** as the *outer* boroughs; borough residents refer to Manhattan as *the city*. A great deal of attitude is implied therein. The truth is that although they are outside the skyline's media limelight, the boroughs do more than play supporting roles to Manhattan. They lend the city a fair portion of its vitality and character—much of Manhattan's work force commutes from one borough or another—and they hold their own on many fronts, including restaurants, theaters, parks and architecture. Following are highlights from all 4.

Brooklyn, with over 300 years of history and more than 75sq mi of land, has always been a city in its own right. It has been a step up the ladder for immigrant groups, an oceanfront resort, a shipping capital, a cultural mecca, a teeming slum and the front runner of an urban renaissance.

Its national reputation is built on vaudeville jokes, a renegade baseball team (the erstwhile **Brooklyn Dodgers**), an imitable accent, urban conflict and a host of famous and often comedic natives—**George Gershwin, Woody Allen, Mel Brooks** and **Beverly Sills** among them. Impressive as it may be, this esteem doesn't begin to do justice to the diverse immensity of what would be, were it still autonomous, America's fourth largest city. Independent until its annexation into New York City in 1898 (Brooklyn-born author **Pete Hamill** calls this *the great mistake*), it has all the earmarks of a major metropolis.

1 Parker's Lighthouse ★$$ An attractive interior and lovely views of the harbor and the East River supplement the standard seafood fare. ♦ Seafood ♦ 1 Main St (Plymouth-Water Sts) Brooklyn Hts. Reservations recommended. 718/237.1555

The River Café

2 River Café ★★★$$$$ The backdrop is unequaled—the towering, glittering Manhattan skyline seen from the foot of the Brooklyn Bridge. Huge bouquets of flowers and a well-dressed crowd offer other visual distractions on this handsome, anchored barge, but only until the food arrives. Chef **David Burke** has gained a national reputation for creating dishes using the most interesting and freshest American ingredients. Buffalo meat, quail, wild greens, intensely flavored berries and fruits, caviar and wild mushrooms are just

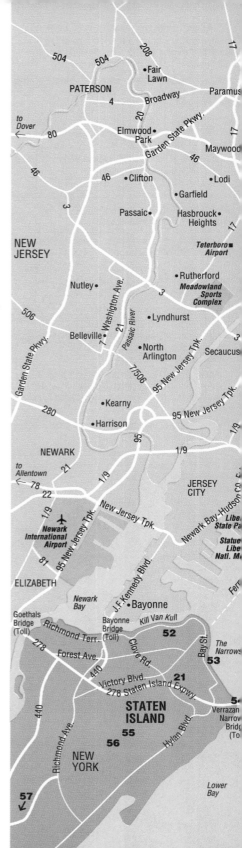

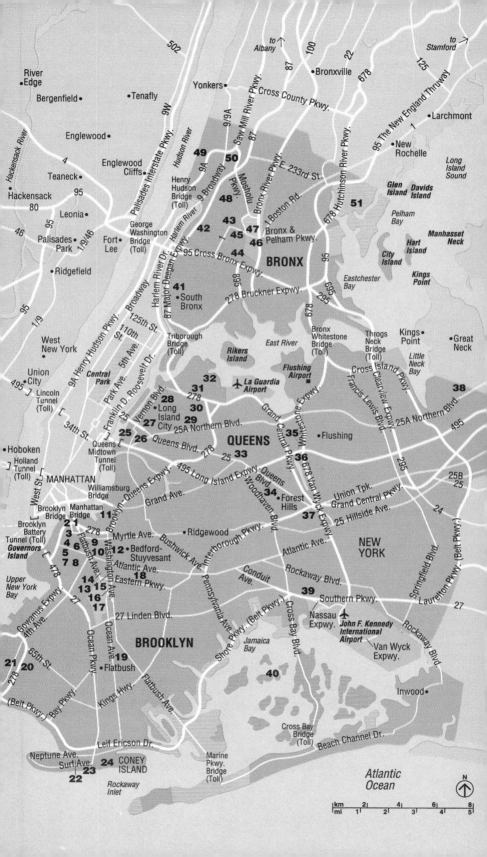

some of the bounty with which his kitchen creates. ♦ American ♦ 1 Water St (East River under Brooklyn Bridge) Brooklyn Hts. Jacket and reservations required. 718/522.5200

3 Henry's End ★$$ This small bistro prepares wild game dishes like elk chops and venison, as well as alligator stew and kangaroo cutlet (really!) with competence and an inventive style. They also do nice things with fish and fowl. ♦ Continental ♦ 44 Henry St (Cranberry St) Brooklyn Hts. Reservations required for 3 or more. 718/834.1776

4 Foffes ★★$$ Veal in any form is good here, as are the pastas—linguini with lobster and shrimp sauce, for example—and desserts. Outdoor seating during the warmer months. The restaurant is housed in a landmark brownstone. Notice the large Art Deco window trimmed in brass. ♦ Italian ♦ Closed Su. 155 Montague St (Clinton-Henry Sts) Brooklyn Hts. Reservations recommended. 718/625.2558

4 Leaf & Bean ★$$ This restaurant is Montague St at its best: intimate yet lively and filled with neighborhood regulars. The wide selection of coffees and teas offered at breakfast, brunch and lunch are for sale, along with a wide assortment of kitchen accessories in the retail store. Food is served until late afternoon. ♦ American ♦ 136 Montague St (Henry-Clinton Sts) Brooklyn Hts. 718/855.7978

4 Montague Street Saloon ★$ This local hangout has a friendly, casual atmosphere. The basic pub fare is good, as is the live entertainment (usually a singer with guitar) Monday through Thursday evenings. The quaint outdoor cafe is open during the warmer months. ♦ American ♦ 122 Montague St (Henry-Hicks Sts) Brooklyn Hts. 718/522.6770

5 Tripoli $$ Atlantic Ave is the center for Middle Eastern cuisine, and among the numerous small restaurants this one is probably the best and most authentic. Excellent lamb kebab, falafel, hummus and heavily honeyed desserts. Live music and entertainment Friday and Saturday nights. ♦ Middle Eastern ♦ 156 Atlantic Ave (Clinton St) Brooklyn Hts. Reservations required F and Sa nights. 718/596.5800

When inventor **Robert Fulton** began steam ferry service to Manhattan in 1814, **Brooklyn Heights** became the first suburban retreat for Manhattan executives. *Fulton's Folly* proved vital on both sides of the river, making him something of a hero: witness the streets renamed in his honor both here and in Manhattan. While the rest of Brooklyn continues to boom, the

Boroughs

Heights remains free of the uglier aspects of *progress* —in 1965 the neighborhood came under the protection of the Landmarks Preservation Commission, and the **Brooklyn Heights Historic District** (America's first) was born. Visit **Montague Street**, a pretty stretch packed with restaurants, boutiques and cafes.

6 Brooklyn Borough Hall (1851, **Gamaliel King**) A palatial sweep of stairs rises to the entrance of this Greek Revival hall of government. The building, originally fashioned after **Dr. William Thornton**'s competition-winning design, was supposed to mimic Manhattan's City Hall, but subsequent design changes dulled the effect. The Victorian cupola was added in 1898 (**Stoughton & Stoughton**). ♦ 209 Joralemon St (Fulton St) Downtown. 718/802.3700

6 Gage & Tollner ★★★$$$ The menu, famous for its length, promises *...to serve the nostalgic atmosphere that serves to bring back fond recollections*, and the place does. The oldest restaurant in the city is still turning out superb seafood. Now at the helm in the kitchen is the celebrated chef **Edna Lewis**, whom Gage & Tollner lured back up north from South Carolina. Among her specialties are Charleston she-crab soup, pan-fried quail, shrimp and crab gumbo and the famed chocolate soufflé she originated at Cafe Nicholson. The gaslights, arched mirrors, dark wood paneling and well-worn mahogany tables are all 19th century. The waiters, proudly wearing the gold eagles, stars and bars awarded for 25-, 5- and 1-year service, are all professionally humble. Local political powers are here for lunch; a more genteel group gathers at night. Among the extensive list of oyster and clam specialties—clam *bellies* (the main section of steamer clams) coated in cornmeal and broiled. ♦ Seafood ♦ 372 Fulton St (Jay St-Boerum Pl) Downtown. Reservations recommended. 718/875.5181

7 Casa Rosa $$ Good home-style cooking, and inexpensive to boot. Have porkchops or lobster *fridilo* (half lobster with mussels, clams and shrimp on a bed of linguini). ♦ Italian ♦ Closed M. 384 Court St (Carroll St) Carroll Gardens. Reservations recommended. 718/625.8874

8 Two Toms $ There's no sign, and at night from the outside the place looks like a workingman's tavern in a deserted warehouse district. Inside, it's just as plain, and there are no menus. The waiters sometimes forget to wear more than an undershirt, and they may come up to the unsuspecting diner and ask, *Well, what'll youse have?* Why bother, you ask. Because it's one of the better Italian restaurants in the borough. ♦ Italian ♦ Closed M. 255 3rd Ave (Union-President Sts) Carroll Gardens. No credit cards. 718/875.8689

9 Junior's ★$ The cheesecake here has the reputation of being the best in New York, and it just may be. The trick is to leave room for it, because copious portions are the house rule. Order simply, and leave some room for that edible velvet. ♦ Deli ♦ 386 Flatbush Ave Ext (DeKalb Ave) Downtown. 718/852.5257

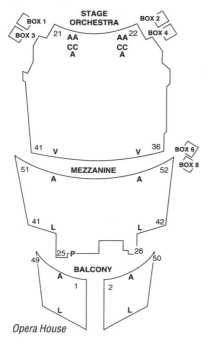

Opera House

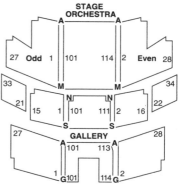

Majestic

10 Brooklyn Academy of Music (1908, **Herts & Tallant**) This organization, affectionately known as *BAM*, was founded in 1859 on Montague St. Among the superlative performers who have appeared at BAM's current home are **Edwin Booth** as *Hamlet* and **Sarah Bernhardt** as *Camille*. **Pavlova** danced and **Caruso** sang in the **Opera House**. BAM is the home of the **Brooklyn Philharmonic**. Over the last decade, impresario **Harvey Lichtenstein** has introduced many innovative programs in music and dance. His annual **Next Wave Festival** has been the launching pad for artists like **Philip Glass, Laurie Anderson** and choreographer **Mark Morris**. In 1987, BAM reopened the **Majestic**, an 83-year-old theater-turned-movie house that had been lying dormant for nearly 20 years. Interestingly, the shell of the theater was left intact—the wear and tear of the years exposed—while 2 semicircular tiers of seats around a large stage were built, creating an intimate amphitheaterlike space with an exciting medieval feel (**Hardy, Holzman & Pfeiffer**). Successful engagements at the Majestic (located on Fulton St, a block away from BAM's main structure) have included choreographer/director **Martha Clarke**'s *Endangered Species*—an elephant, horses and a goat were among the cast—and the musical *Township Fever*, from **Mbongeni Ngema**, the director of *Sarafina*. A shuttle bus leaves from Lexington Ave at 51st St in Manhattan; call BAM for schedule. ♦ Seats: Opera House 2100; Helen Carey Playhouse 1078; Lepercq Space 750; Majestic 900. 30 Lafayette Ave (St. Felix St-Ashland Pl) Downtown. 718/636.4100

Peter (EST. 1887) **Luger**

11 Peter Luger ★★★$$$ One of the oldest and still one of the better, more colorful steakhouses in the city. I come here for one thing, only: well-charred Porterhouse steak made from prime, aged Iowa corn-fed beef. The hefty Porterhouses, ordered for 2 or more, are always cooked perfectly to order and come presliced unless you request otherwise. Potato side dishes are all serviceable, but skip the other vegetables. For dessert, cheesecake or ice cream. *An RSW recommendation.* ♦ Steakhouse ♦ 178 Broadway (Driggs Ave) Williamsburg. Reservations required. No credit cards. 718/387.7400

12 Pratt Institute Architecture, business, science and especially fine arts are the strong suits of this 3500-student school. This 20-acre campus has a satellite in Manhattan. ♦ DeKalb-Willoughby Aves (Classon Ave-Hall St) Downtown. 718/636.3600

13 Thai Taste ★$$ This 2nd-floor restaurant is jam-packed with all sorts of Oriental ornamentation. But don't let that distract you from the *garipup* (puffed dumplings filled with chicken, potatoes, onions and garlic). ♦ Thai ♦ 125 7th Ave (Carroll St) Park Slope. 718/622.9376

14 The New Prospect At Home If you'd rather take out than eat in at the nearby **New**

Prospect Cafe, stop here and pick up a salad or muffin. One of the first of such places to pop up in this increasingly upscale neighborhood. ♦ Takeout ♦ 52 7th Ave (Lincoln-St. John's Pl) Park Slope. 718/230.8900

14 Santa Fe Grill ★★$$ A popular spot for the young after-work crowd. The bar offers a variety of fancy concoctions, and the Cajun food is quite respectable for this far north. ◆ Cajun/Tex-Mex ◆ 62 7th Ave (Lincoln Pl) Park Slope. 718/636.0279

15 Grand Army Plaza (1870, **Frederick Law Olmsted** and **Calvert Vaux**) Monuments have been added since the plaza was first laid out. The Roman-style **Soldiers' and Sailors' Arch** was raised as a tribute to the Union Army in 1892. It was later encrusted with **Frederick MacMonnies'** massive sculptures and some less exuberant bas-relief forms. The **Bailey Fountain** was added in 1932 (**Edgerton Swarthwout**, architect; **Eugene Savage**, sculptor); **Morris Ketchum & Associates** designed the 1965 **John F. Kennedy Memorial**. ◆ Plaza St at Flatbush Ave (Eastern Pkwy-Prospect Park W) Park Slope-Prospect Hts

15 The New Prospect Cafe ★$ Always crowded with folks being served tasty meals at very good prices. The spicy corn-and-shrimp chowder is not to be missed. ◆ American ◆ 393 Flatbush Ave (Plaza St-Sterling Pl) Park Slope. 718/638.2148

16 Brooklyn Botanic Garden (Master plan 1910, **Olmsted Brothers**; landscaping 1912, **Harold Caparn**; Steinhardt Conservatory 1988, **Davis, Brody & Associates**) Not as large or as celebrated as the **New York Botanical Garden** in the Bronx. This one, however, has such celebrated plantings as a Japanese hill-and-pond garden, an herb garden with over 300 specimens and one of the largest public rose collections in America. A conservatory houses the largest bonsai collection in the country. The 50 acres of flora include a fragrance garden for the blind. ◆ Grounds: free; parking fee. Tu-F 8AM-6PM, Sa-Su, holidays 10AM-6PM, Apr-Sep; Tu-F 8AM-4:30PM, Sa-Su, holidays 10AM-4:30PM, Oct-Mar. Steinhardt Conservatory: admission Apr-Nov; parking fee. Tu-Su 10AM-5PM, Apr-Sep; Tu-Su 10AM-4PM, Oct-Mar. 1000 Washington Ave (Empire Blvd-Eastern Pkwy) Prospect Hts. 718/622.4433

16 Brooklyn Museum (1893–1924, **McKim, Mead & White**; 1978, **Prentice & Chan, Ohlhausen**; 1987, **Joseph Tonetti**; addition in progress, **Arata Isosaki** and **James Stewart Polshek & Partners**) This massive 5-story museum is still expanding. Expected to be completed for the Columbus Quincentenary of 1992, the latest renovation will include the addition of 3 floors of new galleries in the West Wing (which, since 1924, has been

reserved for administrative and storage needs); the new 460-seat **Iris and B. Gerald Cantor Auditorium** (which will serve as the museum's first formal gathering place since the original auditorium was converted into the Grand Lobby in the early 1930s); and 2 floors of additional art storage space. Excellent collections include the arts of Egypt, the Classical Middle East and the Orient. Exhibitions of primitive arts come from Africa, the South Pacific and the Americas; other displays feature Greek and Roman antiquities. Costumes, textiles, decorative arts and period furniture dating from the late 17th century are all beautifully laid out for viewing. The museum's permanent collections of paintings and sculpture include works by **Rodin, Modigliani, Cassatt, Degas, Monet, Chagall, Gauguin, Toulouse-Lautrec, Homer, Sargent** and **Bierstadt**. The continuing series of exhibitions by contemporary artists has included **Joseph Kosuth, Alfredo Jarr** and **Reeva Potoff**. ◆ Voluntary contribution. M, W-Su 10AM-5PM. 200 Eastern Pkwy (Washington Ave) Prospect Hts. 718/638.5000

17 Aunt Sonia's ★★$ Small, crowded restaurant perfect after a late-afternoon stroll through Prospect Park or a long visit to the Brooklyn Museum. The menu is eclectic and depends on the chef's mood; the food is dependably excellent and sometimes quite extraordinary. The service is uneven, but good-humored. ◆ Eclectic ◆ 1123 8th Ave (12th St) 718/965.9526

18 Brooklyn Children's Museum (1976, **Hardy, Holzman Pfeiffer Associates**) Children visit a greenhouse, work with butterflies and fossils and learn about how animals get energy from food. They can also participate in a dream sequence inside of a 25ft model of a sleeping head and use their 5 senses to unlock the mystery of objects, using as tools 20,000 cultural artifacts and natural history specimens from the museum's collection. Special events include films, workshops, field trips, concerts and storytelling sessions. ◆ Free. M, W-F 2-5PM; Sa-Su, holidays 10AM-5PM. 145 Brooklyn Ave (St. Mark's Ave) Crown Hts. 718/735.4432

19 City University of New York, Brooklyn College Renovations have been stalled by state budget cuts at this liberal arts college established in 1930, where bachelor's degrees are offered in 95 disciplines and master's degrees are offered in 50. Over 16,000 students attend the 26-acre campus. ◆ Ave H at Bedford Ave, Flatbush. 718/780.5485

20 I Kleinfeld & Son The largest bridal shop in the world stocks 800-1000 models from all the major manufacturers, including **Priscilla of Boston, Carolina Herrara** and **Scassi**. The mother-of-the-bride shops in the PM Department, and bridesmaids go down the street to 8209 3rd Ave. A New York institution and an interesting place to study mother/daughter dynamics. Appointments preferred. ◆ 8202 5th Ave (82nd-83rd Sts) 718/833.1100

21 Areo ★$$ Solid Italian fare. The impressively titled Ram's Feast—veal and filet mignon served with mushrooms and fried zucchini—will satisfy nearly every gourmand. Good cheesecake and tiramisu. ♦ Italian ♦ Closed M. 8424 3rd Ave (85th St) Bay Ridge. Reservations recommended. 718/238.0079

22 Nathan's Famous $ Indeed, it is probably the most famous and elaborate hot dog stand in the world, having served up spicy franks and fabulously greasy, crinkle-cut fried potatoes for nearly a century. ♦ American ♦ Surf Ave at Stillwell Ave, Coney Island. 718/946.2202

23 New York Zoological Society, New York Aquarium (1955, **Harrison & Abramovitz**) Exotic tarpon and turtles and other bizarre creatures of the **Bermuda Triangle Display** and dramatic denizens of the shark tank are on exhibit in the **Native Sea Life** building. Penguins and sea lions provide comic relief, and **Aquatheater** shows provide great entertainment: dolphins in the summer and whales, walruses and sea lions, in the winter. There's also a **Children's Cove**, where kids can touch sea stars and horseshoe crabs. ♦ Admission; parking fee. Daily 10AM-4:45PM. Surf Ave at W 8th St, Coney Island. 718/265.3400

24 Primorsky ★$$ Every night is a party at this lively Russian/Georgian restaurant. Come hungry. The food—tender vegetable appetizers, shish kebab, Georgian breads—is irresistible and filling. Dancing and music nightly. ♦ Russian/Georgian ♦ 282 Brighton Beach Ave (2nd-3rd Sts) Brighton Beach. No credit cards. 718/891.3111

24 Odessa ★★$$$ You can come for lunch, but better to plan on making a night of it. The Eastern European regulars put on their best duds and indulge in vodka on ice, and more vodka on ice, and endless *appetizers* (by the seemingly endless amounts of food brought to your table, you'll find that the word has a decidedly different meaning in Russian). Joining in on the dance floor will help you work it all off. All in all, an extraordinary experience. *An RSW recommendation.* ♦ Russian ♦ 1113 Brighton Beach Ave (13th-14th Sts) Brighton Beach. Reservations required. 718/332.3223

Sprawling **Queens** has always been a conglomeration of towns, villages, model communities and real-estate developments. Suburban in spirit and design, it has become far too dense to be anything but urban in essence. And it has, of late, become the type of immigrant staging ground that Manhattan, Brooklyn and the Bronx used to be (next to Athens, Queens has the world's largest Greek community). But unlike these older boroughs, it is oriented toward the highways that lace it together,

toward the airports (**Kennedy** and **La Guardia**) that sit on either shore, and toward the suburban reaches of Nassau County.

25 Water's Edge ★★★$$$$ Built with 3 sides of glass, and tables that all have a spectacular view of Midtown and Lower Manhattan, this swank river restaurant attracts a well-threaded clientele. The menu is heavy on beautifully grilled and sautéed fish with rich and light sauces, as well as a few unexpected touches like tempura vegetables and, at lunch, potpies. ♦ Seafood ♦ 44th Dr at East River, Long Island City. Jacket, tie and reservations required. 718/482.0033

26 Manducatis ★$$ Family atmosphere, bravado and warmth give Manducatis a real Italian trattoria feeling; chef **Ida**'s fine, straightforward hand with fresh ingredients brings people from Manhattan to this out-of-the-way spot. ♦ Italian ♦ Closed Su. 13-27 Jackson Ave (47th Ave) Long Island City. Reservations recommended. No credit cards. 718/729.4602

26 P.S. 1 An alternative space of the **Institute for Contemporary Art** (see **Clocktower**, page 52). Under the directorship of **Alanna Heiss**, this 19th-century school is used for film, video and exhibitions of new as well as established artists. Call for schedule. ♦ Voluntary contribution. 46-01 21st St (Jackson Ave-45th Rd) Long Island City. 718/784.2084

27 Silvercup Studios In 1983, the **Silvercup Bakery** was converted into a movie studio. Fourteen soundstages are contained within a mammoth 3-block-long building; another 26 are planned. In addition to providing space for work on movies (*Garbo Talks*, *Street Smart*, *The Purple Rose of Cairo*), commercials (which account for most of the studio's activity), and music videos, Silvercup rents screening rooms, production offices and a party room on the 4th floor, where windows overlook the NY skyline. ♦ 42-22 22nd St (Bridge Plaza So-43rd Ave) Long Island City. 718/784.3390

28 Isamu Noguchi Garden Museum (Renovations and addition 1985, **Isamu Noguchi**) One of the few museums dedicated to the work of a single artist, created by that artist. Isamu Noguchi (1904-88) had a controversial career filled with projects that ranged from immense sculpture gardens to *akari* lamps to set designs for choreographers **Martha Graham** and **George Balanchine**. Some of the

Boroughs

greatest examples of Noguchi's work are on display in the museum's 12 galleries and outdoor sculpture garden. *An RSW recommendation.* ♦ Voluntary contribution. W, Sa 11AM-6PM, Apr-Nov. 32-37 Vernon Blvd (33rd Rd) Long Island City. 718/204.7088

29 American Museum of the Moving Image (1988, Gwathmey Siegel & Associates)

All that its name advertises and more. No snobbish distinctions between film and TV or technology and art, but it's not about junk culture, either. Extensive archives, special showings and exhibitions; the artifacts displayed leave an indelible impression of Pop history. ♦ Admission. Tu-F noon-4PM; Sa-Su noon-6PM. 36-01 35th Ave (36th St) Astoria. 718/784.0077; tours 718/784.4160

29 Kaufman Astoria Studio/U.S. Army Pictorial Center

Rudolph Valentino and Gloria Swanson starred in silent films made here in the heyday of New York City's motion picture boom. Edward G. Robinson made the early talkie *Hole in the Wall* here, and the Marx Brothers used the studio for the filming of *The Cocoanuts*. After the studio's 1932 bankruptcy, the property passed through several hands. During WWII, it was used by the Army for training and propaganda films done by Frank Capra. Now a historic landmark, the studio is back in business; it is a favorite location of director Sidney Lumet. Don't miss it! ♦ 34-12 36th St (34th-35th Aves) Astoria. 718/392.5600

30 Piccola Venezia

$$$ Fish dishes are especially good at this off-the-beaten-track Italian restaurant. ♦ Italian ♦ 42-01 28th Ave (Steinway St) Astoria. 718/721.8470

31 Taverna Vraka

$$ Don't be surprised if your waiter suddenly appears in authentic Greek costume to perform folk dances in the middle of the dining room. This is the *real* thing—patrons are known to shower the dancers with dollar bills. ♦ Greek ♦ Closed Tu. 23-15 31st St (23rd-24th Aves) Astoria. 718/721.3007

32 Steinway Mansion (1856) William

Steinway was a great friend of President Grover Cleveland and presented him with a grand piano as a wedding gift. The Steinway home, now an apt setting for Gothic fiction, was once a lively setting for very real fairy tale social events. ♦ 18-33 41st St (Berrian Blvd) Astoria

33 Jai Ya Thai

★$$ Extensive, original Thai menu (300 choices). Try the pork with chili peppers (hot!) and onions. ♦ Thai ♦ 81-11 Broadway (81st-82nd Sts) Elmhurst. Dinner reservations required F-Sa. 718/651.1330

34 London Lennie's

$$ Comforting chowder, pan-fried oysters and big pots of steamers attract hordes of locals to this wood-paneled, nautically decorated fish house. Large wine

list. ♦ Seafood ♦ 63-88 Woodhaven Blvd (63rd Dr-Fleet St) Forest Hills. 718/894.8084

Restaurants/Nightlife: Red Hotels: Blue
Shops/Parks: Green Sights/Culture: Black

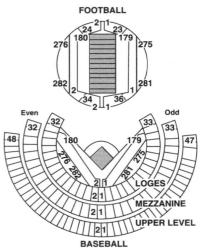

FOOTBALL

BASEBALL

35 Shea Stadium (1963, Praeger-Waterbury)

Home of the New York Mets, this 55,300-seat stadium also hosted Pope John Paul II in 1979 and the history-making 1965 Beatles concert. The stadium opened for the Mets' 1964 season, which coincided with the World's Fair next door at Flushing Meadow Park. For its 25th anniversary in 1988, the stadium underwent a modest renovation that features large neon figures on the outside, new plastic seating to replace old wooden benches and a DiamondVision video screen. Traffic around the stadium is quite congested before and after games; call for directions by public transportation. ♦ 126th St at Roosevelt Ave, Flushing. 718/507.8499

36 Flushing Meadow-Corona Park

A triumph of reclamation! Once a garbage dump, this site, smack dab in the geographic center of New York City, was later chosen for the 1939-40 and 1964-65 New York World's Fairs. ♦ Union Turnpike-44th Ave (Van Wyck Expwy-Peartree Ave) Flushing

Within Flushing Meadow-Corona Park:

Hall of Science (1964, Wallace K. Harrison)

Built as a science pavilion for the 1964-65 World's Fair, this is New York's only hands-on science and technology museum. A sophisticated collection of 150 interactive exhibits focusing on color, light, microbiology, structures, feedback and quantum physics. ♦ Admission. W-Su 10AM-5PM. 47-01 111th St (48th Ave) 718/699.0675

Queens Museum

Excellent art and photography shows and the world's largest scale model: a 9335sq ft Panorama of New York City that includes just about every street, building, bridge and park—at a scale of 1 inch to 100 feet. The World Trade Center measures 18 inches. ♦ Admission. Tu-F 10AM-5PM; Sa-Su noon-5PM. 718/592.5555

37 Pastrami King

$$ Manhattanites reminisce about neighborhood delis as good as this one. ♦ Deli ♦ 124-24 Queens Blvd (82nd Ave) Kew Gardens. No credit cards. 718/263.1717

38 Patrick's Pub ★$$ The cozy, rustic atmosphere is perfect for enjoying Irish coffee and shepherd's pie. ♦ Irish ♦ 252-12 Northern Blvd (Little Neck Pkwy) Little Neck. 718/423.7600

39 Aqueduct Thoroughbred racing from January to May, October to December. ♦ Rockaway Blvd at 108th St, Ozone Pk. 718/641.4700

40 Jamaica Bay Wildlife Refuge Within the Center Gateway National Recreation Area, these vast man-made tidal wetlands and uplands have become a haven for hundreds of species of birds and plants. The fall migratory season, starting in mid-August, is a particularly good time to come. Dress appropriately. ♦ Free. Daily 8:30AM-5PM. Cross Bay Blvd at Broad Channel. 718/474.0613

The Bronx not only stands as a study

in contrasts, it typifies the rapid succession of growth and decline experienced throughout New York City— a microcosm of American urban change squeezed into just over half a century. Today it is a mélange of devastated tenements, suburban riverfront mansions, seaside cottages, massive housing superblocks and fading boulevards of grand Art Deco apartment towers. Although in recent years the Bronx has become a synonym for urban decay, some of the borough remains stable, and heavy philanthropic and governmental investment as well as active, community-based groups are helping to restore the more devastated areas.

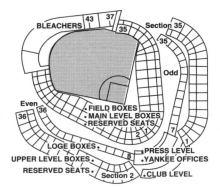

41 Yankee Stadium (1923, **Osborn Engineering Co**; rebuilt 1976, **Praeger-Kavanagh-Waterbury**) In 1973, the **Yankees** celebrated their 50th anniversary in this 57,545-seat horseshoe arena. Remodeling has kept this home of the frequent World Series champs one of the most modern baseball facilities in the country: the first night game was played here in 1946; the first message scoreboard debuted here in 1959. The park is 11.6 acres, 3.5 of which are taken up by the field itself. Within the park are monuments to Yankee greats such as **Lou Gehrig, Joe DiMaggio, Casey Stengel** and, of course, **Babe Ruth**. ♦ E 161st St at River Ave, Highbridge. 293.6000

42 Hall of Fame for Great Americans (1901, 1914, **McKim, Mead & White**) Bronze busts of nearly 100 of America's greatest scientists, statesmen and artists. Sculptures by **Daniel Chester French, Frederick MacMonnies** and **James Earle Fraser**. Classic arcade by **Stanford White**. ♦ Free. Daily 10AM-5PM. W 181st St (University Aves) Bronx Community College, University Hts. 220.6003

43 Edgar Allan Poe Cottage (1812) The writer and his dying wife lived here from 1846–48. *Annabel Lee* was among the works written here. The museum displays many of Poe's manuscripts and other memorabilia. ♦ Nominal admission. W-F 9AM-5PM; Sa 10AM-4PM; Su 1-5PM. Grand Concourse at E. Kingsbridge Rd, Fordham. 881.8900

44 Arthur Avenue Retail Market This section of the Bronx is still a vibrant Italian community, in some ways more so than Manhattan's Little Italy. An indoor farmers' market and lovely bakeries and import shops provide a great diversion before or after a visit to the zoo. ♦ Closed Su. Arthur Ave (E 183rd-E 186th Sts) Fordham. 367.5686

44 Calandra Salted braids and unsalted balls of very fresh mozzarella. Don't forget to keep them in water. ♦ 2314 Arthur Ave (E 184th-E 187th Sts) 365.7572

44 Dominick's ★★$$$ Don't bolt when you see the lines outside. Once inside, the happy crowd will be greeted with terrific, home-style Southern Italian fare—pastas, seafood, meats—and a solicitous staff. Children are welcome. ♦ Italian ♦ Closed Tu. 2335 Arthur Ave (E 184th-E 186th Sts) Fordham. No credit cards. 733.2807

44 Calabrea Pork Store Just try and choose among the 500 kinds of sausage dangling from the ceiling. ♦ 2338 Arthur Ave (E 187th St) 367.5145

44 Mario's $$ Open since 1919, Mario's is big, noisy, gaudy, friendly and filled with families out for a good Italian meal. The large menu specializes in dishes from the Neapolitan region. ♦ Italian ♦ Closed M. 2342 Arthur Ave (E 184th-E 187th Sts) Fordham. Reservations recommended. 584.1188

45 Fordham University Considered by many the nation's foremost Jesuit school, this 85-acre campus has over 13,000 students studying a traditional arts and sciences curriculum. **Rose Hill Manor** (1838), which now forms part of the **Administration Building**, was the home of the original school, **St. John's College**, begun in 1841 by **John Hughes**. Hughes later became New York State's first Catholic arch-

bishop. The campus is a classic collection of Collegiate Gothic structures, most notably **Keating Hall** (1936, **Robert S. Reiley**). ♦ Webster Ave (E. Fordham Rd-Dr. Theodore Kazimiroff Blvd) Fordham. 579.2000

46 The Bronx Zoo
(New York
Zoological Park)
Housing 3800 animals on 265 acres, this is the largest—many believe the best—of New York City's 5 zoos, and certainly one of the top in the nation. At its northernmost end is **Astor Court** (1901–22, **Heins & La Farge**), a collection of formal zoo buildings that contains the elephant house, monkey house and sea lion pool. These structures, influenced by

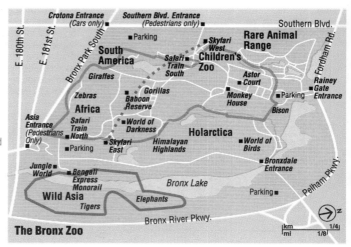

The Bronx Zoo

the 1893 Chicago World's Fair, were built contrary to the original plan, which envisioned an open, natural park setting for the zoo grounds. The balance of the zoo's acreage is less-structured parkland, where African and Asian wildlife roam in open habitat exhibitions. ♦ Admission. M-F 10AM-5PM, Sa-Su, holidays 10AM-5:30PM, Mar-Oct; daily 10AM-4:30PM, Nov-Feb. Bronx River Pkwy (Fordham Rd) Northeast. 367.1010

Within the Bronx Zoo:

Paul Rainey Memorial Gate (1934, **Charles A. Platt**; sculpture, **Paul Manship**) Images of bears and deer decorate these imaginative Art Deco gates, which open onto a 200-year-old Italian fountain donated by **William Rockefeller**. ♦ Fordham Rd at Pelham Pkwy

World of Birds (1972, **Morris Ketchem Jr. & Associates**) Visitors can observe over 500 birds in the 25 environments of this well-designed aviary, with no bars or fences to obscure the view.

Children's Zoo A participatory experience for children, who can explore prairie dog tunnels or hop like a wallaby. Children must be accompanied by an adult. ♦ Nominal admission. Last visitors admitted 1 hour before zoo closes.

Jungle World An award-winning indoor rain forest with 5 habitats, 5 waterfalls, giant trees and Asian animals separated from human beings by bridges and small rivers. Look out for proboscis monkeys, silver-leaf langurs (monkey family), white-cheeked gibbons (ape family) and Indian gharials (alligators that are believed to have roamed the earth 180 million years ago).

World of Darkness (1972, **Morris Ketchem Jr. & Associates**) Day and night are reversed for the nocturnal animals who live here, so they are awake and active for daytime visitors.

Baboon Reserve Two troops of gelada baboons vie for territory and entertain visitors with amazing facial expressions, movements and noises.

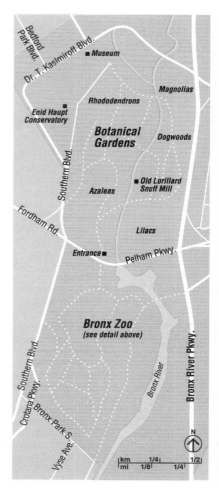

Wild Asia Take a monorail ride through 38 acres of wilderness inhabited by the Siberian tiger, Asian elephant, Formason sika deer, blackbuck antelope, Indian rhino, black leopard and white-cheeked gibbon.

47 New York Botanical Garden One of the world's outstanding botanical gardens, its 250 acres include a 40-acre virgin hemlock forest, formal gardens and the **Enid A. Haupt Conservatory** (1902; restored 1978, **Edward Larrabee Barnes**), which was modeled after the **Great Palm House** at **Kew Gardens** in England. A museum houses a herbarium of 5.5 million dried plants, accessible only to members, and a shop that sells plants and gardening books and supplies. The **Lorillard Snuff Mill** (1840) was converted into a cafe in the 1950s. Last admission is one hour before closing. ◆ Grounds: free. Daily 10AM-7PM, Apr-Oct; 10AM-6PM, Nov-Mar. Conservatory: admission. Tu-F 10AM-5PM, Sa-Su 10AM-6PM, Apr-Oct; Tu-Su 10AM-5PM, Nov-Mar. 200th St at Southern Blvd, Bronx Park. 220.8700

48 City University of New York, Herbert H. Lehman College More than 10,000 students attend this school, founded in 1931 as **Hunter College**, now at 68th St and Lexington Ave in Manhattan. The campus combines Gothic (1928, **Thompson Holmes & Converse** and **Frank Meyers**) and modern structures. The **Lehman Center for the Performing Arts** (1980, **David Todd & Associates** and **Jan Hird Pokorny**), which includes a 2300-seat concert hall, experimental theater, recital hall, library, dance studio and art galleries, has become for the Bronx a kind of scaled-down Lincoln Center and has attracted many of the same events that normally would play Manhattan only. ◆ Bedford Park Blvd W (Jerome-Goulden Aves) Bedford Park. 960.8000

49 Wave Hill The 28-acre Hudson River estate of financier **George W. Perkins** was given to the city in 1965. **Arturo Toscanini, Theodore Roosevelt** and **Mark Twain** each lived here for a short time. The 19th-century mansion hosts a chamber music series, family-arts projects and presents vintage recordings of Toscanini concerts. The dazzling gardens and greenhouses put on a display each season. ◆ Admission. Daily 10AM-4:30PM; free M-F. 675 W 252nd St (Independence Ave at W 249th St) Riverdale. 549.2055

50 Van Cortlandt Museum (1748) This Georgian-Colonial mansion is one of those where **George Washington** actually slept—it was his military headquarters on several occasions. Now it is restored with Dutch, English and Colonial furnishings. ◆ Nominal admission. Tu-F 11AM-3PM; Su 1-5PM. Broadway at W 246th St, Riverdale. 543.3344

51 Bartow-Pell Mansion Museum (1836-42) A Federal home on beautifully manicured grounds, with views of Long Island Sound and outstanding formal gardens. It is run by the **International Garden Club**. A rare treat. ◆ Nominal admission. Tu-Su by appointment. Shore Rd (Pelham and Split Rock Golf Course) Pelham Bay Park. 885.1461

Staten Island, geographically distant from the rest of New York, seems to be more a spiritual cousin to New Jersey, only a narrow stretch of water away. In fact, Staten Island's political ties to New York City are but a historical accident: the island was ceded to Manhattan as a prize in a sailing contest sponsored by the **Duke of York** in 1687. Before 1964, access was possible only by ferry from Manhattan or by car through NJ. In 1964, the **Verrazano-Narrows Bridge** opened, tying Staten Island to Brooklyn. With a new frontier so close at hand, settlers poured over the bridge and changed the rugged face of the island forever. In 1990, tired of being ignored, residents of the *forgotten borough* voted to create a charter commission to provide for the separation of Staten Island from the rest of New York City; a heated debate has begun.

52 Snug Harbor Cultural Center This 83-acre center for the performing and visual arts—a retirement village for sailors from 1833 until the mid 1970s—is composed of 28 historic buildings, many of which are fine examples of Greek Revival, Beaux-Arts, Italianate and Victorian architecture. Stop by the **Visitors Center** for historical exhibitions and information on current and upcoming events, including indoor and outdoor classical, pop and jazz concerts. A historical tour is held every Saturday at 2PM. Trolley buses cart visitors to and from the ferry every 30 minutes Wednesday-Sunday, noon-5PM; later when there are evening performances. ◆ Daily dawn to dusk. 1000 Richmond Terr (Fillmore-Clinton Sts) 718/448.2500

Within Snug Harbor Cultural Center:

The Newhouse Center for Contemporary Art Shows new and emerging artists not often seen in Manhattan galleries, and hosts an indoor/outdoor sculpture exhibition in the summer. ◆ W-Su noon-5PM. 718/448.2500

Staten Island Children's Museum Hands-on exhibits and related workshops and performances for 5 to 12 year olds. A recent program gave children the opportunity to study bugs from both the scientist's and the artist's perspective. Call for extended summer hours. ◆ Free. W-F 1-5PM; Sa-Su, school holidays 11AM-5PM. 718/273.2060

Veterans Memorial Hall A restored chapel used for indoor performances in the fall and winter. ◆ Seats 210. 718/448.2500

New York Bay is really a tidal estuary and the world's southernmost fjord.

Staten Island Botanical Garden Within are an English perennial garden, an herb and butterfly garden, a White Garden (all blooms in shades of gray and white) patterned after the famous English garden in Sissinghurst, and a greenhouse with a permanent display of tropicals, including the **Neil Vanderbilt Orchid Collection**. Best to visit May-October, when the flowers are in bloom. ◆ Free. Dawn to dusk. 718/273.8200

53 The Alice Austen House One of the finest records of turn-of-the-century American life from Alice Austen, a photographer whose work was first discovered in *Life* in 1949. ◆ Suggested donation. Th-Su noon-5PM. 2 Hylan Blvd (Bay St) 718/816.4506

54 Verrazano-Narrows Bridge (1964, **Othmar Amman**) This exquisite 4260ft Minimalist steel ribbon is the world's longest suspension bridge (San Francisco's **Golden Gate** comes in a close second at 4200ft). It flies across the entrance to New York Harbor and is especially beautiful when seen from the Atlantic, against the city's skyline. It is named for **Giovanni de Verrazano**, the first European to see Staten Island (1524). The bridge has become familiar as the starting point for the **New York City Marathon**. ◆ Staten Island Expwy, Staten Island to Gowanus Expwy, Brooklyn

55 Jacques Marchais Center of Tibetan Art (1947, **Jacques Marchais**) An unexpected outpost of Asian culture and tranquility in this small museum on a hill, founded by the late Jacques Marchais and her husband, **Harry Klauber**. One of the largest private collections of Tibetan art in the Western Hemisphere is shown in 2 stone buildings resembling a Tibetan temple. Also art of other Asian countries. ◆ Admission. W-Su 1-5PM, Apr-Nov; groups by appointment, Dec-Mar. 338 Lighthouse Ave (Windsor Ave) Richmond. 718/987.3478

56 Richmondtown Restoration New York City's answer to Williamsburg is a continuing restoration of 29 buildings that shows a picture of 17th- through 19th-century village life. Fourteen are open to visitors, including the 17th-century **Voorlezer House** (1695), the oldest surviving elementary school; the

General Store (1840); and the **Bennet House** (1839), which is home to the **Museum of Childhood**. There are demonstrations of Early American trades and crafts, and working kitchens with cooking in progress. The **Museum**

Store (in the **Historical Museum**) sells reproductions made by village craftspeople. ◆ Admission. W-F 1-5PM, Jan-Mar; Su 1-5PM, Apr-Dec; 441 Clarke Ave (Richmond-Arthur Kill Rds) Richmond. 718/351.1611

57 The Conference House Also called the **Billopp House**. Built in the 1670s, it was the scene of the only peace conference held to try to prevent the Revolutionary War. **Admiral Lord Howe**, in command of the British forces, hosted the parley on 11 September 1776 for 3 Continental Congress representatives—**Benjamin Franklin, John Adams** and **Edward Rutledge**. The house is now a National Historic Landmark with period furnishings and various demonstrations. The rolling lawn is ideal for picnicking. ◆ Nominal admission. W-Su 1-4PM, 15 Mar-15 Dec. 7455 Hylan Blvd (Satterlee St) Tottenville. 718/984.2086

Before the 1850s, immigrants afflicted with diseases were kept on a remote spot on Staten Island. Many local residents became sick and died as a result, and others retaliated by setting fire to the quarantined buildings. This action prompted the state to build **Hoffman** and **Swinburne** islands to house the afflicted. The islands are between Staten Island and Brooklyn, and date from 1872. They were abandoned in the 1920s following the new immigration laws, and serve no purpose today.

John Neary
Head Concierge, Carlyle Hotel

The Promenade Bar in the **Rainbow Room**. If Manhattan's a ship, this is Captain's Bridge.

Watching it snow from the balcony of the **Metropolitan Opera**.

Anchoring a sailboat in **New York bay**. It's very quiet and you see all the lights.

Boathouse Cafe in autumn—all the colors.

Max L. Raab
Chairman of the Board, J.G. Hook, Inc.

Gramercy Park area for its small-town atmosphere. **Pete's Tavern** for acceptable cuisine but cozy ambience. **Gramercy Hotel** bar for earthiness. **Brandywine**, crowded but very good if you can get a table in the SW corner. **Café Nicholson** for delightful strangeness. **Murray Hill** because it reminds me of Philadelphia. All the downtown jazz joints for their embarrassment of riches. **Lions Head** for raunchiness. Upper East Side from 86th St, north on Madison, where you'll find **Island Restaurant**—a culinary and social oasis. **Chez Josephine** for old-shoe comfort and congeniality. Any view from 17 stories or higher, especially in the East 20s. The magnificent panorama from **Windows on the World** (facing north) from sunset until the diamonds bloom.

Robert T. Buck
Director, The Brooklyn Museum

Brooklyn Bests:

River Café. Classic cuisine—one of New York's outstanding menus combined with an unrivaled view from your table of the Manhattan skyline.

Boerum Hill Cafe. A limited but superb menu, served in perhaps the most beautiful 19th-century atmosphere remaining in New York. Noteworthy is its 30ft mahogany bar and its steamboat revival carving.

Aunt Sonia's. A large choice of inventive pasta dishes—original combination of New York savvy and California ingredients. Desserts not to be believed.

Raintree. Beautiful, sitting on Prospect Park in an old soda shop (now pub) basically Italian cuisine—outdoor dining in warm weather.

Tartine & Wine, Inc. Small in-spot. Beautiful interior with lace cafe curtains across the glass front. Home-cooked French-style classics with a nice choice of California wines. In fast-changing Park Slope.

Gage & Tollner. For decades, Brooklyn's best restaurant. Outstanding American cuisine served to generations

of happy clients along with a gem of an authentic Diamond Jim Brady interior, sometimes lit with the original gaslight fixtures. One dines surrounded by mahogany and mirrors—outstanding seafood.

New Prospect Cafe. Near the Brooklyn Museum, a delightful Art Deco touch on a small storefront yields California nouvelle: delicious dishes and salads with featured European ales, beers and beverages.

Seppi Renggli
Head Chef, The Four Seasons

Romantic dinner cruise around Manhattan with **World Yacht Enterprise**.

Best hot dog while watching a New York Rangers game against New York Islanders at **Madison Square Garden**.

Don't miss *Cats* on Broadway.

3AM visit to **Fulton Fish Market**.

Play soccer in **Central Park**.

Helicopter flight around Manhattan each and every season.

Thanksgiving dinner at the **Four Seasons**.

Touring New York

Adventure on a Shoestring *Walking tours that celebrate everything that is wonderful and positive about the city*, according to company founder, **Howard Goldberg**. Chats with members of the community toured are often scheduled. Twelve months a year, rain or shine. ♦ Modest fee. Call for schedule. 265.2663

Doorway to Design Customized behind-the-scenes tours of the interior design, fashion and art worlds as well as walking tours with an architectural historian. ♦ Fee. Call for schedule. 221.1111

Gray Line of New York Two to 8^1/2 hr Manhattan tours. ♦ Fee. Call for schedule. Departure: 900 8th Ave (53rd St) 397.2600

Harlem Gospel & Jazz Tours Tours include visits to historic sites, gospel church services, soul-food restaurants and jazz clubs. ♦ Fee. 302.2594

History Walks Manhattan historian **Joyce Gold** conducts walking tours of Lower Manhattan, Greenwich Village, Chelsea and the Ladies' Mile. ♦ Fee. Call for schedule, departures. 242.5762

Municipal Art Society Walking tours (1hr to all day) with an architectural orientation. Meet in neighborhood of walk. ♦ Fee. Call for schedule. Reservations required. 935.3960

Museum of the City of New York Walks of varying lengths

geared to the museum's current exhibitions. Once or twice a month. Departure from neighborhood of walk. ♦ Fee. Su 1PM. Reservations recommended. 534.1672 ext 206

92nd Street YM/YWHA Neighborhood walking tours, holiday theme tours, visits to artists' studios and other inventive destinations. Also bus tours to Manhattan environs. Most tours (1hr to full weekend) begin at the Y. ♦ Fee. Call for schedule. Reservations required. 415.5600

River to River Downtown Walking Tours. Ruth Alscher-Green will tailor a tour of Lower Manhattan (from the Hudson River to the East River) to the individual or group participating, and is flexible about scheduling. ♦ Fee. 321.2823

Shortline Bus Tours From 2^1/2 hr to all-day tours of Manhattan, plus an evening tour of Christmas lights, in season. ♦ Fee. Call for schedule. Departure: 166 W 46th St (6th-7th Aves) 354.5122

Urban Park Rangers Visitor services for the city's parks, and walking tours of parks in all 5 boroughs. The emphasis is on botany, geology and wildlife. ♦ Free. Call for schedule. Reservations required for workshops and bicycle or bus tours. 427.4040

Chinatown

East Side

Lower Manhattan

MIDTOWN

Central Park

SoHo

Chelsea

HARLEM

East Village

Boroughs

Architectural Highlights

Art Deco

Art Deco, associated with the high society of the 1920s, is strictly codified with reference to the **International Exposition** in Paris in 1925. It has since become more loosely identified as the stylized ornament and streamlined form rooted in the decorative arts movements throughout Europe during the first quarter of this century. Art Deco was manifested in a wide variety of gestures, from the outline of a building (or piece of furniture) to the detail of a smoothly draped swag. The buildings here are a small representation of the Art Deco to be found in the city, the cream of New York's crop. For a more in-depth look, contact the **Art Deco Society** at 925.4946.

Two prime specimens in the Financial District are **McKenzie, Voorhees & Gmelin's New York Telephone Company (Barclay-Vesey) Building** (140 West St) of 1926, and the tower at **60 Wall St**, designed by **Clinton & Russell** in 1932. Also south of 42nd St are the north building of the **Metropolitan Life Insurance** pair (11-25 Madison Ave) by **Harvey Wiley Corbett** and **D. Everett Waid**, 1932; **261 5th Ave** (29th St), a loft building by **Buchman & Kahn**, 1927; the brilliant **2 Park Ave** (34th St) by **E.J. Kahn**, 1927; and, of course, the **Empire State Building** (350 5th Ave), inside and out (1931, **Shreve, Lamb & Harmon**).

Forty-Second St is the heart of the matter, with a concentration of both overall form and intense detailing. The **McGraw-Hill** (now **Group Health Insurance**) **Building** by **Raymond Hood** stands at one end (330 W 42nd St); Hood's **Radiator** (now **American Standard**) **Building** (40 W 40th St) can be seen across Bryant Park. The queen of them all is the **Chrysler Building** by **William Van Alen**, 1930 (405 Lexington Ave). The more ornate and equally wonderful **Chanin Building** (122 E 42nd St) by **Sloan & Robertson** was built in 1929. Last, but by no means least, is the **Daily News Building** (220 E 42nd St) by **Howells & Hood**, 1930.

On 5th Ave, there is the little gem of the **Goelet Building** (608 5th Ave), designed in 1932 by **E.H. Falle & Co.**; **Rockefeller Center** (48th-51st Sts); and the classic **Tiffany & Co.** (727 5th Ave) by **Cross & Cross**, 1940. And do not forego the masterful **Waldorf-Astoria Hotel** (301 Park Ave) by **Schultze & Weaver**, 1931.

Another treasure hunter's strip includes the apartment buildings of Central Park West, from the **Century** (No. 25 Central Park West) by **Irwin Chanin/Jacques Delamarre**, 1931, to the **Eldorado** (No. 300 Central Park West) by **Margon & Holder**, also 1931.

Interiors

Architectural lists generally focus on the exterior qualities of buildings, but perhaps people are more directly touched by their insides—the places and spaces where they work, worship, shop and socialize. Here, then, is a rundown of some of the best of these places in New York:

The lobby of the **Woolworth Building** at 233 Broadway. Two grand banking spaces: the **Bowery** branch at 130 Bowery and **Citibank** at 55 Wall St. **Knoll** furniture showroom at 105 Wooster St; **D.F. Sanders** at 386 W. Broadway; the auditorium at the **New School for Social Research**, 66 W 12th St; the **Salvation Army Centennial Memorial Temple** at 120 W 14th St. **Saks Fifth Avenue** at 50th St is the pride of the department stores. The **Empire State Building**, 350 5th Ave; the main **Reading Room** and the **Great Hall** of the **New York Public Library** at 42nd St and 5th Ave. The **Century Cafe**, 132 W 43rd St, and the restrooms at the **Odeon**, 145 W. Broadway. At **Grand Central Terminal**, not only the main concourse but the vaulted rooms of the **Oyster Bar**. On 42nd St, a wealth of elevator lobbies beckons: **McGraw-Hill** (330 W 42nd St), **Chrysler** (405 Lexington Ave), **Chanin** (122 E 42nd St), **Daily News** (220 E 42nd St) and the **Ford Foundation** (320 E 43rd St). Both the public lobby and the **Ambassador Grill** at **1 UN Plaza**; the **Goelet** (Swiss Center) **Building** elevator lobby, 608 5th Ave. At **Rockefeller Center**, the **RCA** and **International Building** lobbies, **Radio City Music Hall** and all the below-ground concourses. The **Seagram Building** (375 Park Ave) and the **Four Seasons** restaurant (99 E 52nd St). **Le Cygne** restaurant (53 E 54th St). The atrium at **Citicorp** and **St. Peter's Church**, both at 53rd St at Lexington Ave. The 82ft-high skylit atrium of **Edward Larrabee Barnes and Associates' Equitable Life Assurance Building** at 55th St at 7th Ave, which contains murals by **Roy**

Lichtenstein, Sol LeWitt and Sandro Chia, and *America Today,* a series of 10 murals by Thomas Hart Benton. Mr. Chow, behind the Lalique doors at 324 W 57th St; the grand street-level arcade of the AT&T Building, 550 Madison Ave, and the bamboo greenhouse of the IBM Building across the street. The Palm Court at the Plaza is a bit much, but the Oak Room is a haven. The Café des Artistes and the lobby of the accompanying apartment building, 1 W 67th St. The Tiffany rooms at the Seventh Regiment Armory, Park Ave between 66th and 67th Sts; Sointu, and all the objects in this gem at 20 E 69th St. The Frick Collection, 1 E 70th St, and the Morgan Library, 33 E 36th St. Bemelman's Bar at the Carlyle, 35 E 76th St. Half a dozen galleries, courts or halls at the Metropolitan Museum of Art, 5th Ave at 82nd St. The Guggenheim Museum (presently undergoing extensive renovations), 5th Ave at 88th St.

Certainly any house of worship has a special quality on the inside, but say you could visit only 6: St. Thomas, 5th Ave at 53rd St, and St. Patrick's Cathedral, 5th Ave at 50th St; Temple Emanu-El, 1 E 65th St, and Central Synagogue, 652 Lexington Ave; St. Paul's Chapel at Columbia University and the Cathedral of St. John the Divine, Amsterdam Ave at 112th St.

Skyscrapers

Consider the skyscraper: it is the quintessential American building form, and it matured in New York (well, some credit is due Chicago—if you must). The following is an outline of the players in the history of the city's tall buildings as they may still be found (some of the earliest are long gone). First, a note on the building type: skyscrapers dominate the people who build them, yet they remain only a small element of the urban fabric as a whole. The formal qualities and paradoxes of the tall building may be considered with reference to a Classical column: *base, shaft* and *capital.* The base is the part that relates to the street: it is the front we see and the lobby we enter. The shaft is the body of the tower: it has grown taller and changed clothes and outlines as fashions and zoning laws have prescribed. The capital, the articulated top, is the building's distinguishing feature on the cityscape. The relationship of these parts to each other, to people and to the city has changed substantially through the years. But the romance of the early skyline remains and can now be remembered at night, when the little buildings at the top of the tall buildings are illuminated (Metropolitan Life, Chrysler, Empire State, etc). It is another city up there.

In 1903, the Flatiron Building (5th Ave at 23rd St), designed by Daniel Burnham of Chicago, rose 22 stories—to the consternation of many. It is exemplary of the palazzo form of base, body and cornice adapted for many of the early tall buildings. More usual, however, was the exuberant column with the fanciful capital that was a symbol identifying the individual building and animating the skyline, forming a separate city above the street. The best of these are the Metropolitan Life Tower (11-25 Madison Ave); the campanile of St. Mark's Square, transferred to Madison Square by Napoleon Le Brun (1909); Cass Gilbert's 1913 *Cathedral of Commerce,* the Woolworth Building (233 Broadway); and McKim, Mead & White's Beaux-Arts Municipal Building at Chambers and Center Sts. In 1915, Ernest Graham designed the Equitable Building, which filled every imaginable square inch of its site at 120 Broadway. Its bulk caused such concern that zoning laws were written in 1916 specifying building setback and site coverage restrictions. The prescribed new forms can be seen in one tower downtown: the New York Telephone (Barclay-Vesey) Building; and in one uptown: the Shelton Towers Hotel (now Halloran House, 525 Lexington Ave), 1924, by Arthur Loomis Harmon.

Midtown also sprouted an outburst of imaginative design in the '20s. Spires adorned with fanciful crowns embellished the skyline with messages at every turn: 1924, the *Deco-rative* Radiator Building (40 W 40th St); 1927, the medieval Sherry Netherland Hotel (5th Ave at 59th St) by Schultze & Weaver; 1928, the streamlined Gothic Panhellenic Hotel (now Beekman Tower, 3 Mitchell Pl) by Hood's sometime partner, John Mean Howells; 1929, the black-and-white Art Deco Fuller Building (45 E 57th St) by Walker & Gillette; and the Rococo New York Central (now Helmsley) Building at the north end of Park Ave by Warren & Wetmore.

In 1930, *both* the Chrysler Building by William Van Alen (405 Lexington Ave) and the Empire State Building by Shreve, Lamb & Harmon (350 5th Ave) became the *world's tallest building.* The distinctive twin towers of the Waldorf-Astoria and the lacy, radio-waved crown of the RCA Victor (now General Electric) spire by Cross & Cross (570 Lexington Ave) were completed in 1931. Rockefeller Center was under construction throughout the decade around the tower of the masterful RCA Building. The center's chief designer, Raymond Hood, contributed other definitive buildings: the supremely modern Daily News (220 E 42nd St) in partnership with John Howells, of 1930; and the exquisite proto-jukebox

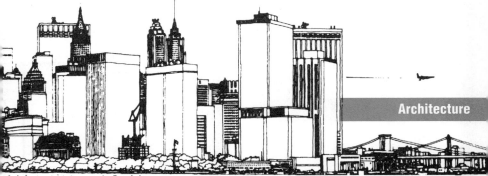

McGraw-Hill (now **Group Health Insurance**) **Building** at 330 W 42nd St, of 1932. These, for a long while, were the last gasp of individuality as building slackened during the Depression and WWII. Then concrete wedding cakes arose during the '40s and '50s to meet the specifications of zoning laws. Typical of the drought is the **Universal Pictures Building** at 445 Park Ave, designed in 1947 by **Kahn & Jacobs**.

A new era began in 1950, with the glass-skinned **United Nations Secretariat** (43rd St, east of 1st Ave), closely followed by **Skidmore, Owings & Merrill**'s **Lever House** (390 Park Ave) in 1952—each in its own way representative of Corbusian tenets. The glass box to beat all glass boxes, however, is the supremely elegant **Seagram Building** of 1958 (375 Park Ave) by **Mies van der Rohe**.

SLS

885 3rd Ave

MHC

Chanin Building

The '60s also produced the problematic **Pan Am Building** (1963, **Walter Gropius**); the mysterious monolith/object/symbol of the **CBS Building** by **Eero Saarinen** in 1965 (51 W 52nd St); and numerous unsavory, static descendants of the Seagram glass-box-on-plaza along 6th Ave—note particularly the **Rockefeller Center extensions** by **Wallace Harrison** in the early 1970s. All were radical departures from the earlier Deco style typified by the **Chanin Building** (shown above). In 1970, height again knew no bounds as the **World Trade Center** towers were topped off (**Minoru Yamasaki**). In 1976, the glass skin as brilliant

Architecture

mask and glittering gown was perfected by **Kevin Roche/John Dinkeloo** at **1 UN Plaza** (44th St at 1st Ave). Variations on this theme include the glossy setbacks

on the facade of **Trump Tower**, by **Swanke, Hayden, Connell & Partners**, 1983 (725 5th Ave), the multi-colored, spandral glass tower rising above the **Museum of Modern Art** by **Cesar Pelli & Gruen Associates**, 1984 (15 W 53rd St), and **I.M. Pei & Partners**' **Jacob K. Javits Convention Center**, 1987 (655 W 34th St). The slick glass skin has a counterpart in the slick granite skin of the IBM tower by **Edward Larrabee Barnes**, 1982 (590 Madison Ave); the **E.F. Hutton Building**, covered in Finnish coral granite by **Roche, Dinkeloo & Associates**, 1987 (31 W 52nd St); the pristine aluminum cladding of the 1977 **Citicorp Center** by **Hugh Stubbins** (153 E 53rd St); and the designs for the **World Financial Center** at Battery Park City by **Cesar Pelli**, 1988. Deviating completely from the square or rectangular base are the wedge of the **Metropolitan Tower** by **Schuman, Lichtenstein, Claman and Efron**, 1985 (146 W 57th St); the so-called *Lipstick Building* (shown above) by **John Burgee Architects** with **Philip Johnson**, 1986 (885 3rd Ave); **Helmut Jahn**'s rounded blue-glass tower with its conical top (750 Lexington Ave); and **Kohn Pederson Fox**'s gray, granite-clad tower, which is set back from the sidewalk in a concave shape that rises the full 34 stories, 1988 (135 E 57th St). **Gwathmey & Siegel**'s renovation and extension to the **Guggenheim Museum** (scheduled completion, fall 1991) will substantially alter the appearance of New York's sole **Frank Lloyd Wright** building and provide improved accommodations for the museum's permanent collection. A fairly sensitive addition to the existing Carnegie Hall is the **Carnegie Hall Tower** (1991, **Cesar Pelli**). It sets off a dramatic tension with the Metropolitan Tower; the 2 tall buildings are separated only by the width of the Russian Tea Room. Not located in Manhattan, but nonetheless profoundly affecting New York's skyline, is Long Island City's **Citicorp Building** by **Skidmore, Owings & Merrill**, 1988 (44th Dr at Jackson Ave, Queens).

Timeline

The **Ice Age** creates one of the world's finest harbors. For thousands of years before European explorers find New York Bay, dozens of Indian tribes inhabit the area.

1500s

1524—Thirty-two years after **Columbus** discovers the New World, **Giovanni da Verrazano**, the Florentine explorer, sails into New York Harbor.

1600s

1609—British captain **Henry Hudson**, in search of a shortcut to India for the **Dutch West India Company**, sails up the river that will bear his name.

1621—The city's history begins with a permanent Dutch settlement named **Nieuw Amsterdam**.

1625—The **first black settlers** are brought as slaves to build the city, and are eventually given land of their own in an area later known as Greenwich Village.

1626—**Peter Minuit**, the first governor, reportedly buys Manhattan Island from the Indians for a trunkful of relatively worthless trinkets.

1647—**Peter Stuyvesant** brings law and order to the town. A municipal code, police force and fire brigade are established.

1654—The **first Jewish settlers** land.

1660—The city's first hospital is established; one of its physicians, **Dr. Lucas Santomee**, was the son of a slave, and New York City's first black doctor.

1664—**Nieuw Amsterdam** becomes **New York** when Stuyvesant cedes control to **Charles II** of England and his brother, **James, Duke of York**.

1700s

1725—Printer **William Bradford** founds New York's first newspaper, *The Gazette*.

1754—**Kings College** (now **Columbia University**) is established at Park Pl and Church St.

1765—The British impose taxes, the harshest of which is the **Stamp Act**.

1774—The *New York Tea Party* takes place when the

Sons of Liberty board the *London* and dump 18 cases of tea into the East River.

1776—The American Revolution starts, and **General George Washington** sets up quarters at No. 1 Broadway. As the Declaration of Independence is adopted by Congress, the Revolutionary forces are driven out of Manhattan by **Lord Howe**. **Nathan Hale** is executed by the British as a spy.

1788—**New York Medical Society** is founded.

1789—New York City becomes capital of the United States. **George Washington** is inaugurated in front of **Federal Hall**. The **Stock Exchange** is established.

1790—The **official population** for New York: 33,000.

1799—The **slave market** closes.

1800s

1804—**Aaron Burr**, the vice president of the US, kills **Alexander Hamilton**, the first secretary of the treasury, in a duel.

1812—War. The British blockade Manhattan. The new **City Hall** opens.

1825—The **Erie Canal** is inaugurated. **Governor DeWitt Clinton**'s brainchild revolutionizes commerce.

1826—**Lord & Taylor** is founded.

1830—With the arrival of new **German immigrants** throughout the previous decade, the population doubles to 202,000.

1831—The first railroad opens: the **New York and Harlem Line**.

1835—**Washington Irving**, the city's first author, publishes *The Legend of Sleepy Hollow* and *Rip Van Winkle*. **James Fenimore Cooper** recounts **John Jay**'s Revolutionary War exploits in his novel, *The Spy*. Newspaper editors **William Cullen Bryant** and **Horace Greeley** found *The New York Evening Post*

and *The New York Tribune*. **Samuel F.B. Morse** develops the telegraph. **Edgar Allan Poe** writes *Annabel Lee* in a small house in the Bronx.

1840s—The local Democratic organization, **Tammany Hall**, directs strong appeals to immigrants and gains massive power, eventually becoming a national symbol for political *bossism*.

1851—*The New York Times* publishes its first edition.

1858—**Calvert Vaux** and **Frederick Law Olmsted** design **Central Park**. **Macy's** department store is founded.

1859—Voters register for the first time.

1860s—**Irish immigrants**, escaping the famine in their homeland, begin to arrive in the city, touching off another period of expansion.

1861—The **Civil War** (then called *The War Between the States*) begins, with New York on the Union side.

1863—Anti-draft mobs riot for 4 days. Troops are brought in to the city to quell the disturbance.

1865—**Abraham Lincoln's** body lies in state at **City Hall** and is viewed by 120,000 people.

1869—Infamous **Black Friday** rocks the financial world. **Rutheford Stuyvesant** erects the first modern apartment building at 142 E 18th St.

1870—A city charter approved by the state legislature gives the notorious **William Marcy *Boss* Tweed** financial control over New York City. Incredible sums of money disappear from city coffers.

1871—*The New York Times* and **Thomas Nast** of *Harper's Weekly* expose and highlight the machinations of *Boss* Tweed and his cohorts.

1873—Banks fail, **Wall Street** panics.

1876—Baseball organizes the **National League**.

1878—The **Bell Telephone Company** opens the first telephone exchange.

1880—**Sarah Bernhardt** makes her American debut at Booth's Theater.

1882—**Thomas Edison's** electric plant opens on Pearl St, making lighting by electricity available to commerce and industry.

1883—The **Brooklyn Bridge**, the structural wonder of the age, opens.

1884—New immigrants from the Orient develop **Chinatown**. The world's first **long-distance telephone** line connects New York to Boston.

1885—**Southern Europeans**, including large numbers of Italians, begin to arrive.

1886—The *Statue of Liberty* is unveiled. **Samuel Gompers** organizes the **American Federation of Labor** (AFL).

1890—**Jewish immigrants** begin to arrive from Eastern Europe, many settling on the Lower East Side.

1891—**Carnegie Hall** is inaugurated with a concert featuring **Peter Tchaikovsky** as conductor.

1892—**Ellis Island** becomes the city's immigration depot.

Timeline

1898—**The 5 boroughs unite** to form **Greater New York**. The population is now over 3 million, making New York City the largest city in the world.

1900s

1900—The banking firm of **J.P. Morgan** organizes the **United States Steel Company**, the first billion-dollar corporation.

1904—The **first subway system** begins operation. Fare is 5¢.

1905—The **Staten Island Ferry** begins operation.

1907—**Wall Street** panics, **J.P. Morgan** helps restore faith in the market by buying vast amounts of gold.

1910—The **National Association for the Advancement of Colored People** (NAACP) is formed.

1911—The **New York Public Library** opens at 42nd St and 5th Ave. **Triangle Shirtwaist Co.** sweatshop fire leads to new labor laws and public safety measures.

1913—The **Armory Show**, with works by **Marcel Duchamp** and **Pablo Picasso**, shocks New Yorkers. The **Woolworth Building** is constructed.

1919—A New York State proposal finally results in the **19th Amendment** to the Constitution: women get the right to vote.

1920—With unpopular **Prohibition** in effect, speakeasies open all over New York City.

1921—New York and New Jersey form the **Port of New York Authority**. (The name is changed in 1972 to **The Port Authority of New York and New Jersey**.)

1925—Playboy **James Walker** is elected mayor by popular vote. **A. Philip Randolph** organizes the **Brotherhood of Sleeping Car Porters**, the country's first all-black union.

1926—Choreographer **Martha Graham** presents her first solo dance concert.

1927—**Charles A. Lindbergh** returns to New York City after his solo flight to France. **Babe Ruth** becomes baseball's home-run king, scoring 60 homers in one year. **Al Jolson** appears in *The Jazz Singer*, the first successful sound film. The **Holland Tunnel**, the first Hudson River vehicular tunnel, opens and connects Manhattan with Jersey City.

1928—**Goethals Bridge** and **Outerbridge Crossing** connect Staten Island with New Jersey.

1929—*Wall Street Lays an Egg...* reads *Variety*. The stock market crashes as banks fail. The **Chrysler Building** and the **Museum of Modern Art** open.

1931—The **Empire State Building**, the **George Washington Bridge** and the new **Waldorf-Astoria Hotel** are completed.

1932—**Mayor James Walker** resigns and sails for Europe. It becomes evident that he and his administration are involved in municipal corruption.

1933—New Yorker **Franklin D. Roosevelt** becomes president. **Fiorello La Guardia** is elected mayor. Under both administrations, top priority goes to coping with unemployment. President Roosevelt's **New Deal WPA** supplies funds for the metropolitan area and suburbs. Lawyer **Thomas Dewey** investigates the rackets and deports crime leader *Lucky* **Luciano**.

1934—Choreographer **George Balanchine's**

American Ballet (now the New York City Ballet) debuts at the White Plains estate of industrialist Felix M. Warburg.

1935—The Hayden Planetarium opens.

1937—*Brown Bomber* Joe Louis becomes the world heavyweight champion. The Lincoln Tunnel opens connecting Midtown Manhattan with Weehawken NJ.

1939—With the onset of WWII, millions of dollars worth of tanks, trucks, guns, planes and ammunition are shipped out of New York City Harbor.

1940—The Queens-Midtown Tunnel opens. After the fall of France, New York City becomes home to many European artists—Mondrian, Léger, Ernst, Moholy-Nagy and Breton among them. A new American modern art, Abstract Expressionism, emerges and becomes known as the *New York School*; practitioners include Jackson Pollock, Arshile Gorky, Hans Hofmann, Willem de Kooning and David Smith.

1941—Mayor Fiorello La Guardia initiates work on a giant air terminal in Queens (later named John F. Kennedy Airport).

1944—Adam Clayton Powell Jr. is elected to Congress. Choreographer Merce Cunningham presents his first solo concert at the Humphrey/Weidman Studio on 16th St; composer John Cage provides the music.

1945—WWII ends. William O'Dwyer is elected mayor.

1946—The United Nations decides to establish headquarters in Manhattan on 17 acres donated by the Rockefellers.

1950—The Brooklyn Battery Tunnel and the Port Authority Bus Terminal open. William O'Dwyer resigns as mayor after disclosures of scandal and fraud in his administration. After 46 years at a nickel, subway fare rises to 10¢.

1953—The Rosenbergs are executed for selling atom bomb secrets to Russia. Robert F. Wagner is elected mayor. Subway fare rises to 15¢.

1954—Edward R. Murrow confronts Joseph McCarthy on the CBS television program *See It Now*.

1956—The Brooklyn Dodgers leave New York City. Ebbets Field is sold for a housing site.

1959—The Guggenheim Museum opens on 5th Ave.

1961—City University of New York (CUNY) is created.

1964—The Verrazano-Narrows Bridge connects Staten Island and Brooklyn.

1965—New York City is paralyzed by an East Coast power blackout. John V. Lindsay is elected mayor.

1966—A race riot breaks out in the East New York section of Brooklyn. Subway fare rises to 20¢.

1967—Rioting and disorder break out in East Harlem.

1968—The Vietnam War Moratorium is held in New York City.

1970—The World Trade Center is topped off and its first tenants move in. Subway fare rises to 30¢.

1972—Subway fare rises to 35¢.

1974—Abraham D. Beame is elected mayor.

1975—Subway fare rises to 50¢.

1978—Ed Koch is elected mayor. A 4-month strike deprives New Yorkers of their newspapers.

1979—Woody Allen romanticizes New York City in his movie *Manhattan*. *New Yorker* writer S.J. Perelman, considered by many America's greatest humorist, dies.

1980—Subway fare rises to 60¢.

1981—Picasso's *Guernica* leaves the US for Spain; the anti-war mural goes home after 42 years on loan to the Museum of Modern Art. A ticker-tape parade salutes 52 American hostages held captive in Iran for 444 days. Mayor Koch is re-elected by a landslide. Former Beatle John Lennon is killed outside the Dakota apartments. Subway fare rises to 75¢.

1982—Over half a million demonstrators against nuclear arms march to Central Park.

1983—A record snowfall of 17.8 inches blankets the city. Philip Johnson's Postmodern AT&T Corporate Headquarters opens on Madison Ave, part of the '80s office building boom.

1984—Subway fare rises to 90¢.

1986—Developer Donald Trump revamps Wollman Rink in Central Park. The *Statue of Liberty* renovation is completed. The Mets win the World Series against the Boston Red Sox. Subway fare rises to $1.00.

1987—Black Monday: the stock market crashes on 19 October. Wall Street doesn't panic. Andy Warhol, the *Father of Pop*, dies in New York Hospital.

1988—The Williamsburg Bridge closes temporarily, due to a crumbling infrastructure. Soviet premier Mikhail Gorbachev's history-making visit to New York is cut short by a devastating earthquake in Armenia.

1989—Mikhail Baryshnikov makes his Broadway debut as Gregor Samsa in Franz Kafka's chilling *Metamorphosis*. Francis Ford Coppola, Woody Allen and Martin Scorsese collaborate in *New York Stories*–3 short films about New York. David Dinkins wins the mayoral campaign to become the first black mayor in New York City history. Subway fare rises to $1.15.

1990—Ellis Island reopens as The National Museum of Immigration after an 8-year, 156-million-dollar renovation. *A Chorus Line*, the longest running show on Broadway, closes after 6137 performances over a 15-year period. Drexel Burnham Lambert investment banker Michael Milken is fined $600 million and sentenced to 10 years in prison for insider trading, the most severe of the convictions in Wall Street banking scandals. The fashion community bands together and slashes prices for Seventh on Sale, a week-long fundraising sale to benefit AIDS research. New Yorkers flock to the American Museum of Natural History to say good-bye to their dinosaur friends, who are undergoing extensive cosmetic surgery and renovations for the next 5 years.

1991—Carnegie Hall celebrates its 100th anniversary.

A

Restaurant Index

Only restaurants with star ratings are listed below. All restaurants are listed alphabetically in the main index. Always telephone as far in advance as possible to confirm your table and ensure that a restaurant has not closed, changed its hours, or booked its tables for a private party.

Index

317